Using Symphony®,
2nd Edition

David Paul Ewing
Geoffrey T. LeBlond

Revised for Release 2.0
by Rebecca Bridges

Que™ Corporation
Carmel, Indiana

Dedication

To Sheila
D.P.E.

To my grandfather
G.T.L.

Product Director
David Ewing

Editorial Director
David F. Noble, Ph.D.

Acquisitions Editor
Pegg Kennedy

Editors
Kelly Currie
Lloyd J. Short

Technical Editor
David Maguiness

Book Design and Production
Dan Armstrong
Sharon Hilgenberg
Jennifer Matthews
Cindy L. Phipps
Joe Ramon
Dennis Sheehan
Mae Louise Shinault
Peter Tocco
Carrie L. Torres

Composed in Garamond and American Typewriter
by Que Corporation.

Screen reproductions in this book were created by means of the
InSet program of INSET Systems Inc.

About the Authors

David Paul Ewing

David P. Ewing is Publishing Manager for Que Corporation. He is author of Que's *1-2-3 Macro Library*, *The Using 1-2-3 Workbook*, and *Using 1-2-3 Workbook Instructor's Guide*; co-author of Que's *Using Q&A*, *Using Javelin*, and *1-2-3 Macro Workbook*; and contributing author to *Using 1-2-3*, Special Edition.

Mr. Ewing received his B.A. from Duquesne University and his M.A. from North Carolina State University. He is currently completing his Ph.D. at Purdue University. Prior to his position at Que, he was the Assistant Director of the Business Writing Program at Purdue University, where he developed course materials and trained instructors. For eight years, Mr. Ewing taught college-level writing and business communications courses. He has published articles in leading business communications books and journals and given numerous presentations at national conferences on writing and business communications.

Geoffrey T. LeBlond

Geoffrey T. LeBlond, president of LeBlond Software, received his B.A. degree from Brown University and his M.B.A. in finance from Indiana University's Graduate School of Business. Mr. LeBlond is co-author of *Using 1-2-3* and a contributing author to *1-2-3 for Business*, both published by Que Corporation. Mr. LeBlond was also a technical editor at Que Corporation for the *IBM PC Update* magazine and Editor-in-Chief of *Absolute Reference: The Journal for 1-2-3 and Symphony Users*.

Contents at a Glance

Part I   **Understanding and Getting Started with Symphony**

An Overview of Symphony   9
Getting Started   31

Part II   **Learning Symphony Worksheet Basics**

The Symphony SHEET Window   77
SHEET Window Commands   97
@Functions   155
File Operations   209
SHEET Window Hands-On Practice.........................   229

Part III   **Using the Symphony Word Processor**

Word Processing: Working in a Symphony DOC Window   247
DOC Window Hands-On Practice   301
Word-Processing Add-Ins: Spelling Checker and Text Outliner   321

Part IV   **Creating Symphony Reports and Graphs**

Printing Spreadsheets and Word-Processing Documents   361
Creating and Displaying Graphs   383
Printing Graphs   429
Creating and Printing Graphs: Hands-On Practice   441

Part V   **Data Management with Symphony**

Data Management   459
Data Management Hands-On Practice   515

Part VI   **Symphony Communications Module**

Communications   531
Communications Hands-On Practice   553

Part VII   **Symphony Macros and the Command Language**

Creating and Using Macros   567
Introduction to the Command Language   601

Troubleshooting Section   661

Appendix   A   Installing Symphony   743
              B   Symphony Release 2.0: New Commands and Features   751

              Index   757

Table of Contents

Introduction 1

Using Symphony 1
Who Should Use This Book? 2
About This Book 2
More Symphony Knowledge 5

I Understanding and Getting Started with Symphony

1 An Overview of Symphony 9

What Is Symphony? 9
Symphony at a Glance 15
Symphony's Capabilities 16
    The Spreadsheet 16
    Playing "What If . . . ?" 18
    Data Management 19
    Creating Graphs 20
    Word Processing 21
    Communications 22
    Window Features 23
    Command Menu System 24
    Settings Sheets 24
    Functions 24
    International Formats and Character Set 25
    Security System 25
    The Command Language and Macros 26
    Naming in Symphony 28
New with Symphony Release 2.0 29
Chapter Summary 30

2 Getting Started 31

The Symphony Menus....................................... 31
  The Symphony Access System 32
    Entering and Exiting from Symphony................... 33
    Tutorial 34
    PrintGraph 34
    Install.. 34
    File-Translate 35
  The SERVICES Menu 35
    Window... 36
      Windows and Files 37
      Function Keys for Window Operations.............. 38
      The Window Menu............................... 38
      Creating, Using, and Deleting Windows 38
      Removing and Redisplaying Windows 39
      Changing Window Shape and Size................. 40
      Restricting Ranges in Windows 41
    File 42
    Print... 43
    Configuration 43
    Application 45
    Settings 46
    New 46
    Exit.. 47
  The Command Menu 47
  Settings Sheets....................................... 47
  The TYPE Menu 50
Automatic Exit versus "Sticky Menu" 50
The Symphony Keyboard 51
  The Alphanumeric Keyboard 53
  The Numeric Keypad................................... 54
  The Lock Key Indicators 55
  The Function Keys 56
    Function Keys Working in All Windows 56
    Function Keys for Specific Windows 58
  Other Special Key Combinations 59
  Cursor-Movement Keys and the Cell Pointer 59
    Moving the Cell Pointer in a SHEET Window 59
    Moving the Cursor in a DOC Window 61
    Moving the Cursor in a FORM Window 62
The Symphony Display 63
  The Control Panel 63

The Mode Indicators 65
Other Indicators 67
Using the Tutorial Disks................................ 68
The Tutorial Lessons Disk............................. 69
Accessing the Tutorial 71
The Help and Tutorial Disk 72
Chapter Summary 73

II Learning Symphony Worksheet Basics

3 The Symphony SHEET Window 77

Worksheet Size and Its Effect on RAM 78
Expanded Memory Specification (EMS) 81
Speed 81
Entering Data 82
Entering Labels 82
Entering Numbers...................................... 84
Entering Formulas..................................... 85
Entering Cell Addresses in Formulas 86
Operators 86
Functions 87
String Formulas 88
Editing 89
Ranges 91
The Shape of Ranges 92
Designating Ranges.................................... 93
Integrating SHEET Windows with Other Applications 93
Chapter Summary 96

4 SHEET Window Commands 97

SHEET Command Menu 97
Range Commands 99
Naming Ranges (**Range Name**) 99
Creating Range Names 99
Deleting Range Names 100

Creating a Table of Range Names...................... 100
Using Range Names 101
Transposing Rows and Columns (**Range Transpose**)........ 103
Copying Values (**Range Values**)........................... 104
Protecting Ranges (**Range Protect**) 104
Filling Ranges with Numbers (**Range Fill**) 108
Creating Frequency Distributions (**Range Distribution**) 109
"What-If" Analysis (**Range What-If**)...................... 111
Cut-and-Paste Commands 114
Moving Cell Contents 114
A Warning about **Move**............................. 115
Pointing to Cells: The Expanding Cell Pointer........... 116
Using the End Key To Point 117
Erasing 118
Inserting Blank Columns and Rows..................... 119
Deleting Columns and Rows 122
Copying.. 124
Relative versus Absolute Addressing 127
Relative Addressing 129
Absolute and Mixed Addressing 130
Setting Cell References 134
Miscellaneous Comments on Copying 135
Adjusting Column Width 136
Formatting the Worksheet 137
Settings Sheets and Commands for Controlling Formats 138
General 140
Currency... 141
Punctuation Format 142
Fixed... 143
% (Percent).. 144
Date 144
Time 145
Scientific.. 146
Bar-Graph... 146
Literal 146
Hidden 147
Other Settings Options................................. 147
Zero 147
Titles... 148
Recalculation 150
Method: Automatic versus Manual Recalculation......... 150
Order: **Optimal**, **Natural**, **Column-by-Column**,
or **Row-by-Row** 151

    Iterations 152
    Chapter Summary 154

5 @Functions 155

Function Basics 155
Mathematical Functions 156
Special Mathematical Functions 157
    Generating Random Numbers: @RAND 158
    Rounding Numbers: @ROUND 158
    Returning a Remainder: @MOD 159
Trigonometric Functions 160
Statistical Functions................................ 160
    Computing a Sum: @SUM 161
    Finding the Maximum and Minimum Values:
        @MAX and @MIN 163
    Counting Nonblank Entries: @COUNT................. 163
    Calculating the Mean: @AVG 163
    A Quick Review of Statistics..................... 164
    Finding Variance and Standard Deviation: @VAR
        and @STD 164
Financial Functions 166
    Net Present Value: @NPV 166
    Present Value of an Annuity: @PV 168
    Future Value of an Annuity: @FV 168
    Number of Time Periods of an Annuity: @TERM....... 169
    Internal Rate of Return: @IRR 169
    Payment per Period: @PMT 171
    Periodic Interest Rate for an Investment: @RATE 171
    Number of Time Periods for an Investment: @CTERM...... 172
    Depreciation Functions 173
        Straight-Line Depreciation: @SLN 173
        Sum-of-the-Years'-Digits Depreciation: @SYD 173
        Double-Declining-Balance Depreciation: @DDB 174
Data Management Functions 174
    Selecting from a List: @CHOOSE 174
    Looking Up Values: @VLOOKUP and @HLOOKUP 175
    Retrieving Data from Specified Locations: @INDEX........ 179
Logical Functions.................................... 180
    Creating Logical Statements: @IF 180
        Using Simple Logical Operators 180
        Adding Complex Operators 182

Notes on Strings.. 184
Error-Trapping Functions 185
@NA and @ERR 185
@ISERR and @ISNA 186
Determining the Aspect of a Cell: @ISSTRING and
@ISNUMBER 187
Special Functions.. 188
Determining the Aspect of a Cell: @CELL................ 188
Determining the Aspect of the Current Cell:
@CELLPOINTER 191
Describing Ranges: @ROWS and @COLS 191
Referring to Cells Indirectly: @@ 191
Documenting Errors: @TRUE and @FALSE 192
String Functions... 192
Locating the Position of One String within
Another: @FIND 192
Extracting One String from Another: @MID 194
Extracting Strings: @LEFT and @RIGHT 194
Replacing Characters in a String: @REPLACE 195
Finding the Length of a String: @LENGTH 195
Comparing Strings: @EXACT 196
Converting Case: @LOWER, @UPPER, and @PROPER 196
Repeating Labels: @REPEAT 197
Eliminating Unwanted Blank Spaces: @TRIM 197
Converting Strings to Numbers and Numbers to Strings..... 197
@STRING 198
@VALUE 198
Converting Numeric Values to String Values
and Vice Versa: @N and @S 199
Functions Used with the ASCII/LICS 199
Producing LICS Characters: @CHAR..................... 200
Nonprintable Characters in the LICS 200
Finding the LICS Code Number: @CODE 201
Removing Unwanted Characters: @CLEAN 201
Date and Time Arithmetic 201
Symphony's Serial Numbering System 202
Date Functions 202
Converting a Date to an Integer: @DATE................ 202
Converting a String to a Date: @DATEVALUE 203
Extracting the Day, Month, or Year 204
Displaying Dates....................................... 204
Today's Date and Time: @NOW 205
Time Functions 205

Converting Time Values to Serial Numbers: @TIME 206
Converting a String to a Time: @TIMEVALUE 206
Extracting the Second, Minute, or Hour 207
Displaying Times 207
General Comments on Date and Time Arithmetic 207
Chapter Summary 208

6 File Operations 209

A General Description of Symphony Files 209
File Management 210
File Bytes 210
File List 211
File Table 211
Simple Storage and Retrieval 212
Making Backup Copies of Files 214
Partial Loads and Saves 215
Combining Files 216
Deleting Files 220
Changing a Drive and Directory 221
Transferring Files 222
Transferring Standard ASCII Files 222
Using the Translate Utility To Transfer Files 223
Transferring Symphony and WordStar Files 225
From WordStar to Symphony 225
From Symphony to WordStar 226
Chapter Summary 228

7 SHEET Window Hands-On Practice 229

Building the Model 230
Entering Labels 230
Entering Numbers 232
Entering and Copying Formulas 233
Expanding the Model 236
Creating Windows 236
Copying between Windows 237
Changing the Spreadsheet 237
Moving Cells 237
Using the Edit Key 238

Inserting and Deleting Rows 238
Protecting the Model 239
   Preventing Accidental Overwrite 240
   Password-Protecting the File 241
Working with Large Spreadsheets 242
   Recalculating the Spreadsheet 243
   Xtracting to Separate Files 243
Chapter Summary 244

III Using the Symphony Word Processor

8 Word Processing: Working in a Symphony DOC Window 247

Creating a DOC Window 248
The DOC Display 249
DOC Function Keys 250
Getting Started in a DOC Window 251
   The DOC Command Menu 251
   DOC Accelerator Keys 252
   Print Attributes 253
   Format Settings 254
      Format Settings in Symphony's Configuration File 254
      DOC Window Format Settings 255
      Guidelines for Using Format Settings 256
Entering Text and Moving the Cursor 258
   Wordwrap 258
   Insert and Overstrike Modes 258
   Moving the Cursor in a DOC Window 259
      A Character or Space at a Time 260
      From Word to Word 261
      From Line to Line 262
      To the Beginning and End of a Line 262
      To the Beginning and End of a Paragraph 262
      From Screen to Screen 262
      To the Beginning or End of a Document or
         Restrict Range 264
      To the Next Carriage Return......................... 264
      To the Top of a Page and Next Page 264

To Specific Lines and Page Numbers 264
To Named Lines 264
Erasing and Editing Text 267
Erasing and Editing: Characters and Words 267
Erasing and Editing: Lines, Sentences, Paragraphs,
and Groups of Words 267
The Erase Command and Key 268
Accelerator Keys for Deleting Text 269
Unerasing Text 269
Moving Text within the Same File 269
Copying Text within the Same File 272
Copying Text from One File to Another 274
Moving Text to a Document in Another File 278
Searching and Replacing 278
The Search Command 280
The Replace Command 281
Formatting Your Document 281
Setting Paragraph Justification 282
The Justification Settings 282
Automatic Justification 287
The Justify Command and Key 287
Setting Tabs, Spacing, and Margins 289
Controlling Page Length and Page Breaks 292
Indenting Sections and Varying Format within the Text 293
Creating, Editing, and Storing Format Lines 294
Integrating Symphony's DOC Window with Other Types 297
Chapter Summary 299

9 DOC Window Hands-On Practice 301

Creating a Document 301
Typing 301
Moving the Cursor 303
Correcting Mistakes 304
Formatting the Document 307
Changing the Format Settings 307
Using Print Attributes 308
Including a Spreadsheet in a Document 310
Entering Labels, Values, and Formulas 311
Formatting the Spreadsheet 313
Additional Editing and Formatting 314

Inserting Format Lines 314
Moving Text 315
Replacing Text 316
Chapter Summary 319

10 Word-Processing Add-Ins: Spelling Checker and Text Outliner 321

Spelling Checker 321
Attaching and Invoking the Speller 322
Spell-Checking a Document 323
Setting Spell-Check Options 324
Correcting Mistakes 324
The Correction Menu 325
Other Spelling Checker Menus 326
Auxiliary Dictionaries 327
Creating an Auxiliary Dictionary 328
The Maintenance Menu 328
Looking at an Auxiliary Dictionary 329
Settings Sheets 331
Spell-Checking a Spreadsheet 331
Text Outliner 332
Attaching and Invoking the Outliner 333
Creating an Outline 334
Inserting Headings 334
Moving around in an Outline 337
Displaying Outline Numbers 337
Hiding and Exposing Headings 337
Printing an Outline 339
Modifying an Outline 340
Editing Headings 341
Inserting Additional Headings 341
Removing Headings 342
Merging Outline Sections 343
Copying Outline Sections 345
Moving Outline Sections 345
Changing Levels 345
Formatting an Outline 347
Changing Indentation 349
Using an Outline To Create a Document 350

Switching between OUTLN and DOC 350
The Outline in the DOC Window 350
Removing Outline Numbers........................... 352
Outlining an Existing Document...................... 352
Printing an Outlined Document 354
Table of Contents 356
Chapter Summary 357

IV Creating Symphony Reports and Graphs

11 Printing Spreadsheets and Word-Processing Documents 361

SERVICES Configuration Printer and SERVICES Print 362
The Print Menu 363
When and How To Print 365
Printing to a File..................................... 365
Printing to a Range 365
Printing Reports: A Few Examples 366
Designating a Print Range 368
Setting Print Options 368
Setting Headers and Footers 369
Setting Margins 370
Repeating Labels on Multipage Printouts 372
Sending an Initialization String to the Printer 373
Setting the Page Length............................... 374
Printing Cell Formulas 374
Naming, Using, and Deleting Print Settings Sheets 375
Controlling the Printer 377
The Printed Results 378
Chapter Summary 381

12 Creating and Displaying Graphs **383**

SHEET and GRAPH Windows 383
Types of Graphs.. 384
  Simple Bar Graphs 385
    Making a Simple Bar Graph in a SHEET Window 385
      Selecting the Type of Graph 386
      Entering Data..................................... 386
      Choosing the Data Range 387
      Viewing the Graph 387
    Adding Titles and Labels 388
    Switching between 1st- and 2nd-Settings Sheets 390
    Changing the Automatic Scale Settings 390
      Overriding Automatic Scaling 391
      Formatting Numbers................................ 391
      Fitting the Graph to the Scales 392
      Changing to Nonzero Origin 393
      Using Other Scale Options 393
    Saving and Recalling Graph Settings................... 393
      Using Graph Settings Catalogs 394
      Deleting Graph Settings 395
      Resetting All the Current Graph Settings 396
      Resetting a Portion of the Current Graph Settings 396
    Saving Graphs for Printing 397
    Creating a More Complex Bar Graph 398
      Adding More Data Ranges 398
      Controlling Bar Graph Crosshatches 399
      Using Legends 401
      Displaying the Graph in Color 401
      Changing Colors in Bar Graphs 402
  Stacked-Bar Graphs................................... 403
  Line Graphs 404
    Controlling Lines and Symbols 408
    Using Data-Labels................................... 409
    Adding Grids.. 412
  Pie Charts... 412
    The Aspect Ratio 414
    Pie Chart Crosshatches.............................. 414
    Color in Pie Charts 416
    Exploded Pie Charts 417
  XY Graphs 417

High-Low-Close-Open Charts 419
Advanced Graphics Topics.................................. 421
  More on GRAPH Windows 422
    Using Current Graph Settings 422
    Changing from One GRAPH Window to Another 422
    Deleting a GRAPH Window 423
  "What If" Graphing 423
  The Draw Key.. 423
  Special Command Options 425
    Using Logarithmic Scale Override 425
    Changing the Y-Axis Scale Width 426
    Controlling Symphony's Automatic Scaling Labels 426
    Hiding Parts of a Graph 428
Chapter Summary 428

13 Printing Graphs 429

Access to the PrintGraph Program......................... 430
Configuration of PrintGraph 430
  Printer Selection 431
  Graph and Font Directories 432
  Specifying an Interface Card 432
  Configurations to Save and Reset 433
  The Image Settings.................................... 433
    Adjusting Graph Size and Orientation 433
    Choosing Fonts...................................... 433
    Choosing Range-Colors 433
    Choosing Page Size 437
  Selection of Files for Printing.......................... 437
Batch Printing 438
  Pause and Eject Options 438
  Align and Page Options................................. 438
Printing and Exiting 439
Chapter Summary 440

14 Creating and Printing Graphs: Hands-On Practice 441

Creating Graphs.. 441
  Creating a Bar Graph 442
  Creating a Pie Chart................................... 444

Working with Named Graphs 447
   Using a Graph 447
   Attaching a Graph.................................. 449
Printing Graphs 451
   Saving Graphs for Printing 451
   Using Default PrintGraph Settings 452
   Changing PrintGraph Settings...................... 453
Chapter Summary 454

V Data Management with Symphony

15 Data Management 459

Attention 1-2-3 Users 460
Database Fundamentals................................. 461
   Organization of a Database 461
   What You Can Do with a Database................... 462
The FORM Window for Creating Databases 462
   Building a Simple Input Form 463
   Using the FORM Generate Command................. 464
   Entering a Record.................................. 466
      Modifying the Current Record before Insertion......... 469
      Modifying Previous Records......................... 469
      Undoing Changes to a Record....................... 469
      Adding New Records 469
      Deleting Records 470
   Sorting the Database 470
   Working with the Settings Sheets 473
      Naming Settings Sheets.,.......................... 473
      Attaching Settings Sheets 474
      Creating a Catalog of Settings Sheets 474
   Searching for Records 474
      Using Formulas in Criteria 475
         Using AND to Combine Criteria 476
         Using OR to Combine Criteria 477
      Adding a Criterion Range.......................... 477
      Approximate Matching 479
      Using Wildcards 480
      Modifying and Deleting Records While Searching........ 480

Using Advanced FORM Features 481
   Creating Special Input Forms 481
   Modifying the Entry Range 481
   Changing Underscores 484
   Modifying the Definition Range 484
   Creating Defaults 485
   Computing Fields 486
   Transforming Fields 487
   Performing Edit Checks 488
   Performing Value Checks 489
   Changing Prompts 490
   Changing Formats 490
   Adding a Field to the Database 490
   Deleting a Field 491
   Using Multiple Input Forms 491
The SHEET Database Commands 491
  Query Record-Sort 492
  The Query Settings Sheet 492
  Ways of Searching for Records........................ 493
   Query Find 494
   Query Extract...................................... 496
   Query Unique...................................... 497
   Query Delete 498
  Query Parse 500
Database Statistical Functions 500
Database Reports 503
  Printing the Entire Database.......................... 503
   The Above Report Range 503
   The Main Report Range 503
  Directing the Report to the Printer 504
  Printing a Portion of a Database to a Range 505
  Creating Database Subtotals 505
   The Below Report Range 507
  Printing Mailing Labels 509
  Printing a Form Letter 510
Chapter Summary 513

16 Data Management Hands-On Practice 515

Creating the Database 515
    Viewing the Database Ranges 518
    Entering Formulas 519
    Entering Records 520
Maintaining the Database 520
    Sorting the Data 521
    Finding a Record 521
    Deleting a Record 523
    Editing a Record 523
Creating Reports 524
    Printing the Default Report 524
    Modifying the Report 525
Chapter Summary 527

VI Symphony Communications Module

17 Communications 531

Guidelines for Successful Communications 532
    Modems and Acoustic Couplers 532
    Asynchronous and Synchronous Transmission 532
    Protocol Methods 533
    Protocol Parameters 533
    Proper Driver Choice 534
Connection to a Bulletin Board System 534
    Changing the Default Settings 535
        The Interface Settings 536
        The Phone Settings 536
        The Terminal Settings 538
    Setting Up a Log-in Sequence 540
        Entering Send and Receive Strings 541
        The Maximum-Time Option 541
        The Repeat-Time Option 542
        Changing Handshaking Settings 543
    Starting Communications 543

Phoning 543
  Starting the Log-in Sequence 544
Copying to the Printer 544
Capturing Data in a Range 545
  Converting Numbers to a Usable Form 545
  Setting the Capture Range Column Widths 546
  Using Functions To Convert Data 547
  Using Query Parse 547
Saving Settings 548
Ending a Session 549
Communications with Another Microcomputer 549
Matching the Interface Settings 549
Making the Connection 549
Sending Messages 550
Sending Ranges 550
Transferring Files 551
Chapter Summary 552

18 Communications Hands-On Practice 553

Settings 554
  Modifying a Communications Configuration File 554
  Automating Your Log-in Sequence 556
Connecting with CompuServe 558
  Capturing Data in a Range 559
  Downloading a File 560
Chapter Summary 563

VII Symphony Macros and the Command Language

19 Creating and Using Macros 567

What Is a Macro? 567
The Elements of Macros 568
Creating Macros 568
  Learn Mode 571
  Function Key Grammar 572

Where To Put the Macros 572

Documenting Your Macros 573

Naming Macros 573

   Using **Range Name Create** 573

   Using **Range Name Labels Right** 575

Executing Macros 575

Automatic Macros 576

Debugging Macros....................................... 576

   Common Errors 577

   Stepping through a Buggy Macro...................... 578

Editing the Macro 579

Some Simple Macros..................................... 580

   Utility Macros for Any Environment 581

      Save Macros 581

      Print Macros 582

      An Autoexecuting Macro 582

   Macros in the SHEET Environment 583

      A Macro To Draw Horizontal Lines 583

      A Macro To Draw Vertical Lines 584

      A Macro To Sum a Column 584

      A Macro To Set Column Widths...................... 585

      A Data-Entry Macro 585

   Macros in the DOC Environment 585

      Letter-Transposition Macro 587

      Word-Transposition Macro........................... 587

      Paragraph-Moving Macro 587

      Paragraph-Erasing Macro............................ 588

      Memo Macro 588

   Spelling Checker Macros 588

   Macros in the GRAPH Environment 589

      Graph Preview Macro 590

      Choose-a-Graph Macro 590

      Graph-Printing Macro 590

   Macros in the COMM Environment 591

      Auto-Dialing Macro 592

      Hangup Macro 592

      Log-in Macro...................................... 592

      Capture Macros 593

   Macros for the FORM Environment 593

      Search Macros 593

      Sort Macro 594

The Macro Library Manager 595

   Accessing the Macro Library Manager 595

Creating a Macro Library in Hyperspace 596
Invoking Macros from the Library 596
Modifying a Library.................................... 597
Removing a Macro 598
Using Range Names and Cell Coordinates 598
Chapter Summary 599

20 Introduction to the Command Language 601

Why Use the Command Language? 601
What Is the Command Language? 602
    The Elements of Command Language Programs 603
    Command Language Syntax............................ 604
Creating, Using, and Debugging Command
Language Programs 604
The Command Language Commands........................ 606
    Commands for Accepting Input 606
        The {?} Command 606
        The GET Command................................. 607
        The GETLABEL Command 607
        The GETNUMBER Command......................... 609
        The LOOK Command 610
    Commands for Program Control 611
        The BRANCH Command 611
        The MENUBRANCH Command 614
        The MENUCALL Command 616
        The RETURN Command 617
        The QUIT Command................................. 618
        The ONERROR Command 619
        The BREAKOFF Command............................ 621
        The BREAKON Command 621
        The WAIT Command 621
        The DISPATCH Command 622
        The DEFINE Command............................. 623
        The RESTART Command 626
    Decision-Making Commands 627
        The IF Command.................................. 627
        The FOR Command................................. 629
        The FORBREAK Command 630
    Data Manipulation Commands 630
        The LET Command 630

The PUT Command 632

The CONTENTS Command 633

The BLANK Command 635

Program Enhancement Commands 635

The BEEP Command 636

The PANELOFF Command 637

The PANELON Command 637

The WINDOWSOFF Command 637

The WINDOWSON Command 639

The INDICATE Command 639

The RECALC and RECALCCOL Commands 639

The PHONE Command 641

The HANDSHAKE Command 642

File Manipulation Commands 642

The OPEN Command 643

The CLOSE Command 645

The READ Command 645

The READLN Command 647

The WRITE Command 647

The WRITELN Command 648

The SETPOS Command 648

The GETPOS Command 649

The FILESIZE Command 649

A Command Language Application 650

Other Command Language Programs 653

A Copy Program To Skip Columns or Rows 653

A Program To Image-Save a Series of Graphs 654

A Program To Auto-Dial 655

A Program To Redial 656

A Program To Create Entry Forms 656

Programs for Changing Default Values 658

Chapter Summary 658

Troubleshooting Section 661

Troubleshooting Installation 664

Problems with Drivers 664

Troubleshooting the Symphony Spreadsheet 668

Problems with Data Entry 668

Problems with Circular References 670

Avoiding ERR 674

Problems with Memory Management 677

Troubleshooting Symphony Commands 680

Problems with Range Names 680
Problems with Relative and Absolute Addressing 684
Problems with Recalculation 685
Miscellaneous Problems............................... 691
Troubleshooting Functions 693
Troubleshooting File Operations 698
Troubleshooting Windows................................. 703
Troubleshooting Word Processing 707
Troubleshooting Printing 712
Troubleshooting Graphing................................. 719
Troubleshooting Data Management 728
Troubleshooting Communications 732
Troubleshooting Macros................................... 735

A Installing Symphony 743

Installing Symphony on a Hard Disk 744
Creating a Symphony Subdirectory 744
Copying the Program Files 744
Using Symphony on a Floppy Disk System 745
Initializing Symphony 746
Making Working Copies of the Symphony Disks 746
Installing Drivers 746
Configuring the Printer and the Data Disk.................. 749
Preparing Data Disks..................................... 749

B Symphony Release 2.0: New Commands and Features 751

New Spreadsheet Commands 751
New Database Features 752
New Database Commands............................... 752
New Word-Processing Features 752
New Word-Processing Commands........................ 753
New Communications Features 754
New Communications Commands........................ 754
Other New Features 755
Macro Keynames....................................... 755
Translate Program..................................... 756

Index 757

Trademark Acknowledgments

Conventions Used in This Book

Using Symphony, 2nd Edition, uses several conventions to help you learn the program.

Boldface letters indicate that the word is a Symphony command and that you can select the command by typing the boldface letter after you have retrieved the appropriate menu. For example, SERVICES **W**indow **C**reate indicates that you retrieve the SERVICES menu, type w, and then type c to select this command.

Words printed in all capital letters signify the following:

Function keys for retrieving Symphony menus: ACCESS SYSTEM, SERVICES, TYPE, and MENU. (When the book refers to specific menus for spreadsheet, word processing, graphics, data form, or communications environments, then SHEET, DOC, GRAPH, FORM, and COMM are used.) For example, SHEET **E**rase indicates that you retrieve the spreadsheet menu and select the **E**rase command.

Mode indicators that appear on the screen in all capital letters are printed in all capital letters.

Range names, including those used for macros, appear in all capital letters.

In general, words appearing in all capital letters within the Symphony control panel are printed in all capital letters.

Function key names are used in the text with function key numbers appearing often in parentheses after the name. GoTo(F5), for example, indicates to press the GoTo key, which is F5 on the keyboard. Whenever the Symphony function requires that you press the Alt key and a function key simultaneously, the function key name is given, followed by the Alt and function key in parentheses—for example, Learn (Alt-F5).

Worksheet cell addresses are indicated as they are in the Symphony control panel; for example, A1..G5, or a range name (SALES).

Introduction

Symphony® is the exciting, fully integrated software package released by Lotus® Development Corporation, creators of the best-selling integrated software 1-2-3®. Symphony gives you not only the best of 1-2-3—the popular electronic spreadsheet, business graphics, and personal data management—but also word processing, data-form capability, and communications. Symphony's outstanding capability of integrating all applications makes this program one of the most powerful and sophisticated programs on the market. And with the latest Release (2.0), Symphony's word-processing and database modes are even easier to use.

Although 1-2-3 users will find Symphony similar to 1-2-3 in many ways, Symphony is much more versatile and more powerfully integrated than its forerunner. First, Symphony's word processor gives you the features of many stand-alone word-processing programs. Second, Symphony's full data-form capabilities go well beyond 1-2-3's data-management operations. And third, Symphony's communications program gives you complete flexibility to connect to time-sharing services and send or receive data to and from other microcomputers.

Using Symphony

With the added capabilities of Symphony comes complexity. Although learning how to use some of Symphony's individual applications may be easy, learning how to use Symphony's window feature, to integrate applications, and to take advantage of the program's special functions and Command Language can take months to master. Many users, therefore, may not be taking full advantage of the program.

Using Symphony, 2nd Edition, helps both the experienced 1-2-3 user and the new user of Lotus products to learn all of Symphony's powerful features. This

1

book explains Symphony's command menu system and special features in a clear, easy-to-understand style. You will particularly appreciate the detailed discussions of Symphony's word processing, data-form capability, communications, window capability, and Command Language. Your learning is made easy by numerous figures showing spreadsheets, word-processing text, databases, and graphs that illustrate command operations. Many examples of commands and functions will help you apply the program to your business problems.

Who Should Use This Book?

If you own Symphony, you should own this book. *Using Symphony*, 2nd Edition, picks up where the Symphony manual leaves off. This book explains both the basics and fine points of the program. Every chapter includes clear explanations and examples, and special care has been taken to cover in detail those topics that are not thoroughly explained in the Symphony manual. For example, many chapters give specific examples of how one of Symphony's features can be integrated with others. Chapter 15 demonstrates how you can use the full capabilities of Symphony's data-management function with the program's data form. And Chapters 19 and 20 cover Symphony's keyboard macro capabilities and Command Language by providing sample macros that you can create for each of Symphony's five applications.

If you do not own Symphony but are considering purchasing the program, this book is also for you. It will help you understand Symphony's unique features.

About This Book

Using Symphony, 2nd Edition, is divided into seven parts according to the structure of Symphony itself. The book also includes a Troubleshooting Section and two appendixes.

Part I: Understanding and Getting Started with Symphony

Chapter 1, "An Overview of Symphony," explains Symphony's basic concepts. This chapter describes in detail the five environments and their capabilities, and illustrates with a practical example how you can integrate the different applications.

Chapter 2, "Getting Started," covers the Symphony menu system, features of the display screen and keyboard, and the program's special window capability. Chapter 2 also discusses the exceptional Symphony tutorial and the program's help-screen facility.

Part II: Learning Symphony Worksheet Basics

Chapter 3, "The Symphony SHEET Window," introduces the foundation application of the program—the spreadsheet—and covers its size and memory capacity. If you are new to spreadsheet programs and to Lotus products, this chapter teaches you the fundamentals of entering data into the Symphony worksheet.

Chapter 4, "SHEET Window Commands," discusses the basic Symphony spreadsheet commands, including **Range**, **Copy**, **Move**, **Erase**, and **Format**.

Chapter 5, "@Functions," explains all of Symphony's sophisticated functions, including mathematical, trigonometric, statistical, financial, data-management, logical, and string functions. Particular attention is paid to Symphony's date and time arithmetic functions, functions that are used with the ASCII/LICS, and other special functions that give you information about the contents and locations of cells (or ranges) in the worksheet.

Chapter 6, "File Operations," covers the important commands for saving and retrieving files. The chapter also explains those commands you will use for file management, consolidating and merging worksheets, and transferring files.

Chapter 7, "SHEET Window Hands-On Practice," is the first of a series of hands-on practice chapters that provide you with practical experience in working with Symphony's various environments. Chapter 7 takes you step by step through procedures for developing, storing, retrieving, and expanding a simple spreadsheet.

Part III: Using the Symphony Word Processor

Chapter 8, "Word Processing: Working in a Symphony DOC Window," introduces you to Symphony's word-processing capabilities by explaining special features of the display screen, function keys for word processing, and keys used for cursor movement. The chapter also covers word-processing commands, showing how you use them for setting formats and editing your text.

Chapter 9, "DOC Window Hands-On Practice," gives you the opportunity to practice entering, editing, and formatting a document in Symphony's word-processing environment.

Chapter 10, "Word-Processing Add-Ins: Spelling Checker and Text Outliner," introduces you to two add-in applications that are included with Symphony Release 2.0. This chapter shows you how to use these applications to extend Symphony's word-processing capabilities.

Part IV: Creating Symphony Reports and Graphs

Chapter 11, "Printing Spreadsheets and Word-Processing Documents," introduces you to Symphony's printing commands, which are for printing reports generated from Symphony's spreadsheets and printing text created by Symphony's word-processor. Through examples of printed reports and a list of the print commands used for each, Chapter 11 shows you how to take advantage of Symphony's special print capabilities.

Chapters 12 and 13, respectively entitled "Creating and Displaying Graphs" and "Printing Graphs," cover in detail Symphony's graphics capabilities. Chapter 12 not only provides examples of all the types of graphs that you can create, but also explains how you can integrate Symphony's GRAPH window with the other features of the program. Chapter 13 describes how to use the PrintGraph program to print graphs. Examples help you to use the program's special settings.

Chapter 14, "Creating and Printing Graphs Hands-On Practice," gives you a chance to practice the commands and procedures you learned in Chapters 12 and 13.

Part V: Data Management with Symphony

Chapter 15, "Data Management," explains how you can use Symphony's full data-management capabilities by integrating the data-form features with the data-management commands and database statistical functions.

Chapter 16, "Data Management Hands-On Practice," takes you through the basics of generating a database; entering, sorting, and locating data; and producing reports.

Part VI: Symphony Communications Module

Chapter 17, "Communications," provides the guidelines for connecting with many kinds of computers. The chapter also explains how to access a bulletin board system and how to communicate with another person's microcomputer.

Chapter 18, "Communications Hands-On Practice," provides a practice session for using Symphony's communications capabilities. In this chapter, you connect with a popular time-sharing service called CompuServe Information Service.®

Part VII: Symphony Macros and the Command Language

Chapters 19 and 20, respectively entitled "Creating and Using Macros" and "An Introduction to the Command Language," go beyond the Symphony manual by presenting examples of macros that you can use with each of Symphony's five applications—spreadsheets, word processing, graphics, data management, and communications. Chapter 19 introduces you to the concept of macros by explaining how to create, use, and debug macros. Chapter 20 covers in depth the features of Symphony's special programming language—the Lotus Command Language.

The **Troubleshooting Section** that follows Chapter 20 can be a valuable resource for you. This section addresses many of the problems you may encounter while using Symphony, and offers a variety of solutions.

Using Symphony, 2nd Edition, also includes two appendixes. Appendix A will help you install Symphony, and Appendix B provides a thumbnail sketch of what commands and features are new with Symphony Release 2.0.

More Symphony Knowledge

Que produces additional publications that are excellent companions to *Using Symphony*, 2nd Edition. *Symphony Macros and the Command Language* provides in-depth coverage of Symphony's macro capabilities and the Lotus Command Language. *Absolute Reference*, Que's monthly journal for Symphony and 1-2-3 users, provides up-to-date Symphony and 1-2-3 applications, tips, and macros, as well as product reviews from readers and industry experts.

For more on each of these titles, see the product information in the back of this book. If you own Symphony, you should also own these books.

PART I

Understanding and Getting Started with Symphony

Includes

An Overview of Symphony

Getting Started

1

An Overview of Symphony

What Is Symphony?

Symphony is an expansion of 1-2-3, the popular integrated spreadsheet program from Lotus Development Corporation. To 1-2-3's three business applications programs—electronic spreadsheet, business graphics, and data management—Symphony adds word-processing, data-form, and communications capabilities. Symphony makes all these expanded applications available in one sophisticated program.

Symphony is an impressive integration of five microcomputer software applications: spreadsheet, word processing, graphics, data management, and communications. All five of these environments are available as soon as you access the program, and they are identified on the screen as the types of windows in which you can work.

Symphony's exciting window feature enables you to create bordered areas on the screen and to perform different applications within these areas with a great deal of flexibility (see fig. 1.1). You can create a spreadsheet in one window, word-processing text in another window, a database in a third window, and a graph in a fourth window. At the same time in a fifth window, you can receive data from another computer or send data to that computer. You can make these different windows appear on the screen simultaneously. (Whether graphs will appear on the screen with other applications depends on your equipment.) Or you can use the full screen area to work on one application and then, by pressing one key, retrieve any other window you have created in the worksheet.

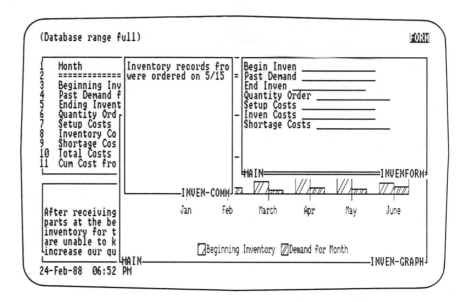

Fig. 1.1

*An example of
Symphony's
window feature.*

The five Symphony environments include the following features:

1. In the SHEET window, you can create numerous kinds of spreadsheets by using Symphony's incredibly large worksheet area (256 by 8,192 cells), sophisticated SHEET command menu, and many functions.

2. In the DOC window, you can draft, revise, and edit documents through Symphony's word-processing capability.

3. In the GRAPH window, you can create and save graphs, display them in color (with the right kind of equipment), and also display them on the screen with other applications, such as spreadsheets, databases, and word-processing text.

4. In the FORM window, you can create a data form, generate a database, and perform sort and query operations.

5. In the COMM window, you can send and receive data through telecommunications lines.

Each of the five Symphony environments, used singly, is an extremely potent tool. Symphony's real power, however, is best illustrated by the program's capability to integrate applications. If you use Symphony to create a spreadsheet and then retrieve the spreadsheet, create a new window, and build a graph on the screen while your spreadsheet still displays, you are using Symphony's integrative power. Whenever you create a database and then use it on the screen to help you compose an important report, you are also using Symphony's integrative power. And if you use Symphony's communications environment to receive on-line data, transfer it into a spreadsheet, graph the information to help you analyze it, then use both the spreadsheet and the graph to prepare a report, you are taking further advantage of Symphony's capability to integrate.

The best way to introduce you to Symphony is to present a simple example showing how you can use and then coordinate four of the environments (data management, spreadsheet, graphics, and word processing).

Let's suppose that you want to use Symphony at home to maintain a record of payments you have made on household bills. You can begin by creating a data form like the one in figure 1.2, which was made in Symphony's FORM environment. In this environment, you can create a data form and then enter records into it. From the information you supply in the form and from the records themselves, Symphony creates a database similar to that in figure 1.3.

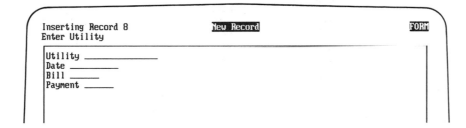

Fig. 1.2

A data form.

Fig. 1.3

A database created from a form.

Now suppose that you want to find out how much your gas bills increased during the fall and winter months of 1988-89 over the previous year's bills. Using Symphony's spreadsheet feature (referred to as SHEET in the top right corner of the screen), you can view a database that includes only gas utility costs (see fig. 1.4). Such a database, although originating from records entered in a FORM environment, can be changed within a SHEET environment by using Symphony's Query commands. The database in figure 1.4 was created from the larger database in figure 1.3, which contains not only gas but also electric, water, and telephone utility costs.

Fig. 1.4

Viewing a database in the SHEET environment.

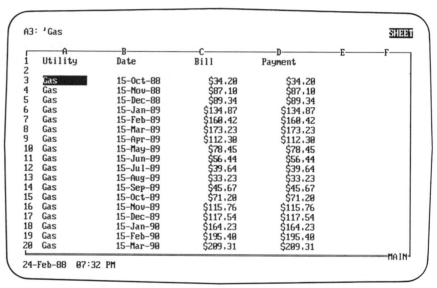

```
A3: 'Gas                                                          SHEET

     ─A────────B─────────C─────────D────────E───────F─
  1  Utility   Date        Bill       Payment
  2
  3  Gas       15-Oct-88      $34.20       $34.20
  4  Gas       15-Nov-88      $87.10       $87.10
  5  Gas       15-Dec-88      $89.34       $89.34
  6  Gas       15-Jan-89     $134.87      $134.87
  7  Gas       15-Feb-89     $160.42      $160.42
  8  Gas       15-Mar-89     $173.23      $173.23
  9  Gas       15-Apr-89     $112.30      $112.30
 10  Gas       15-May-89      $78.45       $78.45
 11  Gas       15-Jun-89      $56.44       $56.44
 12  Gas       15-Jul-89      $39.64       $39.64
 13  Gas       15-Aug-89      $33.23       $33.23
 14  Gas       15-Sep-89      $45.67       $45.67
 15  Gas       15-Oct-89      $71.20       $71.20
 16  Gas       15-Nov-89     $115.76      $115.76
 17  Gas       15-Dec-89     $117.54      $117.54
 18  Gas       15-Jan-90     $164.23      $164.23
 19  Gas       15-Feb-90     $195.40      $195.40
 20  Gas       15-Mar-90     $209.31      $209.31
                                                          MAIN
  24-Feb-88   07:32 PM
```

When you shift from Symphony's FORM environment to the SHEET environment, you can perform data query and sort operations on the database that was created in the FORM environment. You can also apply to the database the same functions used to create spreadsheets. For example, Symphony's spreadsheet environment allows the formatting of columns in your database and the adjusting of column width. Sorting the database, extracting certain categories (or fields), changing the format of values, and changing column width are all operations provided by Symphony's spreadsheet function.

The database of gas costs in figure 1.4 provides a much better idea of how your gas bills have increased than does the database in figure 1.3. But Symphony's GRAPH environment enables you to view quickly the relationship of gas costs for the fall and winter of 1988-89 to costs for the fall and winter of 1989-90. Using the values in the "Gas Costs" database, Symphony created the graph shown in figure 1.5. As the graph indicates, your gas costs are steadily and significantly increasing.

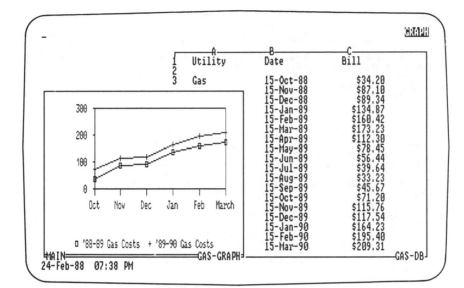

Fig. 1.5

Creating a graph from a database.

Now let's assume that your discovery of this steady increase prompts you to write a letter to your state's public service commission to voice your concern about rising utility rates. While leaving both your database and graph on the screen, you can write your letter and even include with it a copy of the database that emphasizes so dramatically how much gas costs have increased (see figs. 1.6 and 1.7). And to make your point even more emphatic, you can attach to the letter a printing of the graph pictured in figure 1.8.

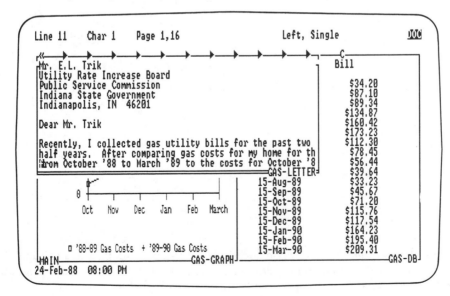

Fig. 1.6

Three windows displayed on-screen simultaneously.

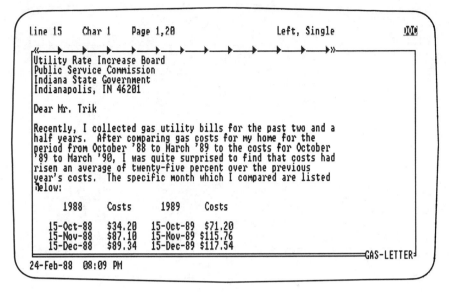

Fig. 1.7

Incorporating database material in a word-processing document.

```
Line 15     Char 1     Page 1,20              Left, Single           DOC
«———►——►——►——►——►——►——►——►——►——►——►——►——»
Utility Rate Increase Board
Public Service Commission
Indiana State Government
Indianapolis, IN 46201

Dear Mr. Trik

Recently, I collected gas utility bills for the past two and a
half years.  After comparing gas costs for my home for the
period from October '88 to March '89 to the costs for October
'89 to March '90, I was quite surprised to find that costs had
risen an average of twenty-five percent over the previous
year's costs.  The specific month which I compared are listed
below:

        1988     Costs     1989     Costs

     15-Oct-88   $34.20   15-Oct-89   $71.20
     15-Nov-88   $87.10   15-Nov-89  $115.76
     15-Dec-88   $89.34   15-Dec-89  $117.54
                                                    GAS-LETTER
24-Feb-88   08:09 PM
```

Fig. 1.8

A printed graph.

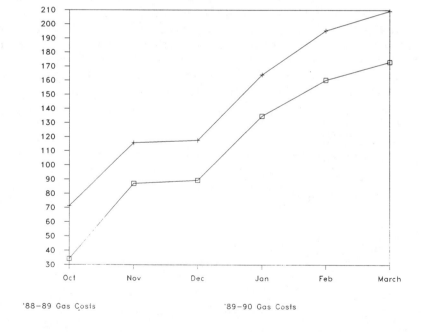

'88–89 Gas Costs   '89–90 Gas Costs

If this simple example hasn't convinced you of Symphony's power and capabilities, read on. The following sections, containing background to the program and an introduction to Symphony's features, provide further evidence.

Symphony at a Glance

Symphony requires 384K of memory, or 512K when you use the Spelling Checker. To take full advantage of Symphony's capabilities, you need equipment for displaying graphs, for displaying text and graphs on the screen at the same time, and for using Symphony's communications feature. Table 1.1 provides a summary of the system requirements.

Table 1.1
Symphony at a Glance

Published by:	Lotus Development Corporation 55 Cambridge Parkway Cambridge, Massachusetts 02142
System requirements:	*Computer:* IBM® PC, IBM PC XT™, IBM AT, IBM Portable, IBM PS/2, COMPAQ® Portable, COMPAQ Plus, and other IBM-compatibles
	Display: color or monochrome
	Minimum disk capacity: one double-density, double-sided disk drive
	Memory size: 384K; 512K when used with Spelling Checker
	Operating system: PC DOS V2.0, V2.1, V3.0, V3.1, V3.2, V3.3; OS/2 V1.0
	Optional hardware: color/graphics adapter, printer, plotter, modem or acoustic coupler, additional monitor, add-on memory board, and expanded memory board
Price:	$695

Appendix A includes the procedure for installing your Symphony disks so that they can operate with your equipment. Before you begin this installation procedure, though, keep these points in mind: You can use Symphony only with DOS versions 2.0, 2.1, and later and with OS/2 1.0 and later. If you want to display graphs on the screen simultaneously with other environments—such as spreadsheets, databases, and word-processing text—you need to check the equipment requirements listed within the Symphony Install program.

Symphony's Capabilities

As mentioned previously, Symphony is an integrated collection of five micro-computer software applications: spreadsheet, word processing, data management, graphics, and communications. These applications are combined with the additional features of windows and a programming language called the Lotus Command Language.

The Spreadsheet

Symphony's spreadsheet component is the most powerful of its features. The spreadsheet environment is an electronic replacement for the traditional financial modeling tools: the accountant's columnar pad, pencil, and calculator. In some ways spreadsheet programs are to these tools what word processors are to typewriters. Spreadsheets offer dramatic improvements in creating, editing, and using financial models.

The typical electronic spreadsheet configures the memory of a computer to resemble an accountant's columnar pad. Because this "pad" exists in the dynamic world of the computer's memory, the pad is different from paper pads in some important ways. For one thing, electronic spreadsheets are much larger than their paper counterparts. Symphony has 8,192 rows and 256 columns.

Each row in Symphony's spreadsheet environment is assigned a number, and each column is assigned a letter or a combination of letters. The intersections of the rows and columns are called cells, which are identified by their row-column coordinates. For example, the cell located at the intersection of column A and row 15 is called A15. The cell at the intersection of column X and row 55 is called X55. You can fill these cells with three kinds of information: numbers; mathematical formulas, as well as special spreadsheet functions; and text (or labels).

A cell pointer allows you to write information into the cells in much the same way that a pencil lets you write on a piece of paper. In the Symphony spreadsheet environment, the cell pointer looks like a bright rectangle on the computer's screen. Typically, the cell pointer is one row high and one column wide.

Because the Symphony grid is so large, you cannot view the entire spreadsheet on the screen at one time. The screen thus serves as a "window" on the worksheet. As mentioned at the beginning of this chapter, this window can contain within it other windows. To view other parts of the sheet, you can scroll across the worksheet with the cursor-movement keys; or if you have created multiple windows on the worksheet, you can retrieve another window to take you to that part of the worksheet. In Symphony, you can create different windows in the worksheet area, all containing different applications, such as word processing and data management.

The spreadsheet feature is the foundation of the program. For example, when you are working in a word-processing (DOC) window or data form (FORM) window, all data is entered and stored within the worksheet boundaries. Because of this setup, entries and changes in a DOC or FORM window can affect a spreadsheet entered on the same worksheet.

To understand this concept, you might imagine a large grid containing 256 columns across the top and 8,192 rows along the side—which is the size of the Symphony worksheet. Then imagine various work areas that you have created on this worksheet (see fig. 1.9). In the upper left corner of the worksheet is a balance sheet. Directly to the right of the balance sheet is a database (created either by you or by Symphony through its FORM capability). Then below the balance sheet are a few of your notes—important points relating to the information in the balance sheet or database.

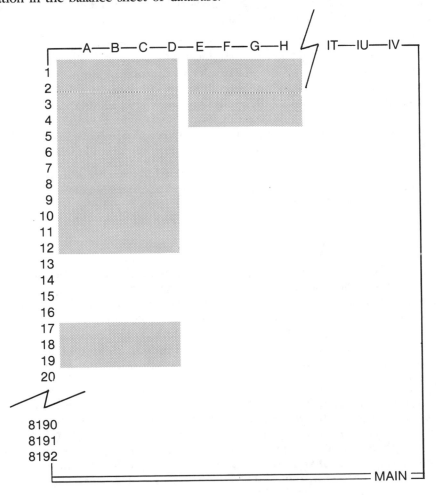

Fig. 1.9
Symphony's worksheet area.

Furthermore, to prevent one range of data from affecting another, you can restrict each work area or window so that the cell pointer doesn't move outside the window and so that some command operations affect data only within the restricted area.

Symphony's window feature makes it possible for you to create a spreadsheet, a database, and word-processing text on the same worksheet within the worksheet's 256 by 8,192 boundaries. How much of this worksheet area you can use and how far apart you can keep one application from another depend on your machine's memory. (Chapter 3 provides a discussion of Symphony's SHEET window and its effect on random access memory.)

Releases 1.1, 1.2, and 2.0 support the new Lotus/Intel/Microsoft® Expanded Memory Specification (EMS) that allows you to use up to four megabytes of memory. If you add to your system a memory board that meets the EMS, your worksheets can hold much more data.

Symphony incorporates numerous functions and commands. For instance, Symphony contains statistical and date functions and offers a wide variety of formats for numeric entries. These formats also let you display or print numbers with embedded commas, dollar signs, parentheses, and percent signs. You can also specify the exact number of digits that will be displayed to the right of the decimal. For example, Symphony can format the number 12345 to look like $12,345.00, 12,345, 1.23E3, or 12345. You can have the number -12345 appear as ($12,345.00) or -12,345. And the number .45 can look like 45% or $.45.

Symphony provides the full range of commands for entering and changing individual cells and ranges, adjusting columns and rows, creating and using range names, and recalculating a worksheet (see Chapters 3 and 4).

Playing "What If . . . ?"

The act of building a model on a spreadsheet establishes all the mathematical relationships in the model. Until you decide to make changes, every sum, product, division, subtraction, average, and net present value remains the same. Each time you enter data into the model, computations are calculated at your command with no effort on your part. All these computations are calculated correctly; spreadsheets don't make math errors. And next month, when you decide to use the same model again, the formulas will still be set, ready to calculate at your command.

Even more important, spreadsheet software allows you to play "What if . . . ?" with your model, particularly when you use Symphony's command, function, and graphics capabilities. Once you have built a set of mathematical relationships into the sheet, Symphony can recalculate it with amazing speed, using different sets of assumptions. If you use only paper, a pencil, and a calculator to build a model, every change to the model requires recalculating every relationship in it. If the model has 100 formulas and you change the first one, you must make 100 calculations by hand to flow the change through the entire model. If, on the other hand, you use a spreadsheet, the same change requires the press of only a few keys—the program does the rest. This capability permits extensive "what if" analysis.

Two specific parts of the Symphony program that allow you easily to perform "what if" analysis are the "what if" graphing capability and the SHEET Range What-If command. Symphony's graphics can be an integral part of "what if" analysis by enabling you to fine-tune projections, budgets, or projects. Symphony's GRAPH window helps you understand the impact on your model of changes in your data. For example, you can create one window to display spreadsheet data and another window to display a related graph. You can then display both windows simultaneously on the screen. When you make a change in the data, the GRAPH window immediately reflects the change.

Symphony's SHEET Range What-If command, on the other hand, enables you to conduct extensive sensitivity analysis and to display the results in a tabular form. The SHEET Range What-If command lets you do the kind of thorough analysis that you might not do otherwise, given the time required to perform the analysis.

These are only two examples of how Symphony can help you with "what if" analysis. As you use the program, you will find numerous ways for conducting sophisticated "what if" analysis through the power of Symphony's functions and Command Language.

Data Management

The integration capability of Symphony, which was mentioned earlier, allows you to perform database operations within the program's spreadsheet environment. Some of the tasks you will want to perform on a Symphony database can be accomplished with the Symphony SHEET commands. For instance, you can add records to a database with the SHEET Insert Rows command. Editing the contents of a database is like editing the contents of any other cell in the worksheet.

In Symphony, you can also sort data. You have three options for sorts: primary key, secondary key, or third-order key. You can conduct a sort in ascending or descending order by using alphabetical or numeric keys. In addition, Symphony allows you to perform various kinds of mathematical analyses on a field of data over a specified range of records. For example, you can count the number of items in a database that match a set of criteria; compute a mean, variance, or standard deviation; and find the maximum or minimum value in the range.

The full power of Symphony's data-management capabilities is especially evident when you make use of the data-form environment (FORM window), the data-management commands included in Symphony's spreadsheet menu, and the database statistical functions.

With its data-management capabilities, Symphony can handle many chores for you, such as setting up database ranges, criterion ranges, and output ranges. When you work in a FORM window, much work is done for you by the program itself.

While you are in a FORM window, you rarely see the entire database at one time. You view the records through a special data form that you build with Symphony's help. To create a data form, such as the one shown earlier in the chapter, begin in a SHEET or DOC window and enter the field names you want in your form. After you enter the field names, shift to a FORM window to have Symphony generate an actual data form and then to begin entering records in the form. (The specific procedures for creating and using a data form are covered in Chapter 15.)

After you enter records into your data form, you can use the data commands in the FORM menu to perform data sort operations. You can also sort records by using the SHEET environment. In fact, when you switch from a FORM window to a SHEET window, Symphony provides a number of data-management operations that you can use on the database you have created. In a spreadsheet environment, for example, you can have Symphony (1) find records that match the given criteria, (2) copy to a specified area of the worksheet all or some of the records in certain fields that match given criteria, and (3) delete records in a database. In a SHEET environment, you can also change the column width of columns in the database, change the format of values, and insert or delete columns or rows.

After you begin using Symphony's data-management operations, you will find how high-powered they are.

Creating Graphs

You can create graphs in two parts of the program. You will find graph commands in Symphony's spreadsheet menu and also in the GRAPH environment of the program.

Symphony is capable of creating bar, stacked-bar, line, scatter, and pie (including exploded pie) graphs and high-low-close-open charts. The exploded pie graph is like a standard pie graph, except that one or more of the slices are separated from the pie for emphasis. High-low-close-open charts are useful for graphing the prices of stocks over time and for evaluating trends.

Other graphics features in Symphony include cross-hatchings, nonzero origins, logarithmic graph scales, and allowing you to control scaling factors manually.

With the right equipment and the correct driver set, you can display both the graph and the spreadsheet on-screen at the same time. If your system cannot display the graph and spreadsheet simultaneously, you can shift back and forth between the spreadsheet and the graph by pressing one key repeatedly.

Word Processing

When you use Symphony's DOC environment, you have the full range of commands and operations that are included in sophisticated stand-alone word-processing programs. And when you use Symphony's Command Language to create macros for simplifying word-processing operations, you will find that the word processor is not only easy to use but also very powerful.

Symphony's word processor provides a number of capabilities. You can move the cursor forward or backward character by character, word by word, or from the beginning to the end (and vice versa) of a line, paragraph, or page. In addition, Symphony enables you to move the cursor to any character by pressing the End key and then pressing that character. Furthermore, a command for naming lines in your text allows you to use Symphony's GoTo key for moving quickly from any location in your text to the named line.

Besides being able to move the cursor in various ways, you can also regulate and change the format of your text. You can set and store configuration settings for margins, spacing, tabs, and paragraph justification. When you store these settings in Symphony's configuration file (see the section on Configuration in Chapter 2), the margins, spacing, tabs, and paragraph justification are automatically set for your text every time you begin a new word-processing session.

If you want to change these configuration settings temporarily for a particular document, you can use Symphony's DOC Format Settings command. And if you need to change format in the middle of a document, Symphony's format lines enable you to change margins, spacing, paragraph justification, and tabs for only one section, then return to the original settings for your document.

Symphony's word processor also includes complete editing and revising capabilities. With Symphony's Erase command or Erase key (a special function key for initiating erase operations), you can erase any number of characters, from single characters to large blocks of text. Symphony makes possible the marking and erasing of large blocks of text with a couple of keystrokes. And when you create macros for erase operations, the number of keystrokes is reduced to one. (See Chapter 19 for more information on creating word-processing macros.)

In addition, Symphony's Search and Replace commands can help you edit text. When you use Search, you can search either forward or backward and easily exit from the search at any time. Although the Replace command performs only forward search-and-replace operations, you can incorporate this command with a macro that automatically moves the cursor to the top of your file to begin a search. (See Chapter 19 for more information on macros.)

For composing and revising, you can use Symphony's Copy, Move, File Xtract, and File Combine commands to create form letters, combine parts of one document with another, and reorganize sections of text.

Symphony's DOC environment is an integral part of the program for many reasons. First, using Symphony's word-processing environment is similar to using the other program applications—spreadsheet, graphics, data management, and communications. Second, you can easily integrate a DOC window with other types of windows. Being able to display a SHEET or GRAPH window along with a DOC window can help you to draft certain kinds of reports. In addition, you can readily incorporate parts of spreadsheets and databases into your text and have your text printed with tables or figures inserted right where you want them.

Beginning with Release 2.0, Symphony includes two word-processing add-in applications: Spelling Checker and Text Outliner. When the Spelling Checker is attached, you can check your documents for spelling errors and typing mistakes. An additional option appears on the DOC menu: Verify. When the Text Outliner is attached, you can use the OUTLN window type to create and edit text outlines.

Communications

Symphony's communications capability (COMM environment/ window) is quite sophisticated, rivaling that of many stand-alone packages. With Symphony, you can use your personal computer to receive database information from a corporate mainframe computer or minicomputer. You can also connect to a time-sharing service to get current news, stocks, weather, and other information. Finally, Symphony's communications capability enables you to exchange information with another microcomputer. You can even connect with many different kinds of computers.

Symphony supports asynchronous communications transmission and several types of protocol for file transfer. With asynchronous transmission, a clock in the computer is used to time the sampling of incoming data and the recording of the number of bits in each sample. You specify the transmission speed (the baud rate or bits per second) for the clock. Protocol, a special system of rules established for exchanging information between computers, is specified during installation. You can select from three different types: XMODEM, BLAST, or B Protocol. XMODEM, developed by Ward Christensen, has become a standard in the microcomputer industry for communications protocols. BLAST (Blocked Asynchronous Transmission) is used on some large systems, while B Protocol can be used to communicate with CompuServe Executive Information Service.

Like other Symphony environments, the communications environment enables you to enter settings for a specific COMM window in the Settings selection from the COMM menu. In the COMM Settings sheet, for example, you enter such settings as the protocol parameters: baud rate, byte length, stop bits, and parity. Included in the COMM Settings sheet are also selections for automatic dialing (if your modem has an auto-dial feature) and settings for matching the characteristics of the COMM window you are using with the service or computer you are calling.

Available through CompuServe, the time-sharing service, is a source of information called "The World of Lotus." When you access CompuServe's Executive Information Service (EIS), you can receive messages from Lotus Development. These messages may contain, for example, information on Symphony product services, tips and techniques for Symphony users, a Symphony user newsletter, and a library of Command Language programs, worksheet models, and add-in applications. In addition, you can send and receive messages to and from other Symphony users.

When you mail in the CompuServe card included in your Symphony package, you will receive a list of CompuServe's services and one hour of free connect time. This on-line time will give you an introduction to The World of Lotus. One other benefit is that the free on-line time will give you a chance to try out Symphony's COMM environment.

Window Features

As indicated at the beginning of this chapter, with Symphony's window capability you can move among any of the five applications (spreadsheet, word processing, data management, graphics, and communications) and view different parts of the same worksheet. In other words, you can create and work within multiple windows on a single screen.

Symphony keeps track of the windows you create by labeling each one with a name that either you assign or Symphony assigns automatically. And whenever you are working in a particular window, it is bordered at the bottom with a double line. The double line tells you that the window is the currently "active" window—the one in which you can perform command operations, enter data, and make changes.

The Window command menu and special window function keys enable you to change the type of window, create new windows, change the size and shape of windows, and split a window horizontally and vertically. You can also restrict a window to a specific range in the worksheet so that data you enter and changes you make won't interfere with data entered in other windows on the worksheet.

As mentioned earlier, you can organize a single worksheet into different parts, or applications, by creating multiple windows of different types. And if you store the worksheet with the SERVICES File Save command, these different windows are stored in one file.

Once you begin using Symphony's window features, you will discover unlimited possibilities for integrating various types of windows on one screen. Creating windows allows you, for example, to compare and analyze spreadsheet data from different areas of the worksheet. You can also write memos and short reports while you view spreadsheets and databases. And you can see data displayed in graphs and modify those graphs as you change the data.

Command Menu System

When you access Symphony through the Access System, the first menu to appear is the Access System menu, which provides options for starting Symphony, the Tutorial, PrintGraph, Install, and File Translate.

Seven command menus are also available. These menus include (1) a SERVICES menu for global operations such as File Save, Retrieve, and Erase, (2) a TYPE menu for changing the type of window you are working in (SHEET, DOC, GRAPH, FORM, and COMM), (3) a SHEET menu for spreadsheet work, (4) a DOC menu for word processing, (5) a GRAPH menu for graphics, (6) a FORM menu for data-form operations, and (7) a COMM menu for communications. If the Text Outliner application is attached, an OUTLN menu is also available.

Many of Symphony's command menus are multilevel (menus within menus). After you select a choice from a menu, Symphony, if it needs more information, provides you with another menu from which to choose.

Settings Sheets

In the seven Symphony menus listed, you will find settings sheets. Except for the DOC menu, all command menus contain settings sheets at the first level. These settings sheets enable you to enter settings for such operations as creating graphs, printing reports and documents, or using Symphony's communications capability.

Symphony displays multiple settings on a single screen. This feature is helpful when you need to remember special print or graph settings. Another advantage of settings sheets is that you can create a catalog of some types of sheets and retrieve these types when needed. To store and reuse a settings sheet, you must assign a name that Symphony will attach to the sheet.

Functions

Symphony includes a wide assortment of built-in mathematical, statistical, financial, logical, date, time, and string functions. In addition, a set of special functions is available that gives you detailed information about the contents of cells (or ranges) and their locations in a spreadsheet. In Chapter 5 you will find a detailed explanation of all the Symphony functions. Here, however, is a brief introduction.

Symphony has a variety of string functions that give you significantly more power to manipulate strings than do earlier integrated packages. The @FIND function, for example, allows you to locate the starting position of one string within another string. The @MID, @LEFT, and @RIGHT functions let you extract one string from another. You can use these string functions, only a few of the many functions available in Symphony, to increase the power of Symphony's database and Command Language capabilities.

The date and time functions in Symphony include @DATEVALUE, @NOW, @TIME, and @TIMEVALUE. @DATEVALUE, a variant of the @DATE function, accepts a date-string rather than a numeric argument. With @DATEVALUE, you can enter @DATEVALUE("6/21/88"), and the function produces a serial number, just as @DATE does when you enter @DATE(88,6,21). The @TIME function arrives at a serial number for a specified time of day that you enter in numeric arguments: @TIME(3,12,30). @TIMEVALUE, on the other hand, uses string arguments to produce a serial number from the information you provide for the hour, minute, and second: @TIMEVALUE("12:30:59").

The special functions in Symphony include @CELL, @CELLPOINTER, @ROWS, @COLS, @TRUE, and @FALSE. All of these provide information about the contents of cells or ranges and their locations in a spreadsheet. For example, if you enter @CELL("width",B12..B12), Symphony returns the width of column B as viewed in the current window. In addition to indicating width, the @CELL function can indicate the address of a cell, the type of value, the label prefix, the format, and the row or column number location. (See Chapter 5 for a listing of the special functions' capabilities.)

Symphony offers a comprehensive set of built-in functions. And when you use these functions with Symphony's Command Language, you will have the ingredients of a sophisticated programming language.

International Formats and Character Set

One other special feature of Symphony is the availability of international formats and an international character set. First, through the configuration settings, you have the options of changing **Currency**, **Date**, and **Time** formats to international formats. The **Currency** option, for example, enables you to change the default dollar sign ($) to a foreign currency sign, such as the British pound (£), if you are going to use that format regularly throughout your worksheet. Second, the international character set, referred to as the Lotus International Character Set (LICS), provides characters from many languages. You can enter these characters at any keyboard. In Symphony's *Reference Manual*, you will find a complete list of international and special characters available in LICS.

Security System

Symphony lets you protect cells in a worksheet so that changes cannot be made in cells containing, for example, important formulas. Symphony's range protection capability, however, also extends to protecting a section of word-processing text in a DOC window. In addition, you can use a special password security system to lock an entire worksheet or range of cells.

Whenever you protect an area of your worksheet, whether the area is part of a spreadsheet or part of word-processing text, you use two commands: Symphony's SERVICES Settings Global-Protection command and the SHEET Range Protect command. These two commands, which enable you to protect a range of cells, prevent users from erasing, moving, or changing the cells, although the cell contents are displayed on the screen. If you want not only to protect cell contents from being changed but also to keep them from being displayed on the screen, you can use the two commands mentioned previously along with the SHEET Format Other Hidden command. (See Chapter 4 for details on protecting a range in the worksheet.)

In addition to the range protection capability, Symphony enables you to "lock" an entire worksheet or range of cells. With Symphony's security system, you create a password for locking and unlocking the worksheet. Only by using the password can a user make changes or even see cell contents.

The last form of security that Symphony provides is the ability to password-protect a file when you save it. This system prohibits anyone even from retrieving the worksheet without the password.

To use the security system, you must select a number of commands in a specific order. The commands and steps for locking a worksheet are provided in table 1.2.

After you have completed the first four steps listed in table 1.2, they will have certain effects on your worksheet. A user cannot change the cell protection setting that you entered in SHEET Range Protect. The SERVICES Settings Global-Protection setting also cannot be changed. Finally, a user cannot redisplay "hidden" cells. With the security system, cell contents do not appear either in the worksheet or in the control panel. If you choose to File Save the file with a password, a user who doesn't know the password cannot retrieve the file. When you do a File Retrieve of a file that has been saved with a password, Symphony prompts you to enter the password.

Whenever you want to unlock a worksheet that you have locked, retrieve the worksheet and select SERVICES Settings Security Unlock. At the Password prompt, enter your password. As long as you enter the password in the exact form in which you created it, you can control any of the settings that were previously frozen.

Symphony's security system goes beyond simply protecting ranges. With the security system, you can not only protect ranges from change but also prevent users from viewing important data or even from retrieving a worksheet.

The Command Language and Macros

Symphony provides not only a keyboard macro capability but also a sophisticated programming language. The Symphony Command Language is the programming

Table 1.2
Steps for Using the Security System

1. Turn on global protection (SERVICES Settings Global-Protection **Yes**) and set SHEET Range **P**rotect.

2. Hide cells from being displayed on the screen by selecting **Format Other Hidden** from the SHEET menu. This command applies to cell entries that you made in a SHEET environment, so don't use **Format Other Hidden** with entries made in a DOC or FORM environment.

3. Once you go through the steps for locking a worksheet, you can unlock it only with the password you have created. You may therefore want to create a backup file of your worksheet at this point, in case you forget the password. To create a backup, save your worksheet under a file name different from the one containing the security system.

4. Lock the worksheet by selecting the SERVICES Settings Security Lock command. Enter a password when the `Password` prompt appears. Before pressing Enter, write down the password and check the spelling closely. To unlock a worksheet, you must enter the password exactly as you originally created it, including upper- and lowercase letters. Symphony accepts a password only in the exact upper- or lowercase specified. For example, if you create the password *MYBUDGET*, Symphony will not retrieve the file if you enter the password as *mybudget* or *MYbudget*.

5. You can further protect the worksheet by saving it with a password. Select SERVICES File Save, type a **P** (at least one space after the specified file name), and press Enter. Symphony prompts you for a password and, after you press Enter, prompts you to verify the password by typing it again.

language available to you for automating repetitive keyboard tasks.

The Symphony Command Language contains a nearly full-featured programming language, including the capability to call subroutines, iterative looping, improved conditional logic, and error trapping. Through these tools, you can develop special applications programs to run using Symphony.

Another feature of Symphony's Command Language is the program's capability to store commands automatically. With Symphony's Learn mode, you can easily create keyboard macros that are usable with little or no editing. When you use the Learn mode, Symphony converts into Command Language statements the commands and keystrokes you enter and then stores the statements in a special worksheet range that you set. Through a name that you assign to this range of statements, you can invoke the macro to simplify an operation.

If you want to go beyond the Learn mode capability and build your own macros to perform many types of complex operations, Symphony's Command Language enables you to do so. These commands do not simply duplicate keystrokes, as does creating a macro with the Learn mode. The Command Language allows you to program, which is much like using a programming language such as BASIC.

Symphony's Command Language has its own special grammar and set of keywords. For example, if you want to enter a command in your macro to cause it to stop processing temporarily so that you can enter a label, you use the following:

{GETLABEL "Enter label: ",FIRST FIELD}

GETLABEL is one of the Command Language's keywords. The items that come after the keyword are examples of arguments that you include in Command Language statements. (For a detailed look at Symphony's Command Language, see Chapter 20.)

Symphony can place macros into separate macro libraries that you can call from any worksheet. These libraries load into a separate area of memory (nicknamed "hyperspace" by Lotus) where they remain resident until explicitly removed. In addition to removing the "clutter" of many macros from your worksheets, this capability allows for more efficient use of memory; commonly used macros need not appear in every worksheet.

Naming in Symphony

Besides Symphony's window and integration features, another important feature for you to know before you jump into the program is "naming." You will do a lot of naming when you use Symphony. Naming, in fact, is fundamental to the program. Naming files, of course, is one kind of naming, but file naming is only the beginning.

By using range names, you can get around the worksheet quickly and enter ranges in commands. When you are working in the word-processing environment, you can name lines in your document. These lines may include lines of text or special lines you insert in a document whenever you want to vary the format of the text. You can also name settings sheets for printing, creating graphs and databases, and communications.

In some cases, Symphony gives you the option of providing names for all the windows you create on the screen for different applications. And when you don't name the windows, Symphony takes the initiative and names them for you, using numbers.

Whenever you assign names, Symphony keeps track of them for you. By keeping track of named print settings, lines of text, format lines, and so on, Symphony helps you get more out of the program. If you want to use a name again and again, Symphony saves the name (and what's attached to it) for you. Then when you want to print, for example, a letter with most if not all of the same print settings you used in another letter in the worksheet, you can call up those original settings—but only if you gave them a name.

As you begin using Symphony, watch out for the special commands that refer to names. When you become accustomed to Symphony's naming feature, you will find that it is quite an advantage.

New with Symphony Release 2.0

Symphony Release 2.0 includes a number of additions and enhancements. Those of you who have upgraded to this version will appreciate the many different improvements to the program. (See Appendix B for a complete description of these new features.)

Most of the Release 2.0 changes were made to the word-processing environment. Here are some of the most important improvements:

- You can now see page breaks and page numbering on-screen.
- Paragraphs automatically reformat after editing changes.
- You can undelete text.
- Print attributes (underlining, for example) are easier to enter.
- Print attribute codes do not display in your text; the attributed text stands out on your screen.
- Short-cut, or "accelerator," keys are offered for most commands.

In addition, Symphony 2.0 includes two add-in programs for use with the DOC environment: a Spelling Checker and a Text Outliner.

Two significant enhancements appear in the database environment. The maximum size of a database has been expanded, and Symphony Release 2.0 has made databases much easier to modify. The spreadsheet also offers a few new features, including faster and more efficient recalculation, global suppression of zeros, and a choice of how negative numbers are displayed.

Release 2.0 did not modify the graphics environment at all, and the communications mode has only a few minor changes. Note, however, that beginning with Release 2.0, Lotus has removed Symphony's copy-protection system used in earlier releases.

Chapter Summary

This chapter summarizes what Symphony is all about. The chapter gives you a comprehensive view of Symphony by introducing you to the program's main features and capabilities. As a first step in learning Symphony, you now have an overview of the features and concepts that make Symphony what it is—an outstanding integrated software package.

For a more specific idea of the power of Symphony's spreadsheet, word-processing, graphics, data management, and communications applications, turn to the following chapters. In the next chapter, you will learn how to get started, by understanding the program's command system, special screen display features, and uses of the keyboard. You will also learn in later chapters how to use each of Symphony's five environments (SHEET, DOC, GRAPH, FORM, and COMM), how to print reports and graphs, how to use Symphony's Command Language, and how you can integrate Symphony's five applications.

2

Getting Started

Getting started in using your Symphony program requires two kinds of preparation. First, you need to copy and install your disks. These operations are detailed in Appendix A. Second, you need a general understanding of the Symphony program. This chapter gives you the kind of background you'll need for getting started with Symphony. You will learn about the menu structure, special uses of the keyboard, general features of the Symphony display screen, the functions and operations of Symphony's windows, and the Tutorial disks.

The Symphony Menus

Possibly the best way to begin learning the Symphony program is by examining the menu system, understanding the various levels, and being aware of the locations of certain commands and operations. Four main menus make up the Symphony menu system: the Access System menu, the SERVICES menu, the command menu system, and the window TYPE menu. Here's how you retrieve each of the four main menus:

- To retrieve the Access System, you must type **access** (plus the name of the driver set if you are not using the default "Lotus") at the DOS prompt.

- To retrieve the SERVICES menu, you press the Services key (the F9 function key).

- To retrieve the command menu for each application (SHEET, DOC, FORM, GRAPH, and COMM), you press the Menu key (F10).

- To retrieve the window TYPE menu, you press the Type key (Alt-F10).

The menus are hierarchical (menus within menus) and allow you easily to generate a command with several steps. To select a command from any menu, you can either move the cursor to the selection and press Enter, or you can type the first letter of the command. If you want to move out of a command menu completely, you press Ctrl-Break. To move back to a prior command-menu level, you press Esc.

Throughout the book, whenever directions are provided for completing an operation, references are to the menu names rather than the corresponding function keys. For example, "press SERVICES" means press the F9 key.

The Symphony Access System

Symphony contains a main access menu that provides options for accessing programs on the separate Symphony disks (see fig. 2.1). With the Access System, you can move back and forth between the Symphony, Tutorial, PrintGraph, Install, and Translate programs.

Fig. 2.1

Symphony's Access System menu.

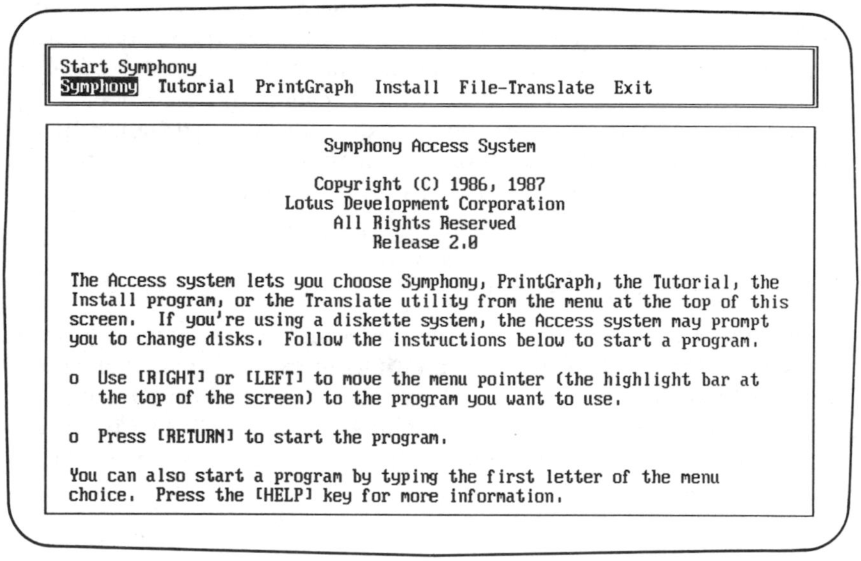

```
Start Symphony
 Symphony  Tutorial  PrintGraph  Install  File-Translate  Exit


                    Symphony Access System

                  Copyright (C) 1986, 1987
                 Lotus Development Corporation
                     All Rights Reserved
                       Release 2.0

The Access system lets you choose Symphony, PrintGraph, the Tutorial, the
Install program, or the Translate utility from the menu at the top of this
screen.  If you're using a diskette system, the Access system may prompt
you to change disks.  Follow the instructions below to start a program.

o  Use [RIGHT] or [LEFT] to move the menu pointer (the highlight bar at
   the top of the screen) to the program you want to use.

o  Press [RETURN] to start the program.

You can also start a program by typing the first letter of the menu
choice.  Press the [HELP] key for more information.
```

Entering and Exiting from Symphony

If you are using a system with two disk drives, you should load the System disk into drive A and load a formatted disk into drive B. Then at the A> prompt, type **access** (or **access** and the name of the driver if you are not using the default driver name "Lotus"). You can also enter Symphony without going through the Symphony Access System by simply typing **symphony**. But entering through the Access System gives you quicker access to the other Access System menu functions. If you have Symphony on your hard disk, first change to your Symphony directory (for example, type **cd \symphony**); then type **access** or **symphony**. The following six functions are available on the Symphony Access System command menu:

Symphony   Tutorial   PrintGraph   Install   File-Translate   Exit

The first option in the Symphony Access System menu is to enter Symphony. To do so, either point to Symphony in the menu by using the cursor-movement keys (→ ←) and then press Enter, or simply type **S**. (As mentioned previously, all Symphony menus enable you to select commands either by moving the cursor and pressing Enter or by typing the first letter of the command.) Several seconds will pass before the next screen appears. Figure 2.2 shows the next screen for a two floppy disk drive system. For a hard disk system, you will see only the SYMPHONY box and then the first spreadsheet window.

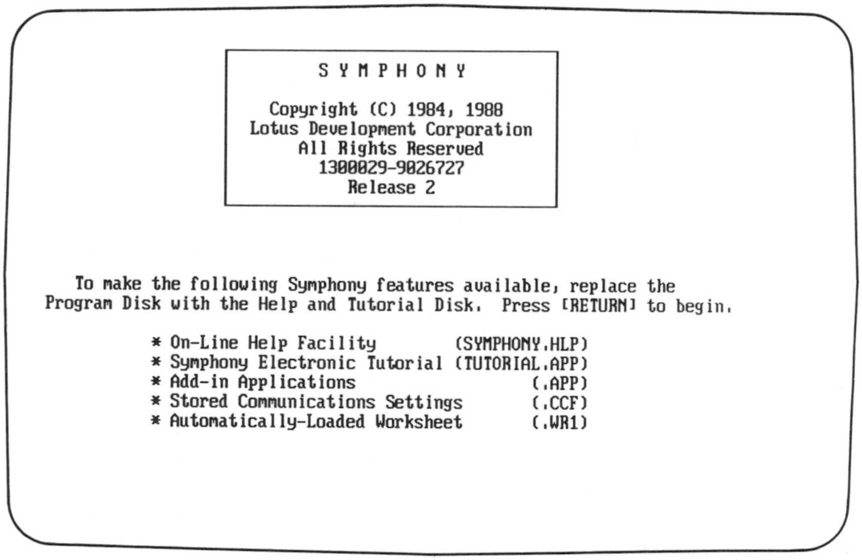

Fig. 2.2

The Symphony copyright screen.

The second screen lists the following five features, which are available if you replace the Program disk with the Help and Tutorial disk (these features are available automatically on a hard disk system):

On-Line Help Facility
Symphony Electronic Tutorial
Add-in Applications
Communications Settings
Automatically Loaded Worksheets

If you want to use any of these options when working with symphony, you must replace your Symphony Program disk with the Help and Tutorial disk. If you don't want to use any of these options, press Enter, and a Symphony window appears.

To exit the Symphony program, select **Exit** from the SERVICES menu. Afterward, Symphony reminds you to save your work if you haven't done so beforehand. If you entered Symphony from the Access System, **Exit** returns you to the Access System. To exit from the Access System, again select **Exit**.

Tutorial

The Access System menu's **Tutorial** option loads Symphony and automatically starts up the Symphony tutorial. If you have a two 5 1/4-inch floppy disk system and select this option, you must replace the Program disk with the Help and Tutorial disk when prompted to do so. You can also execute this option at the system prompt by typing **tutorial** (and the name of the driver set if it is not the default "Lotus") and pressing Enter.

PrintGraph

The **PrintGraph** option in the Access System menu initiates the PrintGraph program for printing graph files. When you choose this option for a two floppy drive system, you must load the PrintGraph disk before you can run the program. (See Chapter 13 for a detailed discussion of the PrintGraph program.)

As with other programs, you can proceed directly to the PrintGraph program without going through the Symphony Access System. Type **pgraph** at the operating system prompt. If the driver name is not "Lotus," you must enter the driver name after typing **pgraph**.

Install

You can also start up the Install program from the Access System menu. If you have a two floppy drive system, Symphony prompts you to replace the Program disk with the Install disk. Alternatively, you can run the Install program from the system prompt by simply typing **install** and pressing Enter.

File-Translate

The File-Translate option accesses the Translate utility. This utility provides a link between Symphony, 1-2-3, Jazz, and outside programs, including VisiCalc and dBASE III. The Translate utility is located on the Translate disk (5 1/4-inch) or PrintGraph with Translate disk (3 1/2-inch). As with the other programs, you can access the Translate utility directly from the operating system prompt. To access the program from the system prompt, type **trans** and press Enter. If the name of your driver is not "Lotus," you must type **trans** and the driver name. (The Translate utility is discussed in detail in Chapter 6.)

The SERVICES Menu

Once you have selected the main Symphony program, three types of command menus are available for retrieving commands and performing operations: SERVICES, TYPE, and command menus specific to each Symphony application.

Within the SERVICES and application command menus you will find a number of settings sheets. (Fig. 2.3 shows an example of a database settings sheet in the FORM environment. Also refer to this chapter's section on "Settings Sheets.") These settings sheets contain various parameters that either relate to a particular environment or are global to the Symphony program. Always easily accessed for viewing, you can change most of the parameters in the settings sheets.

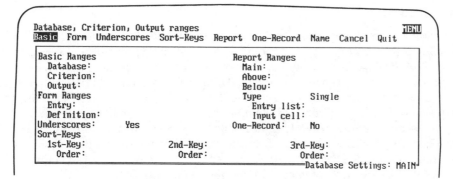

Fig. 2.3

A sample database settings sheet.

The SERVICES menu provides the major operations controlling the five Symphony environments and also provides configuration, special settings, and add-in program options. You can retrieve this menu, which contains the major commands operating in all windows (see fig. 2.4), while you are working in any window.

The first selection in the SERVICES menu is Window. Window enables you to retrieve a window already created; create and name new windows; delete windows; change window size or location; hide, isolate, or expose windows; or split one window into two or four. The File selection contains commands for saving,

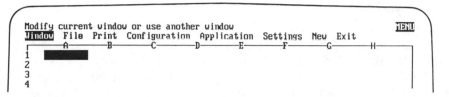

retrieving, and erasing files, as well as commands for special file operations, such as copying files (or parts of files) into worksheets (see Chapter 6). The **Print** selection provides the commands for printing all Symphony documents except graphs. **Configuration** allows you to change default settings.

Another selection, **Application**, lets you access add-in programs and use them when needed. For example, adding DOS through **Application** enables you to perform such operations as copying or formatting disks without having to exit from the Symphony program.

The **Settings** selection displays and enables you to change operations for (1) creating and using macros, (2) locking a worksheet, (3) protecting cells in a worksheet, and (4) automatically loading a communications file. The final two commands in the SERVICES menu, **New** and **Exit**, let you create a new worksheet (after you have saved the current one) and exit from Symphony.

Now let's discuss the SERVICES menu options in more detail.

Window

One of the most important selections in the SERVICES menu is **Window**. As mentioned in Chapter 1, Symphony consists of five applications: spreadsheet, word processing, data management, graphics, and communications. Each of these operates through the window system. At any time you may shift from one type of window to another by pressing the Type key (Alt-F10), then selecting the type of window you want. For example, if you want to shift from working in a spreadsheet window to working in a word-processing window, press Type and select DOC; if you want to work in the data forms window, select FORM; and so on. (See the section entitled "Function Keys Working in All Windows" for a detailed explanation of specific **Window** commands.)

With Symphony's window capability, you can move among any of the five components—spreadsheet, word processing, data management, graphics, and communications—and view different parts of the same worksheet. In figure 2.5, all five types of windows are on-screen at the same time.

Through the SERVICES **Window** command menu, you can change the type of window, create new windows, change the size of windows, split windows horizontally and vertically, and easily change the number of windows that appear on the screen at any one time. Included also are capabilities for restricting a

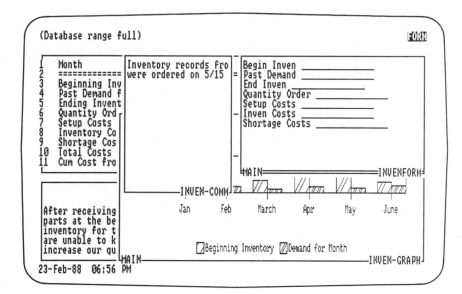

Fig. 2.5

Multiple windows on the screen.

SHEET or DOC window to a specific range in the worksheet, changing the type of border around a window, and automatically redisplaying a worksheet after changes. Both the function keys and the SERVICES Window menu make possible the many window operations.

Windows and Files

Once you begin using Symphony's window feature, you will see that it enables you to organize a single file into many different parts, displaying information in different forms. With the Symphony window feature, you can create multiple windows of different types or shift easily from one type of window to another.

If, for example, your file contains a spreadsheet beginning at cell A1 and ending at cell M90, and a database beginning at cell AA1 and ending at cell AT300, you can easily display sections of both the spreadsheet and the database in two separate windows. If you want to view a graph that analyzes the spreadsheet data, you can add a third window to your screen. Finally, if you want to use the information from your spreadsheet, database, and graph to prepare a word-processed report, you can create a fourth window.

All these windows are created and can be stored within the same file. Although you may be writing the report in a separate window, the text is entered into the same worksheet file in which you created your spreadsheet and database. Changes that you make in one window can affect all other windows, unless you have set restrict ranges (see the section on restricting ranges). When you are working within a window, make sure that different spreadsheets, databases, and texts are far enough away from each other so that one doesn't erase part of or interfere with another. Remember also that when you initiate the **File Save** command, windows are saved within a file as they appear on the screen. You can store windows, like data, within individual files, unless you delete the window by using the **Window Delete** command.

You can also create two or more separate screens and view data from different files. If you want to view data from different files, use the **File Combine** command to pull data from one file into another (see Chapter 6).

After you begin using Symphony's window feature, you will find the possibilities limitless for integrating various types of windows onto one screen. Creating windows allows you to compare and analyze spreadsheet data from different areas of the worksheet. Windows enable you to write memos and short reports, while at the same time viewing spreadsheets and databases. And with windows, you can not only see data displayed in graphs but can also watch graphs change as you modify the data.

Function Keys for Window Operations

Five function keys control special window operations, such as changing the type (TYPE—Alt-F10), switching between two types of windows (SWITCH—Alt-F9), moving the cursor from one window to another (WINDOW—F6), zooming from a small-screen window to a full-screen window (ZOOM—Alt-F6), and redrawing a window (DRAW—Alt-F8).

The Window Menu

The **Window** menu, like other primary menus from the SERVICES menu, contains numerous levels that require different types of responses (see fig. 2.6). And like other menus, the **Window** menu contains a settings sheet, which indicates the current settings for the present window: the name, the type, the range for which pointer movement and data entry are restricted, the display of borders, and the redisplay of a window after spreadsheet changes are made. In addition to the **Settings** command, other commands control creating, retrieving, and deleting windows; removing and redisplaying windows; changing the size and position of windows; and dividing a window into two or four parts.

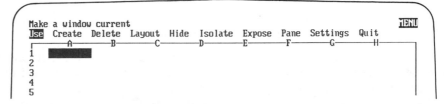

Creating, Using, and Deleting Windows

Within the **Configuration** selection of the SERVICES menu, both window type and name are preset. When you first enter Symphony, you will find that the initial window type is SHEET, and the window name is MAIN. You can change these settings if you want, but an initial window type and name must be set at all times. If, for example, you find yourself using the FORM window more frequently than the SHEET window, you can change the Configuration setting to FORM. Then every time you enter Symphony, a FORM window appears as the first one.

For creating new windows, Symphony provides two procedures. In the first procedure, you (1) select Create from the Window menu, (2) provide a name for the new window, (3) select the window type (SHEET, DOC, GRAPH, FORM, or COMM), (4) identify the size and shape of the new window, and (5) make changes in the Window settings sheet.

The second procedure is to select Pane from the Window menu and indicate the type of split—vertical, horizontal, or both. Symphony automatically names each window and creates each one in the same size and shape. If you want to change the type or name of a window, select Window Settings; if you want to change the size and shape of the window, select Window Layout.

To use windows you have previously created, select the Use command from the Window menu, then indicate which window you want displayed on-screen. When you retrieve another window, the cursor moves from the current window to the window just retrieved. To return the cursor to the other window, press the Window key (F6). This function key also retrieves previously created windows and displays multiple windows on the screen at the same time. The Switch key (Alt-F9), on the other hand, switches the current window type, such as DOC, to a previous window type, such as SHEET.

To delete windows, select Window Delete. If you want to remove a window from the screen only temporarily, use the Window Hide command.

Removing and Redisplaying Windows

Sometimes you may want to create three or four windows and be able to use any of them when needed but also have access at times to a full screen. Three commands—Hide, Isolate, and Expose—and a function key enable you to remove any or all windows from the screen and to expand a single window to full-screen size. Using Hide and Isolate does not delete a window; you can at any time redisplay the window on-screen. If you use the Hide and Isolate commands and then save your file, all previously created windows still exist when you retrieve the file later. As illustrated in figures 2.7A and 2.7B, you can easily change from a screen containing three or four windows to a screen with one window expanded to full-screen size, then redisplay all windows again. If you remove all but your main window, use the Zoom key (Alt-F6) to expand the remaining window to full-screen size.

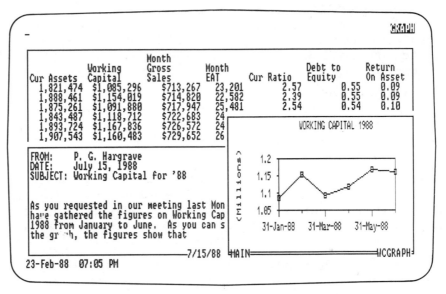

Fig. 2.7A

A screen with three windows.

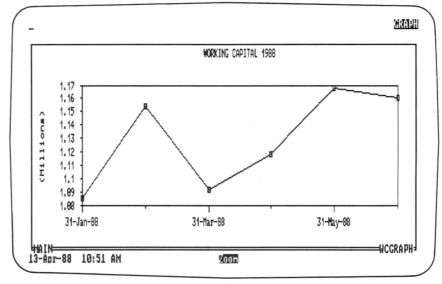

Fig. 2.7B

Zooming to a full-screen window.

Changing Window Shape and Size

In addition to using the Zoom key (Alt-F6) to expand a window, you can use the **W**indow **L**ayout command to expand or decrease the size of any window as well as regulate its shape and position on the screen. When you select **W**indow

Layout, you can position the window anywhere on the screen by anchoring the cursor at a spot that will become one of the four corners of the new window.

Position the cursor in any corner of the window by pressing either the period (.) or Tab key. (Pressing Home moves the cursor to the top left corner of the current window.) Next, highlight the size and shape of the screen you want, using the cursor-movement and PgUp and PgDn keys (see fig. 2.8). Then press Enter. If you decide to change the position of a window but want to retain the current size and shape, select **W**indow Layout, press the Scroll Lock key, and move the cursor.

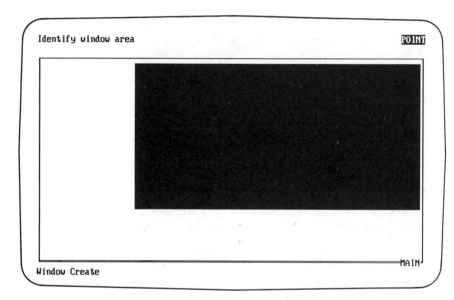

Identify window area   POINT

Window Create   MAIN

Fig. 2.8

Regulating the size and shape of a window.

As mentioned earlier, one quick way to create multiple windows is by using the **W**indow **P**ane command. This command enables you to divide an existing window into two parts, horizontally or vertically, or into four windows (see fig. 2.9). After you have created two or four windows with the **W**indow **P**ane command, you can then change the position, shape, and size of any of the windows. If window size or location causes one window to overlap another, the window in which you are currently working remains on top of the other one until you move to work in another window. That window then cycles to the top of the stack.

Restricting Ranges in Windows

Restricting your work area within a SHEET, DOC, FORM, or COMM window is an important step in creating windows for two reasons. First, restricting the area in which you can enter text in a DOC window, or data in a SHEET window,

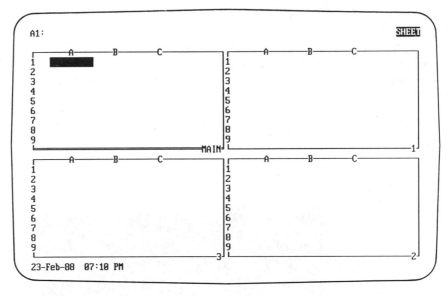

Fig. 2.9

After selecting
SERVICES Window
Pane.

prevents you from accidentally erasing or changing work in another part of the worksheet. Second, restricting the work area can speed up the operation of certain commands. Restricting your work area is particularly important when you are working within a DOC window on a worksheet containing spreadsheet data, because changes in the DOC window can affect the spreadsheet.

To restrict a window area, (1) press the Services key (F9); (2) select **Window**, then **Settings**; (3) select **Restrict**; (4) select **Screen** if you are going to use only the space in the current window, but select **Range** if your work area will be larger than the current window; (5) select **Quit** to enter the restrict range; and (6) then select **Quit** once more to return to DOC mode. Note that when you select **Range**, you also must indicate the area either by typing the beginning and end points or by moving the cursor.

File

The File menu in Symphony contains **Save**, **Retrieve**, **Combine**, **Xtract**, **Erase**, **Bytes**, **List**, **Table**, **Import**, and **Directory** selections. You most often will use **Retrieve** and **Save**, respectively, to load from and save to disk your worksheets. **Combine** and **Xtract** allow you to load or save selected portions of worksheets. With **Import**, you can bring into a worksheet ASCII print files created by Symphony or another program. The other commands, as you will see, provide additional file management capabilities. For instance, **Bytes** indicates the available disk space on the current drive. The **Table** selection creates in a specified range of the worksheet a table with information on files in the specified directory. This information includes file names and extensions, the date and time that each file was last changed, and the number of bytes for each file. (For more information on the Symphony File menu, see Chapter 6, "File Operations.")

Print

You can use the SERVICES **Print** menu to print all documents—spreadsheets, databases, and word-processing documents—but not graphs. The Symphony **Print** menu contains a settings sheet (see fig. 2.10) that displays print options and either default or changed settings. Because the settings sheet is displayed as soon as you retrieve the **Print** menu, you can tell immediately what settings you need to change before saving a print file or printing your report.

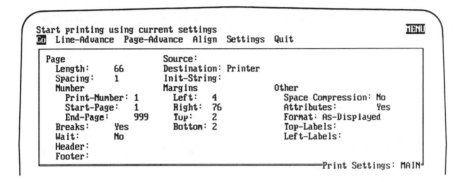

```
Start printing using current settings                    MENU
GO Line-Advance  Page-Advance  Align  Settings  Quit

  Page                  Source:
    Length:     66      Destination: Printer
    Spacing:    1       Init-String:
  Number                Margins                 Other
    Print-Number: 1       Left:   4               Space Compression: No
    Start-Page:   1       Right:  76              Attributes:        Yes
    End-Page:     999     Top:    2               Format: As-Displayed
  Breaks:       Yes     Bottom: 2               Top-Labels:
  Wait:         No                              Left-Labels:
  Header:
  Footer:
                                          ═Print Settings: MAIN═
```

Fig. 2.10

*The SERVICES **Print** settings sheet.*

Symphony allows you to name and save **Print** settings sheets so that you won't have to reset a sheet every time you need to change margins, headings, and so on. (See Chapter 11, "Printing Spreadsheets and Word-Processing Documents," for specific explanations of commands.)

Configuration

Configuration, the fourth selection from the SERVICES menu, provides an easy way for viewing and changing default settings (see fig. 2.11). Configuration settings affect numerous operations, from changing the type of window that initially appears after you access Symphony to changing the size of margins for printing reports. When you display the configuration settings for the first time (press F9 and select **Configuration**), you see the default settings provided by Lotus. You can easily change any setting by selecting the appropriate category in the menu, entering the change(s), and then choosing **Update** to store the new setting.

Symphony stores configuration settings in a configuration file named SYMPHONY.CNF. Whenever you make a change in these settings, you have the option of updating the configuration file. To update the file, you select **Update** from the **Configuration** menu after you have entered all the changes you want to make. Whenever you select **Update**, Symphony stores all current settings in

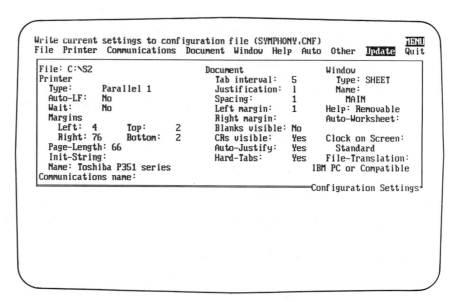

Fig. 2.11

*The SERVICES
Configuration
settings sheet.*

```
Write current settings to configuration file (SYMPHONY.CNF)              MENU
 File  Printer  Communications  Document  Window  Help  Auto  Other  Update  Quit

 File: C:\S2                         Document              Window
 Printer                               Tab interval:   5     Type: SHEET
   Type:      Parallel 1               Justification:  1     Name:
   Auto-LF:   No                       Spacing:        1       MAIN
   Wait:      No                       Left margin:    1     Help: Removable
   Margins                             Right margin:         Auto-Worksheet:
    Left:  4        Top:    2          Blanks visible: No
    Right: 76       Bottom: 2          CRs visible:    Yes   Clock on Screen:
   Page-Length: 66                     Auto-Justify:   Yes     Standard
   Init-String:                        Hard-Tabs:      Yes   File-Translation:
   Name: Toshiba P351 series                                 IBM PC or Compatible
 Communications name:
                                                        Configuration Settings
```

the file. If you do not select **Update**, all newly entered settings are in effect only until the end of your current work session or until you exit from the Symphony program.

Throughout the remaining chapters of the book, various configuration settings are mentioned. Here are the types of settings you can enter in **Configuration**:

File	Stores the disk drive and current directory for the start of a Symphony session (see Chapter 6)
Printer	Contains the configuration settings for the type of printer, line advance, pause between printing pages, margins, page length, initialization string, and printer selection (see Chapter 11)
Communications	Indicates which communications configuration file should be loaded at the beginning of a session; also used to cancel an existing file (see Chapter 17)
Document	Stores default format settings for Symphony's DOC (word-processing) environment; these default settings are for tabs, paragraph justification, spacing, margins, automatic justification of paragraphs, and display of hard spaces, carriage returns, and hard tabs (see Chapter 8)

Window	Controls what window type and name are first displayed when you begin a Symphony session or create a new worksheet file by selecting SERVICES **N**ew (see the section earlier in the chapter on "Creating, Using, and Deleting Windows")
Help	Controls whether the Symphony Help file remains open throughout a session (**I**nstant), or opens only when you press the Help key and closes once you return to Symphony (**R**emovable)
Auto	Enables you to load automatically a worksheet file as soon as you begin a Symphony session
Other	Contains the default settings for (1) **C**lock, which regulates the date and time format, appearing in the bottom left corner of your screen; (2) **F**ile-Translation, which regulates character-code translation tables; (3) **I**nternational, which regulates **P**unctuation and **N**egative display in values, and arguments in functions and in **C**urrency, **D**ate, and **T**ime formats (see Chapter 4); and (4) **A**pplication, which regulates automatically loaded add-in programs
Update	Updates the Symphony configuration file (.CNF) to include any changes in settings

Although the SERVICES **C**onfiguration settings provide global default settings, you can override many of these settings within the specific type of window in which you are working. Settings sheets in the SHEET, DOC, GRAPH, FORM, and COMM environments enable you to override the default settings (see the section called "Settings Sheets").

Application

The **A**pplication selection in the SERVICES menu allows you to add in outside programs and retrieve and use those programs without leaving Symphony. The Application selection enhances Symphony in two ways. First, the selection enables you to use operating system commands, as well as the tutorial, without having to leave Symphony. Second, Application provides the flexibility for adding in other programs, such as the Macro Library Manager, Spelling Checker, and Text Outliner.

Four Application commands control the loading and unloading of add-in programs: Attach, Detach, Invoke, and Clear. The Application Attach command loads an add-in program into main memory, except when you have entered add-in programs into the Configuration Other Application setting of the SERVICES menu. In that case the add-in program(s) automatically load when you select Application. Whenever you add in a program, Symphony adds the file extension .APP when the program is attached.

After you load a program into main memory (either automatically or with Attach), you select Invoke. This command activates the program so that you can begin to use it. Detach and Clear are necessary when you need to free up the memory space being used by add-in programs. Detach unloads a single add-in program, and Clear unloads all add-in programs, completely freeing the memory space for add-ins.

The function of the Application selection is illustrated in Chapter 6. The "Making Backup Copies of Files" section of that chapter describes the procedure for using the DOS add-in application to access the operating system without leaving Symphony.

Settings

The Settings selection indicates the amount of both conventional and expanded memory available as you work within Symphony, indicates whether a coprocessor math chip is installed in your system to speed up certain calculations, and permits you to enter special global settings. The following chapters present specific applications of the Settings options. Provided here, however, is a brief description of each selection.

With the Settings menu, you can change and save special settings for creating and executing macros (see Chapter 19 on keyboard macros). To create keyboard macros automatically, select Learn. To execute a macro automatically at the beginning of a worksheet, select Auto-Execute.

Settings also enables you to secure a worksheet so that the only way to view and change the worksheet is by entering a password that you have created (see Chapter 4 on SHEET window commands). If you want to prevent someone else from viewing and modifying a worksheet, use the Security selection in combination with Global-Protection, and the Range Protect and Format Other Hidden commands of the SHEET menu (see Chapter 4). Finally, through the SERVICES Settings Communications selection, you can automatically load a communications configuration file. (Communications is discussed in Chapter 17.)

New

If you finish working in a worksheet and want to begin a new one, as well as a new file, you select New from the SERVICES menu. Be certain that you save your current worksheet first. Once you have selected New, Symphony asks whether you want to erase everything. If you select Yes, the current worksheet data is lost, unless you first use the File Save command.

Exit

The Exit selection returns you to the main Symphony Access System (or the operating system prompt, if you started up the program by typing **symphony**). Here again, you need to make sure that you have saved your work before exiting. Symphony does not automatically save your file, so you must select File Save before exiting the program.

The Command Menu

Although the SERVICES menu contains the primary operations relating to all applications, each application also has its own command menu, invoked by the Menu key (F10). Although the command menus of the different applications are somewhat similar, each is tailored to a particular environment. The SERVICES menu is used for all windows and remains the same no matter which one you are working in, but the second kind of menu, the command menu, changes with each type of window (see fig. 2.12). You can retrieve the primary command menu for each window by pressing the F10 function key. (When working within a SHEET window, you can retrieve the command menu either by pressing F10 or by pressing the slash (/) key in the lower right corner of the alphanumeric keyboard.)

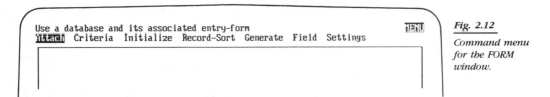

Fig. 2.12

Command menu for the FORM window.

Settings Sheets

In both the SERVICES menu and the command menus, you will find settings sheets. Figure 2.13 shows an example of a SHEET settings sheet. These sheets enable you to store settings for everything from Global-Protection in a worksheet to Spacing settings in a word-processing work area.

Except for the DOC command menu, all command menus contain settings sheets on the first command line. Settings is the final selection in the SHEET, FORM, and COMM menus; 1st-Settings and 2nd-Settings are the second and third selections in the GRAPH menu. Special settings sheets, however, are located within first-level commands. For example, the SHEET Graph command contains two

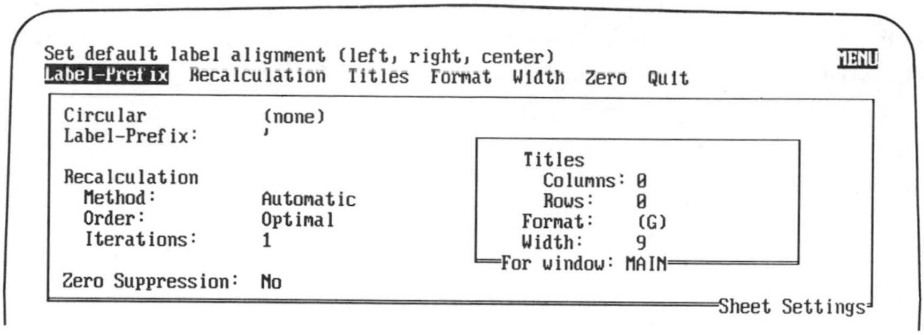

Fig. 2.13

A sample settings sheet in the SHEET environment.

```
Set default label alignment (left, right, center)                    MENU
Label-Prefix  Recalculation  Titles  Format  Width  Zero  Quit

   Circular          (none)
   Label-Prefix:     '
                                              Titles
   Recalculation                                 Columns:  0
     Method:         Automatic                   Rows:     0
     Order:          Optimal                   Format:    (G)
     Iterations:     1                         Width:      9
                                             For window: MAIN
   Zero Suppression: No
                                                      Sheet Settings
```

settings sheets, the SHEET Query command contains one, and the DOC Format command contains one.

If, for instance, you want to set horizontal or vertical titles in a worksheet, you will find Titles within the SHEET Settings window. In addition, you enter numerous kinds of DOC format changes, including changes in tabs, margins, and spacing, through the Format Settings sheet.

Settings sheets provide two major advantages. First, Symphony displays multiple settings on-screen at once. This feature is particularly helpful when you are trying to remember special print or graph settings. Another major advantage of settings sheets is that you can create a catalog of some types of sheets and retrieve them when needed. Such a catalog is useful when you have various kinds of document formats to print, such as memos or letters, each with its own special margin, heading, and spacing formats.

A catalog of print settings sheets can make the job of printing these documents quite simple. As you read other chapters in this book, you will find examples of specific settings sheets and suggestions on how you can use them to make your tasks easier in spreadsheets, word processing, graphics, data management, and communications.

You will find in many cases that settings sheets located in the specific menus of the SHEET, DOC, GRAPH, FORM, and COMM environments contain the same settings as those in the Configuration settings of the SERVICES menu. The effect of SERVICES Configuration settings on settings sheets in the SHEET, DOC, GRAPH, FORM, and COMM windows may be a bit confusing at first. But to help you understand this effect, consider the following example.

Suppose that the SERVICES Configuration setting for the left margin of a DOC window is 5 spaces, and the right margin setting is 65 (see fig. 2.14). Suppose also that you are just beginning a new worksheet and have created a DOC window for writing a memo. When you create the DOC window, the setting for the left margin is 5 spaces, and for the right margin the setting is 65. If you begin entering text into this DOC window, all lines will be indented 5 spaces on the left, as in figure 2.15.

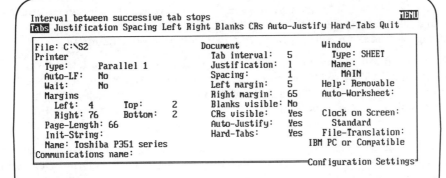

Fig. 2.14

The left margin at 5, right margin at 65.

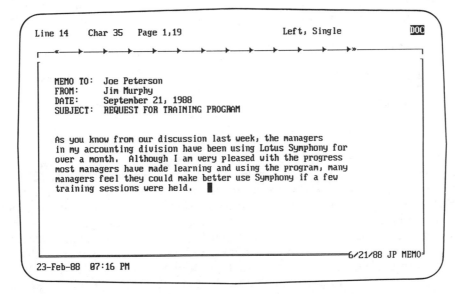

Fig. 2.15

Margin appearing in the document.

If, however, you decide to change the default left margin setting to 10 spaces, you do so by changing the settings sheet in the DOC menu. To change the DOC settings sheet, retrieve the DOC menu by pressing the Menu key (F10), select Format from the menu, and then choose Settings. After you select Settings, Symphony displays a settings sheet containing format settings. If you compare the settings in the settings sheet in SERVICES Configuration Document with the settings in Format Settings, you will see that the settings are the same. After you change the left margin setting in the DOC settings sheet, however, the new setting overrides the setting in SERVICES Configuration Document.

When you finish the memo, suppose that you decide to write a letter. You then create another DOC window on the same worksheet. When you create the new window, it inherits the settings sheet of the previous (memo) window. The DOC settings sheet still overrides the SERVICES Configuration settings, even though you have shifted to a new window.

It is possible to change the Format Settings for the second window. When you do, the first DOC window retains its format settings, and the second DOC window retains its settings. If you create a third DOC window, it will inherit the format settings of the second window. But once you save the worksheet file and begin a new worksheet in a later session, the SERVICES Configuration Document settings will be in effect for the first DOC window in that later session.

The TYPE Menu

In addition to the SERVICES and command menus, one other menu, called TYPE, is part of the Symphony menu tree. The TYPE menu is shown in figure 2.16.

Fig. 2.16

The TYPE menu.

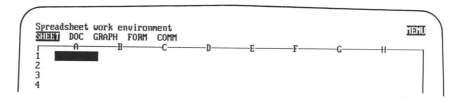

The TYPE menu enables you to change the window environment in which you are working. To retrieve this menu, press the Type key (Alt-F10) and either move the cursor to the new window type and press Enter or type the first letter of the window. Besides using the Type key to change window type, you can use two other methods. One is to use the SERVICES Window Settings Type command. The other method is to press the Switch key (Alt-F9), but only when you already have been using different types of windows in one worksheet. The Switch key returns you to the window type you used previously.

Automatic Exit versus "Sticky Menu"

Symphony contains two ways to exit from a menu. Many menus return you to the current window mode—SHEET, DOC, GRAPH, FORM, or COMM—once you have finished selecting commands or entered a response. Other menus, however, require that you select **Quit** to exit and return to the current window mode. Selecting **Quit**, like pressing Enter, tells Symphony that you have entered a command or changed a setting. To assure yourself that a command has been entered, you need to complete the following:

- Move the cursor to the appropriate selection and press Enter, or type the first letter of the selection.

- To change a setting, such as for margins in **Print Settings**, press Enter or select **Quit** after making the changes.

Remember that you can move out of a command menu by pressing Esc or Ctrl-Break. If you select either Esc or Ctrl-Break before you enter a change in a setting by pressing Enter or selecting **Quit**, however, the change is not entered.

Suppose, for example, that you are working in Symphony's word-processing environment (a DOC window) and want to change margin settings. You first retrieve the DOC command menu. Second, you select **Format** by moving the cursor to `Format` on the menu and pressing Enter or by typing **F**. The following options appear:

Create   Edit   Use Named   Settings

Then you select **Settings**, again either by moving the cursor and pressing Enter or by typing **S**. When the next screen appears, you select **Left** and then enter the new margin when Symphony indicates `Default Left Margin:1`. You enter the new margin simply by typing in the number, such as 4, and pressing Enter. If you were to press Esc or Ctrl-Break at this point rather than Enter, your new setting would not be entered. Once you have pressed Enter and Symphony returns to the prior menu (see fig. 2.17), you can exit by selecting **Quit**, pressing Esc three times (to exit to each previous menu level one at a time), or pressing Ctrl-Break.

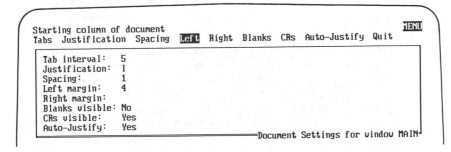

Fig. 2.17

After typing a new margin and pressing Enter.

The Symphony Keyboard

Symphony makes considerable use of the various parts of the IBM keyboard, particularly function keys and the Alt and Ctrl keys used in combination with others. The keyboard is divided into three sections: (1) the alphanumeric keyboard in the center, (2) the numeric keypad on the right, and (3) the special-function key section on the left. With this arrangement in mind, you can more easily understand the functions of the Symphony keyboard.

The IBM Personal Computer keyboard is shown in figure 2.18. Although the keyboard layout is almost the same for the IBM Personal Computer AT, shown in figure 2.19, some minor differences exist. The IBM Enhanced Keyboard, shown in figure 2.20, differs considerably from the others, but the actions of the keys are the same. (Function keys F11 and F12, unique to the Enhanced Keyboard, have no effect in Symphony.)

Fig. 2.18

The IBM Personal Computer keyboard.

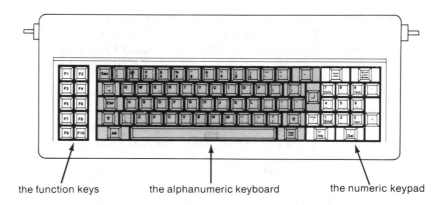

the function keys   the alphanumeric keyboard   the numeric keypad

Fig. 2.19

The IBM Personal Computer AT keyboard.

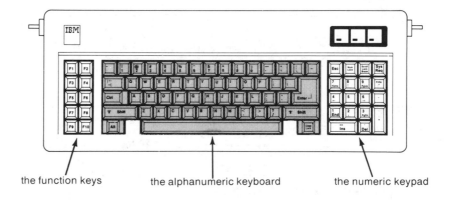

the function keys   the alphanumeric keyboard   the numeric keypad

the function keys

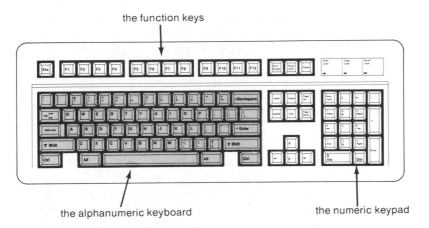

Fig. 2.20

The IBM Enhanced Keyboard.

the alphanumeric keyboard

the numeric keypad

Although the functions of certain keys change as you change windows, the Symphony keyboard sections have certain general characteristics.

Most of the keys in the alphanumeric section at the center of the keyboard are found on any common typewriter. These keys maintain their normal functions in Symphony. Keys that take on unique functions, however, are Esc, Tab, Shift, Ctrl, and Alt.

The numeric keypad on the right side of the keyboard is normally used for entering numbers in most programs on the IBM PC. You can use this keypad for numbers whenever the Num Lock key is set. In Symphony, however, the main purpose of the numeric keypad is cursor movement.

The special-function keys on the left side of the keyboard (on the IBM PC and compatibles) are designed for special uses ranging from getting help (the F1 function key) to retrieving the command menus (the F10 function key).

The Alphanumeric Keyboard

Although most of the alphanumeric keys (see figs. 2.18-2.20) have the same functions as those on a typewriter, several keys have special functions in Symphony. If some of the functions do not make much sense the first time through, don't worry. Their meanings will become clearer as you read more of this chapter and those that follow.

Key	*Function(s)*
Esc	Erases current entry when you specify a command line or range, erases a command menu, or returns from a help screen; removes a graph from the screen and returns you to the graph menu in SHEET mode

Tab	Moves the cursor to each tab setting in DOC mode; moves the cursor to the left when you use Tab with the Shift key; anchors cells or the cursor when you are indicating a range
Alt	When used in combination with the function keys, changes function key operations; used simultaneously with other alpha keys to invoke keyboard macros (Alt is covered in detail in Chapter 19.)
Shift	Changes the central section of the keyboard to uppercase letters and characters; allows you to key in numbers by using the numeric keypad on the right when you are working in a SHEET window. (Shift is equivalent to a temporary Num Lock.)
Ctrl	When used with Break, takes you out of a command operation and back to the SHEET, DOC, GRAPH, or COMM mode; used simultaneously with other alpha keys to invoke accelerator keys in DOC mode (see Chapter 8)

The Numeric Keypad

The keys in the numeric keypad on the right side of the keyboard (see figs. 2.18-2.20) are used primarily for cursor movement. You can also use them for scrolling the screen up or down, deleting characters, and inserting records into a database. In some cases a key's function is specific to the type of window in which you are working. These specific functions are indicated subsequently.

(See the later section on "Cursor-Movement Keys and the Cell Pointer" for detailed explanations of the Home, End, PgUp, and PgDn keys used alone or in combination with other keys.)

Key	*Function(s)*	*Windows*
Backspace	When you are defining the contents of a cell, erases the character to the left of the cursor; erases characters in DOC and FORM windows	SHEET DOC FORM
/ (Slash)	Retrieves the SHEET command menu; used in its normal function as a division sign	SHEET

(Period)	Separates cell addresses when you designate ranges of cells; anchors cell addresses or the cursor when you are pointing; also used as a decimal point (See the section called "Ranges" in Chapter 3.)	SHEET DOC FORM GRAPH COMM
Home	Returns to cell A1 or the beginning of a restrict range from any location in the worksheet in the SHEET window; used after the End key to position the cursor at the active end of the worksheet or restrict range; used in EDIT mode to jump to the beginning of the edit line; returns to the beginning of the file or restrict range from any location in the DOC window; moves to the first record in the FORM window (See the section on "Cursor-Movement Keys and the Cell Pointer.")	SHEET DOC FORM
PgUp	Moves the cursor 20 rows up in the column where it currently resides in a SHEET window; moves the cursor one window up in a DOC window; moves to a previous record in a FORM window	SHEET DOC FORM
PgDn	Moves the cursor 20 rows down in a SHEET window and one window down in a DOC window; moves to the next record in a FORM window	SHEET DOC FORM
Ins	Inserts a record into the FORM database; clears form for next entry; used to switch from Insert to Overstrike mode in a DOC window	FORM DOC

The Lock Key Indicators

Three "lock" keys are on IBM and compatible computers: Num Lock, Caps Lock, and Scroll Lock. Whenever you use any of these keys, Symphony indicates that the keys are operating. Each key has its own reverse-video indicator that appears in the lower right corner of the screen when the key is on (see fig. 2.21).

Fig. 2.21

The lock key indicators in lower right corner.

```
16
17
18
19
20
                                                               MAIN
23-Feb-88  07:18 PM                              CapsNumScroll
```

The Function Keys

The special-function keys in Symphony generally do the same thing regardless of the window type. A few special-function keys change their functions, however, when you change the window environment. You use the F2 function key, for example, to edit cell entries when you are working in a SHEET window, but this same key justifies paragraphs when you are in a DOC window.

Lotus Development provides for Symphony users a function key template that fits over the function keys of your computer. Figure 2.22 is a diagram of this template. The figure distinguishes those keys that operate by pressing a function key alone and those keys that operate by pressing simultaneously the Alt key and a function key. On the template, operations in light tan are initiated by pressing the function key alone. Operations with a gray background are initiated by pressing simultaneously the Alt key and the function key. Like the lock keys, some function keys toggle on and off. In other words, the particular function remains "turned on" until you press the key(s) a second time. Such toggle keys include Alt-F6 (Zoom), Alt-F7 (Step), and F7 (User).

Function Keys Working in All Windows

Some keys operate in all types of windows, whereas other keys function only with specific window types. The three keys that you will probably use most frequently for all window types are the Services key (F9), the Type key (Alt-F10), and the Menu key (F10). Function keys operating in all windows include the following:

Key	*Function(s)*
F1 (Help)	Retrieves the help screens (On a system with two 5 1/4-inch disk drives, you need to replace the Symphony Program disk with the Help and Tutorial disk before pressing F1.)

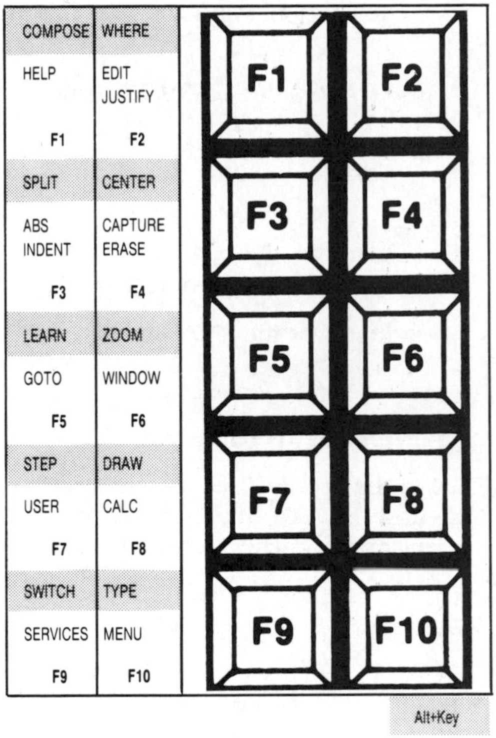
COMPOSE
WHERE
HELP
EDIT JUSTIFY
F1
F2
SPLIT
CENTER
ABS INDENT
CAPTURE ERASE
F3
F4
LEARN
ZOOM
GOTO
WINDOW
F5
F6
STEP
DRAW
USER
CALC
F7
F8
SWITCH
TYPE
SERVICES
MENU
F9
F10
F1
F2
F3
F4
F5
F6
F7
F8
F9
F10
Alt+Key

Fig. 2.22

The function key template.

Alt-F1 (Compose)	Creates special characters by combining two standard characters
Alt-F5 (Learn)	Records keystrokes for creating macros
F7 (User)	Initiates a macro
Alt-F7 (Step)	Operates a macro in single-step mode for debugging
F6 (Window)	Rotates windows; brings a bottom window to the top; moves the cursor from one window to another; rotates the settings sheets for windows of the same type
Alt-F6 (Zoom)	Creates a full screen after isolating a window

Alt-F8 (Draw)	Redraws all windows after making changes
F9 (Services)	Retrieves the SERVICES menu
Alt-F9 (Switch)	Changes window to previous type
F10 (Menu)	Retrieves the command menus for each Symphony environment
Alt-F10 (Type)	Retrieves the TYPE menu

Function Keys for Specific Windows

The function keys listed in the previous section are available for any Symphony window (SHEET, DOC, GRAPH, FORM, and COMM). As mentioned earlier, many function keys have particular uses for specific window types. Here are these keys and their functions:

Key	Window	Function(s)
Alt-F1 (Compose)	DOC FORM SHEET	Inserts special print commands (such as those for boldfacing and underlining) in the text; creates special characters
F2 (Justify)	DOC	Justifies paragraphs
F2 (Edit)	SHEET FORM	Edits a cell entry in a spreadsheet; edits entries in a form
Alt-F2 (Where)	DOC	Indicates page and line location on printed copy of current on-screen line
F3 (Indent)	DOC	Indents lines
F3 (Abs)	SHEET	Changes a formula to absolute reference
Alt-F3 (Split)	DOC	Splits a line without leaving carriage return

F4 (Capture)	COMM	Captures data to a worksheet range or printer
F4 (Erase)	DOC	Erases a block
Alt-F4 (Center)	DOC	Centers a line
F5 (GoTo)	SHEET DOC FORM	Goes to a range
F8 (Calc)	SHEET	Calculates formulas in a worksheet

Other Special Key Combinations

Besides the special uses of the Alt key with function keys, many other key combinations have special functions, particularly in the DOC and SHEET windows. In many cases, these combinations involve moving the cell pointer in a SHEET window or moving the cursor in a DOC or FORM window.

In addition, many special key combinations, called "accelerator keys," are available in DOC mode. For example, rather than selecting the Move command from the DOC menu, you can press Ctrl-M. A complete list of these accelerator keys appears in Chapter 8.

Cursor-Movement Keys and the Cell Pointer

Cursor movement occurs in all Symphony environments. In some cases, cursor movement within a window is primarily for identifying ranges; in other windows, cursor movement is important for entering, editing, and deleting data and for making selections from menus. Cursor movement occurs when you use keys alone and in combination with others, as listed in the following tables. (In a SHEET environment, note that the cursor is referred to as the cell pointer.)

Moving the Cell Pointer in a SHEET Window

Symphony provides several ways for moving around a worksheet, whether you are identifying a range or entering or changing data. Eleven keys in all, used alone and in combination, control cell-pointer movement throughout the worksheet. These keys include the following:

The cursor keys: ←, →, ↓, ↑
The PgDn and PgUp keys
The Home key
The End key
The F5 function key
The Ctrl key (used only in combination with others)
The Scroll Lock key (used only in combination with others)

Here's how to use these keys to move the cell pointer around the worksheet (fig. 2.23 illustrates how the keys operate):

To move the cell pointer:	*Use the following:*
One cell up	↑
One cell down	↓
One cell left	←
One cell right	→
To the upper left corner	Home
To the lower right corner	End + Home
One window up	PgUp
One window down	PgDn
One window left	Ctrl-←
One window right	Ctrl-→
Window up one row	Scroll Lock on, then ↑
Window down one row	Scroll Lock on, then ↓
Window left one column	Scroll Lock on, then ←
Window right one column	Scroll Lock on, then →
To jump the cell pointer to:	*Use the following:*
Specific cell position or named range	F5 function key
Next filled cell above	End then ↑
Next filled cell below	End then ↓
Next filled cell to left	End then ←
Next filled cell to right	End then →
First row of window restrict range	End then PgUp
Last row of restrict range	End then PgDn
First column of restrict range	End then Ctrl-←
Last column of restrict range	End then Ctrl-→
Upper right corner of restrict range	Scroll Lock on, then Home

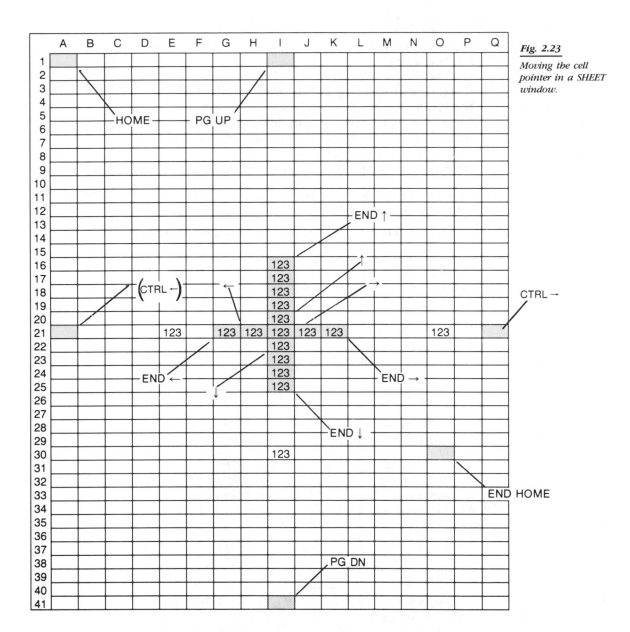

Fig. 2.23

Moving the cell pointer in a SHEET window.

Moving the Cursor in a DOC Window

Moving the cursor in a DOC window is similar to moving the cell pointer in a SHEET window. You can use many more keys, however, to move the cursor in a DOC window. These keys include the following:

The cursor keys: ←, →, ↓, ↑
The PgUp and PgDn keys
The Home key
The End key
The Ctrl key (used only in combination with others)
The Scroll Lock key (used only in combination with others)
The F2 function key (used with the End key)
The Alt-F2 key combination (used with the End key)
Enter (used with the End key)
Any typed character (used with the End key)

These keys enable you to move the cursor around a DOC worksheet in the following ways:

To move the cursor:	*Use the following:*
One line up	↑
One line down	↓
One format line up	End then Alt-F2
One format line down	End then F2
To preceding character	←
To next character	→
To any specific character	End then specific character
To next word	Ctrl-→
To preceding word	Ctrl-←
To beginning of paragraph	End then ↑
To end of paragraph	End then ↓
One window up	PgUp
One window down	PgDn
Window up one line	Scroll Lock on, then ↑
Window down one line	Scroll Lock on, then ↓
Window 25% to left	Scroll Lock on, then ←
Window 25% to right	Scroll Lock on, then →
To upper left corner of a document or restrict range	Home
To end of a document or restrict range	End then Home
To next carriage return	End then Enter

Moving the Cursor in a FORM Window

Cursor movement is important not only for operating within a SHEET or DOC window, but also for the work you do in a FORM window. When you enter information into data forms and criterion records, use the following keys for cursor movement:

The cursor keys: ←, →, ↓, ↑
The Tab key
The Home key
The End key
The Ctrl key (used only in combination with others)

These keys enable you to move the cursor in a FORM window in the following ways:

To move the cursor:	*Use the following:*
To the previous field	↑ or ←
To the next field	↓, →, or Tab
To the first field of a record	Ctrl-←
To the last field of a record	Ctrl-→
To the first record	Home
To the last record	End

The Symphony Display

Descriptions of the Symphony display, like those of many other features of the program, vary according to the type of window being used. Some general remarks, however, can be made about the Symphony display. For all types of windows, the work or display area is bordered on all four sides. You can change this border or remove it completely by using the SERVICES Window Settings Borders command. The border for a SHEET window contains letters and numbers that mark columns and rows (see fig. 2.24).

A particularly important part of the border of any window is the bottom line. The double line indicates the current window. Important areas outside the window border include the control panel, the mode indicator, the date-and-time indicator, the error message area, and the lock key indicator.

The Control Panel

The area directly above the top line of the border is the menu area for all windows,. In Symphony, the command menu line appears in this position, but the explanation of the command appears on the first line above the command menu line (see fig. 2.25).

Whenever a SHEET, DOC, or FORM window is in the mode ready to receive data, the area above the top border contains information about the data or the operations that you must complete before you can enter data.

Fig. 2.24

The border for a SHEET window.

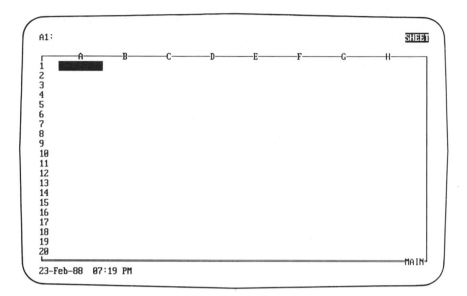

Fig. 2.25

The command menu line with explanations above it.

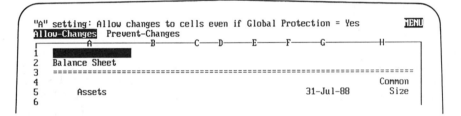

In the SHEET window mode, this first line contains all the information about the current cell, which is the cell where the pointer is currently located (see fig. 2.26). The first item is the address of the cell, such as A10. And the second item is the display format, such as (D1), which is always displayed in parentheses. (Display formats are covered in detail in Chapter 4.) The last item is the actual contents of the current cell, such as @DATE(88,3,31).

The line underneath the current cell information is the edit line. As you enter or edit data, characters display on this line. It is blank in figure 2.26 because the formula has already been entered.

In the DOC window mode, the first line indicates the line, character, and page position of the cursor, as well as the type of justification and spacing that are set (see fig. 2.27). Whenever an asterisk (*) appears in the middle of the control panel, the asterisk indicates that the cursor is positioned on data which was entered in another type of window, or positioned on a special DOC format symbol (see Chapter 8).

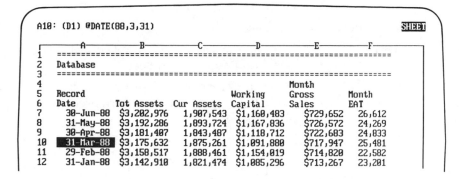

Fig. 2.26

Current cell information displayed in the first line of a SHEET window.

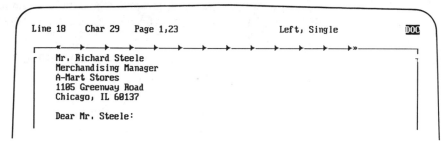

Fig. 2.27

Information displayed in the first line of a DOC window.

In the FORM window mode, the control panel is reserved as a special message area (see fig. 2.28). For example, this area tells you that you need to set a range for creating a form. But more important, the control panel tells you which record is being entered or edited and indicates the entry slot where the cursor is currently positioned.

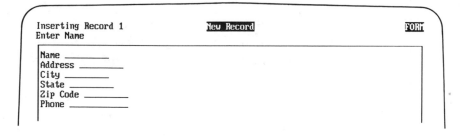

Fig. 2.28

A special message area in the first line of a FORM window.

The Mode Indicators

Symphony provides several modes, one of which is always in effect, depending on what you are doing. The mode indicator is located in the upper right corner of the screen and always shows the current mode. The mode indicators and related modes include these:

Modes Indicating Current Window

Mode Indicator	Description
SHEET	You can enter a command or make a cell entry in the spreadsheet.
DOC	You can enter a command or text or perform editing operations in a word-processing window.
GRAPH	You can enter a command to create graphs and charts and attach them to a GRAPH window.
FORM	You can enter a command or data and change data in the forms you have created in a FORM window.
COMM	You can enter a command or data in the COMM window.
OUTLN	When the Outliner application is attached, you can enter headings and subheadings, or commands, in the OUTLN window.

Modes Working in All Windows

Mode Indicator	Description
MENU	You must select from the SERVICES menu or from a SHEET, DOC, GRAPH, FORM, COMM, or OUTLN menu. (Or you can press Esc to return to a window mode.)
POINT	A range is being pointed to.
HELP	You are using a help screen.
ERROR	An error has occurred, and Symphony is waiting for you to press Esc or Enter to acknowledge the error.
WAIT	Symphony is in the middle of an operation and cannot respond to commands.
EDIT	A settings sheet or cell entry is being edited.

SHEET Window Modes

Mode Indicator	Description
VALUE	A number or formula is being entered.
LABEL	A label is being entered.
FIND	Symphony is in the middle of a **Query Find** operation and cannot respond to commands.
NAMES	A range name (or line marker in a DOC window) is being pointed to.

FORM Window Mode

Mode Indicator	Description
CRIT	A criterion record is being edited.

Other Indicators

In addition to the mode indicators in the top right corner, other indicators are displayed in the area at the bottom of the screen (see fig. 2.29). On the left, Symphony displays date and time whenever you are in a window mode. When you have selected a command, the command name is displayed in the bottom left corner. Also displayed here are error messages and the Memory full message. In the bottom right corner, a number of other indicators appear. These inform you of certain conditions, such as lock keys being on, and also of operations for creating, editing, and using macros.

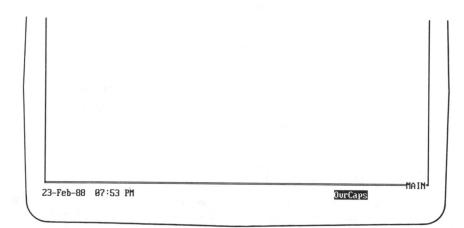

23-Feb-88 07:53 PM

OurCaps

MAIN

Fig. 2.29

Indicators at the bottom of the screen.

Following is a list of other indicators:

Indicator	*Description*
Calc	You need to recalculate the worksheet.
CAPS	The Caps Lock key is on.
Capture	Data from a COMM environment is being logged in a worksheet range to the printer.
Circ	Symphony has found a circular reference in the worksheet.
Draw	You need to update windows because of changes in one of them.
End	The end key is on.
Learn	You can store keystrokes automatically for creating macros.
Macro	A macro is in operation.
Mem	Only a small amount of memory remains.
New Record	A new record is being entered (FORM window).
Num	The Num Lock key is on.
OnLine	In the COMM window, a connection with another computer is signified.
Ovr	You are in the Overstrike mode in a DOC window.
Pause	You need to input something so that a macro can continue.
Scroll	The Scroll Lock key is on.
Step	Step mode is set for running macros.
User	You can execute a macro by entering the macro name.

Using the Tutorial Disks

Whether you are a veteran Lotus user or new to Lotus software, the Tutorial Lessons disk and the Help and Tutorial disk will acquaint you with Symphony and enable you to understand better its command structure, capabilities, and operations.

The Tutorial Lessons Disk

The Tutorial Lessons disk is an excellent introduction to the Symphony program. The tutorial is comprehensive in its treatment of all Symphony applications—spreadsheet, word processing, graphics, database management, and communications. A series of lessons covering the five applications, windows, and macros are presented in separate sections of the disk. You can select any one of the sections as well as particular lessons within that section. If, for example, you want to view the lessons on database management, you can select that item from the menu. You can then choose to begin with either the basic lessons or the more advanced lessons. The Symphony Tutorial disk is excellently conceived, written, and presented.

The following applications and lessons are included on the disk:

A	Introduction	Included are lessons on (1) Using the Tutorial, (2) A Demonstration of Symphony Features, (3) Working in Different Environments, and (4) Performing Tasks Common to All Environments.
B	Spreadsheet	Lessons include (1) Moving around in the Spreadsheet Environment, (2) Entering and Editing Cell Entries, (3) Copying Text and Numbers, (4) Writing Formulas, (5) Copying Formulas, (6) Formatting, (7) Organizing the Spreadsheet, and (8) Using @Functions.
C	Word Processing	Included are (1) Moving around and Entering Text in a Document, (2) Editing a Document, (3) Moving and Copying Text, (4) Including Print Attributes and Unusual Characters, (5) Using Format Lines, (6) Refining a Document's Appearance, (7) Searching and Replacing, and (8) Using the Document Accelerator Keys.

D	Business Graphics	Lessons include (1) Learning the Basics of Creating a Graph, (2) Enhancing a Graph, (3) Changing Graph Settings, (4) Creating a Pie Chart, and (5) Creating a Line Graph.
E	Database Management	Included are (1) Using Entry Forms, (2) Using the Criterion Record, (3) Creating an Entry Form, (4) Editing an Entry Form with the Form Field Command, (5) Editing an Entry Form in the SHEET Environment, (6) Using Database Settings Sheets and Sorting Data, and (7) Using the Database in the SHEET Environment.
F	Communications	Lessons include (1) Setting Up a Communications Session, and (2) Sending and Receiving Data.

If you work through Symphony's tutorial, you are guaranteed a complete introduction to all the major operations and features of the program.

The tutorial is too long and detailed to review all in one sitting. You will do best if you work on one section at a time, particularly because the organization of lessons enables you to begin and end at any point. A number of features make the tutorial an excellent learning aid; it often presents a clearer introduction to the program than does the documentation. Here are a few of the tutorial's strengths:

- The tutorial emphasizes the integrated features of the program by introducing all of Symphony's capabilities.

- Each lesson is based on hands-on exercises that enable you to practice using many of Symphony's keys, commands, and operations.

- At the end of each lesson, you are encouraged and given the opportunity to practice on your own the commands and operations covered in the lesson. If you press the space bar at this point, Symphony puts you in control, allowing you to roam the tutorial's sample worksheet and try out anything you want. Then, when you are ready to return to the tutorial lesson, you press Ctrl-Z.

- Each exercise clearly explains what the goal of each procedure is, what keys you should press, and what part of the screen you should focus on as changes occur (see fig. 2.30).

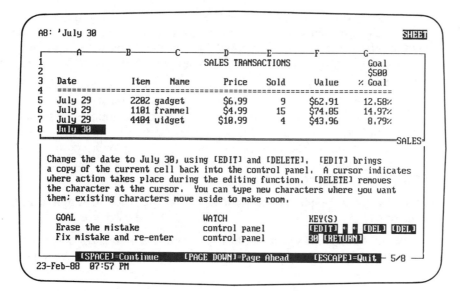

Fig. 2.30

A sample exercise in the tutorial.

- The tutorial is user friendly, not only because it provides clear and complete instructions, but also because it acknowledges the needs of different users, both beginning and advanced.

- If you want to speed up the process of working through a lesson, you can press the space bar, which will enter each of the keystrokes for you. Thus, you get the benefit of the tutorial without having to do all the work. If you want to pass through part of a lesson even more quickly, pressing the PgDn key enables you to do so. One problem, however, is that you cannot return to a prior screen without starting again at the beginning.

The Symphony Tutorial disk is highly recommended as one resource for introducing you to the general capabilities, menus, commands, and operations of Symphony.

Accessing the Tutorial

The tutorial is one of Symphony's add-in applications and must be Attached and then Invoked, using the SERVICES command menu. If you have not started up the Symphony program but want to access the tutorial, you can do so easily and automatically by taking the following steps:

1. Load the Symphony Program disk (if you're on a system with two floppy disk drives) or start from the appropriate directory (if you're working with a hard disk system).

2. Type **tutorial** and press Enter, or type **access** and, at the main Access System menu, move the cursor over to Tutorial and press Enter. (This method does the work for you of calling up Symphony, automatically **Attaching** the tutorial application, and then **Invoking** it.)

3. For a system with two 5 1/4-inch disk drives, you must also do the following: after you load Symphony, and the screen appears as shown earlier in figure 2.2, replace the Symphony Program disk with the Help and Tutorial disk, then press Enter. Symphony next prompts you to replace the Help and Tutorial disk with the Tutorial Lessons disk and press Enter.

If you are already in Symphony and want to access the tutorial, simply take the following steps:

1. Press SERVICES and select Application from the menu. For a system with two floppy disk drives, be sure that the Help and Tutorial disk is in drive A.

2. Select Attach, move the pointer to TUTORIAL.APP, and press Enter.

3. Select SERVICES Application again.

4. Select **Invoke**. At this point, Symphony warns you that your current worksheet, if any, will be wiped out. If you need to save your work, press Esc to get back to it. Otherwise, press Enter.

5. For a system with two floppy disk drives, replace the Help and Tutorial disk with the Tutorial Lessons disk, and press Enter.

The Help and Tutorial Disk

Symphony makes available a series of help screens to which you can easily refer while you're working in the program. If you are using a system with two 5 1/4-inch disk drives, you need to replace the main Symphony Program disk with the Help and Tutorial disk and press the F1 function key to access a help screen while working in the program.

Each screen contains information on a topic listed in the Help Index (see fig. 2.31). To retrieve the Help Index, simply move the cell pointer to the bottom of the screen, position it over Help Index, and press Enter. When the Help Index appears, you will notice that it is arranged alphabetically according to general topics. To select a help screen topic, position the cursor over a heading and press Enter.

Each heading within the Help Index consists of a series of screens, which are organized in two ways. First, screens are organized according to the topics in

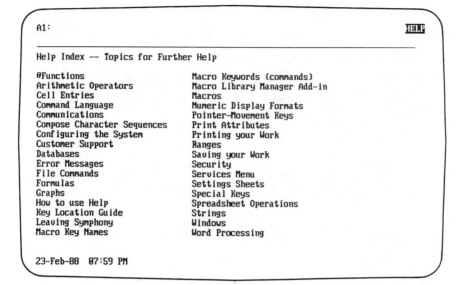

Fig. 2.31
The Help Index.

the Help Index; the @Function help screen, for example, lists all the types of functions. Second, many help screens contain cross-references listed in the bottom left corner of the help screen. If, for example, you select the Database Statistical Functions help screen, it contains cross-references to Database Ranges and Criterion Ranges, among other things (see fig. 2.32). By positioning the cursor on either of these cross-references, you can retrieve the help screen for either Database Ranges or Criterion Ranges.

You can also invoke help immediately after you encounter an error. If you press the F1 function key while the ERROR indicator is still flashing in the upper right corner, a Help screen pops up with detailed information concerning the error.

Chapter Summary

This chapter has provided information for helping you begin to use Symphony. The chapter has presented an overview of Symphony: the Symphony Access System, the menu structure, the window feature, the keyboard, the display, and the Tutorial disks. Now that you have had a chance to discover Symphony, read the following chapters for a closer view of Symphony's capabilities. These include creating spreadsheets; using file commands; using word processing; printing reports; creating and displaying graphs; and using data-management, communications, and macro features.

Fig. 2.32

*Cross-references in
the Help Index.*

```
A1:                                                                    HELP
─────────────────────────────────────────────────────────────────────────
Database Statistical Functions

@DAVG(db_range,col_num,crit_range)      average of selected values
@DCOUNT(db_range,col_num,crit_range)    number of selected values
@DMAX(db_range,col_num,crit_range)      maximum of selected values
@DMIN(db_range,col_num,crit_range)      minimum of selected values
@DSTD(db_range,col_num,crit_range)      standard deviation of selected values
@DSUM(db_range,col_num,crit_range)      sum of selected values
@DVAR(db_range,col_num,crit_range)      variance of selected values

Note:   You must structure the db_range and crit_range like actual Database
        and Criterion ranges, but you need not specify the ranges on a
        Database settings sheet.  Each function uses a crit_range argument
        to select certain records from the db_range and then perform a
        statistical analysis on one field (col-num).


─────────────────────────────────────────────────────────────────────────
Database Ranges        Criterion Ranges      @Functions
@Function Syntax       Help Index

23-Feb-88  08:05 PM
```

PART II

Learning Symphony
Worksheet Basics

Includes

The Symphony SHEET Window

SHEET Window Commands

@Functions

File Operations

SHEET Window Hands-On Practice

3

The Symphony SHEET Window

If you have used 1-2-3, the Symphony spreadsheet application (SHEET window) will be familiar to you. Examining this feature is a good way to begin learning about Symphony. Entering and editing data, moving the cell pointer, and identifying and using ranges are much the same in 1-2-3 and Symphony. Like its counterpart in 1-2-3, Symphony's spreadsheet application is the foundation of the program. And even without the other applications—word processing, data management, graphics, and communications—Symphony is an amazingly powerful program.

The spreadsheet is the basis for the whole Symphony product. Even when you are working in the word-processing window (DOC) or the data-form window (FORM), all data is stored within the worksheet boundaries. Because of this arrangement, entries and changes in a DOC or FORM window can affect a spreadsheet that is entered on the same worksheet.

All of Symphony's other applications depend on the spreadsheet also. For instance, to create a data form, you enter the form in a spreadsheet window and then switch to a FORM window. The database created from form entries is viewed within the spreadsheet environment and can be changed in a SHEET window. Although a separate GRAPH window exists, the spreadsheet menu contains its own commands for creating graphs. In fact, all commands for displaying graphs refer to entries in the spreadsheet and use these entries to draw graphs on the screen. Finally, macros and the Command Language depend on the SHEET environment. To edit a macro, you need to work in a SHEET window.

Worksheet Size and Its Effect on RAM

Symphony's worksheet contains 8,192 rows and 256 columns (2,097,152 cells). Each column is assigned a one- or two-letter name ranging from A for the first column to IV for the last. A good way to visualize the worksheet is to imagine a giant sheet of grid paper about 21 feet wide and 176 feet high!

Compared to the tremendous overall size of the Symphony worksheet, the video display is capable of showing on-screen only 20 rows and 72 characters at a time. As illustrated in figure 3.1, the screen represents one small window on the Symphony worksheet. Because of the worksheet's size, you have plenty of room to create many windows within the same worksheet: windows containing different kinds of spreadsheets; databases; and notes, memos, or short reports.

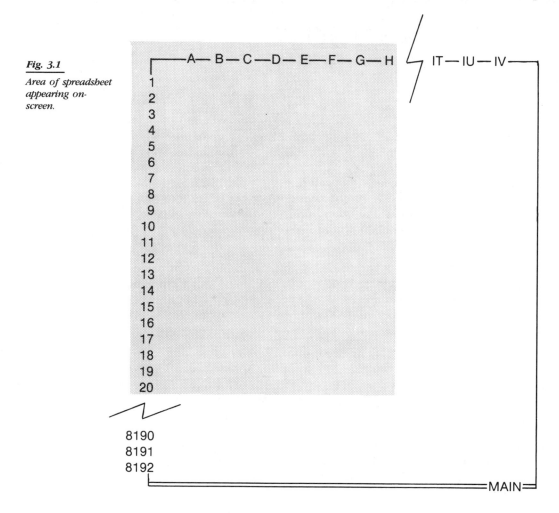

Fig. 3.1

Area of spreadsheet appearing on-screen.

Symphony has some limitations, however, to using the entire sheet. In practical terms, you must consider memory limitations when you are determining the size and complexity of a spreadsheet or database.

The Symphony program with DOS requires approximately 350K of RAM. Symphony's large size stems primarily from the programming required for all the extra features that Symphony provides. Such features as windows, settings sheets, and extensive use of range names require memory on top of the memory required for your data.

In addition to the size of the Symphony program, you must consider the size of the worksheet in RAM. The number of active cells in a worksheet cannot simply be equated to its RAM requirements, because the contents of cells can vary greatly. Perhaps the best way to get a realistic notion of the potential size of a worksheet is to conduct two simple tests. In the first test, you can relate the size of the worksheet to the number of standard 8 1/2-by-11-inch pages that can fit into the worksheet. In the second test, you can experiment with filling cells in the worksheet, using the Copy command, and then see when you run out of main memory. From these two tests, you can draw realistic conclusions about the worksheet size.

To begin the first test, use a configuration of 640K of RAM. After you subtract 350K for the Symphony program and DOS, a worksheet size of 290K remains. If you divide the remaining RAM by the number of characters that fit on a standard 8 1/2-by-11-inch page with pica type (approximately 3,000 characters), you get approximately 96 pages. This figure points out the theoretical capacity of the Symphony sheet. In the second test, again use the configuration of 640K. Begin by entering the label **ABCDEF** in cell A1. Then duplicate this cell until you run out of main memory.

These tests indicate that you can fill columns A, B, and most of C—approximately 24,000 cells. Assuming that 448 cells are on a printed page (8 columns by 56 rows), you could build a 53-page spreadsheet. The results from these two tests demonstrate the difference between theory and reality. Because of the way Symphony allocates memory, in reality your worksheets may be approximately half the size that you might expect.

As you can see, an important consideration when using Symphony is the size of the worksheets you will be creating. Symphony requires a computer with at least 384K of memory; if you are operating Symphony with 384K, you will be limited in the amount of space you can use on your worksheet. You will particularly find memory restricted when you create multiple windows in various sections of your worksheet.

A few guidelines, however, will help you get the most from the amount of memory you have available. First, try to monitor your memory use by periodically checking how much memory is available for your worksheet. You can easily check memory by selecting **S**ettings from the SERVICES menu.

Second, you need to understand how Symphony allocates and consumes memory. Symphony takes a columnar view of things. In other words, space is consumed from the first nonblank cell in a column down to the last nonblank cell in that column. Although blank cells between the first and last nonblank cells in a column still take up space, each column is viewed independently. Although Symphony's memory allocation scheme uses an efficient columnar orientation, strive to keep the active areas within any column packed as close as possible. If you spread out your entries too much, you may find yourself running out of memory because RAM is required to store the contents of cells between entries, even though only blanks may be in the cells. For example, the spreadsheets in figures 3.2 and 3.3 contain the same information, but the first spreadsheet requires about 8 percent more RAM than the second.

Fig. 3.2

A spreadsheet that doesn't economize on space.

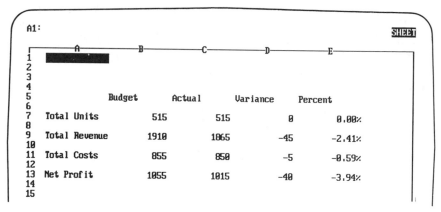

Fig. 3.3

A spreadsheet that economizes on space.

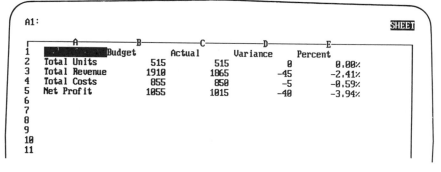

Finally, remember that when you delete a part of a worksheet, the main memory requirements for that worksheet do not diminish completely until you save it to your disk, then load the worksheet back into RAM. Symphony's optimization routines are not totally activated until you store a worksheet. Also, using the SERVICES File Xtract command to shrink the memory requirements further may help. (The commands for storing and retrieving worksheets are covered in Chapter 6, "File Operations.")

Expanded Memory Specification (EMS)

Releases 1.1 and higher of Symphony can take advantage of the Lotus/Intel/Microsoft® Expanded Memory Specification, a combination hardware/software trick to fool the operating system into recognizing more memory than it usually can. Until this method was developed, any program (including Symphony) that operated under normal DOS could not access more than 640K of RAM; Symphony worksheet creation was thus limited to about 290K of memory.

Plug-in memory boards that support expanded memory are now available. By adding one of these boards to your computer, you can break through the DOS memory barrier of 640K RAM. In fact, Releases 1.1 and higher of Symphony can address up to about four megabytes of memory under EMS. That is quite a jump.

EMS is not, however, the perfect solution to the need for more memory. Even with plenty of expanded memory available, you can fill conventional memory (up to 640K) to the point that Symphony will not allow you to proceed. Expanded memory stores only certain kinds of information, and conventional memory is needed to do much of the "bookkeeping" associated with keeping track of such information. Furthermore, depending on the exact nature of your worksheets, you will notice that speed decreases as your worksheet expands to fill the available space.

Speed

Symphony's recalculation speed is an outstanding feature of the program. The speed of Symphony's cell pointer movement is also quite remarkable if you take into account Symphony's large worksheet size. The pointer moves instantly, with almost no visible delay, from the top left corner of the worksheet to the bottom right corner. In contrast with several other spreadsheet programs in which the screen flickers whenever the pointer is moved, Symphony shows almost no flickering. The screen reacts fast enough for you to move quickly to a cell without overshooting and ending up several cells beyond your mark.

Symphony can also "recognize" that a coprocessor microchip exists in your computer. Thus, if you install an 8087 chip in your PC or an 80287 in the AT (and set the appropriate system switch), Symphony can use the chip to speed up certain mathematical calculations. This speed increase applies more to such complex calculations as powers, roots, and algebraic and statistical functions than to standard addition and subtraction.

Entering Data

If you have worked with spreadsheets before, you will recall that you can make three different types of cell entries: labels, numbers, and formulas (including functions). You enter data in a cell simply by positioning the cell pointer in the cell and typing the entry. From the first character that you enter, Symphony interprets the type of cell entry you are making. If you start with one of these characters:

0 1 2 3 4 5 6 7 8 9 + - . (@ # $

Symphony treats your entry as either a number or a formula. If you begin by entering a character other than one of those listed, Symphony treats your entry as a label.

Entering Labels

As you enter a value into the cell, if the first character is not one of those listed previously for entering numbers and formulas, Symphony shifts to LABEL mode.

In spreadsheets, labels commonly are used for row and column headers. A label can be up to 240 characters long and can contain any string of characters and numbers. If a label is too long for the width of a cell, the label will display across the cells to the right, as long as these neighboring cells contain no other entries (see fig. 3.4).

Fig. 3.4

How a label continues across cells.

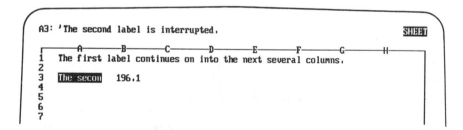

Symphony offers a handy feature: you can left-, center-, or right-justify labels when you display them (see fig. 3.5). You must precede the label with one of the following label-prefix characters:

Character	Action
'	Left-justifies
^	Centers
"	Right-justifies
\	Repeats

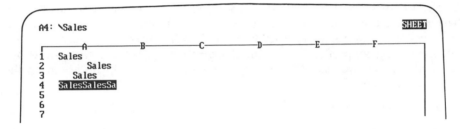

Fig. 3.5

Left-aligned, right-aligned, centered, and repeating labels.

The display default is left-justification. Symphony automatically enters the label prefix. For example, when you enter

Net Income

Symphony stores

'Net Income

If you want to enter a header that begins with a numeral, such as 1988 Sales, you must type the prefix before 1988 ('**1988 Sales**). Symphony then interprets 1988 as a label and automatically left-justifies, as the program does for other labels. If you want to center this header, you enter ^**1988 Sales**.

The most unusual label prefix is the backslash (\ ), which is used for repetition. One of the most frequent uses of this prefix is to create a separator line. The first step is to enter \= in the cell where you want the line to begin (cell A3 in fig. 3.6). This entry causes the equal sign to appear across the entire cell. Once you have set up the first cell, you then use the Copy command from the SHEET menu to replicate the cell across or to other parts of the worksheet (see fig. 3.7). For more information about the Copy command and replication, see Chapter 4.

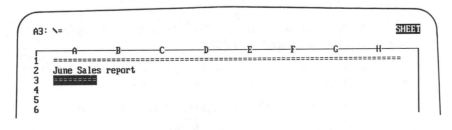

Fig. 3.6

A repeating label prefix.

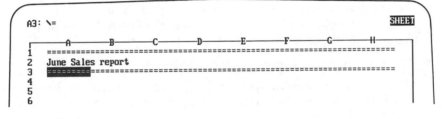

Fig. 3.7

Creating a separator line.

You can control label prefixes in several ways. For example, suppose that you have entered a series of labels, using the standard default of left-justification, but you decide that you would rather have the labels centered. You can manually change each label prefix, or you can change them all at once with the **Range Label-Alignment** command. When you select this command, you are given the following choices:

Left   Right   Center

Each choice gives you the appropriate label prefix (for example, **Left** produces the ' prefix). After you choose **Left**, **Right**, or **Center**, Symphony asks you to designate a range of cells to change. When you specify a range and press Enter, the cells in that range are displayed according to the justification choice you made.

Another option for changing label prefixes is to change the default setting for text justification. The command for this operation is **Settings Label-Prefix** from the SHEET command menu. This command gives you the same options as **Range Label-Alignment**. But after you change label justification with the **Settings Label-Prefix** command, the labels entered before you changed the setting remain as originally aligned. Labels entered after you changed justification appear as set until you change Label-Alignment again.

Entering Numbers

If you begin an entry with any of these characters:

0   1   2   3   4   5   6   7   8   9   +   -   .   (@   # $

Symphony interprets the entry as a number or formula, and you can use cell entry to perform numerous operations. Here are some simple rules for entering numbers:

1. You can begin a number only with the characters 0 through 9, a decimal point, or a dollar sign ($).

2. You can end a number with a percent sign (%), which indicates to Symphony to divide by 100 the number that precedes the sign.

3. You cannot have more than one decimal point in a number.

4. Although you may not use commas when you enter a number, you can display commas with the Format command. You can also suppress the display of a number, or you can display the formula rather than the value itself. (See Chapter 4.)

5. You can enter a number in scientific notation.

If you do not follow these rules when entering a number, Symphony beeps when you press Enter. Symphony also automatically shifts to EDIT mode just as if you had pressed F2. (See this chapter's "Editing" section for an explanation of how to respond.)

Entering Formulas

A special feature of Symphony is that it can process not only formulas relating values but also formulas connecting text strings. The capability to process formulas involving strings is uncommon in spreadsheet programs; computing mathematical formulas, however, is primary to these programs. Generally, electronic spreadsheets allow you to create mathematical relationships among cells. For example, if cell C1 contains the formula

   +A1+B1

then C1 displays the sum of the contents of cells A1 and B1. The cell references serve as variables in the equation. No matter what numbers you enter in A1 and B1, cell C1 always returns their sum. For example, if cell A1 contains the number 5 and cell B1 contains the number 10, the formula in C1 returns the value 15. If you change the number in cell A1 to 4, C1 also changes—to 14. Of course, spreadsheet formulas can be much more complex than this simple example. A cell can be added to, subtracted from, multiplied by, or divided by any other cell. You also can apply spreadsheet functions to the cells.

To enter a formula into a cell, you need to follow certain rules. Suppose, for example, that you want to create a formula which adds a row of numbers—in figure 3.8, the amounts in cells B1, C1, D1, and E1—and place the result in cell F1.

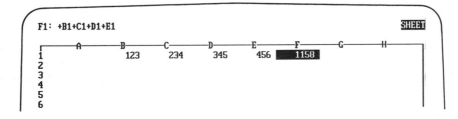

Fig. 3.8

A formula that adds a row of numbers.

One formula that will perform the addition is +B1+C1+D1+E1. The plus sign (+) at the beginning of the formula tells Symphony to interpret the entry as a formula, not a label. For Symphony to recognize an entry as a formula, the entry must begin with one of the following characters:

   0   1   2   3   4   5   6   7   8   9   +   -   .   (@   # $

Entering Cell Addresses in Formulas

You can use two methods to enter cell addresses in formulas: typing and pointing. Both accomplish the same result, and you can mix and match the two techniques within the same formula. Typing cell addresses is self-explanatory, but pointing to cell addresses requires some explanation. The method used is the same as that used in pointing to cell ranges (see the section entitled "Pointing to Cells: The Expanding Cursor" in Chapter 4), but in this case the range is only a single cell.

To enter the formula +B1+C1+D1+E1 by pointing, place the cell pointer in F1, press the plus sign, and move the cell pointer to B1. Notice that the address for the cell (B1) appears after the plus in the second line of the control panel, and that the mode indicator in the upper right corner of the screen shifts from VALUE to POINT mode.

To continue to the next address in the formula, type another plus sign. The cell pointer moves immediately from cell B1 back to the cell where the pointer was located when you began entering the formula—in this case, cell F1. Also, the mode indicator shifts back to VALUE. You continue this sequence of pointing and entering plus signs until you have the formula you want. Remember that nothing prohibits you from using a combination of the two methods of pointing and typing. Use whatever works best for you.

Usually, you will find that it is easier to point to cells that are close to the cell you are defining but simpler to type references to distant cells. Symphony makes pointing to distant cells quite simple, however, because of the End, PgUp, PgDn, and Ctrl keys that help you move quickly around the spreadsheet.

Operators

Operators indicate arithmetic operations in formulas. These operations can be classified as three types: mathematical, logical, and string. Logical operators are discussed in Chapters 5 and 15. The mathematical and string operators are listed here:

Operator	Meaning
^	Exponentiation
+,-	Positive, Negative
*,/	Multiplication, Division
+,-	Addition, Subtraction
&	String Concatenation

Important to understanding operators is knowing their order of precedence. The previous list is arranged in order of precedence. Operators with the highest order of precedence are at the top; operators with equal precedence are listed on the same line and evaluated from left to right. You can always use parentheses, though, to override the order of precedence.

Determine the order of precedence in the following formulas, where B3 = 2, C3 = 3, and D3 = 4. Are your answers the same as those given? In the first two formulas, notice particularly how parentheses affect the order of precedence as well as the answer.

Formula	Answer
+C3-D3/B3	1
(C3-D3)/B3	(.5)
+D3*C3-B3^C3	4
+D3*C3*B3/B3^C3-25/5	(2)

Symphony can process complex formulas that involve many levels of nested parentheses. However, the number of levels is limited. If Symphony is unable to process a formula because it contains too many levels of nested parentheses, ERR, rather than the answer, is displayed. If the formula is too long, the computer beeps and the EDIT indicator appears. In the unlikely event that this message occurs, you should split the formula into one or more intermediate calculations.

Functions

Symphony includes a large assortment of built-in functions that you can use in the worksheet. All Symphony functions are considered formulas by the program. In fact, the functions are simply abbreviations for long or complex formulas. Each function consists of three parts: the @ sign, a function name, and an argument or range. The @ sign signals to Symphony that a function is being entered, the name indicates which function is being used, and the argument or range is the data required by Symphony to perform the function. (Ranges are discussed later in this chapter and also in Chapter 4.) Although Chapter 5 provides a detailed discussion of Symphony functions, a brief illustration is provided here to help you begin to understand them.

In figure 3.8, four cell references were used to create the desired formula. But you could use the @SUM function to "sum" the numbers in the example. (The concept of ranges is important to the @SUM function. For now, think of a range as simply a continuous group of cells.) When you use the @SUM function, the equivalent to the +B1+C1+D1+E1 formula is @SUM(B1..E1). The only difference between the two formulas is one of convenience. Had several more entries extended across the row, the @SUM function would change only slightly in order to use the address of the last cell to be summed. For example, @SUM(B1..Z1) would sum the contents of the first row all the way from B to Z.

String Formulas

As mentioned earlier, Symphony's string arithmetic permits you to create formulas for joining words, phrases, or even sentences. Special functions enable you to perform various operations on strings, including joining them together, converting strings to numbers, and indicating the total number of characters in a string. (These special functions are discussed in Chapters 5 and 15.)

String formulas can join words, phrases, and sentences originally entered in SHEET, DOC, or FORM windows; the string formula, however, must be entered in a SHEET or DOC window. String formulas also are discussed in Chapters 5 and 15, but the following general principles should be mentioned here:

- Like formulas for values, formulas containing strings must begin with the plus sign (+).

- The ampersand (&), which is the special operator for strings, tells Symphony to join items together.

- Like formulas involving values, string formulas also use cell addresses. For example, if you enter **John** in cell B1 and **Smith** in cell B2, the formula +B1&B2 results in JohnSmith.

- To add a space between the first and last name, you indicate within the formula that a space belongs between the two cell entries, as in

    +B1&" "&B2

    Whenever you want to include in a formula an element that is not the cell address itself or a range name, you must enclose that element in double quotation marks. In the previous example, the space is enclosed in double quotation marks, telling Symphony to add a space between B1 and B2.

- You can indicate cell addresses by either typing or pointing.

- String formulas involving functions follow the same rules as mathematical formulas. That is, string functions begin with an @ sign, followed by the function name and an argument or range in parentheses.

Symphony's string arithmetic enables you to apply many types of functions to strings stored in databases, in spreadsheets themselves, and in text produced through Symphony's word-processing capability. In the following chapters, you will find specific explanations of the many string arithmetic functions and suggested applications for using these functions.

Editing

Because of Symphony's complexity, four kinds of editing are possible. First, you can edit data that you are entering in response to a command. For example, you can edit range names, cell addresses, or special entries that you are making in settings sheets. You can edit this data if you have not pressed Enter and "locked in" the entry. The other three kinds of editing involve data that you are entering or have already entered in SHEET, DOC, and FORM windows. This section covers the keys and procedures for editing in a SHEET window, which includes editing labels, values, and formulas. (The procedures for erasing ranges and deleting rows and columns are discussed in Chapter 4.)

Editing an entry in a SHEET window is easy to do in Symphony. To edit an entry in a Symphony worksheet, you begin by moving the cell pointer to the appropriate cell and pressing the F2 function key (the Edit key). If you are in the process of typing the entry, simply press F2.

When you press F2, Symphony switches from SHEET mode to EDIT mode. (The mode indicator in the upper right corner of the screen changes to EDIT.) The cell contents are duplicated in the second line of the control panel (in this book, called the "edit line") and are then ready for editing.

In EDIT mode, the following keys function differently than they do in SHEET mode:

Key	Action in EDIT Mode
←	Moves the cursor one position to the left
→	Moves the cursor one position to the right
Home	Moves the cursor to the first character position of the edit line
End	Moves the cursor one position to the right of the last character
Ctrl-→	Moves the cursor five characters to the right
Ctrl-←	Moves the cursor five characters to the left
Backspace	Deletes the character just to the left of the cursor
Del	Deletes the character above the cursor
Esc	Clears the edit line (will also cancel data that you haven't finished typing)

To show how these keys are used, let's consider two examples. First, suppose that you want to edit an entry in cell E4 that reads Sales Comparisson. After you position the cell pointer in cell E4, here are the keys to press:

Key	Edit Line	Explanation
F2	'Sales Comparisson_	The cursor always appears at the end of the edit line when you press F2.
← ← ←	'Sales Comparisson	The cursor now appears below the extra *s*.
Del	'Sales Comparison	The Del key deletes the character above the cursor.
Enter		You must press Enter to update the entry in the spreadsheet and return to SHEET mode.

One thing to remember about using EDIT mode is that you can use it also when you are entering a cell for the first time and you make a mistake. With EDIT mode, you can eliminate retyping.

Now suppose that you want to change the formula in cell G6 from +D4/H3*(Y5+4000) to +C4/H3*(Y5+4000). After you move the cell pointer to cell G6, press the following keys:

Key	Edit Line	Explanation
F2	+D4/H3*(Y5+4000)_	Again, the cursor always appears at the end of the edit line when you first press F2.
Home	+D4/H3*(Y5+4000)	The Home key takes you to the first position in the edit line.
→	+D4/H3*(Y5+4000)	The → key moves the cursor one position to the right.

C	+CD4/H3*(Y5+4000)	Whenever you enter a character in EDIT mode, the character is inserted to the left of the cursor. Entering a character will never cause you to write over another one. You can eliminate unwanted characters with the Del and Backspace keys.
Del	+C4/H3*(Y5+4000)	The Del key deletes the character above the cursor.
Enter		Again, you must press Enter to update the entry in the spreadsheet and return to SHEET mode.

You can use the F2 (Edit) and F8 (Calc) function keys together to convert a formula stored in a cell to a simple number. Normally, F8 is used for recalculating when **Settings Recalculation** in the SHEET menu is set to **Manual**. (The Recalculation command is covered in Chapter 4.) When you are in EDIT mode, however, pressing F8 causes a formula to be converted to a number that is its current value.

For example, suppose that you want to use F8 to convert the formula in the previous example to its current value (assumed to be 64,000) and store the result. You should take the following steps:

Key	Edit Line	Explanation
F2	+C4/H3*(Y5+4000)_	F2 puts Symphony in EDIT mode.
F8	64000_	F8 converts the formula to its current value (64,000).
Enter	Enter stores the entry in the current cell and shifts the program back to SHEET mode.	

Ranges

In Symphony, the commands and functions often require that you deal with a group of cells in aggregate. This group is called a range. A *range* is one or more cells in a rectangular group. The smallest possible range is one cell and the largest range is the size of the worksheet itself.

Using ranges definitely makes your work in Symphony easier and faster. Because of the worksheet size and the possibility that you may have spreadsheets, databases, and word-processing text in various parts of the worksheet, using range names and indicating ranges in settings sheets saves you from having to hunt all over your worksheet for ranges. Ranges also allow you to process blocks of cells in commands and formulas at the same time.

Although you can choose when to use ranges, you soon will learn that using ranges frequently can simplify and speed up many operations. (Ranges are covered in more detail in Chapter 4.) Once you begin using Symphony extensively, you will find that the range feature is more than a convenience; ranges often are necessary for processing commands and moving to various parts of the worksheet. All the commands that use ranges in a SHEET window are included in the next chapter.

The Shape of Ranges

As you can see from figure 3.9, ranges are rectangles. Symphony's expanding-cursor feature allows you to see the shape of ranges. When you designate a range, Symphony displays it in reverse video. As the cell pointer moves, the reverse-video rectangle expands. Defining a range is easy because you can always tell where its borders are.

Fig. 3.9

A reverse-video expanding rectangle.

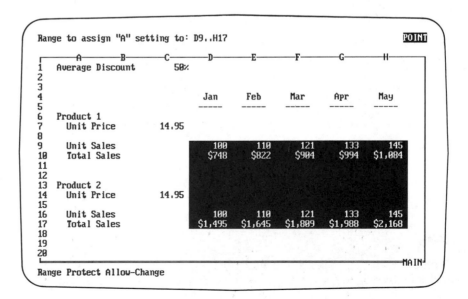

Designating Ranges

You can designate ranges in three ways: by entering cell addresses, pointing to cells, and specifying range names. These methods allow you to indicate the corners of the rectangular group of cells that the range represents.

Ranges are specified by diagonally opposite corners—usually the upper left and lower right cells (see fig. 3.10). Indicating the other set of corners, however, is also permissible. For example, the range shown in figure 3.10 can be identified as A1..D5 or D1..A5.

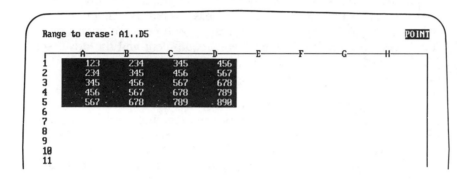

Fig. 3.10

Range specified by diagonally opposite corners.

Cell addresses that specify the corners usually are separated by one or more periods, as in

A7..D10
AA1.AB20
J2...K4

If you separate cell addresses with one period or with three or more, Symphony automatically changes the number of periods to two.

Integrating SHEET Windows with Other Applications

So far, most of this chapter has focused on the SHEET window as a separate application in the Symphony program. But even though you can use the SHEET window apart from the DOC, FORM, GRAPH, and COMM environments, you will get the most from Symphony by integrating your spreadsheet work with the four other applications.

Many possibilities are available for integrating SHEET windows with other types of windows. Some suggestions for coordinating the work that you do in a SHEET window with your work in other kinds of windows follow:

- You can integrate SHEET windows with DOC (word-processing) windows in two ways. First, you can draft reports directly from the data you have collected in a SHEET window. Having a SHEET window with a spreadsheet or database on the screen at the same time you are drafting a report helps you organize your thoughts and present your analysis in the report (see fig. 3.11). Second, as you draft a report in a DOC window, you can easily incorporate figures and charts by using spreadsheets and databases stored in SHEET windows (see fig. 3.12).

- Symphony provides the capability of creating graphs instantly from data collected in spreadsheets and databases. GRAPH windows, moreover, offer the capability of displaying two or more graphs on the screen at once. Depending on your equipment and the driver set, you can display a SHEET window and GRAPH window(s) on the screen simultaneously (see fig. 3.13).

- Once you begin using the FORM environment, you quickly will see how FORM and SHEET environments are integrated. In fact, you will see that getting the most out of Symphony's data-form capability requires working in both environments. These environments are related for two reasons. First, you begin the creation of a data form in a SHEET window. Second, the database created in a FORM window is viewed in a SHEET window. Figure 3.14 shows the relationship of the FORM, SHEET, and GRAPH environments. Also within the SHEET command menu, discussed in Chapter 4, are the primary data-management commands.

Fig. 3.11

Viewing SHEET window while drafting memo in DOC window.

```
 Line 93    Char 33    Page 2,42                  Left, Single          DOC

         Working      Gross      Month              Debt to      Return
Cur Assets Capital    Sales      EAT     Cur Ratio  Equity       On Asset
 1,821,474 $1,085,296 $713,267  23,201      2.57      0.55        0.89
 1,888,461 $1,154,819 $714,820  22,582      2.39      0.55        0.89
 1,875,261 $1,091,880 $717,947  25,481      2.54      0.54        0.10
 1,843,487 $1,118,712 $722,683  24,833      2.61      0.53        0.89
 1,893,724 $1,167,836 $726,572  24,269      2.55      0.53        0.89
                                                        1/88-6/88DB

TO: Jim Swenson, General Manager
FROM: P. G. Hargrave
DATE: July 15, 1988
SUBJECT: Working Capital for '88


As you requested in our meeting last Monday, I
have gathered the figures on Working Capital for
1988 from January to June. As you can see from
the graph, the figures show that
                                                         7/15/88 MEMO
 01-Feb-88   08:31 AM
```

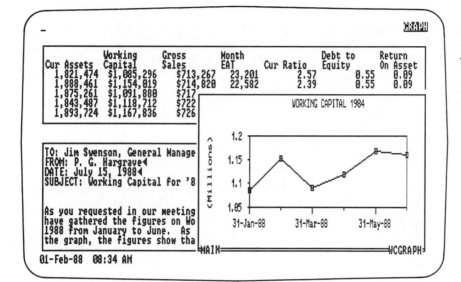

Fig. 3.12

Incorporating figures and charts in DOC reports by using spreadsheets and databases stored in SHEET windows.

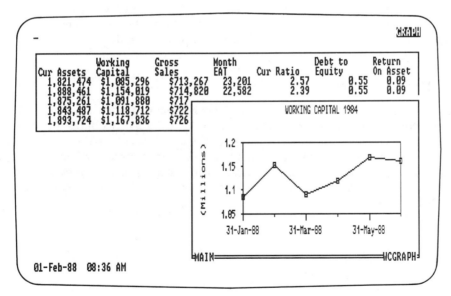

Fig. 3.13

Displaying SHEET and GRAPH windows simultaneously.

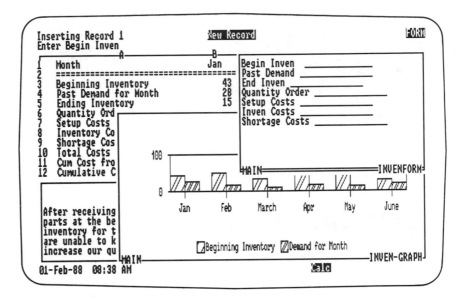

Fig. 3.14

Viewing a related inventory form, database, and graph.

- Symphony's COMM capability depends on the SHEET environment. To use this capability fully, you will need to read-in data transferred through the COMM environment into a SHEET window.

Chapter Summary

As an overview of the Symphony SHEET environment, this chapter has defined the environment's capabilities and described the general procedures for working in a SHEET window. Using these procedures, you will be able to enter and format labels and values easily, build various kinds of sophisticated formulas, edit any cell entry, and integrate SHEET windows with other types of windows. Chapter 4 shows specifically how you can use Symphony's SHEET environment and the SHEET window commands.

SHEET Window Commands

Symphony has a sophisticated command system that provides the full capability of spreadsheet-only programs. Commands are the instructions you give Symphony to perform a variety of tasks, such as formatting a worksheet, creating a graph, or accessing a database. These commands also include replicating formulas, inserting and deleting rows and columns, moving data, switching rows and columns, changing formulas to values, and "hiding" cell contents.

If you have used 1-2-3 for creating spreadsheets, you will find that Symphony's spreadsheet application is much like 1-2-3's. Procedures are similar for entering and editing data, moving the cell pointer, and identifying and using ranges. One major difference should be kept in mind as you use Symphony's SHEET environment: operations that you complete in a SHEET window can affect other windows which you have created on your worksheet. Suppose, for example, that you have created a SHEET window, a DOC window, and a second SHEET window containing a database. Unless you restrict the ranges for each of these windows, changes in one of the SHEET windows may affect the data in the other two windows. In the discussion of the spreadsheet commands, mention is made of those operations that can affect data in other windows.

SHEET Command Menu

Command menus, which are the devices Symphony uses to present command alternatives, allow you to complete a spreadsheet operation easily. You select spreadsheet commands by first retrieving the SHEET command menu. To retrieve the menu, you press either the slash key (/) or the Menu key (F10), hereafter referred to as the SHEET menu key.

The command menu's display makes the system easy to use. As shown in figure 4.1, the menu is visible on the second line of the control panel, while an explanation or list of options appears on the line above. Once you have selected a command, the command name appears in the lower left corner until you have completed all selections or responses.

Fig. 4.1

The SHEET command menu.

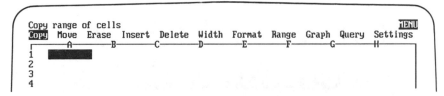

Selecting commands is fairly easy. You can either point to the option you want or enter the first letter of the command name. To point to the command-menu item, use the space bar or the ← and → keys on the right side of the keyboard. When the cursor is positioned at the proper item, press Enter. If you move the cursor to the last item on the list and press the → again, the menu cursor will "round the horn" and reappear on the first item in the list. Similarly, if the menu cursor is on the first item in the menu, pressing the ← moves the cursor to the last option. Pressing the Home key moves the menu cursor to the first option on the menu; the End key moves you to the last option.

Entering the first letter of the command-menu item is another way to select a command. For example, to select the **R**ange **T**ranspose command to switch a column and a row, you press the SHEET menu key (F10) or type /, then type **R** to select **R**ange. At this point, the menu in figure 4.2 appears.

Fig. 4.2

The SHEET Range menu options.

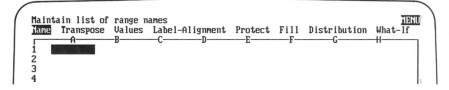

From the line in the menu, you select **T**ranspose by typing **T**. You are then asked to provide information so that Symphony can complete the operation. Throughout this book, the first letter of each word in a command name appears in boldface, emphasizing that you can type the first letter to select the command.

If you find that you have made the wrong command selection, you can press Esc at any time to return to the previous command menu. For instance, if you meant to enter **D**istribution rather than **T**ranspose, press Esc to return to the SHEET **R**ange menu. To move to prior command menus or to move out of MENU mode altogether, enter a series of escapes. You also can hold down the Ctrl key and press the Break key to move out of MENU mode and back to SHEET mode.

If you look back at the Symphony SHEET command menu shown in figure 4.1, you can see that the menu includes commands specifically related to creating spreadsheets (**C**opy, **M**ove, **E**rase, **I**nsert, **D**elete, **W**idth, **F**ormat, **R**ange, and **S**ettings) and graphs (**G**raph) and to conducting database query and sort operations (**Q**uery). This chapter contains the commands for creating spreadsheets. Graphics commands are covered in Chapter 12, and database commands are explained in Chapter 15.

This discussion of spreadsheet commands does not follow the order in which they appear in the menu. The **R**ange commands are discussed first because setting and storing ranges through range names are fundamental tasks in many spreadsheet operations. Following **R**ange commands, the SHEET commands covered in this chapter are **M**ove, **E**rase, **I**nsert, **D**elete, **C**opy, **W**idth, **F**ormat, and three of the **S**ettings options (**Z**ero, **T**itles, and **R**ecalculation).

Range Commands

The commands that operate on ranges are organized in Symphony under the SHEET **R**ange menu. These commands give you the ability to name or protect a range or change the label justification in a range. In SHEET mode, when you press F10 or type /, then type **R**, the menu shown in figure 4.2 appears.

The **L**abel-Alignment command is covered in Chapter 3 in the section entitled "Entering Labels." The other range commands are discussed here.

Naming Ranges (Range Name)

In Symphony, you can assign a name to a range of cells. Range names can be up to 15 characters long and should be descriptive to help you recall what range the name represents. The advantage to naming ranges is that range names are easier to understand and remember than cell addresses, and range names allow you to work more intuitively. For example, describing gross margin with the phrase *SALES - COGS* is more understandable than using *+A17-B10*.

Creating Range Names

You create range names with the **R**ange **N**ame **C**reate and **N**ame **L**abels commands. Once you establish names, you can easily apply them in both commands and formulas. The **R**ange **N**ame **C**reate command allows you to specify a name for any range, even one cell. In executing this command, you can specify ranges by one of two methods: entering the cell address or pointing. You can also use **Range Name Create** to respecify a range if its location has changed. (If a range is affected by minor changes, however, such as the deletion of a column or row of numbers, Symphony handles these changes internally without any respecification.)

You can also use range names when naming macros. A macro is named with **Range Name Create**, as is any other range. (Keyboard macros are discussed in detail in Chapter 19.)

The **Range Name Labels** command is similar to **Range Name Create**, except that with **Range Name Labels**, the names for ranges are taken directly from adjacent label entries. For example, look at figure 4.3. If you use the **Range Name Labels** command and specify that the appropriate name for cell B1 is to the left in cell A1, you can assign the name *Cash* to the range B1. If you assign the label *Accounts Receivable* as a range name, Symphony stores *Accounts Receiv*. Symphony accepts only up to 15 characters (including spaces) for any range name or range name label.

Fig. 4.3

Using the Range Name Labels command.

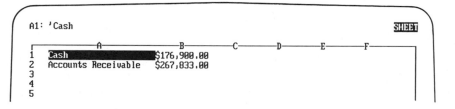

Deleting Range Names

You can delete range names individually or all at once. The **Range Name Delete** command allows you to delete a single range name. The **Range Name Reset** command causes all range names to be deleted. Because of the command's power, you should use **Range Name Reset** with caution.

Creating a Table of Range Names

With the **Range Name Table** command, you can create a list of range names on the current worksheet. The **Range Name Table** option enables you to print a list of range names or see on the screen all the range names you have created (see fig. 4.4).

Creating a range name table is simple, although you should be careful about where you tell Symphony to put the table. To create it, first select the **Range Name Table** command. Then when Symphony asks for the table's location, indicate the range on your worksheet where you want the table and press Enter. Be certain to tell Symphony to place the table in an area that won't interfere

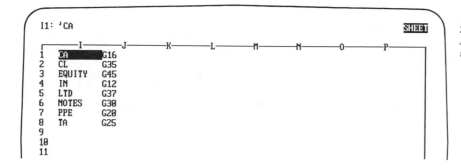

Fig. 4.4

A table of existing range names.

with any other worksheet data. Otherwise, the table will overwrite previously entered data.

Using Range Names

After you've created range names, they can be useful tools in processing commands and generating formulas. In both cases, whenever you must designate a range, you can enter a name instead. Using names eliminates the repetitive task of either entering cell addresses or pointing to cell locations each time a range specification is called for. Suppose that you had designated SALES as a range name for the range A5..J5 in one of your worksheets. The simplest way to compute the sum of this range would then be to use the formula @SUM(SALES). Similarly, to determine the maximum value in the range, you could use the formula @MAX(SALES). You can always use range names in place of cell addresses in functions and formulas.

Symphony also lets you use multiple names for the same range. For example, you can give a cell the range names 1987 SALES and SALES PREV YR in the same worksheet.

Still another advantage is that once you have established a range name, Symphony automatically uses that name throughout the worksheet in place of cell addresses. If you delete a range name, Symphony no longer uses that name but reverts to cell addresses.

Let's look at a few examples of using range names. Figure 4.5 illustrates a simple case of summing two rows of numbers.

If you assigned the range name SALES to the range D3..G3, and the name CGS to range D4..G4, you can define cell H3 with the formula

@SUM(SALES)

Similarly, cell H4 can be assigned the formula

@SUM(CGS)

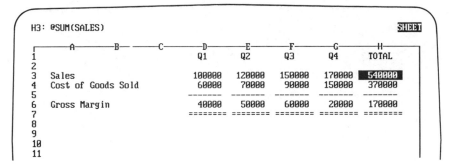

Fig. 4.5

*Range name used
in a formula.*

```
H3: @SUM(SALES)                                                    SHEET
     ┌───A────────B────────C────────D────────E────────F────────G────────H──────
     1                               Q1       Q2       Q3       Q4     TOTAL
     2
     3    Sales                    100000   120000   150000   170000   540000
     4    Cost of Goods Sold        60000    70000    90000   150000   370000
     5                            ───────  ───────  ───────  ───────  ───────
     6    Gross Margin              40000    50000    60000    20000   170000
     7                            ======== ======== ======== ======== ========
     8
     9
    10
    11
```

Finally, cell H6 can contain the formula

@SUM(SALES)-@SUM(CGS)

Another example uses names to designate the ranges of cells to be printed or saved. Suppose that you set up special names corresponding to different areas and want to print or save to another worksheet those special ranges. When Symphony prompts you for a range, you can enter a predefined name rather than actual cell addresses. For example, in response to the print range prompt, you can enter the range name *PAGE 1* or the name *PAGE 5*.

A third range-name example involves the GoTo key (F5). You will recall that the GoTo key allows you to move the cell pointer directly to a cell when you specify the cell's address. An alternative is to provide a range name rather than a cell address. For example, suppose that you create a "help" screen, similar to the one shown in figure 4.6, and name that range INSTRUCT. You can then enter INSTRUCT in response to Address to go to: whenever you want to see your set of instructions on the screen.

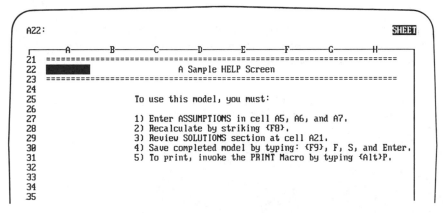

Fig. 4.6

*A sample Help
screen.*

```
A22:                                                               SHEET
     ┌───A────────B────────C────────D────────E────────F────────G────────H──────
    21  =====================================================================
    22  ▮▮▮▮▮▮▮▮▮               A Sample HELP Screen
    23  =====================================================================
    24
    25                   To use this model, you must:
    26
    27                   1) Enter ASSUMPTIONS in cell A5, A6, and A7.
    28                   2) Recalculate by striking {F8}.
    29                   3) Review SOLUTIONS section at cell A21.
    30                   4) Save completed model by typing: {F9}, F, S, and Enter.
    31                   5) To print, invoke the PRINT Macro by typing {Alt}P.
    32
    33
    34
    35
```

To see a list of range names when you are prompted for a range, press the SHEET menu key (F10). For example, you can press the GoTo key followed by the

SHEET menu key and then select from the list the range name to which you want to go.

Using the SALES example of figure 4.5 again, suppose that you assign the name CGS to the range D4..G4. You can erase this portion of the worksheet by pressing F10 or typing /, selecting **Erase**, then entering the range name **CGS** rather than cell coordinates D4..G4.

Suppose that after you select the **Erase** command, you cannot remember the name of the range you want to erase. You can press the SHEET menu key to produce a list of the range names in the current worksheet. If you have more range names than will fit across the control panel, press the SHEET menu key a second time. Symphony displays a complete list of range names on the screen. Figure 4.7 shows the screen with the two range names displayed in the control panel. After the list appears, you can use the cursor to point to the first alternative (CGS) and select it by pressing Enter.

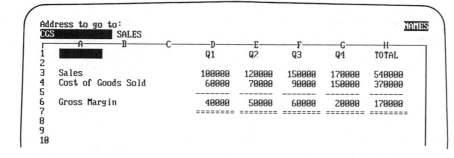

Fig. 4.7

Range names listed in the control panel.

Transposing Rows and Columns (Range Transpose)

With the **Range Transpose** command, you can transform rows to columns or columns to rows. This feature is particularly useful if, for example, you want to convert a monthly inventory sheet, with items listed in column A, to a database that displays each item in a separate column with its monthly figure totaled below it. Figure 4.8 shows such a database.

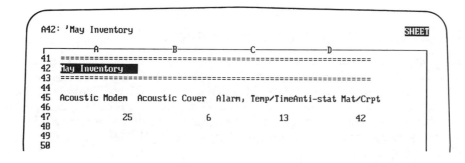

Fig. 4.8

Transposing columns to rows.

As indicated by this example, the **Range Transpose** command allows you to copy labels, values, and formulas and to reverse their positions from rows to columns or from columns to rows. To use this command, select **Range Transpose**, indicate the range of the original column or row, and then specify the range for the new column or row.

When using **Range Transpose**, you should be aware of the following possibilities. First, if you are transposing values or formulas, Symphony either recalculates or indicates that you should press the Calc key when copying is completed. If, however, the range you are transposing contains relative cell addresses (discussed in the section on "Copying"), Symphony cannot convert the cell addresses. In this case, formulas do not recalculate correctly. Second, make sure that the TO range won't interfere with other worksheet data. Otherwise, the transposed columns and rows will overwrite previously entered data.

Copying Values (Range Values)

With **Range Values**, you can copy a range of values from one part of a worksheet to another. This feature is useful when you want to preserve current values that will be changed when new values are entered. What is particularly important about the **Range Values** command is that it converts formulas to values. You don't have to worry, therefore, about formulas that depend on cell references. (Copying formulas with cell addresses is discussed in more detail in the section entitled "Copying.")

Now consider the following illustration of the use of the **Range Values** command. Suppose that you calculate monthly totals from values entered into an income statement, as in figure 4.9. As you change the sheet every month, the Year-to-Date (Y-T-D) totals change as well. If, however, you want to save the Y-T-D totals to compare them with previous years or quarters, the **Range Values** command enables you to do so, as illustrated in figure 4.10.

To copy values in Symphony, select **Range Values**. When Symphony asks for Range to copy FROM:, indicate what range of values you want copied. Then indicate where you want the values copied, being careful that the newly copied values don't overwrite existing data.

Protecting Ranges (Range Protect)

You can use the **Range Protect** command simply to "freeze" a range, thus preventing changes. In addition, when used with the SERVICES **Settings Global-Protection** and SHEET **Format Other Hidden** commands, **Range Protect** permits you to hide a range of cells and prevent another user from making changes in these cells unless that user enters a password especially created by you. (For more on range protection, see the section entitled "Security System" in Chapter 1.)

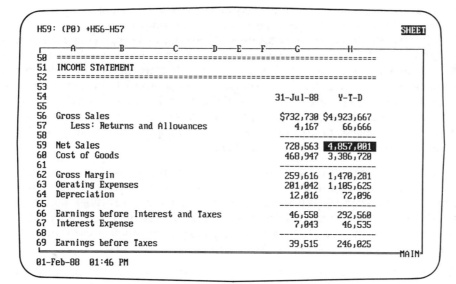

Fig. 4.9

A monthly income statement.

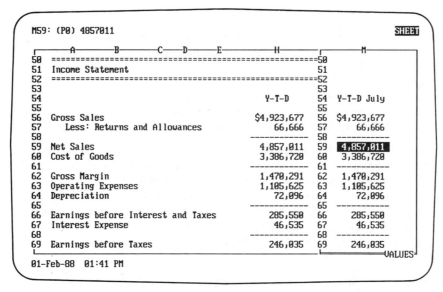

Fig. 4.10

Copying a range of values.

In Symphony, you can use a series of commands to set up ranges of cells that can be changed only with special effort. In fact, rows and columns containing protected cells cannot be deleted from the worksheet. The **Range Protect** command is particularly beneficial when you are setting up worksheets that other people will use but which you don't want changed.

When a worksheet is first created, every cell has the potential of being protected, but no cell is protected unless you invoke the **Settings Global-Protection** command in the SERVICES menu. Lotus uses the analogy of a series of electric fences erected around all the cells in the worksheet. The "juice" to these fences is turned off when the sheet is first loaded. In other words, all the cells in the worksheet can be modified. This arrangement is appropriate because you want to have access to everything in the worksheet while you are creating it. Once you have finished building the worksheet, however, you may have areas that you don't want changed, or you may want to set up special form-entry areas and disallow cell-pointer movement elsewhere.

To protect a range of cells in your worksheet, you need to take certain steps. First, you must provide cell protection for your worksheet. To set **Global-Protection**, evoke the SERVICES menu by pressing F9, select **Settings**, then choose **Global-Protection**. Next, position the cursor on `Yes` in response to `Allow changes only to cells with 'A' setting`, and then press Enter. Once you have issued this command (**Yes**), all cells are protected.

To continue the "electric fence" analogy, the **Global-Protection** command is the switch that activates all the electric fences in the worksheet. After you turn on this switch, your next step is to tell Symphony which fences should be "turned off" so that you can enter data.

Turn off the protection on certain cells by choosing the **Range Protect** command and then selecting **Allow-Changes**. Then indicate the range of cells where changes are to be allowed. You can reprotect these cells at any time by issuing the **Range Protect Prevent-Changes** command. If you want to make changes possible in any cell in the worksheet, select **Settings Global-Protection No** from the SERVICES menu. The chart in figure 4.11 may help you understand the relationship between the **Global-Protection** and **Range Protect** commands.

Suppose that you create a worksheet which includes a number of long and important formulas. You may want to protect these formulas against accidental deletion by using Symphony's protection capability. But what if you need to make a change in several of these formulas? You can allow the formulas to be changed, then prevent the cells from being changed again. Or you can use the **Global-Protection No** setting to "lower the fences" around all the cells. After you make the necessary changes, the **Global-Protection Yes** setting restores protection to all cells.

For even more protection, you can limit the movement of the cell pointer by using the **Window Settings Restrict** selection from the SERVICES menu. Setting a restrict range allows cell-pointer movement only to those cells within the range you set. Suppose, for example, that you want to restrict cell-pointer movement to the area occupied by the data in figure 4.12. To restrict this area, you select **Window** from the SERVICES menu, then **Settings**, then **Restrict**, and finally **Range**. When Symphony asks `Restrict range for this window:`, you type

	SERVICES **G**lobal-Protection **N**o: allow changes to all cells	SERVICES **G**lobal-Protection **Y**es: allow changes to cells with only "A" setting
SHEET **R**ange **P**rotect **A**llow-Changes "A" setting: Allow changes to cells even if **G**lobal-Protection = **Y**es	No Restriction Changes can be made in all cells	Restricted Changes can be made in only "A" cells
SHEET **R**ange **P**rotect **P**revent-Changes Remove "A" setting: Prevent changes to cells when **G**lobal-Protection = **Y**es	No Restriction Changes can be made in all cells	Restricted The "A" marker is removed; no changes can be made

Fig. 4.11

The relationship between Global-Protection and Range Protect.

A57..H76 or move the cell pointer to highlight that range. The restrict range remains in effect in the window where you have set the range until you reset **Restrict**.

```
 Restrict range for this window: A57..H76                    POINT
  ┌──A────B────C────D──E──F────G───────H──────
  57    Less: Returns and Allowances      4,167    66,666
  58
  59  Net Sales                         728,563 4,857,001
  60  Cost of Goods                     468,947 3,386,720
  61
  62  Gross Margin                      259,616 1,470,281
  63  Oerating Expenses                 201,042 1,105,625
  64  Depreciation                       12,016    72,096
  65
  66  Earnings before Interest and Taxes 46,558   292,560
  67  Interest Expense                    7,043    46,535
  68
  69  Earnings before Taxes              39,515   246,025
  70  Income Taxes                       10,342    62,816
  71
  72  Earnings after Taxes               29,173   183,209
  73  Cash Dividends                          0    76,389
  74
  75  Earnings after Dividends          $29,173  $106,820
  76                                    ================
                                                   ─MAIN─
 Window Settings Restrict Range
```

Fig. 4.12

Setting a restrict range.

The **Window Settings Restrict** and the **Range Protect** commands are important features for eliminating the possibility of lost data.

Filling Ranges with Numbers (Range Fill)

The **R**ange **F**ill command has a number of applications throughout the Symphony program, particularly in any SHEET environment where you require a range of values listed in sequence. This range of values can include simply a table of numbers listed in increments of one, or even a list of years, as in figure 4.13. Although you must use **R**ange **F**ill in SHEET mode, you can apply the command in a number of projects: memos or reports that contain long itemized lists, or anything involving a sequence of values or dates.

Fig. 4.13

Two examples of using Range Fill.

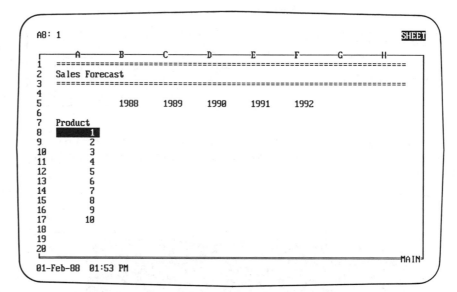

After you choose **R**ange **F**ill, Symphony first asks you where to put the range. Then the program prompts you for the number at which you want the sequence to start and for the step or incremental value that you want to add to the previous value. Finally, you are asked for the ending value at which the filling operation should stop.

Here are the specific steps for entering a sequence of numbers. First retrieve the SHEET menu, select **R**ange, and then select **F**ill when the **R**ange menu appears. Symphony next asks for the Fill range:. Here you indicate the range in the worksheet where the numbers should be listed. In the example in figure 4.13, you would indicate A8..A17. Next, Symphony asks for the Start Value, which in this case is 1, and then the Step Value, or the increment, which is also 1. Finally, you must respond to Stop Value. In this example, you would enter 10. The Symphony default stop value is set at 8191, so it is possible to create a list running the length of the total worksheet area.

One valuable use for the **Range Fill** command is for databases that will be sorted. When you use this command, if you attach consecutive numbers to each record in a database (thereby placing the numbers in a separate field), no matter how much you change the order of the database, you can re-create the original order. You simply sort your database according to the numbers that you attached with **Range Fill**. Using **Range Fill** in this way is particularly helpful if the database you began with has a relational order rather than a numeric one, such as the names of the months in a year. Figures 4.14 and 4.15 show an example before and after resorting. Figure 4.14 shows a database that has been sorted in alphabetical order by first name. Figure 4.15 shows the same database resorted to its original order by the **Range Fill** numbers.

Creating Frequency Distributions (Range Distribution)

Another SHEET command that is valuable when working with databases is the **Range Distribution** command, used to create frequency distributions. For those who are not familiar with this term, a *frequency distribution* is a representation of the relationship between a set of measurement classes and the frequency of occurrence of each class. A simple example of a frequency distribution and the **Range Distribution** command is shown in figure 4.16. This example contains a list of consumers and their product preferences.

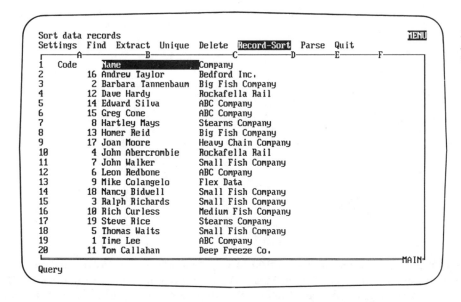

Fig. 4.14

A database before resorting.

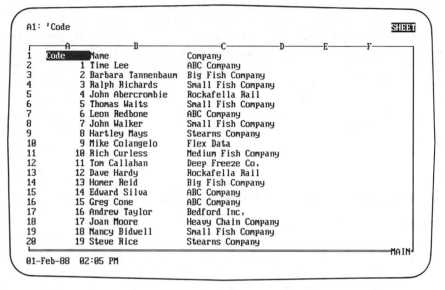

Fig. 4.15

The database resorted to original order.

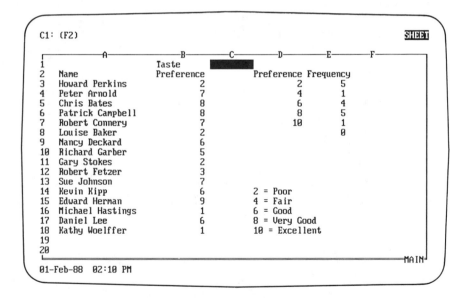

Fig. 4.16

A frequency distribution.

To create the frequency distribution in this example, you need to take the following steps. First, select the **R**ange **D**istribution command from the SHEET menu. Then specify a Values range, which corresponds to the range of numbers listing the "Taste Preference" ratings in column B of figure 4.16. In this example, B3..B18 is the Values range. The next step is to set up the range of intervals, or what Symphony calls the Bin range. Here the Bin range is D3..D7. If you want evenly spaced intervals, you can use the **R**ange **F**ill command to specify the values to be included in the Bin range.

When you specify these ranges and enter the **R**ange **D**istribution command, Symphony returns the Results column (E3..E8) to the right of the Bin range. The Results column is a frequency distribution, which is always in the column segment to the right of the Bin range and extending one row down.

The values in the Results column represent the frequency of occurrence of numbers in the Values range that fall within the interval. The first interval in the Bin range is for values greater than 0 and less than or equal to 2, the second interval is for values greater than 2 and less than or equal to 4, and so on. In the Results column the last value, in cell E8, just below the corresponding column segment, is the frequency of what is left over (that is, the frequency of anything that doesn't fit into an interval classification).

You can use the **R**ange **D**istribution command to create understandable results from a series of numbers, especially in the analysis of surveys. The results are easily graphed, as shown in figure 4.17. According to this graph, the manufacturer of the product should be searching for another product or at least improving the taste of the current one.

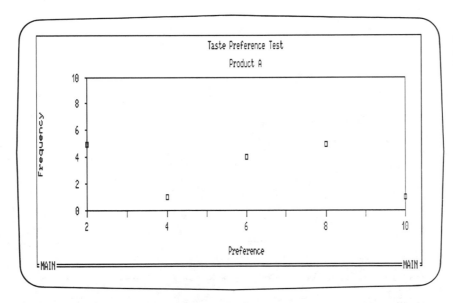

Fig. 4.17

A frequency distribution graph.

"What-If" Analysis (**R**ange **W**hat-If)

Symphony's SHEET **R**ange **W**hat-If command enables you to conduct an extensive analysis with a minimal amount of effort. This command works through iteration.

That is, Symphony takes sets of values and substitutes them one at a time into the worksheet. The results of the substitution are automatically recorded by Symphony. You provide Symphony with the values to substitute and also tell it where to substitute them.

This procedure may sound mysterious, but it is actually very simple. Symphony does most of the work internally. All you have to know is how to set the appropriate ranges. Symphony takes care of the rest.

You may find the **Range What-If** command difficult to use at first. But once you have learned how to use it, you will find that it is one of the most powerful commands in Symphony's SHEET command menu. In fact, the power of this command rivals similar commands in some of the most sophisticated mainframe decision systems. When you consider the ease of implementation, the **Range What-If** command can be one of your most frequently used SHEET commands.

The purpose of the **Range What-If** command is to structure the "what-if" process. The command allows you to build a table of values and have Symphony input them one at a time into a model you have developed. Symphony then records the results in the table, next to the input values.

A simple example of how the command works is illustrated in figure 4.18 in a table of interest rates and their effects on the monthly payments of a 30-year mortgage.

Fig. 4.18

What-if analysis with Range What-If.

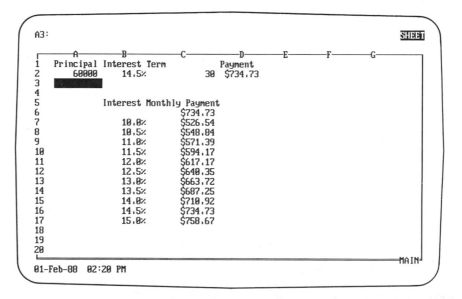

By using the **Range What-If 1**-Way command, you can have Symphony substitute the interest rates you have entered in a column into the appropriate input cell (B2). The input cell is the cell referenced in the original formula into which you want each of the input values substituted. After a few seconds, Symphony lists the corresponding monthly payments in the column next to the interest rates.

Before issuing the **Range What-If** command to calculate the payments shown in figure 4.18, you must enter the principal, interest, and term values in cells A2, B2, and C2, respectively. Then enter in cell D2 the formula for calculating payment: @PMT(A2,B2/12,C2*12). Next, you must enter the interest rate values in a column. (You can use the **Range Fill** command to do so.) Cells B7..B17 hold the interest rates.

The next step is to enter the appropriate formula for calculating the results, or cell address from which to draw them, next to the column of interest rates and one row above the first entry. In the figure 4.18 example, you could enter in cell C6 either the actual formula—@PMT (A2,B2/12,C2*12)—or references to the cell address that contains the formula—+D2.

When you execute the **Range What-If** command, Symphony asks you to indicate a Table Range, which is the range of cells that includes the column of interest rates to be substituted as well as the column where you want the results to appear. The entry for this example is B6..C17. Notice that the formula's row has also been included in the range specification. You are then asked for the input cell. Specify B2 as the input cell, because that is where you want each of the interest rates substituted.

While Symphony is calculating the results, a WAIT sign flashes in the upper right corner of the screen. When Symphony has finished—and sometimes it takes a while—the screen returns to SHEET mode. At this point, the table is complete with all the payment values.

A more involved analysis uses the **Range What-If 2-Way** command. This command requires two input variables rather than one. The advantage to the two-way command is the increased breadth-of-sensitivity analysis.

The **Range What-If 2-Way** command calls for a Table Range and Input Cells for Variables 1 and 2. After you enter this information, Symphony begins building the table of results. The waiting time for the **Range What-If 2-Way** command is substantial, but when you consider what Symphony is accomplishing, the wait is worth it. To duplicate manually what Symphony does would take quite a bit longer.

The advantages of the **Range What-If** command are the abilities to conduct extensive sensitivity analysis and to display the results in a tabular format. The **Range What-If** command lets you do the kind of thorough analysis that you might not do otherwise, given the time required to perform the analysis. Furthermore, the power of the command in combination with macros and special database statistical functions can be outstanding.

Cut-and-Paste Commands

Four primary commands from the SHEET command menu cover the operations that "electronically cut and paste" a spreadsheet. In other words, these commands accomplish what cutting and pasting did in the days of manual spreadsheets: deleting and moving data around on the worksheet. Symphony's cut-and-paste commands include **Move**, **Erase**, **Insert**, and **Delete**.

With these four commands, you have complete control over the appearance of worksheets because the commands allow you to rearrange items in almost any manner. The **Move** command, as its name indicates, moves the contents of cells. The **Erase** command deletes a single cell, row, column, or range of cells. **Insert** enters blank rows and columns in the worksheet, and **Delete** removes rows and columns.

Moving Cell Contents

With **Move**, you can move ranges of cells from one part of the worksheet to another. For example, suppose that you created the sheet shown in figure 4.19 but now want to move the contents of range C1..D3 to the range E1..F3. After you select **Move** from the SHEET menu, Symphony displays the prompt `Range to move FROM:`. You will notice that a range is already specified after this message. To help you enter ranges, Symphony indicates the cell where the cell pointer is presently positioned. If the cell pointer was at cell D7 when you started, the range specified is D7..D7. If the FROM range is different from this range, you can enter the new range in two different ways: either type the addresses of the range's upper left and lower right corners, or move the cell pointer to indicate the range. Instead of typing the addresses, you can type the range name, or press the F10 (Menu) key and then select the range name. To designate the proper FROM range for the example in figure 4.19, type **C1..D3** and press Enter.

Fig. 4.19

The worksheet before using Move.

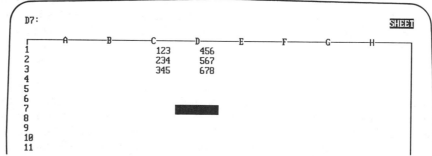

Symphony then asks you to indicate the `Range to move TO:`. Again, a range is already specified for you, and, just as before, it corresponds to the address of the cell where the pointer rests when you initiate the command. To enter your own range, start typing again. For the TO range, you can specify just the single cell E1. Symphony will know that E1 refers to the beginning of the range where you want your list of numbers placed. As soon as you finish designating the TO range and press Enter, the cell pointer returns immediately to where it was when you initiated the command. Figure 4.20 shows the results of the Move operation.

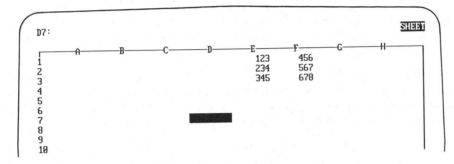

Fig. 4.20

The result of using Move.

When setting ranges, remember that you don't have to position the cell pointer at the beginning of the TO or FROM range when you initiate a command. You can designate a range while the cell pointer is positioned anywhere on the sheet.

A Warning about Move

Whenever you move a range that includes formulas, all the formulas are updated automatically. For example, suppose that you define a simple three-cell worksheet that contains the following data:

    A1 = +D1*100
    C1 = 15
    D1 = +C1

Now suppose that you move the contents of cell D1 to cell E1. The formulas become the following:

    A1 = +E1*100
    C1 = 15
    E1 = +C1

You must be careful about the finality of the Move command. When you move a range of cells into other cells, the TO range is completely overwritten by the FROM range, and the previous contents of the TO range are lost forever. If other cells exist whose formulas depend on the cell addresses of the lost cells, those other cells will be given the value ERR rather than the cell addresses. For example, if you add the cell

    E2 = +E1

to the previous example and repeat the move operation (move D1 to E1), the value of cell E2 changes from 0 to ERR, and the contents of that cell become ERR. The cell E2, once referred to as E1, has been removed and replaced as a result of the move operation.

Pointing to Cells: The Expanding Cell Pointer

Chapter 2 provides a discussion of the keys used for moving the cell pointer in a SHEET window. A few tips and techniques are offered here for defining ranges by pointing to cells.

Suppose that you want to shift the contents of the range C1..D3 to E1..F3, but this time you don't want to enter the cell addresses from the keyboard. Again, assume that the cell pointer was positioned in cell D7 before you initiated the command. When Symphony asks for the FROM range, press Esc.

You must use Esc because Symphony has automatically "anchored" cell D7 for you. In other words, Symphony has automatically designated D7 as one corner of the FROM range. If you do not press Esc and move the cell pointer, you will see the reverse-video field begin to expand, starting at cell D7. Because you do not want to have cell D7 as one corner of the range, you press Esc.

You also can anchor cells yourself by entering a period (.) or by pressing the Tab key. Because you want C1 to be one corner of the FROM range, move the cell pointer to this cell. As you move the cell pointer upward from cell to cell, you will see a change in the address designation in the command field. After you move the cell pointer to C1, type a period to anchor the cell. (Cell C1 may be referred to as the "anchor" cell, and the cell diagonally opposite the anchor cell is called the "free" cell.)

You will notice that cell C1 contains in the middle of it the blinking underscore character. At this point, cell C1 is both the anchor cell and the free cell. But as you move the cell pointer down to cell D3 to point to the other corner of the range, you will see the reverse-video field expand as you shift the free cell. You will also see a change in the second part of the range designation as you move from cell to cell. For example, C1..C2 appears when the cell pointer is at cell C2.

When you reach cell C3, start moving over to cell D3. Now you will see the cell pointer expand in a columnar manner. When you reach cell D3, lock in the range by hitting Enter. The designation of the FROM range appears as though you entered it from the keyboard.

The process for designating the TO range is similar. Once you have specified the FROM range, the cell pointer automatically returns to cell D7. Move the cell pointer to E1 and press Enter. You can designate the TO range by pointing to the entire range, but remember that Symphony knows what you are implying when you enter just E1.

Besides helping to avoid an unwanted cell anchor, the Esc key also can be used when you are in the middle of a command sequence. Pressing Esc returns you to the previous command step. If you are in the middle of a formula, pressing the Esc key erases the cell address from the end of the formula and returns the cell pointer to the current cell.

You can also use the Backspace key in pointing to ranges. Pressing Backspace cancels the range specification, whether or not a cell has been anchored, and returns the cell pointer to its location when you began the command or formula. The Backspace key is slightly more powerful than the Esc key in returning Symphony to your location when you began entering a command or formula.

Using the End Key To Point

By using the End key, your job of pointing to ranges is made fairly easy. Suppose, for example, that you want to move the contents of range A1..C5 to the range that begins at cell A7. When the range prompt A1..A1 appears after you select the Move command, press the End key followed by the →. The cell pointer jumps to cell C1, and the prompt reads A1..C1. Next, move the cell pointer by pressing End and the ↓. The prompt then reads A1..C5.

The End key can speed up the process of pointing to ranges. In this example, you were able to define the range with only four keystrokes. If you had used the two arrow keys rather than the End key, the process would have taken seven keystrokes. The difference becomes even more dramatic when you work with larger ranges.

You can even use the End key in some cases when it appears to be of little value. For example, figure 4.21 shows a worksheet consisting of two rows of information: one continuous and one broken. Suppose that you want to erase the contents of the broken row. Select the Erase command, and Symphony then prompts you for a range to erase. You can enter the range by either typing or pointing to the coordinates.

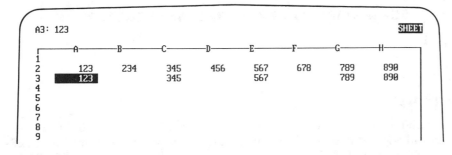

Fig. 4.21

A broken row next to a complete row.

If you point, you may want to try using the End key. But because the range is not continuous, the End key will not easily move you from one end of the range to the other. Try this trick. When you specify the range, first move the cell pointer up one row to cell A2, use End and the → to move the cell pointer to the end of the range, then move the cell pointer down one row. Presto! The correct range is specified. Figures 4.22A, 4.22B, and 4.22C show this process. Although the technique appears to waste keystrokes, it is actually much more convenient than simply using the → to point. You should use this technique often when you define ranges.

Fig. 4.22A

The first step in using the End key on a broken row.

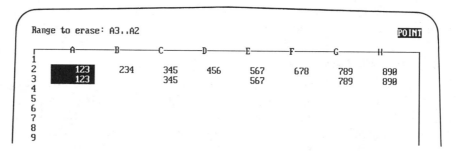

Fig. 4.22B

The second step in using the End key on a broken row.

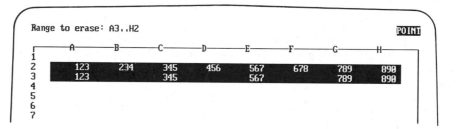

Fig. 4.22C

The final step in using the End key on a broken row.

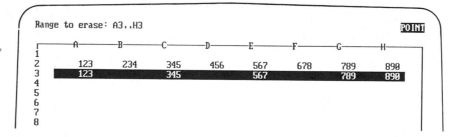

Erasing

In Symphony, two types of erasing commands are available: the SERVICES **New** command and the **Erase** command in the SHEET environment. Symphony's SERVICES **New** command clears the entire worksheet. When you select SERVICES **New**, the command not only erases the worksheet but also restores all global settings to their default conditions, erases range or graph names, and clears any title lock or windows in the sheet. You can use the SERVICES New command in any window environment to wipe the worksheet clean.

On the other hand, the SHEET Erase command erases only those unprotected cells that are within the range you set. But Erase does not alter any of the global settings, including column widths or label prefixes.

To use the Erase command, simply display the SHEET command menu by pressing F10, select Erase, indicate the range you want to erase, and press Enter. When you erase a range, values are recalculated. Whenever you erase a value that is used in a formula that remains in the worksheet, the formula will, depending on the type of address, read ERR. (See the later section entitled "Copying.")

Keep in mind the differences between the two types of commands. Remember also that the SERVICES New command restores the Symphony worksheet to its default configuration. Symphony reduces your chances of mistakenly selecting New instead of Erase by having the two commands in different menu systems.

Inserting Blank Columns and Rows

Insert, the fourth command in the SHEET command menu, is quite valuable for adding blank rows and columns. Suppose that you have finished building a model in a worksheet, but you want to "dress up" its general appearance before you show the model to anyone. One technique for improving a worksheet's appearance is to insert blank rows and columns in strategic places to highlight headings and other important items.

After you select Insert, Symphony asks whether you want to insert a column or a row. Insert also gives you two options: (1) to insert a column or row only within the restrict range of the window in which you are working, or (2) to insert the column or row beyond the restrict range. If you want to insert the column or row within the restrict range, select either Columns or Rows and then enter the range. If you want to insert the column or row beyond the window's restrict range, select Global, then indicate whether you want a column or row inserted, and finally enter the range.

Symphony's capability of inserting columns and rows only within restrict ranges is a tremendous advantage. Restricting the insert prevents you from unknowingly changing data in windows other than the one in which you are currently working. If you have created multiple windows, and you insert a row or column in one of them, using Columns or Rows limits the inserted column or row to the currently active window. Selecting Global, on the other hand, inserts columns or rows in all windows. Remember also that the Insert Global command affects those windows displayed on the screen as well as "hidden" windows. (See the discussion of the Window Hide command in Chapter 2.)

Inserted columns appear to the left of the specified range, and inserted rows appear above the specified range. For example, let's assume that you created the worksheet shown in figure 4.23. If you issue the **Insert Columns** command and enter an insert range of A10..A10, you will get a single blank column inserted to the left of the values in column A, as shown in figure 4.24. Symphony automatically shifts everything over one column and modifies all the cell formulas to reflect the change. If you then repeat the command, but specify the **Rows** option and a range of A10..A10, Symphony inserts one blank row below row 9. Figure 4.25 illustrates the results of this operation.

Fig. 4.23

A sample worksheet.

Fig. 4.24

Inserting a column.

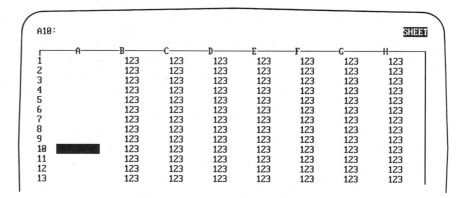

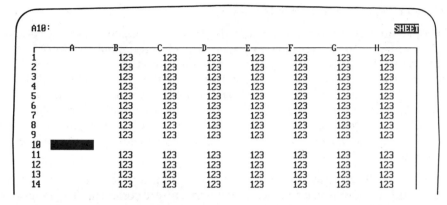

Fig. 4.25
Inserting a row.

Whenever you insert a column or row, Symphony automatically adjusts range settings. Suppose, for example, that you have created two named ranges in the spreadsheet shown in figure 4.26. These range names include CA at cell G16 for "Current Assets" and TNCA at cell G23 for "Total NonCurrent Assets." Once you have entered these range names, Symphony remembers the cell address for each name.

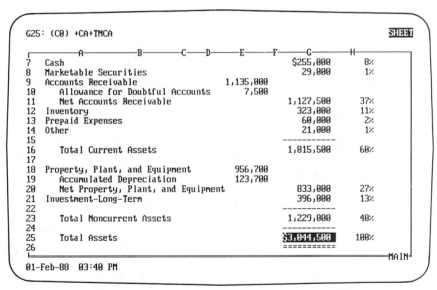

Fig. 4.26
Named ranges at cells G16 and G23.

If, however, you decide to insert a column at column D, Symphony automatically changes CA and TNCA to cells H16 and H23, respectively. This adjustment of remembered ranges occurs whether you use the global Insert or the restrict range Insert, with one exception: only the Insert Global command changes the restrict range of a window.

Deleting Columns and Rows

The opposite of the **Insert** command is the **Delete** command. It deletes columns and rows either in restrict ranges of a window or throughout the whole worksheet. With the **Delete** command, you can delete multiple columns or rows at the same time. After you select this command, you then choose Columns, **Rows**, or **Global** from the menu. Like Insert, **Delete** allows you to restrict the column or row deletion to the current window or to delete columns or rows globally. If you have created multiple windows, the **Delete Global** command will affect all windows, whether or not they are displayed on-screen when you initiate the command.

If you choose **Rows**, Symphony then asks you to indicate the range to be deleted within the window restrict range. As with the **Insert** command, the range you specify should include one cell from a given row. For example, to delete rows 2 and 3 from the worksheet in figure 4.27, you could enter A2..A3. Other acceptable range designations are B2..B3, A2..B3, and C2..G3. The results of the deletion are shown in figure 4.28. Notice that the worksheet is automatically readjusted so that all the contents below row 3 are shifted up. In addition, Symphony adjusts all the formulas, command ranges, and named ranges for the deletion. Formulas that contain references to the deleted cells are given the value ERR.

The easiest way to designate the range to be deleted is by pointing to the appropriate cells. Although you can also enter the cell addresses from the keyboard, pointing to cells helps you to avoid choosing the wrong range inadvertently. Remember that when you use the **Delete** command, the rows or columns you delete are gone for good. If you choose **Columns** or **Rows** from the first menu, the cells in the columns or rows of the window restrict range are deleted. If you choose **Columns** or **Rows** after choosing **Global**, all the cells in the rows or columns, not just the range you specify, are deleted. You may be able to get the values back if you have previously saved a copy of the model on disk. But if you have not saved a copy, the rows and columns are lost.

Fig. 4.27

The worksheet before deleting rows 2 and 3.

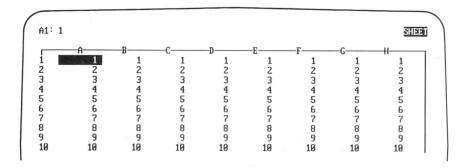

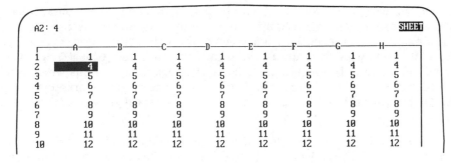

Fig. 4.28

The worksheet after deleting rows 2 and 3.

The process of deleting one or more columns is similar to the procedure for deleting rows. After you select the **C**olumns option from the **D**elete menu, you then specify a range of columns within the window's restrict range to delete. The range you specify should include one or more cells from each column to be deleted.

For example, suppose that you want to delete column B in figure 4.29. A suitable range to designate for the **D**elete command is B1..B1. Again, pointing is the best way to designate the range so that you can avoid selecting the wrong column. Figure 4.30 shows the worksheet after column B is deleted.

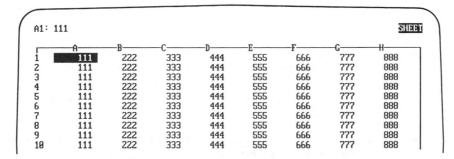

Fig. 4.29

The worksheet before deleting column B.

Fig. 4.30

The worksheet after deleting column B.

Remember that just as you have two options for deleting rows, you also have two options for deleting columns: only within a window's restrict area, or throughout the worksheet. To delete columns throughout the worksheet, choose the **Global** command from the **Delete** menu. After selecting Global, select Columns and indicate the range to be deleted. Here again, be cautious when using the **Global** command. If you have various kinds of data on your worksheet, using the **Delete Global Columns** command may affect areas that you want to keep intact.

In Symphony, you'll find two differences between deleting cells with **Delete** and erasing cells with **Erase**. First, the **Delete** command deletes entire columns and rows within a worksheet, but the **Erase** command erases particular ranges of cells that may be as small or large as you want. Second, when you use **Delete**, the worksheet is automatically readjusted to fill in the gaps created by the deleted columns or rows. But with **Erase**, the cells in the erased range are merely blanked.

The marked difference between **Delete** and **Erase** is best illustrated by using the analogy of a paper spreadsheet. The manual equivalent of **Delete** is to use scissors to cut apart the columnar sheet, remove the unwanted columns and/or rows, then paste the sheet back together again. The **Erase** command, on the other hand, is similar to an eraser that erases ranges of cells on the sheet. Don't forget the distinction between these powerful commands.

Copying

The first command in the SHEET command menu is **Copy**. This command not only replicates data but also copies formulas from one cell to another. You will find yourself frequently using the **Copy** command to copy the contents of cells to other locations in a worksheet. The uses of the **Copy** command can be divided into four categories.

The first type of copy operation is to copy *from one cell to another*. In the worksheet shown in figure 4.31, you can copy the contents of cell A1 to cell A2. Just issue the command **Copy**. Symphony then prompts you to supply a FROM range with the message Range to copy FROM:. Because you want to copy from cell A1, enter **A1**. (If the cell pointer is on cell A1, you can simply press Enter.) Next, Symphony asks for a TO range with the message Range to copy TO:. Because you want to copy the contents of cell A1 to cell A2, enter **A2** as the TO range. Figure 4.32 shows the results of this operation.

As illustrated in this example, the steps required for all copy operations are basically these: (1) select **Copy**, (2) specify the FROM range, and (3) specify the TO range. The only elements that change from time to time are the size, shape, and locations of the TO and FROM ranges.

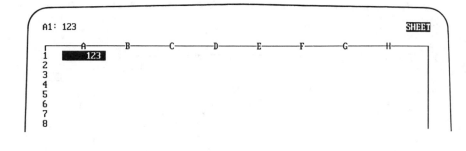

Fig. 4.31

A sample worksheet before using the Copy command.

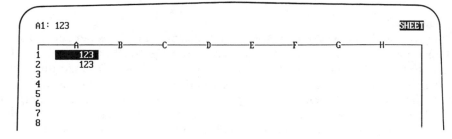

Fig. 4.32

Copying from one cell to another.

A second type of copy operation is to copy *from one cell to a range of cells*. Using the same worksheet shown in figure 4.33, let's suppose that you want to copy the contents of cell A1 into the range B1..H1. To do this, issue the Copy command, specify A1 as the FROM range, and indicate B1..H1 as the TO range. Remember that you can either type the coordinates of the range from the keyboard or point to the range by using Symphony's POINT mode. The results of this copy operation are shown in figure 4.33.

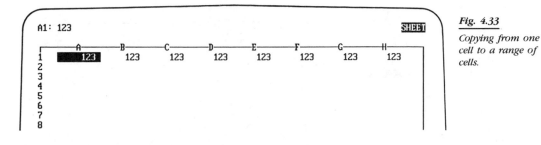

Fig. 4.33

Copying from one cell to a range of cells.

The third type of copy operation is a little more complicated. You may want to copy *a range of cells to another place* in the worksheet. Using the results of your copy in figure 4.33 as an example, now suppose that you want to copy the range A1..H1 to the range A2..H2. As always, begin by issuing the Copy command. Then specify the FROM range—in this case, A1..H1. Next, you must specify the TO range. Now things get a bit tricky. Even though you are copying to the range

A2..H2, the TO range is the single cell A2. The result of this operation is shown in figure 4.34.

Fig. 4.34

Copying a range of cells.

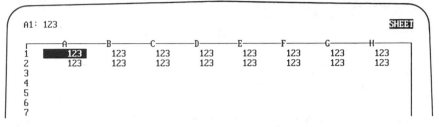

Although the TO range does not seem to make sense, it really is perfectly logical. Think about it this way. You want to Copy to the eight-cell partial row A2..H2. Because the FROM range is an eight-cell partial row, the TO range must also be an eight-cell partial row. Thus the first cell in that partial row is sufficient to define the range. Given a starting point of A2, the only possible destination for the copy is the range A2..H2. Similarly, to specify the single cell H3 as the TO range implies a destination of H3..O3. In other words, Symphony deduces the rest of the destination from the single cell provided as the TO range.

The same principle applies to copying partial columns. Look back at figure 4.32, which shows the results of the first copy example. Now suppose that you want to copy the range A1..A2 to the range B1..B2. The first two steps should be familiar by now. Issue the Copy command and specify the FROM range A1..A2. What should the TO range be? Because you want to copy the two-cell partial column A1..A2 into the two-cell partial column B1..B2, you need to supply only the starting point of the target, which is B1, to create figure 4.35.

Fig. 4.35

Another example of copying a range.

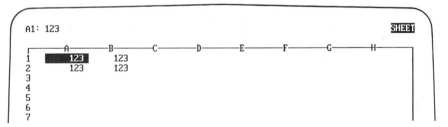

Finally, in the fourth kind of copy operation, you may want to copy *a range of cells to an even larger range of cells* elsewhere in the worksheet. Using figure 4.33 once again as an example, let's assume that you want to copy the range A1..H1 into the rectangular block A2..H20. As before, you issue the command Copy and specify the FROM range as A1..H1. But then indicate the TO range as A2..A20. Figure 4.36 shows the results of this copy.

You can think of this last kind of copy operation as an extension of the third type. Essentially, you can also create the screen shown in figure 4.36 by repeating the Copy command 19 times and specifying 19 different single-row TO ranges. The first TO range would be A2; the second, A3; the third, A4; and so on. Regardless of which method you use, the result is the same, but you can save much time by using the A2..A20 range.

```
A1: 123                                                        SHEET
        A        B        C        D        E        F        G        H
1      123      123      123      123      123      123      123      123
2      123      123      123      123      123      123      123      123
3      123      123      123      123      123      123      123      123
4      123      123      123      123      123      123      123      123
5      123      123      123      123      123      123      123      123
6      123      123      123      123      123      123      123      123
7      123      123      123      123      123      123      123      123
8      123      123      123      123      123      123      123      123
9      123      123      123      123      123      123      123      123
10     123      123      123      123      123      123      123      123
11     123      123      123      123      123      123      123      123
12     123      123      123      123      123      123      123      123
13     123      123      123      123      123      123      123      123
14     123      123      123      123      123      123      123      123
15     123      123      123      123      123      123      123      123
16     123      123      123      123      123      123      123      123
17     123      123      123      123      123      123      123      123
18     123      123      123      123      123      123      123      123
19     123      123      123      123      123      123      123      123
20     123      123      123      123      123      123      123      123
                                                              MAIN
01-Feb-88   03:55 PM
```

Fig. 4.36

Copying a range of cells to an even larger range.

The concept of TO ranges can be complicated. The best way to become familiar with the effects of different TO and FROM ranges is to experiment on your own. After a while, the rules of copying will become "old hat."

Relative versus Absolute Addressing

One of the important features of the Copy command is its capability to copy formulas and to adjust them whenever necessary. But for Symphony to know how to adjust a formula as it is copied to another part of the worksheet, the original formula must contain the right kind of address. You can use two different methods of addressing cells in replication: relative and absolute. These two methods are also important in building formulas. In fact, a discussion of either method of addressing is difficult unless you treat both topics at once. Following are general definitions of these two types of addressing.

In *relative addressing*, when a formula is copied, the cells in the formula change relative to the new cell(s) where the formula has been duplicated. Suppose, for example, that cell A5 contains the formula +A2+A3, meaning that Symphony should add the contents of the cells located two and three cells above A5. If you copy +A2+A3 to cell B5, the formula (in cell B5) reads +B2+B3, as indicated in figure 4.37. When you copy the formula +A2+A3 to cell B5, Symphony interprets the copy this way: the cells located two and three cells above *B5* should be added. One way to understand relative addressing is to remember that when formulas are copied, their operators, their functions, and the relationships of cells, but not the specific cell addresses of the original formulas, are copied.

Fig. 4.37

Copying a formula with relative addresses.

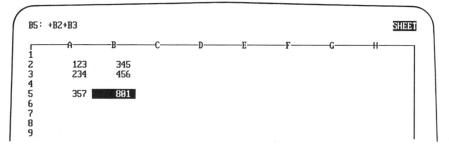

In *absolute addressing*, when a formula is copied, the original cell addresses are copied. For example, if you want to copy the formula in cell A5 (+A2+A3) to cell B5 and have the formula remain as originally entered, you enter the original formula this way:

+$A$2+$A$3

When you copy this formula to cell B5, you still have +$A$2+$A$3, as indicated in figure 4.38. The dollar signs tell Symphony to copy the formula with its original cell addresses.

Fig. 4.38

Copying a formula with absolute addresses.

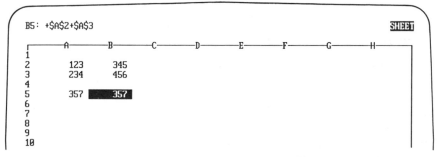

Now let's explore the concepts of relative and absolute addressing in a bit more detail.

Relative Addressing

Suppose that you want to sum the contents of several columns of cells, but you don't want to enter the @SUM function over and over again. Figure 4.39 shows a sample worksheet with five columns of numbers. Only column C has been summed, with the formula @SUM(C3..C7) in cell C8.

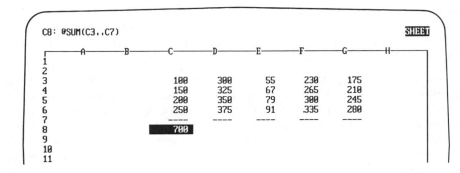

Fig. 4.39

A sample worksheet with an @SUM formula in column C.

You want to add the contents of the cells in columns D, E, F, and G in the same way in which the contents of the cells in column C were added. To perform this addition, use the **C**opy command, which is the command for replicating cells, no matter what their contents.

To initiate the command, choose **C**opy from the main command menu. Symphony then asks for a range of cells to copy FROM. Type **C8** for the range and press Enter. Next, Symphony asks for a range of cells to copy TO. Here you enter D8..G8 by either pointing to or typing the cell addresses. When you hit Enter, Symphony replicates the @SUM formula in cell C8 to the other cells, as shown in figure 4.40.

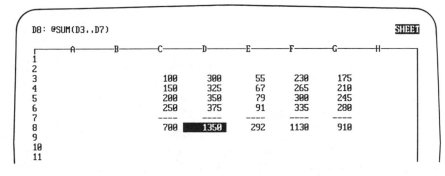

Fig. 4.40

Copying the @SUM formula.

If you look at the formula in the first line of the control panel in figure 4.40, you will see that the formula contains the proper cell addresses for adding cells in column D but not in column C. Symphony knows that when you copied you wanted the relative addresses of cells in column C and not their absolute addresses.

Absolute and Mixed Addressing

Sometimes a formula has an important address that shouldn't be changed as the formula is copied. In Symphony you can create an address that will not change at all as it is copied. Remember that this address is called an absolute address. But you can also create a mixed address, which will sometimes change, depending on the direction of the copy. The following examples will help clarify the concepts of absolute and mixed addresses.

Mixed cell addressing refers to a combination of relative and absolute addressing. Because a cell address has two components—a row and a column—you can fix (make absolute) either portion while leaving the other unfixed (relative). For example, suppose that for Product 1 you want to do a projection of monthly sales in dollars. In the first pass, you want to use a specific retail price, an average discount rate, and a unit volume for the projection. Later you will want to change these parameters to see what happens. Figure 4.41 shows how you can set up the projection.

Fig. 4.41

An example of mixed cell addressing.

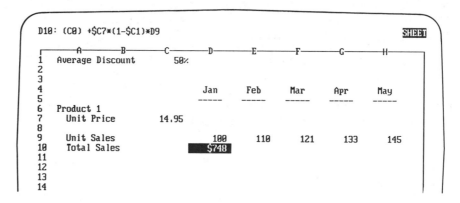

Notice the dollar signs in the formula for cell D10 in the first line of the control panel. The dollar signs signal Symphony to use absolute addressing on the column portion of the addresses. Because dollar signs do not appear in front of the row portion of the addresses, Symphony will use relative addressing there.

To see the importance of this type of referencing, now Copy the contents of cell D10 into the range E10..H10. As before, you first issue the Copy command and designate the FROM range (D10) and the TO range (E10..H10). Figure 4.42 shows the results of this operation.

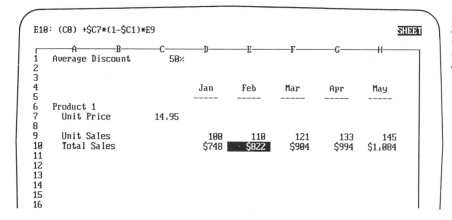

```
        A        B        C        D        E        F        G        H
1   Average Discount     50%
2
3
4                            Jan      Feb      Mar      Apr      May
5                            -----    -----    -----    -----    -----
6   Product 1
7     Unit Price      14.95
8
9     Unit Sales               100      110      121      133      145
10    Total Sales            $748     $822     $904     $994   $1,084
11
12
13
14
15
16
```

Fig. 4.42

Copying a formula with mixed addresses.

Now compare the formula in cell E10 with the original formula in cell D10:

E10 = $C7*(1-$C1)*E9
D10 = $C7*(1-$C1)*D9

Notice that the formulas are identical except for the last item. Symphony holds constant the addresses for C7 and C1. Only the reference to cell D9 is altered. Essentially, this formula says: using a constant price (C7) and a constant discount (C1), compute the dollar sales for Product 1 at each month's sales volume (D9..H9).

Now suppose that you want to create a projection for a second product. You duplicate the labels in column A and change the product name to Product 2. Finally, you copy the contents of the range C7..H10 to the range C14..H17. Figure 4.43 shows the results of this copy operation.

Notice that the numbers in row 17 are not correct. Even though the same price and unit sales volumes have been assigned to Product 2, that product shows monthly dollar sales which are double those for Product 1. To figure out why, look at the formula in cell D17:

+$C14*(1-$C8)*D16

The references to cell C14 and cell D16 are correct—these cells contain the unit price and unit sales for Product 2. But notice that the reference to cell C1 has changed so that it refers to cell C8. This change occurred because the row designation (8) in that address was relative and not absolute. When you copied the formulas containing the address $C1 down the worksheet, Symphony assumed that you wanted to adjust the row component of the address.

You can correct the problem by changing the reference to cell C1 from a mixed to an absolute reference. Edit cell D10 and change the formula to

+$C7*(1-$C$1)*D9

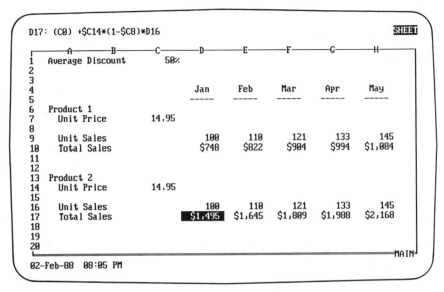

Fig. 4.43

*A formula
containing an
incorrect reference
to cell C8.*

The only difference between this formula and its predecessor in the model in figure 4.41 is the addition of a dollar sign in front of the 1 in the address $C$1. The added dollar sign changes this address from mixed to absolute.

Now you must copy the new formula in cell D10 to the range E10..H10 so that all the formulas in the row are the same. You can then recopy the area D9..H10 into the range D16..H17. Figure 4.44 illustrates the adjusted worksheet.

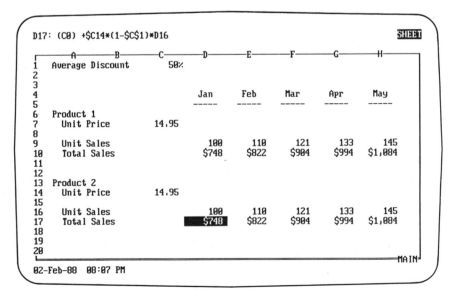

Fig. 4.44

*Adjusting the
reference to an
absolute address.*

Notice that the numbers in cells D17..H17 are now correct. If you look at the following formula in cell D17:

+$C14*(1-$C$1)*D16

you can see that the reference to cell C1 has remained fixed as you copied it.

Another example of mixed cell addressing appears in figure 4.45. This figure contains a table for exploring the effect of different interest rates and years to maturity on the present value of an annuity that pays $1,000 a year. (See the @PV built-in function in Chapter 5 for an explanation of present value.) The general form of the @PV function is

@PV(payment, interest, term)

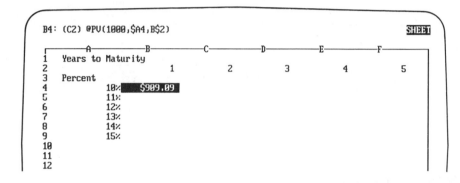

Fig. 4.45

Another example of mixed addressing.

You can see in the command line of figure 4.45 the special places where the dollar signs appear. The idea in this example is to use a single formula for the entire model, with absolute addressing on the column portion of the interest-rate address, and relative addressing on the row portion ($A4). Conversely, you want to use relative addressing on the column portion of the years-to-maturity address, and absolute addressing on the row portion (B$2).

Compare the cell B4 formula in the control panel in figure 4.45 with the formula for cell D8 in figure 4.46. Notice that column A for the interest rate and row 2 for the years-to-maturity have not changed, but the other portions of the addresses have.

A third way you can use mixed cell addressing is to accumulate a running total across a row of numbers. You can type the formula @SUM($A$1..B1) in cell B2 and copy the formula across cells C2 through H2, as shown in figure 4.47. Watch how the relative address in the formula changes as you copy it.

The best way to become comfortable with mixed cell addressing is to experiment with it. Try several different uses and examine your results.

Fig. 4.46

The worksheet after copying the formula.

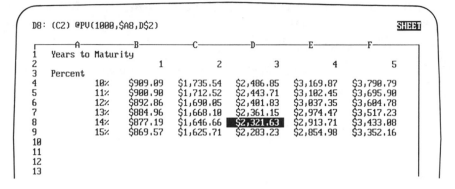

```
D8: (C2) @PV(1000,$A8,D$2)                                    SHEET
   ┌────A────────B─────────C─────────D─────────E─────────F───
 1 │ Years to Maturity
 2 │                   1         2         3         4         5
 3 │ Percent
 4 │          10%  $909.09  $1,735.54  $2,486.85  $3,169.87  $3,790.79
 5 │          11%  $900.90  $1,712.52  $2,443.71  $3,102.45  $3,695.90
 6 │          12%  $892.86  $1,690.05  $2,401.83  $3,037.35  $3,604.78
 7 │          13%  $884.96  $1,668.10  $2,361.15  $2,974.47  $3,517.23
 8 │          14%  $877.19  $1,646.66  $2,321.63  $2,913.71  $3,433.08
 9 │          15%  $869.57  $1,625.71  $2,283.23  $2,854.98  $3,352.16
10 │
11 │
12 │
13 │
```

Fig. 4.47

Accumulating a running total.

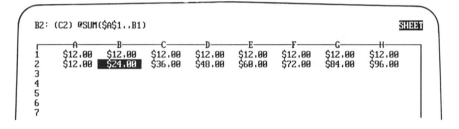

```
B2: (C2) @SUM($A$1..B1)                                       SHEET
   ┌────A────────B────────C────────D────────E────────F────────G────────H───
 1 │ $12.00   $12.00   $12.00   $12.00   $12.00   $12.00   $12.00   $12.00
 2 │ $12.00   $24.00   $36.00   $48.00   $60.00   $72.00   $84.00   $96.00
 3 │
 4 │
 5 │
 6 │
 7 │
```

Setting Cell References

To use absolute addressing to copy cells in Symphony, you must prepare the formula before initiating the Copy command. That is, you must enter dollar signs in strategic places when you define the cell.

You can enter the dollar signs in a formula in two ways. You can type the dollar signs as you enter the formula, or you can use the Abs key (F3) to have Symphony automatically enter the dollar signs for you. One limitation of the Abs key is that you must be in POINT mode to use it. As you will recall from the section in Chapter 3 on entering formulas, in POINT mode you must use the cell pointer to enter addresses.

Here is the procedure for using the Abs key to enter dollar signs. Using the formula in cell D17 in figure 4.44 as an example, begin by entering the first part of the formula; in this case, enter +. To change the formula to an absolute address, shift to POINT mode by moving your cell pointer to cell C14; then press the Abs key. The formula in the control panel shows the address $C14. Pressing the Abs key again changes the address to C$14. A third press of the Abs key changes the address to $C14, which is the result you want. Finish entering the formula by using the pointing method and the Abs key to enter dollar signs for absolute references.

Notice what happens to a cell address when you press the Abs key in POINT mode:

First press	$C$14
Second press	C$14
Third press	$C14
Fourth press	C14

Miscellaneous Comments on Copying

When using the Copy command from Symphony's SHEET menu, keep the following points in mind:

1. When you copy a cell, Symphony automatically copies the format of the cell with it. (See the section entitled "Formats" for more information.) This copying saves you from having to preset the format for an entire range of cells before copying them.

2. Sometimes the TO and FROM ranges will overlap when you copy. Here's the general rule: If you do not overlap the end points for the FROM and TO ranges, you will be okay; if you do overlap them, you may get mixed results. The one time that it is legitimate to overlap the ranges is when the FROM and TO ranges have the same upper left boundary.

3. Remember the finality of the Copy command. If you copy over the contents of a cell, even a cell in another window, you cannot retrieve the contents. Make sure that you have your ranges designated properly before you press Enter.

4. You can copy between two windows, from one SHEET window to another SHEET window, or even from a SHEET window to a DOC window and vice versa. To copy from one SHEET window to another, select Copy and indicate the FROM range. When Symphony asks for the TO range, specify the range within the other window. You can press the Window key (F6) if you want to point to the range. If you want to copy from a DOC window to a SHEET window, shift the window type from DOC to SHEET, initiate the Copy command, indicate the FROM range, and then indicate the TO range within the spreadsheet area. If you want to copy from a SHEET window to a DOC window, you must switch the DOC window to SHEET before initiating the Copy command.

Adjusting Column Width

One of the problems in earlier spreadsheet programs was that you could control the widths of worksheet columns only as a group. If you were setting up a projection of expenses for the next five years and wanted to display full descriptions of the expense items (some of them 20 characters), you would have to set all the columns to a width of 20 characters. Otherwise, you had to abbreviate or truncate the labels.

In Symphony, you don't have this problem. You can separately control the width of each column. You can set the first column of your expense projection at 20 characters wide and the rest of the columns to whatever you need. If a value is wider than the column in which you enter the value, then Symphony displays the value as a series of asterisks (*********). On the other hand, Symphony fully displays a label that is wider than its column, as long as blank cells appear to the right of the label.

The command used to set individual column widths is SHEET Width Set. You can indicate the column width by either entering a number or using the ← and → keys followed by Enter. The advantage of using the left- and right-arrow keys is that you can see the column width actually expand and contract on-screen each time you press these keys. To get a good idea of what your width requirements are, try experimenting when you enter the command.

You should remember two things about the SHEET Width Set command. First, you must locate the pointer in the proper column before you initiate the command. Otherwise, you will have to start over. Second, to reset the column width to the standard setting, you can use the SHEET Width Restore command. This command changes a column width to the width value stored within the window's settings sheet. (See the discussion of the SHEET Settings Width command later in this chapter.)

You even can hide a column. The SHEET Width Hide command prompts you for the range of columns you want hidden. You can respond either by "stretching" the cell pointer across the columns or typing the cell addresses. The indicated columns disappear from your worksheet screen but retain their contents and format. Any cells that depend on cells in hidden columns retain that dependence. Hiding columns is a handy way to blot out temporarily a range of cells while you print the spreadsheet.

To display the columns again, use the SHEET Width Display command. Symphony prompts you for a range of cells whose columns you want displayed. The currently hidden columns are displayed temporarily (with an asterisk next to the column's alphabetic label), allowing you to decide what to display.

As in earlier spreadsheet programs, including 1-2-3, in Symphony you can control all the column widths at once. The command is SHEET Settings Width. The standard setting for column width is 9, but you can change this setting to whatever width you want for the current worksheet.

Any column width that you set previously with the SHEET **W**idth command is not affected by a change in the global setting. For example, if you use SHEET **W**idth to set the width of column A to 12, and then you select SHEET **S**ettings **W**idth to change all the columns in the worksheet to a width of 5, every column except A changes to 5. Column A remains at a width of 12 and must be reset to 5 with the SHEET **W**idth **S**et or **R**estore command.

Both the SHEET **W**idth and SHEET **S**ettings **W**idth commands affect only the current window in which you are working. Note, for example, the three windows in figure 4.48. Each window contains different column widths. The column widths in window 1 are set at the default setting of 9. The column widths in window 2 are set at a width of 6. And the column widths in window 3 are set at various widths. Each window also has a different width setting for its settings sheet. If you were to scroll each window, you would find that the column width of one does not affect the column width of another. Each window maintains its width setting until you either delete the window by using the SERVICES **W**indow **D**elete command or change the width in the settings sheet.

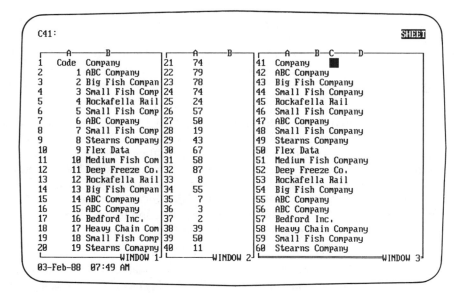

Fig. 4.48

Three windows with different column widths.

Formatting the Worksheet

Format, the seventh command on the SHEET menu, controls how cell contents are displayed on the screen. Symphony has surpassed earlier spreadsheet programs by improving and expanding their format capability. In all, Symphony offers 11 format settings.

Symphony Formats

Currency
Punctuated
Fixed
% (Percent)
General
Date (Including two options for International formats)
Time
Scientific
Other
    Bar-Graph
    Literal
    Hidden

Settings Sheets and Commands for Controlling Formats

The basic command for changing formats in a worksheet is the SHEET Format command. The SERVICES Configuration Other International and SHEET Settings Format commands also control formats. Before beginning a discussion of the various formats, a brief explanation is provided of the functions of the SERVICES Configuration Other International, SHEET Settings Format, and SHEET Format commands.

The SERVICES Configuration Other International selection controls the display of punctuation, including decimal points and commas, within numeric values and functions. This command allows you to use either a dot or a comma to separate the integer part of a number from the fractional part. The command also provides three format options for displaying thousands. Finally, Configuration Other International contains various options for displaying Currency, Date, Time, and Negative number formats. Although you may not find it necessary to change any of the default settings provided by Lotus, you should know that Symphony gives you the flexibility of changing standard numeric formats if you need to.

Although the SERVICES Configuration Other International selection controls numeric, date, and time formats globally, SHEET Settings Format enables you to set a controlling format for each SHEET window you create. For example, suppose that you create two different SHEET windows: one containing values in Currency format with no decimal places, and one containing values in % (Percent) format with two decimal places (see fig. 4.49).

For each window, you can enter a separate setting in the settings sheet. If you do not change the setting for each window, Symphony accepts the default setting

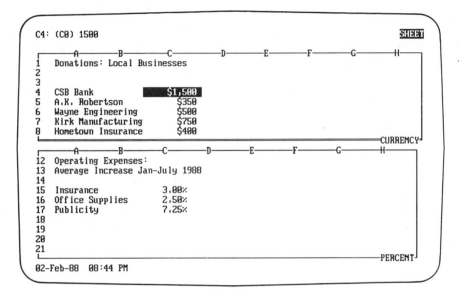

Fig. 4.49

A window formatted in Currency format, and another window in % (Percent) format.

or the setting entered for the first window as the setting for all others. Keep in mind, though, that settings sheets are controlled by the SERVICES Configuration Other International option.

Generally, you will use the SHEET Settings Format option when you are just starting to enter a worksheet in a particular window. You will want to choose the format that the majority of cells will take. Once you have set all the cells to that format, you can use the SHEET Format command to override the window format setting for specific cell ranges. When you select the SHEET Format command, the menu shown in figure 4.50 appears.

The SHEET Format command enables you to set the format for any range, regardless of the format in SHEET Settings. In the example in figure 4.49, column C in window 1 contains values in currency format. These values are formatted automatically because the settings sheet for window 1 has been adjusted for the "currency with no decimal places" format, represented in the sheet as (C∅). If, however, you need to display values in column D in percent format, the SHEET Format command enables you to set the percent format for column D in window 1.

The SHEET Format command has precedence over the SHEET Settings Format command. That is, whenever you change SHEET Settings Format, all the affected numbers and formulas change automatically unless you previously formatted them with SHEET Format. If, however, you have changed the format of a range of numbers by using the SHEET Format command, you can restore the range to the window's SHEET Settings Format by selecting **Reset** on the SHEET Format menu.

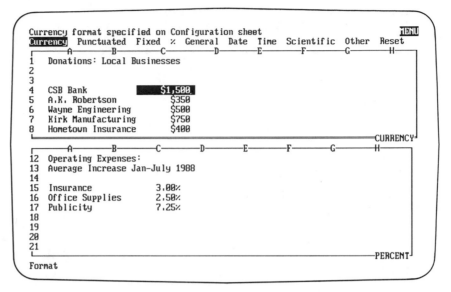

```
Currency format specified on Configuration sheet                MENU
Currency  Punctuated  Fixed  %  General  Date  Time  Scientific  Other  Reset
┌────A────────B────────C────────D────────E────────F────────G────────H────
 1    Donations: Local Businesses
 2
 3
 4    CSB Bank              $1,500
 5    A.K. Robertson          $350
 6    Wayne Engineering       $500
 7    Kirk Manufacturing      $750
 8    Hometown Insurance      $400
└──────────────────────────────────────────────────────────────CURRENCY┘
┌────A────────B────────C────────D────────E────────F────────G────────H────
12    Operating Expenses:
13    Average Increase Jan-July 1988
14
15    Insurance             3.00%
16    Office Supplies       2.50%
17    Publicity             7.25%
18
19
20
21
└───────────────────────────────────────────────────────────────PERCENT┘
Format
```

In addition, the SHEET Format command affects the format of values entered in other windows. In figure 4.49, suppose that you want to format column C in window 1 for currency with no decimal places. The range to format in window 1 is C4..C8. If, however, you accidentally type in the range to format as C4..C18, cells C15..C17 in window 2 will also be displayed in the format for currency with no decimal places.

General

Although General is the fifth command in the SHEET Format menu, the discussion begins with General because it is the default setting for all new worksheets. That is, once you begin a new worksheet, the SHEET Settings Format entry will be General, represented on the settings sheet as (G).

When numbers are displayed in the General format, insignificant zeros to the right of the decimal point are suppressed. If numbers are too large or too small to be displayed normally, Symphony uses scientific notation. Following are some examples of the General format:

123.456
5.63E+14
-22.1
1.9E-09

In the General format, labels are displayed as left-justified. Each is preceded by a single quotation mark that signals Symphony to left-justify. As mentioned in

Chapter 3, you can use the SHEET Settings Label-Prefix or SHEET Range Label-Alignment command to change the default of left justification.

Currency

You can modify and control the Currency format with the two settings sheets and the SHEET Format command mentioned earlier. First, the SERVICES Configuration Other International Currency option enables you to change the currency sign and position. If, for example, you need to create a worksheet with British pound currency values entered, you can change the default currency sign from $ to £ by following these steps: (1) choose Configuration from the SERVICES menu; (2) when the Configuration menu appears, select Other; and (3) select International. Then you have five choices: Punctuation, Currency, Date, Time, and Negative.

When you choose Currency, Symphony displays Currency Sign: $ in the top left corner. To change the sign from $ to £, press the Backspace key to erase $. Next, press the Compose key (Alt-F1) to tell Symphony that you want to create a special figure. Then type the letter *L* and the hyphen (-). The Compose key, the *L*, and the hyphen tell Symphony that you want to create the British pound sign. After changing the currency sign to £, press Enter. Symphony then gives you the option of having the currency sign placed before or after the value.

In some cases, you may want to place the currency sign after the value. To change the position of the currency sign, select Suffix when Symphony displays the options Prefix and Suffix.

You also can control how negative numbers are displayed. Select Configuration Other International Negative and specify Parentheses or Minus. If you want to update the configuration to the new settings, select Update from the SERVICES Configuration menu.

The other settings sheet that controls the Currency format is SHEET Settings Format Currency. Using this command, you can set a worksheet's or a specific window's default format setting to Currency, represented in the settings sheet as (C∅), (C2), and so on, depending on the number of decimal places. If you enter into the settings sheet the format for currency, values in the worksheet or window are displayed in this format unless you use the SHEET Format command to change the format of a range within the worksheet or window.

The SHEET Format Currency command enables you to format a range in the worksheet or window and override the SHEET Settings Format. If, for example, you format a range with the SHEET Format Currency command, then setting the SHEET Settings Format to % (Percent) does not affect the range you formatted with Currency.

Both SHEET Settings Format Currency and SHEET Format Currency give you the option of controlling the number of places to the right of the decimal point. This feature can be helpful if you are having trouble displaying values because they are a little too large for the column width. One solution is to override the default of two places to the right of the decimal point.

If the value you want to display in Currency format is too large for the column width, a series of asterisks appears across the cell instead. In fact, these asterisks will appear for all formats when values exceed column widths. The problem of space is particularly acute with the Currency format, however, because the dollar sign and commas take up quite a bit of space. The best way to handle this problem is to experiment with the formatting parameters and the column width until you get the appearance you want. You may recall that you can control column width through either the SHEET Width or SHEET Settings Width command. The former controls specific columns in the worksheet or window, and the latter controls all the columns at the same time.

When numbers appear in the command line after you enter them, they are preceded by the format indicator for Currency. In fact, all number formats other than General show format indicators in the command line. You do not have to enter them yourself. Symphony automatically provides these indicators, based on the format you have specified.

The format indicator for Currency is C, followed by an integer to indicate the number of decimal places you have chosen; both the C and the integer appear in parentheses. Following are some examples of how numbers appear in the command line after you enter them, and how they are displayed in the worksheet with the Currency format.

In the Command Line	In the Worksheet
(C2)45	$45.00
(C2)1612.3	$1,612.30
(C3)22.805	$22.805
(C1)105.56	$105.6
(C2)-201.99	($210.99)

Punctuation Format

Symphony's punctuation format, like the Currency format, is controlled by four different commands: SERVICES Configuration Other International Punctuation, SERVICES Configuration Other International Negative, SHEET Format Punctuated, and SHEET Settings Format Punctuated. The Configuration settings provide the global settings for the type of punctuation to be used in values. The SHEET Format Punctuated command enables you to format as punctuated a range of values within the worksheet or window. And the SHEET Settings Format Punctuated command allows you to set **P**unctuated as the default setting for a worksheet or specific window.

The SERVICES Configuration Other International Punctuation command gives you eight options for the punctuation used both to display values and to separate arguments in functions. The default setting uses the period (.) to separate the integer part of a number from its fraction part; the comma (,) to separate arguments in functions; and the comma (,) to separate thousands. You will probably use the default setting most frequently, but keep in mind that the other settings are available. The options are listed in a menu that appears after you issue the command.

When you use Symphony's punctuation format in its default setting, this format displays values in the same way as the Currency format, except that no dollar signs appear in punctuation format. Commas separate hundreds from thousands, thousands from millions, and so on.

Punctuation format can be particularly useful in financial statements for displaying all numbers (except those on the very top and bottom of the statement) with commas but without dollar signs. For example, a portion of a balance sheet is shown here:

Cash	$1,750
Receivables	3,735
Inventories	9,200
Current Assets	$14,685

The numbers corresponding to Receivables and Inventories are displayed with the **P**unctuated format, and those corresponding to Cash and Current Assets are displayed with the **C**urrency format.

Fixed

In some ways the **F**ixed format is similar to the **G**eneral format in that Fixed does not display commas or dollar signs. The difference is that the Fixed command lets you control the number of places to the right of the decimal point. When you select Fixed, Symphony prompts you for the number of decimal places you want displayed. After you choose a number, Symphony pads the cells you have selected with zeros to the right of the decimal to the number of places you indicate. Conversely, if you decide to display fewer than the number of decimal places you have entered, Symphony rounds the number to the specified number of places. Following are examples of how numbers appear in the Fixed format:

In the Command Line	*In the Worksheet*
(F0) 15.1	15
(F2) 1000.2145	1000.21
(F3) -21.405	-21.405

Remember: you do not have to enter the format indicator (for example, F0) in the command line. Symphony automatically enters the indicator for you when you format the cell.

The Fixed command can be helpful when you want to control specifically the number of places to the right of the decimal point, without the automatic removal of insignificant digits that occurs in the General format. The Fixed format is particularly appealing when you have columns of numbers and want all the numbers to show the same number of decimal places.

% (Percent)

The % format displays percentages, with the number of decimal places controlled by you. When you choose % format, Symphony multiplies by 100 the value you enter and attaches a percent sign.

In the Command Line	*In the Worksheet*
(P0) .12	12%
(P4) 12.134	1213.4000%
(P2) .5675	56.75%

One of the difficulties with this format is that it seems natural to want to enter integers rather than decimals (such as 12 rather than .12 in the previous example). Symphony persists, however, in its method of storing cell contents in only one way and allowing you to control only the display of the output.

Date

Symphony represents any given Gregorian date as an integer equal to the number of days from December 31, 1899, to the given date. For example, January 1, 1900, is represented by 1; December 31, 2099, which is the last date in Symphony's calendar, is represented by 73050. To enter a date into the worksheet, use one of the date functions: @DATE, @DATEVALUE, or @NOW. (See Chapter 5 for more discussion of the date functions.)

To display a date in its proper Date format, use either the SHEET Format Date or SHEET Settings Format Date command. When you choose SHEET Format Date, any range you have set using the Date format will appear in one of five ways. When you select SHEET Settings Format Date, dates, as well as integers between 1 and 73050, in any cell in the worksheet or window will also be displayed in one of these five ways. You choose one of the five formats after you select **Date**. The five formats include the following:

1. (DD-MMM-YY)   Day-Month-Year   11-Jul-88

2. (DD-MMM)   Day-Month   11-Jul

3. (MMM-YY)   Month-Year   Jul-88

4. Full International   07/11/88
   (See the following paragraph.)

5. Partial International   07/11
   (See the following paragraph.)

With the Full and Partial International formats, the date is displayed according to the setting entered in **Configuration Other International Date** of the SERVICES menu. Four options for Full International and four options for Partial International format are available, all displaying numeric values for months rather than month abbreviations. For more information on date formats, see Chapter 5.

Time

The **Time** format is much like Symphony's **Date** format. The time, like the date, is represented as an integer. To tell Symphony that you are entering a time value into the worksheet, you use one of the time functions: @TIME, @TIMEVALUE, or @NOW.

To display time in hours, minutes, and seconds, use either the SHEET **Format Time** or the SHEET **Settings Format Time** command. Four options are available for **Time** formats, including two International formats. These International Time formats are determined by the setting in the **Configuration Other International Time** option of the SERVICES menu. The **Time** formats available in SHEET **Format Time** and SHEET **Settings Format Time** are the following:

1. (HH:MM:SS AM/PM)   Hour-Minute-Second   11:37:43 PM

2. (HH:MM AM/PM)   Hour-Minute   6:33 PM

3. Full International   18:33:43
   (See the following paragraph.)

4. Partial International   18:33
   (See the following paragraph.)

Four **Time** formats are available in the International settings. These differ from the first two **Time** options according to the punctuation separating hours, minutes, and seconds. Also available is a **Time** format using *h*, *m*, and *s* abbreviations following hours, minutes, and seconds. For more information on time functions and formats, see Chapter 5.

Scientific

The **Scientific** format causes Symphony to display numbers in exponential scientific notation. You may recall that Symphony employs this notation in the **General** format when numbers are too large or too small to be displayed any other way. One small difference between the way the **General** format defaults and the way the **Scientific** format controls scientific notation is found in their treatment of precision. You control the number of decimal places in **Scientific**, whereas Symphony controls them in **General**. Following are some examples.

In the Command Line	In the Worksheet
(S2) 27.1	2.71E+01
(S4) 453.235	4.5324E+02
(S1) -21	2.1E-01
(S0) -1	-1E+00

Bar-Graph

The **Bar-Graph** format, located in the **Other** option of the SHEET **Format** and SHEET **Settings** Format commands, creates a horizontal bar graph of plus or minus signs, depending on the value of the number you enter in the cell. Symphony displays asterisks if the size of the bar graph exceeds the column width. If you enter zero in a cell, a period (.) appears on the graph.

In the Command Line	In the Worksheet
(+) 6	++++++
(+) -4	----
(+) 0	

Unless you develop some unusual applications, you will probably not find much use for the **Bar-Graph** format. Because Symphony's graphics capability is available, you can create a high-quality bar graph as easily as you can a simple graph with the **Bar-Graph** format.

Literal

The **Literal** format is also located in the **Other** option of the SHEET **Format** and SHEET **Settings** Format commands. Literal displays formulas as they are entered in the command line, not the computed values that Symphony normally displays. Numbers entered with this format are displayed in the same way as in the **General** format. In addition, Symphony displays range names rather than cell addresses on the worksheet whenever a formula in the **Literal** format involves range names.

One important application of the Literal format is debugging. Because you can display all the formulas on-screen by selecting Literal, you can more easily find problems and correct them. Some examples of the Literal format are given here.

In the Command Line	*In the Worksheet*
(L) +C4/B12	+C4/B12
(L) (A21*SALES)	(A21*SALES)
(L) 567.6	567.6

Hidden

Another option on the SHEET Format Other and SHEET Settings Format Other menus is the Hidden option, a powerful addition to Symphony's spreadsheet environment. Used alone, Hidden enables you to prevent a cell's contents from displaying on the screen. The cell's contents will appear in the control panel, however, unless you use the SERVICES Settings Security selection in combination with Hidden. (See the section in Chapter 1 entitled "Security System" for more information on protecting a worksheet's contents.)

Hidden suppresses the display of cell contents for any range you indicate after you have retrieved the Format Other Hidden selection from the SHEET menu. If you want to "hide" all cell contents in a window, select SHEET Settings Format Other Hidden. Even though a cell's contents are not displayed on the screen when you have used the Hidden format, Symphony can nevertheless calculate and readjust all formulas and values when values are changed.

Other Settings Options

Three other options on the SHEET Settings menu are worth mentioning here. Zero, Titles, and Recalculation all help control the appearance of your spreadsheet.

Zero

The SHEET Settings Zero command controls the display of zeros on the spreadsheet. If you choose Yes, cells with a value of zero will not display or print; these cells will appear as if they are blank. If you choose No (the default), zeros will display and print. Be aware that Zero is a temporary sheet setting. If you always want to suppress zeros, you must reset Zero to Yes every time you retrieve the file.

Titles

The SHEET Settings Titles command is similar to Symphony's SERVICES **Window Create** command. Both commands allow you to see one area of a worksheet while working on another. The unique function of the **Titles** command, however, is that it freezes all the cells to the left of and above the current cell pointer position so that these cells cannot move off the screen.

If you use the **Window Create** command with the **Settings Titles** command, you can view two different parts of the worksheet while freezing one section in one of the windows. This setup is especially valuable when you want to keep row or column labels in view as you continue to work away from these labels. The **Settings Titles** command is also useful whenever you simply want to freeze part of the worksheet without having to create a new window to do so.

You can see a classic illustration of the advantage of this option when you are entering the items on a pro forma balance sheet and income statement. Suppose that you are trying to set up a budget to project the levels of the financial statement items, month by month, for the next year. Because the normal screen (without any special column widths) shows 20 rows by 8 columns, you will undoubtedly have to shift the screen so that cell A1 is no longer in the upper left corner. In fact, if you enter the month headings across row 1 and the balance sheet and income statement headings down column A, as shown in figure 4.51, you have to scroll the screen several times in order to enter all the items.

Fig. 4.51

A sample balance sheet and income statement.

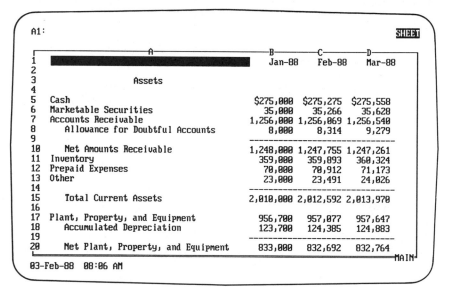

To keep the headings in view on the screen, even when you scroll, select SHEET Settings Titles when the cell pointer is in cell B2. When you enter this command, the following menu items appear:

Both   Horizontal   Vertical   Clear

If you select **Both**, Symphony freezes the rows above the cell pointer and the columns to the left of the cell pointer. That is, neither the rows nor columns move off the screen when you scroll up and down or left and right. If you select **Horizontal**, the rows on the screen above the cell pointer become frozen. If you select **Vertical**, the columns to the left of the cell pointer are frozen and move only when you scroll up and down (but not when you move left and right). **Clear** unlocks the previously set **Titles**.

In the pro forma example, the **Both** option was selected. In this case, when you scroll right and left as well as up and down, the headings always remain in view. Figure 4.52 shows an example of how **Both** works.

```
 G26: (P0) +G24+G15                                          SHEET

 |                 A                    E         F         G
 1                                    May 88    Jun 88    Jul 88
 8        Allowance for Doubtful Accounts   9,725    10,501    10,941
 9                                        ----------  ----------  ----------
 10        Net Amounts Receivable         1,248,592  1,247,974  1,248,420
 11   Inventory                             360,917    360,962    361,241
 12   Prepaid Expenses                       72,677     72,905     73,566
 13   Other                                  25,215     25,964     26,959
 14                                        ----------  ----------  ----------
 15        Total Current Assets           2,020,872  2,022,281  2,025,131
 16
 17   Property, Plant, and Equipment        956,505    960,452    960,868
 18     Accumulated Depreciation            125,846    126,171    126,438
 19                                        ----------  ----------  ----------
 20   Net Property, Plant, and Equipment    830,659    834,281    834,430
 21
 22   Investment Long-Term                  409,222    409,222    409,222
 23                                        ----------  ----------  ----------
 24     Total Noncurrent Assets           1,239,881  1,243,503  1,243,652
 25                                        ----------  ----------  ----------
 26   Total Assets                        3,260,753  3,265,784  3,268,783
                                                                          MAIN
 22-Apr-88  03:27 PM                                          Num
```

Fig. 4.52

An example of using Settings Titles Both.

When you use the **Titles** command to freeze rows or columns, you cannot move the cell pointer into the frozen area. Again, in the pro forma example, if you try to move the cell pointer into cell A2 from cell B2, Symphony beeps and does not allow the cell pointer to move into the locked area. Similarly, using the Home key moves the cell pointer to the upper left cell in the unlocked area—in the example, cell B2. Normally, the Home function moves the cell pointer to cell A1.

Here's one exception to the restriction on cell-pointer movement: If you use the GoTo key (F5) to jump to a cell within the titles area, you will see two copies of the title rows and columns. Figure 4.53 shows the result when you press the GoTo key to go to cell A1 of the pro forma example.

Fig. 4.53

Results of pressing the GoTo key to move to a titles area.

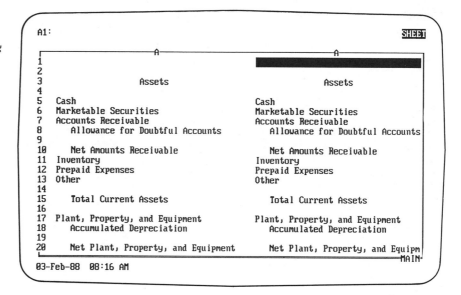

Recalculation

Recalculating all the cells in a worksheet when a value or a formula in one of the cells changes is a primary function of any spreadsheet program. And the SHEET Settings Recalculation command is an important part of Symphony's sophisticated spreadsheet capabilities.

To get to the Recalculation setting, retrieve the SHEET menu and select Settings. After the Settings menu appears, choose Recalculation. (Selecting Settings also causes Symphony to display the default settings for Recalculation and other settings options, as shown in fig. 4.54.) Choosing Recalculation leads to the following three selections:

Method   Order   Iterations

Method: Automatic versus Manual Recalculation

The Method setting tells Symphony that either you want the program to recalculate values automatically when you make changes, or you want to recalculate manually by pressing the Calc key (F8).

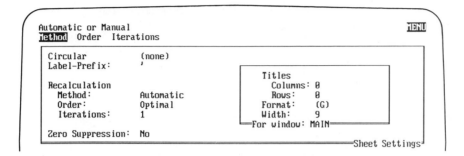

Fig. 4.54

Default settings under the SHEET Settings menu.

When you are working on a large worksheet that involves many formulas, the worksheet may require some time to recalculate. This delay occurs whenever you make a new entry or change a value. One way to get around the problem is to change from the standard Automatic to Manual recalculation.

With Manual recalculation, you can control Symphony so that it recalculates only when you press the Calc key. Manual gives you an advantage only in large worksheets in which you change many values. Otherwise, Symphony is so fast that recalculation occurs almost instantly.

Order: Optimal, Natural, Column-by-Column, or Row-by-Row

If you choose Order from the three Recalculation selections, you can change the order of recalculation from Optimal (the default) to Natural, Column-by-Column, or Row-by-Row. In the Optimal order, Symphony recalculates only the formulas that are affected by changes in the spreadsheet. In the Natural order, Symphony does not recalculate any given cell until the cells on which it depends have been recalculated. Because the relationship is rarely linear, the method of recalculation is not linear. Instead, recalculation occurs in a "topological" manner, starting at the lowest level and working up. The Optimal order also uses this hierarchical method.

With Natural and Optimal recalculation, you no longer have to worry about the order of recalculation and the problem of forward references when a cell refers to another cell that is lower in the worksheet. For example, imagine that you created a sheet with four cells: A1, C1, C2, and C3. Assume that these cells have the following contents:

A1 = +C3
C1 = 100
C2 = 200
C3 = +C1+C2

Here A1 and C3 both have the value 300. Now suppose that you change the number in cell C2 to 100.

If the cells are recalculated by using forward reference, here's what happens. Recalculation starts in the upper left corner of the worksheet, and cell A1 is evaluated first. Because the prior value of C3 (300) has not changed, A1 retains the value 300. Recalculation continues, either column by column or row by row, across the sheet until Symphony comes to cell C3. Because the value of cell C2 has changed, the value in C3 changes to 200.

Clearly, the forward reference order of recalculation causes the value of A1 to be different from that of C3, although the cells are defined to be equal. Even though recalculating the sheet again would eliminate the inequality, it would not remove the basic problem. In large and complex models, undetected forward references are possible.

In one instance you must change from Symphony's **Natural** or **Optimal** order of recalculation to **Column-by-Column** or **Row-by-Row**. The change is needed when you are importing a VisiCalc file that is built around either column-by-column or row-by-row recalculation.

Iterations

Usually, you need only one pass to recalculate a worksheet. But when a worksheet contains a circular reference, one pass does not work. A classic example of a circular reference occurs when you try to determine the amount of borrowing required by a firm. The thought process that is required is this:

1. Borrowings = Assets - (Total Liabilities + Equity). Borrowings represent the difference between projected asset requirements and the sum of total projected liabilities and equity.

2. But the level of equity is a function of net income and dividends.

3. And net income is a function of gross margin and interest expense.

4. Interest expense and gross margin are functions of borrowings.

In this line of thinking you can see the circular pattern. When this kind of reference occurs, Symphony displays a CIRC indicator in the lower right corner of the screen. When you recalculate this type of sheet, using natural or optimal calculation, Symphony does not accurately recompute all the values. Because each value in the circular set depends directly or indirectly on all the other values, Symphony cannot find a "toehold." That is, Symphony cannot find the most fundamental cell in the worksheet because no such cell exists.

Iterative recalculation allows Symphony to overcome this problem. When Symphony is in the Iterative mode, the sheet recalculates a specified number of times each time you strike the Calc key. Normally, the sheet only recalculates once each time you press the Calc key. Although the default number of iterations is 1, you can alter this number in the **Iterations** option of the **R**ecalculation setting. If you have circular references in your sheet, you should keep the number of recalculation passes high.

Iterative recalculation overcomes a circular reference because each recalculative pass through the sheet causes the actual values of the cells to approach more closely their correct values. For example, suppose that you built a sheet with the following set of relationships:

```
A3 = .05*A5
A4 = 100
A5 = +A3+A4
```

When you first enter these formulas, A3 has a value of 0, A4 equals 100, and A5 equals 100. Assume that the number of iterations is set to 5. Here are the values of each cell after each recalculative pass:

	A3	A4	A5
1	5	100	105
2	5.25	100	105.25
3	5.2625	100	105.2625
4	5.263125	100	105.2631
5	5.263156	100	105.2631

Notice that on each pass, the difference between the prior and the current value of cells A3 and A5 becomes smaller. After only 5 passes, the difference is small enough to be insignificant. After 20 passes, the difference would probably be too small for Symphony to recognize. At that point, the problem with the circular reference is eliminated.

You should note two points about iterative recalculation. First, it is possible to create a set of circular references that is too complicated for Symphony to sort out, even in 20 passes. If such a circumstance arises with one of your models, simply set the **Iterations** count to 50 (the maximum). Remember that 20 (and certainly 50) calculations of a large sheet take a long time. Be patient. Control over Symphony will be returned to you soon enough.

Chapter Summary

Using the SHEET environment alone, you will find Symphony an incredibly powerful program. Symphony enables you to build sophisticated spreadsheets and databases with the SHEET window commands. Symphony's real power, however, can best be seen when you combine SHEET window applications with the other environments. In the following chapters, you will discover just how you can integrate the DOC, GRAPH, FORM, and COMM environments with Symphony's SHEET environment.

5

@Functions

You can think of functions (also called built-in functions) as abbreviations of formulas. Symphony's functions are actually quick ways of performing tasks that would otherwise take much longer (or in many cases could not be done at all) with standard mathematical and string concatenation symbols such as +, /, and &.

Symphony includes a comprehensive set of built-in functions. And if you use Symphony's functions with some of its more high-powered features, such as its database or command language, you will find that Symphony has many of the ingredients of a sophisticated programming language.

This chapter begins with an examination of the basics of Symphony's functions. The functions are then covered by application: mathematical, trigonometric, statistical, financial, data management, logical, special, string processing, ASCII/LICS, date, and time.

Function Basics

You announce Symphony's functions to the computer by typing @ before the function name. The @ distinguishes the formula from a normal label entry.

To obtain the values of functions, most functions refer to one or more arguments. An *argument* is one of three different types: a single numeric value, a single string value, or a range. In Symphony, arguments are always written in parentheses after the function. For example, the following function (which we'll assume lies in cell B21) computes the total of a range of eight cells:

@SUM(B12..B19)

Here @ signals that the entry is a function, SUM is the name of the function, and the range B12..B19 is the argument. This function tells Symphony to compute the sum of the numbers located in cells B12, B13, B14, B15, B16, B17, B18, and B19, and to display the result in cell B21.

A few functions, such as @ERR and @NA, do not take arguments. These functions are discussed in detail later in the chapter.

Following are examples of different functions with the three argument types:

@SUM(A2..H14)	Computes the sum of the numbers in the rectangular range A2..H14.
@COUNT(TOTALS)	Returns the number of nonblank cells in the range called TOTALS.
@MAX(C15..H32)	Returns the maximum value in the rectangular range C15..H32.
@SUM(A2..H14,A15)	Computes the sum of the numbers in the range A2..H14 and in cell A15.
@DATEVALUE(AA1)	Converts the string value in cell AA1 (such as "12/23/88") to a serial number representing the number of days since December 31, 1899.
@NPV(.15/12,A1..A17)	Computes the net present value of the 17-month range A1..A17 at the monthly rate of 1.25 percent.
@LOWER("TIMES")	Converts the word TIMES to lowercase.

Like mathematical and string concatenation formulas, functions can be much more complex than those listed. For example, you can combine several functions in a single cell by using functions as the arguments for the original function. This technique is called *nesting*. In practice you will find that you nest functions quite frequently.

Mathematical Functions

Symphony contains several functions that you can use to perform mathematical operations. These functions include the following:

@ABS(number)
Computes the absolute value of a number or cell reference. For example, the function @ABS(-4) returns the value 4, and the function @ABS(-556) returns the value 556. The function @ABS(3) returns 3.

@EXP(number)

Computes the value of the constant *e* (approximately 2.718) to the power specified by the number; often used to reverse the @LN function. For example, the function @EXP(5) returns 148.4131. If cell A1 contains the value 2.75, the function @EXP(A1) returns 15.64263. Also, if @LN(2) is placed in cell AA1, the number that appears in that cell will be 0.693147. If @EXP(AA1) is then placed in cell AB1, the number that appears in that cell is 2. If you use a number greater than 230 with @EXP, Symphony returns asterisks in the cell.

@INT(number)

Computes the integer portion of the number. For example, the function @INT(4.356) returns the value 4. If cell A1 contains the value 55.666, the function @INT(A1) returns the value 55. Notice that unlike the @ROUND function (explained in the next section), @INT simply truncates all the digits to the right of the decimal.

@LN(number)

Computes the natural logarithm (base *e*) of the number or cell reference. For example, the function @LN(17.634) returns the value 2.869828. The number must be positive; otherwise, the function returns the ERR message. (Refer back to the description of @EXP to see how the two functions work.)

@LOG(number)

Computes the logarithm (base 10) of the number or cell reference. For example, the function @LOG(4.56) returns the value 0.658964. If cell A1 contains the value 3.555, the function @LOG(A1) returns the value 0.550839.

@SQRT(number)

Computes the square root of the number or cell reference. For example, the function @SQRT(5) returns the value 2.236067. If cell A1 contains the value 16, the function @SQRT(A1) returns the value 4.

Special Mathematical Functions

The following mathematical functions require special explanation:

@RAND	Generates random numbers
@ROUND	Rounds numbers to a given precision
@MOD	Returns the remainder (the modulus) from division

Generating Random Numbers: @RAND

The @RAND built-in function requires no argument and is used for random number generation. The function generates random numbers between 0 and 1, with up to eight decimal places. If you enter the function @RAND in a cell, that cell displays a different value between 0 and 1 each time the worksheet is recalculated. Figures 5.1A and 5.1B show the same sheet filled with @RAND functions. Notice that in the second sheet, which has been recalculated, each cell has a different value from that in the first.

Fig. 5.1A

An example of @RAND.

```
A1: @RAND                                                        SHEET
┌─────A────────B────────C────────D────────E────────F────────G────────H──────┐
1  0.054059 0.554383 0.530199 0.241763 0.779003 0.603935 0.418282 0.840652
2  0.139802 0.139724 0.685448 0.038902 0.856824 0.373560 0.553594 0.135677
3  0.443549 0.371316 0.353922 0.128959 0.534099 0.216110 0.895260 0.322466
4  0.444313 0.782810 0.669167 0.875216 0.159000 0.932434 0.359635 0.932787
5  0.891609 0.511102 0.534699 0.812932 0.649720 0.791802 0.535911 0.703198
6  0.950949 0.314596 0.139364 0.502688 0.302049 0.137963 0.651078 0.485256
7  0.517686 0.493772 0.560946 0.358935 0.975208 0.494719 0.038912 0.653350
8  0.095770 0.204870 0.247402 0.023325 0.594136 0.892918 0.874426 0.502085
9  0.399329 0.456360 0.217311 0.608279 0.277978 0.892105 0.596665 0.634603
10 0.370764 0.678269 0.409030 0.306274 0.679791 0.786001 0.396492 0.976922
11 0.589145 0.180021 0.012004 0.935240 0.669194 0.682297 0.731524 0.672960
12 0.610805 0.406550 0.493257 0.209936 0.152192 0.646529 0.124070 0.940562
13 0.136826 0.817289 0.269362 0.340349 0.186778 0.983812 0.100481 0.975109
14 0.983271 0.949156 0.527851 0.999164 0.136650 0.131622 0.690015 0.973976
15 0.463798 0.801794 0.721771 0.788145 0.729261 0.379717 0.705688 0.772644
16 0.703137 0.826257 0.760685 0.345602 0.875942 0.612830 0.802806 0.002717
17 0.505400 0.599475 0.975707 0.842977 0.545257 0.045434 0.421829 0.861794
18 0.427035 0.085936 0.190579 0.120522 0.966295 0.294228 0.318517 0.402377
19 0.657586 0.316812 0.561854 0.231639 0.542095 0.076328 0.529675 0.319018
20 0.233887 0.353208 0.229144 0.409238 0.034421 0.807456 0.329548 0.851991
└──────────────────────────────────────────────────────────────────MAIN─┘
03-Feb-88  08:28 AM
```

Fig. 5.1B

The same range after the worksheet is recalculated.

```
A1: @RAND                                                        SHEET
┌─────A────────B────────C────────D────────E────────F────────G────────H──────┐
1  0.627676 0.423453 0.271700 0.374965 0.835292 0.360699 0.171859 0.593345
2  0.740426 0.463289 0.624721 0.599474 0.896855 0.913838 0.032907 0.986494
3  0.260595 0.116055 0.074477 0.850658 0.412128 0.285734 0.306598 0.918840
4  0.822423 0.548995 0.772605 0.247783 0.240170 0.951995 0.753216 0.265197
5  0.440080 0.105077 0.710904 0.661224 0.765725 0.767891 0.869845 0.988630
6  0.298486 0.493548 0.590257 0.411198 0.502806 0.463674 0.101965 0.593793
7  0.653362 0.287065 0.825148 0.436787 0.461068 0.933294 0.475548 0.910891
8  0.118780 0.998308 0.124369 0.493974 0.492136 0.134733 0.226404 0.730360
9  0.350142 0.065185 0.562165 0.157713 0.601523 0.284789 0.492582 0.684554
10 0.148129 0.351363 0.889479 0.765989 0.993839 0.295787 0.368259 0.130553
```

Rounding Numbers: @ROUND

The @ROUND built-in function rounds numbers to a specified precision. The general form of the function is

@ROUND(x,numb_digs)

where x is the number to be rounded, and *numb_digs* is a number between 15 and -15 representing the number of digits to the right of the decimal. Here are some examples of this function:

@ROUND(123.456,3) = 123.456
@ROUND(123.456,2) = 123.46
@ROUND(123.456,1) = 123.5
@ROUND(123.456,0) = 123
@ROUND(123.456,-1) = 120
@ROUND(123.456,-2) = 100

The advantage of the @ROUND function over the SHEET Format Fixed command is that with @ROUND you avoid the errors that may appear when you add rounded currency amounts. If you add the following two sets of numbers, the numbers in the right column appear to have the wrong total.

Cell	Value Stored	Value Displayed in Currency Format to Nearest Cent
A1	123.025	$123.03
A2	123.025	$123.03
A4	246.05	$246.05

The @ROUND built-in function gets around this problem by making the columns total properly.

Cell	Value Stored	Value Displayed in Currency Format to Nearest Cent
A1	123.025	$123.03
A2	123.025	$123.03
A4	246.05	$246.06

The total on the right ($246.06) is derived from using the formula @ROUND(A1,2)+@ROUND(A2,2) in cell A4.

Returning a Remainder: @MOD

The @MOD function returns the remainder (the modulus) from a division operation. @MOD's general form is

@MOD(number,divisor)

The following examples illustrate how @MOD works:

@MOD(7,3)   =   1
@MOD(71.3,21)   =   8
@MOD(31,0)   =   ERR

If you specify 0 as the divisor, Symphony displays ERR.

Here's an example of how the @MOD function can be helpful. Suppose that you want to determine the number of parts that will be left over if you run equal-sized batches of 33 items, and the total demand for a product is expected to be 500 items during the course of a year. The result is 5 items, as in

@MOD(500,33) = 5

Trigonometric Functions

Symphony also has a complete set of trigonometric functions. Many of you will never use these functions because they have little application in the world of accounting or finance. But those of you who use Symphony to solve engineering problems will find these functions invaluable. Symphony's trigonometric functions include the following:

@PI
> This function, which requires no argument, returns the value of the constant pi, accurate to 10 decimal places, or 3.1415926536.

@SIN(number), @COS(number), @TAN(number)
> These functions compute the common trigonometric functions. The values returned are expressed in radians. For example, the value of the function @SIN(2) is 0.909297 (radians). The value of @TAN(136) is 1.290401 (radians).

@ASIN(number), @ACOS(number), @ATAN(number),
@ATAN2(number)
> These functions compute the arcsine, arccosine, arctangent, and four-quadrant arctangent of a number or cell reference. The @ASIN, @ACOS, and @ATAN functions reverse the @SIN, @COS, and @TAN functions, respectively. For example, for the @ACOS function, you specify a number between 1 and -1, representing the cosine of an angle; the value of the function is the size of the angle in radians. The value of @ACOS(.33) is 1.234492 in radians. To convert to degrees, you multiply the value by 180/@PI. Therefore, the value of @COS(.33)*180/@PI is approximately 71 degrees.

Statistical Functions

Symphony has several functions that perform simple statistical analyses. These statistical functions are typically used with an argument consisting of a range of cells. As you may recall, a range is a series of contiguous cells, either by row or column. Symphony's statistical functions include @SUM, @MAX, @MIN, @COUNT, @AVG, @VAR, and @STD.

Computing a Sum: @SUM

Perhaps the most important statistical function is @SUM, which computes the sum of a range of entries. The range is usually a partial row or column but can also be an entire block of cells consisting of several rows and columns. For example, in the simple sheet in figure 5.2, the function @SUM(A1..A2) returns the value 1368, or 345+765. The function @SUM(A1..C2) returns the value 3330, which is the total of all the numbers in the six-cell range. Notice that the range in this case consists of two partial rows.

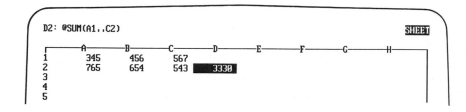

Fig. 5.2

An example of @SUM.

You can even define the argument of the @SUM function as a discontinuous set of cells. For example, the function @SUM(A1,B2,C1) returns the value 1566. This function is equivalent to the formula +A1+B2+C1. A more useful hybrid is the function @SUM(A1..B2,C1), which computes the total of the range A1 to B2 plus the value in C1 for a total of 2787.

In the preceding example, using @SUM takes about the same amount of time as using the longhand arithmetic +A1+A2+B1+B2+C1. But when you have a lengthy range, @SUM can save time.

Another advantage of the @SUM function (and other range functions as well) is that it is more adaptable than a formula to changes made in the sheet with cut-and-paste commands. For example, in the sheet in figure 5.2, the function @SUM(A1..C1) is equivalent to the formula +A1+B1+C1. But if you use the SHEET window's **Delete Column** command to delete column B, the sheet looks like figure 5.3. The formula has changed to +A1+ERR+B1, which returns the message ERR. The function, on the other hand, has changed to @SUM(A1..B1) and returns the correct answer: 912.

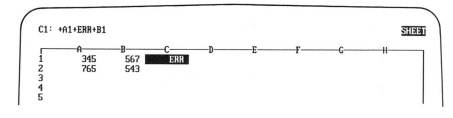

Fig. 5.3

The +A1+B1+C1 formula after deleting column B.

In this example, if you go the other way and insert a column using SHEET Insert Column, what happens? The sheet resembles figure 5.4. The formula is +A1+C1+D1 and still has the value 1368. The function is now @SUM(A1..D1). If you insert a number in the new cell B1, the function includes that number in the new total, but the formula does not.

Fig. 5.4

The +A1+B1+C1 formula after inserting a column.

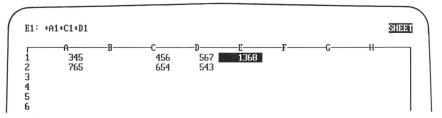

Modeling Tip: Here is a practical application for this insert feature. Whenever possible, define a sum range to include an extra cell at the end of the range. Frequently you can just include the cell that contains the underline to mark the addition in the range. For example, in the sheet shown in figure 5.5, you can enter the formula @SUM(A1..A4) in cell A5. Because the label in cell A4 has a mathematical value of 0, the label does not affect the sum. But because you include the label in the formula, you can add an extra item to the list simply by inserting a row at row 4. The sheet then looks like figure 5.6.

The formula in cell A6 is now @SUM(A1..A5). If you insert the number 114 in cell A4, the formula immediately picks up the number and displays the value 2100 in cell A6.

Fig. 5.5

Including an extra cell in the @SUM formula.

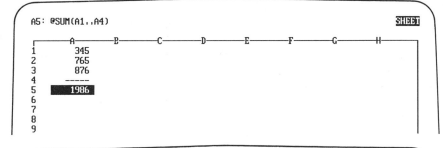

Fig. 5.6

Adding another item to the list.

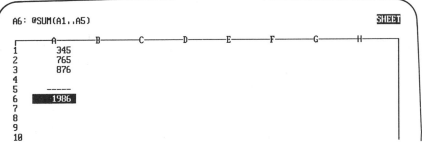

Finding the Maximum and Minimum Values: @MAX and @MIN

The @MAX and @MIN functions return the maximum and minimum values in a range. As with the @SUM function, the range can be a partial row or column, a block of several partial rows and columns, a named range, or a discontinuous group of cells joined by commas. Both @MAX and @MIN assign a value of 0 to labels but completely ignore empty cells. For example, in the simple sheet in figure 5.7, the function @MAX(A1..A5) returns the value 777. The function @MIN(A1..A5) returns the value 134, and the function @MIN(A1..A6) also returns 134, because cell A6 is blank. But if you enter the label *ABCD* in cell A6, the function @MIN(A1..A6) returns the value 0, because Symphony evaluates labels as zero.

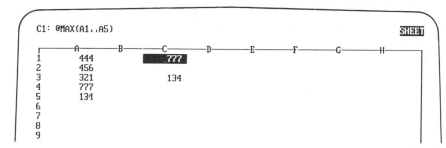

Fig. 5.7

An example of @MAX.

Counting Nonblank Entries: @COUNT

The @COUNT function is similar to the @MIN, @MAX, and @SUM functions. @COUNT returns the count of the number of nonblank entries in a range. In the worksheet in figure 5.7, the function @COUNT(A1..A6) returns the value 5. If you had entered a label or number in cell A6, the value of the function would be 6. Cells containing spaces also increment the @COUNT.

One interesting feature of the @COUNT function is the way it reacts to a single blank cell. If cell A1 is blank, the function @COUNT(A1) returns the value 1. The function @COUNT(A1..A1), however, returns the value 0. In fact, every @COUNT function that refers to a single cell without specifying a range (such as A1..A1) has a value of 1. The most reliable technique for avoiding the single-cell problem is always to specify a range with the @COUNT function.

Calculating the Mean: @AVG

Another simple statistical function is @AVG. This function computes the mean, or average, of all the cells in a range. Essentially, the @AVG function is similar to the @SUM function divided by the @COUNT function. Because @AVG ignores blank cells, an @AVG function that refers to a range with all blank cells returns the value of ERR.

A Quick Review of Statistics

A quick review of statistical concepts may be worthwhile at this time. If you are already quite familiar with the concepts of mean, variance, and standard deviation, as well as population and sample statistics, you may want to skip to the next section.

The *mean*, often called the arithmetic average, is commonly used to mark the midpoint of a group of data items. The mean is calculated by adding the items in a group and dividing the total by the number of items. Don't confuse the mean with the median or mode, which are also measures of central tendency. The *median* is the value midway between the highest and lowest value in the group in terms of probability. Half the items in the group have values above the median, and half have values below. The *mode* is the most commonly occurring value in a group of items (that is, the value you see most often).

Variance and *standard deviation* are related dispersion statistics. To calculate the variance, you subtract the mean of a group of numbers from each number in the group and square each result. You then add the squares and divide the total by the number of items in the group. To compute the standard deviation, you take the square root of the variance. Symphony's @VAR and @STD functions automatically make these calculations for you.

What does the standard deviation tell you? As a general rule, about 68 percent of the items in a normally distributed population fall within a range that is plus or minus one standard deviation of the mean. About 95 percent of the items fall within plus or minus two standard deviations of the mean.

To understand Symphony's @VAR and @STD statistical functions, you should know the difference between population and sample statistics. Population statistics are used when you know the values of all the items in a population. When the number of items is quite large and you don't know them all (which is usually the case), you cannot compute the population statistics. You must instead rely on sample statistics as estimates of the population statistics.

Finding Variance and Standard Deviation: @VAR and @STD

These slightly more complex statistical functions have the following formats:

@VAR(list)	Computes the population variance
@STD(list)	Computes the standard deviation of a population

A simple example that uses both functions is shown in figure 5.8, which includes a list showing the number of items each salesperson sold during a given period. The list of the number of items sold is the population in this example. The population is used as the range for all the statistical functions.

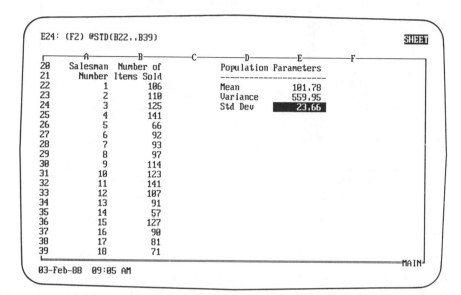

```
E24: (F2) @STD(B22..B39)                                    SHEET
    ┌──A──────B────C──────D──────E──────F──
20   Salesman Number of      Population Parameters
21   Number  Items Sold      --------------------
22      1       106          Mean           101.78
23      2       110          Variance       559.95
24      3       125          Std Dev         23.66
25      4       141
26      5        66
27      6        92
28      7        93
29      8        97
30      9       114
31     10       123
32     11       141
33     12       107
34     13        91
35     14        57
36     15       127
37     16        90
38     17        81
39     18        71
                                                   MAIN
03-Feb-88  09:05 AM
```

Fig. 5.8

A practical application of @VAR and @STD.

The mean of the population (101.78, shown in cell E22) is computed by using the @AVG function. The standard deviation, shown in cell E24, is about 24, which means that roughly 68 percent of the salespeople sold between 77 and 125 items.

If you do not have the entire population of sales figures but only a small portion of it, you can compute the sample statistics. This approach is more realistic because you are more likely to be told that the actual population is all the monthly sales for the year and to be given only one month's worth of sales. You can see that moving into the realm of sample statistics involves more sophisticated concepts.

To calculate the sample variance for the sales data used in the previous example, multiply the population variance by $n/n-1$ (degrees of freedom), where n equals the number of items in the sample. Multiplying by n/n-1 adjusts the variance for the size of the sample used in the calculation. Because n/n-1 is always less than one, multiplying this figure by the population variance has a conservative influence on the sample variance. The results of this calculation are shown in figure 5.9.

Fig. 5.9

Calculating the sample statistics.

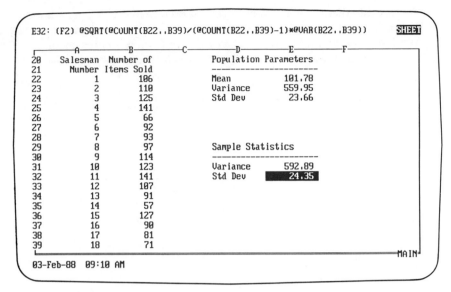

```
E32: (F2) @SQRT(@COUNT(B22..B39)/(@COUNT(B22..B39)-1)*@VAR(B22..B39))   SHEET

┌───────A────────B────────C────────D────────E────────F────
│ 20   Salesman  Number of         Population Parameters
│ 21   Number  Items Sold          ─────────────────────
│ 22      1        106             Mean          101.78
│ 23      2        110             Variance      559.95
│ 24      3        125             Std Dev        23.66
│ 25      4        141
│ 26      5         66
│ 27      6         92
│ 28      7         93
│ 29      8         97             Sample Statistics
│ 30      9        114             ─────────────────────
│ 31     10        123             Variance      592.89
│ 32     11        141             Std Dev        24.35
│ 33     12        107
│ 34     13         91
│ 35     14         57
│ 36     15        127
│ 37     16         90
│ 38     17         81
│ 39     18         71
└──────────────────────────────────────────────────────MAIN
  03-Feb-88  09:10 AM
```

To compute the sample variance in figure 5.9, you can use @COUNT to determine the degrees of freedom, as in

Sample Variance = @COUNT(list)/(@COUNT(list)-1)*@VAR(list)

To compute the standard deviation of the sample, you can take the square root of the sample variance. A convenient way to do this is to use the built-in @SQRT function, as in

Sample Standard Deviation = @SQRT(Sample Variance) =
    @SQRT(@COUNT(list)/(@COUNT(list)-1)*@VAR(list))

Financial Functions

Symphony also has several financial functions. These functions include @NPV, @PV, @FV, @TERM, @IRR, @PMT, @RATE, @CTERM, and the depreciation functions @SLN, @SYD, and @DDB.

Net Present Value: @NPV

The @NPV function computes the net present value of a stream of cash flows. The form of this function is

@NPV(discount_rate,range)

The *discount_rate* is the interest rate that Symphony will use to compute the net present value; the *range* is the stream of flows to be discounted. The interval between the flows must be constant and is determined by the specified rate. For example, if the flows occur one year apart, you should use an annual discount rate. If the rates occur every month, you should use a monthly rate.

You can use the @NPV function to evaluate a variety of investment opportunities. For instance, suppose that you have a chance to buy a piece of property that will create the following stream of income in the next five years:

Year 1	100,000
Year 2	120,000
Year 3	130,000
Year 4	140,000
Year 5	50,000

To evaluate this investment, you can create a simple worksheet, as illustrated in figure 5.10. The function @NPV(A42,A40..E40) returns the value 368075.1631, which is the net present value of that stream at the discount rate of 15 percent. If this rate accurately represents the rate you earn on the investment, and the price of the property is equal to or less than $368,075, the property would be a good investment.

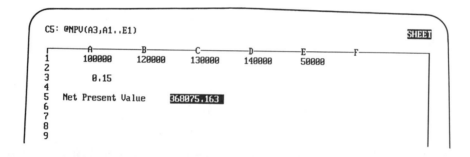

Fig. 5.10

Calculating net present value.

Notice that a cell reference, A42, is used to enter the discount rate into the function. Because the formula @NPV(.15,A40..E40) is just as easy to enter, why wasn't it used instead? In fact, neither method has an advantage until you want to make a change in the rate.

For example, assume that you want to evaluate this same investment with a rate of 14 percent. With the method in figure 5.10, all you need to do is enter the number .14 in cell A42, and Symphony automatically recalculates the worksheet. If you embedded the rate in the formula, you would have to edit the formula, replacing the .15 with .14. As you can see, if several changes are required, this operation would unnecessarily consume much time. You can apply the simple technique of using a cell reference to enter a rate in a variety of situations to facilitate changing a worksheet.

Present Value of an Annuity: @PV

The @PV built-in function calculates the present value of an ordinary annuity, given a payment per period, an interest rate, and the number of periods. An *ordinary annuity* is a series of payments made at equally spaced intervals. *Present value* is the value today of the payments to be made or received later, with the value discounted at a given interest or discount rate. Calculating the present value of an ordinary annuity gives you a way to compare different investment opportunities or potential obligations while taking into account the time value of money. The general form of the @PV formula is

@PV(payment,interest,term)

The actual equation for calculating the present value of an ordinary annuity is

$$PV = payment * \frac{1-(1+interest)^{-n}}{interest}$$

Figure 5.11 shows an example of how you can use the @PV function.

Fig. 5.11

Calculating present value.

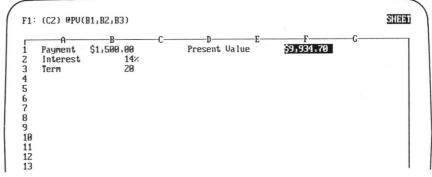

The difference between @NPV (the built-in function for net present value) and @PV stems from the difference in cash flows and the way they are laid out in the worksheet. @NPV calculates the net present value of a series of flows that may or may not be equal but which are all contained in a range of cells in the worksheet. The cash flows in the @PV function must all be equal, and the amount of the flows must be contained in a single cell or entered as a value in the @PV function.

Future Value of an Annuity: @FV

The @FV built-in function is similar in form to the @PV function, but @FV calculates the future value of an ordinary annuity. *Future value* is the value at a given day in the future of a series of payments or receipts, discounted at a given interest or discount rate. Calculating the future value of an annuity allows you to compare different investment alternatives or potential obligations. The form of the @FV function is

@FV(payment,interest,term)

The @FV function uses this equation for calculating the future value of an ordinary annuity:

$$FV = payment \quad * \quad \frac{(1+interest)^{n-1}}{interest}$$

An example using the @FV built-in function is shown in figure 5.12.

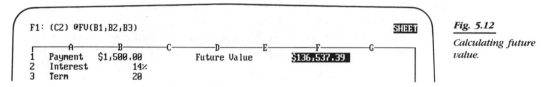

```
F1: (C2) @FV(B1,B2,B3)                                    SHEET
       A         B         C         D         E         F         G
  1  Payment  $1,500.00            Future Value        $136,537.39
  2  Interest      14%
  3  Term          20
```

Fig. 5.12

Calculating future value.

Number of Time Periods of an Annuity: @TERM

You can use the @TERM function to calculate the term (number of time periods) of an ordinary annuity, given the payment, periodic interest rate, and future value. The form of the @TERM function is

@TERM(payment,interest,future-value)

For example, you can use this function to compute the length of time necessary for a periodic investment to grow at a given interest rate to some predetermined amount.

The equation for calculating the number of time periods is

TERM=ln(1+(futurevalue*interest)/payment)/ln(1+interest)

where *ln* equals the natural logarithm.

You use @TERM for an annuity in which payments are made at the end of each time period. For payments made at the beginning of each time period, you must adjust the @TERM function by dividing it by the factor *(1+interest)* as in

@TERM(payment,interest,future-value)/(1+interest)

Internal Rate of Return: @IRR

Internal rate of return (IRR) is the discount rate that equates the present value of the expected cash outflows with the present value of the expected inflows. In simple terms, IRR is the rate of return, or profit, that an investment is expected to earn. Like the other financial calculations, IRR determines the attractiveness of an investment opportunity.

The function for internal rate of return is built around an iterative process in which you provide an initial "ballpark" guess for a discount rate (somewhere between 0 and 1), and Symphony calculates the actual discount rate that equates the present value of a series of cash outflows with the present value of a series of inflows. Symphony's method may seem awkward, but it is actually very logical. The same iterative method is used to calculate IRR manually.

Given the format of the equation, all the inflows and outflows must be in the same range. The general form of the @IRR function is

@IRR(guess,range)

After 20 iterations, Symphony should reach convergence on a discount rate within .0000001, or the program returns ERR. Figure 5.13 shows an example of how the @IRR built-in function is used. The internal rate of return, or profit, for the project illustrated in figure 5.13 is about 16 percent.

Fig. 5.13

Finding the internal rate of return.

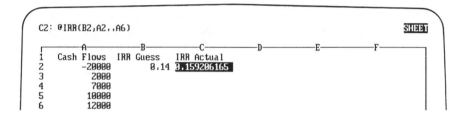

You may encounter two possible problems with the @IRR function. First, Symphony may not converge on a value for one of two reasons. One reason is that you have more than a single sign change between negative and positive cash flows. For example, you may have the sporadic cash flows that appear in figure 5.14. Because Symphony is unable to reach convergence on a single IRR value, the program returns ERR.

Fig. 5.14

The result of using a sporadic cash flow.

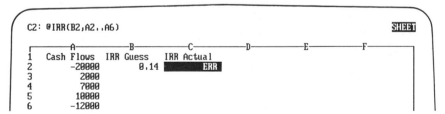

Another possible problem with the @IRR function is that, depending on the guess value you enter, the value returned may be unreasonable. For example, figure 5.15 shows a series of 11 cash flows, an IRR guess of .20, and an IRR of approximately -289 percent. Even though Symphony has not reached the proper convergence, the ERR message is not displayed. The proper IRR for this series of cash flows is approximately 138 percent. To get Symphony to display 138 percent, your guess must be between .74 and 1.0.

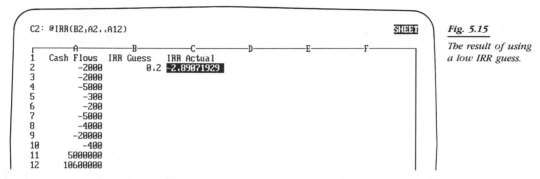

Fig. 5.15

The result of using a low IRR guess.

A good way to avoid this problem with the @IRR function is to guess on the high side. You should also double-check any answer you get by trying two or more guess values.

Payment per Period: @PMT

Another Symphony financial function calculates the mortgage payment required for a given principal, interest rate, and number of periods. The format of this function is

@PMT(principal,interest,n)

where *n* equals the number of periods.

Again, the formula behind the function calculates the present value of an ordinary annuity, but the formula is rearranged to yield the period payment as the result:

$$PMT = principal * \frac{interest}{1-(1+interest)^n}$$

You can use @PMT to build a table of mortgage rate payments similar to those in the SAMPLES.BAS program supplied with DOS. Such a table is easy to construct and appears in figure 5.16.

Periodic Interest Rate for an Investment: @RATE

The @RATE built-in function computes the interest rate per period for an investment. The form of this function is

@RATE(future-value,present-value,number of periods)

As with all investment or annuity functions, the periodic interest rate (not necessarily the annual rate) is the rate calculated. For example, to calculate a monthly interest rate for an investment of $1,000 to grow to $10,000 in eight years, you use

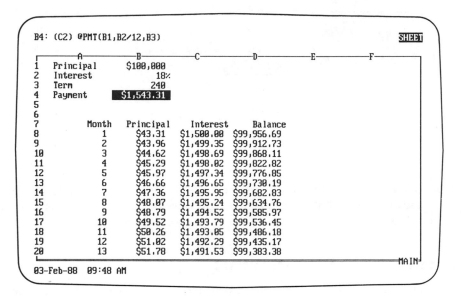

Fig. 5.16

A table of mortgage rate payments created with @PMT.

```
B4: (C2) @PMT(B1,B2/12,B3)                                        SHEET
    ┌───────A────────B────────────C────────D────────E────────F──────
  1  │   Principal      $100,000
  2  │   Interest            18%
  3  │   Term               240
  4  │   Payment       $1,543.31
  5  │
  6  │
  7  │            Month    Principal    Interest      Balance
  8  │              1        $43.31    $1,500.00    $99,956.69
  9  │              2        $43.96    $1,499.35    $99,912.73
 10  │              3        $44.62    $1,498.69    $99,868.11
 11  │              4        $45.29    $1,498.02    $99,822.82
 12  │              5        $45.97    $1,497.34    $99,776.85
 13  │              6        $46.66    $1,496.65    $99,730.19
 14  │              7        $47.36    $1,495.95    $99,682.83
 15  │              8        $48.07    $1,495.24    $99,634.76
 16  │              9        $48.79    $1,494.52    $99,585.97
 17  │             10        $49.52    $1,493.79    $99,536.45
 18  │             11        $50.26    $1,493.05    $99,486.18
 19  │             12        $51.02    $1,492.29    $99,435.17
 20  │             13        $51.78    $1,491.53    $99,383.38
    └───────────────────────────────────────────────────────MAIN┘
    03-Feb-88   09:48 AM
```

@RATE(10000,1000,8*12) or 2.4275 percent

The annual interest rate equivalent would be 12*2.4275 percent, or 29.13 percent.

The @RATE function uses this formula for computing the periodic interest rate:

$$RATE=((futurevalue/presentvalue)^{(1/term)})-1$$

Number of Time Periods for an Investment: @CTERM

The @CTERM function is basically a mirror image of the @RATE function. You can use @CTERM to calculate the number of periods based on the present value, future value, and periodic interest rate of an investment. The form of the function is

@CTERM(periodic interest rate, future-value,present-value)

If you already know the interest rate (from the previous example) and want to compute the number of years needed for the investment to grow from $1,000 to $10,000, you can use @CTERM.

@CTERM is a variation of the @TERM function. Whereas @TERM deals with a series of constant periodic payments (an annuity), @CTERM works from a one-time investment (the present value).

The formula underlying the @CTERM calculation is

CTERM=ln(futurevalue/presentvalue)/ln(1+interest)

where *ln* equals the natural logarithm.

Depreciation Functions

Symphony includes three depreciation functions for dealing with different methods of depreciation: straight-line, sum-of-the-years'-digits, and double-declining-balance. An asset's depreciation expense is calculated based upon the asset's cost, useful life, and salvage value.

Straight-Line Depreciation: @SLN

As the name implies, straight-line depreciation simply takes the depreciable cost (initial cost less salvage value) and divides it evenly over the asset's useful life. The form of this function is

@SLN(cost,salvage value,life)

Thus, a $100,000 asset with a salvage value of $20,000 and a useful life of 10 years would be depreciated at

@SLN(100000,20000,10) or $8,000 per year

The formula used by @SLN is

SLN=(cost-salvage value)/useful life

Sum-of-the-Years'-Digits Depreciation: @SYD

The @SYD function computes depreciation based on the so-called sum-of-the-years'-digits formula. This method accelerates depreciation; greater depreciation occurs in the early periods. The form for this function is

@SYD(cost,salvage value,life,period)

Unlike straight-line depreciation, the sum-of-the-years'-digits depreciation amount varies by period, and thus the time period must be one of the arguments specified. Using the previous example's numbers, the depreciation amount for the fifth year would be

@SYD(100000,20000,10,5) or approximately $8,727

The underlying formula for @SYD is

SYD=(cost-salvage value)*(life-period+1)/(life*(life+1)/2)

Double-Declining-Balance Depreciation: @DDB

Like the sum-of-the-years'-digits method, the double-declining-balance method of depreciation generates amounts that are higher in earlier years than in later years.

The function syntax also is like that of @SYD:

@DDB(cost,salvage value,life,period)

Again, you must specify the period for which you want the depreciation calculated.

The formula for calculating double-declining-balance depreciation is

DDB=(Cost−total depreciation taken in earlier periods)*2/life

Using this formula as is, however, could lead to a situation in later time periods in which the asset's book value (cost less cumulative depreciation) would exceed its salvage value. The @DDB function in Symphony has been modified to ensure automatically that such a situation does not occur. Thus, when the cumulative depreciation equals the asset's cost less its salvage value, the function results in a zero value.

Data Management Functions

Symphony has four simple data management functions: @CHOOSE, @VLOOKUP, @HLOOKUP, and @INDEX. These functions are called "special" functions by Lotus, but in this book they are called data management functions because the functions retrieve data from lists and tables. Do not confuse these functions with Symphony's database statistical functions, which operate only on databases. (Database statistical functions are discussed in Chapter 15.)

Selecting from a List: @CHOOSE

The @CHOOSE function uses a key value, which you provide, to select a number from a list. The form of this function is

@CHOOSE(key,argument0,argument1,...,argumentN)

wherein the first argument is 0, the second argument is 1, and so on.

@CHOOSE displays the argument whose position in the list matches the key. For example, the function @CHOOSE(2,3,4,5) returns the number 5 because 5 is in the second argument position in the list. If the key is changed to 1, as in @CHOOSE(1,3,4,5), the function returns 4.

As with other functions, the arguments in the @CHOOSE function can be numbers, formulas, or functions. You can also use @CHOOSE to select formulas **that** will vary in different situations. For example, the percentage rate used to **compute** depreciation under the ACRS depreciation system varies with the useful life **of** the asset. Thus, an asset with a three-year life is depreciated in the first year of the asset's life at a rate different from that of an asset with a five-year life. **A** function like the following one dramatically simplifies the computation:

@CHOOSE(Year of life,Rate for 3-year asset,Rate for 5-year asset...)

Looking up Values: @VLOOKUP and @HLOOKUP

@VLOOKUP and @HLOOKUP are two variations of a basic LOOKUP function. As their names suggest, these functions, based on the value of a test variable, "look up" a value from a table. The forms of these functions are

@VLOOKUP(test variable,range,column offset-number)

@HLOOKUP(test variable,range,row offset-number)

The first argument, which is the *test variable*, can be either a number or a string.

The second argument is a *range* containing at least two partial rows or columns. This range includes the entire lookup table from the top left corner of the comparison column to the bottom right corner of the last data column. (You can also use a range name here rather than the actual cell references.)

The third argument, called the *offset-number*, determines which data column should supply the data to the function. In every case the comparison column, which is the first column in a vertical lookup table, has an offset-number of 0 (zero); the first data column has an offset-number of 1; and so on. An offset-number can be negative in Symphony, and the number can also exceed the number of columns or rows in the lookup table. (Some examples of negative and excessive offset-numbers will be shown later.)

If you want to use the lookup functions, the worksheet needs to have a lookup table, which must consist of two or more adjacent partial rows or columns. An example of a *numeric* vertical lookup table is illustrated in figure 5.17.

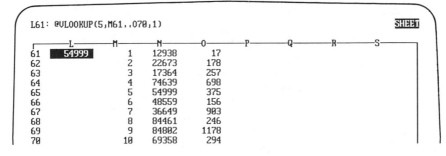

Fig. 5.17

A numeric vertical lookup table.

What differentiates this table from a *string* vertical lookup table is the contents of the first column, M. In a numeric vertical lookup table, the comparison column must contain numbers arranged in ascending order. In a string vertical lookup table, the comparison column can contain labels in any order.

In figure 5.17 the comparison column (M) contains the values that Symphony uses to look up the data shown in the second and third columns (N and O). To access this columnar table, you use the @VLOOKUP or vertical lookup function.

In this table the function @VLOOKUP(5,M61..O70,1) returns the value 54999. To return this result, Symphony searches the comparison column for the largest value that is not greater than the key and returns the corresponding value from the data column which has an offset-number of 1 (in this case, column N). Remember that the comparison column has an offset-number of 0. Column N, therefore, has an offset-number of 1, and column O has an offset-number of 2.

Because the lookup table does not search for a specific match, but for the largest key in the table that is not greater than the search variable, the function @VLOOKUP(5.5,M61..O70,1) also returns 54999. Similarly, a key of 100 returns 69358, the number that corresponds to the largest key in the list. If you use 0 as the key, an ERR message appears because no key in the table is less than or equal to 0.

You can also look up the data in column O. For example, the function @VLOOKUP(10,M61..O70,2) returns the value 294.

Lookup tables must follow specific rules. As mentioned earlier, the comparison column values for numeric lookups must be arranged in ascending order. (In other words, a comparison value cannot be repeated.) For example, the lookup table in figure 5.18 does not work because the comparison values in column M are not in ascending order. The table in figure 5.19 is also not allowed because the key 5 is repeated.

Fig. 5.18

Using comparison values that are not in ascending order.

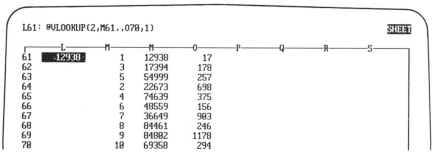

```
L61: @VLOOKUP(2,M61..O70,1)                                    SHEET

      ──L──────M──────N──────O──────P──────Q──────R──────S──
 61   -12938       1     12938      17
 62                3     17394     178
 63                5     54999     257
 64                2     22673     698
 65                4     74639     375
 66                6     48559     156
 67                7     36649     983
 68                8     84461     246
 69                9     84802    1178
 70               10     69358     294
```

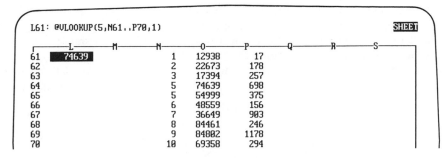

Fig. 5.19

An unacceptable list of comparison values.

A slight modification of the table in figure 5.19 illustrates the effects of using a negative offset-number. Using the statement @VLOOKUP(5,N81..P90,-1) for the vertical lookup table in figure 5.20, you can see that Symphony selects the appropriate value from the column just to the left of the lookup table. Here the value returned from the table lookup is "Shelf 8" (see cell L81).

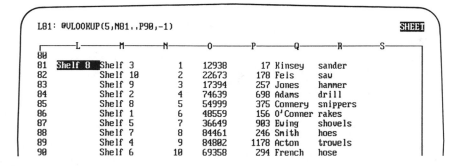

Fig. 5.20

Using a negative offset-number.

Similarly, an offset-number that exceeds the last column in the lookup range is also acceptable. Figure 5.21 shows the result of setting the offset-number to 4. In this case the value returned is "snippers," a value taken from the column that is two columns to the right of the rightmost column in the lookup table.

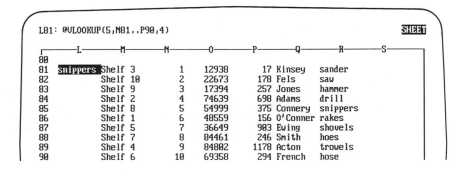

Fig. 5.21

Using an offset-number that exceeds the last column in the lookup range.

Besides numeric table lookups, Symphony can also perform string table lookups. In performing string table lookups, Symphony looks for a perfect match between a value in the comparison column and the test variable. For example, in figure 5.22, Symphony uses the function @VLOOKUP("Shelf 1",M81..O90,1) to search for the value in column N corresponding to Shelf 1. Notice that the string argument is enclosed in double quotation marks in the @VLOOKUP statement.

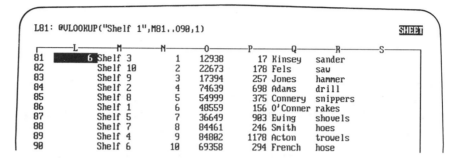

Fig. 5.22

A string vertical lookup table.

If you use 0 as the offset-number for the @VLOOKUP statement in figure 5.22, the value returned is 5. This number corresponds to the position of the matched string in the lookup range. The first entry (nails) is 0, the second entry (hammers) is 1, and so on. If the search of the lookup table fails to produce a match, Symphony returns ERR.

The @HLOOKUP function is essentially the same as @VLOOKUP, except that @HLOOKUP operates on tables arranged across rows rather than columns. The rules here are the same as those for vertical tables. Now look at an example of how the @HLOOKUP function works for a numeric lookup. (Again, the same rules apply for a string lookup.) If you build the table in figure 5.23, the function @HLOOKUP(5,L123..S125,1) returns the value 567. The function @HLOOKUP(8,L123..S125,1) returns the value 890. And the function @HLOOKUP(3,L123..S125,2) returns the value 765.

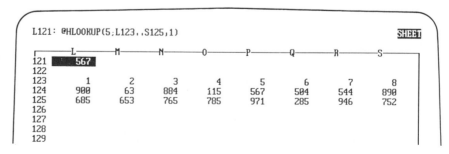

Fig. 5.23

A numeric horizontal lookup table.

A useful application for the @VLOOKUP and @HLOOKUP functions is the creation of tax tables that automatically retrieve the appropriate rate based on income. In fact, this application is the one for which the lookup function was originally developed. You can also use these functions for simple data management, such as handling inventory and employee lists, although in Symphony these tasks can be performed better with the database commands.

Retrieving Data from Specified Locations: @INDEX

The last data management function, @INDEX, is similar to the table lookup functions described previousiy; however, @INDEX has some of its own unique features. The general form of the function is

@INDEX(range,column-number,row-number)

Like the table lookup functions, the @INDEX function works with a table of numbers. But unlike the table lookup functions, the @INDEX function does not use a test variable and a comparison column (or row). Instead, @INDEX requires you to indicate the *column-number* and *row-number* of the *range* from where you want to retrieve data. For example, if you use the function @INDEX(L142..S145,3,2) in figure 5.24, you get the value 2625.

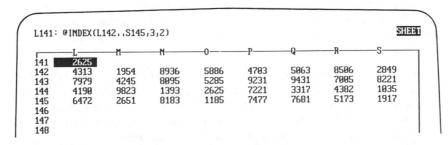

Fig. 5.24

An example of @INDEX.

```
L141: @INDEX(L142,,S145,3,2)                              SHEET
         L       M       N       O       P       Q       R       S
141    2625
142    4313    1954    8936    5886    4703    5063    8506    2049
143    7979    4245    8095    5285    9231    9431    7005    8221
144    4190    9823    1393    2625    7221    3317    4382    1035
145    6472    2651    8183    1185    7477    7681    5173    1917
146
147
148
```

Notice that the number 0 corresponds to the first column, 1 corresponds to the second column, and so on. The same numbering scheme applies to rows. Therefore, using 3 for the column-number and 2 for the row-number indicates that you want the item from the fourth column, third row.

Although the behavior of the @VLOOKUP and @HLOOKUP functions may lead you to believe otherwise, with the @INDEX function you cannot use column and row numbers that fall outside the relevant range. Using either negative numbers or numbers too large for the range causes Symphony to return the ERR message.

The @INDEX function is useful when you know the exact position of a data item in a range of cells and want to locate the item quickly. For instance, the @INDEX function works well for rate quotation systems. Figure 5.25 shows an example of a system for quoting full-page magazine advertising rates.

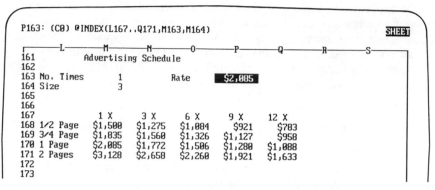

Fig. 5.25

Using @INDEX in a rate quotation system.

In this example the function @INDEX(L167..Q171,M163,M164) returns a value of $2,085. This value corresponds to the amount in the first column and the second row of the index range. If you enter a 6 for the frequency, the ERR message rather than a valid dollar amount appears.

Logical Functions

Symphony, like its predecessor 1-2-3, includes logical functions. You can think of these as a subset of the mathematical functions. In all cases, Symphony analyzes logical functions as either true or false. If a logical function is true, it has a numeric value of 1. But if the logical function is false, it has a numeric value of 0. The importance of a logical function's numeric value will be clarified shortly.

Logical functions are advantageous because they allow you to build conditional tests into cells. These tests return different values depending on whether the tests are true (1) or false (0). Symphony's primary conditional function is @IF. Lotus has added several other logical functions, however, to increase the power of the program over earlier integrated packages (see table 5.1).

Creating Logical Statements: @IF

The general form of the @IF function is

@IF(a,vtrue,vfalse)

where the first argument *a* is tested as true or false. If the result of the test is true (1), the function assigns the cell the value of the second argument, *vtrue*. If the value of the first argument is false, however, the function assigns the cell the value of the third argument, *vfalse*.

Using Simple Logical Operators

In many instances, conditional functions require logical operators, which help to determine the relationship between two different numbers or among several. Following is a list of "simple" logical operators and their meanings:

Table 5.1
Logical Functions

Function	Description
@IF(*cond,a,b*)	If *cond* is TRUE, then *a*; if *cond* is FALSE, then *b*
@ISERR(*cell reference*)	If *cell reference* contains ERR, then TRUE; otherwise, FALSE
@ISNA(*cell reference*)	If *cell reference* contains NA, then TRUE; otherwise, FALSE
@ISNUMBER(*cell reference*)	If *cell reference* contains a numeric value, then TRUE; otherwise, FALSE
@ISSTRING(*cell reference*)	If *cell reference* contains a string value, then TRUE; otherwise, FALSE
@TRUE	Returns a value of 1
@FALSE	Returns a value of 0

Operator	Meaning
=	Equal
<	Less than
<=	Less than or equal to
>	Greater than
>=	Greater than or equal to
<>	Not equal

Simple logical operators have lower precedence than any mathematical operator, but all logical operators have equal precedence within their group.

As mentioned earlier, logical functions are either true (1) or false (0). Conditional statements follow this same line of reasoning. For example, the statement 5<3 is clearly false (0), whereas the statement 16<27 is true (1). Symphony's @IF function tests the conditional statement as either true (1) or false (0) and then assigns a cell value based on the results of the test.

Following are examples of logical statements that use the @IF function, along with their English-language equivalents:

@IF(B4>=450,B5,C7)
    If the value in cell B4 is greater than or equal to 450, then use the value in cell B5. Otherwise, use the value in cell C7.

@IF(A3<A2,5,6)
> If the value in cell A3 is less than the value in cell A2, then assign the number 5. Otherwise, assign the number 6.

@IF(G9<>B7,G5/9,G7)
> If the value in cell G9 is not equal to the value in cell B7, then use the value in cell G5 divided by 9. Otherwise, use the value in cell G7.

@IF(A9<>"January",45,"wrong entry")
> If the value in cell A9 is not the string "January", then assign the number 45. Otherwise, assign the string "wrong entry". Note that if you enter a string value in cell A9, Symphony assigns either the vtrue or the vfalse argument. Note also that you must enter January with double quotation marks in A9. If you enter a number in cell A9, or if the cell is left blank, Symphony returns the ERR indicator.

@IF(@FALSE,"ok","not ok")
> If false (0), then assign "not ok"; otherwise, assign "ok". The value of this function is always "not ok" because the value of @FALSE is always 0. (See a discussion of the @FALSE function.) This example emphasizes the numeric character of the @IF function.

Adding Complex Operators

Relationships get more complicated when another set of logical operators, the complex operators, is introduced:

Operator	Meaning
#NOT#	Not (logical)
#AND#	And (logical)
#OR#	Or (logical)

The complex logical operators have lower precedence than the simple logical operators. Among the complex operators, the #AND# and #OR# have equal precedence.

Now that you have a complete set of logical operators, you can combine simple and complex operators to create the following @IF functions:

@IF(A1<>1#AND#G5="yes",E7,E6)
> If the value in cell A1 is not equal to 1, and the value in cell G5 is "yes", then use the value in cell E7. Otherwise, use the value in cell E6. The values in cells E6 and E7 can be either numbers or strings.

@IF(#NOT#(COST=50)#AND#A1=1,L10,K10)
> If the amount entered in the cell named COST is not $50, and the value in cell A1 is equal to 1, then use the value in cell L10. Otherwise, use the value in cell K10.

Symphony's conditional functions are quite sophisticated. You can use the @IF function in a wide variety of instances to allow Symphony to make decisions. Figure 5.26 provides an example of how you can employ the @IF function.

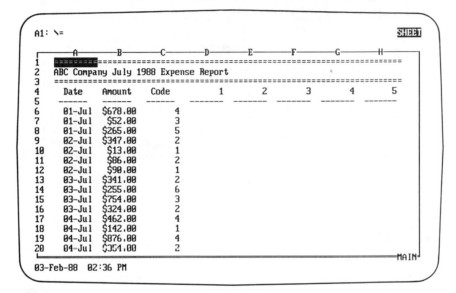

Fig. 5.26

A schedule of expenditures.

Figure 5.26 shows a simple worksheet that summarizes a company's expenditures for the month of March 1988. Column A contains the date of each expenditure, and column B contains the amounts of the disbursements. Notice that column C has been labeled `Code` and that row 4 contains a sequence of numbers, beginning with 1 in column D and ending with 5 in column H. These numbers represent the accounts. Now suppose that the following formula is entered in cell E6:

@IF($C6=E$4,$B6,0)

Similarly, the formula

@IF($C6=F$4,$B6,0)

is entered in cell F6. You can translate these formulas as: If the number in cell C6 (the code) equals the number in cell E4 (or cell F4) (the account), then enter the value in cell B6 here. Otherwise, enter 0 here.

Let's assume that similar formulas exist in all the cells in range D6..H20. Suppose that you enter a code for each check recorded in column A. The code for each disbursement should be a number less than 6. With all the proper codes entered, the result looks like figure 5.27.

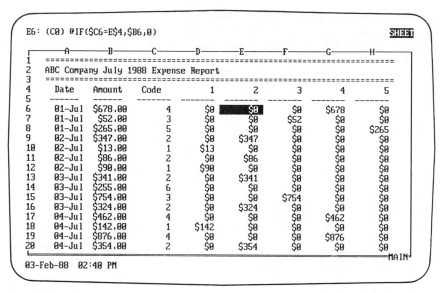

Fig. 5.27

*Using @IF to check
for matching
accounts and
codes.*

```
E6: (C0) @IF($C6=E$4,$B6,0)                                    SHEET
     A-------B-------C-------D-------E-------F-------G-------H-----
1  ================================================================
2  ABC Company July 1988 Expense Report
3  ================================================================
4    Date    Amount   Code      1       2       3       4       5
5    ------  ------   ------  ------  ------  ------  ------  ------
6    01-Jul  $678.00    4       $0      $0      $0    $678      $0
7    01-Jul   $52.00    3       $0      $0     $52      $0      $0
8    01-Jul  $265.00    5       $0      $0      $0      $0    $265
9    02-Jul  $347.00    2       $0    $347      $0      $0      $0
10   02-Jul   $13.00    1     $13      $0      $0      $0      $0
11   02-Jul   $86.00    2       $0     $86      $0      $0      $0
12   02-Jul   $90.00    1     $90      $0      $0      $0      $0
13   03-Jul  $341.00    2       $0    $341      $0      $0      $0
14   03-Jul  $255.00    6       $0      $0      $0      $0      $0
15   03-Jul  $754.00    3       $0      $0    $754      $0      $0
16   03-Jul  $324.00    2       $0    $324      $0      $0      $0
17   04-Jul  $462.00    4       $0      $0      $0    $462      $0
18   04-Jul  $142.00    1    $142      $0      $0      $0      $0
19   04-Jul  $876.00    4       $0      $0      $0    $876      $0
20   04-Jul  $354.00    2       $0    $354      $0      $0      $0
                                                              MAIN
   03-Feb-88  02:40 PM
```

Notice that in each cell, Symphony has compared each code to the accounts located in row 4. In the cells where the code and account match, Symphony has recorded the amount of the disbursement. In all the other cells, Symphony has entered 0. This result is exactly what you can expect from the conditional tests that you used in these cells.

Notes on Strings

Strings have created an additional level of complexity in Symphony's logical functions. When using strings in conditional functions, be aware of how Symphony reacts to your entering numbers or leaving cells blank. The results can be quite different from those of similar numeric conditional tests. The cases that follow illustrate some of the differences:

In case 1, cell C1094 is left blank:

Function	*Value Displayed on the Screen*
@IF(C1094="1","lambda","beta")	ERR
@IF(C1094=1,"lambda","beta")	beta
@IF(C1094=1#OR#C1094="1","lambda","beta")	ERR

In case 2, cell C1094 has the numeric value 1:

Function	Value Displayed on the Screen
@IF(C1094="1","lambda","beta")	ERR
@IF(C1094=1,"lambda","beta")	lambda
@IF(C1094=1#OR#C1094="1","lambda","beta")	ERR

In case 3, cell C1094 has the string "1":

Function	Value Displayed on the Screen
@IF(C1094="1","lambda","beta")	beta
@IF(C1094=1,"lambda","beta")	ERR
@IF(C1094=1#OR#C1094="1","lambda","beta")	ERR

Some of these results may seem counterintuitive when you first look at them, particularly the final function in case 3. You might expect that Symphony would display "lambda" rather than the ERR message. These examples illustrate, however, that you need to have a good idea of what type of entry you are using in a logical function (numeric or string) before you use the entry. The discussion of the @ISSTRING, @ISNUMBER, and @CELL functions should help you evaluate entries.

Error-Trapping Functions

Error-trapping functions test for and evoke NA and ERR messages in a spreadsheet. NA can be translated as "Not Available" and ERR as "Error."

@NA and @ERR

If you have an instance in which you simply don't know what number to use for a value, but you don't want to leave the cell blank, you can use NA instead. Simply enter @NA in the cell. Symphony then displays NA in that cell and in any other cell depending on that cell.

Another problem you may run across, particularly when you are setting up templates for other people to use, is unacceptable values for cells. For example, suppose that you are developing a checkbook-balancing macro, and checks with values less than or equal to zero are unacceptable. One way to indicate unacceptance of these kinds of checks is to use ERR to signal that fact. You might use the following version of the @IF built-in function:

@IF(B9<=0,@ERR,B9)

In simple English, this statement says that if the amount in cell B9 is less than or equal to zero, then display ERR on the screen; otherwise, display the amount. Notice that the @ERR function has been used to control the display in almost the same way as @NA.

Symphony also uses ERR as a signal when the program finds unacceptable numbers—for example, a division by zero or mistakenly deleted cells. ERR often shows up temporarily when you are reorganizing the cells in a worksheet. If errors persist, however, you may have to do some careful analysis to figure out why.

Just as for NA, Symphony displays ERR in any cells that depend on a cell with an ERR value. Sometimes many cells will display ERR after you have made only one or two small changes to a worksheet. To correct this problem, you must trace back down the chain of references to find the root of the problem.

@ISERR and @ISNA

@ISERR and @ISNA relate closely to the @ERR and @NA functions. @ISERR and @ISNA, which are commonly used with the @IF function, allow you to test a cell for the value ERR or NA.

Like the logical operators discussed earlier, the @ISERR and @ISNA functions are always either true (1) or false (0). The function @ISERR(A1) is false (0) if cell A1 does not contain the value ERR, and true (1) if cell A1 is equal to ERR. Similarly, @ISNA(A1) is true (1) if A1 contains the value NA, and false (0) if the cell does not.

You may want to use the @ISERR function frequently to keep ERR messages that result from division by zero from appearing in the worksheet. For example, at one time or another as you use Symphony, you will create a formula that divides a number by a cell reference, as in

23/A4

If A4 contains a value, the formula simply returns the value of the division. But if A4 contains a label or a 0, or if A4 is blank, the function returns the value ERR. The ERR is passed along to other cells in the sheet, creating an unnecessary mess.

Using the formula

@IF(@ISERR(23/A4),0,23/A4)

eliminates the ERR result. This function says that if the value of 23/A4 is ERR, then enter a 0 in this cell; otherwise, enter the value of the division 23/A4. The function effectively traps the ERR message and keeps it from displaying on the worksheet.

@ISNA works in much the same way. For example, the formula

@IF(@ISNA(A4),0,A4)

tests cell A4 for the value NA. If the value of A4 is NA, the formula returns a 0. Otherwise, the formula returns the value in A4. You can use this type of formula to keep an NA message from spreading throughout a worksheet.

Determining the Aspect of a Cell: @ISSTRING and @ISNUMBER

Before you use the contents of a cell, you will sometimes want to use functions to test its *aspect*. One part of a cell's aspect is its type—whether the cell contains a number or a label or is empty. Other parts of a cell's aspect are its address (the row and column at which the cell resides), its label prefix (if any), the width of its column, and its format. Depending on the characteristics of a cell's aspect, you may need to use different methods to process the cell.

Symphony has several different functions for determining a cell's aspect. Which functions you use depends on the particular situation. Symphony does, however, provide some redundancy in this area; usually, you can accomplish what you need to do in more than one way.

Two functions that determine the type of value stored in a cell are @ISSTRING and @ISNUMBER. Both of these functions are most often used with the @IF function. But you can use them with other types of functions as well.

You can use @ISNUMBER to verify whether a cell entry is a number. The general format of the function is

@ISNUMBER(argument)

If the argument is a number, the numeric value of the function is 1. But if the argument is a string, including a blank (" ") string, the numeric value of the function is 0.

As a simple example, suppose that you want to test whether the value entered in cell B3 is a number. If the value is a number, then you want to show the label number in the current cell; otherwise, you want to show the label string. The function you can use is

@IF(@ISNUMBER(B3),"number","string")

With this function you can be fairly certain that the appropriate label will appear in the current cell. But the @ISNUMBER function also gives blank cells a numeric value of 1. Obviously, the function is incomplete as it stands because it will assign the label "number" to the current cell if cell B3 is empty. Before the function is fully reliable, it must be modified to handle the case of blank cells.

At this point you may consider using the @ISSTRING function. @ISSTRING works in nearly the same way as @ISNUMBER. @ISSTRING, however, determines whether a cell entry is a string value. The general format of the command is

@ISSTRING(argument)

If the argument for the @ISSTRING function is a string, then the value of the function is 1. If the argument is a number or blank, however, the value of the function is 0. One nice feature of @ISSTRING is that it stops what Lotus calls the "ripple-through" effect of NA and ERR.

Returning to the earlier example, you can now complete the function with the help of @ISSTRING by using the following formula:

@IF(@ISSTRING(B3),"string",@IF(@COUNT(B3..B3)>0,"number","blank"))

The first step that this function performs is to test whether string data is present. If it is, then the function assigns the label "string". Otherwise, the @COUNT function tests for a number. If the data is a number, then the label "number" is assigned. Otherwise, the label "blank" is assigned.

Notice that the @ISNUMBER has been eliminated from the function. Because @ISNUMBER does not recognize the difference between numbers and blank cells, the @COUNT function has been used instead. (Recall that @COUNT assigns a value of 0 to blank cells, and a value of 1 to cells containing an entry, when the argument used has the range rather than the single-cell format. See the discussion of @COUNT earlier in this chapter for more explanation.) @ISNUMBER's incapability to recognize blank cells is its principal weakness. In many applications, however, @ISNUMBER provides sufficient testing of values, especially when you are certain that a cell is not blank.

Special Functions

These functions are included in a separate category because of their special power to give you detailed information about the contents and locations of cells (or ranges). @CELL and @CELLPOINTER are two of Symphony's most powerful special functions.

Determining the Aspect of a Cell: @CELL

Another, more efficient way to determine the aspect of a cell is to use the @CELL function. @CELL is one of the most comprehensive of Symphony's functions because this function gives you many different options from which to choose. The general form of @CELL is

@CELL(string,range)

The first argument is a string value that you code into the function, indicating to Symphony in what aspect of the cell you are interested. The second argument represents a cell in the range format (such as A1..A1). If you use just the single-cell format, Symphony returns the ERR message. If you specify a range that is larger than a single cell, Symphony uses the upper left corner cell for evaluation.

Table 5.2 shows all the string arguments you can use with @CELL and the corresponding results from Symphony.

Table 5.2
@CELL String Arguments

String	*Symphony Provides:*	
address	The address of the current cell expressed in absolute terms (for example, $G$19)	
contents	The cell value	
row	The row number (1 to 8192)	
col	The column number (1 to 256)	
type	The type of value stored in a cell	
	b	Indicates a blank cell (even if the cell is formatted)
	v	Indicates a number or numeric formula
	l	Indicates a label or string formula
prefix	The label prefix of the current cell	
	'	Indicates a left-aligned label
	"	Indicates a right-aligned label
	^	Indicates a centered label
	|	Indicates a special label such as a word-processing format line or a page break
	blank	Indicates a number, formula, or blank cell (Note: Formula may be a label formula.)
protect	The protection status of the cell	
	1	Indicates that the cell is protected
	0	Indicates that the cell is unprotected

width	The column width of the column in which the cell resides (1 to 240) (Note: Width may be different for each window.)
format	The numeric display format

G	General format
F0 to F15	Fixed decimal (0 to 15 decimal places)
P0 to P15	Punctuated (0 to 15 decimal places) (Equivalent to 1-2-3's comma [,] format)
C0 to C15	Currency (0 to 15 decimal places)
S0 to S15	Scientific (0 to 15 decimal places)
%0 to %15	Percent (0 to 15 decimal places)
D1 to D5	Date (formats 1 to 5)
T1 to T4	Time (formats 1 to 4)
L	Literal (Equivalent to 1-2-3's Text format)
H	Hidden format

Here are some examples of how you can use the @CELL function:

@CELL("address",SALES)
If the range named SALES is C187..E187, Symphony returns the absolute address $C$187. This feature provides a convenient way of listing the upper left corner of a range's address in the worksheet. To list all the range names and their addresses, see the SHEET **Range Name Table** command.

@CELL("prefix",C195..C195)
If the cell C195 contains the label *'Chicago,* Symphony returns ' (indicating left alignment). If, however, cell C195 is blank, Symphony returns nothing; in other words, the current cell appears blank.

@CELL("format",A10)
Symphony returns the ERR indicator because the second argument is not in the range format.

@CELL("width",B12..B12)
Symphony returns the width of column B as viewed in the current window regardless of whether that width was set with the SHEET **Width** command (for the individual column) or the SHEET **Settings Width** command (for the default column width).

Determining the Aspect
of the Current Cell: @CELLPOINTER

The @CELLPOINTER function is similar to the @CELL function, except @CELL-POINTER works with the current cell. The *current* cell is the cell where the cell pointer was sitting when the worksheet was last recalculated. The general format of the command is

@CELLPOINTER(string)

The strings you can use for this function are the same as those for the @CELL function. (See table 5.2.) For example, to determine the address of the current cell, suppose that you enter @CELLPOINTER("address") in cell B22. If recalculation is set to Automatic, the value displayed in that cell is the absolute address $B$22. This same address remains displayed until you make another entry elsewhere in the sheet or press the Calc key. Either action causes the worksheet to be recalculated, and the address that appears in cell B22 changes to reflect the position of the cell pointer when the sheet was recalculated. If recalculation is set to Manual, pressing the Calc key is the only action that causes the address to change.

Describing Ranges: @ROWS and @COLS

@ROWS and @COLS are two other special functions that Symphony offers. They both describe the dimensions of ranges. The general form of these commands is

@ROWS(range)   @COLS(range)

Suppose that you want to determine the number of columns in a range called EXPENSES and to display that value in the current cell. The function you enter is @COLS(EXPENSES). Similarly, you can enter @ROWS(EXPENSES) to display the number of rows in the range.

One rule to remember about @ROWS and @COLS is that you cannot specify a single cell as the argument unless that cell is in the range format (for example, C3..C3). Otherwise, Symphony displays ERR.

Referring to Cells Indirectly: @@

The @@ function refers to the contents of one cell by way of another cell. The form of the function is simply

@@(cell address)

where the cell address can be a single cell address or a range name referring to a single cell. Thus, if cell B10 contains the label A5, and cell A5 contains the number 12000, @@(B10)=12000.

Documenting Errors: @TRUE and @FALSE

Symphony's remaining two special functions are @TRUE and @FALSE. Neither of these functions requires an argument. The numeric value of @TRUE is 1, and the numeric value of @FALSE is 0. Typically, these functions are used with @IF and @CHOOSE, mainly for documentation purposes. For example, the function @IF(B3<30,@TRUE,@FALSE) is exactly equivalent to @IF(B3<30,1,0). In this case, the @TRUE and @FALSE functions provide better documentation than their numeric counterparts.

String Functions

Symphony has a variety of functions that give you significant power to manipulate strings. These string functions are especially useful when you are performing database queries. When you use Symphony's string functions, however, particular caution is necessary to guard against mixing data types. For instance, some functions produce strings, and other functions produce numeric results. You must be careful not to combine functions from these two different groups unless you have taken all the necessary precautions. The proper techniques for mixing data types are discussed throughout this section on string functions.

One other thing to consider about string functions is the numbering scheme used for the positions of characters in a label. These positions are numbered beginning with zero and continuing to a number that corresponds to the last character in the label. For example, the following illustration shows the position numbers for a long label:

```
                    111111111122222
          Ø1234567890123456789Ø1234
          'two chickens in every pot
```

Notice that the label prefix (') at the beginning of the label does not have a number; the prefix is not considered part of the label. Nor are negative position numbers allowed. The importance of position numbers will become clear in the next section.

Locating the Position of One String within Another: @FIND

One of the simplest string functions is @FIND. It is also one of the most convenient functions for illustrating the use of position numbers in strings. You can use the @FIND function to locate the starting position of one string within another string. For instance, using the string from the previous illustration, suppose that you want to find at what position the string "every" occurs in this string. The general format of @FIND is

@FIND(search-string,overall-string,start-number)

The *search-string* is the string you want to locate. In the example, "every" is the search-string. The *overall-string* is the target string to be searched. In the example, "two chickens in every pot" is the overall-string. Finally, the *start-number* is the position number in the overall-string where you want to start the search. Suppose that you want to start the search at position 6. If the overall-string you are searching is located in cell B5, the function you use is

@FIND("every",B5,6)

The result of this example is the number 16, which is the position of the first (and only) occurrence of "every" in the overall-string. If the search-string "every" had not been found in the overall-string, then Symphony would have displayed the ERR message.

Notice that in this example the choice of a start-number of 6 had no bearing on the outcome of the function. You could just as easily have chosen 0, or any other number less than or equal to 16, for the starting position of the search-string. Had "every" appeared more than once in the overall-string, however, you could have used the start-number to locate the search-string's occurrence elsewhere. Suppose that the following overall-string appears in cell B5:

'two chickens in every pot, two cars in every garage

Now suppose that you want to locate all the occurrences of "every" in the overall-string. You can start with the function @FIND("every",B5,0). Just as before, this function returns a value of 16. You can then change the start-number by adding 1 to the result of the original function (as in 1 + 16 = 17). The appropriate function is then @FIND("every",B5,17). This function returns the number 39, which is the starting location of the second occurrence of "every". Next, you can add 1 to the second result (1 + 39 = 40) and use @FIND("every",B5,40). The result of this function is ERR. When you see the ERR message, you can be sure that you have found all the occurrences of the search-string.

One rule to remember about @FIND, and generally about strings, is that the maximum number of characters in a string is 240. Another rule is that Symphony truncates the start-number to a whole number if the number includes a decimal portion.

You should also be aware that @FIND does not perform approximate searching as does the DOC Search command. In the previous example, if you had used a search-string of "Every" rather than "every", you would get the ERR message and not a number value. See Chapter 8 for more information on the DOC Search command.

Extracting One String from Another: @MID

Whereas @FIND helps you to locate one string within another, the @MID function lets you extract one string from another. This operation is called *substringing*. The general form of the function is

@MID(string,start-position,length)

The *start-position* is a number representing the character position in the string where you want to start extracting characters. The *length* argument indicates the number of characters you want to extract. For example, if you want to extract the first name from a label containing the full name "Laura Mann", you can use @MID("Laura Mann",0,5). This function extracts the string starting in position 0 (the first character) and continuing for a length of 5 characters.

Now suppose that you have a column containing a list of full names, and you want to extract the first and last names, putting them into separate columns. To accomplish this task, you can use the @MID and @FIND functions together. Because you know a blank space always separates the first and last names, you can use @FIND to locate the position of the blank in each full name. With this value, you can then set up the functions to extract the first and last names.

Suppose that cell A1 contains the full name "Gerald Frankel". In cell B1, you place the following function:

@MID(A1,0,@FIND(" ",A1,0))

The value of this function is "Gerald" because

@FIND(" ",A1,0)

returns a value of 6 for the length argument. Next, you place in column C the function

@MID(A1,@FIND(" ",A1,0)+1,99)

With the @FIND function, you are indicating that the start-position is one character beyond the blank space. In addition, the length of the string to be extracted is 99 characters. Obviously, using a length of 99 is overkill, but Symphony does not penalize you for this excess. The string that Symphony extracts is "Frankel".

Now that you have seen how to use the @MID and @FIND functions to separate first and last names, you may want to try using these functions in a case with a name containing a middle initial.

Extracting Strings: @LEFT and @RIGHT

@LEFT and @RIGHT, special variations of the @MID function, are used to extract one string of characters from another, beginning at the leftmost and rightmost positions, respectively, in the underlying string. The general format of the functions is

@LEFT(string,length)   @RIGHT(string,length)

The *length* argument is the number of character positions that you want to extract from the *string*. For example, if you are given the string "Cincinnati, Ohio 45243", and you want to extract the ZIP code, you can use @RIGHT("Cincinnati, Ohio 45243",5).

@LEFT works the same way as @RIGHT, except that @LEFT extracts from the beginning of a string. For instance, you can extract the city in the previous example by using @LEFT("Cincinnati, Ohio 45243",10).

Replacing Characters in a String: @REPLACE

The @REPLACE function removes a group of characters from a string and replaces the characters with another string. @REPLACE uses the same numbering scheme as @FIND. That is, @REPLACE numbers the character positions in a string starting with 0 and continuing to the end of the string (up to a maximum of 239). The general form of the command is

@REPLACE(original-string,start-number,length,replacement-string)

The *start-number* argument indicates the position where Symphony is to start removing characters in the *original-string*. The *length* indicates how many characters to remove, and the *replacement-string* contains the new characters that should replace the removed ones. For example, suppose that the string "Now is the time for all good men" appears in cell C1, and you want to replace "men" with "people". The function to use is

@REPLACE(C1,29,3,"people")

Instead of starting at 0 and counting up the 30 positions of the start-number, you may want to use the @FIND function. For instance, you can enter

@REPLACE(C1,@FIND("men",C1,0),3,"people")

This example is just one of many in which combining functions can save you much time and effort.

Finding the Length of a String: @LENGTH

The @LENGTH function simply returns the length of a string. The general form of the function is

@LENGTH(string)

For example, suppose that cell E9 contains the string "Credit policy"; then the value of @LENGTH(E9) is 13. If, in the same spreadsheet, cell J6 contains the formula

+E9&" "&"respondents"

the value of @LENGTH(J6) is 25.

A rule to remember about the @LENGTH function is that the length of numeric strings, as well as empty or null strings, is ERR.

Comparing Strings: @EXACT

The @EXACT function compares two strings. If the strings are alike, @EXACT returns a value of 1. If the strings are not alike, the function returns a value of 0. The general form of the function is

@EXACT(string1,string2)

The method of comparison for @EXACT is similar to the = operator that you use in formulas. But whereas the = operator checks for an approximate match, the @EXACT function checks for an exact match. For example, if cell A2 contains the string "Marketing Function", and cell B2 contains the string "marketing function", the numeric value of A2=B2 is 1 because the two strings are an approximate match. Conversely, the numeric value of @EXACT(A2,B2) is 0 because the two functions are not an exact match.

You must remember one rule when you use @EXACT: You cannot use the function to compare nonstring arguments. For instance, if you are comparing two cells—A2, which is empty, and B2, which contains a valid string—the value of @EXACT(A2,B2) is ERR. In fact, if either argument is a nonstring value of any type (including numbers), Symphony returns the ERR message.

Converting Case: @LOWER, @UPPER, and @PROPER

Symphony offers three different functions for converting the case of a string value. First, @LOWER converts all the letters in a string to lowercase. If letters are already in lowercase, they remain so. For instance, if cell B3 contains the string "ALL iN GooD tiME", the value of @LOWER(B3) is "all in good time".

Second, @UPPER, nearly the opposite of @LOWER, converts all the letters in a string to uppercase. For example, the value of @UPPER("ALL iN GooD tiME") is "ALL IN GOOD TIME".

Finally, @PROPER capitalizes the first letter in each word of a label and converts all other letters in each word to lowercase. (Words are defined as groups of characters separated by blank spaces.) For example, the value of @PROPER("when IS tHE meeTING?") is "When Is The Meeting?"

As you might expect, @UPPER, @LOWER, and @PROPER do not work with nonstring values. For instance, if cell E9 contains a number or a null string, Symphony returns ERR for each of these functions.

Repeating Labels: @REPEAT

@REPEAT repeats strings within a cell, in much the same way as the backslash
(\ ) repeats characters. But @REPEAT has some distinct advantages over the
backslash. The general form of the function is

@REPEAT(string,number)

The *number* argument indicates how many times you want to repeat the *string*
in a cell. For example, if you want to repeat the string "COGS" three times, you
can enter @REPEAT("COGS",3). The resulting string is "COGSCOGSCOGS".
@REPEAT follows Symphony's rule for long labels. That is, if the width of a
column is 9 (the default column width), the string displays beyond the rightmost
boundary of the column, provided no entry is in the cell to the right. The technique for repeating labels with the \ is different from that of @REPEAT. With
\, Symphony fills the column exactly to the existing column width.

By using the @CELL and @LENGTH functions, you can set up a function to fill
a cell almost exactly. If A3 is the cell you want to fill by repeating the string
"COGS", the first step is to enter @CELL("width",A3..A3) in an out-of-the-way
cell, say K4. The next step is to enter @LENGTH("COGS") in another distant
cell, like K5. Then enter @REPEAT("COGS",K4/K5) in cell A3. If the width of
column A is 9 (the default column width), the label that appears in cell A3 is
COGSCOGS. Notice that because @REPEAT uses only the integer portion of the
number argument, "COGS" is repeated only twice rather than 2.25 times.

Eliminating Unwanted Blank Spaces: @TRIM

The @TRIM function trims unwanted blank spaces from a string. The spaces
may occur at the beginning, end, or middle of a string. If more than one consecutive space occurs in the middle of a string, Symphony removes all but one
of the blank spaces. For instance, if the string " When in the course of
human events " resides in cell A3, @TRIM(A3) appears as "When in the course
of human events". Notice that the extra blank spaces have been removed. Notice
also that the value of @LENGTH(A3) is 40, but @LENGTH(@TRIM(A3)) equals
34. (For trimming other characters besides blank spaces, see the section on
@CLEAN later in this chapter.)

Converting Strings to Numbers
and Numbers to Strings

Two of the most important and powerful functions that Symphony offers are
@STRING and @VALUE. The @STRING function converts a number to a string,
and @VALUE changes a string to a number.

@STRING

You can use @STRING to override Symphony's automatic right-justification of numbers and to display a number justified to the left. The general form of the @STRING function is

@STRING(number-to-convert,decimal-places)

Because Symphony uses the fixed-decimal display format for the @STRING function, the *decimal-places* argument represents the number of places that you want to display in the string. For example, if the *number-to-convert* argument is 9.482 and resides in cell J7, you can enter @STRING(J7,2) in the current cell. The result of this function is 9.48, displayed with left-justification.

If the number-to-convert argument is 9.478 rather than 9.482, Symphony rounds the number to 9.48, just as Symphony rounds any number displayed in the fixed-decimal format.

If you want to display a number in its string version with a percent sign or punctuated format, you can use the CONTENTS statement from the Symphony Command Language. See Chapter 20 for more information on the CONTENTS command.

@VALUE

You may want to use the @VALUE function when you have been entering labels in a FORM window but later decide that you prefer to use the data as numbers. For example, suppose that you enter part numbers and their quantities, using Label as the default setting. (If you are not familiar with the FORM window at this point, see Chapter 15.) Now suppose that the information on part numbers works fine in the label format, but you want to change the format of the quantity data in order to sum different part quantities. You can convert the quantity data with @VALUE. The general form of the function is

@VALUE(string)

If cell K11 contains a database entry for the quantity data in the string format, you can enter @VALUE(K11) in an out-of-the-way cell in the worksheet, say Z11. If the string in cell K11 is "23", then the number displayed in cell Z11 is 23. You can now use the number in cell Z11 in any kind of numeric operation. For more examples of converting database entries, see Chapter 15.

Another nice feature of @VALUE is that besides converting strings that appear in the standard number format (for example, 23.445), you can also convert strings with fractions and with numbers displayed in scientific format. For example, if cell T10 contains the string "12 31/32", @VALUE(T10) appears as 12.96875. Even if cell T10 contains the string "12 54/32", @VALUE still performs the appropriate conversion of the string to the number 13.6875. Similarly, if a number is displayed as the string "1.37E+1", @VALUE converts the string to the number 13.7.

You should remember a few rules when you use @VALUE. First, if you leave extra spaces in a string, Symphony does not object. The program, however, has trouble with some extra characters, although trailing percent signs and currency signs (such as $) that precede the string are okay. If you are interested, you should experiment with different character signs to see how Symphony reacts. Finally, if you use numbers as the argument (string) for @VALUE, Symphony simply returns the original number value.

Converting Numeric Values to String Values and Vice Versa: @N and @S

The ability to combine string and numeric arguments in one formula is sometimes useful. Ordinarily, Symphony does not allow you to combine such arguments; instead, the program gives you an error. The way around this "error" problem is to use the @N or @S functions. The general form of these functions is

> @N(cell range) or @S(cell range)

Although Symphony looks only at the upper left corner cell of the range argument, you must specify the argument as a range.

This process becomes particularly useful in a database report (see Chapter 15). You may want to use a formula to refer to a field that contains either a string value or nothing. If you were to use the formula +B20, and B20 were empty, the formula would give you a 0. If you use the formula @S(B20..B20), however, Symphony evaluates that formula as a blank.

Similarly, you can use @N to give you either the cell's numeric value or 0 (if the cell contains a label, string formula, or nothing). The important thing to remember is that these functions do require a range argument. If you specify a single cell, you will get ERR. By the way, an @N or @S formula is a good place to use the "!" as shorthand to turn a single cell into a single cell range, as in @N(!E10).

Functions Used with the ASCII/LICS

Symphony offers a few special functions for interfacing with the Lotus International Character Set (LICS), what Lotus calls "an extension of the ASCII printable character set." (Be aware that the ASCII code number for a given character may not correspond to its LICS code number.) You can best think of the LICS as a new character set created by Lotus and superimposed on top of the ASCII character set.

The complete set of LICS characters is listed at the back of Symphony's *Reference Manual* and includes everything from the copyright sign to the lowercase *e* with the grave accent. More characters are available than you will probably ever use, but you should still know how to use them if the need ever arises.

Producing LICS Characters: @CHAR

You can use the @CHAR function to produce on-screen the LICS equivalent of a number between 0 and 255. The general form of the function is

@CHAR(number)

Suppose that you want to make the cent sign (¢) appear on the screen. You can enter @CHAR(162) in a cell, and the cent sign should appear. What is more, you can use a string formula to concatenate the cent sign to a number. For instance, you can enter the formula +"12"&@CHAR(162) to produce the string "12¢".

You should remember only two simple rules when using @CHAR. First, if the numeric argument you are using is not between 1 and 255, then Symphony returns the ERR message. Second, if your argument is not an integer, Symphony disregards the noninteger portion of the argument.

Nonprintable Characters in the LICS

Be aware that not all the LICS characters are printable, nor will they always show up on the screen. More specifically, codes 1 through 31 comprise the problem area. Because these codes include all the characters necessary for making boxes and arrows in Symphony, you may want to gain access to these characters. You can do so in one of two ways.

First, you can use the Edit key (F2) while you are in a SHEET window. Start with a SHEET window in a new worksheet. Next, use the **Range Fill** command to enter the numbers 1 through 31, starting in cell B1 and moving down column B. Then, after moving one column to the left, enter **@CHAR(B1)** in cell A1 and copy that function to the cells below. Finally, use the **Range Values** command to convert the cells in column A to their actual string values. Even though the cells in column A appear blank, you can see any one of the characters by moving the cell pointer to any cell in column A and pressing Edit. Figure 5.28 shows how the screen should appear.

Fig. 5.28

Viewing the nonprintable LICS characters.

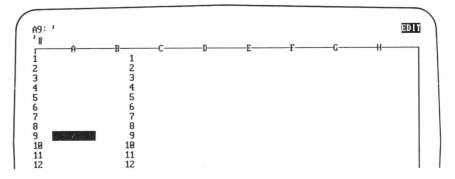

Another way to see the nonprintable characters is to use the SHEET window as it appears in figure 5.28 and change the window to a DOC window. Then you can see all the nonprintable characters corresponding to ASCII/LICS codes 1 to 31. You can continue to use these characters in a DOC window, but because they are nonprintable, only blanks will appear when you try to print the characters.

Finding the LICS Code Number: @CODE

The @CODE function is nearly the opposite of @CHAR. Whereas @CHAR takes a number between 0 and 255 and returns an ASCII/ LICS character, @CODE goes the other way. That is, it examines an ASCII/LICS character and returns a number between 0 and 255. The general form of the function is

@CODE(string)

Suppose that you want to find the ASCII/LICS code number for the letter *a*. Enter @CODE("a") in a cell, and Symphony returns the number 97. If you had entered @CODE("aardvark"), Symphony would still return 97, the code of the first character in the string.

If you specify a number as the argument for @CODE (expressed as a number and not a string), Symphony returns the ERR message.

Removing Unwanted Characters: @CLEAN

Sometimes when you receive strings during a communications session, the strings arrive with nonprintable characters (ASCII codes below 32) interspersed throughout. The @CLEAN function removes the nonprintable characters from the strings. The general format of the function is

@CLEAN(string)

You can also use @CLEAN to remove the carriage-return characters from a string created in a DOC window. (A carriage-return symbol is the equivalent of an ASCII/LICS code 13.) Before you use in a concatenation formula or a function a string you created in a DOC window, it's a good practice to use @CLEAN first.

Date and Time Arithmetic

One of Symphony's most advanced features is its capability to manipulate dates and times. You can use this feature for such things as mortgage analysis, aging of accounts receivable, and time management.

Symphony's Serial Numbering System

All aspects of Symphony's date-handling capability are based on Symphony's capability to represent any given date as a serial integer equal to the number of days from December 31, 1899, to the date in question. With this scheme, January 1, 1900, is represented by the number 1; January 2, 1900, is represented by the number 2; and so on. The maximum date that Symphony can handle is December 31, 2099, represented by the serial number 73050.

Symphony's time-handling capability is based on fractions of serial numbers. For instance, 8:00 a.m. is represented by the decimal fraction 0.333333 (or 1/3). Similarly, the decimal fraction for 10:00 p.m. is 0.916666. Symphony's serial numbering system allows you to devise an overall number representing both date and time.

Date	Time	Serial Number
January 3, 1900	01:00 AM	3.041666666
December 9, 1935	12:00 PM	13127
December 30, 1983	12:00 AM	30680
June 25, 1984	09:21 AM	30858.38958
December 31, 2099	11:00 PM	73050.95833

The serial numbering system also allows you to manipulate dates and times just as you would any other number in Symphony. For example, after setting the beginning date for a project and adding to that date the number of days that the project should take, you can easily determine the completion date. Working with time values is just as easy. For example, you can set up a complete schedule for the day by dividing it into hour increments.

Date Functions

Symphony's date functions include @DATE, @DATEVALUE, @DAY, @MONTH, @YEAR, and @NOW.

Converting a Date to an Integer: @DATE

Perhaps the most commonly used date function is @DATE. This function allows you to change a date to an integer that Symphony can interpret. The form of the @DATE function is

@DATE(year-number,month-number,day-number)

Here are some examples showing how you can use the @DATE built-in function:

@DATE(55,12,30)=   20453

@DATE(12,1,1)=   4384

@DATE(C7,C8,D10)=   integer equivalent of the date represented by these cells. If the cells contain the values 83, 12, and 25, respectively, the function has the value 30675.

The numeric arguments have certain restrictions. First, the *year-number* must be between 0 (indicating the year 1900) and 199 (the year 2099). Second, the *month-number* must be between 1 and 12. Third, the *day-number* must be one of the actual values for a given month (for example, 30 days for September and 31 days for December). Finally, Symphony truncates all but the integer portion of each numeric argument.

Once Symphony has interpreted a date as an integer, you can then use the Format command to display the date in a more recognizable way (such as 06/26/88). For a discussion of Symphony's date and time formats, see the sections in this chapter entitled "Displaying Dates" and "Displaying Times" and also Chapter 4.

Converting a String to a Date: @DATEVALUE

@DATEVALUE is a variant of @DATE because, like @DATE, @DATEVALUE produces a serial number from the month, day, and year information that you provide. But unlike @DATE, which expects numeric arguments, @DATEVALUE accepts a string as the argument. The general form of the function is

@DATEVALUE(date-string)

The *date-string* must be in any one of the available **Date** formats—**D1**, **D2**, **D3**, **D4**, or **D5**. (See this chapter's section on displaying dates.) If the string conforms to one of the formats, Symphony displays the appropriate serial integer.

Function	Date Format	Number
@DATEVALUE("26-JUN-88")	D1	32320
@DATEVALUE("26-JUN")	D2	32320
@DATEVALUE("JUN-88")	D3	32295
@DATEVALUE("09/12/88")	D4	32398
@DATEVALUE("09/12")	D5	32398

Notice that for the second function, Symphony automatically supplied 88 as the year. You can assume that a date in 1988 was entered when DOS prompted the user for a date at the start of the day's session. Note also that for the third function, Symphony defaults to the first day in June for the day value. You may prefer to enter the date-string in one of what Lotus calls the International date formats. (These formats are called **D4** and **D5** in Symphony. See the section entitled "Displaying Dates.")

Extracting the Day, Month, or Year

The built-in functions of @DAY, @MONTH, and @YEAR allow you to extract parts of a date in integer form. In the example

@DAY(32476) = 29
@MONTH(32476) = 11
@YEAR(32476) = 88

the three functions, taken together, are nearly the reverse of the @DATE built-in function because they allow you to convert from the integer format back into Gregorian format. You can use these functions for various time-related chores, such as aging accounts receivable and setting up a table for amortizing a loan.

Displaying Dates

The five date functions discussed thus far are extremely useful for entering dates in the worksheet in a form that Symphony can understand. But there is a problem. The results of these functions are integers that don't look like dates and are therefore hard to comprehend. For example, do you know the dates represented by the numbers 30124 and 32988?

The SHEET Format Date command allows you to display these integers in one of the following five arrangements (Lotus calls them **D1** through **D5**):

Number	Arrangement	Example
1	DD-MMM-YY	26-Jun-88
2	DD-MMM	26-Jun
3	MMM-YY	Jun-88
4	MM/DD/YY	06/26/88
5	MM/DD	06/26

Note that for all the examples shown above, the integer displayed in the worksheet before formatting is 32320.

Notice, too, that the first option (**D1**) creates a string which is 9 characters long—too long to be displayed in a column with the default width of 9. In general, you will need to expand any column containing dates formatted in the DD-MMM-YY format so that the column width is 10 or more characters. Because you can display the other date formats in columns of normal width, you can frequently use these formats (especially **D4**) in place of the more detailed, but wider **D1** format.

The default separation character for the International date formats (**D4** and **D5**) is / (for example, 6/26/88). But you can also use periods or dashes as the separation characters. To indicate to Symphony that you plan to use something other than the default setting for the International formats, however, you must modify one of the configuration settings. To modify the setting, use the SERVICES Configuration Other International Date command; then you can select the format you like.

Suppose that you have chosen the default setting for the separation character, and you want to enter the date-string in the **D4** (MM/DD/YY) format. You can enter @DATEVALUE("6/26/88"), and Symphony displays the number 32320. If you enter @DATEVALUE("6-26-88"), Symphony returns the ERR message. (Symphony does not expect the hyphen [-] as the separation character unless you change the configuration settings.)

Today's Date and Time: @NOW

The @NOW function returns today's date and time as an integer representing the number of days since December 31, 1899, and a fraction representing the time elapsed since 12:00 a.m. of the previous day. This built-in function is particularly useful for taking advantage of an IBM PC's (and compatible's) time-keeping capability. If you have a clock that automatically supplies the date and time, or if you simply enter the date and time when you are prompted by DOS at the start of the day, the @NOW function gives you access to the date and time in the current worksheet. For example, if you enter the date **6-26-88** in response to the DOS date prompt and **16:00** to the DOS time prompt (corresponding to 4:00 p.m.), the @NOW function has the value

@NOW = 32320.66

Because the @NOW function depends on the PC DOS or MS-DOS system date and time for its value, unless your machine has a system clock you must always remember to enter at least the date, and more preferably the date and time, in response to the operating system prompt before you enter Symphony. (If you want to modify the operating system date and time while you are in midsession, see the discussion on exiting to DOS in "Making Backup Copies of Files" in Chapter 6.)

Time Functions

Until this point, the discussion of how Symphony deals with time has been brief. As mentioned earlier, time is expressed in fractions of serial numbers between 0 and 1. For example, .5 is equal to 12 hours (or 12:00 p.m.). You should think of Symphony as a military timekeeper. That is, 10:00 p.m. in normal time is 22:00 in military time.

Symphony's timekeeping system may seem a little awkward at first, but you should get used to it quickly. Here are some general guidelines:

1 hour	=	0.041666
1 minute	=	0.000694
1 second	=	0.000011

Converting Time Values to Serial Numbers: @TIME

The @TIME built-in function arrives at a serial number for a specified time of day. The general form of the function is

@TIME(hour-number,minute-number,second-number)

Here are some examples of how you can use @TIME:

@TIME(3,12,30)=	0.133680
@TIME(23,0,0)=	0.958333
@TIME(C7,C8,D10)=	integer equivalent of the time represented by these cells. If the cells contain the values 23, 12, and 59, respectively, the function has the value 0.967349.

The numeric arguments have certain restrictions. First, the *hour-number* must be between 0 and 23. Second, both the *minute-number* and *second-number* must be between 0 and 59. Finally, Symphony truncates all but the integer portion of each numeric argument.

Once Symphony has interpreted a time as a fraction of a serial number, you can then use the Format command to display the time in a more recognizable way (for example, 10:42 PM). See the section entitled "Displaying Times" for a discussion of Symphony's **Time** formats.

Converting a String to a Time: @TIMEVALUE

Just like @DATEVALUE and @DATE, @TIMEVALUE is a variant of @TIME because @TIMEVALUE produces a serial number from the hour, minute, and second information you provide. But unlike @TIME, which uses numeric arguments, @TIMEVALUE uses a string argument. The general form of the function is

@TIMEVALUE(time-string)

The *time-string* must appear in one of the four **Time** formats—**T1** through **T4**. (See this chapter's section entitled "Displaying Times.") If the string conforms to one of the appropriate formats, Symphony displays the appropriate serial number fraction. (If you then format the cell, Symphony displays the appropriate time of day.)

Function	Time Format	Number
@TIMEVALUE("1:30:59 PM")	T1	0.5631828704
@TIMEVALUE("1:30 PM")	T2	0.5625
@TIMEVALUE("13:30:59")	T3	0.5631828704
@TIMEVALUE("13:30")	T4	0.5625

Extracting the Second, Minute, or Hour

The @SECOND, @MINUTE, and @HOUR built-in functions allow you to extract different units of time from a numeric time fraction. In the examples

@SECOND(30284.4432)	=	12
@MINUTE(30284.4432)	=	38
@HOUR(30284.4432)	=	10

notice that the argument includes both an integer and a decimal portion. Although the integer portion is important for date functions, time functions disregard that part. You can use @SECOND, @MINUTE, and @HOUR for various time-related chores, the most important of which is developing a time schedule.

Displaying Times

You have now examined all the time functions that Symphony has to offer, but the results of these functions are serial number fractions that don't look at all like the times you usually see. The SHEET Format Time command allows you to display times in a more recognizable format. Lotus offers the following four different formats, called **T1** through **T4**:

Number	*Arrangement*	*Example*
1	HH:MM:SS AM/PM	11:51:22 PM
2	HH:MM AM/PM	11:51 PM
3	HH:MM:SS (24 hours)	23:51:22
4	HH:MM (24 hours)	23:51

For all these examples, the fractional number displayed in the worksheet before formatting is 0.994.

Note that the first option (**T1**) creates a string 11 characters long and thus requires a column width of 12. For this reason, unless you need to display seconds, you may prefer the **T2** format.

The International formats (**T3** and **T4**) use the colon as the default separation character. But you can also use periods, commas, or other characters as separation characters. When you change the separation characters, you must modify one of the configuration settings, as you do for the **Date** formats. To modify the setting, use the SERVICES Configuration Other International Time command. Afterward, you can select the separation characters you prefer.

General Comments on Date and Time Arithmetic

Notice that Symphony's date and time arithmetic capabilities incorporate both a set of functions and a set of formats. Don't be confused by this mix. The functions, like @DATEVALUE, enter dates or times in the worksheet; the formats display these functions in an understandable form. Although you can use the format without the function, or the function without the format, the two tools are not very meaningful when used apart.

In most cases date and time arithmetic requires simply subtracting one number from another. By subtracting, you can easily determine the number of days between dates, or hours between times. For example, subtracting @DATE(88,7,31) from @DATE(88,8,15) results in the value 15 (days). Similarly, subtracting @TIME(10,4,31) from @TIME(12,54,54) results in a value of 0.11832175 (2 hours, 50 minutes, and 23 seconds).

You even can determine the number of minutes, hours, weeks, and years between two serial numbers by dividing the difference by an appropriate number. If you need only a rough idea, you can use the banker's convention of 7 days in a week, 30 days in a month, and 360 days in a year. If you want to be more exact, you can use the @MOD function for remainders. You can even build in odd-numbered months and leap years. Symphony's date keeping and timekeeping allow you to simplify the analysis or make it as sophisticated as you like.

As mentioned earlier, besides using date and time functions in arithmetic calculations, you can also use them in logical expressions, such as @IF(@DATE(88,15,05)>B2,C3,D4). In simple English this statement says: If the serial number equivalent to May 15, 1988, is greater than the value in cell B2, then assign the value in cell C3 to the current cell; otherwise, use the value in D4. You can use this kind of test to help keep track of investment portfolios or time performance.

Chapter Summary

In this chapter, you have seen examples of Symphony's SHEET functions at work. In the next chapter, you'll examine Symphony's file-handling commands. You will learn how to save and retrieve worksheet files and how to use the program's other, more sophisticated file-management tools.

6

File Operations

One of the commands you will use quite often is the File command from the SERVICES menu. File provides the important operations for storing, retrieving, and deleting files to and from disks. In addition, Symphony's file operations enable you to combine entire files, to combine a range from one file with a range in another file, to extract part of a file and place it in another file, and to import text or numbers.

A General Description of Symphony Files

Before you use the file commands, keep in mind several rules concerning files. Symphony file names can be up to eight characters long; that is, Symphony stores only eight characters. Following are three basic rules for file names:

1. File names may not include blank spaces.

2. You can use either letters (A through Z) or numbers (0 through 9) to create file names. Symphony does not accept many other characters, including

    < > , . *

3. In file names, Symphony automatically converts lowercase letters to uppercase.

In addition to the eight-character name, all files are designated with a three-character extension. Although you determine the eight-character name, Symphony controls the extension, which varies with the type of file. The six possible file extensions are the following:

.WR1	For worksheet files (Symphony Release 1.1 and higher)
.PRN	For print files
.PIC	For graph files
.CCF	For communications configuration files
.CTF	For character-translation files
.APP	For add-in application files
.MLB	For macro library files

If you have used 1-2-3, you will notice that the file extension for 1-2-3's worksheet files is different from the extension used in Symphony. Release 2 of 1-2-3 uses .WK1; Release 1A uses .WKS. Release 1.0 of Symphony uses .WRK. The extent of compatibility among different worksheets is described later in this chapter in the section entitled "Transferring Files."

Each file contains only one worksheet, and you work on a worksheet only when it is in main memory. But you can create many windows within one file. As explained in Chapter 2, you can set up your worksheet so that it contains a window for entering a spreadsheet, a window for word processing, a window for graphics, a window for data management, and a window for communications. When you save your file after having created and entered data in all five windows, the file stores all window settings. When you next retrieve the file, the windows are available with their individual settings. But if you use the SERVICES Window Delete command to delete any windows before saving your file, those windows are lost.

File Management

The following file commands in the SERVICES File menu are available to enable you to perform several file-checking and management operations: **File Bytes**, **File List**, and **File Table**. It's particularly important to perform these commands before initiating the **File Save**, **File Erase**, and **File Combine** commands.

File Bytes

The **File Bytes** command provides a quick and simple way for you to check the available disk space on the current disk drive. **File Bytes** is important for checking disk space when you are creating new files on a disk that already contains many files or a few large files.

File List

When you use **File List**, Symphony displays one of four types of file lists on the screen: a list of worksheet files (.WRK or .WR1), print files (.PRN), graph files (.PIC), or all files including those not created by Symphony. For instance, after you select **File List Worksheet**, Symphony displays all worksheet files on the screen. During any session in which you have attached the Macro Library Manager add-in, you will have an additional choice—Macro Library files (.MLB).

Figure 6.1 presents an example of a file list. Notice in the control panel that Symphony displays in the top line the current drive and directory. The second line of the control panel displays the file name of the file on which the cursor is positioned, as well as the date and time when the file was last modified and the number of bytes in the file.

```
Directory: A:\*.wr1                                              FILES
          FIG4_12.WR1    02/01/88      13:51        18715

FIG4_12.WR1   FIG4_15.WR1   FIG4_43.WR1   FIG4_44.WR1   FIG4_45.WR1
FIG4_46.WR1   FIG4_47.WR1   FIG4_48.WR1   FIG4_49.WR1   FIG4_5.WR1
FIG4_52.WR1   FIG4_53.WR1   FIG4_6.WR1    FIG4_8.WR1    FIG4_9.WR1
FIG5_15.WR1   FIG5_16.WR1   FIG5_20.WR1   FIG5_22.WR1   FIG5_23.WR1
FIG5_24.WR1   FIG5_25.WR1   FIG5_27.WR1   FIG5_8.WR1
```

Fig. 6.1

A file list.

To return to your current window, press Enter. Remember that issuing a command such as **File List** replaces a current SHEET, DOC, FORM, GRAPH, or COMM window, but only temporarily. The command does not affect the data that you have entered into that window.

File Table

You may find it convenient at times to have a printed copy of the file names that are located on a particular disk or to have a list available within your worksheet area. The **File Table** command creates a list of files in a worksheet area specified by you. You can therefore save the list you have created or print a copy to keep with your floppy disks.

When you select **File Table**, Symphony gives you two different options for the list. First, Symphony asks you to specify the directory from which you want the list created. If you press Enter, Symphony accepts the current directory. The second option is whether to create a list of worksheet files (.WR1), print files (.PRN), graph files (.PIC), or all files, including those not created in Symphony. If you have attached the Macro Library add-in, you are offered the additional option of Macro Library files (.MLB).

To place the file table into the worksheet, Symphony asks you to indicate a range for the table. Here you need to indicate only the first cell where the table should begin. Be careful when you specify where the table should be located, because it will overwrite any existing cell contents. Keep in mind that each entry in the table occupies three columns, as illustrated in figure 6.2. The first column contains the file name, the second column contains the date and time when the file was last modified, and the last column contains the number of bytes in the file.

Fig. 6.2

A file table.

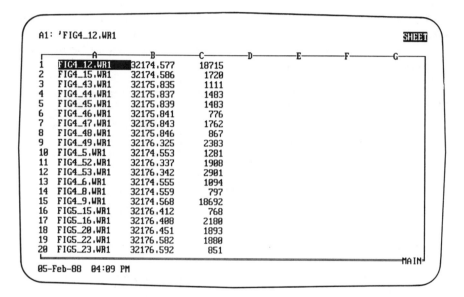

```
A1: 'FIG4_12.WR1                                                    SHEET

         A           B           C        D       E       F       G
 1  FIG4_12.WR1   32174.577    18715
 2  FIG4_15.WR1   32174.586     1720
 3  FIG4_43.WR1   32175.835     1111
 4  FIG4_44.WR1   32175.837     1483
 5  FIG4_45.WR1   32175.839     1483
 6  FIG4_46.WR1   32175.841      776
 7  FIG4_47.WR1   32175.843     1762
 8  FIG4_48.WR1   32175.846      867
 9  FIG4_49.WR1   32176.325     2383
10  FIG4_5.WR1    32174.553     1281
11  FIG4_52.WR1   32176.337     1908
12  FIG4_53.WR1   32176.342     2901
13  FIG4_6.WR1    32174.555     1094
14  FIG4_8.WR1    32174.559      797
15  FIG4_9.WR1    32174.568    18692
16  FIG5_15.WR1   32176.412      768
17  FIG5_16.WR1   32176.408     2180
18  FIG5_20.WR1   32176.451     1893
19  FIG5_22.WR1   32176.582     1880
20  FIG5_23.WR1   32176.592      851
                                                                   MAIN
05-Feb-88  04:09 PM
```

Simple Storage and Retrieval

In Symphony the basic file functions of storing and retrieving entire files are easy to perform. The **File Save** command in the SERVICES menu allows you to save an entire worksheet in a disk file.

When you choose File Save, Symphony displays the file name for the worksheet in which you are currently working if you have previously created a file (see fig. 6.3).

To save all data entered in the worksheet since you last saved it, press Enter. When Symphony displays A file with that name already exists -- replace it? No Yes, type **Y** or move the cursor to Yes, making sure that you do want the worksheet currently on the screen to replace your previously saved file.

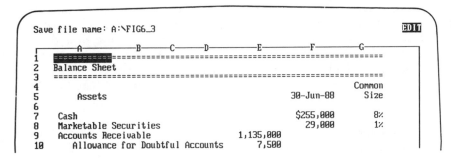

Fig. 6.3

Selecting File Save.

If you want to create a new file, type the file name after the drive and directory name (for example, c:\symphony\filename). If you want to change the disk drive or create the file in another directory, press Esc twice or Backspace the necessary number of times to clear the drive, directory, and file name; then type the appropriate disk drive followed by a colon (:), a backslash (\), the directory name, another backslash, and finally the name of the file. As mentioned earlier, when you enter a file name, you do not need to type the period (.) or a .WR1 extension. Symphony automatically supplies these items. The **File Save** command makes an exact copy of the current worksheet, including all the formats, range names, settings, and windows that you have specified.

To call a file back into main memory from the disk, use the **File Retrieve** command. When you issue this command, Symphony displays a menu of all .WR1 or .WRK file names currently on the disk.

Often the list extends beyond the single line on the first page. You have two options for seeing the entire list of file names. The first option is to use the cursor keys. For example, you can use the right-arrow key to move the cursor to the right, beyond the last file name in the current line. The Home and End keys are also useful tools for locating a file name. Home returns you to the first file name on the list, and End sends you to the last file name.

The second option is to have Symphony list a complete menu of all file names (see fig. 6.4). To have a complete list of files displayed, select SERVICES File **R**etrieve and then press the Services key (F9) a second time after the Name of file to retrieve: message appears in the control panel.

```
Name of file to retrieve: A:\*.wr1                              FILES
        FIG4_12.WR1     02/01/88      13:51         18715

  FIG4_12.WR1    FIG4_15.WR1    FIG4_43.WR1    FIG4_44.WR1    FIG4_45.WR1
  FIG4_46.WR1    FIG4_47.WR1    FIG4_48.WR1    FIG4_49.WR1    FIG4_5.WR1
  FIG4_52.WR1    FIG4_53.WR1    FIG4_6.WR1     FIG4_8.WR1     FIG4_9.WR1
  FIG5_15.WR1    FIG5_16.WR1    FIG5_20.WR1    FIG5_22.WR1    FIG5_23.WR1
  FIG5_24.WR1    FIG5_25.WR1    FIG5_27.WR1    FIG5_8.WR1
```

Fig. 6.4

Displaying a complete list of files with File Retrieve.

Just as when saving a file, you can override the default disk and indicate a directory when you retrieve a file. To change the disk drive and indicate a directory, select SERVICES File Retrieve. When Symphony displays the prompt and the current file name, for example, `Name of file to retrieve: B:\*.WR?`, press Esc twice or the Backspace key several times to erase `B:\*.WR?`. Then indicate the disk drive, the file directory, and finally the file name, as in

> c:\sales\junetot

Notice that the disk drive is indicated by the c: and that the drive and directory are separated by the backslash (\), as are the directory name and file name.

Making Backup Copies of Files

You can use two procedures in Symphony for making backup copies of files. The first procedure involves running the File Save operation on two separate disks. The second procedure involves copying files by using the Application Attach option in the SERVICES menu. (See Chapter 2 for directions for using the SERVICES Application command.)

In the first procedure, you can use the File Save command to make backup copies of files whenever you want to copy files one at a time. First, save your file once by following the directions given previously for File Save. After Symphony has saved your file, remain in the Symphony program. Then insert another formatted blank disk (or a disk that has enough space for the file you want to save) into the disk drive. Finally, repeat the File Save operation, saving the file to the disk you just inserted.

The second procedure for making backup copies is to use the DOS add-in application whenever you want to copy one or more files. First, make sure that you have saved your current worksheet to a file. Second, if you have set DOS to attach automatically (see Chapter 2 for directions on automatically attaching an add-in application), select DOS from the SERVICES menu. Otherwise, you must first attach the application.

To attach the application, retrieve the SERVICES menu and select Application. (If you are using a system with two 5 1/4-inch disk drives and are using your Help and Tutorial disk for attaching the DOS add-in, be sure that the Help and Tutorial disk is in drive A.) Next select Attach, and the words `Application name:` appear in the control panel. A menu of add-in programs also appears in the second line of the control panel. Move the cursor to DOS and press Enter, or simply press Enter if DOS is the only program or the first one listed in the menu. Now, select DOS from the SERVICES menu.

Finally, once the DOS prompt appears, follow the specific directions for copying files, using your DOS COPY command. Type **exit** to return to Symphony.

Partial Loads and Saves

Often you will want to store only part of a worksheet (such as a range of cells) in a separate file on the disk. Symphony enables you to extract part of a worksheet that has been created in either a SHEET or DOC environment. For example, you may want to extract outlays from an expense report of revenues from an income statement. One of the best uses for partial storage is breaking up worksheet files that are too large to be stored on a single diskette. Or you may want to extract parts of a DOC file to create new reports or form letters.

The **File Xtract** command allows you to save a part of a worksheet file. This command saves either the formulas that exist in a range or the current values of the formulas in the range of a SHEET window, depending on whether you choose **Formulas** or **Values**. Either option creates a worksheet file that you can reload into Symphony with the **File Retrieve** command. If you decide to save only the current values, however, the resulting worksheet file contains numbers but no formulas. Selecting **Formulas** creates a file with all the formulas intact.

After you choose **Formulas** or **Values**, you must either select an existing file or create a new file to which the range can be extracted. After selecting a file or typing the name of a new file, you must then indicate the range you want extracted, whether or not that portion includes a range from a SHEET or DOC window. As is generally the case with Symphony, the range to be saved can be as small as a cell or as large as the entire worksheet.

If you are extracting a range from a DOC window, you will notice that Symphony automatically shifts from the DOC window to a SHEET window when the program asks you to indicate the range to be extracted. Symphony views the text entered in a DOC window in terms of cell contents. (In addition, in a SHEET window Symphony reads DOC lines as long labels entered into column A cells.) If, for example, you want to extract two text paragraphs from a DOC window, you would issue **File Xtract** and press Enter in response to Select Formulas. (Although this option doesn't apply to extracting text, you nevertheless must make a selection in order to set the **File Xtract** range.)

If you select an existing file to which the indicated range is to be extracted, remember that the file's contents will be lost, replaced by the contents of the extract range. Symphony reminds you of losing the original by displaying the following:

    A file with that name already exists -- replace it?
    No Yes

Extracting ranges from DOC windows is covered in more detail in Chapter 8.

Combining Files

Another function you may want to perform is to make copies of certain ranges from other worksheets and place these ranges into strategic spots in the current worksheet. For example, if you work for a large firm, you may want to combine into one all-encompassing worksheet the balance sheets and income statements from different divisions.

A simple technique for accomplishing this kind of consolidation is to keep a copy of an "empty master." Then when the time comes to perform a consolidation, you will always have an empty master from which to work. In addition, when you start with an empty master, you can copy the first divisional worksheet onto the master and leave untouched the original copy of the divisional worksheet.

Copying a range of cells can also be helpful when you want to combine quarterly data into a yearly statement. Again, the forms must be compatible, and you will benefit by keeping an empty master. The command used to combine data is SERVICES File Combine. This command gives you the following options:

Copy	To pull an entire worksheet or a named range into a worksheet and have the new contents write over the existing area.
Add	To pull in the values or formulas from an entire worksheet or a named range and add the new contents to the existing cell contents. (Add is the option you use for consolidating worksheets, as in the earlier examples.) Incoming values are either added to the existing cell values or entered into an empty cell. Instead of having values overlay labels and formulas, Symphony retains any labels and formulas that exist.
Subtract	To pull in an entire worksheet or a named range of cells and subtract the new contents from the existing cell contents. When an existing cell is empty, the incoming value is subtracted from zero, and the result is entered in the cell. As is true for Add, Symphony does not allow incoming values to overlay existing labels and formulas.

For any of these options, place the cell pointer in the upper left corner of the area in the worksheet where you want the incoming data to be entered. Suppose, for example, that you want to add values from two separate files into the spreadsheet in figure 6.5. Because the values in both spreadsheets are stored in the

same cells, you should position the cell pointer in A1 before initiating the File
Combine Add command.

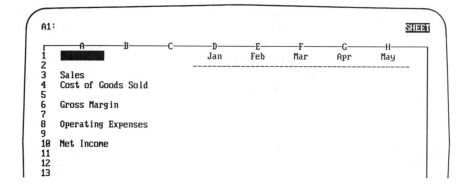

Fig. 6.5

*Preparing to use
File Combine Add.*

If you want to use **File Combine Copy** to copy a file or named range into a DOC
window, you should position the cell pointer in the upper left corner of the
area where the incoming data should begin, as in figure 6.6.

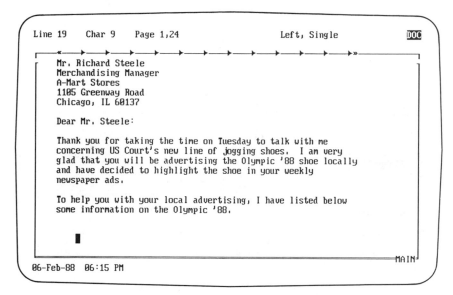

Fig. 6.6

*Copying a file or
range into a DOC
window.*

When using **File Combine Copy**, you need to be particularly careful when positioning the cell pointer so that the incoming data won't overwrite anything in
the worksheet that you want to save. One way of assuring yourself that important
data won't be lost is to use cell protection. Before you issue File Combine, first

use the SERVICES Settings Global-Protection and SHEET **R**ange Protect commands, allowing changes only to that part of the worksheet where incoming data will be overlaid. (See the section in Chapter 4 on protecting ranges.)

Figures 6.7, 6.8, 6.9, and 6.10 show examples of the **C**opy and **A**dd options. Figure 6.7 shows a worksheet that was created and stored on disk. Figure 6.8 shows another worksheet that is stored in Symphony's memory. Figure 6.9 shows the results of combining these two sheets through the **C**opy option, and figure 6.10 shows the results of using the **A**dd option. (The **S**ubtract option is similar enough to the **A**dd option that an example of **S**ubtract has not been included here.)

Fig. 6.7

A worksheet created and stored on disk.

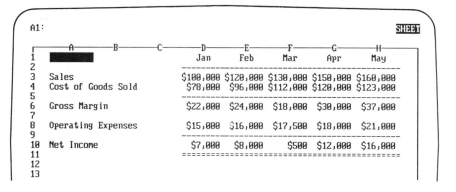

Fig. 6.8

A worksheet stored in memory.

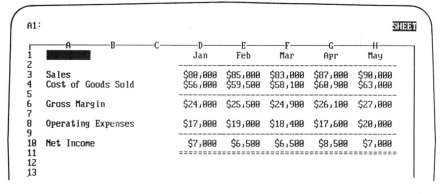

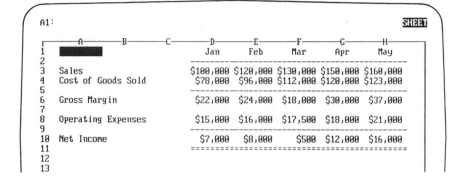

Fig. 6.9

The results of
using File Combine
Copy.

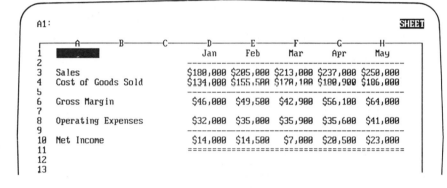

Fig. 6.10

After issuing File
Combine Add.

In addition to using **File Combine** to copy the contents of a spreadsheet into an existing file, you can also use the command to copy text entered in a DOC environment. Incorporating the File Xtract and File Combine commands enables you to create special form letters or document files and to combine parts or all of these files into your current worksheet.

Suppose, for instance, that you frequently write promotional material and sales correspondence, using the same product description for both types of documents. You can store this product description in a special file that you can then combine into the individual sales or promotional letters (see figs. 6.11 and 6.12). For a more detailed discussion of the File Xtract and File Combine commands in a DOC environment, see Chapter 8.

Keep in mind also that you can reduce File Combine operations to two keystrokes by converting frequently used command sequences into keyboard macros. For more information on macros, see Chapter 19.

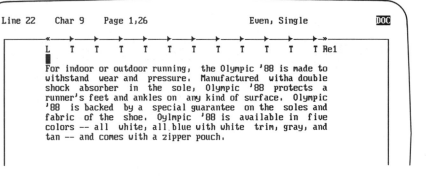

Fig. 6.11

Promotional material in a DOC window.

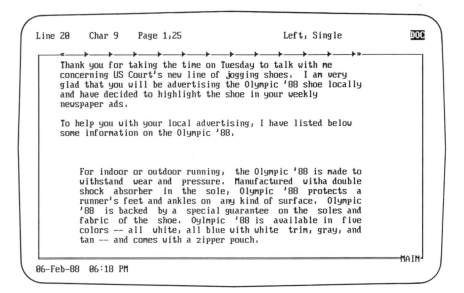

Fig. 6.12

Combining the promotional material into a DOC sales letter.

Deleting Files

When you save files, you sometimes may find that the disk is full. Symphony informs you of this condition by indicating Disk full in the lower left corner of the screen. You can do one of two things when this occurs: swap disks, or delete one or more of the current files that occupy space on the disk.

Deleting files, like making backup copies of files, can be accomplished by either of two procedures. The first is to use the DOS add-in application and then use the DOS ERASE command to erase files. If you want to erase a number of files at one time, this first procedure is easier. The other process for erasing a file is to use the **File Erase** command from the SERVICES menu. When you select

File **Erase** and enter the name of the file to be deleted, Symphony erases that file from the disk. You are given a chance to halt the deletion process when Symphony asks

```
Are you sure you want to erase this file?
No Yes
```

Once you respond with **Y**, the complete file is deleted, and you cannot recover it by conventional means. Always check and double-check before you delete a file to be sure that you really want to delete it. Be careful, too, when you tell Symphony which file to delete. Make sure that the cursor is positioned on the file you want deleted or that you have correctly typed the file name.

When you name files, make file names clearly distinguishable from one another to minimize accidental deletion of the wrong file. For example, consider the following file names:

SALESA.WR1 	SALESB.WR1 	SALESC.WR1 	SALESD.WR1

Because of the different sixth character, Symphony correctly stores all these files. But the similarity in names increases the possibility that you might inadvertently erase the wrong file.

Changing a Drive and Directory

When you select Configuration from the SERVICES menu, the first item on the **Configuration** sheet displayed on the screen is **File**. This item indicates the default setting for the disk drive where files are to be saved and retrieved. In Symphony the default setting is drive C. This drive, then, is the active disk drive for storing and retrieving files. The **Configuration File** setting also permits you to enter a default file directory.

You may sometimes find that you must override temporarily the default disk drive. In such a case, use the SERVICES **File Directory** command. When you select **File Directory**, the words `Current directory:`, followed by the default drive and directory, appear in the control panel, as in

```
Current directory: C:\SYMPHONY\DRAFT
```

If you want to change either the drive or the directory or both, press Esc to erase the drive and directory entry or use the Backspace key to erase part of the entry. Next, type in the new drive and/or directory, then press Enter. At this point, the drive and/or directory is changed—but only until you exit from Symphony. Later, when you reenter the program, **File Directory** is reset to its default setting.

Because Symphony always checks the current default drive when you invoke the **File Directory** command, this method of changing the default does not work if, for instance, drive A malfunctions. In this case, change the default in the Configuration File setting.

Transferring Files

With its expanded capabilities, Symphony gives you access to the most frequently used applications: spreadsheet, word processing, data management, graphics, and communications. Another component of Symphony's integration is the capability of transferring files created from programs outside Symphony. In some cases, the transfer procedure is fairly easy, as in the case of transferring 1-2-3 files into Symphony. At other times, transferring files is a bit more complex. Symphony nevertheless enables you to transfer files into the program and also to convert Symphony files for use in other programs.

Specifically, the SERVICES File Import and SERVICES Print Settings commands and the Translate utility provide the operations for transferring files back and forth between Symphony and another program. The kinds of files that you can transfer with these techniques are limited. This setback, however, is a minor one because you can convert most files to the proper format by using one of the available techniques. The methods described in this section work well and, with a few exceptions, are easy to use.

Transferring Standard ASCII Files

The File Import command copies standard ASCII and LICS files to specific locations in the current worksheet. .PRN (print) files are one example of standard ASCII text files created to print after a current Symphony session. (.PRN files and their uses are covered in detail in Chapter 11.) Other standard ASCII files include those produced by different word-processing programs and BASIC programs. LICS files, on the other hand, are those files created with the Lotus International Character Set. These files are created by using the SERVICES Configuration Other File-Translation command.

In the worksheet, position the cell pointer on the cell where you want the upper left corner of the imported file to be located. Then invoke the File Import command with either Text or Structured. These two options have quite different effects on the worksheet.

The Text designation causes Symphony to create a separate left-justified label in the first cell of a new row for each line of imported text. In other words, everything in a line is placed in just one worksheet cell, called a long label.

Whereas the **Text** option treats numbers as text, the **Structured** option treats numbers as numbers. The rules for the **Structured** option are (1) any number is valid, (2) only text enclosed in double quotation marks is valid, and (3) each valid item in a line is placed in a separate cell within a row.

You also can use the SHEET **Query Parse** command to convert ASCII files into separable text and numbers. (See the "Using **Query Parse**" section in Chapter 17.)

Regardless of which option you choose for **File Import** (**Text** or **Structured**), when the file items are imported into the worksheet, everything that previously existed in that area of the worksheet is written over. Be sure that nothing important is in the affected range of cells.

Using the Translate Utility To Transfer Files

Symphony's Translate utility permits you not only to import Multiplan, VisiCalc, dBASE II, dBASE III, Jazz, DCA, or DIF files but also to translate Symphony worksheet files (.WR1) to DCA, DIF, 1-2-3, or dBASE files. Furthermore, you can translate files from Symphony 2.0 into the earlier Symphony 1.0. You do not need to translate files from the earlier releases of Symphony (1.1 or 1.2) into the current release. Symphony 2.0 automatically makes the translation when the program reads in those worksheets.

This translation capability is one of the many features that demonstrate Symphony's flexibility. For example, the utility is a helpful aid to users who are creating dBASE files and want to process that data through Symphony. The Translate utility is also an important part of Symphony's communications applications.

Before you begin to use the Translate utility, make sure that the files you want to transfer have the correct file-name extensions. If an extension differs from those listed subsequently, use the DOS RENAME command to change the extension. (Refer to your system's directions for using DOS and the RENAME command.)

In general, Symphony's Translate utility translates from and to the following types of files and requires the following file name extensions:

File Type	File Extension
1-2-3 Release 1A	.WKS
1-2-3 Release 2 or 2.01	.WK1
dBASE II or dBASE III	.DBF
DIF	.DIF
DCA RFT format	.RFT

Jazz	.JZZ
SYMPHONY Release 1.0	.WRK
SYMPHONY Release 1.1, 1.2, or 2.0	.WR1
VisiCalc	.VC
Multiplan SYLK	.SLK

After you have checked the file extensions and made corrections if necessary, the translation operation is fairly simple. Follow these steps:

1. Access the Translate utility in one of two ways: through the system prompt or through the File-Translate option on the Symphony Access System menu. If you access the utility at the system prompt, type **trans** after the prompt, or **trans** and the driver name if you are using a driver name other than the default name "Lotus." (If you are using a system with two 5 1/4-inch floppy disk drives, remember to insert the Symphony Translate disk into drive A before you begin to access the utility. If you are using 3 1/2-inch drives, insert the PrintGraph with Translate disk.)

2. After you access the utility, Symphony displays on the left side of the screen a menu of the file translation options (see fig. 6.13). Select one of the displayed options.

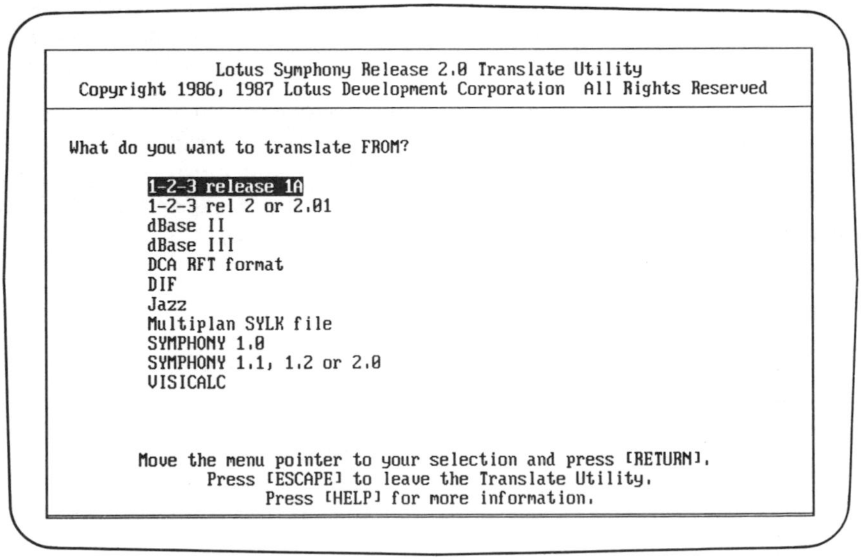

Fig. 6.13

A menu of the file translation options.

```
              Lotus Symphony Release 2.0 Translate Utility
      Copyright 1986, 1987 Lotus Development Corporation  All Rights Reserved


   What do you want to translate FROM?

              1-2-3 release 1A
              1-2-3 rel 2 or 2.01
              dBase II
              dBase III
              DCA RFT format
              DIF
              Jazz
              Multiplan SYLK file
              SYMPHONY 1.0
              SYMPHONY 1.1, 1.2 or 2.0
              VISICALC



         Move the menu pointer to your selection and press [RETURN].
              Press [ESCAPE] to leave the Translate Utility.
                   Press [HELP] for more information.
```

3. Symphony then displays on the right side of the screen a list of file types to which you can translate. Again, select one of the displayed options.

4. At this point, Symphony displays some useful information about your specific source and destination file combination. Read the message and then press Esc to continue.

5. Symphony searches the default drive for the specified file extensions and displays a list of files of the type selected. Highlight the file you want and press Enter. If none are on the default drive, you either insert a new disk in the default drive and continue the search, or press Esc to change the drive specification.

6. By default, Symphony assigns the specified file name, adding to it the destination extension. For example, if you choose to translate a file named SAMPLE1 from Symphony Release 2.0 to 1-2-3 Release 1A, Translate assigns the name SAMPLE1.WKS to the results of the translation. You also can choose to edit that name.

7. In a few cases, you must make an additional choice. To translate a .DIF file to a 1-2-3 or Symphony worksheet, you are asked to choose either **C**olumnwise or **R**owwise translation. To translate from a worksheet to a dBASE file, you must choose to translate either the entire **W**orksheet or a named **R**ange.

8. Initiate the translation operation by selecting **Y**es (or return to the original file list by choosing **N**o. Selecting **Q**uit returns you to the translation menu.

Transferring Symphony and WordStar Files

With Symphony's word-processing capability, you may find that you want to transfer WordStar files or sections of text from WordStar files to Symphony. On the other hand, you may sometimes want to transfer Symphony worksheet files to WordStar. Transferring files between two programs can be quite an advantage when you want to use existing WordStar files to create new documents that incorporate data created in Symphony.

From WordStar to Symphony

Transferring a WordStar file for use in Symphony requires two operations. First, use a utility (available in the public domain) for converting the WordStar file to ASCII. If you don't have such a utility, you can still import the file, but with a much more involved process. You must create a custom character-translation table and then enter and save it in Symphony's **C**onfiguration **S**ettings sheet. Then you can transfer WordStar files with **F**ile **I**mport.

To create a custom character-translation table in Symphony, you must understand how Symphony uses the Lotus International Character Set (LICS) to display characters. Each character in LICS is represented by one of 256 codes (using the numbers 0 through 255). The numbers 32 through 127 represent the same codes as their ASCII equivalents. For example, the LICS (and ASCII) code for the character *b* is 98. (See the Symphony *Reference Manual* for a listing of the LICS characters and their related codes.) For most ASCII files, the conversion from ASCII to LICS requires almost no change in code numbers, but this fact is not true for WordStar files.

Before Symphony can transfer WordStar files, you need to create the custom character-translation table pictured in table 6.1. The left side of table 6.1 shows the default character-code-translation table that appears in the worksheet when you use the SERVICES Configuration Other File-Translation Generate Current command and choose cell A1 as the location for the upper left corner of the table.

Column A of the default table shows the codes that Symphony uses when it sends a character to a print file or a remote computer during a communications session. Column B of the same table shows the default codes used when a file is imported into the program or read in during a communications session. When you are importing WordStar files, you are most concerned with changing the values in column B.

To determine the code that Symphony uses when it receives a character, add 1 to the LICS code number. Symphony uses this number as a row number to look up the appropriate item. For example, to look up the code that corresponds to LICS code 226, Symphony goes to row number 227 and finds code 153—the box or unknown character.

To change the code table to handle WordStar files, use the SHEET Range Fill command to enter the numbers 0 through 127 in cells B129..B256. (See the right side of table 6.1.) This change causes Symphony to convert the last character in each word to a readable LICS character. Use the SERVICES Configuration Other File-Translation Generate Save command to save the new table under a special name, for example, WORDSTAR.CTF. (The .CTF extension indicates a custom character-translation file.) Then use the SERVICES Configuration Other File-Translation Custom command to activate the custom table.

From Symphony to WordStar

Transferring a Symphony .WR1 file to WordStar requires the following steps. First, convert the Symphony .WR1 file to a .PRN file (a print file). To make this change, retrieve the Symphony file to be converted, then select SERVICES Print Settings. Choose Source, then Range, and then indicate the range for the print file. If you want to transfer the complete file, simply set the range to the end of the file by using the End and Home keys.

Table 6.1
Custom Character-Translation Table

The Default Table			A Special Table for Reading in WordStar Files		
A	B	C	A	B	C
1	0	0	1	0	0
2	32	1	2	32	1
3	32	2	3	32	2
4	32	3	4	32	3
.	.	.	.	.	.
.	.	.	.	.	.
32	32	31	32	32	31
33	32	32	33	32	32
34	33	33	34	33	33
35	34	34	35	34	34
.	.	.	.	.	.
.	.	.	.	.	.
127	126	126	127	126	126
128	127	127	128	127	127
129	63	199	129	63	0
130	63	252	130	63	1
131	63	233	131	63	2
.	.	.	.	.	.
.	.	.	.	.	.
226	160	223	226	160	97
227	131	153	227	131	98
.	.	.	.	.	.
.	.	.	.	.	.
253	129	153	253	129	124
254	152	178	254	152	125
255	63	153	255	63	126
256	63	153	256	63	127

After indicating the range of the source, select **Destination** and choose **File**. When Symphony asks for the file name, type only the first part of the name, not the extension, of the file you want to transfer. Next, to eliminate all margin settings, select **Margins** and then choose the No-Margins option. Select **Quit** to return to the main **Print** menu, then select **Go** and wait as Symphony saves the print file. Finally, choose **Quit** to exit from the SERVICES menu. You have now created a .PRN file ready to be used in WordStar.

Chapter Summary

As you use Symphony, you will find yourself frequently performing not only the "necessary" file operations—that is, **File Save** and **File Retrieve**—but also many others. Some **File** commands you will use for file management. For instance, as you begin to create worksheet files containing valuable spreadsheets and databases, you will want to make copies of these files for safekeeping. And as the number of worksheet, print, and graph files increases, you may use **File List**, **File Bytes**, and **File Erase** to keep track of files and disk space and clean out files. Finally, you will want to use such commands as **File Combine**, **File Xtract**, and **File Import** as you apply Symphony to numerous spreadsheet, data management, and word-processing applications.

SHEET Window
Hands-On Practice

This chapter reinforces many of the concepts detailed in Chapters 1 through 6. As you work through this chapter, you will develop, store, retrieve, and expand the sample spreadsheet illustrated in figure 7.1.

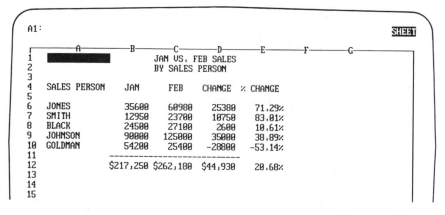

Fig. 7.1

A sample spreadsheet model.

Take a few moments to analyze the model. The titles and headings are entered as labels. The JAN and FEB sales columns contain values you will type in, while the CHANGE and % CHANGE columns contain formulas you will enter and copy. The TOTALS row also contains formulas.

Building the Model

As you build this model, you will enter different types of data, activate several of the function keys, and use the SERVICES and SHEET menus. To create the SALES spreadsheet, begin by typing in the labels, values, and formulas.

Entering Labels

Symphony automatically left-aligns labels in a cell and precedes each label with an apostrophe ('). To right-align a label as you enter it, precede the text with a double quotation mark ("). To center the cell contents, type a caret (^) before you type the label data. If you want a character to repeat across the cell's column width, use the repeating label prefix (\). For example, type \- to create a dashed line in a cell.

To enter the initial label contents in the SALES spreadsheet, follow these steps. Remember that boldface type indicates which keys you should press to execute the command.

1. Load the Symphony program.

2. A blank worksheet should be displayed, and you should be in SHEET mode.

3. Enter the labels as follows or refer to figure 7.2:

   In cell: *Enter:*

A1	JAN VS. FEB SALES
A2	BY SALES PERSON
A4	SALES PERSON

   Note: The label SALES PERSON extends into column B. Ignore this overlap for now. You will fix it later.

A6	JONES
A7	SMITH
A8	BLACK
A9	JOHNSON
A10	GOLDMAN
A12	TOTALS
B4	^JAN
B11	\-
C4	^FEB
D4	"CHANGE
E4	"% CHANGE

Now compare your spreadsheet to figure 7.2. If you made a mistake as you typed the labels, position the cell pointer on the cell containing the error and then

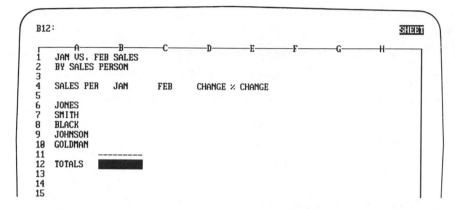

```
B12:                                                    SHEET
    ┌───A────────B───────C───────D───────E───────F───────G───────H────┐
  1  JAN VS. FEB SALES
  2  BY SALES PERSON
  3
  4  SALES PER   JAN      FEB      CHANGE % CHANGE
  5
  6  JONES
  7  SMITH
  8  BLACK
  9  JOHNSON
 10  GOLDMAN
 11            ─────────
 12  TOTALS    ████████
 13
 14
 15
```

Fig. 7.2

Labels for the sales spreadsheet model.

retype the entry. (You will use EDIT mode, the alternative method of correction, later in this chapter.) If you typed an entry into a cell that should be blank, place the cell pointer on this cell and remove the unwanted entry by using SHEET **E**rase.

The dashed line should extend across columns B through E. Copy the repeating label from cell B11 to C11..D11.

1. Place the cell pointer on cell B11.

2. Select SHEET **C**opy.

3. Press Enter to copy FROM B11 (that's the location of the label that you want to copy).

4. Move the cell pointer to cell C11 and type a period (.) to anchor the pointer at the beginning of the TO range.

5. Move the cell pointer to cell D11. The cells of the TO range should be highlighted on your screen. The TO range should read C11..E11. Press Enter to complete the command.

Column A needs to be wider than the other columns to accommodate the SALES PERSON label. Widen this column only.

1. Place the cell pointer anywhere in column A.

2. Select SHEET **W**idth **S**et.

3. Enter **13** as the column width.

Save the spreadsheet by selecting SERVICES **F**ile **S**ave. Type **SALES** as the file name. (The file name can be up to eight characters long; no spaces are allowed.)

Remember to save your work periodically! Symphony does not automatically save for you.

Because you have already saved your file, at this point you can do one of several things:

- Execute SERVICES **Exit Yes** to leave Symphony.

- Begin a new worksheet after invoking SERVICES **New Yes**.

- Select SERVICES **File Retrieve** to retrieve a different file.

- Continue working with the current SALES spreadsheet displayed on the screen.

Now enter the values into the current model.

Entering Numbers

As you enter numbers, Symphony automatically lines them up on the right side of the cell. Although you cannot alter this alignment, you can change how the number is displayed: with commas, percent signs, dollar signs, and decimal places. You can change the overall format settings for the entire spreadsheet or for individual cells. (Refer to Chapter 4 for a complete presentation of the available options.)

For this model, you will establish **Punctuated** as the overall numeric format so that the numbers display commas. But two areas require special formatting. The last row of numbers (the totals) should have dollar signs, so you must individually format this range to **Currency**. You also need to format column E, the % CHANGE column, to **%** (percent) with **2** decimal places. Here are the steps to follow for entering and formatting the values:

1. First, enter the following values in the indicated cells. Remember, do not type commas when entering the numbers; you will add the commas with formatting.

In cell:	Enter:
B6	35600
B7	12950
B8	24500
B9	90000
B10	54200
C6	60980
C7	23700
C8	27100
C9	125000
C10	25400

2. Select SHEET **S**ettings **F**ormat **P**unctuated. Enter **0** for the number of decimals. Then select **Q**uit. Commas are automatically entered in your existing values. Your spreadsheet should look like figure 7.3.

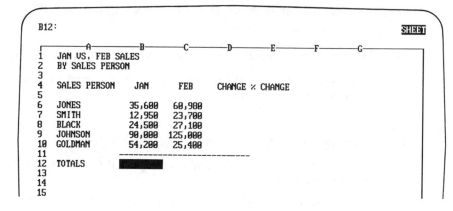

```
B12:                                                         SHEET
   ┌────A────────B────────C────────D────────E──────F──────G──────
   1  JAN VS. FEB SALES
   2  BY SALES PERSON
   3
   4  SALES PERSON   JAN      FEB      CHANGE ⁒ CHANGE
   5
   6  JONES        35,600   60,900
   7  SMITH        12,950   23,700
   8  BLACK        24,500   27,100
   9  JOHNSON      90,000  125,000
   10 GOLDMAN      54,200   25,400
   11              ---------------------------
   12 TOTALS        ████████████
   13
   14
   15
```

Fig. 7.3

*Values formatted in **Punctuated** with 0 decimal places.*

3. To format the TOTALS row as currency, select SHEET **F**ormat **C**urrency. Enter **0** for the number of decimals.

4. Specify the range **B12..D12**. When you enter the totals in this range, the numbers will automatically display with dollar signs.

5. To format the % CHANGE column to percent, select SHEET **F**ormat **%** and enter **2**.

6. Specify **E6..E12** as the range to format. When you enter the % CHANGE formulas in this range, the numbers will automatically display with percent signs.

7. Resave the file with SERVICES **F**ile **S**ave **SALES** Yes.

Your spreadsheet model now contains labels and numbers. To illustrate the true power of an electronic spreadsheet compared to a hand-calculated one, you need to include one other type of input—formulas.

Entering and Copying Formulas

Symphony calculates formulas automatically; you only need to specify which mathematical operations are to be performed and which cell locations are to be involved in those operations. You create a formula by either typing each cell address and mathematical operator involved, or by typing the math operators and pointing to the cells. You can also use any of Symphony's built-in functions. (See Chapter 5 for a detailed discussion of functions.)

To complete the SALES spreadsheet, you need formulas to compute the following three items:

- the change between JAN and FEB sales (in cell D6)

- the percentage change between JAN and FEB sales (in cell E6)

- the total sales (in cell B12)

First enter the formula to calculate the change between JAN and FEB sales:

1. Enter **+C6-B6** in cell D6. The formula displays in the control panel, and the answer appears in the cell.

2. Select SHEET Copy.

3. Press Enter to copy FROM D6 (that's where the formula is).

4. Move the cell pointer to cell D7 and type a period (.) to anchor the pointer at the top of the TO range.

5. Move the cell pointer down to cell D10. The cells D7 through D10 should be highlighted on your screen, and the TO range should read D7..D10. Press Enter to complete the command. Your screen should now resemble figure 7.4.

Fig. 7.4

The model after you enter the CHANGE formula in column D.

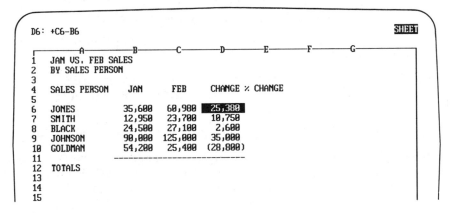

You used the typing method for entering the CHANGE formula. Some users prefer this "typing-only" method for entering relatively short formulas that contain only cells visible on the current screen. But as a general rule, a much safer way to enter formulas is the "type-and-point" method. When building formulas with the type-and-point method, you point to the cells rather than type the cell references. Use this method to build the % CHANGE formula.

1. Place the cell pointer on cell E6.

2. Type + and then press the ← once to point to cell D6.

Note: Do NOT press Enter while you are creating the formula; if you watch the control panel, you will see the formula being built.

3. Type a slash (/). The pointer returns to E6, the cell you are entering the formula into. Then press the left-arrow key three times to point to cell B6.

4. Press Enter to accept the final formula: +D6/B6.

5. Select SHEET **C**opy.

6. Press Enter to copy FROM E6 (where the formula is).

7. Move the cell pointer to E7 and type a period (.) to anchor the pointer at the top of the TO range.

8. Move the cell pointer down to E10. The cells E7 through E10 should be highlighted on your screen, and the TO range should read E7..E10. Press Enter to complete the command. Your screen should now look like figure 7.5.

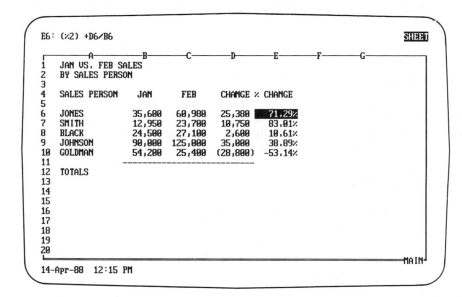

Fig. 7.5

The model after you enter the % CHANGE formula in column E.

Use @SUM, one of Symphony's built-in functions, to total the JAN column; then copy this formula across row 12.

1. Enter the TOTALS formula **@SUM(B6..B10)** in cell B12.

2. Use SHEET **C**opy to copy FROM B12 TO C12..D12.

Also, copy the % CHANGE formula FROM E10 TO E12. Your spreadsheet should look like figure 7.6.

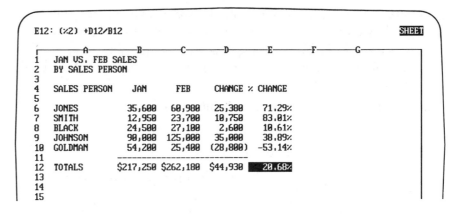

Fig. 7.6

The spreadsheet with all labels, values, and formulas entered.

```
E12: (%2) +D12/B12                                              SHEET
┌───────A────────B────────C────────D────────E────────F────────G──────┐
1   JAN VS. FEB SALES
2   BY SALES PERSON
3
4   SALES PERSON    JAN      FEB     CHANGE % CHANGE
5
6   JONES          35,600   60,980   25,380   71.29%
7   SMITH          12,950   23,700   10,750   83.01%
8   BLACK          24,500   27,100    2,600   10.61%
9   JOHNSON        90,000  125,000   35,000   38.89%
10  GOLDMAN        54,200   25,400  (28,800)  -53.14%
11                        ─────────────────────────
12  TOTALS        $217,250 $262,180 $44,930   20.68%
13
14
15
```

Expanding the Model

This model was designed to compare sales in JAN and FEB, but works equally well for any two months in the year. You can expand your model by creating windows for different month combinations and then copying the model into these windows.

Creating Windows

One of Symphony's most powerful features is its capability of keeping separate information in different windows. You can quickly switch between windows with the press of a key (F6). The windows can be of any size, and you can create as many as you need. Let's expand the sample model by creating two windows: one for January and February, and another for February and March.

1. Select SERVICES **W**indow Create.

2. Enter **JAN-FEB** as the window name.

3. Select SHEET as the window type.

4. Press Enter to select the entire screen as the window area.

5. Select **R**estrict **R**ange and specify **A1..G20**.

6. Select **Q**uit.

Notice the window name JAN-FEB at the bottom of the window. Now create a window for FEB-MAR.

1. Select SERVICES **W**indow Create.

2. Enter **FEB-MAR** as the window name.

3. Select SHEET as the window type.

4. Press Enter to select the entire screen as the window area.

5. Select **Restrict Range** and specify **H1..O20**.

6. Select **Quit**.

Notice the window name, FEB-MAR.

Copying between Windows

The Window key (F6) moves you from one window to the next. You can even use this key in the middle of the Copy command to copy information between windows. Follow these steps to copy the table from the JAN-FEB window to the FEB-MAR window.

1. Press F6 until the JAN-FEB window is displayed. (Look at the window name at the bottom of the screen.)

2. Select SHEET Copy.

3. For the FROM range, indicate **A1..E12**; press Enter.

4. Press F6 until you are in the FEB-MAR window.

5. The cell pointer should be in cell H1. Simply press Enter to complete the copy. Note that the pointer then moves back to the JAN-FEB window.

6. Press F6 until you reach the FEB-MAR window again.

Changing the Spreadsheet

Once you have created your spreadsheet, it's likely that you will want to make changes to it. Because you are using an electronic spreadsheet rather than a paper spreadsheet, making changes is a snap. You can easily move a cell or a range of cells, edit cells, and insert and delete rows and columns. Throw away your scissors and bottle of whiteout!

Moving Cells

In the model, the spreadsheet title would look better if it were centered above the entire table. Use the **Move** command to rearrange the title.

1. Position the cell pointer on cell H1.

2. Select SHEET **Move**.

3. Press the ↓ to move to cell H2; the FROM range is now H1..H2. Press Enter.

4. Move the pointer to cell J1 and press Enter.

5. Repeat these steps to move the titles to cell C1 in the JAN-FEB window.

Using the Edit Key

Although you have copied the table to FEB-MAR, the chart still contains references to January and February and data from those months. Revise the table so that it contains February and March headings. Use the Edit key (F2) to modify the cell contents.

1. Place the cell pointer on cell J1.

2. Press F2 to display the contents of cell J1 in the control panel. Notice the EDIT mode indicator in the upper right corner of the screen.

3. Use the ← or Ctrl-← to move the cursor to the F in FEB.

4. Press the Del key three times to remove FEB.

5. Type **MAR**. Note how the characters are automatically inserted.

6. Use the ← to move the cursor to the J in JAN; delete this word with the Del key.

7. Type **FEB**.

8. Press Enter to exit EDIT mode.

9. Change the column headings from JAN and FEB to FEB and MAR. Simply type over the cell contents, remembering to first type the caret (^) to center the labels.

10. Use SHEET Width Set to widen column H to 13. (See fig. 7.7.)

Figure 7.7 shows how the spreadsheet should look after you edit the labels.

Inserting and Deleting Rows

Simple commands on the SHEET menu enable you to insert and delete easily any number of rows or columns. As long as you don't disturb an end point of a formula range, you can safely insert and delete without having to reenter or edit a formula.

Add two new people to the FEB-MAR table by inserting two rows.

1. Place the cell pointer on cell H9.

2. Select SHEET Insert Row.

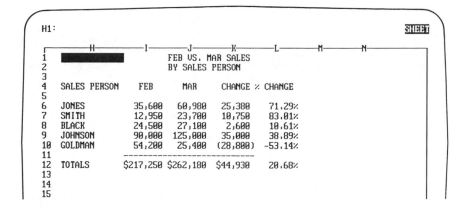

Fig. 7.7

Labels edited for the FEB-MAR window.

3. Press the ↓ once to highlight the range H9..H10; press Enter to complete the row insertions.

4. Enter the following labels:

   In cell: *Enter:*

   H9   THOMAS
   H10   CARMAN

You will enter the values later, when you enter the February/March values for the rest of the salespeople.

Now delete the row containing the sales for SMITH.

1. Position the cell pointer on cell H7.

2. Select SHEET **Delete R**ow.

3. Press Enter to delete the current row.

Your spreadsheet should now look like figure 7.8.

Protecting the Model

A great deal of time and effort goes into developing, testing, and entering data into a model. Although you have saved your file on disk, and you know that you should make a backup copy on another disk, you may want to consider using some additional measures available in Symphony.

You can build protection into your worksheet, preventing entry into some cells (formulas, for example) while permitting entry into others (such as input cells). When the protection is enabled, you needn't worry about accidentally typing over the formulas you worked so hard to create.

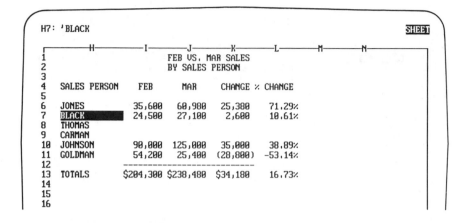

Fig. 7.8

Inserting and deleting rows.

You also may want to password-protect your file so that no one else can retrieve the file without entering the correct password.

Preventing Accidental Overwrite

The only cells that you need to change in the model spreadsheet are the monthly data figures. You should protect all other cells from accidental changes. Protecting a spreadsheet involves two steps: (1) enabling global protection, and (2) unprotecting the cells you want to be able to change.

1. Select SERVICES **S**ettings **G**lobal-Protection **Y**es **Q**uit. Now you've protected all cells.

2. Select SHEET **R**ange **P**rotect **A**llow-Changes.

3. Specify the range of cells you want to be able to change: in this case, **I6.J11**. These unprotected cells appear brighter or in a different color on your screen. The A in these cells indicates the Allow-Changes protection status. Press Enter.

4. Enter the following values into the unprotected range (see fig. 7.9). Simply type over the existing data in these cells.

In cell:	*Enter:*
I6	60980
I7	27100
I8	35000
I9	45000
I10	125000
I11	25400
J6	75000

J7	26000
J8	35000
J9	45000
J10	150000
J11	26000

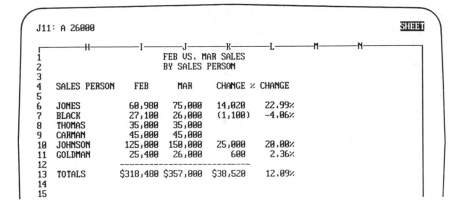

Fig. 7.9

Entering values in the unprotected range (I6..J11).

5. Try typing a value into a protected cell, such as K6. What happens? Press Esc to clear the error.

6. Turn off global protection by selecting SERVICES **S**ettings **G**lobal-Protection **N**o **Q**uit.

You also need to copy the CHANGE and % CHANGE formulas into the inserted rows. You can copy both formulas at once by following these steps:

1. Position the cell pointer on cell K7.

2. Select SHEET **C**opy.

3. Press the → once to highlight K7..L7 as the range to copy FROM; press Enter.

4. For the TO range, indicate the range **K8..K9** and press Enter. Your screen should resemble figure 7.10.

Password-Protecting the File

You can assign a password to a file by typing a **p** after the file name when you save. Keep in mind, though, that if *you* forget the password, you will lock *yourself* out of the file, too!

1. Select SERVICES **F**ile **S**ave.

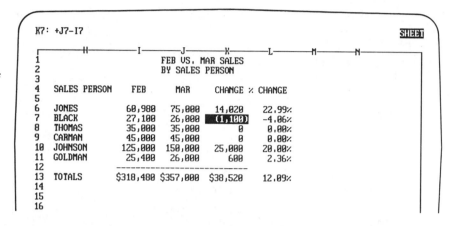

Fig. 7.10

The model after you copy the CHANGE and % CHANGE formulas into the inserted rows.

```
K7: +J7-I7                                                              SHEET
    ┌────H────────I────────J────────K────────L────────M────────N────┐
    1                         FEB VS. MAR SALES
    2                         BY SALES PERSON
    3
    4   SALES PERSON     FEB       MAR       CHANGE % CHANGE
    5
    6   JONES          60,980    75,000     14,020     22.99%
    7   BLACK          27,100    26,000    (1,100)     -4.06%
    8   THOMAS         35,000    35,000         0      0.00%
    9   CARMAN         45,000    45,000         0      0.00%
   10   JOHNSON       125,000   150,000    25,000     20.00%
   11   GOLDMAN        25,400    26,000       600      2.36%
   12                          ----------------------------
   13   TOTALS       $318,480  $357,000   $38,520     12.09%
   14
   15
   16
```

2. Press the space bar and type **p**; then press Enter.

3. Enter the password **test**. Blocks will appear on the screen as you type. Press Enter.

4. Verify the password by typing it a second time. Press Enter.

5. Select **Yes** to replace the file.

To see how password protection works, clear the screen and retrieve the file.

1. Select SERVICES **New Yes**.

2. Select SERVICES **File Retrieve**.

3. Type **SALES** and press Enter.

4. Type the password **test**. Make sure you type it with the same combination of upper- and lowercase you used initially. Press Enter.

Working with Large Spreadsheets

With a small spreadsheet, every change you make is instantly and automatically recalculated. Once your spreadsheets become large, however, you will notice a delay in the time Symphony takes to recalculate the spreadsheet. You can deal with this problem in one of two ways. First, you can turn automatic recalculation off so that the spreadsheet recalculates only when you press the Calc function key (F8). Or, you can divide the large spreadsheet into several smaller ones by Xtracting ranges to new files.

Recalculating the Spreadsheet

Change the **Recalculation Method** to **Manual** and use the Calc key to recalculate the table manually after you've made several changes.

1. Select SHEET **Settings Recalculation Method Manual Quit.**

2. Enter **74000** in cell J6. Notice the Calc indicator at the bottom of the screen (see fig. 7.11).

3. Enter **29000** in cell J7.

4. Press F8 to recalculate the spreadsheet. The Calc indicator disappears, and the formula results reflect the changes in the data.

5. Change back to automatic recalculation by selecting SHEET **Settings Recalculation Method Automatic Quit.**

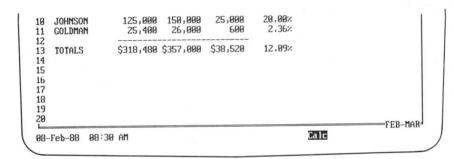

Fig. 7.11

The Calc *indicator with recalculation set to Manual.*

Xtracting to Separate Files

Instead of placing each two-month combination in a separate window, you can put each table in a separate file. With larger models, you would have to use this method. The **File Xtract** command copies sections of a spreadsheet into new files.

1. Select SERVICES **File Xtract Formulas.**

2. Enter **FEB-MAR** as the file name.

3. Indicate the range **H1..L13** and then press Enter.

4. Select SERVICES **New Yes** to clear the screen.

5. Select SERVICES **File Retrieve** and enter **FEB-MAR**. Your screen should look like figure 7.12.

Fig. 7.12

The February/ March table extracted to a new file.

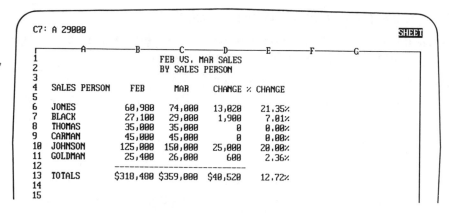

```
C7: A 29000                                              SHEET
┌────A────────B────────C────────D────────E───────F───────G──────
│1                        FEB VS. MAR SALES
│2                        BY SALES PERSON
│3
│4  SALES PERSON     FEB       MAR      CHANGE % CHANGE
│5
│6  JONES         60,980    74,000     13,020    21,35%
│7  BLACK         27,100    29,000      1,900     7,01%
│8  THOMAS        35,000    35,000          0     0,00%
│9  CARMAN        45,000    45,000          0     0,00%
│10 JOHNSON      125,000   150,000     25,000    20,00%
│11 GOLDMAN       25,400    26,000        600     2,36%
│12                       --------------------------
│13 TOTALS       $318,480  $359,000    $40,520    12.72%
│14
│15
```

Chapter Summary

This chapter has given you hands-on practice with Symphony's central application: the spreadsheet. You started building your model by entering labels, values, and formulas. You then expanded the model by creating windows for other versions of the spreadsheet. You changed the spreadsheet by editing, moving, inserting, and deleting. You also learned how to protect your model by password-protecting the file and by protecting sections of the spreadsheet so that you don't inadvertently overwrite formulas or labels. Finally, you learned some tools for working with large spreadsheets: turning automatic recalculation off and extracting sections of the spreadsheet to smaller files.

In the following chapter, you will learn how to take advantage of Symphony's word-processing capabilities.

PART III

Using the Symphony
Word Processor

Includes

Word Processing: Working in a Symphony
DOC Window

DOC Window Hands-On Practice

Word-Processing Add-Ins: Spelling Checker
and Text Outliner

8

Word Processing: Working in a Symphony DOC Window

What are the advantages of having a fully integrated software package that includes word processing? Once you begin to use Symphony's word-processing feature, the Symphony DOC environment, you will find numerous advantages to having this capability. The first is simply one of convenience. Not having to access another program or to change disks whenever you need to compose a letter or memo, draft a report, or put a few notes together is one kind of convenience. But there's also the handiness of learning one program but having five applications available at any time.

Learning to use Symphony's word-processing environment is similar to learning to use the other program applications—spreadsheet, graphics, data management, and communications. The Symphony DOC environment shares a number of features with the other applications, including similarities in the display screen, the use of command menus, and the way Symphony stores text. Except for handling special format lines or print commands within the text, you don't need to master a new way of entering commands in Symphony's DOC window environment; the approach is the same as that for a SHEET, FORM, GRAPH, or COMM window.

The second advantage to having word processing along with spreadsheet, data management, graphics, and communications is Symphony's capability to integrate word processing with the other applications. For instance, you can be working in a DOC window and at the same time have a SHEET or GRAPH window on the screen. You will find that this capability alone may make switching from a single word-processing program to Symphony well worth it.

The third advantage to using Symphony's word-processing capability is the simplification of many DOC operations through the use of macros, which are discussed in Chapter 19. That chapter shows you how to create macros for many moving, erasing, and copying operations. After becoming familiar with Symphony's DOC environment and the process of creating Symphony macros interactively, you will be able to reduce many lengthy operations to one keystroke.

This chapter introduces you to Symphony's word-processing capabilities so that you can make the DOC window environment a regular part of using the program. Included are the following topics:

- Creating a DOC window

- The DOC display

- The DOC function keys

- Getting started in a DOC window

- Entering text and moving the cursor

- Erasing and editing text

- Searching and replacing

- Formatting your document

- Integrating the DOC environment with other Symphony applications

Creating a DOC Window

You can use various methods to create a DOC window. First, if you will be working within a DOC window more frequently than other types of windows (SHEET, GRAPH, FORM, or COMM), then you can begin every work session with a DOC window by updating the SERVICES Configuration Window Type setting to DOC. To change the setting for the window type, retrieve the SERVICES menu by pressing the Services key (F9), select Configuration from the menu, then choose Window. Next, select Type. When the five types of windows are displayed, either type D or move the cursor to DOC and press Enter. Finally, choose Configuration Update. The default window is then set to DOC. Every time you access the Symphony program or create a New worksheet, the window type will be DOC.

If, however, you set the default window type at SHEET, GRAPH, FORM, or COMM, you can shift to a DOC window by pressing the Type key (Alt-F10) and selecting DOC. You also can use Alt-F9 to switch back and forth between a DOC window and the last used window. You can use one other procedure for setting the window type. Whenever you create a new window by using the **Window Create** command from the SERVICES menu, Symphony asks you to choose a window type. If the current window is not DOC, you can select it.

The DOC Display

When you enter the Symphony program for the first time, a SHEET window is the type of window to appear. Symphony has set the default setting for initial window type to SHEET. In the SHEET window, columns are represented by letters at the top, and rows are indicated by numbers down the left side. The SHEET window, which is bordered on all four sides, contains an indicator area in the top right and left corners. When you shift to a DOC window, either by pressing Alt-F10 or by creating a new window with the SERVICES **Window Create** command, the display remains much the same as for the SHEET window—still bordered on all four sides and containing indicators in the upper right and left corners.

In addition, DOC commands are displayed exactly as those for SHEET, GRAPH, FORM, and COMM (see fig. 8.1). When you retrieve the DOC command menu, it appears above the top line of the DOC border, and the explanation of the cursor-highlighted command appears above the menu line.

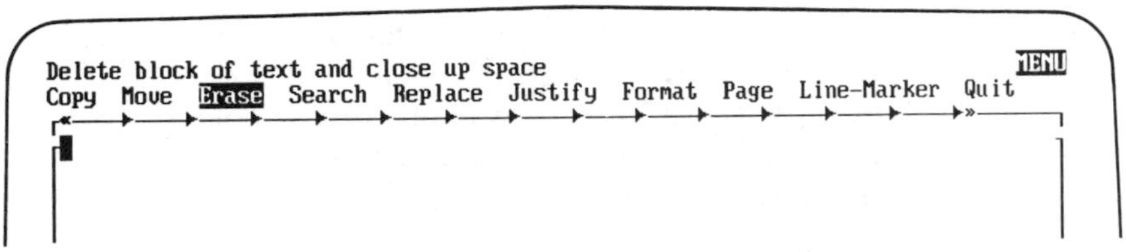

```
Delete block of text and close up space                           MENU
Copy  Move  Erase  Search  Replace  Justify  Format  Page  Line-Marker  Quit
┌─◄──────►─────►────►──────►──────►─────►─────►─────►────►──────►»─┐
│ █                                                               │
```

Fig. 8.1

The DOC commands displayed.

The DOC display screen, however, has some special features. First, the top line of the border indicates the left and right margins and all tab settings. The default setting (shown in the SERVICES Configuration settings sheet) for the left margin is 1 and for the right margin is 72. Tabs are set 5 spaces apart. The top line indicating margins and tabs is always displayed unless you change the border from **S**tandard to **L**ine or **N**one by selecting SERVICES **W**indow **S**ettings **B**orders.

Above the top line are three indicators: the cursor position (line, character, and page), the type of justification and spacing, and the mode indicator. An asterisk in the middle of the control panel indicates that the cursor is presently located on data which has been entered in another type of window.

If you are working in a DOC window and move the cursor to data that you have already entered in a SHEET environment, for example, Symphony displays the asterisk to remind you that DOC commands and operations and SHEET commands and operations are not interchangeable. For example, you cannot edit labels and numbers entered in a SHEET window by using the Backspace and Del keys while you are working in a DOC window. If you include special format lines (discussed later in this chapter) in your text, an asterisk appears when the cursor is positioned at these format lines, again telling you that you cannot change this text as you can other data.

One other indicator to note particularly is the Calc indicator in the bottom right corner. Calc indicates that changes in the DOC window may affect calculations in spreadsheets created in other areas of your worksheet. If you do have spreadsheets in the worksheet, press the Calc key (F8) to recalculate cell values.

DOC Function Keys

Whenever you begin word-processing operations in a DOC window, eight function keys are available, ranging from a key for justifying paragraphs to a key for jumping the cursor from one part of the text to another.

Two of these keys—Justify (F2) and Erase (F4)—perform the same operations as comparable commands from the DOC command menu. The function keys that have special uses for DOC operations are the following:

Key	*Function*
Alt-F1 (Compose)	Used for creating special characters not included on the keyboard. To create a special character, press Alt-F1; then press the key(s) for the symbol. For example, to create a "less than or equal to" symbol, press Alt-F1 and then type = and <.
Alt-F2 (Where)	Indicates in the lower left corner of the screen the page and line location of the cursor's present position. This information is also displayed at the top of the screen (for example, Page 1,6). The Where key is left over from earlier versions of Symphony, which did not display the page number at the top of the screen. This key is not too useful in Symphony 2.0.
F2 (Justify)	Justifies paragraphs; completes the same operation as that of Justify Paragraph from the DOC menu.
Alt-F3 (Split)	Divides a line of text or creates blank lines without leaving hard carriage returns.
F3 (Indent)	Indents a paragraph or section of text. (See the later sections on special formatting.)
Alt-F4 (Center)	Centers a line of text with respect to the margin settings for the line.

F4
(Erase)

Initiates the Erase command; completes the same operation as that of the Erase command from the DOC menu.

F5
(GoTo)

Used for jumping the cursor to another line on the same page, to a line on another page, or to a named line. (See the later section entitled "The GoTo Key and Line-Marker Names.") When you press F5 and then the Menu key (F10), a list of all marked lines appears.

Getting Started in a DOC Window

What do you need to know as you begin using Symphony's word processor? You probably want to know how text is displayed, stored, and finally printed. You also need to know how to enter text on the screen and how to edit and change text.

Getting started in a DOC window requires that you understand the organization of the DOC command menu (fig. 8.2), the "accelerator" keys that are available, the kinds of special commands that are inserted within the text, and the different kinds of settings sheets that affect a DOC window.

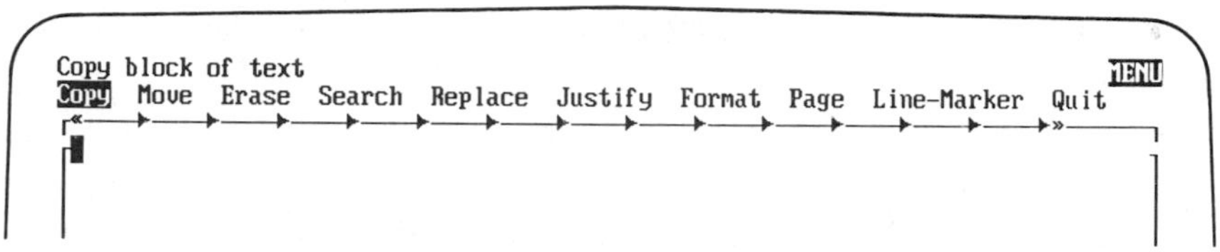

```
Copy block of text                                                    MENU
Copy  Move  Erase  Search  Replace  Justify  Format  Page  Line-Marker  Quit
```

Fig. 8.2

Organization of the DOC command menu.

The DOC Command Menu

Using the DOC command menu requires the same operations as using the command menus for other windows. You simply press the Menu key (F10), move the cursor to the command, and complete the operations required by that command. The DOC commands fall into the following primary categories:

1. Copy, Move, and Erase commands

2. Search and Replace commands

3. Format commands, including those for paragraph justification, spacing, margins, tabs, and operations connected with creating special "format lines," naming lines, and inserting page breaks

DOC Accelerator Keys

As an alternative to using the DOC command menu, you can use "accelerator" keys. For example, you can press Ctrl-C rather than select **C**opy from the DOC menu. Following is a list of the available accelerator keys:

Key	*Description*
Auto (Ctrl-J)	Turns auto-justification on/off
Begin (Ctrl-B)	Begins print attribute
Case (Ctrl-X)	Converts capitalization of characters
Copy (Ctrl-C)	Copies text
Delete Left (Ctrl-T)	Deletes text to start of line
Delete Line (Ctrl-D)	Deletes current line
Delete Right (Ctrl-Y)	Deletes text to end of line
Delete Word (Ctrl-Backspace)	Deletes previous word
Format (Ctrl-F)	Inserts format line
Merge (Ctrl-O)	Inserts merge character
Move (Ctrl-M)	Moves text
Next Page (Ctrl-PgDn)	Moves cursor to next page
Page (Ctrl-N)	Inserts page break
Paste (Ctrl-P)	Inserts last deleted text
Replace (Ctrl-R)	Replaces text

Search (Ctrl-S)	Searches for text
Stop (Ctrl-E)	Ends print attribute
Top Page (Ctrl-PgUp)	Moves cursor to top of page

Print Attributes

You can place special print attributes (indicating boldface, italic, underlining, superscript, subscript, and combinations of these) within the text. For example, if you want Symphony to boldface a character, letter, or word, you enclose it within print attribute commands. Here are the steps to follow:

1. Signal the beginning of a special print attribute by pressing Ctrl-B. (B stands for "Begin Attribute.") The Print Attribute menu displays.

2. Select the appropriate print attribute from the menu. Following is a description of each option:

Attribute Option	*Code*
Boldface	B
Italic	I
Underline	U
Superscript	+
Subscript	-
Strike-through	X
Boldface italic	0 (Zero)
Boldface underline	1
Boldface italic underline	2
Italic underline	3
Boldface superscript	4
Italic superscript	5
Boldface subscript	6
Italic subscript	7
Boldface italic subscript	8
Boldface italic superscript	9
Include spaces in print attributes	S
Do not include spaces	Q

3. Signal the end of the print attribute by pressing Ctrl-E (for "End Attribute").

Before selecting these print attributes, make sure that your driver is set for the right printer(s). (See Appendix A's section on installing drivers.)

If you have a monochrome monitor, the attributed text appears either underlined or in low intensity. If you have a color monitor, the text appears in a different color. To identify which attribute has been selected, move the cursor anywhere within the attributed text and look in the control panel for the code. For example, a U displays in the control panel for underlined text, and a B appears for boldfaced text.

If you find you have selected the wrong attribute or later change your mind about a print attribute you selected, you can change the begin attribute. Place the cursor at the beginning of the attributed text, press Ctrl-B, and select the new attribute. Symphony automatically removes the old attribute.

To eliminate a print attribute entirely:

1. Place the cursor at the beginning of the attributed text.

2. Press the Erase key (F4). The print attribute characters display on the screen.

3. Press Enter to erase the begin attribute character.

4. Place the cursor at the end of the attributed text.

5. Press the Erase key (F4).

6. Press Enter to erase the end attribute character.

Format Settings

The first step in using Symphony's DOC environment is to adjust special format settings. Besides inserting format lines in the text (discussed later in this chapter), Symphony provides two ways for controlling the format of a DOC environment: the default format settings stored in Symphony's configuration file (SYMPHONY.CNF), and the format settings that you can enter for each DOC window you create.

Format Settings in Symphony's Configuration File

The SERVICES Configuration Document setting establishes the default settings for tabs, justification, spacing, margins, display of hard spaces between words, display of carriage returns and hard tabs, and automatic justification of paragraphs. When you first enter Symphony, the following default settings are in operation:

Tab interval: 5
Justification: 1
Spacing: 1
Left margin: 1
Right margin: 72
Blanks visible: No

CRs visible: Yes
Auto-Justify: Yes
Hard-Tabs: Yes

You can change any or all of these settings by selecting Configuration from the SERVICES menu, choosing Document, selecting each item to be changed, and then entering the new settings. Once you have changed the Configuration Document settings, you need to update the settings sheet by selecting Update from the Configuration menu. If you do not update the sheet, the new settings that you enter are in effect only until you finish your current work session and exit from the program.

The SERVICES Configuration Document settings are useful for storing format settings for frequently modified documents. You need to remember that Configuration Document settings control the format settings for the first DOC window that you create in any given file. You may therefore want to change the SERVICES Configuration Document settings to the kind of format you plan to use most often. For example, if you find that you will frequently be using the DOC environment for creating one-page memos, you may want to change the Configuration Document settings to the particular format required by the memos.

DOC Window Format Settings

You can override Configuration Document settings, however, by using the Format Settings command from the DOC menu. When you change Format Settings, these settings control the format of any text you enter. Also, whenever you change Format Settings in one DOC window and then create another DOC window, the second window inherits the format settings of the previous window unless you have deleted that window.

After you enter a DOC window, the next step is to determine whether you need to change format settings. As mentioned earlier, the top line of the border tells you where margins and tabs have been set. Above the top line in the control panel, Symphony indicates the type of justification and spacing. For example, `Left, Single` tells you that the window is set for left-justification and single-spacing.

Whenever you need to change format settings for the current DOC window, use the DOC Format Settings command. This command allows you to enter settings for the current window and to save those settings along with the window. Suppose, for example, that you are creating a table, as shown in figure 8.3. In the window (named TABLE 1), you need a left margin of 15, a right margin of 60, and double-spacing. (Double- and triple-spacing do not appear on the screen, but they do appear in printed copy. See this chapter's section called "Setting Tabs, Spacing, and Margins.")

In addition to checking the settings for margins, tabs, justification, and spacing before you begin to work in a DOC window, you can also check three other

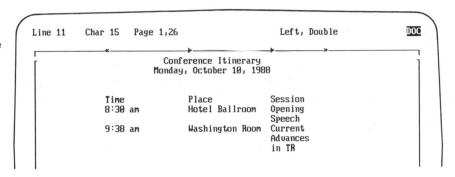

Fig. 8.3

Creating a table in a DOC window.

settings by retrieving the Format Settings sheet from the DOC menu. (You can also change these three settings in the SERVICES Configuration Document settings.) The settings are the following:

- **Blanks.** If you select **Yes,** Symphony displays periods on the screen for every space. Because the default setting is **No,** you need to change this setting only when you want spaces marked.

- **CRs.** Symphony displays hard carriage returns. **Yes** is the default setting.

- **Auto-Justify.** When Auto-Justify is set to **Yes,** which is the default setting, Symphony automatically justifies paragraphs after every editing change. If you select **No,** paragraphs do not justify until you press the Justify key (F2) or select DOC Justify. The Auto accelerator key (Ctrl-J) also turns automatic justification on and off.

Guidelines for Using Format Settings

When you use the SERVICES Configuration Document settings, the DOC Format Settings, and format lines, keep the following guidelines in mind:

1. The Configuration Document settings provide the default settings; however, DOC Format Settings can override Configuration Document settings.

2. A DOC Format Settings sheet is stored with each window you create, and the settings remain with that window until you change them.

3. **Blanks, CRs,** and **Auto-Justify** settings override format lines.

Some examples can help clarify the relationships of the SERVICES Configuration Document settings, a DOC Format Settings sheet, and format lines. You can also note the effect that creating different windows has on these three methods for adjusting format.

When you create the first DOC window for a worksheet, the DOC Format Settings are inherited from the **Configuration Document** settings. Figure 8.4 shows the **Configuration Document** settings stored in the Symphony configuration file (SYMPHONY.CNF). The DOC **Format Settings** for the DOC window, shown in figure 8.5, are the same as those in the **Configuration Document** settings.

```
 Interval between successive tab stops                              MENU
 Tabs Justification Spacing Left Right Blanks CRs Auto-Justify Hard-Tabs Quit

 File: C:\S2                      Document              Window
 Printer                          Tab interval:   5       Type: SHEET
   Type:      Parallel 1          Justification:  1       Name:
   Auto-LF:   No                  Spacing:        1          MAIN
   Wait:      No                  Left margin:    1       Help: Removable
   Margins                        Right margin:           Auto-Worksheet:
     Left:  4      Top:     2     Blanks visible: No
     Right: 76     Bottom:  2     CRs visible:    Yes    Clock on Screen:
   Page-Length: 66                Auto-Justify:   Yes       Standard
   Init-String:                   Hard-Tabs:      No     File-Translation:
   Name: Toshiba P351 series                              IBM PC or Compatible
 Communications name:
                                            Configuration Settings
```

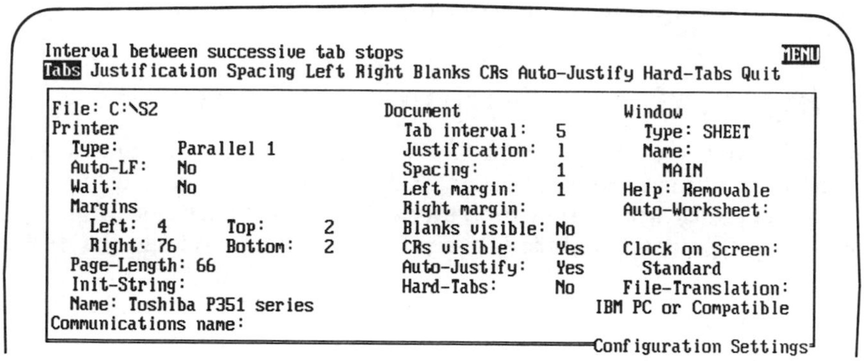

Fig. 8.4

The SERVICES Configuration Document settings.

```
 Interval between successive tab stops                              MENU
 Tabs Justification  Spacing  Left  Right  Blanks  CRs  Auto-Justify  Quit

   Tab interval:    5
   Justification:   1
   Spacing:         1
   Left margin:     1
   Right margin:    1
   Blanks visible:  No
   CRs visible:     Yes
   Auto-Justify:    Yes
                                   Document Settings for window TABLE 1
```

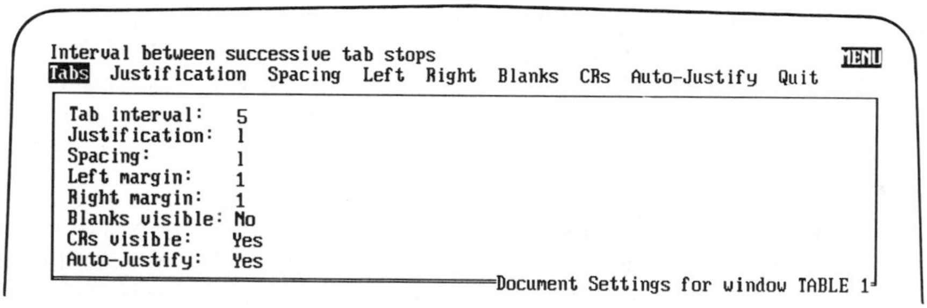

Fig. 8.5

The DOC Format Settings.

Note that the right margin setting is initially left blank; Symphony automatically sets the right margin according to the size of the current window. When you create a second DOC window on the screen, that window inherits the DOC **Format Settings** from the first window. You can, however, change the settings in DOC **Format Settings** for the particular window in which you are working. In the example in figure 8.3, the DOC **Format Settings** have been changed to these:

Tab interval: 17
Justification: 1 (1 = Left)
Spacing: 2
Left margin: 15
Right margin: 60
Blanks visible: No

CRs visible: Yes
Auto-Justify: No

You can also return to your original format settings by using the DOC **F**ormat **E**dit **C**urrent **R**eset command (see this chapter's section called "Creating, Editing, and Storing Format Lines"). If you decide that you don't need the format line at all, use the **E**rase command to delete the format line or the format line marker. Whenever you erase a named format line, the name is also deleted.

Entering Text and Moving the Cursor

After you have made changes in the SERVICES **C**onfiguration **D**ocument settings and the DOC **F**ormat **S**ettings, you are ready to begin entering text in the DOC window. Entering words from the keyboard isn't much different from typing words on a typewriter keyboard, except for wordwrap and Insert/Overstrike modes.

Wordwrap

If you have used word-processing programs before, you are probably familiar with wordwrap. In Symphony, as in other word processors, wordwrap is the capability of maintaining automatically the right margin and moving the cursor to the succeeding line. Whole words, then, are not divided but "wrap around" to the next line. In other words, you do not have to press the carriage return to begin a new line. When wordwrap occurs, Symphony formats each line according to the controlling justification setting—**N**one, **L**eft, **E**ven, or **C**enter.

At times, you may want two words (or letters and numbers separated by spaces) to remain on the same line rather than have one word at the end of a line and the other word at the beginning of the next line. In this case, you can insert a "hard space" between the two words.

For example, you may want a trademark, product name, or company name, such as "J. P. McMurphy," to appear all on one line (see fig. 8.6). To have the entire name wrap around to the next line, take the following steps. Type **J.**, press the Compose key (Alt-F1), then press the space bar twice. Symphony inserts a dot, indicating that a hard space is inserted. Next, type **P.**, press the Compose key, and again press the space bar twice. Symphony inserts another dot. When margins are justified because of wordwrap, "J. P. McMurphy" remains on the same line.

Insert and Overstrike Modes

The Insert mode is the default setting for entering characters from the keyboard. Whenever you enter characters in Insert mode, you can insert any character or

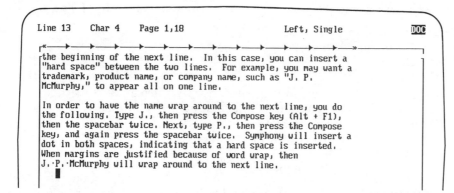

Fig. 8.6

Inserting hard spaces.

a space to the immediate left of the cursor. Also, whenever the DOC environment is set in Insert mode, wordwrap is in effect.

The Overstrike mode is the opposite of the Insert mode. You turn on Overstrike by pressing the Ins key in the lower left corner of the numeric keyboard. In Overstrike mode, you can change characters or add spaces directly over the character or space where the cursor is positioned. Also, wordwrap is turned off in Overstrike mode. Whenever Overstrike mode is on, an Ovr indicator is displayed in the bottom right corner of your screen.

Using the Backspace key in both Insert and Overstrike modes erases the character to the left of the cursor. In Insert mode, however, characters to the right are shifted to the left when you press the Backspace key. In Overstrike mode, characters to the right remain in their original positions.

The real differences between entering text into a DOC window and typing text at a typewriter keyboard are noticeable when you use Symphony's word processor for performing many kinds of editing and formatting operations. These operations range from word-level changes, like correcting spelling, to much larger changes, such as moving blocks of text or transferring text from other files.

Moving the Cursor in a DOC Window

An essential part of performing many editing and formatting operations is being able to move the cursor within a DOC window. You will find cursor movement to be quite convenient when you are working not only in DOC mode as you enter and change text, but also in POINT mode when you are completing such commands as Copy, Move, and Erase.

Moving the cursor in a DOC window is similar to moving the cell pointer in a SHEET window; you use many of the same keys for both kinds of movements. You can use many more keys, however, to move the cursor in a DOC window.

The keys for moving the cursor in a DOC window include the following:

The cursor keys: ←, →, ↑, ↓
The PgUp and PgDn keys
The Home key
The End key
The Ctrl key (used only in combination with others)
The Scroll Lock key (used only in combination with others)
The F2 key (used with the End key)
The Alt + F2 keys (used with the End key)
The Enter key (used with the End key)
Any typed character (used with the End key)

Using these keys in a DOC window enables you to move the cursor from one character or space to another, from one word to another, from one line to another, from the beginning of the paragraph to the end (and vice versa), from one screen to another, and from the beginning of the window restrict range to the end (and vice versa). The sections that follow describe in detail each of these types of cursor movement.

A Character or Space at a Time

You may at times want to move the cursor backward or forward one character or space, particularly when you need to correct a misspelling in a previous word on the current line. The keys listed here are used for moving from one character to another:

To move the cursor:	*Use the following:*
To preceding character	←
To next character	→
To any specific character	End, then specific character

You will find the last option especially convenient when you want to move forward to a specific spot in your text. Although using the Search command is similar to using the End key and a specific character, the latter method saves you keystrokes. The Search command requires six keystrokes, including one to return to DOC mode; the End key followed by a character requires only two.

Suppose that you want to move the cursor forward to a sentence that ends with a question mark. If you use Search, you first retrieve the DOC menu by pressing the Menu key (F10) and then select Search. Next, you type the character (in this case, a question mark), press Enter, and then indicate whether the search should be Forward or Backward. Finally, after the cursor moves to the specific character, you select Quit to move out of MENU mode and back to DOC mode. With the End key, you accomplish the same operation by pressing End and then pressing the Shift and question-mark keys at the same time.

The End-key method is also convenient when you are highlighting a block for completing the Copy, Move, or Erase commands. For example, suppose that you want to erase the beginning of the second sentence shown in figure 8.7A, erasing from `Although` to the comma after `character`. To erase this part of the sentence, first place your cursor at the beginning of the sentence, then select the DOC Erase command or press the Erase key (F4). When the `Erase what block?` prompt appears, press End, then press the comma key (see fig. 8.7B), and finally press Enter.

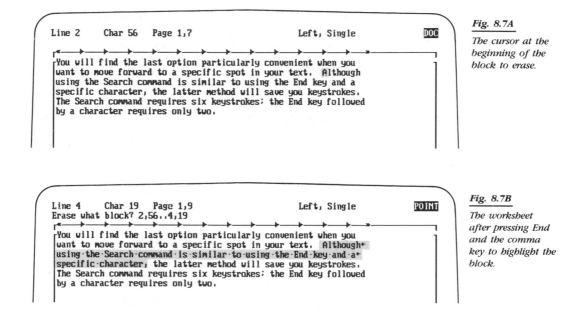

Fig. 8.7A

The cursor at the beginning of the block to erase.

Fig. 8.7B

The worksheet after pressing End and the comma key to highlight the block.

Search does, however, have several advantages over the End key. The Search command enables you to complete not only a forward but also a backward search. The End key followed by a character operates only for forward movement. The Search command can also search for words or phrases, while the End key can search for only one character. (For more information on the Search command, see this chapter's section called "Searching and Replacing.")

From Word to Word

Moving the cursor from the beginning of one word to the beginning of the next or preceding word is convenient when you want to move quickly to the middle of a line or to edit a character at the beginning or end of a word. The keys for moving the cursor from one word to another are listed here:

To move the cursor:	*Use the following:*
To the next word	Ctrl-→
To the preceding word	Ctrl-←

From Line to Line

Two types of cursor movement from one line to another are available in Symphony. These include moving the cursor from one line of text to another and moving the cursor from one format line to another.

To move the cursor:	*Use the following:*
One line up	↑
One line down	↓
One format line up	End then Alt-F2
One format line down	End then F2

To the Beginning and End of a Line

To move the cursor to the beginning or end of a line, use these keys:

To move the cursor:	*Use the following:*
To the beginning of a line	End then ←
To the end of a line	End then →

To the Beginning and End of a Paragraph

To move the cursor to the beginning or end of a paragraph, use the following keys:

To move the cursor:	*Use the following:*
To the beginning of a paragraph	End then ↑
To the end of a paragraph	End then ↓

Moving the cursor to the beginning or end of a paragraph is especially useful when you want to copy, erase, or move a whole paragraph. Suppose that you want to erase a paragraph. First, place the cursor at either the beginning or the end of the paragraph. If you place the cursor at the beginning of the paragraph, next press Erase (F4). Symphony asks, Erase what block? Press the End key and the ↓ key to highlight the paragraph; then press Enter.

From Screen to Screen

Sometimes you will want to move quickly to the previous or next screen. One thing to keep in mind when you use the keys listed here is that Symphony moves the cursor *exactly* one screen. A previous or later screen does not overlap (see figs. 8.8A and 8.8B).

To move the cursor: *Use the following:*

One window up   PgUp
One window down   PgDn

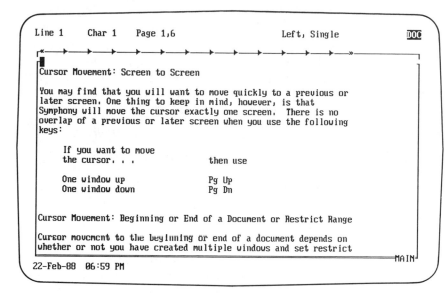

Fig. 8.8A

A screen display.

```
Line 1    Char 1    Page 1,6              Left, Single        DOC

Cursor Movement: Screen to Screen

You may find that you will want to move quickly to a previous or
later screen. One thing to keep in mind, however, is that
Symphony will move the cursor exactly one screen.  There is no
overlap of a previous or later screen when you use the following
keys:

        If you want to move
        the cursor. . .              then use

        One window up                Pg Up
        One window down              Pg Dn


Cursor Movement: Beginning or End of a Document or Restrict Range

Cursor movement to the beginning or end of a document depends on
whether or not you have created multiple windows and set restrict
                                                        MAIN
22-Feb-88  06:59 PM
```

Fig. 8.8B

*The display after
pressing PgDn.*

```
Line 21   Char 1    Page 1,26            Left, Single        DOC

ranges for the one document.  If, for example, you have created
only one DOC window in a particular file, then the keys listed
below will move the cursor to the beginning or end of the
document itself.

If, however, you have created two or more DOC windows each with
its own restrict range, the following keys will move the cursor
to the beginning or end of the Restrict range for the window.  On
the other hand, if you have created two or more windows, but
left the Restrict range setting to None, then the keys will move
the cursor to the beginning of the worksheet and end of the
document.

        If you want to move
        the cursor.  .  .             then use

        To upper left corner of a
        worksheet or Restrict range   Home

        To end of a document          End then Home
                                                        MAIN
14-Apr-88  01:57 PM
```

To the Beginning or End of a Document or Restrict Range

Cursor movement to the beginning or end of a document depends on whether you have created multiple windows and set restrict ranges for the document. If, for example, you have created only one DOC window in a particular file, then the keys listed after the next paragraph move the cursor to the beginning or end of the document itself.

If you have created two or more DOC windows, each with its own restrict range, these same keys move the cursor to the beginning or end of the restrict range for the window. On the other hand, if you have created two or more windows but left the restrict range setting to None, then the keys move the cursor to the beginning of the worksheet and the end of the document.

To move the cursor:	*Use the following:*
To upper left corner of a worksheet or restrict range	Home
To end of a document or restrict range	End then Home

To the Next Carriage Return

If you have hard carriage returns in your text, particularly in key places, such as at the ends of paragraphs or after headings, this method is useful for quickly moving the cursor to key spots in the text. For instance, you may want to highlight an area of text when you are using the Copy, Move, or Erase commands. To move the cursor to the next carriage return, press the End key and then press Enter.

To the Top of a Page and Next Page

When working with multipage documents, you will often want to move from one page to the next or to the top of the current page. You can use these keys:

To move the cursor:	*Use the following:*
To top of current page	Ctrl-PgUp
To next page	Ctrl-PgDn

To move to a specific page and line number, use the GoTo key as explained in the next section.

To Specific Lines and Page Numbers

In addition to using the keys previously listed for moving the cursor from one part of your text to another, you can use the GoTo key for jumping the cursor from one line to another or from one page to another. To move the cursor this way, first press the GoTo key (F5). Symphony asks, Go to where? In response, enter the line number to which you want to move the cursor. If your cursor is positioned at line 535 and you want to jump to line 555, type **555** and press Enter. You can also enter a page number when Symphony asks, Go to where?, but you must still include a line number. For example, to move to the top of page 10, press GoTo (F5) and then enter **10,6** at the prompt.

Using the GoTo key is particularly useful when you are comparing a printed copy of your text with the text on the screen. If, for example, you want to move the cursor to the middle of page 3, type **3**, a comma, and then the line number, which you determine by dividing the SERVICES **Print** Settings **Page** Length setting in half. If the setting is 66, you type **3,33** at the prompt.

To Named Lines

You can also use the GoTo key to move the cursor to lines you have named with the DOC **Line-Marker** command. You may want to create a line marker and name for every key point in your document—each major heading of a chapter, for example (see fig. 8.9).

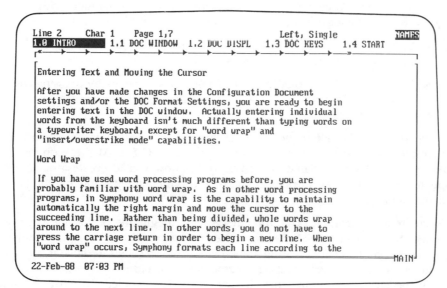

Fig. 8.9

Using line markers in a document.

Keeping a menu of line-marker names for key headings in a document has two applications. First, line-marker names enable you to move back and forth between sections by pressing the GoTo key and entering the name at the prompt (or pressing GoTo and F10, then moving the cursor to the name). Second, a menu of line-marker names can provide you with a key outline to your document (see fig. 8.10). If you create line-marker names for major headings of your text, you need to place numbers before the headings to keep them in their text order;

otherwise, Symphony organizes all names alphabetically. (Symphony orders numbers between 1 and 9, including those with one or more decimal places.)

Fig. 8.10

A menu of line-marker names.

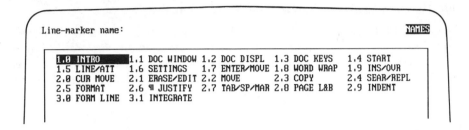

```
Line-marker name:                                                    NAMES

   1.0 INTRO      1.1 DOC WINDOW 1.2 DOC DISPL 1.3 DOC KEYS  1.4 START
   1.5 LINE/ATT   1.6 SETTINGS   1.7 ENTER/MOVE 1.8 WORD WRAP 1.9 INS/OVR
   2.0 CUR MOVE   2.1 ERASE/EDIT 2.2 MOVE       2.3 COPY      2.4 SEAR/REPL
   2.5 FORMAT     2.6 ¶ JUSTIFY  2.7 TAB/SP/MAR 2.8 PAGE L&B  2.9 INDENT
   3.0 FORM LINE  3.1 INTEGRATE
```

Here are some guidelines for creating and using line-marker names:

1. Line-marker names can contain up to 15 characters.

2. Names can consist of any type of characters and can include spaces.

3. Symphony stores names either alphabetically or by number, with numbers taking precedence over letters.

4. You can display a menu of line-marker names by pressing the GoTo key, then pressing the DOC menu key.

5. You can display a complete list of line-marker names by pressing the DOC menu key after line-marker names appear in the control panel (see fig. 8.10).

As illustrated in figure 8.9, when you establish a line marker and create a name, Symphony stores each name. In some ways the DOC Line-Marker command is like the SHEET **R**ange **N**ame command. Both allow you to create a name for a specific location on the worksheet and then use the name for moving the cursor to that location.

To create a line marker, place the cursor at the beginning of the line you want named. Next, select Line-Marker from the DOC menu. When the options appear, choose **A**ssign if you are creating a line-marker name; select **R**emove if you want to delete a name. When creating a name, you can either type a new name or move the cursor to a name that already exists. If you select an existing name, Symphony warns you that another line already has this name and asks whether you want to use the name here instead. If you select **Y**es, Symphony assigns that name to the line where the cursor is currently located. (See also the section entitled "Creating, Editing, and Storing Format Lines.")

Although range names have many other functions in spreadsheets, line-marker names are limited to these two primary functions:

1. Using line-marker names to find specific lines in your document; that is, pressing the GoTo key and then entering the line-marker name.

2. Using line-marker names to create a file of format lines, which you can store and then retrieve whenever you need to change a DOC window's format to a previously created format. If you store format lines in a separate file, you can use the SERVICES File Combine command to add these format lines into your text.

Erasing and Editing Text

As you become accustomed to processing text, you will find yourself juggling many of the following tasks: (1) entering words, sentences, and paragraphs on the screen; (2) correcting misspellings and typographical errors and making other word-level corrections; (3) organizing your sentences, paragraphs, and sections; and (4) editing your text to improve its development and organization.

Symphony's DOC environment enables you to handle all four of these tasks easily and efficiently by combining the cursor-movement keys; the format settings; and the Erase, Move, Copy, and Search commands. This section describes the tools Symphony provides for completing different types of editing and erasing tasks.

Erasing and Editing: Characters and Words

For the most part, simple editing consists of moving the cursor to a character or word and deleting, changing, or moving that character or word. To delete or change individual characters, use the cursor-movement keys, Backspace key, and Del key. The editing functions of the cursor keys and Backspace key depend on whether you are in Insert or Overstrike mode (see the earlier section entitled "Insert and Overstrike Modes").

To move individual characters, you can use the Move command from the DOC menu. In most cases, however, using the Move command for this purpose requires as many, if not more, keystrokes than are required for simply deleting the character, moving the cursor (in the Insert mode) to the right of where you want the character moved, and retyping the character. If you find that you often have to correct letter reversals, such as reversing the *i* and *e* in the misspelled word *recieve*, then you can create a simple macro that reverses letters for you whenever you invoke the macro. (See Chapter 19 for an explanation of how to create this macro.)

Erasing and Editing: Lines, Sentences, Paragraphs, and Groups of Words

When you have to erase or edit segments of text larger than individual characters, use the Copy, Move, and Erase commands from the DOC menu. These commands, combined with the various cursor-movement keys, make your job of changing and correcting text quite easy. You can use these cursor-movement keys to high-light the area you want erased, moved, or copied:

Use the following:	*To highlight:*
Space bar	A word
End →	A line
End, then the end punctuation of the sentence (. ? !)	A sentence (that doesn't contain these marks inside the sentence)
End ↓	A paragraph or portion of text from anywhere in a paragraph to the end of the paragraph
End, then Home	A section that ends with the end of your text or the end of the window's restrict range

The Erase Command and Key

When you need to erase a group of words; one or more lines, sentences, or paragraphs; or larger segments of text; the DOC Erase command and the Erase key (F4) make the procedure easy. Erase also enables you to delete format lines and print attributes from the text. When you use Erase, keep the following points in mind:

1. Only the *last* block you erase can be restored with the Paste key (Ctrl-P). See the section on "Unerasing Text."

2. Because the Erase command can erase data outside the DOC window area in which you are working, be careful when you specify the block to be erased. To prevent erasing data accidentally, set a restrict range for your DOC window and make sure that the restrict range doesn't overlap data that you don't want changed.

3. You can place the cursor at either the beginning or end of the block you want to erase.

4. If **Auto-Justify** is turned on, Symphony automatically justifies paragraphs after you complete the Erase operation.

The procedure for erasing blocks of text requires four steps. First, position the cursor at the beginning or end of the block you want to erase. Second, initiate the Erase command by pressing the Erase key or selecting **Erase** from the DOC menu. Third, highlight the block you want to erase by moving the cursor to the end or back to the beginning of the block. (See the list in the preceding section for ways to highlight blocks.) Fourth, press Enter.

If you are erasing a format line, Symphony automatically highlights the whole line. You cannot erase, move, or copy only part of a format line.

Accelerator Keys for Deleting Text

Instead of pressing the Erase key (F4) and highlighting the area you want erased, you can use accelerator keys to delete words, lines, or parts of lines.

Use the following:	To delete:
Ctrl-Backspace	Word to left of cursor
Ctrl-D	Current line
Ctrl-T	From cursor to left end of line
Ctrl-Y	From cursor to right end of line

Unerasing Text

Because Symphony stores the last text you deleted in a temporary storage area called the "clipboard," you can retrieve accidentally deleted text. The Paste accelerator key (Ctrl-P) pastes the clipboard contents back into your document at the cursor location. You should remember two important points about unerasing text: (1) Symphony can restore only the most previously deleted text, and (2) text deleted with the Backspace or Del key is not stored in the clipboard and thus cannot be retrieved.

Moving Text within the Same File

The **Move** command from the DOC menu enables you to move characters, words, sentences, or larger blocks of text to any area within the DOC window's restrict range if a restrict range is set, or within the worksheet if the restrict range is set to **None**. Be careful, however, when you are using the Move command, because it can affect data in other windows.

Follow these guidelines when using Move:

1. The area where you are moving TO must be within the DOC window's restrict range. If, for example, you are moving 20 lines of text to the end of your present text located at line 590, and you have set your restrict range at 600, Symphony displays the message Not enough room in the Restrict range. To correct this problem, change SERVICES Window Settings Restrict.

2. Whenever you move text to an area within other text, Symphony moves all existing text down. Symphony also automatically justifies the text, if DOC Format Settings Auto-Justify is set to **Yes**. Otherwise, you must justify the text by pressing the Justify key (F2) or using the DOC Justify command.

3. Using the **Move** command can affect data entered in other types of windows on the same worksheet. For example, a spreadsheet entered below the DOC window area can be affected by Move if you do not restrict the range for the DOC window.

4. When you use the DOC **Move** command, it does not overwrite other data, as does the SHEET **Move** command.

With these guidelines in mind, you will find that using the **Move** command is fairly easy. To move any portion of text, you must position the cursor at the beginning of the text you want moved (see fig. 8.11A). Then select **Move** from the DOC menu or press the Move accelerator key (Ctrl-M). When `Move FROM what block?` appears, indicate the area to be moved by highlighting it with the cursor (see fig. 8.11B).

After you indicate the move FROM area, next indicate where to move TO by moving the cursor to the place you want the text to begin. Then press Enter. If DOC **Format Settings Auto-Justify** is set to **No**, you may need to justify the paragraph by pressing the Justify key or selecting **Justify** from the DOC menu (see fig. 8.11C).

Fig. 8.11A

The cursor at the beginning of the block to move.

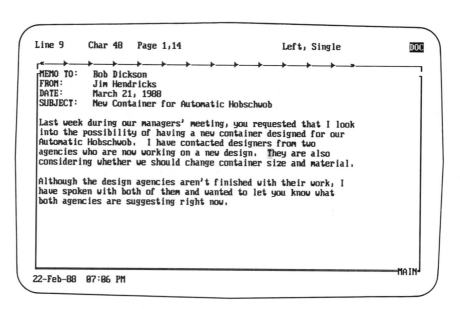

```
Line 9     Char 48    Page 1,14              Left, Single        DOC

MEMO TO:   Bob Dickson
FROM:      Jim Hendricks
DATE:      March 21, 1988
SUBJECT:   New Container for Automatic Hobschwob

Last week during our managers' meeting, you requested that I look
into the possibility of having a new container designed for our
Automatic Hobschwob.  I have contacted designers from two
agencies who are now working on a new design.  They are also
considering whether we should change container size and material.

Although the design agencies aren't finished with their work, I
have spoken with both of them and wanted to let you know what
both agencies are suggesting right now.




                                                              MAIN
22-Feb-88  07:06 PM
```

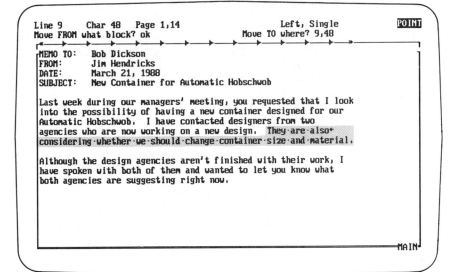

Fig. 8.11B

The worksheet after highlighting the block.

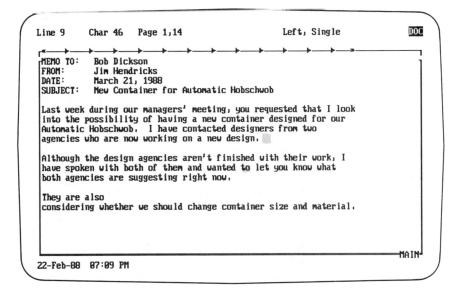

Fig. 8.11C

The worksheet after moving the text.

If you want to move text to an area in another DOC window, when the Move TO where? prompt appears, press the Window key (F6). You may need to press the Window key several times until the window to where you want the text moved appears. Once the cursor is positioned in the correct window, move the cursor to the place where the text should begin. Press Enter to complete the move operation.

Another way of moving text is to erase it from the original location, place the cursor where you want to move the text, and then paste it with the Paste accelerator key (Ctrl-P). Just be careful that you don't erase any additional text before pasting the text you want restored; as you may recall, only the last deleted text is stored in the clipboard.

Copying Text within the Same File

Copy, the first command on the DOC menu, enables you to copy characters, words, lines, or larger blocks of text to another blank area of the worksheet. Following are a few guidelines for using the Copy command:

1. The area to which you are copying must be within the DOC window's restrict range, and the restrict range should be large enough to accommodate the copied text. When you execute the Copy command, text following the copied portion moves down; enough room should be available within the restrict range for the text to move down.

2. After you copy text to another part of the window, Symphony automatically justifies the text and all the following paragraphs if DOC Format Settings Auto-Justify is set to Yes. Otherwise, you must justify the text by pressing the Justify key (F2) or selecting the DOC Justify command.

3. Using the Copy command can affect data entered in other types of windows on the same worksheet. For example, a spreadsheet entered below the DOC window area can be affected by Copy if you do not restrict the range for the DOC window.

4. When you use the DOC Copy command, it does not overwrite other data, as does the SHEET Copy command.

To copy any portion of text, position the cursor at the beginning of the text to be copied. Then select Copy from the DOC menu or press the Copy accelerator key (Ctrl-C). When Copy FROM what block? appears, indicate the area to be copied by moving the cursor (see fig. 8.12A).

After you indicate the copy FROM area, next indicate where to copy TO by moving the cursor to the place you want the copied text to begin (see fig. 8.12B). Then press Enter. If DOC Format Settings Auto-Justify is set to No, you may need to justify the paragraph by pressing the Justify key or by selecting Justify from the DOC menu (see fig. 8.12C).

If you need additional copies of the same text, you can paste them in with the Paste accelerator key (Ctrl-P), because copied text is stored in the clipboard. After you make your first copy with the Copy command, place the cursor where you want the next copy to go, and press Ctrl-P. Continue until you have made all the copies you need.

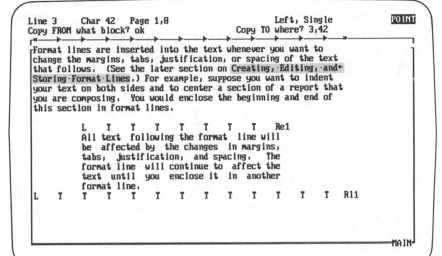

Fig. 8.12A

Highlighting the block to be copied.

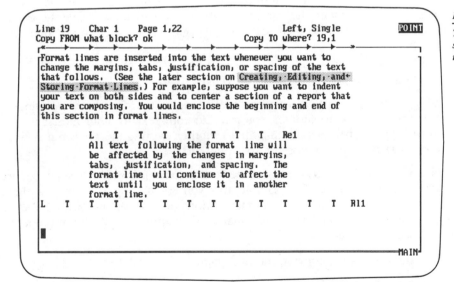

Fig. 8.12B

The cursor at the spot where the text is to be copied.

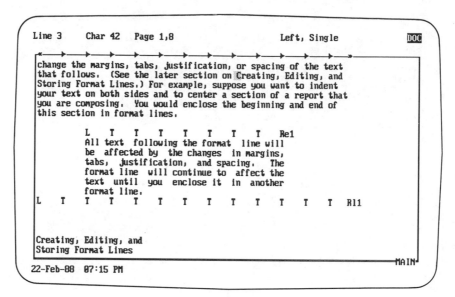

Fig. 8.12C

The worksheet after copying the text.

If you want to copy to an area in another DOC window, when the `Copy TO where?` prompt appears, press the Window key (F6). You may need to press the Window key a few times until the window in which you want the text to be copied appears. Once the cursor is in the correct window, move the cursor to the place where the copied text should begin. Press Enter to complete the copy operation.

Copying Text from One File to Another

In addition to copying text from one area to another within the same window or from one window to another, you can also copy text to other files. You may want to copy text from an existing file to another existing file. Or you may want to copy text from an existing file to a new file.

For copying text from one file to another existing file, follow the first procedure described here. Suppose, for example, that you are writing a letter to a client to promote a new product your company is introducing (see fig. 8.13A). As you begin writing the letter, you realize that a paragraph from text in another file will fit well into your letter.

Follow these steps for copying the paragraph into your letter:

1. Using SERVICES File **S**ave, save the current worksheet that contains the beginning of the letter to the client.

2. Using SERVICES File **R**etrieve, retrieve the file that contains the paragraph you want to copy into the letter.

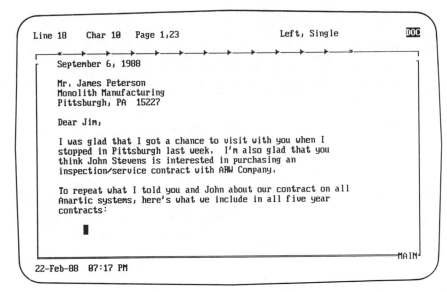

Fig. 8.13A
A sample letter.

3. When the worksheet for the second file appears, move your cursor to the paragraph you want to copy (see fig. 8.13B).

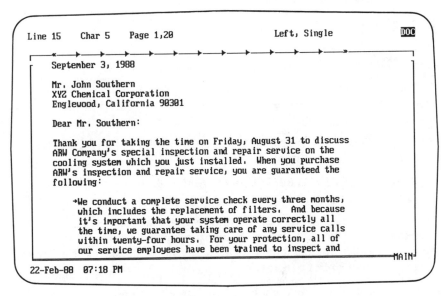

Fig. 8.13B
Placing the cursor at the beginning of the text to copy.

4. Switch from a DOC to a SHEET window by pressing the Type key (Alt-F10) and selecting SHEET.

5. Retrieve the SHEET command menu, select **Range**, then select **Name Create** (see Chapter 4's section called "Creating Range Names").

6. Enter a range name for the paragraph when the Range name: prompt appears.

7. Indicate the range for the paragraph you want to copy. Notice that in SHEET mode, word-processing text appears as long labels originating in column A (see fig. 8.13C).

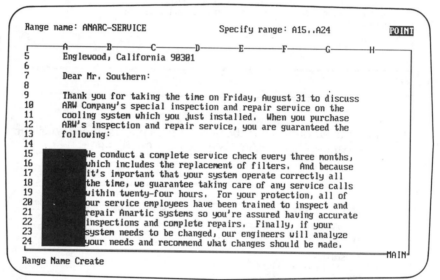

Fig. 8.13C

Text as long labels in SHEET mode.

```
Range name: ANARC-SERVICE          Specify range: A15..A24        POINT
   A        B        C        D        E        F        G        H
 5            Englewood, California 90301
 6
 7            Dear Mr. Southern:
 8
 9            Thank you for taking the time on Friday, August 31 to discuss
10            ARW Company's special inspection and repair service on the
11            cooling system which you just installed.  When you purchase
12            ARW's inspection and repair service, you are guaranteed the
13            following:
14
15            We conduct a complete service check every three months,
16            which includes the replacement of filters.  And because
17            it's important that your system operate correctly all
18            the time, we guarantee taking care of any service calls
19            within twenty-four hours.  For your protection, all of
20            our service employees have been trained to inspect and
21            repair Anartic systems so you're assured having accurate
22            inspections and complete repairs.  Finally, if your
23            system needs to be changed, our engineers will analyze
24            your needs and recommend what changes should be made.
                                                                MAIN
Range Name Create
```

8. Using SERVICES **File** **S**ave, save the file with the same name it had when you retrieved it.

9. Using SERVICES **File** **R**etrieve, retrieve the file containing the letter into which you want to copy the paragraph.

10. Place the cursor at the beginning of where you want to copy the paragraph. Make sure enough blank space is below the cursor to accommodate the paragraph. Otherwise, the paragraph will overwrite existing text (see fig. 8.13D).

11. Select SERVICES **File** Combine Copy Named-Area and type in the range name for the paragraph.

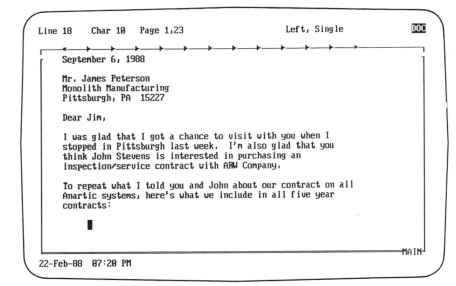

Fig. 8.13D
The cursor at the
spot where the text
is to be copied.

12. Next, indicate whether you want to preserve line markers in the paragraph text.

13. Select the file where the paragraph is stored and press Enter.

The paragraph should now be copied into your letter (see fig. 8.13E).

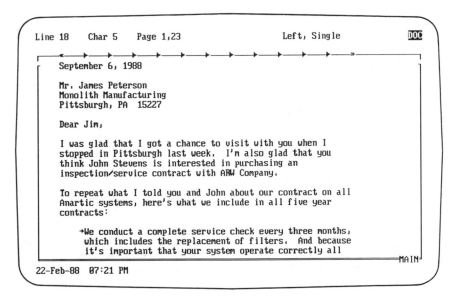

Fig. 8.13E
The worksheet
after copying the
paragraph into the
letter.

If you find that you frequently copy a particular section of text from one file to another, you may want to create a separate file for that special section of text. Copying a section of text involves using the SERVICES File **X**tract command and requires the following steps:

1. To copy a section of text, retrieve the file containing the text you want to copy (use SERVICES File **R**etrieve) and place the cursor at the beginning of that text.

2. Select the File **X**tract command from the SERVICES menu.

3. If you are *not* extracting any spreadsheet data, press Enter at the Preserve Formulas prompt.

4. When the Xtract file name: prompt appears, enter a name for the new file to which you want the text copied.

5. Indicate the range of the text you want copied and press Enter.

Your section of text is then copied into the new file. (If you don't supply an extension, Symphony uses .WR1.) Whenever you want to copy this text into another document, use the SERVICES File **C**ombine command described earlier in this section. If you are copying the entire file into your current file, select SERVICES File **C**ombine **C**opy and then **E**ntire-File rather than **N**amed-Area.

As with many Symphony word-processing operations, you can also create macros for the copy operations described in this section (see Chapter 19).

Moving Text to a Document in Another File

To move text to a document in another file, use the procedure described in the previous section—with one additional step. After you copy a block from one file to another, you can then delete the original block.

Searching and Replacing

One distinguishing feature of word-processing programs is their search-and-replace capabilities. Programs differ in their speed for completing search-and-replace operations, in the options available for performing these operations, and in the ease of using them. In most respects, Symphony's search-and-replace capabilities compare favorably to similar capabilities of many sophisticated word-processing programs.

Symphony, for example, provides both forward and backward search, performs search-and-replace operations quickly, and makes using search-and-replace operations quite easy. **S**earch and **R**eplace are separate commands located in Symphony's DOC menu. You can invoke these commands with the accelerator keys (Ctrl-S and Ctrl-R) as well.

You can search for and replace the following types of strings entered in a DOC window:

- A single character, including those characters in the Lotus International Character set, such as *a, 4, &, ∗*

- A cluster of characters (for example, prefixes and suffixes such as *ed*), with no cluster containing more than 50 characters and spaces

- A single word

- Groups of words and characters, with no group containing more than a total of 50 characters and spaces

- Symphony's word-processing symbols, such as carriage returns, spaces, tabs, and page breaks

You can search for and replace the following word-processing symbols (note that you must enclose each symbol in backslashes):

Special symbol:	*Symphony finds:*
\~\	A carriage return character
\^\	A tab character
\:\	A page break character
\-\	A space, tab, or hard space

For example, if you want to add a tab at the beginning of each paragraph, you can search for \~\ (a carriage return, which precedes each paragraph) and replace it with \~\\^\ (a carriage return and a tab).

You can also use wildcards in the search-and-replacement string if you don't know what character appears in a single character position. For example, if you type **Sm\?\th** as the search string, Symphony finds Smith, Smythe, or Smathers. (Note that, as with the word-processing symbols, you must enclose each wildcard in backslashes.) The basic wildcard is \?\, which finds any character in the indicated position, but additional wildcards are available to narrow down the search to either a letter or number:

Wildcard string:	*Symphony finds:*
\?\	Any character
\&\	Any letter or number
\a\	Any letter
\A\	Any uppercase letter
\#\	Any number

When the string to be searched for is composed of words, the search is affected by whether you enter the words in upper- or lowercase.

If you search for:	*Symphony finds:*
1. All lowercase	Any combination of upper- and lowercase letters
Example: tutorial program	tutorial program Tutorial Program Tutorial program
2. Initial letter capitalized	Initial letter capitalized, but other letters can be either uppercase or lowercase
Example: Tutorial Program	Tutorial Program
3. All uppercase	Only all uppercase
Example: TUTORIAL PROGRAM	TUTORIAL PROGRAM

When you are searching once for a single character and you are performing a forward search, use the End key and then type the character. If, however, you want to search for more than one occurrence, or if you want to search backward for a single character, you need to use the DOC Search command. Although the Search command performs both forward and backward searches, the Replace command searches for and replaces a string only by working forward through the text. To overcome this limitation, you can create a simple macro that automatically moves the cursor to the beginning of your document and initiates the Replace command. (See Chapter 19 for more information on creating macros.)

The Search Command

If you follow the guidelines provided in the previous discussion, you will find the Search command quite easy to use. To begin the search, retrieve the DOC menu and select Search, or press the Search accelerator key (Ctrl-S). When the prompt Search for what? appears, enter the string you want Symphony to find and press Enter. Symphony then provides the following options for searching the text:

Forward   Backward   Quit

Select either of the first two options to initiate the document search. When Symphony finds the first occurrence of the string, the cursor highlights the string. At this point, you have two options. You can continue the search by selecting either Forward or Backward, or you can select Quit. When you select Quit, the cursor remains at the string's location so that you can edit, move, or delete the string. If you press Ctrl-Break before you select **Quit**, the cursor moves back to where it was when you initiated the **Search** command.

If Symphony cannot find the string in the direction you indicated, `String not found` displays in the bottom left corner of your screen. You can then select **Forward** or **Backward** to begin the search in the opposite direction, or choose **Quit** to move from MENU mode back to DOC mode.

The Replace Command

To use the **Replace** command, you must either retrieve the DOC menu and select **Replace**, or press the Replace accelerator key (Ctrl-R). When the prompt `Replace what?` appears, enter the string you want Symphony to replace and press Enter. Symphony then asks, `Replace it with what?` Enter the replacement string and press Enter.

At this point, Symphony begins the search for the first occurrence of the string, conducting a forward search from the cursor to the end of the document. If Symphony does not find the string, the program displays `String not found` in the bottom left corner of the screen and returns you to the `Replace what?` prompt. But if Symphony finds the first occurrence of the string, the following menu appears:

    Once   Continue   Skip   All-Remaining   Quit

If you select **Once**, Symphony replaces the string and returns to DOC mode. If you select **Continue**, Symphony replaces the string and searches for the next occurrence of the string. When the next occurrence is found, Symphony again waits for you to respond by selecting any of the items from the menu. If you select **Skip**, Symphony skips over the string and searches for the next occurrence. When you select **All-Remaining**, Symphony finds and replaces every occurrence of the string, beginning at the cursor's position and finishing at the end of the document. After completing the search-and-replace operation, Symphony displays `No more occurrences found`. Select **Quit** from the menu to return to DOC mode.

Formatting Your Document

For text entered in Symphony's DOC window, you can set the format in three ways. First, you can control format through the SERVICES Configuration Document settings. Second, you can control format through **Format Settings** in the DOC menu. Third, you can control format by creating format lines within the DOC window.

The three formatting methods, including the effects they have on one another, were discussed earlier in the section entitled "Format Settings." This section describes the different kinds of format commands and how they affect text as it appears on the screen and as it is printed.

Setting Paragraph Justification

You can set and regulate paragraph justification in a number of ways. The Justification setting, in both the SERVICES Configuration Document and the DOC Format Settings menus, controls paragraph justification within each window. Remember that Format Settings override Configuration Document settings. In the DOC window in a worksheet, however, format settings are inherited from the Configuration Document settings of the SERVICES menu. Whatever Justification setting is in effect in a format line or Format Settings controls automatic justification when turned on, and controls the changes made when you invoke the Justify key (F2) and the DOC Justify command.

The Justification Settings

You can control justification with the DOC Format Settings Justification command or with the Justification setting for a format line. DOC Format Settings Justification can be determined by either SERVICES Configuration Document Justification, by the DOC Format Settings Justification of a previously created DOC window, or by you.

The Justification setting for a format line, on the other hand, is determined by you if you are creating a new format line or editing one. Also, the Justification setting for a format line can be determined by DOC Format Settings Justification whenever you choose to reset a format line to the DOC Format Settings. In any case, when you want to change justification, you are given the following four options:

None   Left   Even   Center

Whatever option is set in DOC Format Settings Justification controls justification for your DOC window unless you create a format line within the text. If you do, the format line overrides Format Settings Justification. Keep in mind the differences between DOC Format Settings and format lines.

If you change DOC Format Settings Justification after you have entered text, the setting affects all text except that preceded by a format line. For example, the DOC Format Settings Justification setting for the text shown in figure 8.14 is Left. All paragraphs in the text have the same format, so no format lines are entered. If you change DOC Format Settings Justification to Even, the justification automatically changes throughout the text (see fig. 8.15).

If, however, the original text contains a format line, as in figure 8.16, changing DOC Format Settings Justification affects all text except the text after the format line (see fig. 8.17).

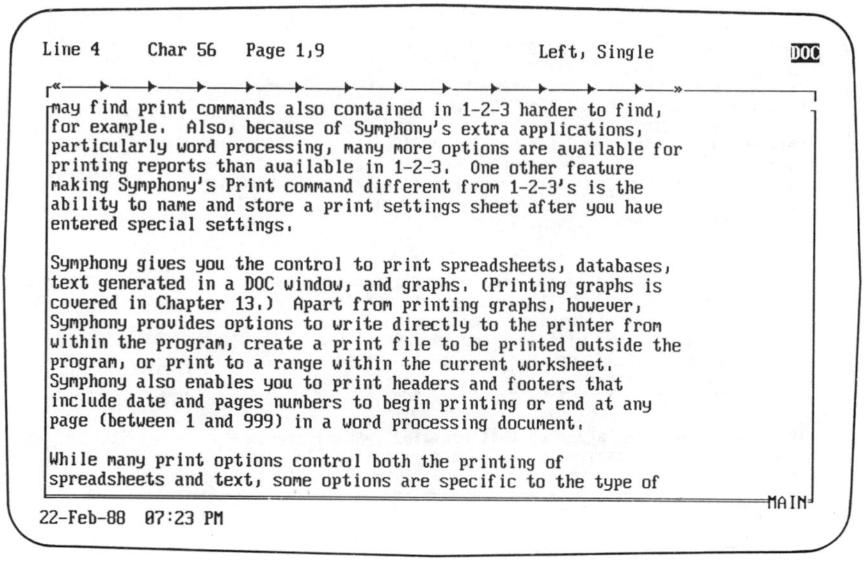

```
Line 4      Char 56    Page 1,9              Left, Single        DOC
r«──▸──▸──▸──▸──▸──▸──▸──▸──▸──▸──▸──▸──»─┐
may find print commands also contained in 1-2-3 harder to find,
for example.  Also, because of Symphony's extra applications,
particularly word processing, many more options are available for
printing reports than available in 1-2-3.  One other feature
making Symphony's Print command different from 1-2-3's is the
ability to name and store a print settings sheet after you have
entered special settings.

Symphony gives you the control to print spreadsheets, databases,
text generated in a DOC window, and graphs. (Printing graphs is
covered in Chapter 13.) Apart from printing graphs, however,
Symphony provides options to write directly to the printer from
within the program, create a print file to be printed outside the
program, or print to a range within the current worksheet.
Symphony also enables you to print headers and footers that
include date and pages numbers to begin printing or end at any
page (between 1 and 999) in a word processing document.

While many print options control both the printing of
spreadsheets and text, some options are specific to the type of
                                                    ─MAIN─
22-Feb-88  07:23 PM
```

Fig. 8.14

Text formatted with DOC Format Settings Justification Left.

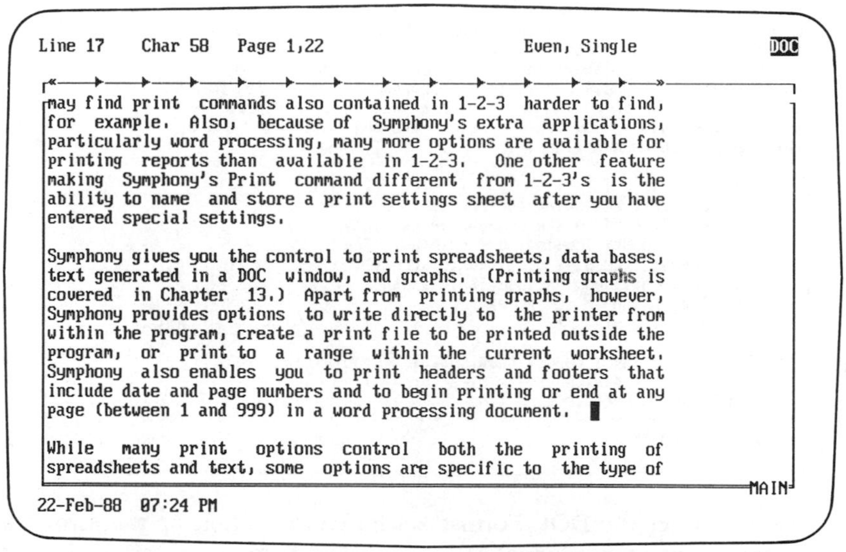

```
Line 17     Char 58    Page 1,22             Even, Single        DOC
r«──▸──▸──▸──▸──▸──▸──▸──▸──▸──▸──▸──▸──»─┐
may find print  commands also contained in 1-2-3  harder to find,
for  example.  Also,  because of  Symphony's extra  applications,
particularly word processing, many more options are available for
printing  reports than  available  in 1-2-3.   One other  feature
making  Symphony's Print  command different  from 1-2-3's  is the
ability to name  and store a print settings sheet  after you have
entered special settings.

Symphony gives you the control to print spreadsheets, data bases,
text generated in a DOC  window, and graphs.  (Printing graphs is
covered  in Chapter  13.) Apart from  printing graphs,  however,
Symphony provides options  to write directly to  the printer from
within the program, create a print file to be printed outside the
program,  or  print to  a  range  within the  current  worksheet.
Symphony  also enables  you  to print  headers  and  footers that
include date and page numbers and to begin printing or end at any
page (between 1 and 999) in a word processing document. ▮

While   many  print   options  control   both  the   printing  of
spreadsheets and text, some  options are specific to  the type of
                                                    ─MAIN─
22-Feb-88  07:24 PM
```

Fig. 8.15

The setting changed to Even.

Fig. 8.16

Adding a format line.

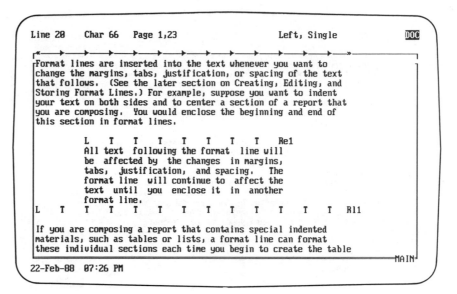

Fig. 8.16

Adding a format line.

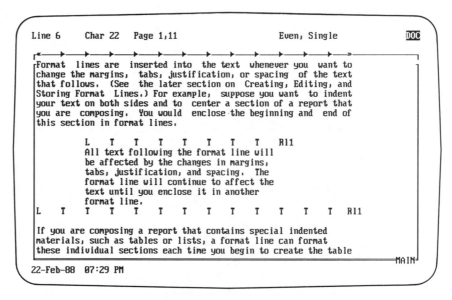

Fig. 8.17

Unaffected format line setting.

When you set either the DOC Format Settings Justification or the format line at None, text no longer wordwraps as you type. Automatic justification, the Justify key, and the Justify command are turned off. When all three are inactive, entering text on the screen is like entering text at a typewriter. You can continue typing to the right-margin limit. In a Symphony DOC window, this limit is a total of 240 characters and spaces.

With the Justification None setting, you control the carriage return and can thus format the section of text however you want. But if you change the Justification setting from None to Left, Even, or Center, then all text, except text following format lines, is changed.

Left is the default setting in SERVICES Configuration Document Justification. When Justification is set to Left in DOC Format Settings or in a format line, text is left-justified against either the default margin (1) or your margin setting. When the Justification setting is Left, lines on the right are ragged (see fig. 8.18).

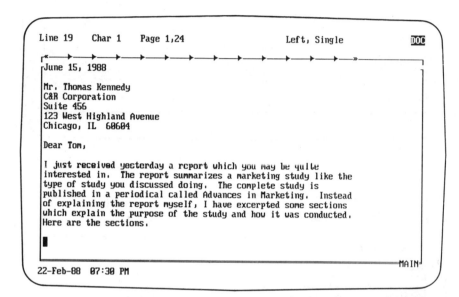

```
Line 19    Char 1    Page 1,24              Left, Single           DOC

June 15, 1988

Mr. Thomas Kennedy
C&R Corporation
Suite 456
123 West Highland Avenue
Chicago, IL  60604

Dear Tom,

I just received yesterday a report which you may be quite
interested in.  The report summarizes a marketing study like the
type of study you discussed doing.  The complete study is
published in a periodical called Advances in Marketing.  Instead
of explaining the report myself, I have excerpted some sections
which explain the purpose of the study and how it was conducted.
Here are the sections.



22-Feb-88  07:30 PM                                              MAIN
```

Fig. 8.18

Left-justified text with ragged-right margin.

When you use the Justification Even setting, Symphony justifies text along both the left and right margins (see fig. 8.19). To justify the text on both sides, Symphony enters extra spaces within each line. In documents where the lines are short, Even justification may leave a number of large spaces within the text (see fig. 8.20).

Center, which is the last option for Justification, centers every line of text according to the left and right margins controlling the section of the document (see fig. 8.21).

While the Justification command controls the paragraph alignment, the Auto-Justify command determines whether the paragraphs are automatically or manually refitted into the margins after you make editing changes.

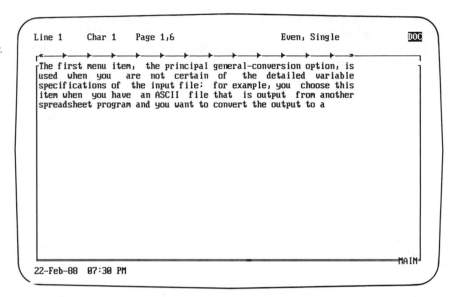

Fig. 8.19

Even-justified text.

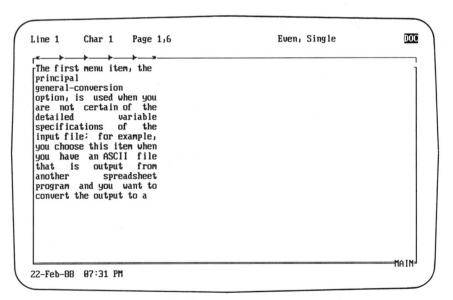

Fig. 8.20

Even-justified text with short lines.

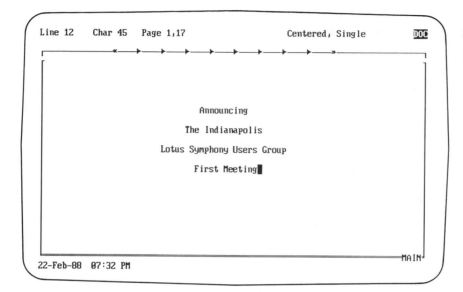

Fig. 8.21
The Justification Center setting.

The figure shows a DOC window containing:

```
Line 12    Char 45   Page 1,17              Centered, Single      DOC

                           Announcing

                         The Indianapolis

                   Lotus Symphony Users Group

                          First Meeting

22-Feb-88  07:32 PM                                          MAIN
```

Automatic Justification

You can set paragraph justification to automatic or manual. The default setting is automatic, set with SERVICES Configuration Document Auto-Justify Yes. The Auto-Justify setting in Format Settings of the DOC menu inherits the default setting. You can override the SERVICES Configuration Document Auto-Justify setting by changing the setting in DOC Format Settings or by pressing the Auto accelerator key (Ctrl-J).

Whenever DOC Format Settings Auto-Justify is set to Yes, paragraphs are automatically justified when you disturb the original justification by using any of the word-processing commands (for example, Copy, Erase, Move, or Replace) or by inserting or deleting text. Paragraphs are justified according to the margin settings and justification settings that control margins—either DOC Format Settings or a format line. If you change the margins or justification manually for any part of your text, the Auto-Justify setting can affect that text, changing it to the margins and justification controlling the text around that portion.

The Justify Command and Key

As mentioned earlier, the Justify key, Justify command, and Auto-Justify command operate according to the justification setting controlling a section of text. If you have turned off auto-justification, you must justify paragraphs or larger units of text by using the Justify key (F2) or the Justify command from the DOC menu. Suppose that you want to erase the second sentence of the paragraph shown in figure 8.22A. If auto-justification is turned off, then after you erase the sentence, you need to press Justify (see fig. 8.22B).

Fig. 8.22A

Erasing text with auto-justification turned off.

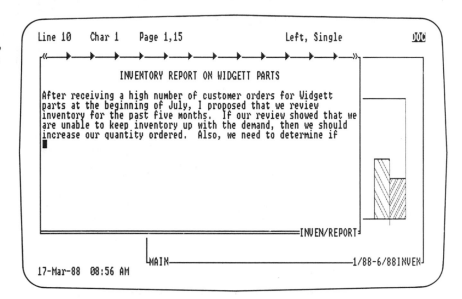

Fig. 8.22B

The worksheet after text is erased.

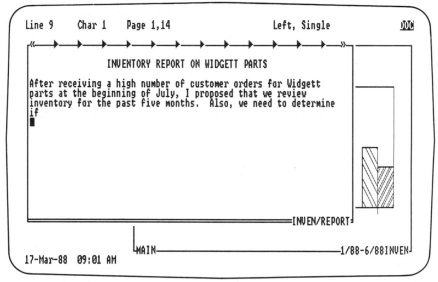

The **J**ustify command in the DOC menu is different from the Justify key in one respect. When you select DOC **J**ustify, you have two choices: **P**aragraph and **A**ll-Remaining. Selecting **P**aragraph performs the same operations that are performed by the Justify key. Selecting All-Remaining justifies not only the paragraph where the cursor is located but all following paragraphs to the end of the document.

Setting Tabs, Spacing, and Margins

As with justification, you can regulate the tab, spacing, and margin settings by entering new settings in the Configuration Document settings of the SERVICES menu, in the Format Settings of the DOC menu, or in a format line. For all three types of settings, the options for changing tabs, spacing, and margins are the same. Also, the effect of one type of setting on another (for example, the effect of DOC Format Settings on SERVICES Configuration Document settings) is the same as that mentioned earlier for Justification.

If you want to modify the tab setting, you can change the default setting of 5 (SERVICES Configuration Document Tabs), change the tab setting for a specific DOC window (DOC Format Settings Tabs), or change the tab setting for a section of text by creating a format line (DOC Format Create or Edit). With the SERVICES Configuration Document Tabs command or the DOC Format Settings Tabs command, you can set the interval between tab stops to any number between 1 and 240, whereas with the DOC Format Create or Edit command, you can set tab stops wherever you like. (See the section on "Creating, Editing, and Storing Format Lines" for specific information on setting and clearing tabs in a format line.)

Tab settings are indicated in the top line of the standard border of a DOC window by right arrows positioned between the left and right margin indicators. In a format line, a tab setting is indicated with a T.

The default setting for spacing is 1 (single). You can, however, change spacing to double or triple in the SERVICES Configuration Document Spacing settings, in the DOC Format Settings Spacing command, or in a format line. Whenever you change from single-spacing to double- or triple-spacing, Symphony does not display either double- or triple-spacing on the screen, but the correct spacing is apparent when you print the document (see figs. 8.23A and 8.23B). Spacing is one of the few settings that control print format but not the screen display.

Even though double- or triple-spacing does not appear on the screen, Symphony still counts your lines according to the spacing you set. The page and line number in the control panel reflect the accurate printed page and line number of the cursor position. If double-spacing is set, the line number increments by two as you move the cursor down a line on your screen (for example, from Page 1,6 to Page 1,8). The control panel also indicates the spacing with Single, Double, or Triple.

The margin settings, indicated as Left and Right on the command menus of SERVICES Configuration Document and DOC Format Settings, are displayed in the top line of the standard DOC border as two less-than and two greater-than

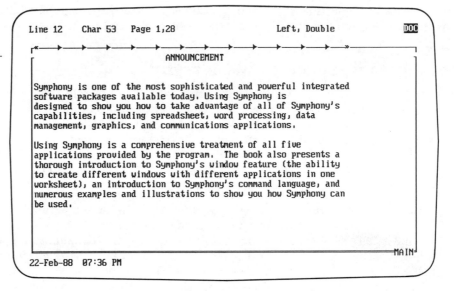

Fig. 8.23A

How double-spacing appears on-screen.

Fig. 8.23B

Printed document with double-spacing.

```
                              ANNOUNCEMENT



    Symphony is one of the most sophisticated and powerful

    integrated software packages available today.  Using Symphony is

    designed to show you how to take advantage of all of Symphony's

    capabilities, including spreadsheet, word processing, data

    management, graphics, and communications applications.


    Using Symphony is a comprehensive treatment of all five

    applications provided by the program.  The book also presents a

    thorough introduction to Symphony's window feature (the ability

    to create different windows with different applications in one

    worksheet), an introduction to Symphony's command language, and

    numerous examples and illustrations to show you how Symphony can

    be used.
```

signs ($\ll$ and $\gg$). In a format line, margins are indicated by the L and R indicators on each side of the line (see fig. 8.24).

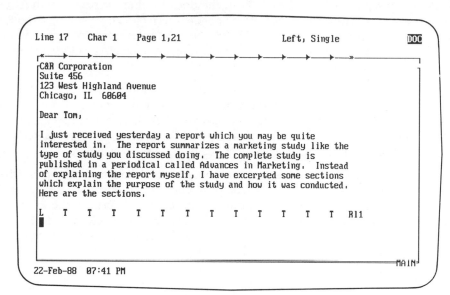

Fig. 8.24

Margins indicated on top border line and format lines.

If you want to set margins in either SERVICES **C**onfiguration **D**ocument or DOC Format **S**ettings, select **L**eft or **R**ight from the appropriate menu. When you are changing the left margin, Symphony displays the prompt `Default Left Margin:`. At this prompt, enter a figure between 1 and 240. To change the right margin, select **R**ight. Two other options then appear: **S**et and **R**eset. Use **S**et when you want to enter a right margin between 1 and 240. Use **R**eset when you want the right margin adjusted to the width of the DOC window in which you are working.

See the section entitled "Creating, Editing, and Storing Format Lines" for instructions on setting left and right margins in a format line.

The left margin on your screen may be different from the left margin on printed pages. Here's how left margin settings for screen and print affect one another. If you have set the left margin for text on the screen to 1 and the left margin print setting to 4, Symphony prints a left margin of 5. In other words, Symphony adds the DOC left margin setting to the left margin setting for print (see Chapter 11 for an explanation of print commands).

Controlling Page Length and Page Breaks

Two settings in the SERVICE menu are available for controlling the number of lines of text for each printed page. First, the default value for page length is set in SERVICES Configuration Printer Page-Length. This page-length setting is stored in Symphony's configuration file (SYMPHONY.CNF). Second, you can change page length for any document you are creating by changing SERVICES Print Settings Page Length.

SERVICES Print Settings Page Length overrides SERVICES Configuration Printer Page-Length for the particular window in which you are working. If you do not change SERVICES Print Settings Page Length, the page-length setting is inherited from either SERVICES Configuration or the SERVICES Print Settings created for another window in the same worksheet.

In the control panel, Symphony displays the page and line number where the cursor is positioned (see fig. 8.25). The page and line numbers are determined by the setting in SERVICES Print Settings Page Length. Consider the example shown in figure 8.25. If the setting for SERVICES Print Settings Page Length is 66, Symphony displays Page 12,51 in the control panel. If you change the page-length setting to 33, however, Symphony then displays Page 29,23.

Fig. 8.25

Page and line number displayed in control panel.

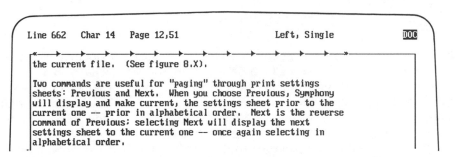

```
Line 662    Char 14    Page 12,51              Left, Single        DOC

the current file,  (See figure 8,X),

Two commands are useful for "paging" through print settings
sheets: Previous and Next,  When you choose Previous, Symphony
will display and make current, the settings sheet prior to the
current one -- prior in alphabetical order,  Next is the reverse
command of Previous; selecting Next will display the next
settings sheet to the current one -- once again selecting in
alphabetical order,
```

When you print text entered in a DOC window, Symphony automatically ends one page and begins another according to the page-length setting in SERVICES Print Settings Page Length. But if you want to control where a page ends and a new one begins, use the DOC Page command.

Suppose, for example, that you want to keep on separate pages certain sections of a report, as in figure 8.26. To break the page between the two sections, place the cursor on the line where you want the break to occur and select Page from the DOC menu. Alternatively, you can use the Page accelerator key (Ctrl-N). Symphony then places a marker (::) in the left margin to indicate that the page will break at that line. If you want to change a page break, simply erase the break by using the Erase key (F4) or the DOC Erase command.

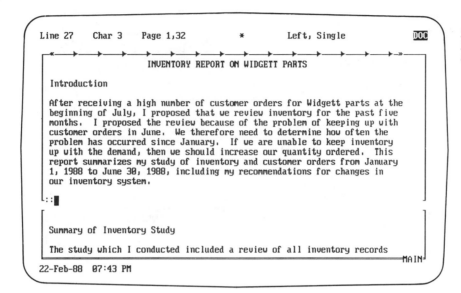

Fig. 8.26
Inserting a page-break marker.

The screen shows:

```
Line 27   Char 3   Page 1,32      *        Left, Single        DOC

                    INVENTORY REPORT ON WIDGETT PARTS

 Introduction

 After receiving a high number of customer orders for Widgett parts at the
 beginning of July, I proposed that we review inventory for the past five
 months.  I proposed the review because of the problem of keeping up with
 customer orders in June.  We therefore need to determine how often the
 problem has occurred since January.  If we are unable to keep inventory
 up with the demand, then we should increase our quantity ordered.  This
 report summarizes my study of inventory and customer orders from January
 1, 1988 to June 30, 1988, including my recommendations for changes in
 our inventory system.
::

 Summary of Inventory Study

 The study which I conducted included a review of all inventory records
                                                                    MAIN
 22-Feb-88  07:43 PM
```

Indenting Sections and Varying Format within the Text

If you are composing a letter, memo, or report in which the format is consistent—that is, the text contains all paragraphs of the same margins, spacing, and so on—then setting the format is easy. But if your document contains sections of text that vary from the regular format (for example, with indented paragraphs, tables, or lists), you can simplify your job by using Symphony's Indent key (F3) and format lines.

You may want at times to indent a section of text underneath another section, as shown in figure 8.27. To indent this way, use the Indent key (F3). To indent a whole section, change from Insert to Overstrike mode if you are not already in that mode. Next, move the cursor to the space where you want each line of indented text to begin. Press the Indent key, then type the section of text. When you finish typing, press the Justify key (F2) or use the Justify command to justify the section of text.

The Indent key is also useful whenever you want to include an itemized list containing items that are preceded by numbers, letters, or bullets (see fig. 8.28). Follow the steps discussed in the previous paragraph, with one variation. Instead of pressing the Indent key before you begin typing a section of text, first type the number, letter, or bullet and then press Indent. Repeat this procedure for each item in your list.

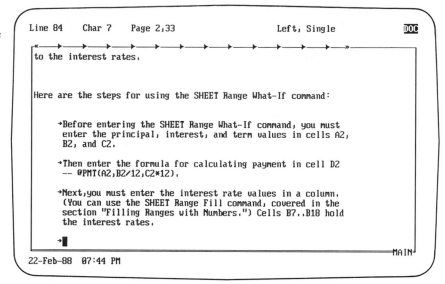

Fig. 8.27

*Indenting sections
of text.*

Fig. 8.28

*Using the Indent
key to create an
indented list.*

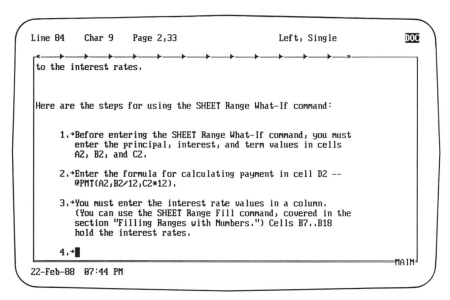

Creating, Editing, and Storing Format Lines

If you find that you repeatedly change the format in the documents you write, then you can create, name, and store format lines for changing the format whenever you want. As mentioned earlier, format lines enable you to change the format settings in a DOC window while you are entering text on the screen. Format lines are particularly useful, for example, whenever you want to indent a block of text or create special lists or tables. Keeping a file of format lines makes it possible for you to retrieve special formats without having to re-create these lines each time. This section describes how to create, name, store, retrieve, and edit format lines.

You can create format lines in your text wherever you want to change margins, tabs, paragraph justification, or spacing. For example, if you want to indent on both the left and right a section of quoted text, you can use a format line to set off the text, as shown in figure 8.29.

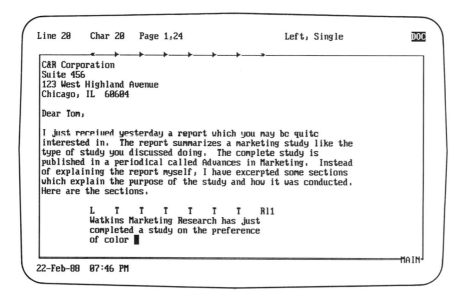

Fig. 8.29

Inserting a format line to indent a section of text.

To create a format line, retrieve the DOC menu and select Format, then choose **Create**, or use the accelerator key, Ctrl-F. Symphony asks, Where should format line(s) be inserted? Move the cursor to the line just before the line where the newly formatted text is to begin, and press Enter. On this preceding line, Symphony then places a format line with the same settings as those controlling the text preceding the format line. For example, if you are creating a format line for the first time in the DOC window, the format line inherits the settings controlling that window. In figure 8.30, the format line settings duplicate the margin and tab settings indicated in the top line of the border and the justification and spacing settings indicated in the control panel.

After displaying a format line on the screen, Symphony provides a menu for changing, naming, and storing format lines; using them; or removing the name of a format line (see fig. 8.31).

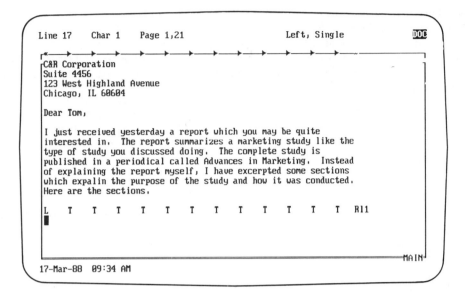

Fig. 8.30

*A format line
inheriting the
settings for the
window.*

Fig. 8.31

*The format line
menu.*

To change a format line, select either **Margins/Tabs**, **Justification**, or **Spacing**. Then press Enter. When you choose **Margins/Tabs**, for example, the control panel clears, and your next step is to change margins and tabs on the format line.

Think of editing a format line as editing text in a document. You insert and delete the L (left margin), T (tab), and R (right margin) symbols and insert and delete spaces until the format line is just as you want it. To set the left margin, delete the existing L and insert an **L** where you want the left margin to be. To shorten the right margin, place the cursor on the R and backspace to the appropriate location. To lengthen the right margin, make sure Insert mode is on, place the cursor on the R, and insert spaces until the R is in the desired spot.

It is best to work in Overstrike mode when setting and clearing tabs in a format line, so that the right margin is not affected by the insertions and deletions you may make. To set a specific tab stop, position the cursor in the format line at the place where you want the tab stop and type a **T**. To clear a tab stop, place the cursor on the tab to clear and press the space bar (Overstrike mode must be on).

After you have changed margin and tab settings, press Enter. The format line menu appears again. At this point, you can make other changes (such as paragraph justification or spacing), assign a name to the format line, or exit from the menu.

If you want to change justification or spacing, simply select one of those choices from the menu and enter the appropriate setting. Symphony indicates justification by displaying the first letter of the type of justification (n = None, l = Left, e = Even, c = Center) after the R (right margin) indicator. Spacing is indicated directly after justification (1 = Single, 2 = Double, 3 = Triple).

Once you have entered all settings for the format line, you have two options. First, you can exit from the DOC menu and return to the text by choosing **Quit**. Second, you can create a name for the format line. When you create a name, the format line settings are stored with that name and can be retrieved and reused whenever you need them.

To create a name and store the format line, select **Line-Marker** from the format line menu. When Symphony displays two options (**Assign** and **Remove**), choose **Assign** and enter a name when the Name to assign: prompt appears. At this point, the format line settings are stored with the line's assigned name. Finally, select **Quit** to exit from the menu and go back to DOC mode.

After you have named a format line, you can reuse the line when needed. Just select **Format** from the DOC menu, then **Use-Named**. Symphony asks, Where should format line(s) be inserted? Move the cursor to the place where you want the line(s). Afterward, press Enter. Symphony displays the name of your format line with an @ sign preceding it. All named format lines are displayed this way when you reuse them.

In addition to creating and naming format lines, you can also edit either a named format line or one that is currently in the DOC window but not named. To edit either type, select **Format Edit**, then either **Current** or **Named**. Whenever you edit either type of format line, you can change any of the format settings (**Margins/Tabs**, **Justification**, or **Spacing**) or have Symphony change the format line to the DOC window's default format settings. To change a format line to the window's default format settings, select **Reset**.

Integrating Symphony's DOC Window with Other Types

One of the advantages of Symphony's word-processing feature, as mentioned earlier, is the capability to integrate word processing with the applications of spreadsheet, data management, graphics, and communications. Here's an example of how you can integrate a DOC window with a SHEET, FORM, and GRAPH window.

In figure 8.32, you can see four separate windows created on the screen. The first is a FORM window containing the data form. The second window, a SHEET window, displays the database created from form entries. The third window, GRAPH, is the graphics representation of one part of the database—column D, "Working Capital." Finally, notice the long rectangular DOC window at the bottom of the screen.

Fig. 8.32

Integrating four different windows.

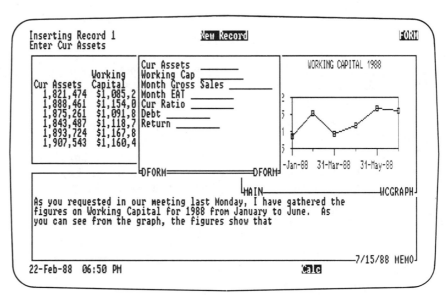

What's the connection of the DOC window to the others? From the text in the DOC window, you can see that the user is beginning to write a report summarizing important conclusions from the data entered and presented in other windows. Having both a SHEET and a GRAPH window at hand helps you analyze and organize text. In addition, you can make a report more effective by combining either a database or graphics into the text. To combine a database or part of the data into the text, you can use the SERVICES File Combine command at the point in the document where the database is to appear. To integrate a graph, you can print a copy of the graph and then insert it into the printed copy of your report.

Chapter Summary

This chapter has introduced you to the power Symphony offers in its word-processing capabilities. You have learned how to create a DOC window, how to enter and edit text in your document, how to move, copy, and erase blocks of text, and how to use Symphony's search-and-replace operations. This chapter also explained formatting a document with the appropriate paragraph justification, tabs, spacing, margins, page length, and format lines. In the next chapter, you can get some hands-on practice for working in a DOC window.

DOC Window Hands-On Practice

In Symphony's DOC environment, you can type letters, memos, reports, and other word-processed documents. Because Symphony is an integrated program, you can even switch modes in the middle of a report and type a spreadsheet table using SHEET mode's extensive calculation capabilities.

In this chapter, you will practice many of the word-processing functions discussed in Chapter 8. You will type a memo, make corrections, format the document, and make other, more extensive changes to the document. This memo will also include a simple spreadsheet. Figure 9.1 shows the memo you will create.

Creating a Document

Creating a document involves two basic steps: typing the text and making corrections. If you have been using a typewriter or a spreadsheet program to type your documents, you will find that Symphony's word processor saves you time in all areas of document creation.

Typing

One convenient feature in word processing is automatic wordwrap. Words automatically wrap to the next line when you reach the right margin. The only time you need to press Enter is when you want to finish a paragraph, leave a blank line, or end a short line.

301

Fig. 9.1

*The final version
of the DOC memo.*

```
                      MEMORANDUM
     DATE:     December 8, 1987
     TO:       Joe Manager
     FROM:     Bill Boss
     SUBJECT:  November Sales


     The November  sales figures for your  division just arrived.
     (Because of  our new Symphony  program, we were able  to get
     the totals in record time!)  It looks like most sales people
     in your division had a  fairly good month.  Sales for Jones,
     Black, and  Johnson were  up from last  month.  I'm  not too
     surprised that Goldman's sales were down because his October
     sales were at such an extraordinary level ($125,000) that it
     would  have been  hard to  top.  I  am worried  about Smith,
     however.  His  sales have been steadily  decreasing over the
     year.  Please call to set  up an appointment to discuss this
     issue.

     Here  is a  summary of  the November  sales figures  for the
     sales people in your division:

              JONES      $75,000
              SMITH       23,000
              BLACK       52,000
              JOHNSON     59,000
              GOLDMAN     85,000
                         ---------
              TOTAL      $294,000

     Remind your sales people about  the following issues as soon
     as possible:

          The  retail  price  of product  line  A  will
          increase  by  10%.  All  other  prices  will
          remain the same until further notice.

          Beginning in January, quotas will increase by
          15% over this year's quotas.

          Because  of cash  flow  problems, no  bonuses
          will be given this year.

     Keep up the good work, Joe.  Talk to you soon.  Don't forget
     to call me about that appointment.
```

In this portion of the exercise, you will type the first half of the memo (see fig. 9.2).

1. Load the Symphony program. A blank worksheet should be displayed.

2. Press the Type key (Alt-F10) to display the TYPE menu.

3. Select **DOC**. The word-processing window should appear, with the default format line at the top.

4. Type the memo shown in figure 9.2. (The arrow-shaped symbols in the document are tab and carriage-return symbols. You should press Tab when you see an arrow pointing to the right, and Enter when the arrow points to the left.) Don't worry about making typing mistakes; you will correct them later. If you prefer, you can correct with the Backspace key as you type. Remember, press Enter only to

- end a short line of text
- create a blank line
- end a paragraph

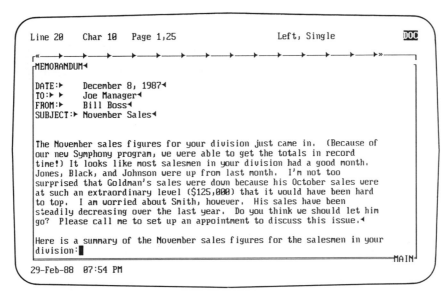

Fig. 9.2

Typing a memo in DOC mode.

5. Select SERVICES **F**ile **S**ave.

6. Enter **MEMO** as the file name.

Note: The document remains on-screen after you save it.

Moving the Cursor

Before you can correct your mistakes in the memo, you need to know how to move the cursor. First of all, you should probably learn how *NOT* to move the cursor: Never use the space bar or the Tab or Enter keys because you will insert spaces or symbols into the document. The basic cursor-movement keys are the arrow keys. When you have a long document, however, the arrow keys get tiresome, so Symphony offers many different, faster ways to move the cursor. (For a detailed description of these commands, refer to Chapter 8's section called "Moving the Cursor in a DOC Window.") You will practice a few of these short-cuts in your document.

1. Use the arrow keys to move the cursor into the first paragraph of the memo.

2. Press Ctrl-→ several times to move the cursor a word at a time to the right.

3. Press Ctrl-← to move the cursor left one word.

4. Press Ctrl-Home to move to the beginning of the line.

5. Press Ctrl-End to move to the end of the line.

6. Press End then Home to move to the end of the document.

7. Press Home to move the cursor to the beginning of the document.

8. Press Ctrl-S to move the cursor to a specific word in the document. Type **Smith** and press Enter.

9. Select **Forward**. The cursor moves to the first occurrence of Smith. This occurrence is the one you wanted (and the only one in the document, for that matter!).

10. Select **Quit**.

Correcting Mistakes

You can correct typing mistakes by: (1) deleting, (2) inserting, and (3) overstriking. Symphony offers an abundance of ways to delete text. The Del key deletes single characters. If you have more than a few characters to remove, you can delete a section of text with the Erase key (F4) or the DOC Erase command. Accelerator keys are available for deleting words, lines, and parts of lines.

The Ins key toggles you between Insert and Overstrike modes. By default, all text is inserted. If you want to type over text (for example, if you transposed two characters), you can temporarily switch to Overstrike mode by pressing the Ins key. Pressing Ins again turns Insert mode back on.

If auto-justify is on (the default setting), paragraphs automatically adjust to the margins when you insert and delete text. If auto-justify is off, you must press the Justify key (F2) to realign each paragraph manually after you make editing changes.

Overstrike the phrase came in with the word arrived.

1. Position the cursor on the c in came in.

2. Press the Ins key to turn on Overstrike mode. The Ovr indicator should display at the bottom of the screen.

3. Type **arrived**.

4. Press the Ins key to turn off Overstrike mode.

Insert several words and phrases in the paragraph.

1. Position the cursor on the g in good month.

2. Make sure Insert mode is on. (The Ovr indicator should *not* display at the bottom of the screen.)

3. Type **fairly** followed by a space. The text pushes to the right, and the paragraph realigns automatically.

    Note: If auto-justify is off, you will need to press the Justify key (F2) to realign the paragraph after inserting text.

4. Position the cursor on the J in Jones.

5. Type **Sales for** followed by a space.

Delete several words using three of the deletion methods: the Del key, the Erase key (F4), and an accelerator key.

1. Position the cursor on the word me in the last sentence of the first paragraph.

2. Press the Del key three times.

    Note: If auto-justify is off, you will need to press the Justify key (F2) to realign the paragraph after deleting text.

3. Position the cursor on the beginning of the sentence Do you think we should let him go?.

4. Press the Erase key (F4).

5. Press the → until the entire sentence (including the two spaces after the question mark) is highlighted. (See fig. 9.3.)

6. Press Enter.

7. Position the cursor on the space after the word last in last year.

8. Press Ctrl-Backspace to delete the word last. The paragraph realigns automatically.

Use the previous techniques to correct any other mistakes you may have made. Your document should now look similar to figure 9.4.

Fig. 9.3

A highlighted block to erase.

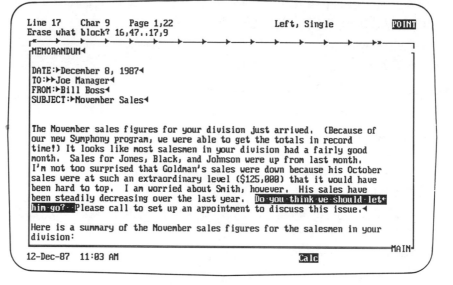

Fig. 9.4

After making deletions and corrections.

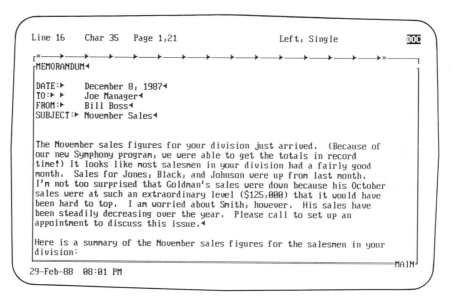

If you accidentally delete text, you can restore it with the Paste accelerator key (Ctrl-P). Experiment by deleting some text and then pasting it back into the document.

1. Position the cursor anywhere on the first line of the paragraph.

2. Press Ctrl-D to delete the current line.

3. With the cursor in the same location, press Ctrl-P to paste it back.

4. Place the cursor in the middle of the line.

5. Press Ctrl-Y to delete from the cursor to the end of the line.

6. Undelete the text by pressing Ctrl-P.

7. Press Ctrl-T to delete from the cursor to the beginning of the line.

8. Undelete with Ctrl-P.

Formatting the Document

Symphony offers many features to enhance your document so that it is much more than just words on the page. You can automatically center lines, boldface and underline text, right-justify the margins, and change the margin settings.

Changing the Format Settings

Format settings control the margins, tabs, line spacing, and justification of the entire document. You can also format individual sections by creating special format lines. You will insert a format line later in this chapter, but for now let's change the document's overall margin and justification settings.

The default right margin is 72. This margin is too wide for your memo. Set a new right margin for the document.

1. The cursor can be anywhere in the document.

2. Select DOC Format Settings.

3. Select **Right Set** to set the right margin.

4. Type **60** and press Enter. The Format Settings menu redisplays.

   Note: You will not see the effect of your margin change until you exit the menu.

Now change the justification of the document.

1. Select **Justification Even**.

2. Select **Quit** to see the formatting changes. Notice that the text reformatted itself to the new right margin. The right margin is smooth because you changed justification from left to even. (See fig. 9.5.)

Fig. 9.5

Reformatted to a new, even margin.

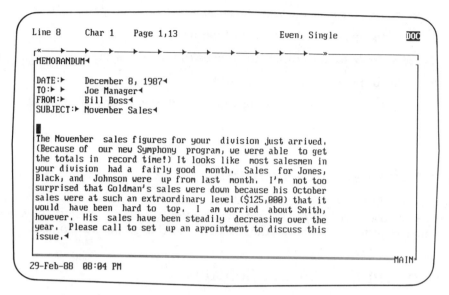

To center a title on a typewriter you had to go to the center of the page and backspace once for every two characters in the title. In Symphony, you type the title at the left margin and press the Center key (Alt-F4).

1. Position the cursor anywhere on the word MEMORANDUM.

2. Press Alt-F4. The title is centered.

Using Print Attributes

Besides centering, another way to make text stand out is with print attributes: boldface, underline, italic, and so on. You must place a "begin attribute" command where the print attribute should begin and an "end attribute" command at the end. The attributes are actually codes embedded in the text that instruct the printer how to print the text. On the screen, the attributed text appears in a different color or shading, depending on your monitor. The attribute codes are only visible when you use the **Erase** command.

Boldface the word MEMORANDUM.

1. Position the cursor at the beginning of the word MEMORANDUM.

2. Press Ctrl-B to begin an attribute. The attribute menu displays in the control panel.

3. Select **B** for Bold.

Note: Begin bold attribute symbols were inserted into the text, though you cannot see them. The text after the cursor should be shaded or colored differently, indicating boldfaced text.

Now you must indicate where boldface should end so that you don't boldface the entire document.

4. Position the cursor after the word MEMORANDUM (on the carriage-return symbol).

5. Press Ctrl-E to end the attribute. Only the word MEMORANDUM should be shaded differently now.

Boldface the memo headings (DATE:, TO:, FROM:, and SUBJECT:).

1. Position the cursor on the beginning of the word DATE:.

2. Press Ctrl-B to begin the attribute. The attribute menu displays in the control panel.

3. Select **B** for Bold.

4. Position the cursor after the colon.

5. Press Ctrl-E to end the attribute.

6. Repeat steps 1 through 5 to boldface TO:, FROM:, and SUBJECT:.

Underlining text involves the same method, except you choose the **U** (underline) attribute. Underline several words in the first paragraph.

1. Position the cursor on the e in the word extraordinary.

2. Press Ctrl-B to begin the attribute.

3. Select **U** for Underlined.

4. Position the cursor on the space after the word.

5. Press Ctrl-E to end the attribute.

6. Repeat steps 1 through 5 to underline the word worried.

If you decide you no longer want the text underlined or boldfaced, you can remove the attributes. You must use the Erase key (F4) or the DOC **Erase** command to delete the attributes, because the codes display only when you choose this command. The Del key does not work.

1. Position the cursor at the beginning of the word worried.

2. Press the Erase key (F4). Notice the attributes before and after each word that has an attribute assigned (see fig. 9.6.).

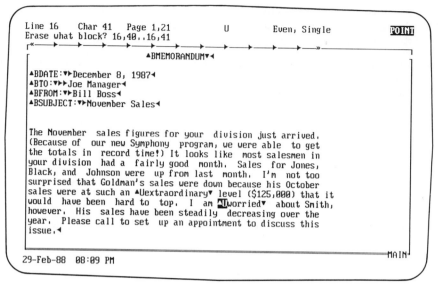

Fig. 9.6

*The print attributes
displayed.*

3. Because the begin attribute codes are already highlighted, press Enter. The underlining is removed.

   Note: Even though the underlining effect is removed, you should still clean up your text and remove the end attribute code.

4. Position the cursor after the word `worried`.

5. Press the Erase key (F4). Notice the end attribute code.

6. Press Enter. The end attribute code is removed.

When printed, your document should look like figure 9.7.

Including a Spreadsheet in a Document

By simply switching to SHEET mode, you can type a spreadsheet table in any word-processing document—it is that easy. SHEET mode offers several advantages over DOC mode for table typing. First, the columns are already established in the spreadsheet. In DOC mode, you would have to calculate where to set the tab stops and then set each tab. Second, the spreadsheet can total your columns and rows for you.

See Chapters 3 through 7 for additional information on using a SHEET window.

Fig. 9.7

The printed result.

```
                         MEMORANDUM

       DATE:      December 8, 1987
       TO:        Joe Manager
       FROM:      Bill Boss
       SUBJECT:   November Sales


       The November  sales figures for your  division just arrived.
       (Because of  our new Symphony  program, we were able  to get
       the totals in  record time!) It looks like  most salesmen in
       your division  had a  fairly good  month.  Sales  for Jones,
       Black, and  Johnson were  up from last  month.  I'm  not too
       surprised that Goldman's sales were down because his October
       sales were at such an extraordinary level ($125,000) that it
       would  have  been  hard to  top.  I  am worried  about Smith,
       however.  His  sales have been steadily  decreasing over the
       year.  Please call to set  up an appointment to discuss this
       issue.

       Here  is a  summary of  the November  sales figures  for the
       salesmen in your division:
```

Entering Labels, Values, and Formulas

If the data were already typed in this or another spreadsheet, you could copy it into the document. In this exercise, however, you need to enter the labels and values yourself. First, you must switch to SHEET mode.

1. Press Switch (Alt-F9) to switch to the last mode you were in (SHEET).

   Note: You can also use the Type key (Alt-F10) and select a **SHEET** window.

2. Type the following labels so that your spreadsheet looks like figure 9.8:

In cell:	*Enter:*
C24	JONES
C25	SMITH
C26	BLACK
C27	JOHNSON
C28	GOLDMAN
C30	TOTAL

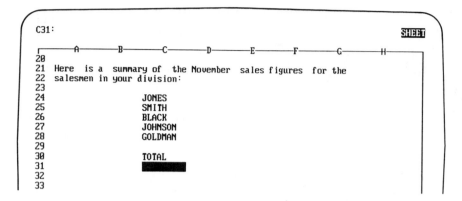

Fig. 9.8

Entering labels in SHEET mode.

3. In cell D29 type \- to create a dashed line.

4. Type the following values:

In cell:	Enter:
D24	75000
D25	23000
D26	52000
D27	59000
D28	85000

Compare your spreadsheet to figure 9.9. If you made a mistake as you typed the cell contents, position the cell pointer on the cell containing the error and then either retype the entry or use the Edit key (F2). If you typed an entry into a cell that should be blank, place the cell pointer on this cell and remove the unwanted entry by using SHEET Erase.

Fig. 9.9

Adding the sales figures.

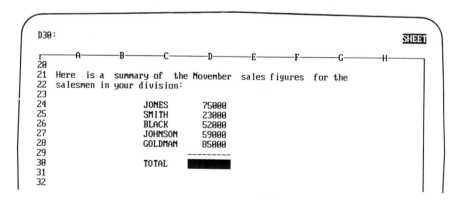

This basic spreadsheet requires only one formula: the total. Keep in mind, however, that your formulas can get as complex as needed.

1. Position the cell pointer on cell D30.

2. Enter **@SUM(D24.D28)**. The total (294000) appears in the cell.

Formatting the Spreadsheet

By default, Symphony doesn't punctuate the numbers. Change the overall format settings to **Punctuated**, and then format the top and bottom numbers in the column to **Currency**. Figure 9.10 displays the formatted spreadsheet.

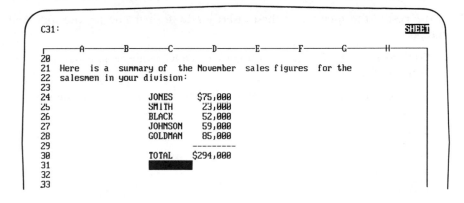

Fig. 9.10

The formatted spreadsheet.

1. Select SHEET **S**ettings **F**ormat **P**unctuated.

2. Enter **0** for the number of decimals. Select **Q**uit. All numbers now have commas.

3. Select SHEET **F**ormat **C**urrency. Enter **0** for the number of decimals.

4. Type **D24** as the range to format. The top number in the column now has a dollar sign.

5. Select SHEET **F**ormat **C**urrency. Enter **0** for the number of decimals.

6. Type **D30** as the range to format. The total now has a dollar sign also.

The table is now finished; you can switch back to the DOC window. If you later need to change any of the labels or values you entered in the spreadsheet, you *must* switch back to SHEET mode. Symphony does not permit spreadsheet changes in DOC mode.

Additional Editing and Formatting

In this final exercise, you will finish typing the memo. Part of the memo will be indented from the left and right margins, so you will need to create a new format line for this text. After this exercise, you will also be able to add two more editing functions to your repertoire: **Move** and **Replace**.

Inserting Format Lines

Each document can have any number of format lines, which control the settings for sections of text. The format lines appear in the document on the screen but do not print. You can change the margins and tabs in an inserted format line by using your regular editing keys (arrow keys, Backspace, Del, Ins, and so on).

Type the rest of the memo and then insert a new format line for the indented paragraphs.

1. Press Switch (Alt-F9) to switch back to DOC mode, if you haven't done so already.

2. Starting two lines below the table, type the text displayed in figure 9.11A.

Fig. 9.11A

Typing the rest of the memo.

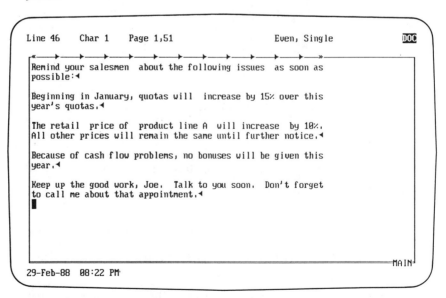

```
Line 46    Char 1    Page 1,51              Even, Single      DOC

Remind your salesmen  about the following issues  as soon as
possible:◄

Beginning in January, quotas will  increase by 15% over this
year's quotas.◄

The retail  price of  product line A  will increase  by 10%.
All other prices will remain the same until further notice.◄

Because of cash flow problems, no bonuses will be given this
year.◄

Keep up the good work, Joe.  Talk to you soon.  Don't forget
to call me about that appointment.◄
█


                                                          MAIN
29-Feb-88  08:22 PM
```

3. Place the cursor on the B in Beginning.

4. Select DOC **Format Create**.

    Note: You can also use the Format accelerator key (Ctrl-F) to insert a format line.

5. Press the Tab key to anchor the range so that you can highlight.

6. Press the ↓ to highlight three paragraphs, as shown in figure 9.11B. Press Enter. Format lines are inserted above and below the three paragraphs.

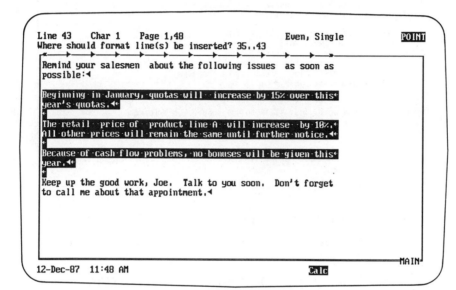

Line 43   Char 1   Page 1,48   Even, Single   POINT
Where should format line(s) be inserted? 35,.43

Remind your salesmen about the following issues as soon as
possible:◄

Beginning·in·January,·quotas·will··increase·by·15%·over·this◄
year's·quotas.◄◄

The·retail··price·of··product·line·A··will·increase··by·10%.◄
All·other·prices·will·remain·the·same·until·further·notice.◄◄

Because·of·cash·flow·problems,·no·bonuses·will·be·given·this◄
year.◄◄

Keep up the good work, Joe. Talk to you soon. Don't forget
to call me about that appointment.◄

12-Dec-87 11:48 AM   Calc   MAIN

Fig. 9.11B

The text to be reformatted.

7. Select **Margins/Tabs**. The cursor moves into the format line.

8. The cursor should be on the left margin symbol (L). Press the space bar five times to move the left margin over five spaces.

9. Move the cursor to the right margin symbol (R).

10. Press the Backspace key until the right margin is at character number 50 (look in the control panel for the Char 50 display).

11. Press Enter when you are finished editing the format line.

12. Select **Quit** to see the effect of your format changes. Your document should look similar to figure 9.11C.

Moving Text

Another common part of the editing process is cutting and pasting. When you need to reorganize text, use Symphony's **Move** command.

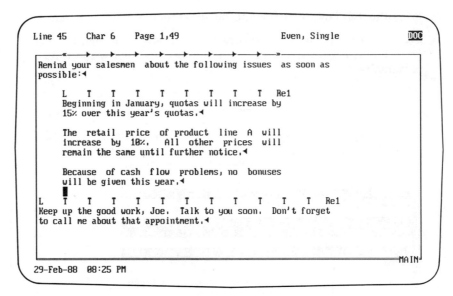

Fig. 9.11C
New format lines.

Move one of the indented paragraphs.

1. Position the cursor at the beginning (Char 1) of the first indented paragraph.

2. Select DOC **M**ove or use the Move accelerator key (Ctrl-M). Symphony asks, Move FROM what block?

3. Press the ↓ twice to highlight the paragraph and the blank line after the paragraph.

4. Press Enter. Symphony asks, Move TO where?

5. Move the cursor to the beginning (Char 1) of the last indented paragraph (Because of cash flow problems...).

6. Press Enter. The paragraph is deleted from the original location and inserted into the new spot. Your document should resemble figure 9.12.

   Note: If you didn't place the cursor at character 1, you may have extra spaces at the beginning of the paragraph. Use the Del key to remove them.

Replacing Text

If you find that you have consistently used the wrong word or phrase throughout a document, you can use Symphony's **R**eplace command to make the corrections for you.

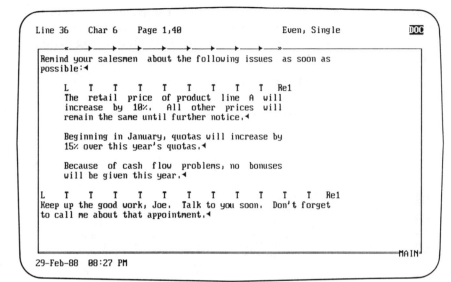

Fig. 9.12

After rearranging paragraphs.

Use **Replace** to replace salesmen with sales people.

1. Press Home to move the cursor to the top of the document.

   Note: The **Replace** command only searches forward from the cursor position, so you should place the cursor at the top of the document before invoking the command.

2. Select DOC **Replace** or use the Replace accelerator key (Ctrl-R) to begin the replacement operation. Symphony prompts you to enter the word to replace.

   Note: The last word you searched for (Smith) displays. You can type over this word.

3. Enter **salesmen**. Symphony then prompts you for the replacement text.

4. Enter **sales people**. Symphony displays the **Replace** menu and finds the first occurrence of salesmen.

5. Select **Continue** to replace the first occurrence and continue the search. Symphony finds the second occurrence of salesmen.

6. Select **Continue** until the message No more occurrences found appears.

7. Press Esc to cancel the error message.

Continue does a discretionary replace; this option stops at each occurrence of the word or phrase and gives you a chance to **Skip** it. If you want to replace all occurrences of the word automatically, select **All-Remaining** rather than Continue.

The final printed document appears in figure 9.13.

```
                        MEMORANDUM

        DATE:      December 8, 1987
        TO:        Joe Manager
        FROM:      Bill Boss
        SUBJECT:   November Sales


        The November  sales figures for your  division just arrived.
        (Because of  our new Symphony  program, we were able  to get
        the totals in record time!)  It looks like most sales people
        in your division had a  fairly good month.  Sales for Jones,
        Black, and  Johnson were  up from last  month.  I'm  not too
        surprised that Goldman's sales were down because his October
        sales were at such an underlined{extraordinary} level ($125,000) that it
        would  have been  hard to  top.  I  am worried  about Smith,
        however.  His  sales have been steadily  decreasing over the
        year.  Please call to set  up an appointment to discuss this
        issue.

        Here  is a  summary of  the November  sales figures  for the
        sales people in your division:

                      JONES     $75,000
                      SMITH      23,000
                      BLACK      52,000
                      JOHNSON    59,000
                      GOLDMAN    85,000
                                ---------
                      TOTAL    $294,000

        Remind your sales people about  the following issues as soon
        as possible:

            The  retail  price  of product  line  A  will
            increase  by  10%.   All  other  prices  will
            remain the same until further notice.

            Beginning in January, quotas will increase by
            15% over this year's quotas.

            Because  of cash  flow  problems, no  bonuses
            will be given this year.

        Keep up the good work, Joe.  Talk to you soon.  Don't forget
        to call me about that appointment.
```

Chapter Summary

In this hands-on practice chapter, you learned the most commonly used features in word processing. You typed a memo, corrected mistakes, enhanced the document with print attributes, formatted the document with new margins and justification, performed an electronic cut-and-paste operation, and used Symphony's search-and-replace feature. You also typed a table in the middle of the document using Symphony's SHEET mode. This step is what integration is all about.

10

Word-Processing Add-Ins: Spelling Checker and Text Outliner

Add-in applications are outside programs that you can attach to Symphony so that the add-ins' commands become part of the Symphony program. In other words, add-in applications enable you to extend Symphony's basic functions. Generally you only attach the application when you need to use a special function and then detach the application when you are finished.

Symphony 2.0 includes two word-processing add-in applications: a spelling checker and a text outliner. These programs were formerly sold as separate products. Spelling Checker locates misspelled words and typing errors so that you can correct them. With Text Outliner, you can create outlines and tables of contents and organize the structure of your documents. Let's first discuss Spelling Checker.

Spelling Checker

Spelling Checker is a valuable addition to Symphony because the add-in checks for typing and spelling mistakes in your word-processing files, thus enabling you to produce more professional-looking documents. But Spelling Checker does more than just find misspelled words. It also locates repeated words (when you accidentally type the same word twice in a row, for example) and makes sure that each sentence begins with a capital letter.

After you issue the command to begin spell-checking, Spelling Checker checks each word in your document against the 80,000 words in the application's standard dictionary. If the word is not in the dictionary, Spelling Checker highlights the word so that you can decide whether the word is misspelled or simply not in the dictionary. Spelling Checker gives you several options at this point.

If the word is incorrectly spelled, you can edit the word yourself or choose from a list of possible correct spellings. If the word is correctly spelled but is just an unusual word or proper noun, you can bypass it and proceed to the next word, or you can add the word to an auxiliary dictionary.

You can check the entire document, any selected portion of the document, or even a single word.

Attaching and Invoking the Speller

Before you can use the Spelling Checker, you must first attach it. The Spelling Checker program, when attached, consumes an extra 137K of memory. Therefore, to use Spelling Checker, your computer must have at least 512K. If you are using other memory-resident programs or have attached other applications, you may not have enough memory to attach Spelling Checker. If you get an insufficient memory message, you will have to detach your other applications or remove your memory-resident programs.

Because Spelling Checker requires so much memory, you probably will not want to load the application automatically when you load Symphony. If you think you can spare the memory, however, it is definitely more convenient not to have to attach the application every time you want to spell-check. Use the SERVICES Configuration Other Application Set command to specify which applications you want to autoload. If you autoload Spelling Checker, the DOC menu includes an extra option, Verify, whenever you load Symphony.

If you are running Symphony on floppy disk drives, you need to insert the Speller and Outliner Add-Ins disk into drive A to attach the application. Use the SERVICES Application Attach command and select **SPELLER.APP** from the list of applications by moving the cursor to **SPELLER.APP** and pressing Enter. The Spelling Checker copyright screen appears, and eventually the Application menu reappears in the control panel. Select **Quit**. Floppy disk users can now remove the Speller and Outliner Add-Ins disk from drive A.

To invoke the Spelling Checker, select DOC Verify. You may be tempted to choose **Invoke** from the Application menu to begin the spell-checking, but if you do, you get the message Select Verify from the DOC menu. To check the spelling of a document, therefore, simply select DOC **Verify**.

Once you have finished spell-checking a document, you may want to detach the application to free up memory for other applications or files. If you will be editing and spell-checking other small documents, you can leave Spelling Checker attached. If you are going to be working on large files or want to use other applications or memory-resident programs, however, you should detach Spelling Checker. Select the SERVICES Application Detach command and choose **SPELLER.APP**.

Spell-Checking a Document

After you have attached Spelling Checker, you are ready to begin spell-checking a document. If the document isn't already on your screen, retrieve the file you want to check. Place the cursor at the beginning of the document, or if you want to check just part of the document, place the cursor at the beginning of the area you want to check. Press the DOC Menu key (F10) and notice the new menu option that appears: **V**erify. Select this new option, and the Verify menu displays, as shown in the control panel of figure 10.1.

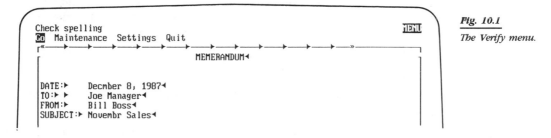

Fig. 10.1

The Verify menu.

At this point, you should make sure that the spell-check settings are correct. Select **S**ettings to view the Spelling Checker settings sheet shown in figure 10.2.

Fig. 10.2

The Spelling Checker settings sheet.

Setting Spell-Check Options

By selecting DOC Verify Settings Options, you can change several spelling defaults: Autocorrect, Sentence, and Hyphens.

Setting Autocorrect to Yes tells Spelling Checker to correct automatically all occurrences of a misspelled word. In other words, if you consistently misspelled a word throughout the document, Spelling Checker stops at the first misspelling so that you can indicate how you want it corrected, and then Spelling Checker automatically corrects any other words misspelled the same way. If Autocorrect is set to No (the default), Spelling Checker stops at each spelling error.

You should be aware that the autocorrect option requires additional memory because all the words you correct are stored in memory. If you run out of memory during spell-checking, you will see the message Cannot add more words for autocorrection. You can continue spell-checking by pressing Esc, but any new misspelled words are not autocorrected. If you quit the session, you clear the memory of all words recorded for automatic correction, and you can then start spell-checking from where you stopped.

The next checking option is Sentence. With a Yes setting (the default), Spelling Checker ensures that each sentence begins with a capital letter. If the application finds a sentence that begins with a lowercase letter, the following options appear in the control panel:

>   Capitalize   Resume   Quit

You then choose Capitalize to have Spelling Checker capitalize the letter, or Resume to leave the letter lowercase.

The last option on the Spelling Checker settings sheet is Hyphens. This option determines whether Spelling Checker considers a hyphenated word as one word or two. With a Yes setting (the default), Spelling Checker looks in the dictionary for two words; the letters before the hyphen are considered one word, and the letters after the hyphen are another. With a No setting, Spelling Checker searches the dictionary for the entire hyphenated word.

Any settings you change remain in effect only while Spelling Checker is attached. Read the section called "Settings Sheets" to see how to store these settings permanently once you have changed them.

Correcting Mistakes

Those of you who are running Symphony from 5 1/4-inch floppy disks need to place the Speller Dictionary disk in drive A before beginning the spell-check. Those of you with 3 1/2-inch drives must insert the Speller and Outliner disk in drive A. To begin the spell-check, select DOC Verify Go. Spelling Checker asks you for a spell-check range, and you must highlight the text you want to spell-check. You can check the entire document, a designated range, or a word.

To check from the cursor to the end of the document, press End and then Home to highlight quickly the rest of the text. (If the cursor is not at the correct starting point, you must first press Esc to unanchor the range; then you position the cursor and reanchor by pressing Tab. Then you can highlight the text.)

The Correction Menu

After you indicate the spell-check range, the correction menu appears, as shown in figure 10.3, and the first misspelled word is highlighted. You choose the appropriate option on the correction menu, depending on whether the word is misspelled or simply not in the dictionary.

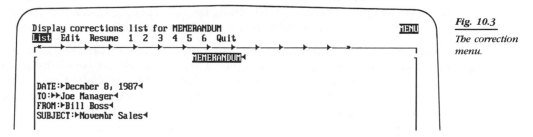

Fig. 10.3

The correction menu.

Use the first two options, List and Edit, to correct a misspelled word. If you are unsure of the correct spelling, choose List. Spelling Checker gives you a list of possible correct spellings (see fig. 10.4). If one of the suggestions is correct, you can highlight it with the pointer and press Enter. Spelling Checker then corrects the word in the document. When the Autocorrect option in the settings sheet is set to Yes, all identical misspellings are also corrected.

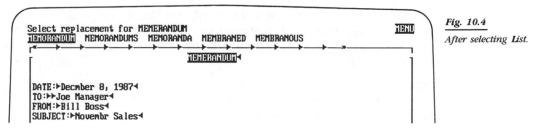

Fig. 10.4

After selecting List.

Spelling Checker does not always list the spelling you are looking for. Press Esc to clear the list and display the correction menu if you don't see the correct spelling listed. Occasionally, Spelling Checker cannot find any possible corrections for the word and thus displays the message No correction words found. You must then find an old-fashioned dictionary and look up the correct spelling yourself.

When the mistake is merely a typo and you know the correct spelling, choose the Edit option. This option displays the misspelled word in the control panel and takes you into EDIT mode. You can use all your regular edit keys (arrows, Del, Backspace) to correct the word. When you press Enter, the misspelled word in your document is replaced by the corrected word. Again, when the Auto-correct option is set to **Yes**, all repeated misspellings are corrected as well.

Often the words that Spelling Checker finds are not actually misspelled; they are words specific to your type of business or company (proper nouns, acronyms, technical terms, and so on). If Spelling Checker highlights one of these words and you rarely use it in any of your documents, choose **Resume**. This option skips over the word and takes you to the next misspelling. On the other hand, if you use the word frequently (your name, for instance), you can add the word to an auxiliary dictionary. The more words you add to auxiliary dictionaries, the faster spell-checking will go in the future, because Spelling Checker never again stops at a word you have added to the auxiliary dictionary.

To add a word to the personal dictionary (the auxiliary dictionary that is auto-matically created for you), choose option **1** on the correction menu. If you have created other auxiliary dictionaries (see the later section entitled "Auxiliary Dic-tionaries"), choose the appropriate number from **2** through **6**. If you have not created and set any auxiliary dictionaries, the message *** not defined in settings sheet *** is displayed when you select a number.

Note that each possible variation of a word (singular, plural, different verb tenses, lowercase, all uppercase, and capitalized) is considered a different word and must be added separately to the dictionary.

The last option on the correction menu is **Quit**. Use this option to exit the verification process before it is complete.

Other Spelling Checker Menus

Besides the correction menu just discussed, you may have several other menus displayed during the spell-checking process. When Spelling Checker encounters a double word (as in *I read the the book*), the menu shown in the control panel of figure 10.5 appears.

If you typed the word twice in error, choose **Erase**, and Spelling Checker elimi-nates one of the words. Choose **Resume** to leave both words in the document. **Quit** cancels the spell-checking process.

The capitalization menu is another menu you may use during spell-checking. As mentioned earlier, with the **Sentence** option set to **Yes**, Spelling Checker looks for sentences that do not begin with a capital letter. When Spelling Checker finds such a sentence, the program displays the following options:

Capitalize   Resume   Quit

Choose **Capitalize** to have Spelling Checker capitalize the letter, or **Resume** to leave the letter lowercase. **Quit** exits the spell-checking process.

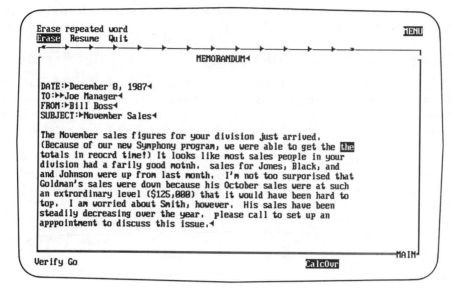

Fig. 10.5

When Spelling Checker finds a double word.

Auxiliary Dictionaries

One auxiliary dictionary, PERSONAL.DCT, is included with the program and is automatically specified on the Spelling Checker settings sheet next to Aux 1 (see fig. 10.6). You can use this dictionary for adding all the words you commonly use that are not in Spelling Checker's standard dictionary (AMERICAN.LEX). Or you may find it more convenient to store your words in separate auxiliary dictionaries.

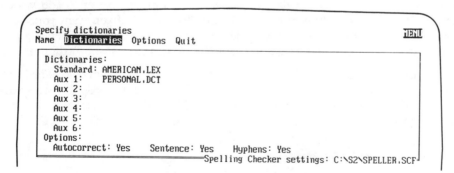

Fig. 10.6

The Spelling Checker settings sheet.

As you can see in the settings sheet in figure 10.6, Spelling Checker has room for up to six auxiliary dictionaries. Each department in a company may want to create its own auxiliary dictionary, and the company itself could have a dictionary of names and acronyms used companywide. In a large company, it makes sense to have one person create the dictionary of special words and then distribute it to the people who need it.

Creating an Auxiliary Dictionary

To add words to an auxiliary dictionary, you must first define the dictionary on the Spelling Checker settings sheet. If you want an auxiliary dictionary (in addition to PERSONAL.DCT), use the DOC Verify Settings Dictionaries Set command. Choose a number from **2** to **6** and then give the dictionary a name (SALES, for example). Spelling Checker tells you that this file is a new file and asks if you want to create it. Choose **Yes**, and Spelling Checker gives the file a .DCT extension (SALES.DCT, for example). This new name appears on the settings sheet, as in figure 10.7. The dictionary's full path name is also specified on the settings sheet.

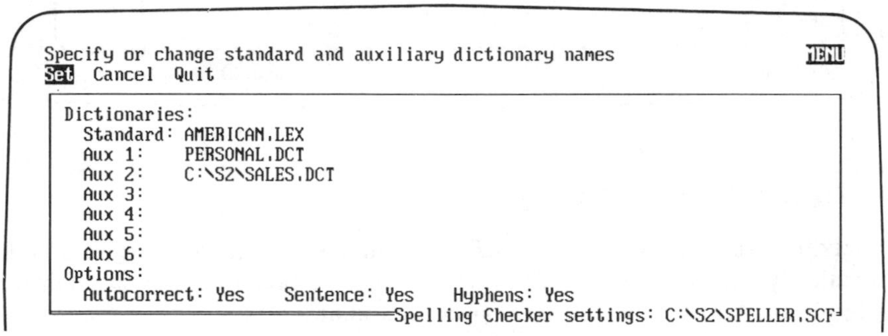

Fig. 10.7

Adding another auxiliary dictionary.

```
Specify or change standard and auxiliary dictionary names          MENU
Set  Cancel  Quit

  Dictionaries:
    Standard: AMERICAN.LEX
    Aux 1:    PERSONAL.DCT
    Aux 2:    C:\S2\SALES.DCT
    Aux 3:
    Aux 4:
    Aux 5:
    Aux 6:
  Options:
    Autocorrect: Yes     Sentence: Yes     Hyphens: Yes
                               Spelling Checker settings: C:\S2\SPELLER.SCF
```

The auxiliary dictionary names you define remain in the settings sheet only as long as Spelling Checker is attached. Thus, you must use the **Dictionaries Set** command to activate an auxiliary dictionary each time you want to add words to it. PERSONAL.DCT, however, is automatically defined. If you want your auxiliary dictionaries to be set automatically when you use Spelling Checker, you can save the settings. See the section entitled "Settings Sheets" for further details.

After the dictionary is listed on the settings sheet, you can add words to the dictionary in three ways. The first method—adding words during spell-checking—was discussed in the previous section on the correction menu. The following two sections discuss the alternative methods for adding words.

The Maintenance Menu

Using the **Maintenance Add** command, you can add words to an auxiliary dictionary by typing them one at a time. Before you can add words to an auxiliary dictionary, however, you must define and list the dictionary in the settings sheet, as explained in the previous section.

To add a word with the **Maintenance** command, select DOC Verify **Maintenance Add**. Select the dictionary to which you want to add the word. Choose **1** to add the word to the PERSONAL dictionary, or select the appropriate previously defined dictionary. To see the dictionary name associated with each number, you can highlight the number and read the description, as shown in figure 10.8. After choosing the dictionary, type the word you want to add.

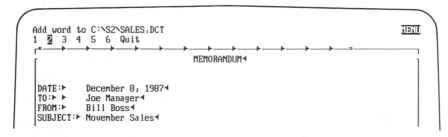

Fig. 10.8

Adding words to an auxiliary dictionary.

The **Maintenance** command also gives you options to **Delete** and **Modify** words in your auxiliary dictionaries. These two options are important in case you accidentally add a misspelled word. To remove a word from an auxiliary dictionary, select DOC Verify **Maintenance Delete**. Select the dictionary from which you want to remove the word and then type the word.

Use the **Modify** command when you want to correct a word you have added to the dictionary. The **Modify** option saves you from having to delete and then add the word. After you select DOC Verify **Maintenance Modify** and choose the right dictionary, Spelling Checker asks for the Current word and the Replacement word. The program assumes that you want to edit the word, so after you provide the current word, Spelling Checker automatically fills in the same word for the replacement word and puts you in EDIT mode.

Looking at an Auxiliary Dictionary

The problem with the **Maintenance** command is that it does not show you the dictionary, so you may not discover that the dictionary contains misspelled words. Or maybe you know that you added a misspelled word, but you do not remember exactly how you misspelled it. None of the **Maintenance** commands provide a list from which you can look up words.

Because the auxiliary dictionaries are stored in a standard text format called ASCII, however, and Symphony can import this type of file, you can look at your auxiliary dictionaries in the spreadsheet. Or, if you prefer, you can view an auxiliary dictionary in any program that can edit and save ASCII files (SideKick, for example).

Before you edit your auxiliary dictionaries, it's wise to make a backup copy of the file. Exit to DOS and copy the file to a floppy disk. For example, go to the drive/directory where your PERSONAL.DCT is located and then copy it to drive A:

    copy personal.dct a:

To look at your PERSONAL.DCT (make sure that you have added some words to it first, because the default file is empty), clear the screen by selecting SER-VICES **New Yes**. Then, to retrieve an ASCII file, use the SERVICES **File Import Text** command. Choose PERSONAL.DCT (or whichever dictionary file you want to view), and the words appear down column A, one word in each cell (see fig. 10.9).

Fig. 10.9

A dictionary file.

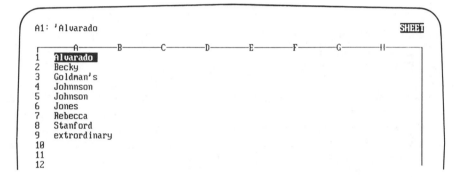

If all you want to do is look at this list to help you correct mistakes with the DOC **Verify Maintenance** command, you can print the list and use it as a reference guide. You can also correct the mistakes right in the spreadsheet. Use the SHEET **Delete Row** command to remove words, and SHEET **Insert Row** to add new words. Use the Edit key (F2) to modify misspelled words. As you insert words, make sure that the list remains alphabetical and that all the words beginning with uppercase letters are alphabetized before the lowercase words (see fig. 10.9). The dictionary does not work properly if the words are not alphabetized in this manner.

To save the dictionary when you are finished with modifications, print the dictionary to a file. Follow these steps:

1. Switch to a DOC window so that you don't have to specify a source range when you print.

2. Select SERVICES **Print Settings Destination File**.

3. Enter the name of your auxiliary dictionary (for example, PERSONAL.DCT).

4. Select **Destination Erase Yes** to erase the old auxiliary dictionary file.

5. Select **Margins No-Margins**.

6. Select **Quit Go Quit**. The dictionary is printed to a file.

Note that you must use the previous steps, not the **File Save** command, to save the dictionary file. **File Save** creates a worksheet file, not an ASCII file.

Settings Sheets

If you want to change the default for your spell-check options (**Autocorrect**, **Sentence**, **Hyphens**) permanently or to have auxiliary dictionaries automatically defined in the settings sheet, you need to save the sheet to a Spelling Checker configuration file. The **Name** command on the **Verify Settings** menu provides an option to **Save** configuration files. The default file is called SPELLER.SCF, which is the configuration file that is automatically pulled up when you attach Spelling Checker. Though you can have multiple configuration files, you will probably only need this one. Therefore, when you want to save changes to your Spelling Checker settings sheet, save the changes to SPELLER.SCF. Symphony warns you that the file already exists and asks if you want to replace the file. Select **Yes**.

If you have several different auxiliary dictionaries, you may want to create separate configuration files for various combinations of the dictionaries. Then you can choose the appropriate configuration for each document you check. Use the **Name Save** command and enter a name to identify the file. Spelling Checker automatically assigns the file extension .SCF. For example, if you name the configuration file SALES, the complete file name is SALES.SCF.

To use other Spelling Checker configuration files that you have previously saved, select the **Name Retrieve** command and enter the appropriate file name. The settings sheet then appears with the name in the lower right corner of the sheet. When you spell-check a document, Spelling Checker uses the options and dictionaries listed in the settings sheet.

To return to the default Spelling Checker settings, select **Name Default-Settings**. The settings sheet then looks similar to figure 10.10. The settings are changed only while Spelling Checker is attached.

The **Name Erase** command deletes Spelling Checker configuration files that you have previously saved.

Spell-Checking a Spreadsheet

In addition to spell-checking documents, Spelling Checker also checks spreadsheets—with one major limitation. Spelling Checker checks only the words entered into the first column of the window. Retrieve the spreadsheet you want to spell-check, and switch to a DOC window. The words that appear in a brighter intensity on your screen are the only ones Spelling Checker considers. Select **DOC Format Justification None** so that each word remains on a separate line.

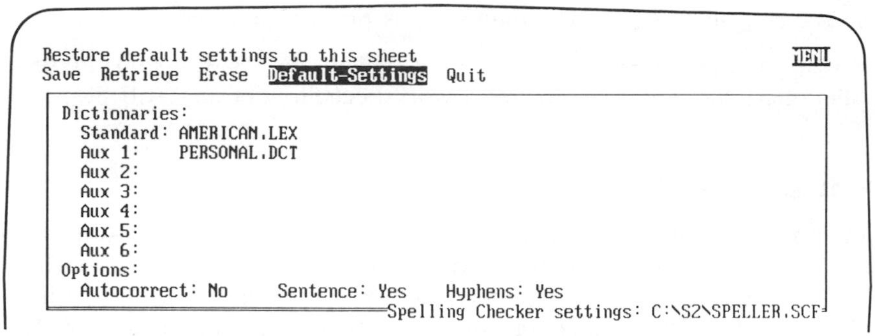

Fig. 10.10

Restoring default Spelling Checker settings.

```
 ┌─────────────────────────────────────────────────────────────────────┐
 │  Restore default settings to this sheet                       MENU    │
 │  Save  Retrieve  Erase  Default-Settings  Quit                        │
 │  ┌──────────────────────────────────────────────────────┐            │
 │  │ Dictionaries:                                          │            │
 │  │   Standard: AMERICAN.LEX                               │            │
 │  │   Aux 1:    PERSONAL.DCT                               │            │
 │  │   Aux 2:                                               │            │
 │  │   Aux 3:                                               │            │
 │  │   Aux 4:                                               │            │
 │  │   Aux 5:                                               │            │
 │  │   Aux 6:                                               │            │
 │  │ Options:                                               │            │
 │  │   Autocorrect: No    Sentence: Yes    Hyphens: Yes    │            │
 │  └──────────────────────────────────┬───────────────────┘            │
 │                    Spelling Checker settings: C:\S2\SPELLER.SCF       │
 └─────────────────────────────────────────────────────────────────────┘
```

If you don't select this option, the lines will jumble together. Once you take these steps, you are ready to begin spell-checking the same way you do with documents.

None of the cells in the spell-check range can be protected. If they are, Symphony displays the message Cannot check protected cells. You should then disable protection with the SERVICES Settings Global-Protection No command.

Text Outliner

Most often the reason for creating an outline is to provide a structure for writing a document, because an outline shows the document's structure at a glance. Consequently, the outline can help you create a more organized document. You can also use outlines to help organize your thoughts for lectures and speeches. For example, you can use an outline as a "cheat sheet" when giving a speech, or give the outline to the audience to let the listeners know what topics you will be discussing.

You may be thinking that you can type outlines just fine in DOC mode so why use Text Outliner? Basically, Text Outliner automates the entire process of creating and modifying an outline. First of all, you don't have to do any tabbing or numbering; the outline format is created automatically. Secondly, in a word processor, you would have to create two separate documents (the outline and the body text), and after creating the outline you would have to retype your outline headings into the text manually. With Text Outliner, you type the outline headings once, and you can view the outline with headings only (no text) or with the headings integrated into the text.

Finally, if you need to reorganize the outline or document, the outlining features make it a much easier process. Working in the OUTLN window, you can quickly move, copy, and delete entire sections (headings, subheadings, and associated text). In a DOC window, you would have to highlight large blocks of text and do a lot of scrolling to accomplish the same thing.

With Text Outliner, you can make global changes to your headings. For example, you can specify print attributes (such as boldface) for all your headings with a single command. You can also change the amount of indentation in the outline levels by pressing a single key. You can't make these kinds of global changes in DOC mode.

Attaching and Invoking the Outliner

Before you can use Text Outliner to create or modify an outline, you must first attach the Outliner add-in application. By attaching the Outliner, you have a sixth window type available (see fig. 10.11A), and when you select OUTLN, the Menu key offers a whole set of new commands (see fig. 10.11B).

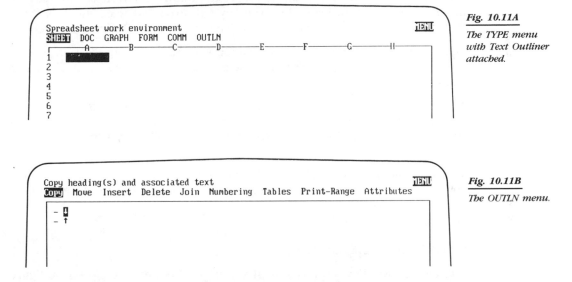

Fig. 10.11A

The TYPE menu with Text Outliner attached.

Fig. 10.11B

The OUTLN menu.

Unlike the Spelling Checker program, Text Outliner consumes very little memory—only about 27K. So you should not encounter the memory problems that are possible with Spelling Checker. If you are outlining a long document and get an insufficient memory message, you may need to free up memory by detaching any other applications or removing any memory-resident programs.

Attaching Text Outliner is similar to attaching Spelling Checker. If you are running Symphony on floppy disk drives, you need to insert the Speller and Outliner Add-Ins disk into drive A before attaching the application. Use the SERVICES Application Attach command and select **OUTLINER.APP** from the list of applications. The Text Outliner copyright screen appears, and eventually the Application menu reappears in the control panel. Select **Quit**. Floppy disk users can now remove the Speller and Outliner Add-Ins disk from drive A.

If you retrieve an outline file without first attaching Text Outliner, you may get the message (must Attach OUTLINER) in the middle of the screen. This message indicates that you saved the file while in the OUTLN window, and because OUTLN is not a valid window type until you attach Text Outliner, Symphony cannot display the outline in an OUTLN window. (You can look at the spreadsheet or document version of the outline in a SHEET or DOC window without attaching Text Outliner, but the text will not look much like an outline.) After you attach Text Outliner, the error message disappears, and the outline displays.

If you use Text Outliner every day, you can have Symphony automatically attach the add-in each time you load Symphony. Use the SERVICES Configuration Other Application Set command to attach the application automatically.

To create an outline or use any of the Text Outliner commands, you must be in an outline window. Press the Type key (Alt-F10) and select OUTLN. Note that the OUTLN window type is only offered when Text Outliner is attached.

You do not invoke the Outliner application with SERVICES Application Invoke. If you try to do so, Symphony displays the message Press [TYPE] and select OUTLN.

After you have finished using Text Outliner, you can detach it to free up memory for other applications or files. Use the SERVICES Application Detach command and select **OUTLINER.APP**, or select SERVICES Application Clear to clear all applications.

The application automatically detaches itself when you exit Symphony, unless you have configured Symphony to attach Text Outliner automatically every time you load Symphony.

Creating an Outline

The OUTLN window displays several special symbols, as you can see in figure 10.12. The ↓ indicates the top of the outline, while the ↑ indicates the bottom. The minus sign (-) indicates that the heading has no subheadings beneath it. The plus sign (+) tells you that the heading does have subheadings.

To create entries in your outline, you invoke the Insert command from the main OUTLN menu.

Inserting Headings

Text Outliner offers two ways to insert headings into an outline: with the OUTLN Insert command or with the Ins key. The Ins key requires fewer keystrokes, so you will probably use this method most of the time.

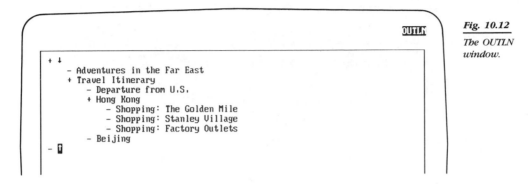

Fig. 10.12
*The OUTLN
window.*

When you select the **Insert** command from the OUTLN menu or by pressing the Ins key, the heading level menu displays:

Same-Level   Lower-Level   Higher-Level   Quit

Figures 10.13A, 10.13B, and 10.13C show how the heading The Forbidden City appears after it is inserted at different levels. If you select **Same-Level**, the new heading is given the same level of indentation as the highlighted heading Beijing (see fig. 10.13A).

Lower-Level makes the new heading a subheading of the highlighted heading and indents the new heading four spaces from the previous heading. (You can adjust the number of spaces in the indentation. The procedure for changing the number is discussed in the section on "Changing Indentation.") The Forbidden City was inserted at a **Lower-Level** in figure 10.13B.

Higher-Level makes the new heading one level higher than the highlighted heading and places the new heading four spaces to the left of the previous heading (see fig. 10.13C).

```
                                                        EDIT
    + ↓
        - Adventures in the Far East
        + Travel Itinerary
            - Departure from U.S.
            + Hong Kong
                - Shopping: The Golden Mile
                - Shopping: Stanley Village
                - Shopping: Factory Outlets
            - Beijing
            - The Forbidden City
    - ↑
```

Fig. 10.13A

Inserting a Same-Level heading.

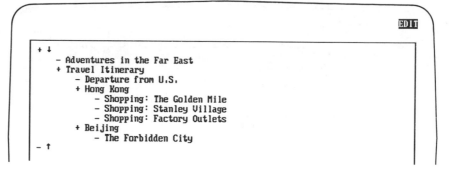

Fig. 10.13B

Inserting a Lower-Level heading.

Fig. 10.13C

Inserting a Higher-Level heading.

After you have indicated the heading level, type the text for the heading. Text Outliner automatically places you in EDIT mode, so you can use your edit keys to correct mistakes (see the section entitled "Editing Headings" for additional information). Press Enter when you are finished typing the heading. The heading level menu reappears so that you can continue adding headings to your outline.

Select **Quit** when you are finished inserting outline entries. If you accidentally exit the Insert command, simply position the cursor and press the Ins key again. See the section entitled "Inserting Additional Headings" for information on inserting headings in an existing outline.

Note that **Higher-Level** moves the heading back only a single level. If you need to move back two levels, select **Higher-Level** and make a blank entry, which you can delete later. (A minus sign appears with no heading next to it.) Then choose **Higher-Level** again and type your heading. Refer to the section on "Deleting Headings" to see how to remove the blank heading.

If you accidentally indicate the wrong level, use the **Move** command to move the heading to the correct level.

Moving around in an Outline

Moving around in an outline is quite different from moving around in a document. First of all, in OUTLN mode, you do not have a single character cursor as you do in DOC mode. Instead, you have a pointer, similar to SHEET mode's cell pointer, except that the OUTLN pointer's length varies according to the length of the heading.

Your cursor-movement keys also work differently in OUTLN mode, as shown in the following list:

Key	Moves pointer to the
↑	Previous heading at the same level
↓	Next heading at the same level
←	Previous heading, regardless of level
→	Next heading, regardless of level
Ctrl-←	Previous heading at higher level
Ctrl-→	Next heading at higher level
Home	Top of the outline
End	Bottom of the outline

The PgUp and PgDn keys work the same way as they do in DOC mode. In OUTLN mode, the GoTo key (F5) does not move to a page or a line number; instead, this key switches you to DOC mode with a single keystroke.

Displaying Outline Numbers

By default the outline is not numbered, but by pressing the Tab key you can get two different types of numbering systems. Press the Tab key once, and each level in the outline is numbered sequentially (1, 2, 3, . . .). See figure 10.14A for an example of sequential numbering.

Press the Tab key a second time, and multilevel (absolute) numbering displays (1, 1.1, 1.2, 1.2.1, . . .). See figure 10.14B for an example of multilevel numbering.

Press the Tab key a third time, and the default outline (no numbering) displays. Unfortunately, Text Outliner does not offer a Roman numeral system (I, A, 1, a).

You must be in OUTLN mode when you press the Tab key. If you are in the middle of inserting entries, you are in EDIT mode, and the Tab key has no effect.

Hiding and Exposing Headings

Sometimes when you create a long outline with many subheadings, you lose sight of what your major topics are (the old "can't see the forest for the trees" syndrome). If this situation occurs, you may want to hide the subheadings so that

Fig. 10.14A

*An example of
sequential
numbering.*

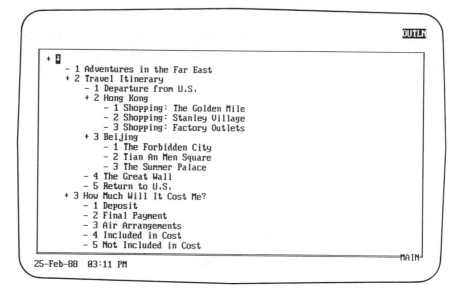

```
                                                          OUTLN
  + ▯
      - 1 Adventures in the Far East
    + 2 Travel Itinerary
        - 1 Departure from U.S.
        + 2 Hong Kong
            - 1 Shopping: The Golden Mile
            - 2 Shopping: Stanley Village
            - 3 Shopping: Factory Outlets
        + 3 Beijing
            - 1 The Forbidden City
            - 2 Tian An Men Square
            - 3 The Summer Palace
        - 4 The Great Wall
        - 5 Return to U.S.
    + 3 How Much Will It Cost Me?
        - 1 Deposit
        - 2 Final Payment
        - 3 Air Arrangements
        - 4 Included in Cost
        - 5 Not Included in Cost
                                                          MAIN
  25-Feb-88  03:11 PM
```

Fig. 10.14B

*An example of
multilevel
numbering.*

```
                                                          OUTLN
  + ▯
      - 1 Adventures in the Far East
    + 2 Travel Itinerary
        - 2.1 Departure from U.S.
        + 2.2 Hong Kong
            - 2.2.1 Shopping: The Golden Mile
            - 2.2.2 Shopping: Stanley Village
            - 2.2.3 Shopping: Factory Outlets
        + 2.3 Beijing
            - 2.3.1 The Forbidden City
            - 2.3.2 Tian An Men Square
            - 2.3.3 The Summer Palace
        - 2.4 The Great Wall
        - 2.5 Return to U.S.
    + 3 How Much Will It Cost Me?
        - 3.1 Deposit
        - 3.2 Final Payment
        - 3.3 Air Arrangements
        - 3.4 Included in Cost
        - 3.5 Not Included in Cost
                                                          MAIN
  25-Feb-88  03:11 PM
```

you can view just the major headings. Text Outliner offers several keys to hide temporarily and expose subheadings:

Key	*Description*
- (on numeric keypad)	Hides all subheadings of highlighted heading
+ (on numeric keypad)	Exposes all subheadings one level under highlighted heading
* (on numeric keypad)	Exposes all subheadings at all levels under highlighted heading

After you have hidden headings, you can look at the special symbols to the left of the headings to determine which headings are hidden. Remember, the minus sign (-) indicates that a heading does not have any subheadings, and the plus sign (+) indicates that subheadings exist. If a heading has a + next to it, but you do not see any subheadings, you can deduce that the subheadings are hidden. For example, in figure 10.15, Adventures in the Far East does not have any hidden subheadings, but Travel Itinerary does.

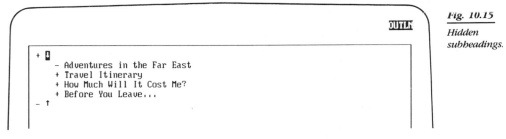

Fig. 10.15

Hidden subheadings.

The quickest way to display just your major headings is to press Home to go to the top of your outline, and then press minus (-) to hide all the headings. Then press plus (+) to expose the headings one level under the current heading, as shown in figure 10.15.

If you have selectively hidden certain subheadings and want to expose them all, you could go to each heading and press plus (+) to expose its subheadings. A faster way, however, would be to go to the top of the outline and press the asterisk (*) to expose all the headings.

Printing an Outline

You cannot directly print your outline as it appears in an OUTLN window. If you do try to print, when you specify a **S**ource **R**ange, you will immediately see that something is wrong. You are switched into SHEET mode, and the outline is triple-spaced with multilevel numbering, a bunch of special codes, and no indentation at the different levels. You could print this version of the outline, but it would not look much like an outline.

You can print an exact copy of the outline, however, as you see it in the OUTLN window. The **Tables Outline** command on the OUTLN menu makes a duplicate of your outline in another part of the spreadsheet so that you can specify this range as the **Source**. To create this copy, select OUTLN **Tables Outline**. You are automatically switched into SHEET mode, and Text Outliner asks you for a destination range. Be sure to indicate an empty part of the spreadsheet. Otherwise, the outline will copy over and replace any cells containing data. Make sure that you *DO NOT* specify the area containing the spreadsheet version of your outline.

After you copy the outline to the spreadsheet (see fig. 10.16), you can use the SERVICES **Print** command to print the outline. Specify the copy you just made as the **Source Range**.

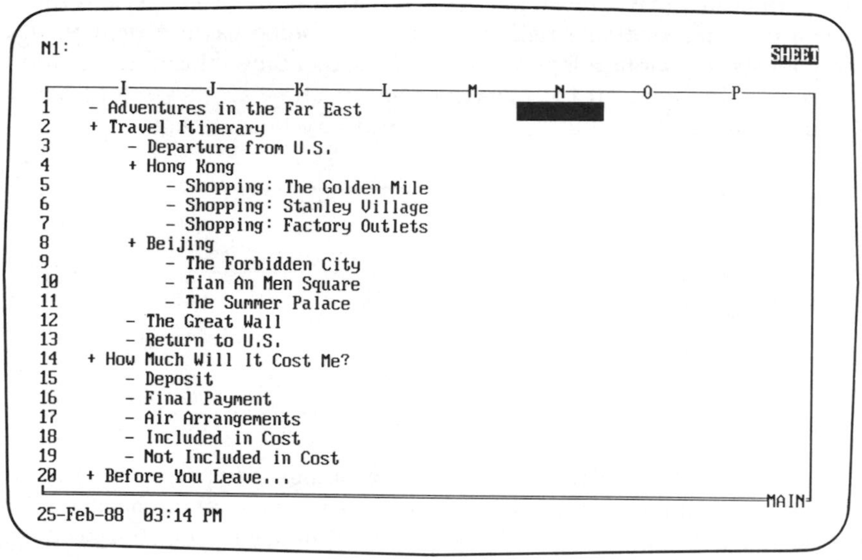

Fig. 10.16

After copying an outline to a spreadsheet.

```
 N1:                                                           SHEET

    ┌────I────────J────────K────────L────────M────────N────────O────────P─────
    1     - Adventures in the Far East                  ████████████
    2     + Travel Itinerary
    3         - Departure from U.S.
    4         + Hong Kong
    5             - Shopping: The Golden Mile
    6             - Shopping: Stanley Village
    7             - Shopping: Factory Outlets
    8         + Beijing
    9             - The Forbidden City
    10            - Tian An Men Square
    11            - The Summer Palace
    12        - The Great Wall
    13        - Return to U.S.
    14    + How Much Will It Cost Me?
    15        - Deposit
    16        - Final Payment
    17        - Air Arrangements
    18        - Included in Cost
    19        - Not Included in Cost
    20    + Before You Leave...
    └                                                                   MAIN
    25-Feb-88  03:14 PM
```

If the outline is part of a document (see the section on "Using an Outline To Create a Document"), you will find the **Tables Outline** command useful for printing only the outline (no text).

Modifying an Outline

One of the benefits of creating outlines in Text Outliner rather than in a word processor is Text Outliner's capacity to manipulate in terms of headings and subheadings rather than in terms of individual characters. For example, if you want to move a section, you do not need to highlight all the text and subheadings that belong with that section. By highlighting just the heading, you automatically move everything underneath it. The same applies for deleting and copying.

In Text Outliner, you can format headings as a group rather than one by one. With the OUTLN Attributes command, you can specify the print attributes either for all levels, for a specific level, or for an individual heading. You can also change the amount of indentation in the outline levels by pressing a single key. In a DOC window, you cannot make global changes like these.

Editing Headings

If you make a mistake in one of your outline entries after you have entered it, you can use the Edit key (F2) to correct. If you are in the middle of inserting an entry, you are automatically in EDIT mode and consequently do not need to press the Edit key. Editing a heading in an OUTLN window is almost identical to editing a spreadsheet cell in a SHEET window. Use the pointer to highlight the heading you want to edit, and press F2. You then get a single-character cursor rather than a rectangular pointer. Use the right- and left-arrow keys to move the cursor, and take advantage of the following editing keys:

Key	Function
Del	Deletes character at cursor
Backspace	Deletes character to left of cursor
Home	Moves to beginning of heading
End	Moves to end of heading
Esc (once)	Clears entry
Esc (twice)	Restores original entry

Characters are automatically inserted to the left as you type. And you cannot overtype characters as you can in DOC mode.

Inserting Additional Headings

To insert a heading after the outline has been created, place the pointer above where you want the new heading to appear. This positioning may not be what you expect, because data is inserted above the cursor in DOC and SHEET modes. In OUTLN mode, though, headings are inserted below the pointer. For example, to insert the heading Cancellations between the headings Final Payment and Air Arrangements, as shown in figure 10.17, you place the pointer on Final Payment.

After you have placed the pointer in the proper location, use the OUTLN Insert command or the Ins key. You must then choose the heading level: Same-Level, Lower-Level (a subheading), or Higher-Level (one level higher). Next, type the heading text and press Enter. If you are finished adding headings, choose Quit. Otherwise, select the heading level for the next insert and then continue.

If the outline was numbered, it dynamically renumbers as you insert new entries.

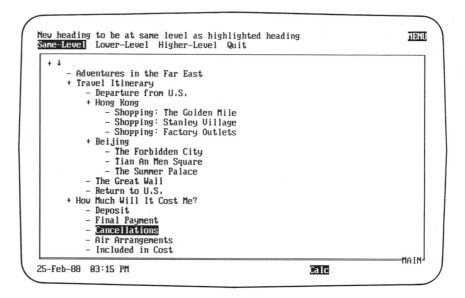

Fig. 10.17

Inserting a new heading.

```
New heading to be at same level as highlighted heading          MENU
Same-Level  Lower-Level  Higher-Level  Quit

  ↑ ↓
        - Adventures in the Far East
        + Travel Itinerary
            - Departure from U.S.
            + Hong Kong
                - Shopping: The Golden Mile
                - Shopping: Stanley Village
                - Shopping: Factory Outlets
            + Beijing
                - The Forbidden City
                - Tian An Men Square
                - The Summer Palace
            - The Great Wall
            - Return to U.S.
        + How Much Will It Cost Me?
            - Deposit
            - Final Payment
            - Cancellations
            - Air Arrangements
            - Included in Cost
                                                         ─MAIN─
 25-Feb-88  03:15 PM                       Calc
```

Removing Headings

To remove a heading, use the OUTLN **D**elete command or the Del key. First place the pointer on the heading you want to remove. Press the Del key or choose OUTLN **D**elete. The message Delete what? appears in the control panel. The heading and all its subheadings (if any) are highlighted. This high-lighting should alert you to the fact that you cannot delete a heading without also deleting its subheadings. Furthermore, if any text falls under the heading or subheadings in the document, this text would also be deleted. Make sure that you want to delete all this material! Fortunately, Text Outliner asks you to confirm your intent to delete heading(s) and associated text, as shown in figure 10.18. If all you want to do is remove a heading, and not the text, you might want to use the **J**oin command (see the next section).

If you have hidden any subheadings with the minus key (-), the hidden headings are also deleted, even though they are not displayed. It's a good idea to go to the top of the outline and press the asterisk (*) to expose all headings before you delete anything. With all headings displayed, you see exactly what headings and subheadings you are deleting. It's also a good idea to save your file before you delete, because the **D**elete command is so convenient that it borders on being dangerous.

You can also delete more than one heading at a time. By default, Text Outliner highlights the single heading on which your pointer rests (and any subheadings), but you can use your arrow keys to highlight additional entries.

If the outline was numbered, it dynamically renumbers as you delete entries.

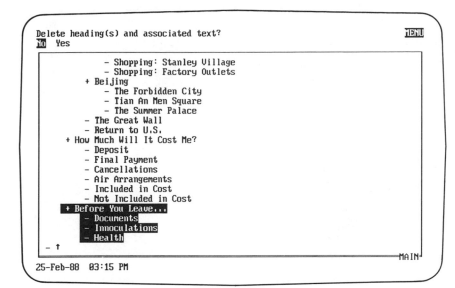

Fig. 10.18

Deleting headings.

Merging Outline Sections

The OUTLN Join command merges together two adjoining sections. In effect, Join deletes the heading and moves its subheadings and associated text to the previous heading. So rather than move the subheadings and then delete the main heading, you can use Join to do it in one step.

The Join command does have its limitations. You can join sections only at the same or higher level. This concept is best explained by example. Refer to figure 10.19A. You can join the headings Adventures in the Far East and Travel Itinerary, because they are at the same level. But Text Outliner does not let you join How Much Will It Cost Me? with Travel Itinerary, because the heading before How Much Will It Cost Me? is at a lower level. If you attempt to perform this operation, you get the message Target must be at same or higher level.

To merge two sections, select OUTLN Join. Text Outliner asks, Merge what section with preceding section?. Move the pointer to the section you want to merge. Text Outliner highlights not only the section you point to but also the preceding section. You are asked to confirm your intention. As you can see in figure 10.19B, all the text and subheadings of the second section are added onto the first section, and the heading for the second section (Travel Itinerary) is deleted. If you had previously hidden any of the headings in the merged section, the Join operation would automatically expose these subheadings.

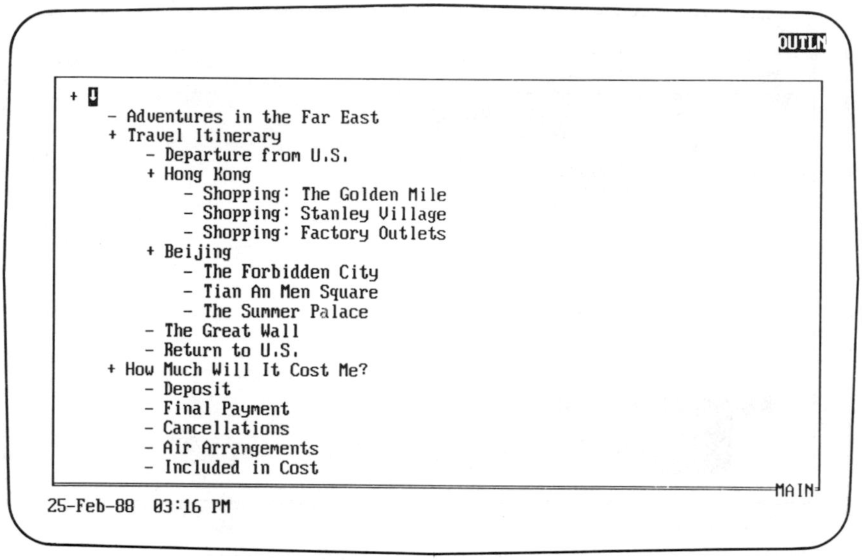

Fig. 10.19A

Before joining
Travel
Itinerary *to*
Adventures in
the Far East.

```
                                                          OUTLN
    + █
        - Adventures in the Far East
        + Travel Itinerary
            - Departure from U.S.
            + Hong Kong
                - Shopping: The Golden Mile
                - Shopping: Stanley Village
                - Shopping: Factory Outlets
            + Beijing
                - The Forbidden City
                - Tian An Men Square
                - The Summer Palace
            - The Great Wall
            - Return to U.S.
        + How Much Will It Cost Me?
            - Deposit
            - Final Payment
            - Cancellations
            - Air Arrangements
            - Included in Cost
                                                      MAIN
    25-Feb-88  03:16 PM
```

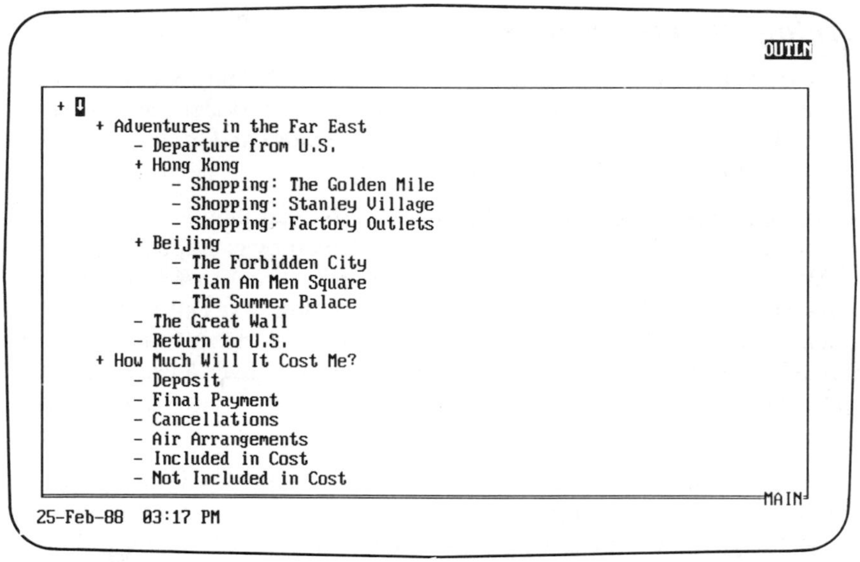

Fig. 10.19B

After using the
Join command.

```
                                                          OUTLN
    + █
        + Adventures in the Far East
            - Departure from U.S.
            + Hong Kong
                - Shopping: The Golden Mile
                - Shopping: Stanley Village
                - Shopping: Factory Outlets
            + Beijing
                - The Forbidden City
                - Tian An Men Square
                - The Summer Palace
            - The Great Wall
            - Return to U.S.
        + How Much Will It Cost Me?
            - Deposit
            - Final Payment
            - Cancellations
            - Air Arrangements
            - Included in Cost
            - Not Included in Cost
                                                      MAIN
    25-Feb-88  03:17 PM
```

If the outline was numbered, it dynamically renumbers after you use the Join
command.

Copying Outline Sections

Use the **C**opy command to copy a section of your outline to another location in the outline. This command copies the heading(s) you highlight, any subheadings (including ones you may have previously hidden), and any accompanying text that exists in the DOC window.

Select OUTLN **C**opy, and Text Outliner asks, `Copy what?`. Highlight the heading or headings you want to duplicate and press Enter. Text Outliner then asks, `Copy after what heading?`. As with the **I**nsert command, the entries are inserted after the pointer. Place the pointer on the line above where you want the copy to go; then press Enter. The heading level menu displays in the control panel. Note that you are asked to choose the level with respect to the highlighted heading, not the level at which the headings were previously. Choose the appropriate level, and the section copies.

If the outline was numbered, it dynamically renumbers after you use the **C**opy command.

Moving Outline Sections

The **M**ove command has two purposes in Text Outliner. First, **M**ove reorganizes your outline if you want to restructure it. Second, you can use the command to change the level of a heading. (See the next section, "Changing Levels.") The **M**ove command relocates the heading(s) you highlight, any subheadings you may have previously hidden, and accompanying text in the DOC window.

Select OUTLN **M**ove, and Text Outliner asks, `Move what?`. Highlight the heading or headings you want to move; then press Enter. Text Outliner asks, `Move after what heading?`. As with the **I**nsert and **C**opy commands, the entries are inserted after the pointer. Place the pointer on the line above where you want the section to be moved and press Enter. The heading level menu displays in the control panel. Note that you are asked to choose the level with respect to the highlighted heading, not the level at which the headings were previously. Choose the appropriate level, and the section moves.

If the outline was numbered, it dynamically renumbers after you use the **M**ove command.

Changing Levels

Because the **M**ove command asks you to specify what level you want the heading to have in its new location, you can use this command to change a heading's level without actually relocating the heading. Suppose that you want the heading `The Great Wall` in figure 10.20A to be a subheading of `Beijing`. Select OUTLN **M**ove. Text Outliner asks, `Move what?`. Highlight `The Great Wall` and press Enter. Text Outliner asks, `Move after what heading?`. Place the pointer on the preceding line, which keeps the heading in the same position in the outline, and press Enter. The heading level menu displays in the control panel. You want the heading to be at the same level as the target heading (The Summer Palace), so select Same-Level. The section moves to the right—it changes level. The outline now looks like figure 10.20B.

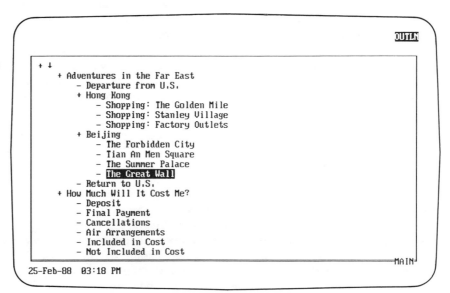

Fig. 10.20A

Before changing heading levels.

```
                                                              OUTLN
┌──────────────────────────────────────────────────────┐
│ + ↓                                                    │
│    + Adventures in the Far East                        │
│       - Departure from U.S.                            │
│       + Hong Kong                                      │
│          - Shopping: The Golden Mile                   │
│          - Shopping: Stanley Village                   │
│          - Shopping: Factory Outlets                   │
│       + Beijing                                        │
│          - The Forbidden City                          │
│          - Tian An Men Square                          │
│          - The Summer Palace                           │
│       - The Great Wall                                 │
│       - Return to U.S.                                 │
│    + How Much Will It Cost Me?                         │
│       - Deposit                                        │
│       - Final Payment                                  │
│       - Cancellations                                  │
│       - Air Arrangements                               │
│       - Included in Cost                               │
│       - Not Included in Cost                           │
└──────────────────────────────────────────────MAIN─────┘
 25-Feb-88  03:19 PM
```

Fig. 10.20B

Moving The Great Wall *to a new level.*

```
                                                              OUTLN
┌──────────────────────────────────────────────────────┐
│ + ↓                                                    │
│    + Adventures in the Far East                        │
│       - Departure from U.S.                            │
│       + Hong Kong                                      │
│          - Shopping: The Golden Mile                   │
│          - Shopping: Stanley Village                   │
│          - Shopping: Factory Outlets                   │
│       + Beijing                                        │
│          - The Forbidden City                          │
│          - Tian An Men Square                          │
│          - The Summer Palace                           │
│          - The Great Wall                              │
│       - Return to U.S.                                 │
│    + How Much Will It Cost Me?                         │
│       - Deposit                                        │
│       - Final Payment                                  │
│       - Cancellations                                  │
│       - Air Arrangements                               │
│       - Included in Cost                               │
│       - Not Included in Cost                           │
└──────────────────────────────────────────────MAIN─────┘
 25-Feb-88  03:18 PM
```

Let's look at a slightly more complicated example. Suppose that you want the subheading Air Arrangements to be a major heading, and you want the two headings below it to be subheadings of Air Arrangements, not of How Much Will It Cost Me?. Figure 10.21A illustrates how you would like to restructure the outline.

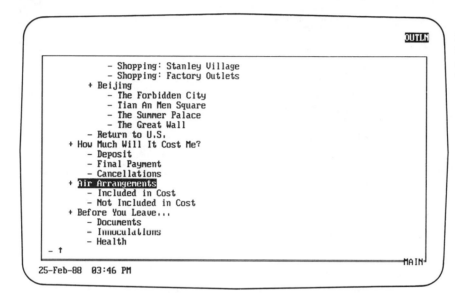

Fig. 10.21A

Changing Air Arrangements *to a major heading.*

You might think that all you have to do is move Air Arrangements to a higher level. But figure 10.21B shows the results of this move. The subheadings still "belong" to the heading How Much Will It Cost Me?, so they stay put, and the new major heading (Air Arrangements) moves after all the subheadings. Consequently, you must perform a second move operation to move the subheadings. Highlight the two subheadings (Included in Cost and Not Included in Cost) and move them after Air Arrangements, specifying a Lower-Level. Now the outline looks like figure 10.21A.

Formatting an Outline

If you were creating an outline in DOC mode, without using Text Outliner, you would have to format each of your headings individually with the appropriate print attribute (such as boldface or underlined). You would have to press Ctrl-B and specify an attribute before each heading, and then press Ctrl-E after each heading. With the Text Outliner's **Attribute** command, however, you can format headings as a group rather than one by one, allowing you to format all your headings quickly and consistently. Furthermore, you can indicate the print

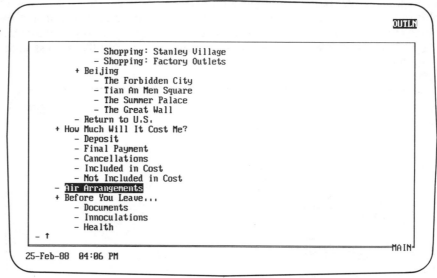

Fig. 10.21B

*The first step of the
move.*

```
                                                                    OUTLN
         - Shopping: Stanley Village
         - Shopping: Factory Outlets
      + Beijing
         - The Forbidden City
         - Tian An Men Square
         - The Summer Palace
         - The Great Wall
      - Return to U.S.
    + How Much Will It Cost Me?
         - Deposit
         - Final Payment
         - Cancellations
         - Included in Cost
         - Not Included in Cost
    -  Air Arrangements
    + Before You Leave...
         - Documents
         - Innoculations
         - Health
  - ↑
                                                               MAIN
 25-Feb-88  04:06 PM
```

attributes for all levels, for all headings at a certain level, or for an individual heading.

By indicating special print attributes for your headings, you can easily discern them from the document text, and from each other, when you print the document or outline. To format your headings, select OUTLN **Attributes**. The following menu displays in the control panel:

Global   **L**evel   **S**ingle

To format all the headings with the same print attribute, choose **G**lobal. To assign a special format for all the headings at a particular level, select **L**evel. Choose **S**ingle to set the attributes for only one heading.

If you choose **L**evel, Text Outliner asks, Attributes for what level?. Place the pointer on any heading in the level you want to format; then press Enter. If you choose **S**ingle, Text Outliner asks, Attribute for what heading?. Point to the appropriate heading and press Enter.

After you choose one of the three options, you see the attribute menu. This menu is similar to the menu you get in DOC mode when you press Ctrl-B, except that the OUTLN version has two additional choices: **N**on-Printing and **C**lear. If you choose **N**on-Printing, the heading(s) do not print in the document, although they do print in the outline. (The section entitled "Outlining an Existing Document" discusses when you might want to use this nonprinting feature.) If you no longer want any attributes for the heading(s), select **C**lear to remove the attributes.

Changing Indentation

By default, each level in the outline is indented four spaces from the previous level. But you are one keystroke away from changing the amount of indentation: you can type a number from 1 to 9 to control the indentation. For example, if you want each level indented 7 spaces from the preceding level, type 7. You instantly see the effect of the new indentation in your outline. Figure 10.22A displays the default indentation, while figure 10.22B shows a 7-space indentation.

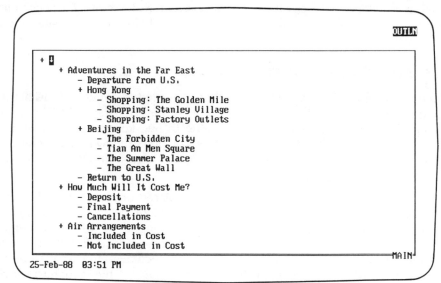

Fig. 10.22A

Default (four-space) indentation.

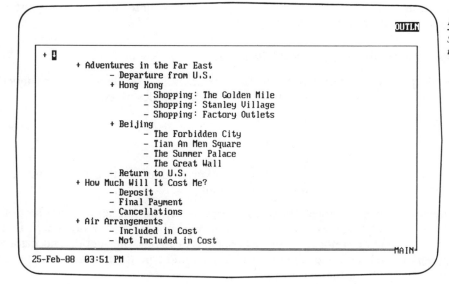

Fig. 10.22B

Seven-space indentation.

You must be in OUTLN mode when you type the number. If you are inserting entries (that is, you are in EDIT mode), you cannot change the indentation.

Using an Outline To Create a Document

So far, this chapter has concentrated on the creation and modification of outlines. Creating the outline, however, is just the first step. Most often the reason for creating an outline is to provide you with a structure for writing a document. This section discusses how to use the outline to help you write and edit a document effectively.

Switching between OUTLN and DOC

When you want to type text into your outline, you need to switch to DOC mode. The quickest way to go to DOC mode is to press the GoTo key (F5). The GoTo key in OUTLN mode switches to DOC mode in one keystroke. You can also press the Type key (Alt-F10) and select DOC, or press the Switch key (Alt-F9) if the last mode you were in was DOC. To switch back from DOC to OUTLN, use the Switch or Type keys.

When you switch to DOC mode, the cursor is placed underneath the heading on which the pointer rested in OUTLN mode. Similarly, when you switch back to OUTLN mode, the pointer is placed at the heading under which the cursor was located. Thus, you can use the outline to move quickly to different sections of a long document. If you are working in your document and want to move to a distant section, switch to OUTLN, move the pointer to the section to which you want to go, and then switch back to DOC. Your cursor will be underneath the desired heading. It's much faster to move the pointer in a compact outline than to scroll in the document.

The Outline in the DOC Window

When you switch from OUTLN to DOC, your outline headings are surrounded by codes, as shown in figure 10.23. The codes are described here:

Code	Description
{B}	Section-begin marker
{E}	Section-end marker
{-B}	Section-begin marker (hidden section in the outline)
{N}	Nonprinting heading

The section-begin marker, {B} or {-B}, appears on the line above each section. The section-end marker, {E}, appears after any subheadings or document text. If the heading does not have any subordinate headings, the section-end marker appears three lines under the heading. You should type the text associated with the heading above the end marker.

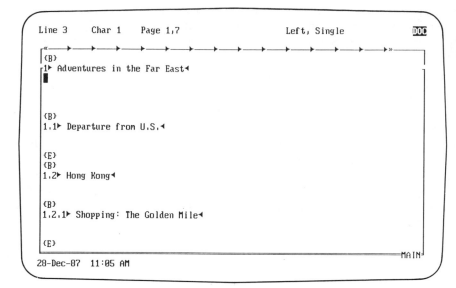

If you place the cursor on a line containing a marker, the control panel displays an asterisk. The asterisk indicates that you cannot edit the line in DOC mode. If you try to type anything on this line, Symphony beeps and displays at the bottom of the screen the message `Cannot alter this area of the docu-ment`. Because in DOC mode you cannot edit the lines containing begin or end markers, you do not need to worry about deleting them accidentally.

These special symbols do not print, nor do they leave blank lines when you print the document. To confirm this fact, look at the page and line number in the control panel as you move the cursor from a line containing a section marker to the line below it. You will see that the line number does not change.

The {N} symbol preceding a heading indicates that this heading will not be included in the printed document. You cannot edit nonprinting headings, as indicated by the asterisk in the control panel.

You *can* edit your headings (except for nonprinting headings) while in a DOC window, and the headings automatically change in the OUTLN window. If you completely erase a heading, the first line of text displays in the outline as a heading. If the line is blank, the following message appears where the heading formerly was in the OUTLN window: [`No heading on line below section-begin marker`]. To correct this error, switch back to DOC mode and type the heading on the line directly underneath the section-begin marker. The heading may no longer be at the right level, so you may have to use the **Move** command to adjust the level. (See the section on "Changing Levels.")

The headings are automatically numbered in DOC mode, regardless of whether the outline is numbered in OUTLN mode. If you do not want the numbers in the document headings, you can remove them, as explained in the next section.

Removing Outline Numbers

By default, the headings in DOC mode are numbered with the multilevel system (1, 1.1, 1.1.1). In most cases, you probably don't want numbered headings in the document. You will therefore want to remove the numbering in the document before you print. Switch to the OUTLN window and select OUTLN **Num**bering **Delete-Numbers**. In addition to removing outline numbers in the DOC window, this command removes the numbering and indentation in the OUTLN window, as shown in figure 10.24A. The document looks like figure 10.24B. To restore numbering and indentation, use the OUTLN **Numbering Renumber** command.

Because the indentation is eliminated from the outline, you will not want to use this command while working in the OUTLN window. You probably will issue the **Delete-Numbers** command before printing and then restore the numbering and indentation with the **Renumber** command the next time you work with the outline.

If you have turned off the numbering in your document, you may lose track of where you are in terms of your outline. When Text Outliner is attached, you have several additional commands available to you in DOC mode. One of these commands, **Format Location**, tells you which outline section your cursor is in. The current section (for example, Section 5.4) displays in the lower left corner of the screen.

The **Format Location** command saves you from switching to OUTLN mode, turning numbering back on to see where you are, then switching back to DOC mode.

Outlining an Existing Document

If you type all or part of a document before creating an outline, it's not too late to outline the document. But why would you want to outline an existing document? First, an outline shows you the document's structure at a glance. Sometimes when writing you get lost in what you are saying and lose track of the document's organization. The outline might lead you to reorganize some of the sections. This line of thought leads directly to the second reason for outlining an existing document: If you do need to reorganize the document, the outlining features make the process much easier. Working in the OUTLN window, you can quickly move, copy, and delete entire sections (headings, subheadings, and associated text).

To create an outline for existing text, you make the outline entries in DOC mode, not OUTLN mode. When Text Outliner is attached, an additional com-

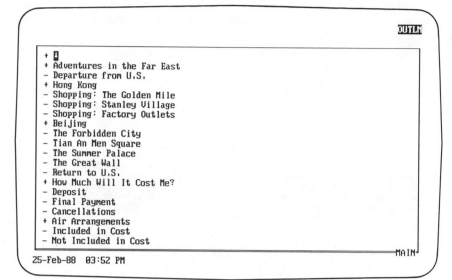

Fig. 10.24A

The results of selecting OUTLN Numbering Delete-Numbers.

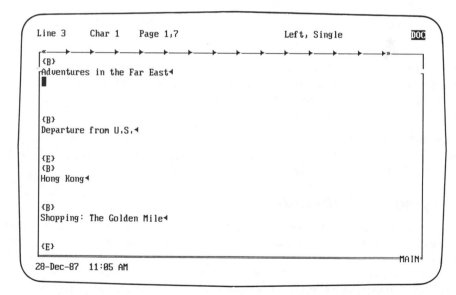

Fig. 10.24B

The document after deleting numbers.

mand appears on the DOC Format menu: **Outline-Section.** With this command, you can indicate the heading and the text to be included with the heading.

Select DOC **F**ormat **O**utline-Section. Highlight the text to be included in this section (including any subsections) and press Enter. Text Outliner asks you to Enter heading for this section. Type the heading and press Enter. The new heading appears, and the begin- and end-section markers are inserted in the appropriate places in the document (see fig. 10.25). Repeat this procedure for each section.

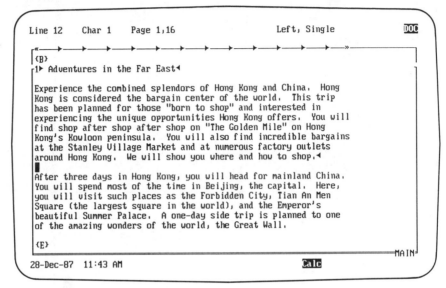

Fig. 10.25

Inserting headings in an existing document.

```
Line 12    Char 1    Page 1,16              Left, Single         DOC

«————▸————▸————▸————▸————▸————▸————▸————▸————▸————▸————»
{B}
1▸ Adventures in the Far East◂

Experience the combined splendors of Hong Kong and China.  Hong
Kong is considered the bargain center of the world.  This trip
has been planned for those "born to shop" and interested in
experiencing the unique opportunities Hong Kong offers.  You will
find shop after shop after shop on "The Golden Mile" on Hong
Kong's Kowloon peninsula.  You will also find incredible bargains
at the Stanley Village Market and at numerous factory outlets
around Hong Kong.  We will show you where and how to shop.◂
█
After three days in Hong Kong, you will head for mainland China.
You will spend most of the time in Beijing, the capital.  Here,
you will visit such places as the Forbidden City, Tian An Men
Square (the largest square in the world), and the Emperor's
beautiful Summer Palace.  A one-day side trip is planned to one
of the amazing wonders of the world, the Great Wall.

{E}
                                                              MAIN
28-Dec-87  11:43 AM                          Calc
```

If you switch to OUTLN mode, you can see the outline you are creating in DOC mode. Switch back and forth between DOC and OUTLN mode frequently so that you can make sure you are indicating the correct range for each section and, hence, structuring the outline properly.

When an existing document contains already-typed section titles, you either need to delete the titles or specify the outline headings as nonprinting (OUTLN Attributes Global Non-Printing).

Printing an Outlined Document

In a DOC window, Symphony prints all the text by default. So to print the entire document, make sure you are in DOC mode and then issue the SERVICES Print Go command. Symphony prints your entire document along with the headings and section numbers. If you do not want the section numbers to print, use the OUTLN Numbering Delete-Numbers command before printing. Any headings specified as Non-Printing with the OUTLN Attributes command do not print at all.

If you want to print a part of the document, select SERVICES Print Settings Source Range and then highlight the appropriate part of the text. An alternative (and faster) way of specifying certain sections to print, though, is Text Outliner's Print-Range command. With this command, you only have to highlight the outline heading(s) of the text that you want to print, as illustrated in figure 10.26A. Figure 10.26B shows how **Print-Range** takes care of entering the appropriate **Source Range** into the current Print settings sheet. This command makes it convenient to print certain sections of a long document selectively.

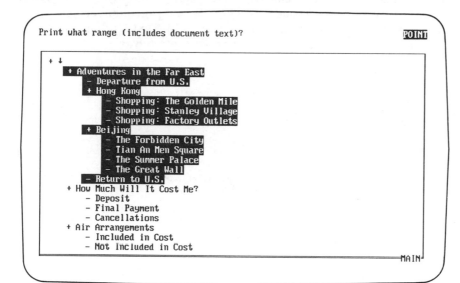

Fig. 10.26A

Highlighting a range to print.

Fig. 10.26B

The source range in the settings sheet.

If you save the document with a **Print-Range** specified, this **Source Range** is permanently stored in the Print settings sheet. The next time you issue the **Print** command, this range prints. To return to the default setting of the entire document, issue the SERVICES **Print Settings Source Cancel** command.

Table of Contents

Another reason for outlining a document is to have Text Outliner create a table of contents for the document. The OUTLN Tables Table-of-Contents command generates a table of contents containing headings, section numbers, indentation, blank lines between level changes, leader dots, and page numbers. Figure 10.27 is an example of a table of contents generated by Text Outliner. The table is stored in the spreadsheet and can be printed separately.

Fig. 10.27

A table of contents.

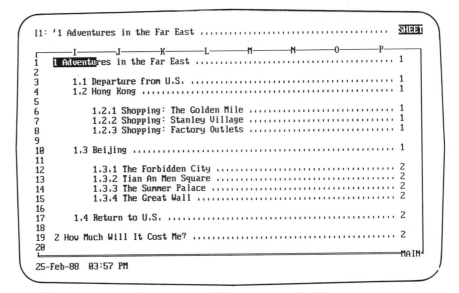

```
I1: '1 Adventures in the Far East ..................................... SHEET

      ─I────────J─────K──────L──────M──────N──────O──────P─
   1  1 Adventures in the Far East ...................................... 1
   2
   3      1.1 Departure from U.S. .................................... 1
   4      1.2 Hong Kong ............................................. 1
   5
   6          1.2.1 Shopping: The Golden Mile ....................... 1
   7          1.2.2 Shopping: Stanley Village ....................... 1
   8          1.2.3 Shopping: Factory Outlets ....................... 1
   9
  10      1.3 Beijing .............................................. 1
  11
  12          1.3.1 The Forbidden City ............................. 2
  13          1.3.2 Tian An Men Square ............................. 2
  14          1.3.3 The Summer Palace ............................... 2
  15          1.3.4 The Great Wall ................................. 2
  16
  17      1.4 Return to U.S. ....................................... 2
  18
  19  2 How Much Will It Cost Me? .................................. 2
  20                                                             MAIN
25-Feb-88  03:57 PM
```

To create a table of contents, select OUTLN Tables Table-of-Contents. Text Outliner then asks you to enter several parameters. The first prompt is Enter width. The number you enter here determines where the page number is placed in the table. If you accept the default (72), Text Outliner places the page number 72 characters from the left margin of the table.

The second prompt is Enter indentation. Regardless of the indentation used in your outline, you can specify a different indentation for the table of contents. You can specify a 1- to 9-space indentation.

Text Outliner nexts asks you to Enter number of heading levels to include in table. The default is 32, or all, heading levels. If you only want your major headings in the table of contents, you can specify 1 or 2 heading levels. Figure 10.28 shows a table of contents that includes 2 heading levels, as contrasted to the table in figure 10.27, which shows all levels.

Text Outliner then switches you into SHEET mode and asks you for a destination range. Make sure you indicate an empty part of the spreadsheet; otherwise, the

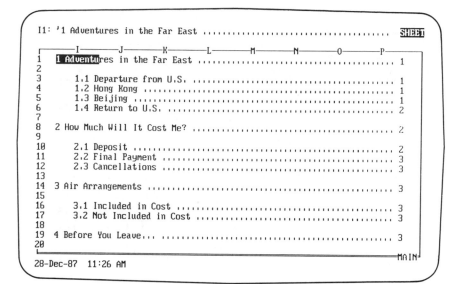

```
I1: '1 Adventures in the Far East ........................................ SHEET
     I───────J───────K───────L───────M───────N───────O───────P──
 1  1 Adventures in the Far East ....................................... 1
 2
 3      1.1 Departure from U.S. ........................................ 1
 4      1.2 Hong Kong ................................................. 1
 5      1.3 Beijing ................................................... 1
 6      1.4 Return to U.S. ............................................ 2
 7
 8  2 How Much Will It Cost Me? ....................................... 2
 9
10      2.1 Deposit ................................................... 2
11      2.2 Final Payment ............................................ 3
12      2.3 Cancellations ............................................ 3
13
14  3 Air Arrangements ............................................... 3
15
16      3.1 Included in Cost ......................................... 3
17      3.2 Not Included in Cost ..................................... 3
18
19  4 Before You Leave... ............................................ 3
20                                                              MAIN
28-Dec-87  11:26 AM
```

Fig. 10.28

A table of contents with only two levels included.

table of contents copies over and replaces any cells containing data. After you copy the table of contents to the spreadsheet, you can use the SERVICES **Print** command to print the table. Specify the table that Text Outliner just created as the **Source Range**.

You can edit the table of contents before you print. Switch to DOC mode and turn off justification with the DOC **Format Settings Justification None** command. If you do not turn off justification, the lines of the table will wrap together, leaving you with a jumbled mess that no longer resembles a table of contents!

Whenever you revise your document, keep in mind that the table of contents may no longer be accurate. If you have made significant revisions, you need to generate a new table of contents. Do not forget to erase the old table before creating the new one.

If you do not want section numbering in the table of contents, turn off numbering with the OUTLN **Numbering Delete-Numbers** command before you generate the table. Bear in mind that this command also turns off indentation, so the different levels in the table will not be indented, and blank lines will not appear between section-level changes. See figure 10.29.

Chapter Summary

By using the Spelling Checker and Text Outliner add-in applications, you can add power to Symphony's word processing. With Spelling Checker, you can re- duce the number of typing and spelling mistakes in your documents and spread-

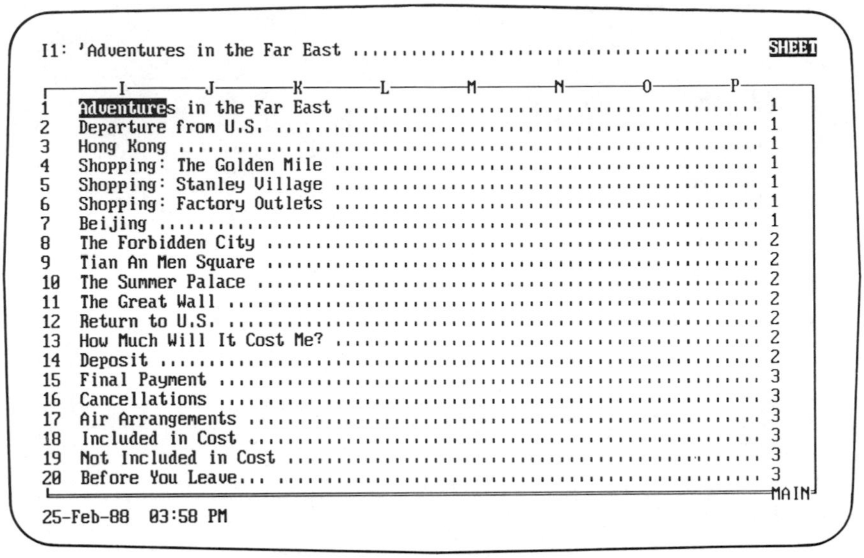

Fig. 10.29

After turning off numbering.

```
I1: 'Adventures in the Far East ....................................... SHEET
 ┌─────I─────J─────K─────L─────M─────N─────O─────P──┐
 1  Adventures in the Far East ........................................ 1
 2  Departure from U.S. .............................................. 1
 3  Hong Kong ........................................................ 1
 4  Shopping: The Golden Mile ........................................ 1
 5  Shopping: Stanley Village ........................................ 1
 6  Shopping: Factory Outlets ........................................ 1
 7  Beijing .......................................................... 1
 8  The Forbidden City ............................................... 2
 9  Tian An Men Square ............................................... 2
10  The Summer Palace ................................................ 2
11  The Great Wall ................................................... 2
12  Return to U.S. ................................................... 2
13  How Much Will It Cost Me? ........................................ 2
14  Deposit .......................................................... 2
15  Final Payment .................................................... 3
16  Cancellations .................................................... 3
17  Air Arrangements ................................................. 3
18  Included in Cost ................................................. 3
19  Not Included in Cost ............................................. 3
20  Before You Leave... .............................................. 3
 └──────────────────────────────────────────────────────────MAIN┘
 25-Feb-88  03:58 PM
```

sheets, enabling you to produce more professional-looking documents. Text
Outliner allows you to create outlines and tables of contents for your documents.
Furthermore, you will probably find that your long documents are easier to revise
and organize with Text Outliner.

PART IV

Creating Symphony Reports and Graphs

Includes

Printing Spreadsheets and Word-Processing Documents

Creating and Displaying Graphs

Printing Graphs

Creating and Printing Graphs Hands-On Practice

11

Printing Spreadsheets and Word-Processing Documents

Symphony lets you control the printing of spreadsheets, databases, documents, and graphs. This chapter discusses the printing of spreadsheets and word-processing documents; printing graphs is discussed in Chapter 13. As explained in that chapter, printing graphs requires that you use a separate program and disk, the PrintGraph disk (5 1/4-inch) or the PrintGraph with Translate disk (3 1/2-inch), rather than the Symphony Program disk. Chapter 15 covers the printing of databases.

Except in the case of printing graphs, Symphony provides options for writing directly to the printer from within the program, creating a print file to be printed outside the program, or printing to a range within the current worksheet. Symphony also enables you to print headers and footers that include dates and page numbers and to begin printing or end printing at any page (between 1 and 999) in a word-processing document.

Although many print options control the printing of both spreadsheets and text, some options are specific to the type of application. For example, within the SERVICES **Print** menu are the options for printing spreadsheets as displayed or as cell formulas. You can tell Symphony to repeat the printing of column and row headings for each page of a spreadsheet you print. Special print options related to printing documents include regulating underlined, boldface, super-script, and subscript characters in text.

SERVICES Configuration Printer and SERVICES Print

If you will be sending data directly to the printer, you will want to make sure that the correct printer driver is set and that you have accessed the Symphony program with the correct driver (see Appendix A for an explanation of setting drivers). Apart from the driver setting, however, two other types of settings affect the output to the printer, print file, or worksheet range (the three output choices you have when using SERVICES Print). These two settings are SERVICES Configuration Printer settings (see fig. 11.1) and SERVICES Print settings (see fig. 11.2).

Fig. 11.1

The SERVICES Configuration Printer settings.

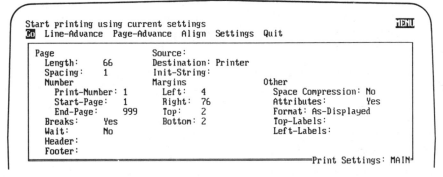

```
Ending column of document                                          MENU
Tabs Justification Spacing Left Right Blanks CRs Auto-Justify Hard-Tabs Quit

File: C:\S2                    Document              Window
Printer                          Tab interval:  5      Type: SHEET
  Type:      Parallel 1         Justification: 1      Name:
  Auto-LF:   No                 Spacing:       1        MAIN
  Wait:      No                 Left margin:   1      Help: Removable
  Margins                       Right margin:         Auto-Worksheet:
    Left:  4      Top:    2     Blanks visible: No
    Right: 76     Bottom: 2     CRs visible:    Yes   Clock on Screen:
  Page-Length: 66               Auto-Justify:   Yes     Standard
  Init-String:                  Hard-Tabs:      Yes   File-Translation:
  Name: Toshiba P351 series                            IBM PC or Compatible
Communications name:
                                                  Configuration Settings
```

Fig. 11.2

The SERVICES Print settings.

```
Start printing using current settings                              MENU
Go Line-Advance Page-Advance Align Settings Quit

Page                    Source:
  Length:      66         Destination: Printer
  Spacing:     1          Init-String:
Number                  Margins              Other
  Print-Number: 1         Left:    4          Space Compression: No
  Start-Page:   1         Right:   76         Attributes:        Yes
  End-Page:     999       Top:     2          Format: As-Displayed
  Breaks:      Yes        Bottom:  2          Top-Labels:
  Wait:        No                             Left-Labels:
  Header:
  Footer:
                                                  Print Settings: MAIN
```

SERVICES Configuration Printer contains the default settings for single sheet versus continuous feed and for margins, page length, and initialization string. These settings are inherited by the first SERVICES Print Settings sheet in a worksheet. For example, if your SERVICES Configuration Printer setting for the left margin is 5 and for the right margin is 65, the first SERVICES Print Settings sheet you retrieve in a worksheet displays these margins. In addition, SERVICES Configuration **Printer** contains settings for printer type (parallel or serial) and automatic line feed, which are necessary settings for sending output directly to the printer.

You can, however, change the SERVICES **Configuration Printer** settings and update the Symphony configuration file to include new settings. Eight choices are available for parallel or serial interface between Symphony and a printer (**Configuration Printer Type**). You can also choose a printer name from the printers you selected during the Install program (**Configuration Printer Name**). This feature is helpful if you have more than one printer attached to your system. Settings are also available for having either Symphony or your printer automatically advance the paper at the end of each line (**Configuration Printer Auto-LF**). When determining which **Configuration Printer** settings to change and how to change them, consult the manual that comes with your printer.

Through SERVICES **Configuration Printer**, you can also regulate whether the printer continuously loads paper after finishing a page or whether the printer waits (**Configuration Printer Wait**). SERVICES **Configuration Printer** contains settings for left, right, top, and bottom margins (SERVICES **Configuration Printer Margins**) and page length (SERVICES **Configuration Printer Page-Length**). Finally, print type and size are controlled by the setting in SERVICES **Configuration Printer Init-String** (see the later section on "Sending an Initialization String to the Printer").

As figure 11.2 indicates, SERVICES **Print** contains many types of options. These include selections for regulating the format for printing spreadsheets to selections for regulating the naming and use of print settings sheets.

The Print Menu

The examples in this chapter provide explanations of many of the options in the SERVICES **Print** menu (see fig. 11.2). A general introduction to the types of commands that are available may help you understand Symphony's print capabilities. **Print** commands fall into the following categories:

1. Commands for indicating what should be printed, stored in a print file, or entered into a range in the worksheet (**Settings Source**)

2. Commands for having source data printed directly, stored in a print file, or entered into a range in the worksheet (**Settings Destination**)

3. Commands regulating the format of the page

   A. Number of lines per page (**Settings Page Length**)

   B. Spaces between lines in spreadsheets or databases (**Settings Page Spacing**)

      C. Headers on each page (**Settings Page Header**)

      D. Footers on each page (**Settings Page Footer**)

      E. Margins (**Settings Margins**)

      F. Boldface, underlining, superscript, and subscript (**Settings Other Attributes**)

      G. Printing of spreadsheet data—as displayed on-screen versus displayed with cell formulas (**Settings Other Format**)

      H. Printing of worksheet labels (**Settings Other Top-Labels**, **Settings Other Left-Labels**, and **Settings Other No-Labels**)

      I. Numbers printed on each page (**Settings Page Number**)

4. Commands controlling printer operations

      A. Page breaks (**Settings Page Breaks**)

      B. Paper feed (**Settings Page Wait**)

      C. Print size and type (**Settings Init-String**)

5. Commands for creating, naming, using, resetting, and deleting print settings sheets

      A. Creating and naming print settings sheets (**Settings Name Create**)

      B. Using print settings sheets (**Settings Name Use**, **Settings Name Previous**, and **Settings Name Next**)

      C. Deleting print settings sheets (**Settings Name Delete**, **Settings Name Reset**, and **Settings Name Initial-Settings**)

The SERVICES **Print** menu is one of Symphony's "sticky" menus. The only way to exit from this menu is to specify the **Quit** option. Whenever you perform one of the functions from the **Print** menu, the program returns to exactly where you were before you made your selection. Be careful not to press the Enter key again at this point unless you want to execute the same function twice. You will find that it is particularly disconcerting to return from printing the worksheet with the **G**o function, only to press Enter again accidentally and print the file a second time. If you want to interrupt a print operation, press Ctrl-Break and then Esc to clear the ERROR message.

Whenever you are printing to a printer, a print file, or a range in a worksheet, you must press SERVICES **Print Go** to initiate the printing operation. When you create a print file (that is, when the **Destination** is a **File**), the operation is not completed until you exit from the **Print** menu by either choosing **Quit** or pressing Esc.

When and How To Print

The first choice you make in printing a file is whether to create a print file. If you want to work with the file in another software program, if the system you are working on doesn't have a printer, if your printer isn't working, or if you want to create a file whose output you can send over data communications lines, then you can set up a print file. The SERVICES **Print Settings Destination File** command stores output in a file either to be sent or to be printed later with the DOS TYPE command or special printing routine. Or use the SERVICES **Print Settings Destination Printer** command if you want to go directly to the printer in the current Symphony session.

Symphony offers an alternative to creating a print file if your printer isn't working or if you don't want to print immediately. In Symphony you can name and store print settings and then retrieve those settings later when you want to print a spreadsheet or word-processing text. Being able to save print settings alleviates having to reset print commands and also enables you to use a print settings sheet for other documents or spreadsheets in your worksheet. (See the section entitled "Naming, Using, and Deleting Print Settings Sheets".)

Printing to a File

Files created with the SERVICES **Print Settings Destination File** command have a .PRN file-name extension. You can call portions of .PRN files back into Symphony from the disk and enter them into specific locations in a worksheet with the **File Import** command. Creating a .PRN file also enables you to transfer a Symphony file to another word-processing program, such as WordStar. Importing .PRN files, however, is not as straightforward as it sounds. (Chapter 6 provides more information on importing .PRN files.)

When you do create a print file, you should be sure to change the margin settings in the print settings sheet with SERVICES **Print Settings Margin No-Margins**. This command eliminates margins and page breaks and sets single-spacing. Also note that if you print repeatedly to the same print file, Symphony appends your report or text to the end of the file. If you want to replace the existing file, you need to erase it (SERVICES **Print Settings Destination Erase**) before you print.

Printing to a Range

In addition to the options of sending data directly to the printer or creating a print file, Symphony provides one other choice. You can send print data to a range in the worksheet. "Printing" data to a range in the worksheet is particularly valuable when you want to import SHEET data into a DOC window. For example, when you transfer spreadsheet data into the DOC window of a worksheet with the SERVICES **Print Settings Destination Range** command, you can edit the data or use DOC commands on the data as you would with data originally entered in the DOC mode.

Printing to a range in the worksheet is different from using the SHEET Copy command. With SHEET Copy, you can copy a spreadsheet or parts of a spreadsheet into a DOC window. But even though the spreadsheet section is copied into a DOC area, you cannot use the Del or Backspace key to change the entries.

Printing Reports: A Few Examples

Shown here to help you understand Symphony's print capabilities are three examples of reports and how you can print them. The first example is a spreadsheet (Mom's Root Beer Company Cash-Flow Projection) that will be printed with the minimum number of print options. In this case, the spreadsheet will be printed much as it appears on the screen, without any of the special options. Figure 11.3 shows a portion of the screen display of the spreadsheet.

Fig. 11.3

An example: Mom's Root Beer Company Cash-Flow Projection.

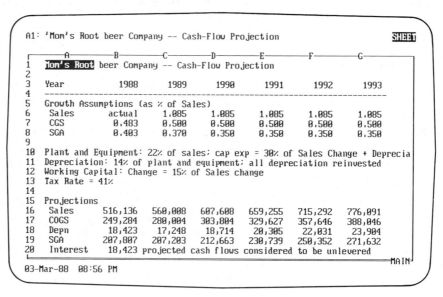

```
A1: 'Mom's Root beer Company -- Cash-Flow Projection          SHEET
┌─────A────────B────────C────────D────────E───────F───────G──────
1  Mom's Root beer Company -- Cash-Flow Projection
2
3  Year           1988     1989     1990     1991     1992     1993
4  ----------------------------------------------------------------
5  Growth Assumptions (as % of Sales)
6    Sales       actual    1.085    1.085    1.085    1.085    1.085
7    CGS          0.483    0.500    0.500    0.500    0.500    0.500
8    SGA          0.403    0.370    0.350    0.350    0.350    0.350
9
10 Plant and Equipment: 22% of sales; cap exp = 30% of Sales Change + Deprecia
11 Depreciation: 14% of plant and equipment; all depreciation reinvested
12 Working Capital: Change = 15% of Sales change
13 Tax Rate = 41%
14
15 Projections
16   Sales       516,136  560,008  607,608  659,255  715,292  776,091
17   COGS        249,204  280,004  303,804  329,627  357,646  388,046
18   Depn         18,423   17,248   18,714   20,305   22,031   23,904
19   SGA         207,807  207,203  212,663  230,739  250,352  271,632
20   Interest     18,423 projected cash flows considered to be unlevered
                                                                   ─MAIN
03-Mar-88  08:56 PM
```

The second example of a report (Inventory Report on Cattuna) has been created in a DOC window; again, the report will be printed much as it appears on the screen. Double-spacing does not, however, appear on the screen (see fig. 11.4).

Finally, the third report example (The Cattuna Distributing Inventory), shown in figure 11.5, will illustrate how to use the special options for printing spreadsheets.

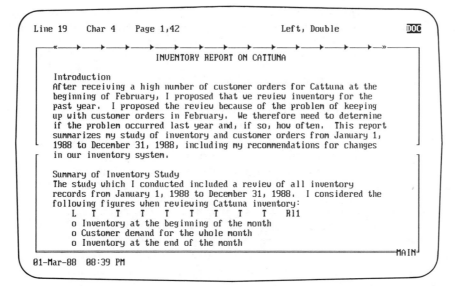

```
 Line 19    Char 4    Page 1,42              Left, Double        DOC
 «━━━▶━━━▶━━━▶━━━▶━━━▶━━━▶━━━━▶━━━▶━━━▶━━━▶━━»
                  INVENTORY REPORT ON CATTUNA

   Introduction
   After receiving a high number of customer orders for Cattuna at the
   beginning of February, I proposed that we review inventory for the
   past year.  I proposed the review because of the problem of keeping
   up with customer orders in February.  We therefore need to determine
   if the problem occurred last year and, if so, how often.  This report
   summarizes my study of inventory and customer orders from January 1,
   1988 to December 31, 1988, including my recommendations for changes
   in our inventory system.

   Summary of Inventory Study
   The study which I conducted included a review of all inventory
   records from January 1, 1988 to December 31, 1988.  I considered the
   following figures when reviewing Cattuna inventory:
        L    T    T    T    T    T    T    T    R11
        o Inventory at the beginning of the month
        o Customer demand for the whole month
        o Inventory at the end of the month
                                                            ━MAIN┘
 01-Mar-88  08:39 PM
```

Fig. 11.4

An example: Inventory Report on Cattuna.

```
 A1: 'Month                                                SHEET
      ┌───────A───────────B───────C───────D───────E───────F──────
   1  │Month                  Jan     Feb     Apr     May    June
   2  ═══════════════════════════════════════════════════════════
   3  Beginning Inventory     43      51      60      42      30
   4  Past Demand for Month    28      16      18      12      20
   5  Ending Inventory         15      35      42      30      10
   6  Quantity Ordered         36       0       0       0      36
   7  Setup Costs ($10 per order) $10.00  $0.00  $0.00  $0.00  $10.00
   8  Inventory Costs ($.2/unit)  $3.00  $7.00  $8.40  $6.00   $2.00
   9  Shortage Costs ($1/unit)    $0.00  $0.00  $0.00  $0.00   $0.00
  10  Total Costs for Month      $13.00  $7.00 $14.80  $6.00  $12.00
  11  Cum Cost from Last Month    $0.00 $13.00 $20.00 $43.20  $49.20
  12  Cumulative Costs to Date   $13.00 $20.00 $34.80 $49.20  $61.20
  13
  14
  15  Order Quantity Input Cell ->    36
  16  Order Point Input Cell ---->    28
  17
  18                          Order   Cumulative    Order   Cumulative
  19                          Quant      Cost       Quant      Cost
  20                          ─────────────────     ─────────────────
                                                            ━MAIN┘
 01-Mar-88  08:41 PM
```

Fig. 11.5

An example: The Cattuna Distributing Inventory.

For the first sample report, called Mom's Root Beer Report, you would probably be more interested in the figures on the cash-flow projection for the next 10 years than in the format of the printed page. The only thing special you might do for the printing of this report is to print all 12 columns on one standard 8 1/2-by-11-inch page.

Whether you decide to print the report immediately or create a print file and print it later, you begin either operation by selecting **P**rint from the SERVICES menu.

Designating a Print Range

One of the first steps in printing any report is to designate a range of cells to be printed. As indicated earlier, the command used to designate a range is SERVICES **P**rint **S**ettings **S**ource **R**ange. In addition to **R**ange, Symphony provides another option for indicating the source of the print output: **D**atabase. You choose **D**atabase whenever the source is a report specified in the database settings sheet (see Chapter 15).

In the first and second print examples, setting the range requires selecting SERVICES **P**rint **S**ettings **S**ource **R**ange. If the source range begins with the upper left corner of the window's restrict range and ends with the lower right corner of the restrict range, first move the cursor to the upper left corner. Then select SERVICES **P**rint **S**ettings **S**ource **R**ange. Symphony prompts you for the Range to be printed:. Press the Tab key followed by the End key, then the Home key. The cursor highlights the complete restrict range. This sequence is also useful for pointing to a print range when the range is the entire sheet. You can temporarily prevent columns from being printed by using the SHEET **W**idth **H**ide command.

In the third print example, setting the print range is somewhat more complicated. Printing the spreadsheet part of this document requires setting multiple ranges in order to print the inventory on two 8 1/2-by-11-inch pages. You must designate and print these ranges one at a time.

Because a print file has been created for this third example, the ranges will be appended one after the other in the file. Symphony lets you control the format of each range that is written. This feature is helpful when you want to control the printing of each part of the inventory. Each time a range is designated and print options are changed, you must select **G**o from the SERVICES **P**rint menu in order to send the range to the print file. **G**o is also required to send a range to the printer. To exit the Print menu, choose **Q**uit or press Esc.

Setting Print Options

Aside from the task of designating print ranges, the only other report-printing task that requires any kind of detailed explanation is that of setting print options. Several print options will be designated for the Cattuna Distributing Inventory, whereas only a few options will be used for Mom's Root Beer Report (to get everything on one page) and the Inventory Report on Cattuna.

Special print options are available for both spreadsheets and text. The options for spreadsheets include the following:

- Spacing

- Printing column and row labels along the top and left on every page

- Printing cell formulas rather than cell entries as displayed

For DOC text, special print options include printing special print attributes: underlined, boldface, superscript, or subscript characters. The DOC Format Settings Spacing command controls spacing for printing text created in a DOC window.

Setting Headers and Footers

For the third report, the first step after designating a print range is to set the header and footer options. These options allow you to specify up to 240 characters of text in each of three positions—left, center, and right—in the header and footer. Realistically, you should use only enough text to fit on an 8 1/2-inch-wide page.

You can enter all the text yourself, but Symphony offers some special characters that control page numbers, the current date, and the location where text is printed in the header and footer lines. These special characters are the following:

#	This character automatically prints page numbers, starting with the number entered in SERVICES **P**rint **S**ettings **P**age **N**umber. If you use **P**rint **A**lign, the page number is reset to the number in SERVICES **P**rint **S**ettings **P**age **N**umber.
@	This character automatically includes the current date in the form 07/24/88 and takes the date from what you entered when you loaded DOS—that is, the current date.
|	Headers and footers have three separate segments: left-justified, centered, and right-justified. Use this character to separate one segment from another. Notice the following examples of entries for header or footer lines.

What you type:

Cattuna Distributing Co. Inventory | | page #
| Cattuna Distributing Co. Inventory, page #
Cattuna Distributing Co. Inventory, @, page # |

What appears on the page:

Cattuna Distributing Co. Inventory   page 1
                        Cattuna Distributing Co. Inventory, page 1
                Cattuna Distributing Co. Inventory, 07/24/88, page 1

You can use these symbols (@ | #) in either headers or footers. Also, the date appears in the format for month, day, and year (MM/DD/YY). Figures 11.14A and 11.14B at the end of this chapter show how the header and footer options are set up with the special characters for the third report. For the header and footer options to work, you must set SERVICES **Print Settings Page Breaks** to **Yes**. Otherwise, Symphony ignores your header and footer entries.

You should note two things about headers and footers. First, Symphony always places two blank lines below the header and two above the footer line. Second, if you use the # special character for page numbers, and if you want to print a report a second time, you must reset the page-number counter by selecting SERVICES **Print Align**. Otherwise, the page counter picks up where it left off.

You cannot change headers or footers in the middle of a report. If you want to print different headers and footers in different sections of a report, you must create a separate print settings sheet, enter the new header or footer, and set **Print Settings Page Number Start-Page** to the number of the first page of the new section.

Setting Margins

Margin settings that control the size of text margins as the text is printed are located in the following three settings sheets:

1. SERVICES **Configuration Printer Margins**, which contains default margin settings

2. SERVICES **Print Settings Margins**, which contains the specific margin settings you enter for a specific print output

3. DOC **Format Settings Left**, which affects the left margin of text entered in a DOC window

Note that when printing the left margins of text created in a DOC environment, Symphony adds the margin settings in DOC **Format Settings Left** to those in SERVICES **Print Settings Margins Left**.

If you are retrieving the print settings sheet (SERVICES **Print Settings**) for the first time in a worksheet, you will notice that the sheet contains the margin settings stored in SERVICES **Configuration Printer Margins**.

When setting your margins for data entered in a SHEET or DOC window, you can either use those provided by SERVICES **Configuration Printer Margins** or enter new margin settings. The SERVICES Print Settings Margins option overrides SERVICES Configuration Printer. The default margin settings (from the edge of the paper) stored in SERVICES Configuration Printer Margins are the following:

Left 4
Right 76
Top 2
Bottom 2

You can change right and left margin settings to settings between 0 and 240, and top and bottom margin settings to settings between 0 and 16. Whenever you change margin settings in SERVICES Configuration Printer Margins, you can update the Symphony configuration file to these new settings by selecting Update from the SERVICES Configuration menu.

The SERVICES Print Settings Margins command operates on both spreadsheets and text entered in a word-processing window. The same margin settings can result in different margins, however, depending on whether you are printing a spreadsheet or printing text from a DOC window.

For the first example, Mom's Root Beer Report, you will want to fit everything on an 8 1/2-by-11-inch page. But the worksheet contains 12 active columns of data, which, when combined, form a total worksheet width of 108 characters. The only way to fit everything on one page is to use compressed print on a dot-matrix printer. You can get up to 136 characters on a line with this type of print. With 5 characters for the left margin and a worksheet width of 108, you can just stay under the limit of 136. You should set the right margin at 136 and send an Init-String to the printer to use compressed print (see the section on "Sending an Initialization String to the Printer").

An alternative to the compressed print is to use the current defaults. You can let the printer print up to 80 columns on one page with either pica or elite type, then continue to another page with what is left over. This solution is not an ideal one, but it is the only other choice.

For the second example, the Inventory Report on Cattuna, you will want a left margin of 5 and a right margin of 72. As you'll recall, for text from a DOC window, Symphony adds the left margin settings from DOC Format Settings Left to the left margin settings in SERVICES Print Settings Margins. The original setting in DOC Format Settings for the left margin is 4; the setting in SERVICES Print Settings Margins is 1. Symphony therefore prints a left margin of 5.

For the third example, the Cattuna Distributing Inventory, the top and bottom margins are set at 8. These margin settings, which are the distance from the top of the page to the header and from the bottom of the page to the footer, should give you a good appearance. The left margin is set at 4 for this report, and the right margin at 76. You may have to try several different combinations to get the setup you want.

Repeating Labels on Multipage Printouts

Symphony allows you to print column and row headings on a multipage printout, such as the spreadsheet in the third example. If, for instance, you want to print a comparative income statement that has several columns of monthly figures carrying beyond the first page, you can have the row headings that usually occur in the first column of the first page repeated on each page. SERVICES **Print Settings Other Top-Labels** is the option you can use to repeat column labels. SERVICES **Print Settings Other Left-Labels** repeats row labels.

You can also use SERVICES **Print Settings Other Top-Labels** or **Left-Labels** whenever you want to extract part of a database and have the correct column and row headings printed with it. For example, suppose that you want to print only one section from a database, such as the one shown in figure 11.6, which extends from column A to column J.

Fig. 11.6

A sample database.

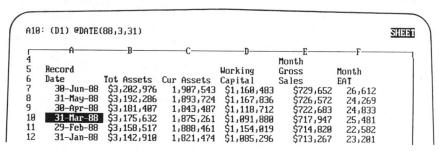

If you want to print only the range from A10..J12 and also print labels with the range, you would follow this procedure. First, select SERVICES **Print Settings Source Range** and indicate the range of the database that you want to print. In this case, enter **A10..J12**. After indicating the range, select **Destination Printer** and make any necessary page or margin changes.

To have labels printed, select SERVICES **Print Settings Other Top-Labels**. To indicate which labels should be your top labels, enter the row range or highlight the row where column headings are located. In figure 11.6, for example, you highlight A4..J6. To indicate which labels should be your left labels, select SERVICES **Print Settings Other Left-Labels** and specify the column of labels you want printed. You are now ready to begin printing, unless you first want to name the settings sheet you just created so that you can use it again. The printed database range is shown in figure 11.7.

Fig. 11.7

A printed portion of the database.

	Record			Working	Month Gross	Month		Debt to	Return	
	Date	Tot Assets	Cur Assets	Capital	Sales	EAT	Cur Ratio	Equity	On Assets	DSO
	31-Mar-88	$3,175,632	1,875,261	$1,091,880	$717,947	25,481	2.54	0.54	0.10	54
	29-Feb-88	$3,158,517	1,888,461	$1,154,019	$714,820	22,582	2.39	0.55	0.09	55
	31-Jan-88	$3,142,910	1,821,474	$1,085,296	$713,267	23,201	2.57	0.55	0.09	57

When you are using the SERVICES Print Settings Other Top-Labels and Left-Labels commands to print labels on consecutive pages after the first page, be careful that you do not include the column and row labels when you set the Source Range. If you set the Source Range to include column and row borders and also enter a range in Top-Labels and Left-Labels, Symphony prints the labels twice on the first page (see fig. 11.8).

```
==========================================================================================
Balance Sheet                    Balance Sheet
==========================================================================================
                                                                              Common
  Assets                           Assets                             31-Jul-88   Size

Cash                             Cash                                  $275,000      8%
Marketable Securities            Marketable Securities                   35,000      1%
Accounts Receivable              Accounts Receivable        1,256,000
  Allowance for Doubtful Accounts   Allowance for Doubtful Accounts     8,000
  Net Accounts Receivable           Net Accounts Receivable           1,248,000     39%
Inventory                        Inventory                              359,000     11%
Prepaid Expenses                 Prepaid Expenses                        70,000      2%
Other                            Other                                   23,000      1%
                                                                     ------------
  Total Current Assets             Total Current Assets              2,010,000     62%

Property, Plant, and Equipment   Property, Plant, and Equipment    956,700
  Accumulated Depreciation          Accumulated Depreciation        123,700
  Net Property, Plant, and Equipmen  Net Property, Plant, and Equipment    833,000     26%
Investment-Long-Term             Investment-Long-Term                   396,000     12%
                                                                     ------------
  Total Noncurrent Assets           Total Noncurrent Assets           1,229,000     38%
                                                                     ------------
  Total Assets                      Total Assets                     $3,239,000    100%
```

Fig. 11.8

Labels printed twice.

Sending an Initialization String to the Printer

If you want to control either print size or type, you can regulate both through the Init-String (initialization string) commands. Two separate Init-String settings are available: one in SERVICES Configuration Printer and one in SERVICES Print Settings. The SERVICES Configuration Printer Init-String is stored in Symphony's configuration file (.CNF) and controls SERVICES Print Settings Init-String, unless you change the SERVICES Print Settings Init-String.

The Init-String option sends a string of up to 39 characters to the printer every time you select Go from the SERVICES Print menu. All printers are different, so you must look carefully at your printer's manual to see what is required for your printer. The string is composed of backslashes (\) followed by the decimal equivalent of special characters in ASCII code.

You can change the print size and type by selecting SERVICES Print Settings Init-String. After you select this command, Symphony asks you to enter the printer-control sequence (see fig. 11.9). At the printer-control sequence prompt, you should enter the special control code(s) for your printer. (Again, consult your printer's manual.)

Like the other SERVICES **P**rint **S**ettings commands, the Init-String is a temporary override of the SERVICES **C**onfiguration **P**rinter setting, unless you name the settings sheet. If you name the settings sheet, it will be saved for you to use again. (For a more detailed description of this option, refer to the *Symphony Reference Manual*, with your printer manual also in hand, and experiment.) If you don't expect to use your printer's special features and just want regular printing, then don't worry about the Init-String command.

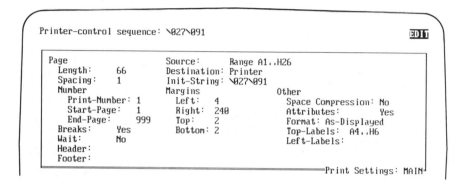

Fig. 11.9

Entering
printer-co
sequence
String.

Setting the Page Length

The SERVICES **C**onfiguration **P**rinter setting for the number of lines printed on one page is 66. You can change this number temporarily or store a new page length in a named print settings sheet. You can set page length to any number between 1 and 100 with SERVICES **P**rint **S**ettings **P**age **L**ength. This option is helpful when you use special forms, paper, or type sizes. Because standard 8 1/2-by-11-inch paper has been used for the three examples in this chapter, however, this option will default to 66 in all three examples.

Printing Cell Formulas

Symphony enables you to print cell contents in more than one way. For the sample reports in this chapter, the contents are printed just as they are displayed on the screen (except for spacing in the second example); also printed is a one-line-per-cell listing of the cell formulas for the Mom's Root Beer Report.

The command SERVICES **P**rint **S**ettings **O**ther **F**ormat controls the way cell formulas are printed. When you enter this command, you are given the following choices:

As-Displayed   **C**ell-Formulas

The **C**ell-Formulas option creates the one-line-per-cell listing of the contents of a worksheet. This option is convenient for debugging and also can be useful for re-creating formulas in other worksheets. Figure 11.10 shows the Cell-Formulas listing of Mom's Root Beer Report.

The **As**-Displayed option reverses the Cell-Formulas option. **As**-Displayed returns to printing the format as it appears on-screen.

Naming, Using, and Deleting Print Settings Sheets

As mentioned several times throughout this book, one of Symphony's advantages is the program's capability to name (and thus save) settings sheets. When you name settings sheets, you can retrieve them and reuse the settings in the worksheet. You can save settings sheets, however, only if you save the file in which they were created.

SERVICES **Print Settings** provides the flexibility of entering the print settings for two different documents at the same time. After you have finished printing the first document, simply retrieve the named settings sheet, align or advance paper if needed, and then select **Go** to begin printing the next document.

Here's how you use the options provided by named print settings sheets. After entering all the settings—margins, headers, footers, and so on—select SERVICES **Print Settings Name**. When you select **Name**, the following menu appears:

    Use   Create   Delete   Previous   Next   Initial-Settings   Reset   Quit

From the **Name** menu, choose **Create**. When Symphony asks for the Name for new Print settings sheet:, enter a name, preferably one that will remind you of the document for which the name was created.

Before exiting from the file, you need to save the file by using the SERVICES **File Save** command; having saved the file, you also retain the print settings sheet. Whenever you decide to use the print settings sheet again, select SERVICES **Print Settings Name Use**. A list of named print setting sheets displays in the control panel of your screen. If you want to see a complete listing of print settings sheets, press the Services key (F9), and Symphony displays a complete listing of sheets for the current file (see fig. 11.11).

Two commands are useful for "paging" through named print settings sheets: **Previous** and **Next**. When you choose **Previous**, Symphony displays and makes current the settings sheet previous to the current one. (The sheets are in alphabetical order by name.) The **Next** command is the reverse of **Previous**; this option displays the settings sheet following the current one.

You can not only create, use, and cycle through print settings sheets, but you can also edit and delete them. One command is available for changing the print settings sheet currently on the screen back to the default settings in SERVICES **Configuration Printer**. To delete a single settings sheet, use the SERVICES **Print Settings Name Delete** command. If, however, you want to erase all named print

Fig. 11.10

A partial Cell-Formulas listing for Mom's Root Beer Report.

```
A1: 'Mom's Root beer Company -- Cash-Flow Projection
A3: 'Year
B3: 1988
C3: 1989
D3: 1990
E3: 1991
F3: 1992
G3: 1993
H3: 1988
I3: 1989
J3: 1990
K3: 1991
L3: 1992
M3: 1993
N3: 1994
O3: 1995
P3: 1996
Q3: 1997
R3: 1998
S3: 1999
T3: 2000
U3: 2001
V3: 2002
A4: \-
B4: \-
C4: \-
D4: \-
E4: \-
F4: \-
G4: \-
H4: \-
I4: \-
J4: \-
K4: \-
L4: \-
M4: \-
N4: \-
O4: \-
P4: \-
Q4: \-
R4: \-
S4: \-
T4: \-
U4: \-
V4: \-
A5: 'Growth Assumptions (as % of Sales)
A6: ' Sales
B6: (F3) "actual
C6: (F3) 1.085
D6: (F3) 1.085
E6: (F3) 1.085
F6: (F3) 1.085
G6: (F3) 1.085
H6: (F3) 1.085
I6: (F3) 1.085
J6: (F3) 1.085
K6: (F3) 1.085
L6: (F3) 1.085
M6: (F3) 1.085
N6: (F3) 1.085
O6: (F3) 1.085
P6: (F3) 1.085
Q6: (F3) 1.085
R6: (F3) 1.085
S6: (F3) 1.085
T6: (F3) 1.085
U6: (F3) 1.085
V6: (F3) 1.085
A7: ' CGS
B7: (F3) +B17/B16
C7: (F3) 0.5
D7: (F3) 0.5
E7: (F3) 0.5
F7: (F3) 0.5
G7: (F3) 0.5
H7: (F3) 0.5
I7: (F3) 0.5
J7: (F3) 0.5
K7: (F3) 0.5
L7: (F3) 0.5
M7: (F3) 0.5
N7: (F3) 0.5
O7: (F3) 0.5
P7: (F3) 0.5
Q7: (F3) 0.5
R7: (F3) 0.5
```

```
S7: (F3) 0.5
T7: (F3) 0.5
U7: (F3) 0.5
V7: (F3) 0.5
A8: ' SGA
B8: (F3) +B19/B16
C8: (F3) 0.37
D8: (F3) 0.35
E8: (F3) 0.35
F8: (F3) 0.35
G8: (F3) 0.35
H8: (F3) 0.35
I8: (F3) 0.35
J8: (F3) 0.35
K8: (F3) 0.35
L8: (F3) 0.35
M8: (F3) 0.35
N8: (F3) 0.35
O8: (F3) 0.35
P8: (F3) 0.35
Q8: (F3) 0.35
R8: (F3) 0.35
S8: (F3) 0.35
T8: (F3) 0.35
U8: (F3) 0.35
V8: (F3) 0.35
A10: 'Plant and Equipment: 22% of sales; cap exp = 30% of Sales Change + Depreciation
A11: 'Depreciation: 14% of plant and equipment; all depreciation reinvested
A12: 'Working Capital: Change = 15% of Sales change
A13: 'Tax Rate = 41%
A15: 'Projections
A16: ' Sales
B16: (P0) 516136
C16: (P0) +B16*C6
D16: (P0) +C16*D6
E16: (P0) +D16*E6
F16: (P0) +E16*F6
G16: (P0) +F16*G6
H16: (P0) +G16*H6
I16: (P0) +H16*I6
J16: (P0) +I16*J6
K16: (P0) +J16*K6
L16: (P0) +K16*L6
M16: (P0) +L16*M6
N16: (P0) +M16*N6
O16: (P0) +N16*O6
P16: (P0) +O16*P6
Q16: (P0) +P16*Q6
R16: (P0) +Q16*R6
S16: (P0) +R16*S6
T16: (P0) +S16*T6
U16: (P0) +T16*U6
V16: (P0) +U16*V6
A17: ' COGS
B17: (P0) 249284
C17: (P0) +C16*C7
D17: (P0) +D16*D7
E17: (P0) +E16*E7
F17: (P0) +F16*F7
G17: (P0) +G16*G7
H17: (P0) +H16*H7
I17: (P0) +I16*I7
J17: (P0) +J16*J7
K17: (P0) +K16*K7
L17: (P0) +L16*L7
M17: (P0) +M16*M7
N17: (P0) +N16*N7
O17: (P0) +O16*O7
P17: (P0) +P16*P7
Q17: (P0) +Q16*Q7
R17: (P0) +R16*R7
S17: (P0) +S16*S7
T17: (P0) +T16*T7
U17: (P0) +U16*U7
V17: (P0) +V16*V7
A18: ' Depn
B18: (P0) 18423
C18: (P0) +C16*0.22*0.14
D18: (P0) +D16*0.22*0.14
E18: (P0) +E16*0.22*0.14
F18: (P0) +F16*0.22*0.14
G18: (P0) +G16*0.22*0.14
H18: (P0) +H16*0.22*0.14
I18: (P0) +I16*0.22*0.14
J18: (P0) +J16*0.22*0.14
K18: (P0) +K16*0.22*0.14
```

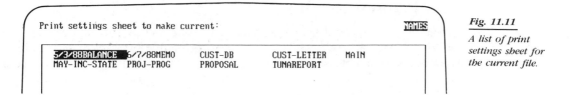

```
Print settings sheet to make current:                          NAMES

   5/3/88BALANCE  6/7/88MEMO    CUST-DB      CUST-LETTER   MAIN
   MAY-INC-STATE  PROJ-PROG     PROPOSAL     TUNAREPORT
```

Fig. 11.11

A list of print settings sheet for the current file.

settings sheets in a particular file, select SERVICES **P**rint **S**ettings **N**ame **R**eset. After you use this command, print settings from SERVICES **C**onfiguration **P**rinter are in effect.

Controlling the Printer

Symphony makes it possible for you to control the printer. In fact, Symphony provides so much control that you hardly ever have to touch the printer except to turn it on just before printing and turn it off when you are done.

The ability to control the printer is important in printing the Cattuna Inventory. Between some of the different sections and text to be printed for this report, you need to space down several lines. The SERVICES **P**rint **L**ine-**A**dvance command makes the printer skip a line each time you enter the command. In this example, the command will be used several times in a row to skip between some of the sections.

The SERVICES **P**rint **P**age-**A**dvance command causes the printer to advance the paper to the top of a new page each time you enter the command. When you use **P**age-**A**dvance at the end of a printing session, Symphony prints the footer on the next page. If you **Q**uit from the SERVICES **P**rint menu before issuing the **P**age-**A**dvance command, the last footer does not print.

Finally, when you start printing this report, you will need a way to signal to the printer where the top of the page is. The command used to align the page is SERVICES **P**rint **A**lign. Again, this command saves you from having to touch the printer control buttons.

You must enter the SERVICES **P**rint **G**o command to start the printer. This command also allows you to send a range to a print file (SERVICES **P**rint **S**ettings **D**estination **F**ile) and to a worksheet (SERVICES **P**rint **S**ettings **D**estination **R**ange).

If you want to interrupt the printing of a report in midstream, simply press the Ctrl key and the Break key simultaneously. The print buffer may take some time to clear, depending on the buffer's size, but Symphony eventually returns you to the worksheet. Press Esc to clear the ERROR message displayed in the MODE indicator.

Now that you understand how to set print options, let's take a look at the three examples.

The Printed Results

In figures 11.12A, 11.12B, 11.13A, 11.13B, 11.14A, and 11.14B, you can see the SERVICES **P**rint **S**ettings sheet and the final printed copy of each of the three reports. Each example requires different commands for printing, which are listed subsequently.

Fig. 11.12A

The print settings sheet for Mom's Root Beer Report.

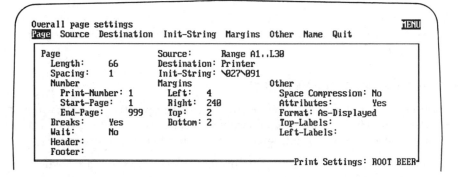

```
Overall page settings                                           MENU
Page  Source  Destination  Init-String  Margins  Other  Name  Quit

  Page                      Source:      Range A1..L30
    Length:      66         Destination: Printer
    Spacing:     1          Init-String: \027\091
  Number                    Margins               Other
    Print-Number: 1           Left:    4            Space Compression: No
    Start-Page:   1           Right:   240          Attributes:        Yes
    End-Page:     999         Top:     2            Format: As-Displayed
  Breaks:       Yes           Bottom:  2            Top-Labels:
  Wait:         No                                  Left-Labels:
  Header:
  Footer:
                                                 Print Settings: ROOT BEER
```

To print the Mom's Root Beer Company Cash-Flow Projection (figs. 11.12A and 11.12B), you enter the following commands:

1. SERVICES **P**rint **S**ettings **S**ource **R**ange **A1..L30** and press Enter

2. SERVICES **P**rint **S**ettings **I**nit-String **\027\091** and press Enter

3. SERVICES **P**rint **S**ettings **M**argins **R**ight **240** and press Enter

4. SERVICES **P**rint **S**ettings **M**argins **Q**uit

5. SERVICES **P**rint **S**ettings **Q**uit

6. SERVICES **P**rint **G**o

The only special entries made in the **P**rint commands for the Mom's Root Beer Report are **I**nit-String and **M**argins. Otherwise, printing this report merely requires setting the range and selecting **G**o when you are ready to begin printing.

To print the Inventory Report on Cattuna (figs. 11.13A and 11.13B), you enter the following commands:

1. SERVICES **P**rint **S**ettings **P**age **F**ooter |# and press Enter

2. SERVICES **P**rint **S**ettings **P**age **Q**uit

3. SERVICES **P**rint **S**ettings **S**ource **R**ange **22..50** and press Enter

4. SERVICES **P**rint **S**ettings **M**argins **L**eft **1** and press Enter

5. SERVICES **P**rint **S**ettings **M**argins **Q**uit

6. SERVICES **P**rint **S**ettings **Q**uit

7. SERVICES **P**rint **G**o

The only special entry for printing the Inventory Report is the footer entry |#. Through this entry, the page number is centered and printed at the bottom of the first page (see fig. 11.13B).

*** FILE: FIG11_12.WR1 ***

Fig. 11.12B
The printed result.

Mom's Root beer Company -- Cash-Flow Projection

Year	1988	1989	1990	1991	1992	1993	1988	1989	1990	1991	1992

Growth Assumptions (as % of Sales)

Sales	actual	1.085	1.085	1.085	1.085	1.085	1.085	1.085	1.085	1.085	1.085
CGS	0.483	0.500	0.500	0.500	0.500	0.500	0.500	0.500	0.500	0.500	0.500
SGA	0.403	0.370	0.350	0.350	0.350	0.350	0.350	0.350	0.350	0.350	0.350

Plant and Equipment: 22% of sales; cap exp = 30% of Sales Change + Depreciation
Depreciation: 14% of plant and equipment; all depreciation reinvested
Working Capital: Change = 15% of Sales change
Tax Rate = 41%

Projections

Sales	516,136	560,008	607,608	659,255	715,292	776,091	842,059	913,634	991,293	1,075,553	1,166,975
COGS	249,284	280,004	303,804	329,627	357,646	388,046	421,030	456,817	495,647	537,776	583,487
Depn	18,423	17,248	18,714	20,305	22,031	23,904	25,935	28,140	30,532	33,127	35,943
SGA	207,807	207,203	212,663	230,739	250,352	271,632	294,721	319,772	346,953	376,444	408,441
Interest	18,423	projected	cash	flows	considered	to	be	unlevered			
EBT	22,199	55,553	72,427	78,583	85,263	92,510	100,373	108,905	118,162	128,206	139,103
Tax	9,724	22,777	29,695	32,219	34,958	37,929	41,153	44,651	48,446	52,564	57,032
EAT	12,475	32,776	42,732	46,364	50,305	54,581	59,220	64,254	69,716	75,641	82,071
Cash Flow	30,898	50,024	61,446	66,669	72,336	78,485	85,156	92,394	100,247	108,769	118,014
Cap Expend	64,757	30,410	32,995	35,799	38,842	42,144	45,726	49,612	53,829	58,405	63,369
Work Cap		6,581	7,140	7,747	8,405	9,120	9,895	10,736	11,649	12,639	13,713
Net CF		13,034	21,312	23,123	25,089	27,221	29,535	32,045	34,769	37,725	40,931

Present Value of Operating Cash Flows

Po	Total	Per/share (21,533 shares)
12%	257,893	11.98
13%	236,999	11.01
14%	218,493	10.15

Present Value of Terminal Value (no growth after 2002)

Po	Total	Per/share (21,533 shares)
12%	143,129	6.65
13%	109,622	5.09
14%	84,597	3.93

Present Value of Terminal Value (constant growth after 2002)

Ke	Total	Per/share (21,533 shares)
14%	233,643	5.42
15%	164,569	3.82
16%	118,915	2.76

Present Value of Tax Shields from Debt

If you compare figure 11.4 (the Inventory Report as it appears on the screen) with figure 11.13B (the printed copy), you will notice a difference in spacing. On the screen the report appears with single-spacing (except for the extra spaces added manually after the first paragraph). The report, however, is printed with double-spacing. Double- and triple-spacing settings do not affect the text on the screen. If DOC Format Settings Spacing or a format line is set with double- or triple-spacing, these settings control the spacing during printing.

Fig. 11.13A

The print settings sheet for Inventory Report on Cattuna.

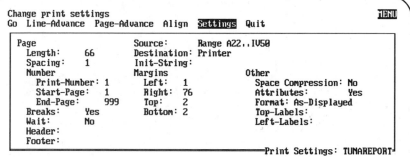

Fig. 11.13B

The printed result.

In addition, for any text created in a DOC window, spacing in the printed copy is controlled by DOC Format Settings Spacing or a format line rather than SERVICES Print Settings Page Spacing. Keep in mind that if you want your document printed with double- or triple-spacing, enter the setting in DOC Format Settings Spacing. Also keep in mind that the spacing you add manually to your document is also added to the spacing setting, as illustrated by the extra spacing after the first paragraph in figure 11.13B.

To print the Cattuna Distributing Inventory (figs. 11.14A and 11.14B), you would enter the following commands:

1. SERVICES **Print Settings Page Spacing 2**

2. SERVICES **Print Settings Page Header Cattuna Distributing Inventory Report** | | **Page#** and press Enter

3. SERVICES **Print Settings Page Quit**

4. SERVICES **Print Settings Source Range A1..G12** and press Enter

5. SERVICES **Print Settings Destination File Cattuna**

6. SERVICES **Print Settings Margins Right 100** and press Enter

7. SERVICES **Print Settings Margins Top 8** and press Enter

8. SERVICES **Print Settings Margins Bottom 8 Quit Quit**

9. SERVICES **Print Go**

This third example requires six special options, as indicated by the previous list of commands. First, to make the sheet easy to read, you must change spacing from single to double. Second, you enter a header identifying the report on the left side and the page number on the right. Third, if you want to use this report in another software program, you can create a print file. Finally, to center the report evenly on the page, you change the top and bottom margins to 8.

Chapter Summary

This chapter has presented an introduction to printing reports and other documents with Symphony's SERVICES Print command. Covered here are all the major print operations that you will need when you begin printing spreadsheets and word-processing documents. Symphony's print capabilities, however, extend beyond what is discussed in this chapter. For example, Symphony is capable of printing database reports, labels, and form letters. These operations require integrating the print functions with Symphony's data-management capabilities (Symphony's FORM window). In Chapter 15, "Data Management," you will find a discussion of the special print functions connected with using Symphony's FORM window.

```
Change print settings                                          MENU
Go  Line-Advance  Page-Advance  Align  Settings  Quit

 ┌──────────────────────────────────────────────────────────────┐
 │ Page                 Source:     Range A1..G12                 │
 │   Length:    66      Destination: File C:\S2\CATTUNA.PRN       │
 │   Spacing:    2      Init-String:                              │
 │ Number               Margins             Other                │
 │   Print-Number: 1      Left:     4          Space Compression: No │
 │   Start-Page:   1      Right:  100          Attributes:      Yes │
 │   End-Page:   999      Top:      8          Format: As-Displayed │
 │ Breaks:      Yes      Bottom:    8          Top-Labels:        │
 │ Wait:         No                            Left-Labels:       │
 │ Header:                                                        │
 │ Footer:                                                        │
 └──────────────────────────────────────────────┐
                                       Print Settings: TUNAREPORT
```

Fig. 11.14A

The print settings sheet for The Cattuna Distributing Inventory.

```
Cattuna Distributing Inventory Report                                     Page 1


Month                         Jan      Feb      Apr      May     June     July
===============================================================================
Beginning Inventory            43       51       60       42       30       46
Past Demand for Month          20       16       18       12       20       13
Ending Inventory               15       35       42       30       10       33
Quantity Ordered               36        0        0        0       36        0
Setup Costs ($10 per order) $10.00    $0.00    $0.00    $0.00   $10.00    $0.00
Inventory Costs ($.2/unit)   $3.00    $7.00    $8.40    $6.00    $2.00    $6.60
Shortage Costs ($1/unit)     $0.00    $0.00    $0.00    $0.00    $0.00    $0.00
Total Costs for Month       $13.00    $7.00   $14.00    $6.00   $12.00    $6.60
Cum Cost from Last Month     $0.00   $13.00   $20.00   $43.20   $49.20   $61.20
Cumulative Costs to Date    $13.00   $20.00   $34.00   $49.20   $61.20   $67.80
```

Fig. 11.14B

The printed result.

12

Creating and Displaying Graphs

Symphony's graphics are designed for quick and easy implementation. Graphs are an integral part of the program, and you can convert data to a graph without transferring data from one program to another. Instead, you can easily display the graph by means of one or two simple commands.

Symphony has a good set of graphics commands, but the program is not as powerful as some of the dedicated graphics packages. If you need graphics principally for analytic purposes rather than for presentations, however, Symphony may have all the power you need.

SHEET and GRAPH Windows

Symphony has the capability to display graphs and text at the same time on the same screen. If you select the Shared mode of display when you create your driver set, Symphony can show a graph in one window and text in another (see Appendix A for more on setting up drivers). In fact, Symphony does not restrict the number of windows you can create; you can show as many different graph or text windows as you can fit on the screen at any one time.

You access all of Symphony's graphing capabilities by using the Graph command within the SHEET environment, or you can set up a separate GRAPH window specifically designed to display graphs. The GRAPH window has all the capabilities of a SHEET window. What's the difference then? When do you want to use a SHEET window for graphing, and when is a GRAPH window more appropriate?

The difference between a SHEET window and a GRAPH window is how long a graph remains displayed on the screen. When you are in a SHEET window, you enter **P**review from the main **G**raph menu to display a graph on the screen. The main **G**raph menu includes these options:

> Preview   1st-Settings   2nd-Settings   Image-Save   **Q**uit

By selecting **P**review, you can display a graph temporarily. The graph remains displayed only until you press another key. Then you return to the SHEET environment, and the main **G**raph menu reappears in the control panel.

On the other hand, when you are in a GRAPH window, the current graph displays automatically in the window. You can use the **A**ttach option to display other graphs on the screen. The GRAPH window menu includes these options:

> Attach   1st-Settings   2nd-Settings   Image-Save

When you select **A**ttach, any graph that you name remains displayed in the window indefinitely. The only way you can eliminate the graph from the window is to attach another graph or delete the graph name (see the section called "Deleting Graphs").

Otherwise, all the commands in the **G**raph menu of the SHEET environment are exactly the same as those in the main menu of the GRAPH environment. You can even pass settings back and forth between the two environments. For example, you can create a pie chart in the SHEET environment and give those settings a name, such as SALESPIE. You can then use the same settings to display SALESPIE in a GRAPH window. Because the settings are shared by the two windows, any changes you make in one environment are also made in the other.

Most of the examples in this chapter illustrate commands that are available for graphing in both SHEET and GRAPH windows. The section entitled "More on GRAPH Windows" (near the end of the chapter), however, includes several examples in which you need to choose one environment.

Types of Graphs

Regardless of the environment, SHEET or GRAPH, Symphony offers six basic types of graphs:

> Simple Bar
> Stacked-Bar
> Line
> Pie
> XY
> High-Low-Close-Open

Simple Bar Graphs

Suppose that you want to create a simple worksheet containing data about store openings over the last five years for the three biggest retailers in the United States, as shown in figure 12.1. You can create many interesting graphs that help make the data more understandable. For example, you can build a simple bar chart to illustrate the data on Sears alone. This graph is illustrated in figure 12.2.

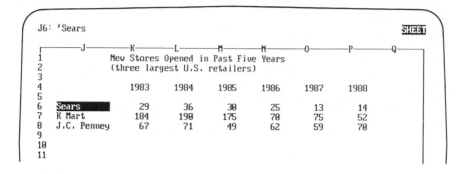

Fig. 12.1

Sample worksheet data.

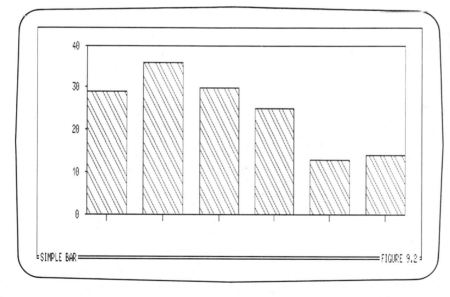

Fig. 12.2

A simple bar graph.

Making a Simple Bar Graph in a SHEET Window

Bar graphs are used to compare different sets of data. A typical bar graph consists of vertical bars that show value by the height of the bar. To create a bar graph, start in a new SHEET window that occupies the entire screen and select SHEET Graph.

Selecting the Type of Graph

After you select **Graph**, then **1st-Settings**, you must choose the type of graph you want to produce. Figure 12.3 shows the 1st-Settings menu and settings sheet. Note that the default graph type is Line.

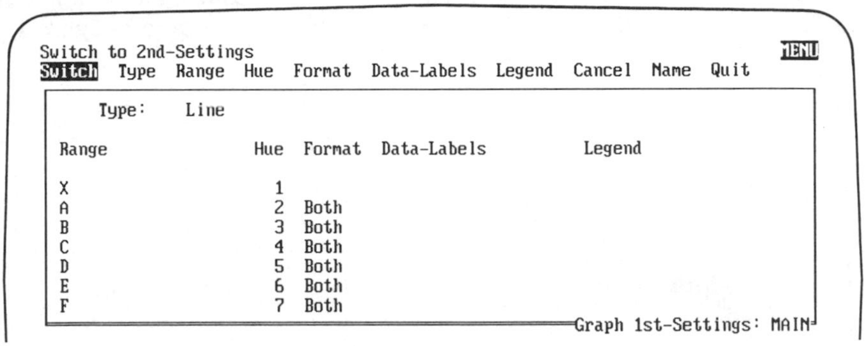

Fig. 12.3

The 1st-Settings menu and settings sheet.

```
Switch to 2nd-Settings                                            MENU
Switch  Type  Range  Hue  Format  Data-Labels  Legend  Cancel  Name  Quit

     Type:     Line

  Range                 Hue  Format  Data-Labels       Legend

  X                      1
  A                      2   Both
  B                      3   Both
  C                      4   Both
  D                      5   Both
  E                      6   Both
  F                      7   Both
                                                   Graph 1st-Settings: MAIN
```

Select **Type** from the 1st-Settings menu. The following menu then appears:

Line   Bar   Stacked-Bar   XY   Pie   High-Low-Close-Open

Because you are creating a bar graph, choose **Bar** from this menu. Notice that Symphony automatically returns you to the 1st-Settings menu and settings sheet. In figure 12.4 you can see that the graph **Type** has changed from the default setting of Line to Bar.

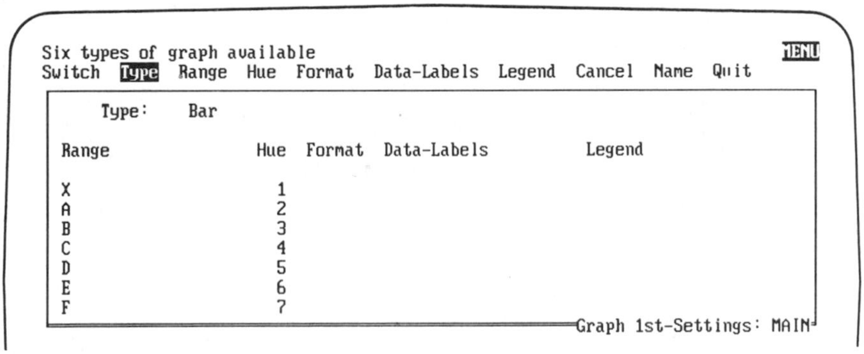

Fig. 12.4

Selecting Bar as the graph Type.

```
Six types of graph available                                     MENU
Switch  Type  Range  Hue  Format  Data-Labels  Legend  Cancel  Name  Quit

     Type:     Bar

  Range                 Hue  Format  Data-Labels       Legend

  X                      1
  A                      2
  B                      3
  C                      4
  D                      5
  E                      6
  F                      7
                                                   Graph 1st-Settings: MAIN
```

Entering Data

Now that you have told Symphony what type of graph to create, you must give the program information to use in creating the graph. You begin this process by selecting **Range** from the 1st-Settings menu. Selecting **Range** brings up the following menu:

X A B C D E F Quit

The appropriate range for the simple bar graph is **A**. After you choose this option, Symphony prompts for a range definition.

Choosing the Data Range

You can define the range with cell references or a range name. In this example, the coordinates are K6..P6 (the Sears data in fig. 12.1). Remember that you can enter this reference by typing the cell coordinates from the keyboard or by using the POINT mode. (If you are in the GRAPH environment when you want to designate a range, Symphony temporarily shifts to the SHEET environment.)

The simple bar graph in the example requires only one range, but Symphony lets you specify as many as six data ranges per graph. The letters **B** through **F** on the **R**ange menu represent the other ranges.

The data range for the sample graph consists of a partial row of data, but the data range can also be a partial column. The graphs in this chapter include examples of both vertical and horizontal data ranges. Remember, however, that the range must be a continuous set of cells. The ranges A2..A6, D3..F3, and F14..F30 are legal ranges; but the ranges A2,A4,D7 and E5,E8,F17,I4 are not.

Viewing the Graph

The final step in producing the graph is to enter **P**review from the main **Graph** menu. The results of selecting this command depend on your hardware and how you configured it during installation. (For more on installing the system, see Appendix A.) If you have a nongraphics screen, nothing happens; all you get is a beep. But don't worry; although you can't see the graph on the display, it still exists in your computer's memory. You can use the PrintGraph program (see the next chapter) to save and print your graph.

If you have a graphics card and either a black-and-white or color monitor, the bar graph displays on the screen after you enter **P**review. Notice that in both cases, the temporary GRAPH window, which is created by your selecting **P**review, replaces the SHEET window on the screen. (This change always happens when you are in the SHEET environment regardless of whether you selected Shared or Toggle mode during installation.) You can return to the worksheet by pressing any key.

Finally, if you are fortunate enough to have a dual monitor system with both a graphics monitor and a monochrome display (and you selected the Dual mode during installation), the bar chart appears on the graphics monitor, and the worksheet remains on the monochrome display. If your graphics monitor can display color, you can format the graph to take advantage of that capability, too. You must have a color printer, however, in order to print the graph in color.

Adding Titles and Labels

Although the picture created so far has graphics appeal, the graph does not offer much information. To complete the graph, you must add titles and labels. For instance, you can enter titles for the graph itself and for the X and Y axes. You first access the SHEET **Graph 2nd-Settings** command menu. Figure 12.5 shows this command menu in the control panel above the **Graph 2nd-Settings** sheet.

Fig. 12.5

*The 2nd-Settings
menu and settings
sheet.*

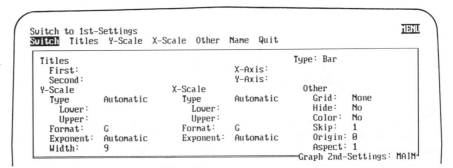

You then select **Titles** from the **2nd-Settings** command menu. The **Graph 2nd-Settings Titles** command produces the following choices:

First   Second   X-axis   Y-axis   Quit

The **Titles** command lets you assign a main title and subtitle to appear at the top of the graph (the **First** and **Second** options) and also titles for the X and Y axes (the **X-axis** and **Y-axis** options). To enter the X-axis label for this sample graph, select **X-axis** and simply type the title **Year** and then press Enter. Then choose **Y-axis** and type **Number of Stores** and press Enter. Figure 12.6 shows the original bar graph with the titles added.

Note the graph titles at the top of figure 12.6. These titles were entered using the **First** and **Second** options. **First** was used for the main title, "New Stores Opened in Past Five Years," and **Second** for the subtitle below it, "(three largest U.S. retailers)."

You usually enter these titles by typing the title from the keyboard. In this case, however, we used the special backslash (\ ) feature available with the SHEET **Graph 2nd-Settings Titles** command (and **Legends** command). This feature lets you enter the contents of cells rather than type in text. To use the contents of a cell for a title (or legend text), place a backslash (\ ) before the cell address when Symphony asks you for a title. For instance, enter **\K1** for **First** and **\K2** for **Second**. Notice that these selections appear in the **2nd-Settings** sheet (see fig. 12.7).

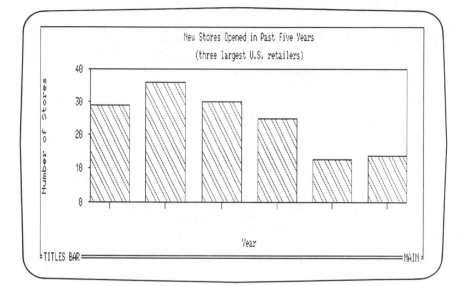

Fig. 12.6

A bar graph with titles added.

Fig. 12.7

Using cell references to enter the First and Second titles.

You can also use a range name for a title or label. To do so, enter the range name rather than the cell reference after the backslash. Incidentally, a Symphony graph title can be no longer than 39 characters.

You should be aware of two particulars of Symphony's graph titles. First, Symphony always disregards label prefixes when setting up titles, so the program automatically centers the First and Second graph titles when displaying the graph. Second, the First and Second titles look very much alike in size and intensity on the screen, but the PrintGraph program prints the First title much larger than the Second. (This facility is explained in the following chapter.)

Another enhancement you may make is to add labels along the X-axis to define the data items you are plotting. Figure 12.8 shows the basic bar graph to which X-axis labels have been added.

Fig. 12.8

The bar graph with X-axis labels.

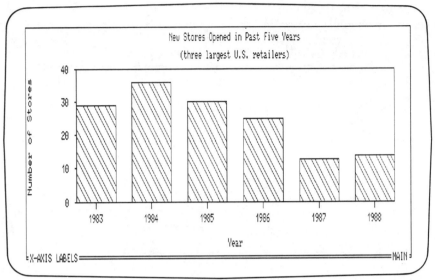

You add these labels by selecting **X** from the **1**st-Settings **Range** menu and pointing to the appropriate range of labels in the worksheet. (See the following section for how to switch from the **2**nd-Settings sheet to the **1**st-Settings sheet.) In this example, the labels are in the range K4..P4 (see fig. 12.1). Symphony uses the contents of the cells in the indicated range as the X-axis labels. (The values in the range K4..P4 are stored as numbers; however, Symphony uses them as labels in this instance.) Symphony automatically centers the X labels.

Switching between 1st- and 2nd-Settings Sheets

Because Symphony offers so many graphing options, the settings are located in two settings sheets: **1**st-Settings and **2**nd-Settings. You can get from the **2**nd-Settings command menu to the **1**st-Settings menu by choosing **Quit** from the **2**nd-Settings menu to return to the main **Graph** menu. You can then select **1**st-Settings. An easier way is available, though. Symphony offers a **Switch** option as the first selection in both the **1**st- and **2**nd-Settings command menus. **Switch** lets you automatically switch back and forth between the two graph settings sheets without having to return to the main **Graph** menu.

Changing the Automatic Scale Settings

Symphony automatically sets the scale (upper and lower limits) of the Y-axis according to the range you designate. This feature is extremely convenient. Symphony uses a scale that shows all the data points in the graph with the graph filling as much of the window as possible. If Symphony did not automatically set the scale, creating graphs would be much more cumbersome.

Sometimes you may want to change the scale that Symphony has chosen for a graph. For example, you may want to focus attention on a certain range of values, such as those surrounding a target goal, or you may want to create a series of graphs that all have the same scale.

Overriding Automatic Scaling

You can override Symphony's automatic scaling in several ways. The commands for overriding automatic scaling are accessed through the **2nd-Settings Y**-Scale and **X**-Scale commands. Suppose that you have selected **2nd-Settings Y**-Scale. The following menu appears:

   Type   Format   Exponent   Width   Quit

The **Type** option selects the kind of scale overriding that you want. Symphony usually uses linear scales, but you can also set logarithmic scales. The options that appear once you have selected **Type** are

   Manual-Linear   Automatic-Linear   Logarithmic

The **Manual-Linear** option manually overrides Symphony's automatic scaling in a linear fashion. With Manual-Linear, you must manually set the lower and upper boundaries of the scale. Logarithmic, on the other hand, lets you override Symphony's automatic linear scaling in a logarithmic fashion; however, Symphony still sets the upper and lower boundaries on its own. (See "Advanced Graphics Options" at the end of the chapter for more on logarithmic scaling.)

When you choose Manual-Linear, Symphony requests upper and lower boundaries for the scale limits. Figure 12.9 shows how this function works. This figure uses the same data as figure 12.8, except that the scale has been changed to show an upper limit of 60 and a lower limit of -60.

If you decide that you want to eliminate the manual overrides you have set up, you can select the Automatic-Linear option to reset the scaling to automatic.

Formatting Numbers

The **Format** option of the **2nd-Settings X**- and **Y**-Scale commands allows you to change the way the numbers on the X-axis and Y-axis are displayed. The alternatives under this option are the same as those for the SHEET Format command. You can specify that the numbers be displayed with a fixed number of digits, with a $ or embedded command, or as a percentage with an appended % sign. For example, figure 12.10 shows the same graph as figure 12.9, except that in figure 12.10 the scale has been assigned the Fixed 2 format.

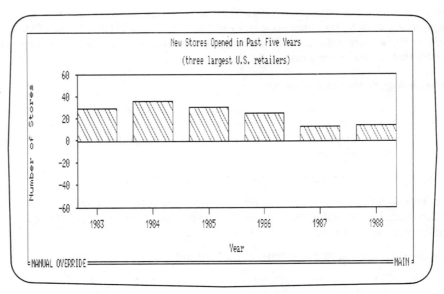

Fig. 12.9

Manually overriding Symphony's automatic scaling.

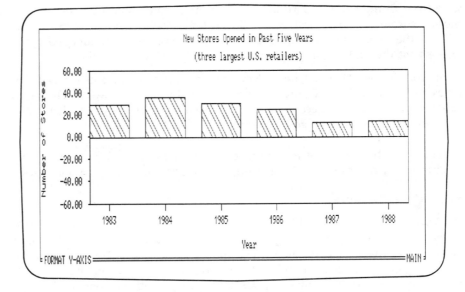

Fig. 12.10

The Y-axis labels formatted to Fixed 2.

Fitting the Graph to the Scales

Symphony always tries to fit the graph into the scales you have specified. If you set the upper limit of a scale too low, the resulting graph simply shows as much of the data as can be squeezed into the allotted space. For example, if you set the upper limit at 10 and the lower limit at 0 and try to graph the sample data, the result is the graph in figure 12.11.

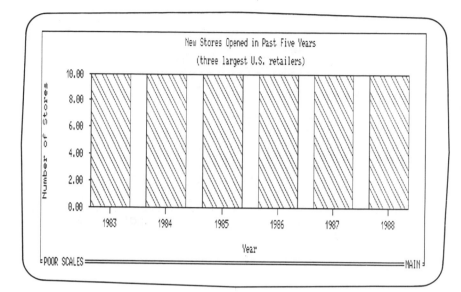

Fig. 12.11

Inadequate upper limits.

Changing to Nonzero Origin

When you use the Manual-Linear option, Symphony always ignores a positive lower limit or a negative upper limit on the Y-axis scale; this feature ensures that zero (the origin) is always on the scale. Symphony offers another option, however, that lets you change a graph's origin. This new option is accessed through the 2nd-Settings **Other Origin** command. For example, you can change the origin of the graph in figure 12.8 from 0 to 10. Figure 12.12 shows how the graph changes. Note that to display the data, you must reset the graph to Automatic-Linear.

Using Other Scale Options

You have several other scale options for formatting a graph. These include logarithmic scaling, controlling the width of Y-axis scale numbers, and controlling Symphony's scaling messages. These options are best applied to more complex graphs and therefore are discussed in the section entitled "Advanced Graphics Options" at the end of the chapter.

Saving and Recalling Graph Settings

Only one set of graph settings can be the *current* graph settings. Before you can build a new set of graph settings sheets, you must store the old ones.

Fig. 12.12

A graph with a nonzero origin.

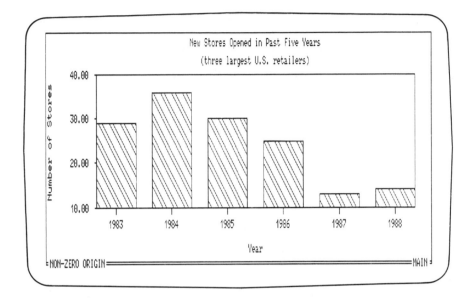

By issuing the **Name** option from either the **1st-** or **2nd-Settings** command menu, you can instruct Symphony to remember the parameters stored in the current graph settings sheets. (The option resides in both menus.) The **Name** command gives you these options:

Use   Create   Delete   Previous   Next   Initial-Settings   Reset   Quit

With the **Create** option, you can create a 15-character name for the current settings. All the settings in both the **1st-** and **2nd-Settings** sheets—the data range settings, graph titles, and axis titles—are saved under this name. The new name appears in the lower right corner of both the **1st-** and **2nd-Settings** sheets; when you save the Symphony file, the name is saved also.

You can recall a named set of **1st-** and **2nd-Settings** sheets at any time by issuing the **Name Use** command. When you issue this command, Symphony presents a list of all the named sets of graph settings stored in the current worksheet (the *settings catalog*). You can select the set you want by typing the name from the keyboard or pointing to the name in the list. Symphony then retrieves the **1st-** and **2nd-Settings** sheets of the named set and makes them the current set.

If you save a file without naming the current graph settings, Symphony still keeps your current graph settings.

Using Graph Settings Catalogs

You can create several different graph settings sheets for a single file, even for a single window. The entire group of settings in a worksheet file is called a catalog. The **Name** Create and **Name** Use commands make it easy to create and use a catalog of settings sheets. For example, the settings sheets for all the various graphs in this chapter are contained in a single catalog. After each settings sheet was created, it was attached to a GRAPH window, and a picture of the graph was taken.

Two other options available in the **Name** menu help you select settings sheets from a catalog. These commands are **Previous** and **Next**. When you select **Previous**, Symphony automatically selects the settings sheet that alphabetically precedes the current settings sheet in the catalog. For example, suppose that you had the following catalog of settings names:

FORMAT Y-AXIS	NONZERO ORIGIN
LOGARITHMIC	OVERRIDE
MAIN TEXT	POOR SCALES
MANUAL	SIMPLE BAR
MANY PARTS	X-AXIS LABELS

If the current settings name is SIMPLE BAR and you select **Previous**, Symphony shifts the current settings to POOR SCALES. If the current settings name is FORMAT Y-AXIS when you choose **Previous**, however, Symphony uses the last entry in the list, X-AXIS LABELS. The **Next** option works just the opposite from **Previous**.

Deleting Graph Settings

To delete a single settings name from the worksheet, use the **1st**- or **2nd-Settings Name Delete** command. As with the **Name Create** command, Symphony prompts you with a list of all the settings names in the current worksheet file. You can point to the name you want to delete, or type the name from the keyboard.

To delete all the settings names, you can issue **Name Reset**. This command automatically deletes all the settings names in the catalog. Be careful. When you delete the settings names, all the settings for all the graphs in the current file are lost. A "Yes/No" confirmation step in the **Name Reset** command gives you a second chance if you accidentally type **R** for **Reset**. After you enter **Yes**, however, all the settings for all the graphs are gone.

You must remember two rules in regard to deleting graph names. First, you cannot delete the current settings name. For example, suppose that FORMAT Y-AXIS is the current graph settings name. You must make another settings name current before you can delete FORMAT Y-AXIS.

A second thing to remember about deleting settings names in Symphony is that the program provides no barrier to deleting a settings name which is attached to a GRAPH window. The GRAPH window then simply appears blank on the screen, and the settings for the GRAPH window are reset to the default configuration settings.

Resetting All the Current Graph Settings

Instead of deleting a settings name, you can completely reset all the settings associated with that name by using the **Name Initial-Settings** command. When you select the **Initial-Settings** option, Symphony resets the current settings sheet to the default settings. For example, suppose that you have created what you thought were the correct settings for a graph of revenue projections and named the settings PROJECT REVENUE. Suppose also that you later discover that the settings in PROJECT REVENUE are all wrong. You can go through a detailed sequence of making current another settings name, deleting PROJECT REVENUE with the **Name Delete** command, and finally re-creating PROJECT REVENUE with **Name Create**. A much easier way to reset all the settings for PROJECT REVENUE, however, is to use the **Initial-Settings** command while the name is still current.

Resetting a Portion of the Current Graph Settings

Besides resetting all the current settings for a particular name, you can also delete selected settings with the **1st-Settings Cancel** command. In fact, you can delete all or just a portion of the **1st-Settings** with this command. Settings that you can delete include range addresses, formats, data labels, legends, and hues (colors). For example, suppose that you have the 1st-Settings sheet that appears in figure 12.13.

Fig. 12.13

An example of a 1st-Settings sheet.

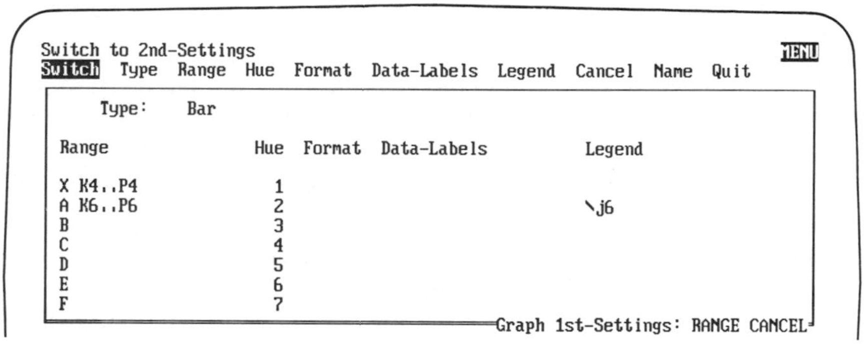

```
Switch to 2nd-Settings                                              MENU
Switch  Type  Range  Hue  Format  Data-Labels  Legend  Cancel  Name  Quit
┌─────────────────────────────────────────────────────────────────────┐
│     Type:    Bar                                                      │
│                                                                       │
│  Range              Hue  Format  Data-Labels       Legend            │
│                                                                       │
│  X K4..P4            1                                                │
│  A K6..P6            2                              \j6               │
│  B                   3                                                │
│  C                   4                                                │
│  D                   5                                                │
│  E                   6                                                │
│  F                   7                                                │
└───────────────────────────────────Graph 1st-Settings: RANGE CANCEL──┘
```

To delete the A range addresses, select **Cancel** from the **1st-Settings** menu. The following options then appear:

> **Entire-Row**   **Range**   **Format**   **Data-Labels**   **Legend**   **Hue**

Select **Range**, which produces the following menu:

> **Graph**   **X**   **A**   **B**   **C**   **D**   **E**   **F**   **Quit**

To cancel the A range, select **A**. The 1st-Settings sheet then appears as shown in figure 12.14.

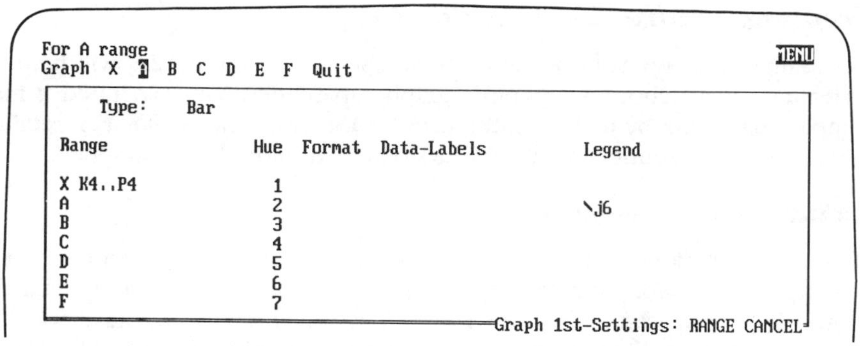

```
For A range
Graph  X  🅰  B  C  D  E  F  Quit                    MENU

     Type:     Bar

   Range              Hue  Format  Data-Labels       Legend

   X  K4..P4           1
   A                   2                           ＼j6
   B                   3
   C                   4
   D                   5
   E                   6
   F                   7
                              Graph 1st-Settings: RANGE CANCEL
```

Fig. 12.14

After deleting the A range addresses.

If you want to delete all the entries for the A range, select the **1st-Settings Cancel Entire-Row A** command. The **1st-Settings** sheet then looks like figure 12.15.

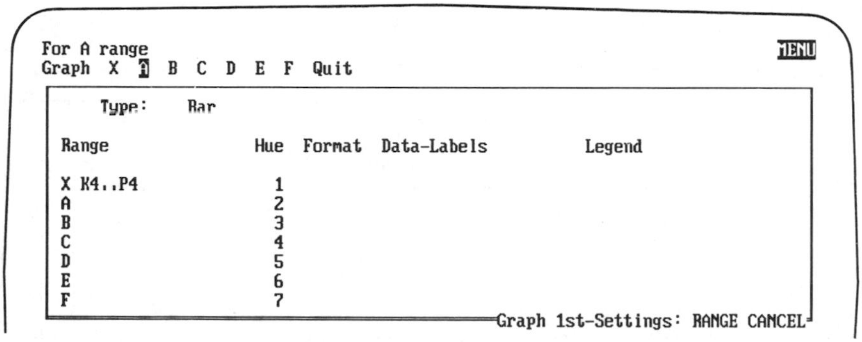

```
For A range
Graph  X  🅰  B  C  D  E  F  Quit                    MENU

     Type:     Bar

   Range              Hue  Format  Data-Labels       Legend

   X  K4..P4           1
   A                   2
   B                   3
   C                   4
   D                   5
   E                   6
   F                   7
                              Graph 1st-Settings: RANGE CANCEL
```

Fig. 12.15

After deleting all entries for the A range.

To delete all the settings for the entire graph, select **1st-Settings Cancel Entire-Row Graph**. Symphony resets all the settings in the **1st-Settings** sheet to the default settings.

Saving Graphs for Printing

As mentioned earlier, the main Symphony program does not have the capability of printing graphs. You must use the PrintGraph program for this task. Before you can print a graph with PrintGraph, however, you must save the graph. The **Image-Save** option from the GRAPH menu or SHEET **Graph** menu causes Symphony to save the current graph settings, including all the selected formatting options. All saved graph files have the extension .PIC.

Once you have created a .PIC file, you can no longer access it from the main Symphony menu, other than to list the file's name. The .PIC file is accessible only from the PrintGraph program. If you want to re-create the graph on-screen from within Symphony, you must give the settings a name in the current worksheet file.

Creating a More Complex Bar Graph

Increasing the complexity of the bar graph shown in figure 12.8 will help you understand more about Symphony's graph capabilities. You can build a more complex bar graph by including the data for the two other major U.S. retailers, K Mart and J. C. Penney, with the Sears data you have already graphed.

Adding More Data Ranges

After you create a new settings name (by using **Name Create**), your next step is to inform Symphony that the new graph should include two additional data ranges. You must first access the **1st-Settings Range** menu. Because you have already created one data range, the next set of data goes into the B range. To enter the data range, select **B** from the **Range** menu and tell Symphony that the data is located in the range K7..P7 (see fig. 12.1). To enter the third data set, select **C** and indicate the location of the data: K8..P8. If you are in a SHEET window, use **Graph Preview** to draw the graph. The graph then appears as shown in figure 12.16.

Fig. 12.16

A bar graph with three data ranges.

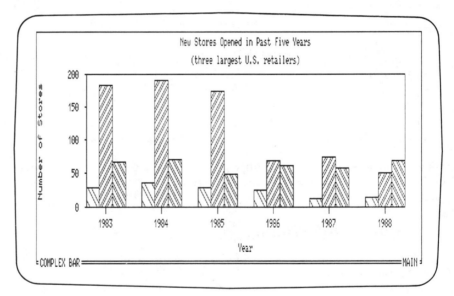

As you can see, the graph groups the data sets. The first data items from each range are grouped together; similarly, the second and third data items are clustered together. This arrangement makes it easy to compare the data in each data set.

For an additional challenge, you may try creating a special graph window. To do so, use the SERVICES **Window Create** command and enter a window name;

you may want to use FIGURE 12.16 for the name. You can then call up the GRAPH menu by selecting the Menu key (F10 on IBM PCs and compatibles). Finally, use the Attach option from the GRAPH menu to attach the settings to the window.

Controlling Bar Graph Crosshatches

Notice the different crosshatches within the bars in figure 12.16. The earlier bar graphs in this chapter also contained crosshatches, but because only one set of data was included, only one pattern of crosshatches appeared. Because the graph in figure 12.16 has several sets of data, the contrast between crosshatches is much greater. Cross-hatching makes it easy to distinguish among different data sets when they are graphed in black and white. Normally, Symphony controls the crosshatches for you.

Although most of the time you will want Symphony to control the cross-hatching, the program does allow you to select patterns yourself. Symphony offers seven different cross-hatching patterns with a numbering scheme of 1 through 7. Figure 12.17 shows the patterns and their respective numbers.

Fig. 12.17

Available bar graph cross-hatching patterns.

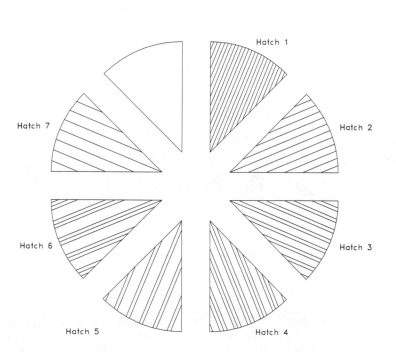

Suppose that you prefer the patterns numbered 5 through 7. To change the patterns for the data sets, use the **1st-Settings Hue** command. If you want to change the patterns for data set A to pattern 5, use **1st-Settings Hue A 5**; to change data set B to pattern 6, use **Hue B 6**; and so on. Figures 12.18A and 12.18B show the **1st-Settings** sheet and associated bar graph with these selected patterns.

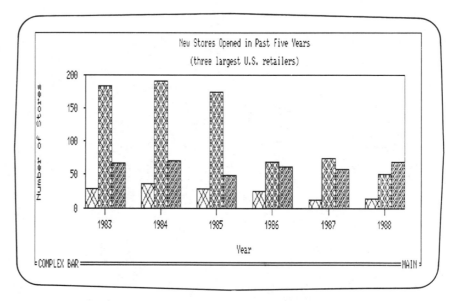

Fig. 12.18A

The 1st-Settings sheet after changing the cross-hatching patterns.

Fig. 12.18B

The resulting bar graph.

On the **1st-Settings** sheet, the **Hue** for range X is 1. Changing the **Hue** selection for range X has no effect when you are displaying a graph in black and white. When you are using color, though, the **Hue** selection allows you to change the color of the labels below the X-axis.

Using Legends

Whenever you have more than one set of data on a graph, you need some method to distinguish one set from another. Symphony has several ways to help you distinguish data sets. Line graphs provide different symbols to mark the different data points. Bar charts use different patterns of crosshatches. If your display is on a color monitor, Symphony can also use color to make the distinction.

Even with the different patterns of color or crosshatches, legends to label the patterns are also useful. At the bottom of figure 12.19B, below the X-axis, are three different legends corresponding to the three different ranges of data already graphed. You enter these legends with the **1st-Settings Legend** command. After you have selected this option, you type the actual legend text. For example, you can enter **Sears** for legend A. Or, as with titles, you can enter legends with a backslash (\ ) and a cell reference or range name. For example, you can enter \J6 for **1st-Settings Legend A**, \J7 for **B**, and so on. The legends in the settings sheet shown in figure 12.19A were entered with this method. The corresponding graph is shown in figure 12.19B.

Displaying the Graph in Color

If you have a color monitor, you can instruct Symphony to display graphics in color. The capability of producing colors is one of the nicest features of the program. Just what colors Symphony uses depends on your hardware. If you have an IBM PC/XT, Symphony can display graphics in only three different colors (white, red, and blue). These colors are not to be confused, however, with the large selection of colors the program can use for printing graphs if you have the appropriate printer or plotter. (Printing graphs and the additional colors available are covered in the following chapter.)

To display the graph from figure 12.19B in color, select **Color Yes** from the **2nd-Settings Other** menu. You can then set the bars and lines for the data and label ranges to different colors. Symphony offers the following hues for computers with Color Graphics Adapters (CGA):

Hue Number	Actual Color
1	White
2	Red
3	Blue
4	White
5	Red
6	Blue
7	White

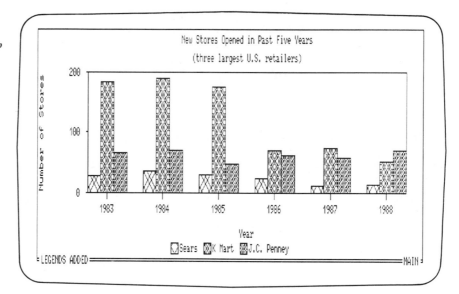

Fig. 12.19A

Using cell references to enter legends.

Fig. 12.19B

A bar graph with legends.

The list of colors available for the IBM PC is obviously somewhat limited, and the colors for your particular machine may be different. Computers with Enhanced Graphic Adapters (EGA) can have up to seven different colors. You should consult your dealer if you have any questions about what colors Symphony can produce on your machine.

Changing Colors in Bar Graphs

If you don't like the colors that Symphony chooses for the different ranges, you can change the hues. For example, suppose that you prefer the outside scales and numbers to be red and the bars to be blue for data range A, white for B, and red for C. Use the **1st-Settings Hue** command to make the appropriate changes. To select red for the outside scales and numbers, choose **1st-Settings Hue X 2**; to have blue for range A, use **1st-Settings Hue A 3**.

You can also use the **Hue** option to control the crosshatches. Whether Symphony uses colors or crosshatches for filling in the bars in a bar graph depends on whether you have invoked color. Unfortunately, on bar graphs you cannot have colors and crosshatches at the same time. (You can with pie charts; see the section entitled "Pie Chart Crosshatches.")

Stacked-Bar Graphs

A slight variation of the basic bar graph is the stacked-bar graph. Stacked-bar graphs are frequently used to compare different sets of data while showing the components and total of each data set. In these graphs, the totals are created by stacking the component data items one on another.

In figure 12.20, you can see the total number of store openings for the three largest U.S. retailers. This graph was created in much the same way as was the graph in figure 12.19B. In fact, the same settings were used to produce both, except the **1st-Settings Type** was changed to **Stacked-Bar** in the second graph. Preview draws the graph in the SHEET environment. Notice that legends, X-axis labels, and titles have also been added. They, too, were added in the same way as they were in the simpler examples.

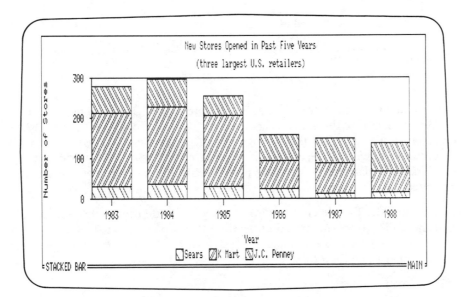

Fig. 12.20

A stacked-bar graph.

Line Graphs

Symphony also offers line graphs, which are particularly useful for showing time-series data but are by no means restricted to this use. Consider the data on "Interest Movements for February 1988" that appears in figure 12.21. This data reflects the Federal Funds Rate and London Interbank Offering Rate (LIBOR) for the indicated dates.

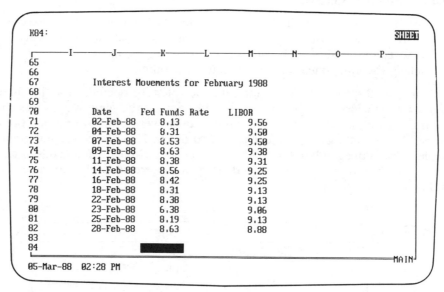

To create a line graph of the Federal Funds Rate plotted against time, first select the **Line** option from the **1st-Settings Type** menu. Next, select **1st-Settings Range A** and enter the range for the A range (in this example, K71..K82). As always, the graph is drawn with **Preview** when you are in the SHEET environment and is automatically displayed when you are in the GRAPH environment. Figure 12.22 illustrates this line graph.

Once again, titles have been added to the graph. To add these titles, select **Titles** from the **2nd-Settings** menu and enter the titles shown for **First**, **X-axis**, and **Y-axis** selections. Figures 12.23A and 12.23B show the **1st-** and **2nd-Settings** sheets for the graph in figure 12.22.

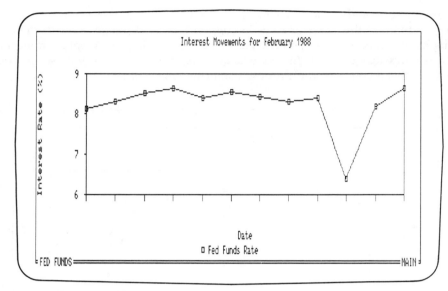

Fig. 12.22

A line graph drawn from the Federal Funds Rate data.

```
Switch to 2nd-Settings                                                    MENU
Switch  Type  Range  Hue  Format  Data-Labels  Legend  Cancel  Name  Quit

      Type:    Line

Range                 Hue  Format  Data-Labels         Legend

X                      1
A K71..K82             2   Both                        \k70
B                      3   Both
C                      4   Both
D                      5   Both
E                      6   Both
F                      7   Both
                                            Graph 1st-Settings: FED FUNDS
```

Fig. 12.23A

The 1st-Settings sheet for figure 12.22.

```
Displayed above graph                                                     MENU
First  Second  X-axis  Y-axis  Quit

  Titles                                        Type: Line
    First:  \j67                      X-Axis: \j70
    Second:                           Y-Axis: Interest Rate (%)
  Y-Scale                  X-Scale                  Other
    Type     Automatic       Type     Automatic       Grid:   None
     Lower:                   Lower:                   Hide:   No
     Upper:                   Upper:                   Color:  No
    Format:  G               Format:  G               Skip:   1
    Exponent: Automatic      Exponent: Automatic      Origin: 0
    Width:   9                                        Aspect: 1
                                            Graph 2nd-Settings: FED FUNDS
```

Fig. 12.23B

The 2nd-Settings sheet for figure 12.22.

Notice also that the line chart in figure 12.22 has no X-axis labels. The next step is to enter the range of dates in column J as the **X** range. As with the bar graphs shown earlier, you enter X-axis labels by selecting the **X** option from the 1st-Settings **R**ange menu. In this example, use the range J71..J82. When you redraw this graph with the **P**review command, you will see figure 12.24.

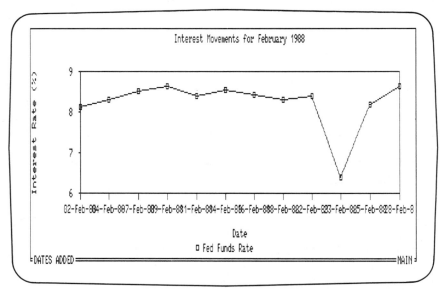

Using the entire set of data labels in column J causes a problem—the graph simply does not have enough room to display all the labels without overlapping them. This problem can occur any time you have many X labels or unusually long ones.

Symphony offers two solutions. One option is to reformat the dates in a shorter form (for instance, format D2—DD/MMM). If you prefer not to change the format, however, you can use the 2nd-Settings **O**ther **S**kip command to skip every nth X label when the graph is displayed. After you enter the command, Symphony prompts you for the skipping factor. In most cases, as in the example shown in figure 12.25, skipping every other label (specifying a factor of 2) is sufficient to clean up the graph. On some graphs, however, it may be necessary to choose a much larger factor. Symphony has the capability to skip as many as 8,192 X labels.

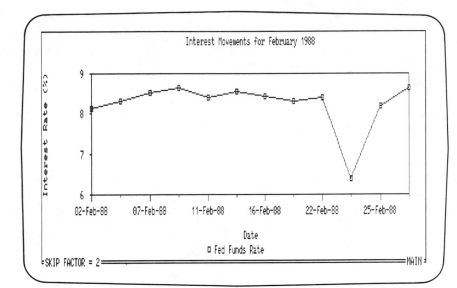

Fig. 12.25

After specifying a skipping factor of 2.

The fact that the date labels are ordered sequentially doesn't matter to Symphony. The program could just as easily have plotted against any other set of labels. Although cells containing date functions were used for the X-axis labels, Symphony can use numbers, labels, or other functions for these labels.

The data set that appears in figure 12.21 suggests a second line graph tp compare the variations in the Federal Funds Rate to the changes in LIBOR during the same period. This graph is really a simple extension of the previous one. To continue the example, you must first create a B range that captures the data in range M71..M82. Also specify the Legend for the B range as \M70. Figure 12.26 illustrates the new graph.

Notice the different symbols (box and plus) at the points of intersection on the graph. So far, you have seen only one of the four ways of displaying a line graph. The command that controls the lines and symbols at the points of intersection on a line graph is **1st-Settings Format A** through **F**. After you choose one of the ranges from A through F, Symphony provides the following options:

Lines **Symbols** **Both** **Neither**

Fig. 12.26

A line graph with two data ranges.

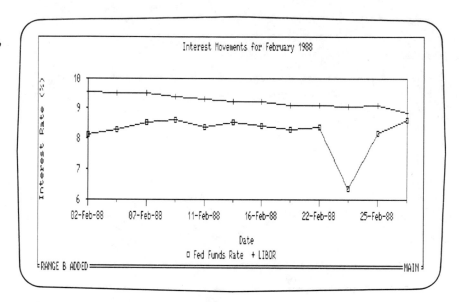

Fig. 12.26

A line graph with two data ranges.

Controlling Lines and Symbols

Lines signals Symphony to connect the different data points with straight lines and no symbols. Figure 12.27 shows the graph from figure 12.26 with lines only.

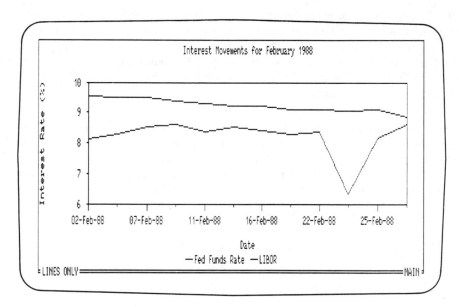

Fig. 12.27

A line graph with lines but no symbols.

The **S**ymbols option tells Symphony to leave out the straight lines and use different graphic symbols for each of up to six data ranges. The symbols are

A □   D ▷
B +   E x
C △   F ▽

Figure 12.28 shows the graph with symbols but no lines. Although you can use this format with line charts, it is more commonly used with XY plots.

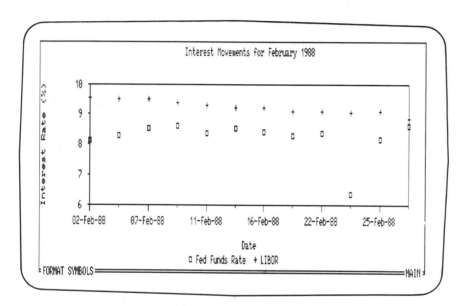

Fig. 12.28

A line graph with symbols but no lines.

The third choice, **Both**, is the default used in figures 12.22 through 12.26 to produce both lines and symbols. Because it is difficult to tell one data set from another without using both lines and symbols, **Both** is the preferred option in most cases.

The **N**either option suppresses both lines and symbols. You may wonder how points of intersection can be shown if neither lines nor symbols appear on the graph. The answer is through **D**ata-Labels.

Using Data-Labels

Symphony's **D**ata-Labels command uses data from a SHEET window as labels in a graph. These labels are placed in the graph near the data points. The **D**ata-Labels option is a part of the **G**raph **1**st-Settings menu. After you choose **1**st-Settings **D**ata-Labels, the following menu appears:

   A   B   C   D   E   F   Quit

Notice that the options here correspond to the data range options; one set of data labels exists for each set of data. In general, you will want to use the same coordinates to define the data labels and the data range. After you indicate the range containing the data labels, Symphony presents the option of placing the data labels above or below the data point, centered on the data point, or to the left or right of the data point.

The data labels can be numbers, values, or text. In most cases, you will want to use numbers as data labels. If you use text, be sure to keep the strings short to avoid cluttering the graph.

Figures 12.29A and 12.29B show the 1st-Settings sheet and sample line graph (one data set) with data labels and without symbols or lines. You can use data labels in a line chart that includes lines and symbols, as well as in a graph that contains no lines or symbols. In fact, in line charts with multiple data sets, you need lines or symbols to differentiate the various data sets. Otherwise, the graph looks like a jumble of numbers. Figure 12.30 shows another line graph with two sets of data and data labels.

Fig. 12.29A

A 1st-Settings sheet with data labels and without symbols or lines.

```
 Switch to 2nd-Settings                                              MENU
 Switch  Type  Range  Hue  Format  Data-Labels  Legend  Cancel  Name  Quit

      Type:     Line

   Range                  Hue   Format  Data-Labels          Legend

   X J71..J82              1
   A K71..K82              2    Neither C K71..K82           \k70
   B M71..M82              3    Both
   C                       4    Both
   D                       5    Both
   E                       6    Both
   F                       7    Both
                                        Graph 1st-Settings: DATA LABELS 1
```

If you are not using lines or symbols (on a line graph), you will probably want to center the data labels on the data points. Otherwise, you'll want to choose one of the other options to avoid cluttering the graph.

Data labels also work with bar graphs. In bar graphs, the labels are centered above each bar. As with line charts, data labels in bar graphs can be helpful in identifying the numeric value associated with each data point.

Sometimes it is easy to get confused about the difference between the X-axis titles, the X labels, and the data labels. An X-axis title usually describes the units of measure used on the X-axis (like dollars or years). X labels distinguish the different data points (for example, 1987 and 1988 data). Data labels describe individual data items.

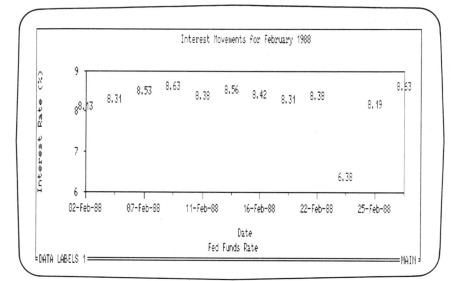

Fig. 12.29B

The line graph with data labels and neither symbols nor lines.

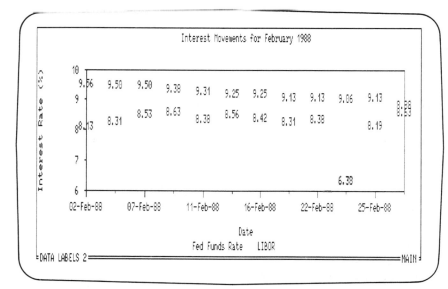

Fig. 12.30

A line graph with data labels and two data sets.

Adding Grids

Symphony offers still another option for formatting graphs: **Grid**. This option lets you impose a grid on a Symphony graph. The command to create a grid is **2nd-Settings Other Grid**. The submenu under this command offers the following options:

Horizontal   Vertical   **Both**   **None**

The first option creates a horizontal grid over the graph; the second, a vertical grid. Option three, **Both**, causes both types of grids to display, as in figure 12.31. The last option, **None**, eliminates all grids from the current graph settings.

Fig. 12.31

Imposing a grid.

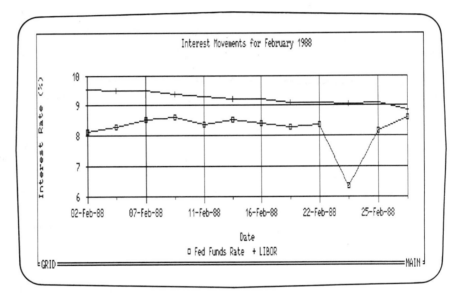

Although grids can be useful, they also can clutter the graph unnecessarily. You may find that using data labels works better than grids for many applications.

Pie Charts

Pie charts, another of Symphony's graph types, show relationships within a single set of data items. Each data item is a slice of the pie, and the entire pie represents the sum of the slices.

In many ways, a pie chart is the simplest of Symphony's graphs. Only one data range can be represented by a pie chart, so only the **1st-Settings Range A** option is needed to define a pie. Because a pie chart has no axes, you cannot use the X- and Y-axis titles. Similarly, grids, scales, and data labels are not used with pie charts.

One convenient way to show the advantages as well as the limitations of a pie chart is to add data to figure 12.1. As you can see in figure 12.32, the additional data is simply the regions and their respective store openings for the year 1988.

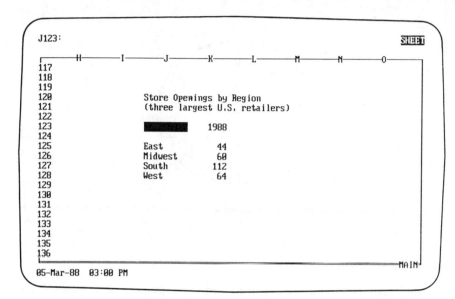

Fig. 12.32

Sample data for a pie chart.

To create a pie chart from the data in figure 12.32, first select **Pie** from the 1st-Settings **Type** menu. Next, indicate K125..K128 as the A range. Because pie charts do not have an X- or a Y-axis, Symphony adopts the convention of using the X-range as the captions for the slices of the pie. Here you designate J125..J128 as the X label range. Figure 12.33 shows the resulting graph.

In this pie chart, you should notice the number of slices in the pie and the percentages next to the labels. The number of slices in the pie corresponds to the number of data items in the A range—in this case, four. The most important limitation on the number of data items used in a pie chart is that the labels tend to get bunched up if you use too many items. Each situation is different, but you might need to collect some of the smaller slices into an "Other" category if you have too many data items.

The point of a pie chart is to show the relationship of each data item to the whole. Symphony automatically calculates the percentage of each slice and places this percentage next to the appropriate label. It would be nice, however, if you could also display the value of each data item next to the percentage. Although the basic Symphony program does not offer this feature, you could use an add-on package such as Freelance Plus® or Graphwriter II.

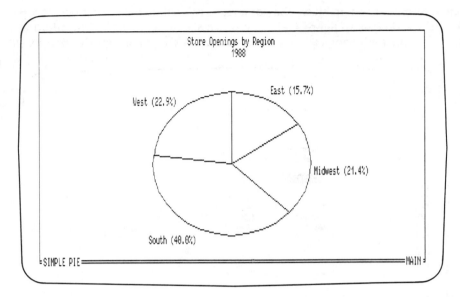

Fig. 12.33

The pie graph based on the data in figure 12.32.

The Aspect Ratio

The aspect ratio is the ratio of height to width in a graph. For most graph types, changing the aspect ratio slightly has no adverse visual effect. When you change the aspect ratio in a pie chart, however, the pie may be noticeably *not* round. In fact, even with the same aspect ratio, some computers may show a round pie chart, but others will show the same pie as an ellipse. Therefore, Symphony offers a special command to control the aspect ratio of pie charts: **2nd-Settings Other Aspect**. If you find that your pie charts do not look round, you may want to use this command.

Pie Chart Crosshatches

Symphony also gives you the option of using crosshatches in pie charts. Pie charts have the same number of cross-hatching patterns as bar charts, but the patterns themselves are different. Figure 12.34 shows Symphony's pie chart cross-hatching patterns.

When setting up cross-hatching patterns for a bar chart, you use the **Hue** option from the **1st-Settings** menu. With pie charts, you must set up a special range of values containing hatching pattern numbers. (Lotus also calls them "hue" numbers.) You then assign the range of pattern numbers to the B range of the pie chart. Because pie charts do not use the B range for assigning other data, this range is free for pattern numbers.

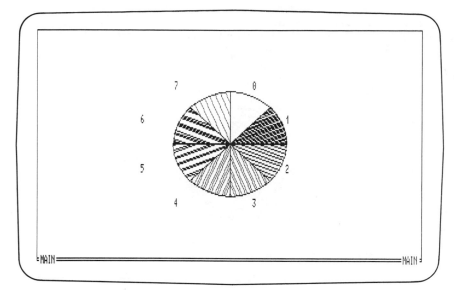

Fig. 12.34

Available pie chart cross-hatching patterns.

For example, suppose that you want to assign pattern 1 to the first slice of the pie chart. Then, starting at the top of the pie chart and moving clockwise, pattern 2 is assigned to slice 2; pattern 3 to slice 3; and so on. To get the proper cross-hatching patterns, you must place the pattern numbers in the worksheet (as they appear in the range M125..M128 in fig. 12.35) and assign them to the B range. If you set Color to No, using the 2nd-Settings Other command, the pie chart then appears as illustrated in figure 12.36.

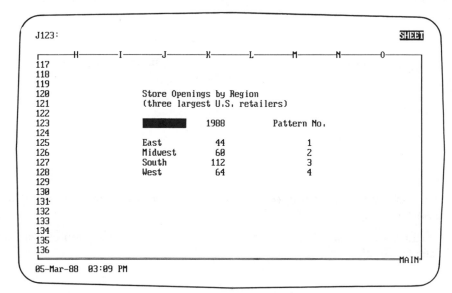

Fig. 12.35

Placing the cross-hatching patterns in the worksheet.

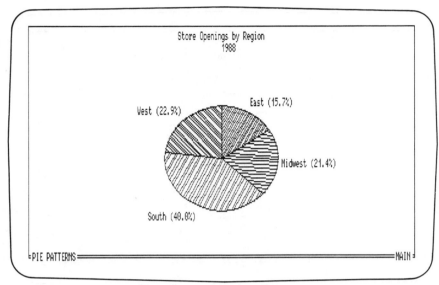

Fig. 12.36

The pie chart after specifying cross-hatching patterns.

Color in Pie Charts

Unlike a bar graph, you can use both color and crosshatches in a pie chart; but whenever you use color in a pie chart, Symphony automatically draws all slices with the same crosshatch pattern. When you use color, the values you code in the B range control the color of the slices but not their crosshatch patterns.

For example, suppose that you want to reproduce in color the pie chart shown in figure 12.36. If you have a Color Graphics Adapter, you assign the colors just as you do for bar charts.

B-Range Value	Actual Color
0 or blank	No color, no crosshatches
1	White
2	Red
3	Blue
4	White
5	Red
6	Blue
7	White

Notice that a B-range value of 0 causes Symphony to omit both color and crosshatches.

You can choose from seven different colors if you have a computer with an Enhanced Graphics Adapter.

Symphony draws the labels, titles, and percentages, using the **Hue** designated for the X range. The slices are outlined with the **Hue** specified in the A range. Remember that the **1st-Settings Hue** numbers have no bearing on the colors in a pie chart. The values in the B range determine the color of the sections inside each pie slice.

Exploded Pie Charts

Exploded pie charts allow you to draw emphasis to one or more slices in a pie chart. By adding a value of 100 to the normal B-range value, you can have Symphony set a slice apart from the others. For example, suppose that you want to produce the graph shown in figure 12.36 but with the slice for the West Coast region exploded. The **1st-Settings** sheet in figure 12.37A shows how you must change the B range, and figure 12.37B shows the exploded pie chart.

You can also explode more than one slice in a pie chart. Simply add 100 to each B-range pattern number that you want to explode.

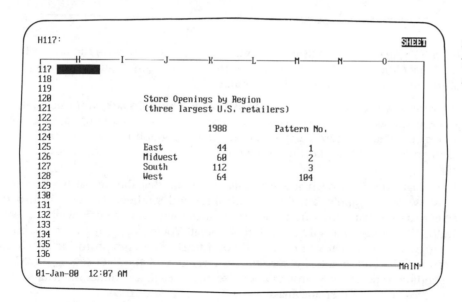

Fig. 12.37A

Adding 100 to the West region's B-range value.

XY Graphs

Symphony also offers XY graphs, which are sometimes called scatter plots. In an XY graph, two or more data items from the same data range can share the same X value. Obviously, this arrangement is not possible with a line chart. XY graphs are not used to show time series data. Instead, XY graphs help to illustrate the relationships between different attributes of data items, such as age and income or educational achievements and salary.

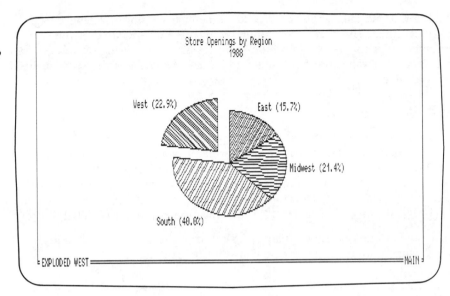

Fig. 12.37B

The pie chart with the West slice exploded.

In an XY graph, the X labels become more than simple labels on the graph. They are, in fact, the X-axis scale, which means that an XY graph requires as a minimum of information an X range and an A range.

In every other respect, an XY plot is like a line graph. In fact, you can think of a line graph as a specialized type of XY graph. For an example of an XY graph, look at the data in figure 12.38A and the resulting graph in figure 12.38B. (The X range is J206..J219, and the A range is L206..L219 in these figures.)

Note that titles have been added to this graph and that the format has been set to show only symbols rather than both lines and symbols. To set this format, select the Format option from the 1st-Settings menu and specify Symbols. Typically, XY graphs are displayed with this format. You can display the graph, however, using any format you choose. If you format an XY graph to include lines between the data points, be sure that at least one of the data sets is sorted in ascending or descending order. Otherwise, the lines that connect the data points will cross one another and make the graph difficult to read.

Frequently, scatter plots also include a line, called the *regression line*, which is an approximation of the trend suggested by the data in the graph. Unfortunately, Symphony cannot produce an XY graph with a regression line.

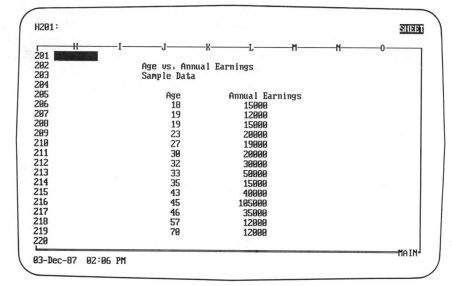

Fig. 12.38A

Sample data for an XY graph.

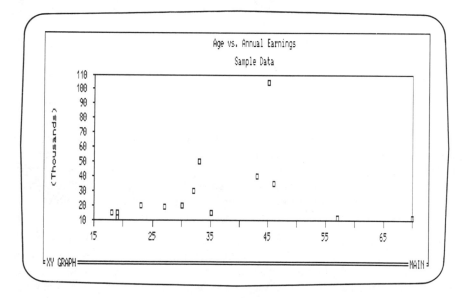

Fig. 12.38B

An XY graph.

High-Low-Close-Open Charts

Finally, Symphony offers high-low-close-open graphs. This type of graph is most often used for illustrating the daily price movements of stocks. But you can also track commodities or other financial data that experience price fluctuations.

When setting up the high-low-close-open graph, you should think of it as a special kind of bar graph. For example, to create a bar graph of just the high prices for a series of days, you enter those values as the A range and enter the graph **Type** as **Bar**. To change the bars to lines, you simply change the graph **Type** to High-Low-Close-Open. Figure 12.39A shows some typical stock quotation data, and figure 12.39B illustrates the graph you produce by designating the A range as K6..K15.

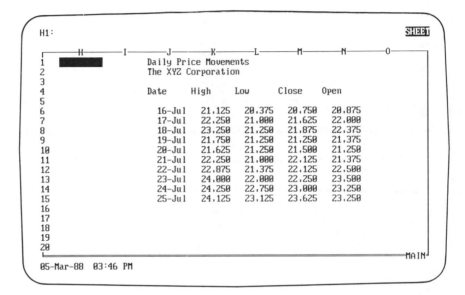

Fig. 12.39A

*Sample stock
quotation data.*

This type of chart, however, is really no more useful than a bar chart of the same data. To add more information to the graph, you must designate a B range and specify the X range as J6..J15. Once again, if the graph were a bar chart, including a B range would simply add another series of bars to the graph. But because the **Type** is **High-Low-Close-Open**, adding a B range has a different effect. Both the high and low prices for each day are combined into a single vertical line.

By adding a third and fourth range to the graph (the C and D ranges), you combine the opening and closing price information into the graph. An example of a high-low-close-open chart is shown in figure 12.39C. The closing prices are represented by the right tick marks and the opening prices by the left tick marks on the vertical lines in the graph.

A good technique to remember when organizing the data for a high-low-close-open chart is to arrange the data in parallel columns in the same sequence as the graph name: high, low, close, open. This method helps to prevent confusion when you must designate ranges for the graph.

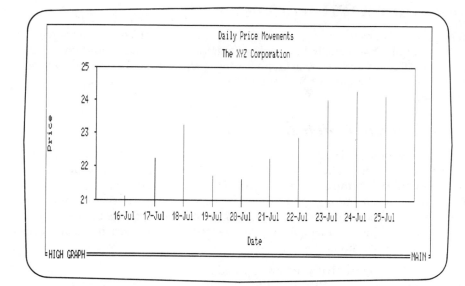

Fig. 12.39B

After designating K6..K15 as the A range.

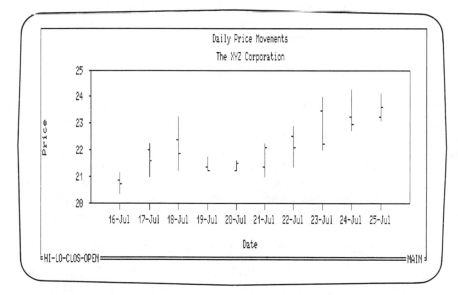

Fig. 12.39C

The high-low-close-open chart.

Advanced Graphics Topics

Symphony has several advanced options relating to GRAPH windows and also some special command options.

More on GRAPH Windows

When you start out with a new file, attaching graph settings to a GRAPH window is fairly simple. You usually have only one graph settings name and one GRAPH window. After you have several graph settings names and GRAPH windows, however, matching the proper settings name with the proper window can be a problem.

Using Current Graph Settings

A typical method for creating graphs is to start in the SHEET environment with the Graph command. Then, after you have all the settings and have decided that you want to Attach the settings to a GRAPH window, the first step is to create the new GRAPH window. Interestingly enough, when you create a new graph window, Symphony automatically attaches the current settings to the new window. Although this automatic feature saves work in many cases, it can also create problems in other situations.

For example, suppose that you have created all the graph settings for a pie chart and named the settings PIE1. You then decide that you want to create a second pie chart, PIE2, which is the same as PIE1 but uses color. The first step you take to create the new PIE2 graph settings is to use the 1st- or 2nd-Settings Name command to create the new name, PIE2. (If you do not create the new name before modifying the current settings, all the changes are made to the PIE1 settings.) You can then make changes to the current settings; these changes will apply to PIE2.

Now, suppose that you want to Attach the named settings to GRAPH windows. If you start by creating a new GRAPH window to display the PIE1 settings, Symphony automatically attaches the current settings to the new window. Because the current settings are those for PIE2, the new window shows those settings immediately. This feature can be confusing. After you attach the PIE1 settings to the new GRAPH window, though, the window appears as you originally intended. Note: You must always remember the name of the current graph settings. If you are not careful, you may wind up using the wrong graph settings.

Changing from One GRAPH Window to Another

When you are changing from one GRAPH window to another, the current graph settings travel with you. Even though the new window usually has named graph settings of its own, those settings do not appear in the 1st- and 2nd-Settings sheets unless you issue the Name Use command.

A frequent mistake is to change windows and immediately start altering graph settings. Again, be careful not to make changes to the wrong graph settings.

Deleting a GRAPH Window

As you may recall, Symphony does not allow you to delete the current named graph settings. But the program provides no barriers to deleting the current GRAPH window. If you do delete the current GRAPH window, the next most recently accessed window appears on the screen.

Unfortunately, Symphony does not have a **Window Rename** option. Therefore, the best technique for renaming a GRAPH window is to start from the original graph window and create a new window with the appropriate name. If you start from the original window, Symphony uses all its settings when you create the new window. You can then delete the old window, using the SERVICES **Window Delete** command.

"What If" Graphing

Symphony's graphics can be an integral part of "what if" analysis. You can use graphics extensively to fine-tune projections, budgets, or projects. You'll be amazed at how graphics will help you understand the impact of changes in your data on the results of your models.

If your hardware has graphics capability, you can use Symphony's windowing to perform outstanding "what if" analysis. For example, you can set up one window to display spreadsheet data and another window with a related graph; you can then display both windows simultaneously on the screen. When you make a change in the data, the GRAPH window immediately reflects the change. You can even show multiple GRAPH windows on the screen at once. Figure 12.40 shows SHEET and GRAPH windows that appear simultaneously on-screen (see Chapter 2 for more on windows).

In figure 12.40 the value for 1988 is $190,311. If you change the value for 1988 by 200,000, the change is immediately reflected in the graph (see fig. 12.41).

Keep in mind that using graphs is a good way to verify the reasonableness of your data. You may be surprised at how much help a simple graph can be for checking your work.

The Draw Key

GRAPH windows have only one special key associated with them—the Draw key (Alt-F8). Pressing the Draw key causes Symphony to redraw automatically all the windows that appear on the screen, GRAPH windows included.

The Draw key is normally used with the **Auto-Display** option of the SERVICES **Window Settings** command. If you set a GRAPH window's **Auto-Display** to **No**,

Fig. 12.40

A SHEET and a GRAPH window on-screen simultaneously.

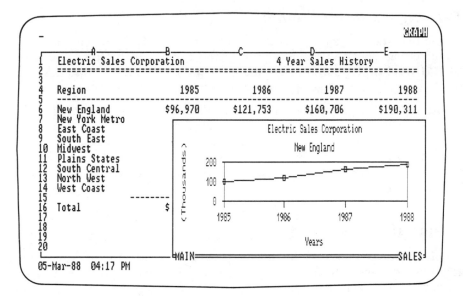

Fig. 12.41

Changes to worksheet reflected in graph.

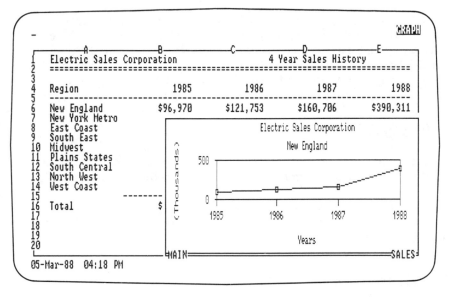

Symphony will not redisplay that window unless you press Draw (or unless that window is made the current window). For example, suppose that you have the windows appearing on the screen as shown in figure 12.40, and you want to change the data as shown in figure 12.41. If you have set the Auto-Display option to **No** for the GRAPH window on the right side of the screen (fig. 12.40), when you make the change in the data for the SHEET window on the left (fig. 12.41), the GRAPH window does not redraw. If you press the Draw key, however, the updated GRAPH window reappears on the right just as in figure 12.41.

Special Command Options

Symphony offers several other special command options. Most of these options involve controlling Symphony's numeric scaling. But some relate to Symphony's capability to hide certain parts of a graph.

Using Logarithmic Scale Override

The advantage of logarithmic scaling is that it allows you to compare very large and very small numbers in a reasonable fashion. Sometimes when you use linear scaling in Symphony, extremely large numbers in a range can dwarf their smaller companion numbers. For example, suppose that you want to create a bar graph of the number of parts produced on a new production process during the first eight months of 1987. Figure 12.42 shows how the graph might appear.

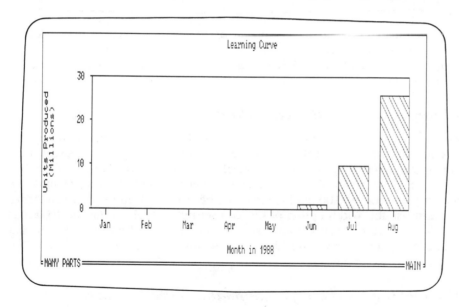

Fig. 12.42

Problems with linear scaling.

Because of the relatively large number of parts produced in August (26 million), the smaller quantities for January through April (53 to 7,420) cannot be seen. Figure 12.43 shows the same numbers graphed with the **2nd-Settings Y-Scale Type** command set to **Logarithmic**.

Note that Symphony creates evenly spaced tick marks along the Y-axis; however, the numbers that are assigned to the marks are not evenly distributed numerically.

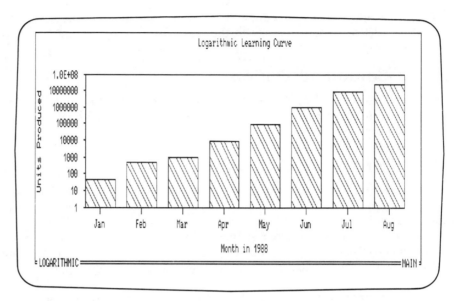

Fig. 12.43

After issuing 2nd-Settings Y-Scale Type Logarithmic.

Each tick mark corresponds to a power of 10. For example, the first tick mark corresponds to $10^1=10$, the second mark to $10^2=100$, the third to $10^3=1{,}000$, and so on. The **2nd-Settings Y-Scale Type Automatic-Linear** command resets the Y-axis to automatic linear scaling.

Changing the Y-Axis Scale Width

Notice in figure 12.43 that the largest Y-axis scale number appears in Symphony's scientific format as 1.0E+08. Because the default width of Symphony's scale numbers is 9 characters, Symphony is incapable of displaying 100,000,000 (the fixed format equivalent of 1.0E+08). Therefore, Symphony opts for the scientific format. If you want the 100 million scale number to appear in its full fixed format, you can use the **Width** option of the **2nd-Settings Y-Scale** command to change the width to 10 or greater. Conversely, if you set the width to less than 9 characters, Symphony shows asterisks. Note: **Width** is not an option for the **2nd-Settings X-Scale** command.

Controlling Symphony's Automatic Scaling Labels

Anyone who graphs very large numbers may experience problems with the program's automatic scaling labels. (Scaling labels are the messages that appear next to the X- and Y-axis labels when the values being graphed are in the thousands or greater.) For example, when you graph numbers in the billions, Symphony uses a scaling factor label of (Times 1E9) rather than (Billions).

If you don't like the automatic scaling labels that Symphony offers, you can select your own—up to a point. The technique is to specify manually an exponent

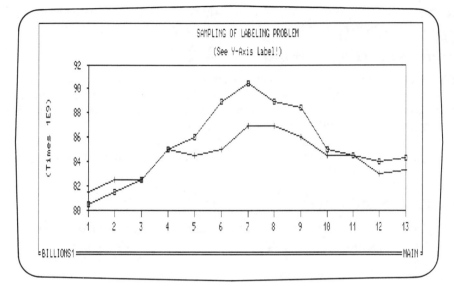

Fig. 12.44

An example of Symphony's automatic scaling labels (see Y-axis label).

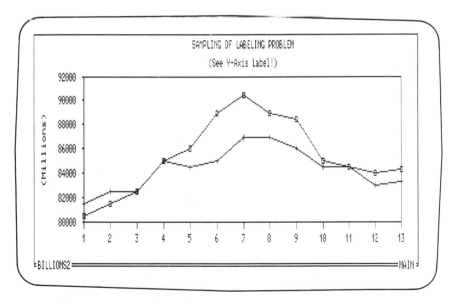

Fig. 12.45

After changing the scaling message with 2nd-Settings Y-Scale Exponent Manual.

(power of ten) representing the number of zeros to be truncated when a range is graphed.

For example, suppose that you have the graph in figure 12.44, and you want to change the scaling message from (Times 1E9) to something more readable. By using the **Manual** option of the **2nd-Settings Y-Scale Exponent** command, you can get Symphony to display (Millions) by selecting an exponent of 6 (see fig. 12.45). Although Symphony will not show the label (Billions), (Millions) certainly beats (Times 1E9).

Hiding Parts of a Graph

Symphony allows you to hide all the different elements of a graph that reside outside the box containing the graph. These elements include titles, scale numbers, exponents, and legends. When you select the Hide option from the 2nd-Settings Other command menu, the box portion of the graph occupies the entire window. You can also hide the X- and Y-axis scale numbers by selecting the Hidden option from the 2nd-Settings X- or Y-Scale Format Other command.

Chapter Summary

Symphony's windowing feature adds a new dimension to the term *business* graphics. To get a good feel for Symphony's power, you should start working with graphics at the earliest possible point in your introduction to Symphony. The more you work with Symphony's graphics, the more you will realize the benefits of the program's integration. The next chapter augments your graphics knowledge by describing Symphony's PrintGraph program for printing graphs.

13

Printing Graphs

Even though Symphony allows you to show graphs and text on your screen simultaneously, your printer cannot print graphs and text in the same operation. Some software packages are capable of printing graphs and text together, but the results may lack sufficient detail for presentation purposes because the programs use graphics block characters that often do not give graphs clear resolution.

Lotus chose the greater detail offered by bit-mapped graphics. This choice means that Symphony can produce presentation-quality graphics, but there is a trade-off: the main program itself is incapable of printing graphics. To print a graph, you must first save the graph to a graph file with a .PIC extension. Then you exit Symphony and enter the PrintGraph program. Finally, you select the file and the options for printing.

Lotus decided to deviate from its customary all-in-one style for reasons of size. By making PrintGraph a separate program, Lotus decreased the total size of the main program. Unfortunately, this move also limited interactive capability in printing graphs in Symphony.

Still, the PrintGraph program has many strengths; for one, it is easy to use. The menus and command structure are similar to Symphony's main program. (Some might even argue they are a great deal simpler.) The PrintGraph program is capable of batch processing, so the program can print several graphs consecutively. Finally, PrintGraph has many special features that would not otherwise be available because of size restrictions. PrintGraph produces high-resolution output on special graphics printers and plotters, makes enlargements and reductions, allows rotations, and offers several colors and font types.

Access to the PrintGraph Program

You can access Symphony's PrintGraph program through the Access System. Most often you will probably use PrintGraph immediately after a Symphony session. Before leaving Symphony, make sure that you have saved the graph file with the Image-Save option from either the SHEET Graph or the GRAPH menu (as explained in the previous chapter). After you use the SERVICES Exit command to leave Symphony, use the Access System menu to enter the PrintGraph program rather than exit to DOS.

If you have sufficient RAM, you also can enter the PrintGraph program through the SERVICES DOS command. The advantage of this technique is that you do not have to reload Symphony after leaving PrintGraph; you can go directly back into Symphony by typing **exit** after the system prompt. Be careful, though. Always save your files before trying this technique.

To use this method, you must first attach the DOS.APP file (as explained in Chapter 6). Next, you should check how much RAM is available by using the SERVICES Settings command. If you have approximately 150K left (a conservative estimate), you should be able to run PrintGraph simultaneously with Symphony and not worry about overwriting Symphony files. You may, however, need more RAM to print several graphs at one time. Once you have left Symphony (using the SERVICES DOS command), type **pgraph** plus the appropriate driver-set name (for example, **pgraph drivs1**) at the system prompt. At this point, you will move into PrintGraph.

If you are starting directly from DOS, you can enter PrintGraph directly or go through the Access System. To enter the program directly, simply type **pgraph** plus the appropriate driver-set name at the operating system prompt. To go through the Access System, enter **access** plus the appropriate driver-set name.

Configuration of PrintGraph

To configure PrintGraph, you must first select the appropriate driver set during installation (see Appendix A). The graphics devices you have access to when you run PrintGraph depend entirely on the devices you select during installation. If you do not select any graphics device during installation, you cannot run PrintGraph.

You can select more than one graphics device during installation. For example, if you have an HP plotter and a Toshiba P351 printer, you can select both as graphics output devices. The only restriction is that a device must be supported by Symphony. If your printer or plotter is not on the list of Symphony-supported graphics devices, you may want to call Lotus Development to see whether a device driver has been released for your printer or plotter.

The second stage of configuring PrintGraph occurs after you are in the program; you need to indicate your particular hardware setup. Figure 13.1 shows an example of the PrintGraph screen when you are running the program for the first time.

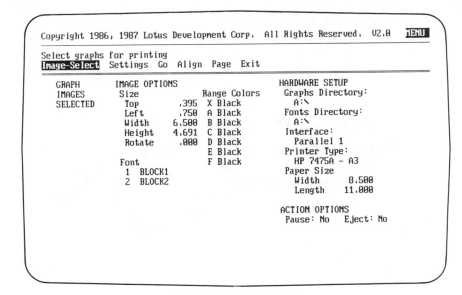

```
Copyright 1986, 1987 Lotus Development Corp. All Rights Reserved.  V2.0  MENU

Select graphs for printing
Image-Select  Settings  Go  Align  Page  Exit

   GRAPH       IMAGE OPTIONS                      HARDWARE SETUP
   IMAGES        Size                Range Colors   Graphs Directory:
   SELECTED        Top       .395    X Black           A:\
                   Left      .750    A Black         Fonts Directory:
                   Width    6.500    B Black           A:\
                   Height   4.691    C Black         Interface:
                   Rotate    .000    D Black           Parallel 1
                                     E Black         Printer Type:
                 Font                F Black           HP 7475A - A3
                   1  BLOCK1                         Paper Size
                   2  BLOCK2                           Width     8.500
                                                       Length   11.000

                                                    ACTION OPTIONS
                                                    Pause: No   Eject: No
```

Fig. 13.1

The PrintGraph screen.

Printer Selection

After you are in the program, you need to choose a device to print the graphs. You select a device from the printer(s) you selected in the Install program. The PrintGraph main menu includes these options:

  Image-Select **S**ettings **G**o **A**lign **P**age Exit

Select **S**ettings, and the following menu choices appear:

  Image **H**ardware **A**ction **S**ave **R**eset Quit

Choose **H**ardware to tell PrintGraph that you want to initiate or change the hardware setting. The Hardware menu includes these options:

  Graphs-Directory **F**onts-Directory **I**nterface **P**rinter **S**ize-Paper Quit

Select **P**rinter. After you have made this choice, a menu of the graphics devices you selected during installation appears on the screen (see fig. 13.2). Just move the cursor to the appropriate line and press the space bar. This action marks the selected printer with a # symbol. When you press Enter, PrintGraph returns to the main PrintGraph settings sheet.

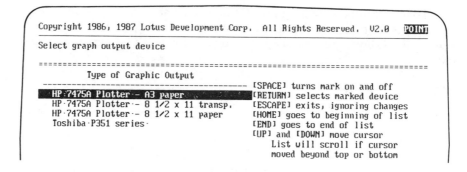

Copyright 1986, 1987 Lotus Development Corp. All Rights Reserved. V2.0 **POINT**

Select graph output device

==

Type of Graphic Output
HP·7475A Plotter·- A3 paper	[SPACE] turns mark on and off
HP·7475A Plotter·- 8 1⁄2 x 11 transp.	[RETURN] selects marked device
HP·7475A Plotter·- 8 1⁄2 x 11 paper	[ESCAPE] exits, ignoring changes
Toshiba·P351 series·	[HOME] goes to beginning of list

[SPACE] turns mark on and off
[RETURN] selects marked device
[ESCAPE] exits, ignoring changes
[HOME] goes to beginning of list
[END] goes to end of list
[UP] and [DOWN] move cursor
          List will scroll if cursor
          moved beyond top or bottom

Graph and Font Directories

When you configure PrintGraph to your hardware, you must also indicate the directories for the graph and font files. The information you supply for the **Graphs-Directory** and **Fonts-Directory** tells PrintGraph which directories to search for the graph and font files. A:\ is the default drive and directory for the graph and font files. If you have a hard disk and have stored all your graph and font files in a subdirectory, you will need to change these default settings. On systems with two disk drives, change the graph directory to B:\ where your data files (worksheets, graphs, and so forth) are stored.

Specifying an Interface Card

The **Interface** option of the **Hardware** menu specifies either a parallel or a serial interface card for your system. You are given eight choices:

1   A parallel interface—the default.

2   A serial interface (RS-232-C-compatible). You must specify a baud rate (see following paragraphs).

3   A second parallel interface.

4   A second serial interface (RS-232-C-compatible). You must specify a baud rate (see following paragraphs).

5-8 One of four possible remote devices, LPT1 through LPT4.

If you specify a serial interface, you must select a baud rate, which determines the speed at which data is transferred. Because each printer has its own requirements, you need to consult your printer's manual for the appropriate rate. Many printers accept more than one baud rate, so a general guideline is to choose the fastest baud rate that the printer will accept without corrupting the data. The available baud rates appear in table 13.1.

Table 13.1
Available Baud Rates

Setting	Baud
1	110
2	150
3	300
4	600
5	1,200
6	2,400
7	4,800
8	9,600
9	19,200

Configurations to Save and Reset

To save the hardware settings, select Save from the Settings menu. The saved settings will then be active for subsequent PrintGraph sessions. PrintGraph saves the settings in a file called PGRAPH.CNF, which is read each time PrintGraph is loaded. You will probably not want to change hardware settings unless you change your hardware.

Another option in the Settings menu, Reset, provides a function almost the opposite of Save. Reset cancels all the Settings made during the current session and returns to the options that were present when PrintGraph was loaded or the options Saved during the current session, whichever occurred last.

The Image Settings

Besides settings for your hardware configuration, other settings affect the way graphs appear on the printed page. These Image settings apply to all the graphs printed in a batch. All the Image settings are saved when you update the .CNF file. If you want different Image settings for different graphs, you must select and print the graphs one at a time.

To specify the Image settings, select Image from the Settings menu. The following choices are then displayed:

   Size   Font   Range-Colors   Quit

Adjusting Graph Size and Orientation

The Size option in the Image menu allows you to adjust the sizes of graphs and to decide where they will be printed on a page. This option also allows you to rotate the axes by as much as 90 degrees. The menu for the Size option gives you the following choices:

Full   Half   Manual   Quit

Full means that the graph will occupy an entire page, and Half indicates that the graph will take up a half-page. PrintGraph automatically handles all the spacing and margins for both these choices unless you specify Manual.

Selecting Manual produces these options:

Left   Top   Width   Height   Rotation   Quit

Use Left, Top, Width, and Height to adjust the respective margins. The numbers you supply are converted from base 10 to base 2 after you enter them, so don't be concerned if they seem to be different when they are displayed. Rotation adjusts the number of counterclockwise degrees of rotation. You must choose a number between 0 and 90. At the one extreme, 0 causes no rotation—the X-axis prints as it normally appears on-screen. At the other extreme, a full 90 degrees of rotation shifts the X-axis to a vertical position.

Interestingly enough, if you choose the Full option, Symphony prints graphs rotated 90 degrees. Thus the X-axis of a bar graph runs along the long edge of an 8 1/2-by-11-inch page. If you choose the Half option, Symphony considers the degree of rotation 0; the X-axis of a bar graph runs along the short edge of a sheet of paper so that you can fit two graphs on a single page.

You need to experiment to get the results you want from Rotation. When you select Half, the default settings for Width and Height are 6.500 and 4.691, respectively. This setting gives an aspect ratio of approximately 1 (X-axis) to 1.385 (Y-axis). If you change the aspect ratio, distortion can, and often does, occur when PrintGraph fits a rotated graph into the specified height and width. Distortion in bar and line graphs is usually not a problem. Distorted pie charts, however, probably will look like ellipses rather than pies. When you change the settings for height and width, the best policy to avoid distortion is to maintain the 1 to 1.385 aspect ratio.

Choosing Fonts

Symphony allows you to print in different character types (fonts). (This includes printing with a dot-matrix printer.) The Font option lets you choose from among 11 different character types (see fig. 13.3). The number after the font name indicates the density—how dark the printed character will be. The fonts followed by a 2 are identical to the fonts with the same names followed by a 1, but the number-2 fonts are darker.

You even can set the first line of text, the graph title, in one font, and the remaining lines of text in another. If you specify only one font, PrintGraph uses this font for all the text in the graph.

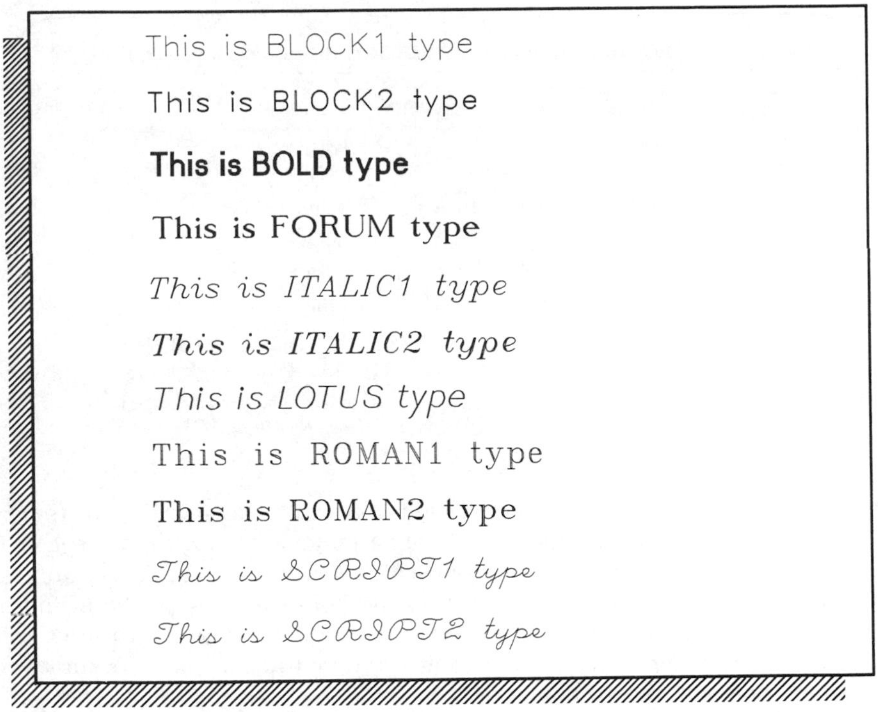

This is BLOCK1 type

This is BLOCK2 type

This is BOLD type

This is FORUM type

This is ITALIC1 type

This is ITALIC2 type

This is LOTUS type

This is ROMAN1 type

This is ROMAN2 type

This is SCRIPT1 type

This is SCRIPT2 type

Fig. 13.3

Fonts available for printing graphs.

An example is the exploded pie chart of retail-store openings from the previous chapter; a dark Forum typeface is used for the first graph title and a lighter Forum for the other lines. To get these fonts, you would specify FORUM2 for **Font 1** (the first line of the title), and FORUM1 for **Font 2**. If another font had not been chosen for **Font 2**, it would have automatically taken on the same value as **Font 1**.

Once you specify the fonts for a graph, they appear in the settings sheet. Figure 13.4 shows a settings sheet in which ITALIC2 was specified for **Font 1**, and ITALIC1 for **Font 2**.

Choosing Range-Colors

If you have a color printing device, you can select **Range-Colors** from the **Image** menu. This option sets the colors for printing or plotting different parts of graphs. If the device you are using does not support color graphics (most printers do not), of course, you have no choice of colors.

PrintGraph assigns a default color of black to every data range and to the grid, axes, and scales. You may assign any color to any data range, however, or you may assign the same color to more than one data range.

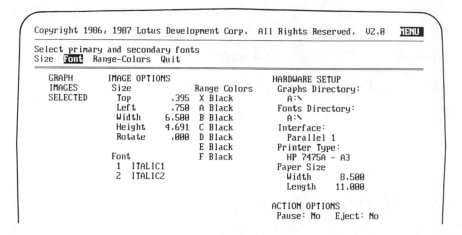

Fig. 13.4

A settings sheet to print a graph in ITALIC2 and ITALIC1 fonts.

When you select **Range-Colors**, PrintGraph asks you to assign colors to the data ranges in Symphony. Each time you specify a range letter (**X** or **A** through **F**), Printgraph displays a list of colors from which you can choose. The colors you use in PrintGraph do not have to be the same colors you use in the main Symphony program. In fact, you don't have to have a color monitor to print color graphs. On the other hand, if the graphics printer you specified does not print in color, your only choice is black.

After you have assigned colors to the ranges, the screen looks similar to figure 13.5.

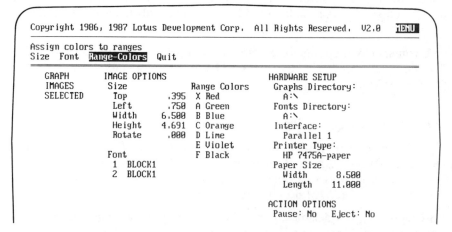

Fig. 13.5

The screen after you assign colors.

You may save the color settings by means of the **S**ave option from the **S**ettings menu. This choice saves Range-Colors settings (and all other image and hardware settings) to PGRAPH.CNF so that the settings will be available for the next PrintGraph session.

Choosing Page Size

You specify the dimensions of the paper your graphics printer uses by selecting **Settings Hardware Size-Paper**. The default settings are 8 1/2 inches wide and 11 inches long.

Selection of Files for Printing

After you have configured PrintGraph, you can return to the main PrintGraph menu and choose **Image-Select**. After your initial use of PrintGraph, **Image-Select** will probably be the first step every time you use the program. This option gives you a list of all the .PIC files on the current **Graphs-Directory**. A typical list of graph files is shown in figure 13.6.

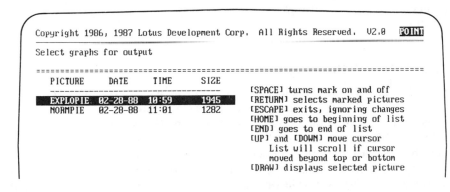

```
Copyright 1986, 1987 Lotus Development Corp.  All Rights Reserved.  V2.0   POINT
───────────────────────────────────────────────────────────────────────────────
Select graphs for output

===============================================================================
   PICTURE     DATE     TIME     SIZE
   ───────────────────────────────────       [SPACE] turns mark on and off
   EXPLOPIE  02-28-88  10:59    1945          [RETURN] selects marked pictures
   NORMPIE   02-28-88  11:01    1282          [ESCAPE] exits, ignoring changes
                                              [HOME] goes to beginning of list
                                              [END] goes to end of list
                                              [UP] and [DOWN] move cursor
                                                 List will scroll if cursor
                                                 moved beyond top or bottom
                                              [DRAW] displays selected picture
```

Fig. 13.6

A sample list of graph files.

The directions for selecting files appear on the right side of the display. To select a graph file to print, use the up- and down-arrow keys to position the cursor at the appropriate entry; then press the space bar. Pressing the space bar causes PrintGraph to place a # next to the graph name to indicate that the graph has been selected for printing. Press Enter to return to the main PrintGraph menu.

You can select as many graphs as you want before you press Enter. A # appears next to each graph you select. To confirm your choice, press Draw (Alt-F8) to see the graphs as they were created and displayed in Symphony. (The graphs will look slightly different when you view them in PrintGraph, because the special font types are used on the printed copies.)

Batch Printing

The way you print graphs in batch depends on your particular graphics device. For instance, if you have a graphics device that accepts only single sheets of paper, such as the HP 7470A plotter, you can configure PrintGraph to run unattended except when you have to load a new piece of paper. Many graphics devices, such as the HP plotter, are smart enough to know when you have room to print the next graph. If you do have room, the device prints. Otherwise, it pauses for you to load another piece of paper.

If, on the other hand, you have a graphics device that accepts continuous-form paper, such as the IBM Color Graphics Printer, you can have graphs printed continuously and unattended. You simply elect not to have the printer pause between graphs.

If the configuration settings that you have set are inappropriate for one of your graphs, you can easily override them. For example, suppose that you want to change the Size settings. You simply call up the Size menu and choose the settings you need. These new settings remain in effect until you change them or exit from the program.

Pause and Eject Options

Action is a Settings menu selection that controls the interval between graphs when you are printing in batch mode. The two choices for Action are Pause and Eject. Pause makes the printer pause between graphs so that you can change settings, and Eject controls whether the printer stops for you to change paper. Your choices of these options depend on how many graphs you are printing and what size they are. For example, if you are printing several full-size graphs on a dot-matrix printer, you will probably want the Eject option set so that the paper advances automatically between graphs.

Align and Page Options

The Align selection in the main PrintGraph menu sets the program's built-in, top-of-page marker. When you choose the Align option, PrintGraph assumes that the paper is correctly aligned in the printer with the top of the form in the right place. PrintGraph then inserts a form feed at the end of every page, using the page-length information you provided when installing the graphics device.

Note: Many printers have controls that allow you to scroll the paper up and down one line at a time. PrintGraph does not recognize these controls. If you, for example, scroll the paper up three lines without realigning, PrintGraph will be three spaces off when it next issues a form-feed command.

The **Page** selection in the main PrintGraph menu advances the paper one page at a time. This useful option advances continuous-form paper to help you remove the printed output at the end of a printing session.

Printing and Exiting

To print a graph, you must select **G**o from the main PrintGraph menu. After you have done so, PrintGraph begins printing. If you are printing several graphs, you may as well have lunch while you wait, because PrintGraph's high-resolution printing takes a long time. Printing the graph shown in figure 13.7 in full size on an HP 7470A plotter took about four minutes. On the other hand, printing the same graph with an IBM PS/2 Model 80 and an HP LaserJet Series II required only about 1 minute.

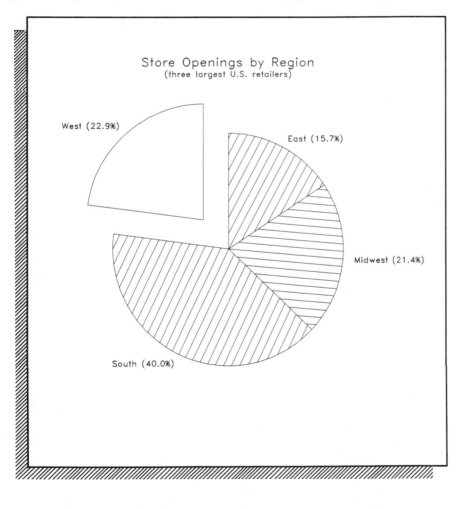

Fig. 13.7
A printed pie chart.

Exiting from PrintGraph is similar to exiting from any other Symphony module. You simply choose **Exit** from the main PrintGraph menu. After you select **Exit**, you are returned to the Access System or to DOS, depending on which way you entered PrintGraph.

Chapter Summary

This chapter showed you how to use the PrintGraph program to produce high-resolution, presentation-quality graphics. PrintGraph is a separate program from Symphony, an arrangement that deviates slightly from Lotus's integrated approach, but the results produced by the PrintGraph program are outstanding, and the program is easy to use.

The next chapter offers you a chance to practice your newfound skills in creating and printing graphs with Symphony and PrintGraph.

14

Creating and Printing Graphs: Hands-On Practice

Symphony's graphing capabilities are directly integrated with the SHEET environment: your graphs are based on data in your spreadsheets. The printing of graphs, however, is accomplished through the separate PrintGraph program.

In this chapter, you will create and print several graphs, using many of the available options to "dress up" the graphs. You will store all the graphs for printing as well as for subsequent recall to the screen. You will first work with graphs in a SHEET window, using the Graph option on the SHEET menu. Then you will display and revise these same graphs in a GRAPH window. If you want to review a concept in greater detail as you work through the practice exercises in this chapter, refer to the following chapters:

- Creating and Displaying Graphs (Chapter 12)
- Printing Graphs (Chapter 13)

Creating Graphs

For the graphs in this practice chapter, you will use data from the SALES spreadsheet you developed in Chapter 7 ("SHEET Window Hands-On Practice"). You will create two graphs: (1) a bar graph displaying January versus February sales, and (2) a pie chart of the January sales data.

Creating a Bar Graph

For the sales bar graph, place the salespeople's names along the X-axis, and use the January and February sales as the two ranges of data. Begin by retrieving the SALES spreadsheet you built in Chapter 7. If you haven't yet created this spreadsheet, you will need to do so before proceeding.

1. Select SERVICES File Retrieve.

2. Type **SALES** and press Enter, or point to the file named SALES and press Enter.

Because you are creating a bar graph of the sales data for January and February, name this graph JAN/FEB-BAR.

1. Press F6 until the JAN-FEB window is displayed (the lower right corner of the screen displays the window name).

2. Select SHEET Graph 1st-Settings Name Create.

3. Enter **JAN/FEB-BAR**.

Specify the ranges for this bar graph.

1. Select **Type** **Bar**.

2. Select **Range** **X**.

3. Enter **A6..A10**. (This range includes the salespeople's names, which will go along the X-axis.)

4. Select **A** for the first data range.

5. Enter **B6..B10** (the January data).

6. Select **B** for the second data range.

7. Enter **C6..C10** (the February data).

8. Select **Quit** **Quit** **Preview** to display the graph. (It should match fig. 14.1.) Notice the graph's name, JAN/FEB-BAR, in the left corner of the window.

Without legends, you don't know which data range is January and which is February. Also, the graph is incomplete without titles.

1. Press any key to return to the Graph menu.

2. Select **1st-Settings** **Legend**.

3. Select **A** for the first data-range legend.

4. Enter **JAN**.

5. Select **B** for the second data-range legend.

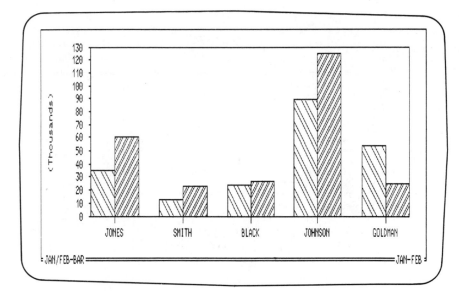

Fig. 14.1

A bar graph with two data ranges.

6. Enter **FEB**.

7. Select **Quit Switch** to go to the **2nd-Settings** sheet, where the **Titles** option is located.

8. Select **Titles**.

9. Select **First**.

10. Enter **\C1** to use the contents of cell C1 (JAN VS. FEB SALES) as the graph's top title.

11. Select **Second**.

12. Enter **\C2** to use the contents of cell C2 (BY SALES PERSON) as the second title.

13. Select **X-axis**.

14. Enter **SALES PERSON**.

15. Select **Y-axis**.

16. Enter **SALES VOLUME**.

17. Select **Quit Quit Preview**. Your graph should resemble figure 14.2.

18. Press any key to display the **Graph** menu.

19. Save and replace the file. (Select SERVICES **File Save**, press Enter to accept the name SALES, and select **Yes** to replace.)

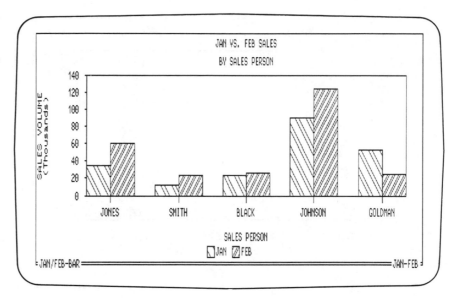

Fig. 14.2

The bar graph after adding titles and a legend.

Creating a Pie Chart

Due to the nature of a pie chart, you can graph only one set of data: the A range. In its most basic form, the pie chart is simply a circle divided into sections of different sizes. By adding a B data range, however, you can indicate cross-hatching patterns for each segment and even explode one or more pieces of the pie.

The pie chart you are going to create will display the January data. Name this new graph before creating the settings.

1. Select SHEET Graph 1st-Settings Name Create.

2. Enter **JAN-PIE**.

The B range from the bar graph you just created does not apply to this graph, so you must cancel this range.

1. Select **Cancel Entire-Row B**.

2. Select **Quit**.

Specify a title for the pie chart.

1. Select **Type Pie**.

2. Select **Switch** to go to the **2nd-Settings** sheet.

3. Select **Titles First**.

4. Press Esc to remove the top title that is left over from the bar graph.

5. Enter **JANUARY SALES**.

6. Select **Quit Quit Preview**. Your graph should look similar to figure 14.3.

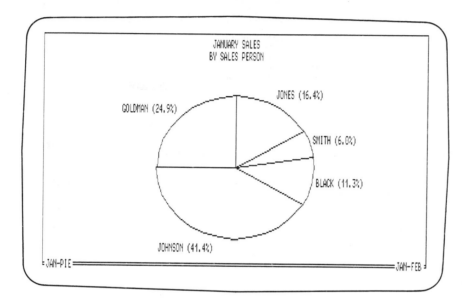

Fig. 14.3

*A pie chart of
January sales.*

What a dull graph! Let's create a B range to specify shading patterns for the different pieces of the pie. You will need to return to SHEET mode to enter this range.

1. Press any key to display the **Graph** menu; select **Quit** to go to SHEET mode.

2. In cells F6..F10, enter the numbers 1 through 5 to specify a different pattern for each section (see fig. 14.4).

3. Select SHEET **Graph 1st-Settings Range**.

4. Select **B** for the second data range.

5. Enter **F6..F10** (the range of shade values).

6. Select **Quit Quit Preview**. The graph now should look like figure 14.5.

Now the graph is much more attractive. You can further enhance a pie chart by exploding one of its sections. To explode one of the segments, you add 100 to the slice's shade value. Return to the spreadsheet and change one of the shade values.

Fig. 14.4

Entering crosshatch pattern numbers in column F.

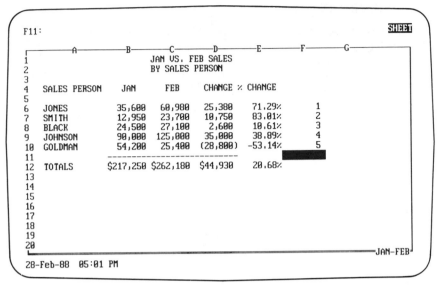

Fig. 14.5

After using the B range to specify crosshatch patterns.

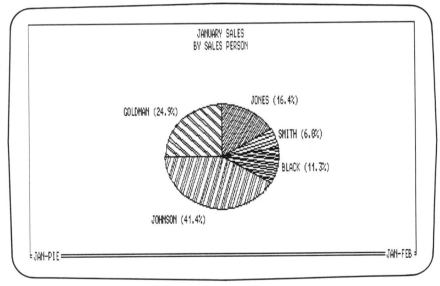

1. Press any key to display the **Graph** menu, and select **Quit** to go to SHEET mode.

2. In cell F7, enter **102**.

3. Select SHEET **G**raph **P**review. Figure 14.6 shows the exploded pie chart.

4. Save and replace the file.

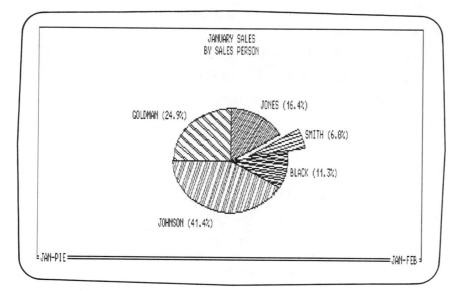

Fig. 14.6
An exploded pie chart.

Working with Named Graphs

Once you have created and named your graphs, you will want to display them so that you can view them and make changes. You can use two ways to call up the various graphs you have named, depending on which window type you are using. In a SHEET window, you recall a named graph by selecting the **Name Use** command. Then you must choose **Preview** to see the graph. If you are working in a GRAPH window, the **Attach** command recalls the specified graph settings and automatically displays the graph.

Using a Graph

To work with the bar graph you created earlier, you first need to **Use** it.

1. Select SHEET **Graph 1st-Settings Name Use**. A list of named graphs appears.

2. Select the name **JAN/FEB-BAR** from the list.

3. Select **Quit Preview** to view the bar graph of January and February data. Your graph should look just like the one in figure 14.2.

4. Press any key to display the **Graph** menu.

The fact that each graph has two settings sheets (**1st-Settings** and **2nd-Settings**) gives you an idea of how many options are available. One option changes the format of the numbers on the Y-axis. Another changes the cross-hatching patterns, or "hue," of the bars.

1. Select **2nd-Settings Y**-Scale **F**ormat **C**urrency.

2. Enter **0** for the number of decimal places.

3. Select **Q**uit **S**witch to move to the **1st-Settings** sheet.

4. Select **Hue.**

5. Select **A** for the first data range.

6. Select **7** to choose pattern 7.

7. Select **B** for the second data range.

8. Select **1** to choose pattern 1.

9. **Q**uit from the submenus and **P**review these changes. (See fig. 14.7.) Notice the dollar signs next to the numbers on the Y-axis, and the different shading patterns of the bars.

Fig. 14.7

After formatting the Y-scale and changing the bar crosshatch patterns.

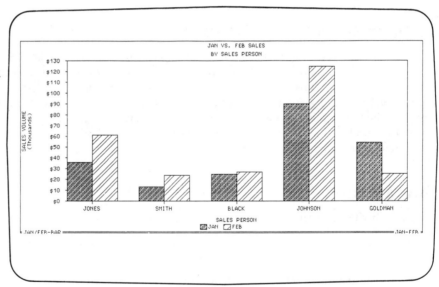

You can also change the spreadsheet data and quickly see the modifications reflected in your graphs. Correct an error in the January data and then view the revised JAN-PIE graph.

1. Select **1st-Settings N**ame **U**se.

2. Select **JAN-PIE.**

3. **P**review the graph and notice that SMITH has 6 percent (6.0%) of the January sales.

4. Go to SHEET mode.

5. In B7, enter **20000**.

6. Select SHEET **Graph Preview**. The graph in figure 14.8 appears.

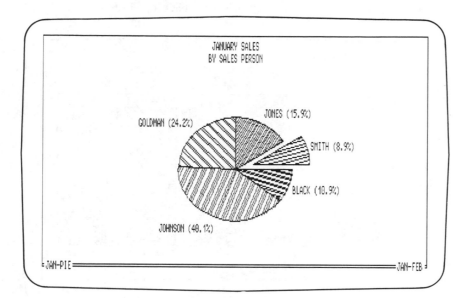

Fig. 14.8

Reflecting changes made to the spreadsheet data.

Note that the graph automatically redrew and recalculated the percentages. Smith now has a larger slice of the pie.

Attaching a Graph

Another way to work with graphs in Symphony is through a GRAPH window. When you are in GRAPH mode, the Menu key (F10) displays the GRAPH menu, and the graph currently attached to the window is automatically displayed. (No Preview command exists.)

Both the JAN/FEB-BAR graph and the JAN-PIE graph belong to the JAN-FEB window, so you will attach each of these graphs to this window.

1. Go to SHEET mode.

2. Press Alt-F10 to display the TYPE menu.

3. Select GRAPH as the window type. (The JAN-PIE graph automatically displays because it was the last graph you used in this window.)

4. Select GRAPH **Attach**. A list of graph names appears.

5. Select **JAN/FEB-BAR** from the list.

The JAN/FEB-BAR bar chart automatically displays in the window. Change this graph to a stacked-bar graph.

1. Select GRAPH **1st-Settings Type Stacked-Bar**.

2. Select **Quit**, and the new graph displays. (See fig. 14.9.)

Fig. 14.9

A stacked-bar graph.

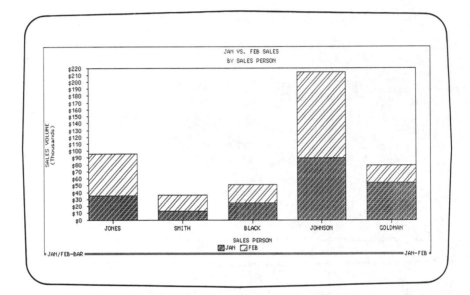

The Y-scale contains too many increments. Change the Y-scale to have a different upper limit (for example, 300,000).

1. Select GRAPH **2nd-Settings Y-Scale Type Manual-Linear**.

2. Press Enter to keep the lower limit at 0.

3. Enter **300000** for the upper limit.

4. Select **Quit Quit** to view the new graph.

Now attach JAN-PIE so that you can change that graph.

1. Select GRAPH **Attach**.

2. Select **JAN-PIE**.

JAN-PIE displays. Change the aspect ratio of the pie so that the circle is wider.

1. Select GRAPH **2nd-Settings Other Aspect**.

2. Enter **.5**.

3. Select **Quit** to view the new graph, which should resemble figure 14.10.

4. Save and replace the file.

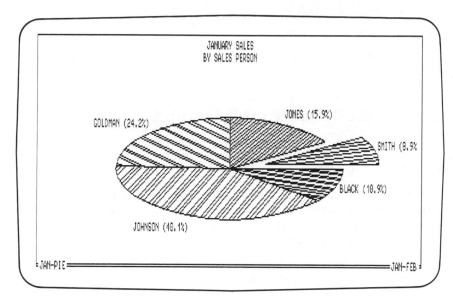

Fig. 14.10

After changing the aspect ratio of the pie chart.

Printing Graphs

Once you have created your graphs and are satisfied with how they look on-screen, you may want to print them. To print graphs, you must access a utility program outside the main Symphony program. This program is called PrintGraph. Because PrintGraph is separate from Symphony, before you exit Symphony you must save in its own graph file each of the graphs you want to print.

Saving Graphs for Printing

The **Image-Save** command on the **Graph** menu is the option you use to save graphs for printing. This command stores the graph in a file with a .PIC extension.

First, save the JAN-PIE graph for printing. (Make sure this graph is the current one.)

1. Change the window type back to SHEET.

2. Select SHEET **Graph Image-Save**.

3. Enter **PIE** as the graph file name. (Symphony stores the file under PIE.PIC.)

Save the JAN-FEB/BAR graph for printing.

1. Select **1st-Settings Name Use**.

2. Select **JAN/FEB-BAR**.

3. Select **Quit Image-Save**.

4. Enter **BAR** as the graph file name. (Symphony stores the file under BAR.PIC.)

Using Default PrintGraph Settings

Once you are in the PrintGraph program, you need only a few keystrokes to produce a default half-size graph displaying block style print. You'll print the PIE graph with the default settings.

Before you begin this practice session, make sure that the PrintGraph hardware setup (**Printer, Interface, Fonts-Directory, Graphs-Directory,** and **Size-Paper**) is appropriate for your equipment. See Chapter 13's section on the "Configuration of PrintGraph" for information on hardware setup.

To print the PIE graph, first make sure that your file is saved and that you have image-saved each of the graphs you want to print. Then use the following command sequences:

1. **Exit** from Symphony.

2. If the Access System menu displays, select **PrintGraph**. Or, if the DOS prompt (C> or A>) appears, make sure that the PrintGraph program is in the current directory or drive and enter **pgraph**.

3. Choose **Image-Select** from the main PrintGraph menu.

4. Position the highlighted bar on PIE and press Enter. (This step automatically marks [with a # symbol] for printing the highlighted file name. The main PrintGraph menu redisplays.)

5. Check the printer, making sure that it is on-line and that the print head is at the top edge of the paper.

6. Select **Align** to ensure that Symphony recognizes the current top-of-page.

7. Select **Go** and wait for the half-size graph to print.

8. Select **Page** from the main PrintGraph menu to advance the paper to the top of the next page.

9. Check the output, which should match figure 14.11.

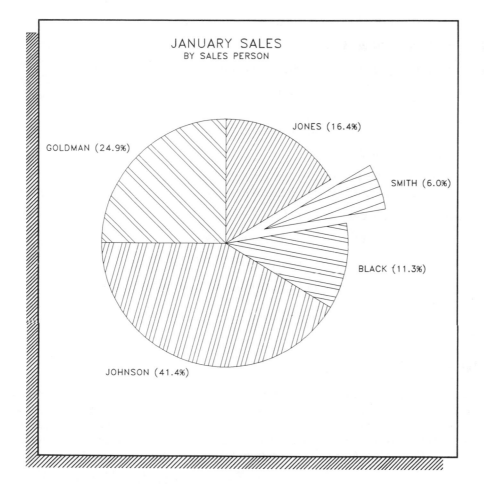

JANUARY SALES
BY SALES PERSON

JONES (16.4%)

GOLDMAN (24.9%)

SMITH (6.0%)

BLACK (11.3%)

JOHNSON (41.4%)

Fig. 14.11

The printed pie chart.

Changing PrintGraph Settings

You use the main PrintGraph menu's Settings option to alter print options. Most of the Settings options deal with establishing a specific print environment (location of files, type of printer, and so on) and are not illustrated here. In this final practice session, you will use two options (Font and Size) to change the default graph's image and produce a full-size graph with two font styles.

To produce this full-size stacked-bar graph, use the following command sequences:

1. Choose Image-Select from the main PrintGraph menu.

2. Position the highlighted bar on PIE and press the space bar to unselect this file.

3. Position the highlighted bar on BAR and press Enter.

4. Select **Settings Image Size Full**.

5. Select **Quit** to exit the **Size** submenu.

6. Select **Font 1** to access a list of Symphony font styles.

7. Position the highlighted bar on FORUM and press the space bar to specify this print style for the top center title. Press Enter.

8. Select **Font 2**.

9. Position the highlighted bar on LOTUS and press the space bar to specify the print style for the remaining descriptive text. Press Enter.

10. Select **Quit Quit** to exit the submenus.

11. Select **Go** and wait while the graph prints.

12. Select **Page** twice to eject the graph from the printer.

13. Check the printed full-size graph to be sure that it matches figure 14.12.

14. Select **Exit**.

Chapter Summary

This chapter has given you a chance to practice creating and working with graphs in Symphony's SHEET and GRAPH windows. You also practiced printing these graphs with the separate PrintGraph program. Review the detailed graphing information in Chapters 12 and 13, and check this book's troubleshooting section for additional tips. And remember: one .PIC is worth a thousand .WR1s!

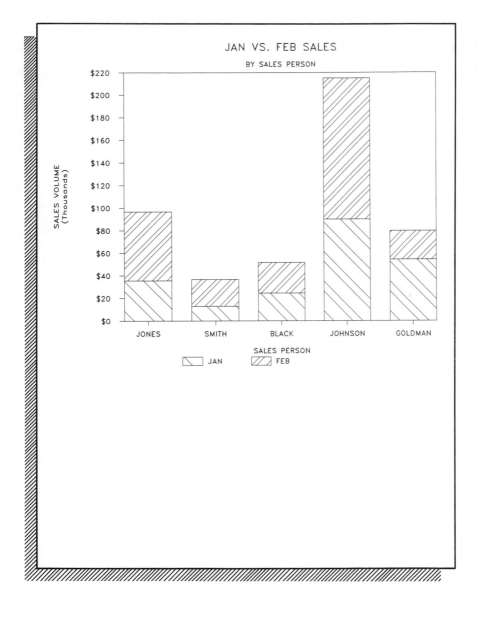

JAN VS. FEB SALES
BY SALES PERSON

SALES VOLUME
(Thousands)

$220
$200
$180
$160
$140
$120
$100
$80
$60
$40
$20
$0

JONES   SMITH   BLACK   JOHNSON   GOLDMAN

SALES PERSON

JAN   FEB

Fig. 14.12

The stacked-bar chart printout.

PART V

Data Management with Symphony

Includes

Data Management

Data Management Hands-On Practice

15

Data Management

Data management involves all the commands and procedures for creating and manipulating a database. Three distinct areas are included: the FORM window, the database commands in the SHEET environment, and database statistical functions. You use data management in a FORM window for setting up and manipulating individual records. The SHEET commands are for working with groups of records. Finally, you use database statistical functions for determining statistics about groups of records within a database.

These three areas are closely interrelated. For example, you can create a database of all your customers' names and addresses by means of a special form you have set up in a FORM window. Once the database is created, you can then use the database commands in the SHEET environment to extract the names of all your customers who operate in a specific location. (Many of the settings used in the FORM window can also be used in the SHEET window.) Finally, you can use database statistical functions to determine the number of customer names you've extracted and their average monthly orders from your company.

Symphony's data-management program has many strengths. First, it's easy to create forms and to add or modify records. Second, when you are using a FORM window, you can hide everything in the database except the input form. Therefore, you can set up a data-entry environment for someone who does not know, or care to know, Symphony. Third, Symphony's data management is fast. Because all the operations are RAM-based, you can perform rapidly almost any database manipulation you want. Finally, the data management is integrated; you can use data-management techniques in all of Symphony's working environments—SHEET, DOC, GRAPH, FORM, and COMM.

Although Symphony's data management is strong in several respects, it is weak in others. Most notably, like everything else in Symphony, the fact that data management is RAM-based places strict limitations on the size and the kinds of applications for which you can use data management.

Modifying an existing database was quite difficult in earlier versions of Symphony. You had to insert and delete columns, create and delete range names, and modify all the different database ranges manually. Fortunately, in Release 2.0, you can easily **Move**, **Insert**, and **Delete** fields with **Field**, the new FORM menu option.

Another drawback is that Symphony's data management is hard to learn. It is probably one of the most complex operations in the program. As you will soon see, many special rules apply. But you will probably find that you need to know only some of those rules in order to accomplish what you want.

The structure of this chapter follows the three natural divisions inherent in Symphony's data management: the use of FORM windows, SHEET database commands, and database statistical functions. Included at the end of the chapter is a section on printing database reports. This topic is a particularly good one to end with because it incorporates many different aspects of Symphony's data-management capability.

Attention 1-2-3 Users

If you are an experienced 1-2-3 user, you have a distinct advantage in learning Symphony's data management—provided you keep an open mind. Many of the important techniques are the same in both programs, but Symphony has added several new techniques. Most of them are associated with Symphony's FORM window, so mastering this window requires patience.

The structure of the FORM environment may seem rigid at first, and lacking some of the flexibility and user control that is so appealing in 1-2-3. Once you get to know the FORM environment, however, you will learn to use it to your advantage. For example, the FORM window has several special ranges. Some are new, others may look familiar, and all have special locations that Symphony automatically chooses. After you have learned all the rules for these special ranges, however, you don't have to stick to Symphony's locations. You can put the special ranges anywhere you want.

You can use Symphony's data management in a way remarkably similar to 1-2-3's data management if you prefer. All the same capabilities are there. But you miss the full power of Symphony's data management if you limit yourself to 1-2-3's ways. You can let Symphony handle many routine chores for you (setting up database ranges, criterion ranges, and output ranges, for instance). You will learn quickly when to let Symphony do the work for you and when to do it yourself.

If you are an experienced 1-2-3 user, you may want to go directly to the section entitled "The FORM Window for Creating Databases." You can expect the FORM window to be somewhat different from what you are used to. By the time you come to the SHEET commands and the database statistical functions, however, you will feel at home. Give special attention to the ranges used in the SHEET environment and the locations of the **Query** commands in the menu structure, but database statistical functions should require only a cursory review. Finally, you will want to pay close attention to the information about printing database reports, particularly if you intend to print form letters or mailing lists.

Keep in mind that Symphony has more severe RAM limitations than 1-2-3. Because the main Symphony program requires approximately 320K of RAM, you have only about 320K left for applications. (This figure assumes you have the maximum of 640K on your computer and no expanded memory.)

Database Fundamentals

A database is a collection of related pieces of information. In its simplest form, a database is a list that can contain any kind of information, from addresses to tax-deductible expenses.

In Symphony, a database is a range of cells that spans at least one column and at least two rows. This basic definition alone contains nothing that sets a database apart from any other group of cells. But because a database is actually a list, another important aspect is its method of organization. Just as a list must be properly organized before you can gain information from it, a database must also be properly organized. Remembering the underlying similarity between a database and any other group of cells in Symphony will help you learn about the different commands presented in this chapter. You will begin to see many other instances where you can use these commands in what might be considered nondatabase applications.

Organization of a Database

As mentioned previously, an important aspect of a database is the way it is organized. This organization relies heavily on the composition of the database itself. To understand this composition, you need certain general definitions. First, databases are made up of *records*. Each record corresponds to an item in a list. In Symphony, a record is a row of cells within a database. Second, records are made up of *fields*. In Symphony, a field is a single cell (or column) within a record. Finally, you use *field names* at the tops of columns to identify fields; field names are required for nearly every database operation. Figure 15.1 illustrates a simple database.

In figure 15.1, a typical database, the second record resides in row 4. The name that is highlighted, `Cotter, James F.`, is one of the four fields for that record. The field name for the items in column I is `Name`.

Fig. 15.1

A sample database.

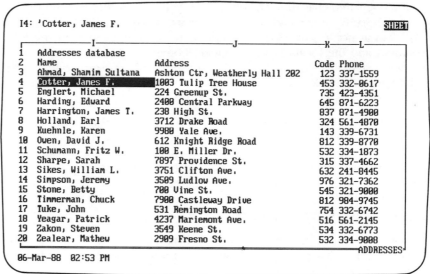

```
I4: 'Cotter, James F.                                          SHEET
┌──────────────I──────────────────────J──────────K───L────────┐
 1  Addresses database
 2  Name                 Address                       Code Phone
 3  Ahmad, Shamin Sultana Ashton Ctr, Weatherly Hall 202 123 337-1559
 4  Cotter, James F.     1003 Tulip Tree House         453 332-0617
 5  Englert, Michael     224 Greenup St.               735 423-4351
 6  Harding, Edward      2400 Central Parkway          645 871-6223
 7  Harrington, James T. 238 High St.                  837 871-4900
 8  Holland, Earl        3712 Drake Road               324 561-4870
 9  Kuehnle, Karen       9980 Yale Ave.                143 339-6731
10  Owen, David J.       612 Knight Ridge Road         812 339-8770
11  Schumann, Fritz W.   100 E. Miller Dr.             532 334-1873
12  Sharpe, Sarah        7897 Providence St.           315 337-4662
13  Sikes, William L.    3751 Clifton Ave.             632 241-8445
14  Simpson, Jeremy      3589 Ludlow Ave.              976 321-7362
15  Stone, Betty         700 Vine St.                  545 321-9000
16  Timmerman, Chuck     7900 Castleway Drive          812 984-9745
17  Tuke, John           531 Remington Road            754 332-6742
18  Yeagar, Patrick      4237 Mariemont Ave.           516 561-2145
19  Zakon, Steven        3549 Keene St.                534 332-6773
20  Zealear, Mathew      2909 Fresno St.               532 334-9000
                                                       └ADDRESSES┘
06-Mar-88  02:53 PM
```

What You Can Do with a Database

If the database in figure 15.1 were your own database, what would you use it for? You might want to sort it by last name to get an alphabetical list. You might also want to *query* the database for a name or group of names. For example, you could search out the street address for a particular person or select all the people in the database with the same telephone exchange. Sorting and querying are the chief methods used in Symphony to get meaningful information from a database. Symphony offers several ways to sort and query, depending on whether you are in a SHEET or a FORM window.

The FORM Window for Creating Databases

One of the nicest features of creating a database in a Symphony FORM window is the amount of work the program does for you behind the scenes. While you are in a FORM window, you rarely see the entire database; yet Symphony constantly keeps track of it. You just browse through the database, looking at one record at a time. You view the records with a special form that you build with Symphony's help.

To gain a better understanding of Symphony's FORM window, suppose that you are a manufacturer of special accessory chips for the semiconductor market, and you want to build a "Customer Priority" database for one of your best-selling but difficult-to-manufacture computer chips. Because demand is far higher than you can supply, you want the database to be the foundation for a priority system that allocates chips as fairly as possible but at the same time maximizes your profit.

Building a Simple Input Form

While planning the database, you decide that you want to use Symphony's forms capability, and you also decide that the database should contain the following fields:

Field Name	Type	Length	Example Value
Order number	Label	7 characters	PO1435
Customer name	Label	21 characters	Amdek Corporation
Phone	Label	13 characters	312-364-1180
Priority	Number	2 decimal	1
Entry date	Serial number	10 decimal	7/23/88
Promise date	Serial number	10 decimal	8/23/88
Amount	Number	8 decimal	23000

The simplest way to build an input form for the database is to use the **Generate** command in a FORM window. Before you can use this command, you need to use either a SHEET or DOC window to enter the field names. Figure 15.2 shows how you enter the field names for the Priority database while you are in a SHEET window.

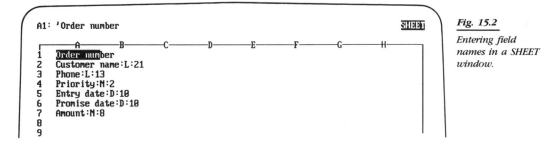

A1: 'Order number   SHEET

```
      A        B       C       D       E       F       G       H
1   Order number
2   Customer name:L:21
3   Phone:L:13
4   Priority:N:2
5   Entry date:D:10
6   Promise date:D:10
7   Amount:N:8
8
9
```

Fig. 15.2

Entering field names in a SHEET window.

Notice that the field names are entered in a single column down the window. You can also enter the names across a row. In a SHEET window, Symphony does not care which way you choose, as long as you place the field names in consecutive cells. Nonconsecutive cells lead to blank columns in the database and therefore waste space.

Immediately after each field name, for all but the field "Order number," you can see a letter followed by a colon and a number. The letters and numbers are used to indicate the field type and the field length, respectively. When you issue the Generate command, Symphony uses the field types and field lengths to set up the database. If you do not indicate a type or length, as is the case with "Order number," Symphony uses the default settings.

The choices you have for the field type are *L* (label), *N* (number), *D* (date), *T* (time), or *C* (computed). The label and number choices tell Symphony whether you want to store entries for those fields as labels or numbers, respectively. The date and time choices are a little different. Symphony uses its special serial-numbering scheme to store date and time values. Therefore, if you enter a date in any one of the valid date formats (D1 through D5), Symphony converts your entry to a serial number. If you select a computed field type, Symphony calculates the value based on a formula you supply. (Computed fields are treated in more depth in the section on "Advanced FORM Features.")

Specifying a field length tells Symphony how wide the columns in the database should be. For example, if you choose a length of 10 for the "Entry date" field, Symphony uses a column width of 10 for that field in the database.

Figure 15.3 shows you how to enter the field names in a DOC window. When you are using a DOC window, you must enter field names down a column. Before you enter the field names, change DOC Format Settings Justification to None. This action prevents Symphony from putting two or more field names on the same line. (When you customize the input form, you may want to combine field names on the same line.)

Fig. 15.3

Entering field names in a DOC window.

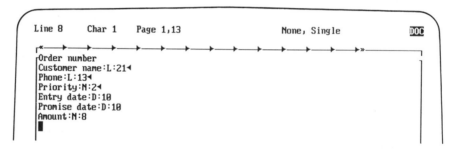

Using the FORM Generate Command

To use the input form you have created, you must change to a FORM window. When you do so, Symphony displays a blank screen with the message No Definition range defined at the top. Disregard the message this first time; it will soon disappear. To initiate the FORM Generate command, first press the Menu key to access the main FORM window menu, which displays

Attach Criteria Initialize Record-Sort Generate Field Settings

When you select Generate, Symphony gives you the following menu options:

Label Number Date Time Computed

These choices give the default field type. If you choose **Number**, for example, you are telling Symphony that any field name without an accompanying field-type indicator should be a number field. In this example, choose **Label** for the default field type.

Next, Symphony asks you for a default field length. The length you choose is the value Symphony uses when a field-length number is not explicitly declared. Enter **7**, which is the default length you want for the "Order number" field. (You already explicitly declared the lengths for all the other fields when you entered the field names.)

After you have selected a length, Symphony asks you for a database name. The name you choose should be clearly descriptive because it will be used for establishing a series of range names. For this database, enter **Priority**.

Finally, Symphony asks you for a Field Names range. So that you can choose the range, Symphony temporarily shifts to the SHEET environment. You can then enter the proper range. In this case, you enter the range **A1..A7**, which is the column of field names shown in figures 15.2 and 15.3.

After you enter the Field Names range, Symphony immediately shifts to an input form, provided you have entered the field-name information correctly. Figures 15.4A and 15.4B show how the input form appears in both FORM and SHEET mode.

```
┌─────────────────────────────────────────────────────────────┐
│ Inserting Record 1          New Record              FORM      │
│ Enter Order number                                            │
│ ┌───────────────────────────────────────────────────────┐    │
│ │Order number _____                                   │    │
│ │Customer name _____                         │    │
│ │Phone _____                                       │    │
│ │Priority __                                             │    │
│ │Entry date _____                                    │    │
│ │Promise date _____                                  │    │
│ │Amount _____                                         │    │
│ │                                                        │    │
│ │                                                        │    │
│ │                                                        │    │
│ │                                                        │    │
│ │                                                        │    │
│ │                                                        │    │
│ │                                                        │    │
│ │                                                        │    │
│ └─PRIORITY───────────────────────────────────────MAIN──┘    │
│ 06-Mar-88  03:03 PM                    Calc                   │
└─────────────────────────────────────────────────────────────┘
```

Fig. 15.4A

The input form in FORM mode.

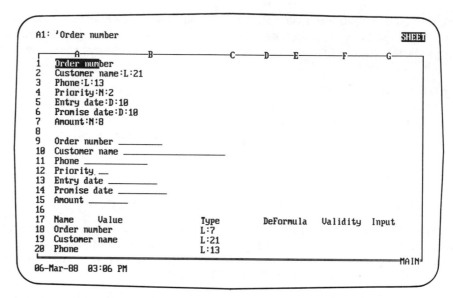

Fig. 15.4B

The input form in SHEET mode.

As mentioned earlier, Symphony uses the lengths you specify for determining the individual column widths in the database. As illustrated in figure 15.4B, however, Symphony also uses the field lengths to determine the number of underscores that follow the field names in the input form.

Entering a Record

At this point you can start entering records. To enter the order number for the first input record, you simply start typing. For example, type **PO1435** and then press Enter. When you press Enter, the cursor shifts down to the second field in the input form, the "Customer name." For this field, type **Amdek Corporation** and press Enter. Continue this process until you have entered the last value for the last field. Then, to insert the record in the database, press the Ins (Insert) key. After you press Ins, Symphony enters the first record in the database and erases the data from the input form so that you can enter another record.

Following is a guide to important keys for entering and revising data records in a FORM window:

Key	Activity
PgDn	Moves sequentially to the next record in the database. When you are editing or entering data, adds current record to the database and displays next record or new blank record.

PgUp	Moves sequentially to the previous record in the database. When you are entering or editing data, adds record to the database and displays previous record.
Enter (or Tab)	Moves cursor to next field.
Home	Adds current record to the database and takes you to the first record in the database. If you are not entering or editing data, displays the first record.
End	Adds current record to the database and takes you to the last record in the database. If you are not entering or editing data, displays the last record. End followed by PgDn positions you at the end of the database and generates a blank form ready for input.
GoTo	Jumps directly to a record if you enter the record number.
Edit (F2)	To revise an existing entry, press Edit to activate the field. You can then use the edit keys, such as Backspace, Esc, and Del, in the same manner as in SHEET mode (see Chapter 2).
Esc	If pressed once, clears the current field. If pressed twice, clears all fields and restores their previous values. If pressed three times, removes current entry and returns to previous record.
Backspace	Clears the current field.
Begin typing	During editing of a field, causes Symphony to erase the current entry and lets you enter a new one.
Ins	During data entry, adds current record to the database and displays a new blank form. When you are editing data, adds current record to the database, leaving record in the form with cursor at the first field.
Del	During editing of data, deletes current record from the database. You are given a Yes/No confirmation step.
↑	Moves cursor to previous field above or to the left of current cell.
↓	Moves cursor to next field below or to the right.
→	Moves cursor to next field.

←	Moves cursor to previous field during entry of new data. Moves cursor to next field during revision of data.
Ctrl-←	Moves cursor to the first field in the form.
Ctrl-→	Moves cursor to the last field in the form.

When you enter a record in a database by pressing the Ins key, Symphony places a copy of the record in a special database area located in the rows below the input form. The exact location of that area is not important for now. What is important is that when you use a FORM window, Symphony automatically does much of the work that you would otherwise have to do yourself.

After you enter a date, Symphony automatically changes the date to the D1 display format. For example, figure 15.5 shows how the screen appears just after you enter the "Entry date" in the D4 (the Full International) format but before you press Enter. Figure 15.6 shows what happens after you press Enter. Just as with the @DATEVALUE function, you can enter the date in a FORM window in any one of the valid date formats: D1 through D5. (You cannot, however, use a formula or a function.) Later you will learn how to change the date to any display format you want.

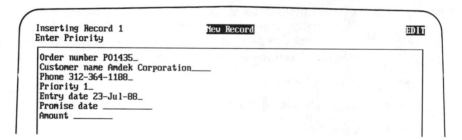

Fig. 15.5

After entering the entry date but before pressing Enter.

```
Inserting Record 1                    New Record                    EDIT
Enter Priority

Order number PO1435_
Customer name Amdek Corporation____
Phone 312-364-1188_
Priority 1_
Entry date 23-Jul-88_
Promise date _____
Amount _____
```

Fig. 15.6

After pressing Enter.

```
Editing Record 1 of 1                                              FORM
Enter Promise date

Order number PO1435_
Customer name Amdek Corporation____
Phone 312-364-1188_
Priority **
Entry date 23-Jul-88_
Promise date _____
Amount _____
```

Modifying the Current Record before Insertion

Sometimes you discover a mistake before you insert a record. You have several ways to modify the entry. Suppose that you discover an error immediately after entering an order number, and you want to go back and change it. One way is to press the ↑, which returns you to the "Order number" field, and start typing. The old entry immediately disappears and clears the way for the new entry. Another method is to use the Edit key. Move the cursor to the "Order number" field and press the Edit key; you can then use the Backspace, Esc, and Del keys just as you would in EDIT mode in a SHEET window (see Chapter 2 for more on the Edit key). Another alternative is to use the Backspace key. When you press Backspace, Symphony erases the field where the cursor is and moves the cursor to the next field. You can then position the cursor and make the correct entry. If you press the Esc key, all fields are cleared.

Modifying Previous Records

If you have already pressed the Ins key when you find the error in a record, you must make that record current again before you can modify it. One way to make the record current is to use the PgUp key to browse through the records until you reach the one you want to modify. Another way is to use the GoTo key. If you can remember the number of the incorrect record, simply press the GoTo key and type the record number. Symphony immediately goes to that record.

Undoing Changes to a Record

If you change a record that you previously inserted in the database and then decide you don't like the changes you've made, you can always recall the original copy of the record. Simply press the Esc key twice. The first time you press Esc, Symphony clears the field where the cursor resides and restores the original value of the field. The second time you press Esc, Symphony restores the entire original record.

Adding New Records

If, after making the initial entries to the database, you decide to add more records, first use the End key to go to the last record in the database. Then press the PgDn key. Symphony then shows a New Record indicator at the top of the screen and a blank entry form below.

Adding new records is similar to making changes in existing records. Simply enter the value you want in a field and press Enter. When you press Enter, Symphony shifts the cursor down to the next field in the input form. After entering your last field, press the Ins key to enter the new record in the database. You can add as many new records as you want up to the practical limitations of RAM. Be sure to press Ins once for each record after you have entered all the fields for that record.

Deleting Records

Deleting records is the easiest operation in a FORM window. Simply use the GoTo, PgUp, or PgDn key to make current the record you want to delete. Then press the Del key. Symphony asks if you are sure you want to delete this record. Answer **Yes**, and Symphony completely erases the record from the database and displays the next record in the form.

Sorting the Database

Suppose that you have entered several records in the Priority database, and you want to sort the database by priority number. To sort the database, you must first select the **Settings** option from the main FORM menu. Figure 15.7 shows a copy of the FORM settings sheet with the **Settings** menu in the control panel.

Fig. 15.7

The FORM Settings sheet and menu.

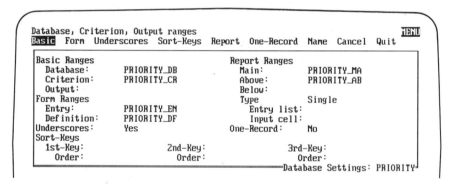

```
Database, Criterion, Output ranges                                    MENU
Basic Form  Underscores  Sort-Keys  Report  One-Record  Name  Cancel  Quit

Basic Ranges                         Report Ranges
   Database:       PRIORITY_DB          Main:        PRIORITY_MA
   Criterion:      PRIORITY_CR          Above:       PRIORITY_AB
   Output:                              Below:
Form Ranges                             Type         Single
   Entry:          PRIORITY_EN          Entry list:
   Definition:     PRIORITY_DF          Input cell:
Underscores:       Yes                One-Record:     No
Sort-Keys
   1st-Key:                2nd-Key:                3rd-Key:
     Order:                  Order:                  Order:
                                               Database Settings: PRIORITY
```

The next step is to select the **Sort-Keys** option from the **Settings** menu. When you choose **Sort-Keys**, Symphony gives you three options:

   1st-Key   2nd-Key   3rd-Key

To sort the database by priority number, choose **1st-Key**. Symphony shifts temporarily to the SHEET environment so that you can select the proper field. Figure 15.8 shows the Database range A34..G53 (corresponding to PRIORITY_DB in the settings sheet in figure 15.7). This range is the same one that would appear if you selected **Basic Database** from the **Settings** menu.

When Symphony shows you the Database range, simply point to any item in the "Priority" field (column D) to designate the **1st-Key**. For example, you might point to cell D35. After you point to the **1st-Key**, Symphony asks whether you want **Ascending** or **Descending** order. Because you want the priority numbers to appear in ascending order, type **A** (for Ascending).

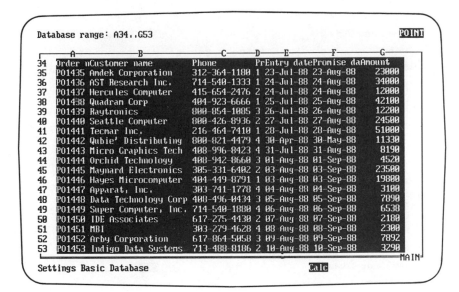

Fig. 15.8

The Database range.

After you set up the **1st-Key**, press the Menu key (F10) to return to the main FORM menu and then issue the **Record-Sort** command. Symphony asks whether you want to sort **All** the records or only the **Unique** records. (If you select Unique, Symphony removes all duplicates.) After you select **All** or Unique, Symphony rearranges the data according to priority number and returns you to the database form. Figures 15.9A and 15.9B show the settings and newly sorted database. The database appears only when you use the **Settings Basic Database** command.

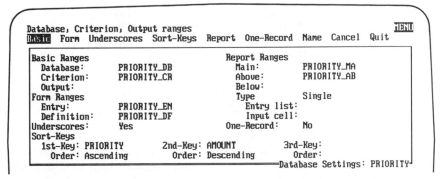

Fig. 15.9A

1ST-KEY setting for sorting by priority number.

Notice that the priority numbers appear correctly, but you have no way of telling the relative priorities within a group. For example, five purchase-order numbers have priority 1, but no priorities are apparent within that group. If you want to

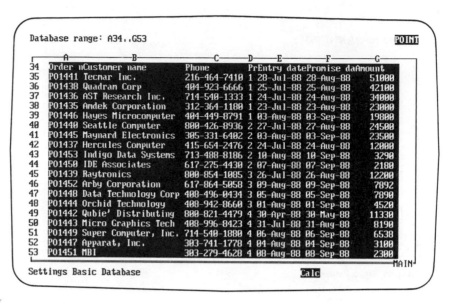

Fig. 15.9B

The database sorted by priority number.

prioritize within each group, you can use the dollar amount of the order (or some other field) as the **2nd-Key** (see fig. 15.10A). Figure 15.10B shows what happens when you select cell G35 as the **2nd-Key** with **Descending** order and re-sort the database with the **Record-Sort** command. Symphony allows you to specify up to three different **Sort-Keys** for sorting records.

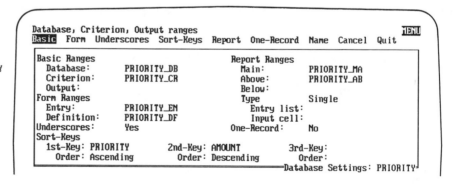

Fig. 15.10A

2ND-KEY setting for sorting first by priority and second by dollar amount of order.

Besides using the **Settings Basic Database** command to see the entire sorted database, you can also browse through the individual records one at a time to check their order. Remember that when you re-sort the database, the first record to appear is the record at the end of the sorting order.

Although you use the FORM window to look at individual records, and the SHEET window to view several records at once, the two windows have a great deal in

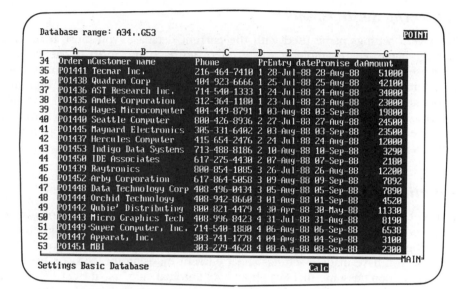

```
Database range: A34..G53                                    POINT
    ┌───A────────B──────────────C──────D────E─────────F───────────G──────
 34 │Order nCustomer name       Phone        PrEntry datePromise daAmount
 35 │P01441 Tecnar Inc.         216-464-7410 1 28-Jul-88 28-Aug-88   51000
 36 │P01438 Quadran Corp        404-923-6666 1 25-Jul-88 25-Aug-88   42100
 37 │P01436 AST Research Inc.   714-540-1333 1 24-Jul-88 24-Aug-88   34000
 38 │P01435 Amdek Corporation   312-364-1180 1 23-Jul-88 23-Aug-88   23000
 39 │P01446 Hayes Microcomputer 404-449-8791 1 03-Aug-88 03-Sep-88   19800
 40 │P01440 Seattle Computer    800-426-8936 2 27-Jul-88 27-Aug-88   24500
 41 │P01445 Maynard Electronics 305-331-6402 2 03-Aug-88 03-Sep-88   23500
 42 │P01437 Hercules Computer   415 654-2476 2 24-Jul-88 24-Aug-88   12000
 43 │P01453 Indigo Data Systems 713-488-8186 2 10-Aug-88 10-Sep-88    3290
 44 │P01450 IDE Associates      617-275-4430 2 07-Aug-88 07-Sep-88    2180
 45 │P01439 Raytronics          800-854-1085 3 26-Jul-88 26-Aug-88   12200
 46 │P01452 Arby Corporation    617-864-5058 3 09-Aug-88 09-Sep-88    7892
 47 │P01448 Data Technology Corp 408-496-0434 3 05-Aug-88 05-Sep-88   7890
 48 │P01444 Orchid Technology   408-942-8660 3 01-Aug-88 01-Sep-88    4520
 49 │P01442 Qubie' Distributing 800-821-4479 4 30-Apr-88 30-May-88   11330
 50 │P01443 Micro Graphics Tech 408-996-8423 4 31-Jul-88 31-Aug-88    8190
 51 │P01449 Super Computer, Inc. 714-540-1800 4 06-Aug-88 06-Sep-88   6530
 52 │P01447 Apparat, Inc.       303-741-1770 4 04-Aug-88 04-Sep-88    3100
 53 │P01451 MBI                 303-279-4620 4 08-Aug-88 08-Sep-88    2300
    └────────────────────────────────────────────────────────────MAIN─
Settings Basic Database                      Calc
```

Fig. 15.10B

The database sorted by priority number and amount of order.

common when it comes to database operations. For example, the SHEET **Q**uery **R**ecord-Sort command is almost exactly the same as the FORM **R**ecord-Sort command. The differences between the SHEET and FORM database commands are presented later in this chapter.

Working with the Settings Sheets

Just as with other types of settings sheets (including GRAPH, DOC, and COMM), you can name and save FORM **S**ettings sheets.

Naming Settings Sheets

The settings sheet that appears in figure 15.9A was stored under the name 1ST-KEY; the sheet that appears in figure 15.10A was stored under the name 2ND-KEY. (If you look at the right corners of both figures, you can see the names of the settings sheets.) To save a group of settings under a name, you use the **C**reate option from the FORM **S**ettings **N**ame menu that appears as follows:

   Use **C**reate **D**elete **P**revious **N**ext **I**nitial-Settings **R**eset **Q**uit

The **N**ame **U**se command recalls the named settings.

Attaching Settings Sheets

To have a settings name used with the current database, you must attach the settings name. For example, if you want to go back and forth in the Priority database between sorting by order number and sorting by priority, you may want to create two different settings sheets: ORDER NUMBER, which contains a sort key (Sort-Keys 1st-Key) from column A; and PRIORITY, which contains a sort key from column D. Depending on how you want the database sorted at any given time, you use the FORM Attach command to attach the appropriate settings sheet to the database and then re-sort the database.

Creating a Catalog of Settings Sheets

Like GRAPH Settings, Symphony offers both **Previous** and **Next** options in its **Name** command menu. These options allow you to browse sequentially through a catalog of settings sheets and select the one you want. Be careful, though. Just because you have made a settings sheet current by using the **Next** or **Previous** command, don't assume that Symphony will automatically use the settings sheet the next time you perform a **Record-Sort** or other database operation. You must attach the settings name to the current database before Symphony can use the settings.

Searching for Records

In addition to sorting a database, Symphony's FORM environment makes it easy for you to search for records. You can search for records individually or in groups. For example, suppose that you are given the Priority database sorted by priority number and amount, and you want to find the record for PO1452.

To find a record in the database, you must enter selection criteria. The criteria can be numbers, labels, or formulas. To enter selection criteria, choose the **Criteria** option from the main FORM menu. Symphony then provides the following options:

> Use **Ignore** Edit

To enter selection criteria and to modify criteria, select **Edit**. Symphony then displays a blank input form with the message Editing Criterion Record 1 of 1 at the top. (Symphony lets you enter as many as four different criterion records.) To select the database record for PO1452, you enter that order number in the "Order number" field. Figure 15.11 shows the input form just after you have entered the order number.

Next, press PgUp to return to the database. Then choose **Criteria Use** to have Symphony use the selection criteria you have established. Symphony selects the record, as illustrated in figure 15.12.

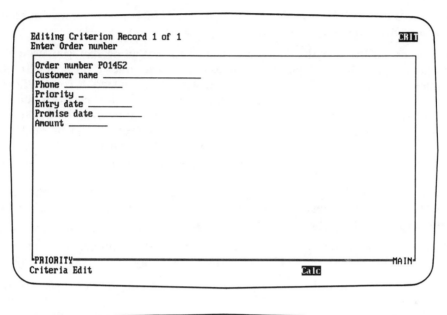

Fig. 15.11

*Entering an order
number in a
criterion record.*

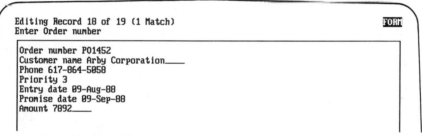

Fig. 15.12

The selected record.

Once you have seen the record for PO1452, and you want to move to another task, choose **Criteria Ignore**. This command returns you to the database, but the criteria you have set up remain in the criterion record. If you want to reinvoke the criteria later, simply select FORM **Criteria Use** again.

Using Formulas in Criteria

Besides choosing individual records, you can also set up criteria to select a group of records. Suppose, for example, that you want to select all records in the database whose amount is greater than $10,000. To enter this criteria, return to the FORM **Criteria Edit** command. Because the criteria for the purchase order still reside in the input form, you must first delete the purchase order number from the "Order number" field. To do so, you can enter a blank space or press the Backspace key while the cursor is in the "Order number" field. Next, move to the "Amount" field and enter the formula +?>**10000**. This entry may not look like a formula, but it has special meaning in a criterion record.

The question mark in the formula indicates to Symphony that you want the program to supply a cell address. Symphony then uses one of the special range names that the program sets up under the **Generate** command. If you look back at figure 15.8, you can see the Database range for the Priority database (PRIORITY_DB). When setting up the database, Symphony uses the field-name headings as range names for the cells directly below (see row 34 of fig. 15.8). In other words, cell A35 is named ORDER NUMBER, cell B35 is CUSTOMER NAME, and so on. Therefore, when you use a question mark in a criterion formula, Symphony automatically substitutes the appropriate range name for the cell where you enter the formula. (In this case, Symphony automatically substitutes AMOUNT for the question mark because you entered the formula in the "Amount" field.)

Because you are entering a formula, you must be sure to precede the question mark with a plus (+) sign. Otherwise, the formula does not work correctly.

After you enter the criteria for records with an amount greater than $10,000, press the PgUp key and select FORM **Criteria Use**; Symphony returns 10 records that meet the criteria. Figure 15.13 shows the first of the 10 and the message that appears at the top of the screen, indicating which record is in the input form. At this point, the Home, End, PgUp, and PgDn keys let you browse through only those records that match the selection criteria. You must use the FORM **Criteria Ignore** command to return to the entire database.

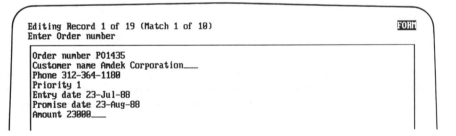

Fig. 15.13

The first of ten selected records.

Using AND To Combine Criteria

Now suppose that you want to select all the records in the database whose amount is greater than $10,000 *and* whose priority number is 2 or below. First, use the FORM **Criteria Edit** command to edit the criterion record you have constructed. Next, move to the "Priority" field and enter the formula +?<=**2**. Don't be concerned if you don't see the entire formula. You can verify it by using the Edit key (F2) even though "Priority" is a two-position field. Because you still want every record whose amount is greater than $10,000, you leave the original formula in the "Amount" field (+AMOUNT>10000).

By combining the two formulas in the same criterion record, you are telling Symphony that you want to combine these two criteria with AND. In other words, for a record to filter through the criteria you have set up, the record must pass both tests. Figure 15.14 shows the second record that meets the new criteria.

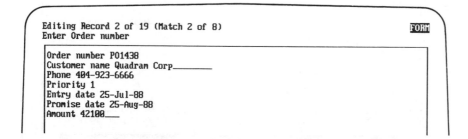

```
Editing Record 2 of 19 (Match 2 of 8)                    FORM
Enter Order number

Order number P01438
Customer name Quadram Corp_____
Phone 404-923-6666
Priority 1
Entry date 25-Jul-88
Promise date 25-Aug-88
Amount 42100___
```

Fig. 15.14

A record meeting the AND criteria.

Using OR To Combine Criteria

Suppose, on the other hand, that you want all the records that have a priority of 2 or below *or* have an amount greater than $10,000. To combine criteria with OR, place them in different criterion records. Keep the original formula in the first criterion record (+AMOUNT>10000) and delete the criterion formula for the "Priority" field; then use the **Criterion Edit** command followed by PgDn to add another criterion record. After placing the proper formula (+?<=2) in the "Priority" field, press PgUp twice to return to the database. Finally, invoke the **Criteria Use** command again to initiate the search. This time you get 12 records that match the criteria (see fig. 15.8 to verify this number).

Adding a Criterion Range

As mentioned earlier, Symphony allows you to construct up to four criterion records, which can give you fairly complex criteria. At times, however, you may want to step outside Symphony's structure. For example, you may want to add a criterion record. To do so, you must know where Symphony stores the Criterion range.

If you use the **FORM Settings Basic Criterion** command, Symphony displays the Criterion range. Figure 15.15 shows the Criterion range for the last example. Notice that the two formulas appear on different lines. Criteria combined with OR reside on different lines in a Criterion range, and criteria combined with AND reside on the same line. Notice also that each formula appears as 1 in the figure. The value of a formula is always true or false (1 or 0). These formulas appear as 1s because both their values are true for the records to which they currently refer. If you shift to the SHEET environment and use the Literal display format on these formulas, they will display in their normal form.

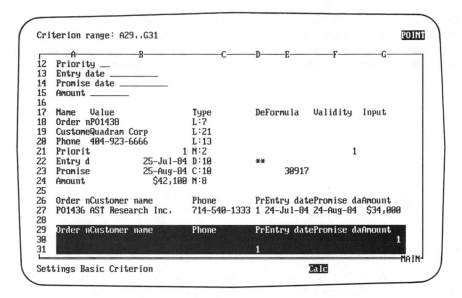

Fig. 15.15

The Criterion range.

When you use the **Generate** command, Symphony automatically sets up the Criterion range and names it according to the database name you choose. The name of the Criterion range in the example is PRIORITY_CR. When you first use the **Generate** command, the Criterion range consists of the field names and one blank row (A29..G30 in the example). As you add criterion records, however, the range grows. You have added two criterion records in the current example, so the Criterion range is now three rows deep (A29..G31). Symphony automatically keeps track of the Criterion range, the Database range, and several other important ranges. This feature is one of the most convenient elements of building a database in the FORM work environment.

Symphony automatically sets up the FORM window to allow enough space for four criterion records. But what if you want five? For example, suppose that you want to select all the records for the following customer names:

> Quadram Corp
> Indigo Data Systems
> Seattle Computer
> AST Research Inc.
> Orchid Technology

To select the records for Quadram Corp, simply place that name in the "Customer name" field of a criterion record. To use all five names, however, requires five criterion records.

If you want to add another record to the Criterion range, first shift to the SHEET environment. Next, move the cursor to the Criterion range by pressing the GoTo key and typing **PRIORITY_CR**. This step places the cursor at the top left corner

of the Criterion range. The easiest way to add a criterion record is to use the
Insert Rows command to insert a blank row below the field-name headings in
the Criterion range. Because this method inserts a row in the middle of the
range, the Criterion range (in FORM **Settings Basic Criterion**) automatically expands. Figure 15.16 shows the new Criterion range.

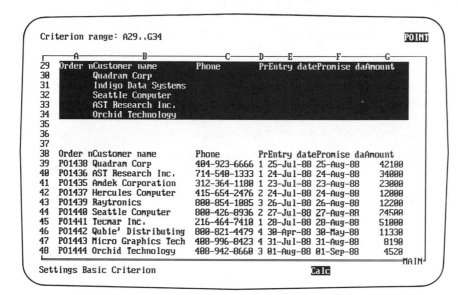

Fig. 15.16

After inserting rows in the Criterion range.

When you make the appropriate change to the Criterion range, Symphony instantly recognizes five criterion records.

Approximate Matching

Symphony uses approximate matching when evaluating the labels in a record.
(The DOC **Search** command uses the same feature.) For example, suppose that
you want to find all the records in the Priority database whose "Customer name"
begins with *A*. When you enter the formula @LEFT(?,1)="A" in the "Customer
name" field of the first criterion record, Symphony returns four database records.
An alternative is to use the same formula but with a lowercase *a*: @LEFT(?,1)="a".
Symphony returns the same results because the program does not recognize the
difference between lowercase and uppercase letters when matching labels.

Note: If you have leading spaces in front of the @LEFT formula, you must delete
them so that Symphony will handle your formula correctly.

Using Wildcards

Symphony also has wildcard provisions for matching labels. The characters ?, *, and ~ have special meanings when used in criterion records.

The ? character instructs Symphony to accept any character in that position (just as the character does in DOS). For example, if you want to find the record for order number PO1452 but suspect that you typed a zero rather than a capital *O* for the second character when you entered the record, you can use the label P?1452.

The * character tells Symphony to accept all characters that follow the *. Suppose again that you want to select the records in the Priority database whose "Customer name" begins with *A*. You can enter A* or a*. Be forewarned: Symphony does not recognize the * character when you put characters after it. For example, *dek* is an invalid use of the wildcard character.

When placed at the beginning of a label, the ~ character indicates that all the values except those that follow it are to be selected. For example, if you want all the records in the Priority database except those that begin with the letter *A*, you can enter ~A* in the first criterion record. In this case, Symphony returns 15 records from the Priority database.

Although the ~ character works well for labels, it doesn't work for formulas and numbers. To get the same results with a number or a formula, you must use either the $<>$ or #NOT# logical operator. For example, if you want to select all the records in the Priority database *except* those whose priority number is 4, you can enter *=?$<>$4. (Note that the ? character is not used as the label wildcard in this case.) Similarly, you can enter the formula #NOT#?=4. Both formulas give the same results.

Modifying and Deleting Records While Searching

Suppose that while you are searching a database, you find a record that requires modification. You can stop the search by using the **Criteria Ignore** command and return to the database to edit the record. But this method is not desirable because you will have to find the record again before you can modify it. A better technique is to modify the record on the spot.

When you are in a FORM window, you can modify any record. If you modify the record to the point where it no longer fits the criteria, Symphony no longer lets you see the record during the search operation (unless you change the selection criteria). If, on the other hand, you are performing a search operation in a SHEET window using the **Query** command, you cannot modify records.

Besides modifying records while searching in a FORM window, you can also delete records. Simply press the Del key just as you would under normal circumstances. Symphony asks for confirmation before deleting the record.

Under no circumstances can you add a record while you are in the middle of a search operation in a FORM window. This statement holds even if one of the records that conforms to the search criteria is the last record in the database. (Recall that under normal circumstances you must move to the last record in the database before adding a record.)

Using Advanced FORM Features

Now that you are familiar with the basics of creating a standard input form and entering a simple database, you are ready to learn some of the more advanced features of Symphony's FORM window. For example, up to this point Symphony has automatically handled the layout of input forms and has entered all the important ranges with little help from you. You will now learn how to create customized input forms and make other modifications to a database to suit better your personal data-management needs.

Creating Special Input Forms

Suppose that you decide that you want to create a special input form for entering additional records in the Priority database. To begin with, you decide that you want to place two fields on the same line in the input form. Assume that you want to put the "Phone" field on the same line as the "Customer name" field. To do so, you can use the FORM Field Move command.

After you choose FORM Field Move, Symphony asks you to Select field to move. Position the cursor on the field you want to move ("Phone," in this example) and then press Enter. Next, Symphony asks you to select the new position for the field. Move the cursor to the appropriate position—in this case, several spaces after the "Customer name" field—and press Enter. Symphony warns you that any data to the right or below the database ranges may move; select Yes to proceed.

The field moves, but you are left with a blank line in the original "Phone" field position (see fig. 15.17). To get rid of this blank line, you must be familiar with another special range that was created when Symphony generated the database: the Entry range.

Modifying the Entry Range

Symphony creates the Entry range when you issue the Generate command. Figure 15.18 shows the Entry range for the Priority database.

The Entry range (A9..A15) contains a column of label entries, the same labels that appear in the input form when you enter data. If you want to remove the blank line, you must modify the Entry range. (*Note:* This range is the entry layout

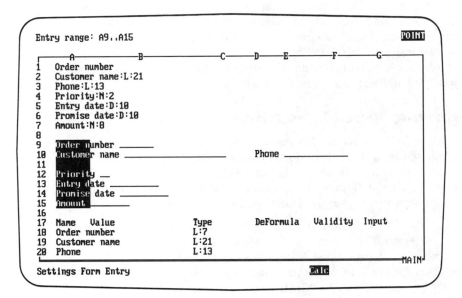

Fig. 15.17

The input form after moving the Phone field.

```
Move a field to a different position in the form          MENU
Insert  Delete  Move  Quit

Order number _____
Customer name _____      Phone _____

Priority _
Entry date _____
Promise date _____
Amount _____
```

Fig. 15.18

The Entry range.

```
Entry range: A9..A15                                      POINT

   A          B          C      D    E      F       G
1   Order number
2   Customer name:L:21
3   Phone:L:13
4   Priority:N:2
5   Entry date:D:18
6   Promise date:D:18
7   Amount:N:8
8
9   Order number _____
10  Customer name _____      Phone _____
11
12  Priority _
13  Entry date _____
14  Promise date _____
15  Amount _____
16
17  Name     Value          Type      DeFormula  Validity  Input
18  Order number            L:7
19  Customer name           L:21
20  Phone                   L:13
                                                          MAIN

Settings Form Entry                          Calc
```

and not the initial data definition.) First, use the Type key (Alt-F10) to change to the DOC environment. (You can use the SHEET environment and the SHEET Delete Rows command, but the procedure is easier in the DOC environment.) Once again, make sure that Format Settings Justification is set to None so that Symphony does not try to justify the Entry range.

After you change to the DOC environment, move the cursor to the Entry range—to the blank line between "Customer name" and "Priority." Use the Del key to remove the blank line. Figure 15.19 shows the Entry range after the change.

The address of the Entry range is stored in the settings sheet under the name PRIORITY_EN. (Symphony assigned this name when you used the Generate command.) If you issue the FORM Settings Form Entry command, Symphony highlights the PRIORITY_EN range. You should not have to change this setting.

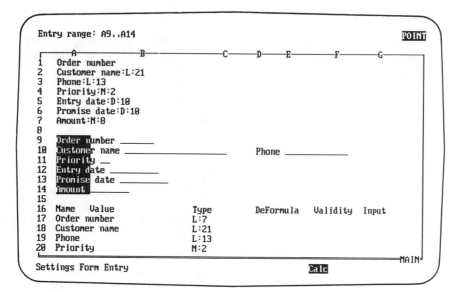

Fig. 15.19

The Entry range after deleting the blank line.

The FORM Field Move command automatically repositions the fields in the Entry and Definition ranges, but not in the Database, Criterion, and Report ranges. (These ranges are discussed later in the chapter.) If you want to move the field in these other ranges, you must use the SHEET Move command. Keep in mind, however, that the SHEET Move command does not insert; you will probably need to make the move in several steps so that you don't overwrite data.

Changing the position of the "Phone" field in the input form does not affect the way Symphony enters records in the database. In fact, you can put several field names on the same line. Symphony processes them sequentially from left to right as though they were all on separate lines. Figure 15.20 shows how the input form appears after this first change.

```
Inserting Record 1            New Record              FORM
Enter Order number
Order number _____
Customer name _____    Phone _____
Priority __
Entry date _____
Promise date _____
Amount _____
```

Fig. 15.20

The new input form.

Changing Underscores

Suppose that you also want to modify the input form to allow longer entries by increasing the size of the "Customer name" field from 21 to 30 characters. To do so, you simply shift to the DOC environment, position the cursor on the "Customer name" label, and add 9 underscore characters to the 21 that are already there. Incidentally, you can stop underscores from appearing at all in the input form. Simply select FORM Settings Underscores No.

Modifying the Definition Range

If you prefer not to change the input form, but you would still like it to be able to handle longer customer names, Symphony offers the scrolling-characters technique. To use this technique, you have to know how to change the Definition range. The Definition range for the Priority database (PRIORITY_DF: A17..H23) appears in figure 15.21.

Fig. 15.21

The Definition range.

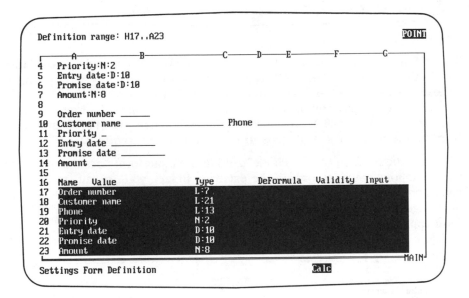

The Definition range, which is the most comprehensive range in the FORM work environment, contains fields for checking the type of entries made and their *validity*; that is, whether they fall within a certain range of values. The Definition range is also where you control the format for displaying entries and other customization.

To change the number of characters that you can enter in the "Customer name" field but not change the input form, you must switch to the SHEET environment.

Next, move the cursor to the "Type" field in the Definition range. The appropriate "Type" field is cell C18 in figure 15.21. (You can always find the correct cell address by looking at the entries in the Name column, the first column in the Definition range.) Notice that the "Type" field is where Symphony stores the type and length information you provided when you created the database. Change the value in cell C18 from L:21 (for label, 21 characters long) to L:30. When you switch back to the FORM environment, you can now enter labels up to 30 characters long in the "Customer name" field. Because the input form does not have enough visible room to display a 30-character string, however, Symphony begins scrolling when you reach the 21st character.

This FORM window scrolling feature also works for number entries. Be fore-warned, however, that because Symphony can store numbers with as many as 15 decimal places, the scrolling feature is practical only up to that point. When you get beyond 15 places, Symphony automatically shifts to the scientific format.

Another mistake to watch out for is eliminating the Definition range address in the settings sheet when you are rearranging the input form. To access the Definition range in the settings sheet, use the FORM Settings Form Definition command. Normally, if you have eliminated the Definition range address, the entry in the settings sheet is blank. You must restore the correct value in order for the FORM window to work properly.

Creating Defaults

Now that you are familiar with the basic concept of the Definition range, you are ready to make more modifications to the input form. Suppose, for example, that you want to set up the current date as the default entry date in the input form. As the default, the current date will show up every time you create a new record. You then have the option of keeping the current date or overriding it with another date.

To set up a default in the input form, you must make the proper entry in the "Default" field of the Definition range. Although the label in cell D16 of figure 15.21 is truncated (De), the label indicates the top of the Default column. To have the current date display as the default in the "Entry date" field, enter the formula **@INT(@NOW)** in cell D21, the cell corresponding to the "Entry date" field in the Default column. [The formula @INT(@NOW) takes the integer portion of the current date/time serial number; see Chapter 5.] Figure 15.22 shows the input form with the new "Entry date" default.

You can also enter labels or numbers as defaults. For example, to have the priority number default to the highest priority, you can enter the number 1 in cell D20.

No matter what default you use (formula, label, or number), you should always make sure that your entry is the correct type. Although Symphony performs a validity check on the default value, the program does not check to see whether

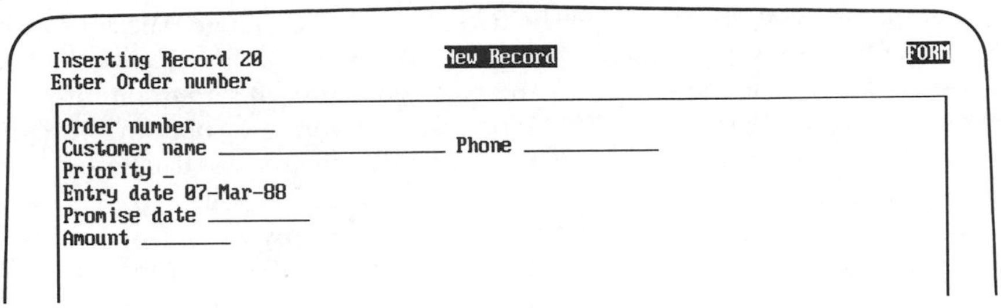

Fig. 15.22

The input form with the entry date default.

```
┌─────────────────────────────────────────────────────────────┐
│ Inserting Record 20           ▐New Record▌            FORM   │
│ Enter Order number                                          │
│  ┌──────────────────────────────────────────────────────┐   │
│  │Order number ─────                                     │   │
│  │Customer name ─────────────────── Phone ───────────    │   │
│  │Priority _                                             │   │
│  │Entry date 07-Mar-88                                   │   │
│  │Promise date ────────                                  │   │
│  │Amount ───────                                         │   │
```

the default is the correct entry type. If you are not careful, you may wind up with character data in a number field, or vice versa.

Computing Fields

Suppose that, as a company policy, you always assign a promise date that is 30 days after the entry date. Therefore, after you have entered the entry date, you prefer to have Symphony compute the promise date. Symphony lets you define a computed field when you first create the database. That time is the best time to define a computed field, but if you decide later that you want to enter one, you simply change the type designation in the Type column of the Definition range to *C* (for computed).

To complete the change, you must enter the formula **+B21+30** in cell E22. Column E is labeled Formula in figure 15.21. Whenever you enter a formula for computing a field or transforming a field, you always enter the formula in the Formula column of the Definition range. Notice that the formula refers to a value in column B, the Value column. Symphony uses the Value column as a temporary holding place for the current record before writing it to the database. (Symphony places the result of the formula in the Value column.) You should always make the formulas for computed fields refer to the appropriate cells in the Value column. Figure 15.23 shows the input form after the "Promise date" is computed from the "Entry date."

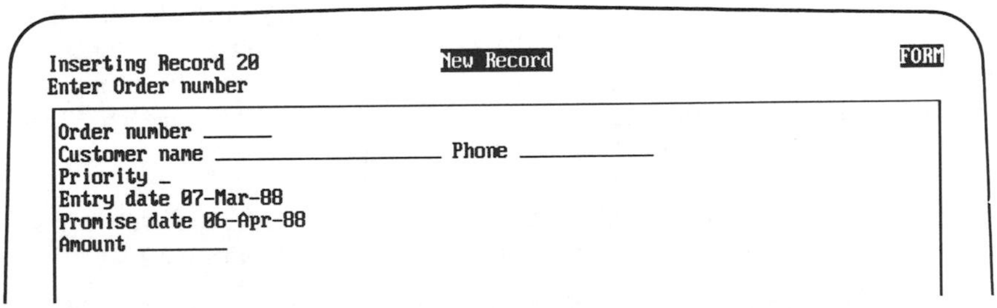

Fig. 15.23

The promise date computed from the entry date.

```
┌─────────────────────────────────────────────────────────────┐
│ Inserting Record 20           ▐New Record▌            FORM   │
│ Enter Order number                                          │
│  ┌──────────────────────────────────────────────────────┐   │
│  │Order number ─────                                     │   │
│  │Customer name ─────────────────── Phone ───────────    │   │
│  │Priority _                                             │   │
│  │Entry date 07-Mar-88                                   │   │
│  │Promise date 06-Apr-88                                 │   │
│  │Amount ───────                                         │   │
```

When you use the input form, you will notice that the cursor jumps past a computed field. Because the field is computed from the values in other fields of the same record, you cannot enter a value manually. Therefore, when you designate a field as the computed type, be sure you will not want to change the field manually.

You should also avoid the mistake of trying to compute fields from other records in the database. The difficulty of creating general formulas for this purpose is beyond the scope of the beginner. You can refer to values outside the Definition range but not formulas; Symphony does not recalculate formulas outside the Definition range during a database operation.

Transforming Fields

Besides computing fields, you can also transform them. The main difference between the two methods is that you can manually modify transformed fields but not computed fields.

Suppose, for example, that you always enter order numbers beginning with PO. Rather than enter the entire order number yourself, you prefer to type only the number portion and have Symphony enter the initial string for you. To arrange this setup, place the formula +"PO"&G17 in cell E17. (Note: Do not be concerned if ERR is generated before the entry of data.) This cell resides in the Formula column, the same column you use whenever you enter a formula for computing a field. But this time the formula refers to a cell in the Input column. Figure 15.24 shows the Input column in the Definition range.

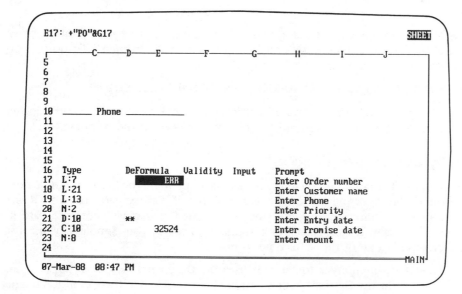

Fig. 15.24

The Input column in the Definition range.

The entries from the input form are stored temporarily in the Input column. You never actually see values in the Input column; however, any formula that transforms an entry must refer to this column.

Figure 15.25 shows the input form after an order number has been entered but before Enter has been pressed. Figure 15.26 shows the input form after Enter has been pressed.

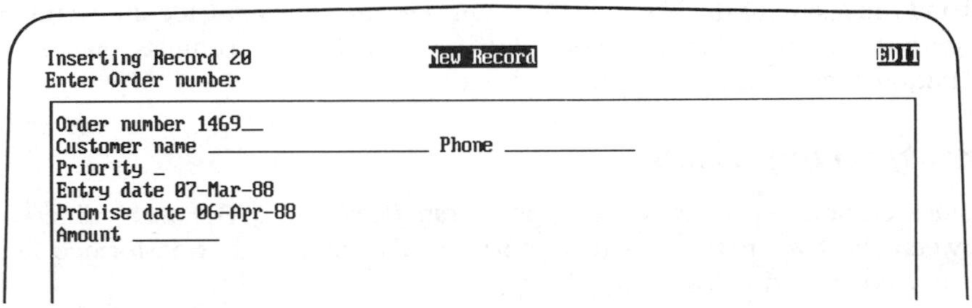

Fig. 15.25

After entering the order number but before pressing Enter.

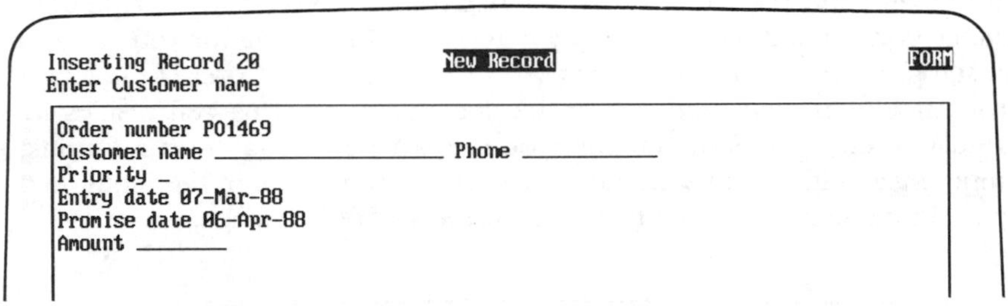

```
Inserting Record 20                    New Record                    EDIT
Enter Order number

Order number 1469__
Customer name _____    Phone _____
Priority _
Entry date 07-Mar-88
Promise date 06-Apr-88
Amount _____
```

Fig. 15.26

After pressing Enter.

```
Inserting Record 20                    New Record                    FORM
Enter Customer name

Order number PO1469
Customer name _____    Phone _____
Priority _
Entry date 07-Mar-88
Promise date 06-Apr-88
Amount _____
```

As another example of transforming an entry, assume that you want to enter customer phone numbers without having to enter the hyphens. To do so, you can enter the following formula in cell E19:

@LEFT(G19,3)&"-"&@MID(G19,3,3)&"-"&@RIGHT(G19,4)

Just as with default and computed entries, transformed entries are stored in the Value column (column B) until the record is placed in the database.

Performing Edit Checks

Symphony offers some simple edit checks that depend on the field-type indicators you use when creating a database. For example, if you indicate that a field is a date field (by entering a *D* after the field name), you must enter the date in one of the valid date formats, or Symphony beeps at you. Similarly, you must enter time in one of the valid time formats.

Incidentally, Symphony automatically uses the D1 format for displaying dates in the input form, the Database range, and the Value column of the Definition range.

Times are displayed in the T1 format. If you want to modify the way in which a date or time is displayed, you must change the format in the Value column of the Definition range. Any change you make is reflected in the input form.

Symphony also checks for valid numbers and labels when you use *N* and *L* field-type indicators. For example, because the "Priority" field in the example database is designated as a two-character field, you must enter a number between 0 and 19. When a field is a label field, however, Symphony accepts just about any entry. About the only edit check that Symphony provides for a label field is to test its length.

Performing Value Checks

Besides the simple edit checks that Symphony provides through field-type indicators, you can also validate inputs by using formulas. For example, suppose that you want to disallow priority numbers greater than 4 in the Priority database. You can enter the formula +**B20**<=**4** in cell F20 of the Definition range. Notice that column F is the Validity column of the range and that the formula also refers to a cell in the Value column. Value-checking formulas must always be written this way.

You need to remember two rules when you are using value-checking formulas. First, any default values you use must pass the check; Symphony does not check default values. Second, value-checking formulas test the value in the Value column, not the values actually input.

Here's an example illustrating the importance of this second rule. Suppose that you want to build a formula to check the four right-hand digits of the order number in the Priority database and also use another formula to enter automatically the "PO" portion of the order number. The formula to transform the order number is +"PO"&G17. This formula refers to a cell in the Input column, and Symphony places the result in the Value column. Therefore, because the value-checking formula tests the value in the Value column, you must use a formula that works with the transformed order number. The following is such a formula:

@IF(@ISERR(@VALUE(@RIGHT(B17,4)))=0, @TRUE,@FALSE)

This formula converts the four right-hand digits of the order number from characters to numbers. Next, the function tests for an ERR message indicating that the conversion has not taken place. If the conversion does take place, no ERR message is produced, and the value of the function is 1. Otherwise, the value of the function is 0.

Changing Prompts

In column H in figure 15.24, you can see the prompts that Symphony uses when you enter data in the input form. Symphony automatically supplies these prompts when you create the database.

Suppose that you want to change the prompt for the priority number from Enter Priority to Priority?. Simply enter the new label in cell H20 of the Definition range, and Symphony uses the new prompt for the next record you enter.

Changing Formats

You can change the format of the "Amount" field in the Priority database to the Currency **0** format. Move the cursor to cell B23 in the Definition range and change the format there. A simple way is to switch to the SHEET environment and use the SHEET Format command. Symphony then displays in the new currency format the amounts you enter in the Input form.

Changing the display format in the input form does not change the format in the records stored in the Database range (PRIORITY_DB). Because most of the time you see the records only as they appear in the input form, however, you don't really care how they appear in the Database range. If you do want to format the Database range, you can use the SHEET Format command and indicate the column of values.

Adding a Field to the Database

No matter how well you have thought out and planned your database, it's likely you will need to add a field at a later date. Symphony 2.0's FORM Field Insert command makes this type of structural change easy. (Earlier versions of Symphony required that you insert the field manually into each of the special database ranges.)

In the customer database you have been building in this chapter, assume that you want to add a "Comment" field after the "Amount" field. In the FORM window, select FORM Field Insert. Symphony then asks you to supply a series of items. Enter **Comment** in response to the Specify field name: prompt, select **Label** for the field type, and enter **20** for the field length. When asked to Select position for field, put the cursor under Amount and press Enter. Symphony warns you that any data to the right or below the database ranges may move; select **Yes** to proceed.

Symphony automatically inserts the new field in the input form and all other database ranges (Criterion, Report, Definition, and Database).

Deleting a Field

The FORM Field command also has an option to Delete a field. After you select the field to delete (choose "Comment" for this example), Symphony asks you to confirm the deletion by answering **Yes** or **No**. Like moving a field, deleting a field leaves a blank line in the input form. Because in this example you deleted the "Comment" field from the end of the form, you do not notice the blank line. If the blank line were in the middle of the form, however, you would want to delete it in SHEET or DOC mode. (See the earlier section on "Modifying the Entry Range" for details.)

The **Field Delete** command deletes the field from the Entry and Definition ranges but not the Database, Criterion, and Report ranges. You must remove these columns yourself with the SHEET **Erase** or **Move** commands. You then may need to adjust column widths with SHEET **Width Set**.

Using Multiple Input Forms

When you create an entry form, the **Generate** command automatically attaches the form to the database. But you can activate different input forms for the same database by means of the **Attach** command. For example, you can use two different input forms when you need to keep certain fields confidential in a database. You also need to use the **Attach** command when you create more than one database settings sheet and you want to switch to these alternate settings.

The SHEET Database Commands

As mentioned earlier, SHEET database commands are used to manipulate groups of database records. For database operations in the SHEET environment use, if possible, the settings that are automatically created in the FORM environment so that you don't have to re-create the settings yourself. You always, however, have the option of creating or modifying the settings in the SHEET environment. Determining when to use Symphony's automatic capabilities and when to use your own is an acquired art. As you become more familiar with Symphony, you should find this choice increasingly easier to make.

A good time to use the SHEET environment is after you have built a database with Symphony's FORM environment. For example, suppose that you have the name and address database that was used at the beginning of the chapter and appears again in figure 15.27, and you want to make a copy of all the records whose area code is 812. Symphony's SHEET commands give you a way to accomplish this task.

The main command for performing database operations in the SHEET environment is the **Query** command. (*Query* is just another word for search.) The simplest **Query** command option is **Record-Sort**.

Fig. 15.27

A sample Addresses database.

```
I1: 'Addresses database                                              SHEET
          ──────I─────────────────────J───────────K────L──
  1   Addresses database
  2   Name                    Address                         Code Phone
  3   Ahmad, Shamim Sultana    Ashton Ctr, Weatherly Hall 202   123 337-1559
  4   Cotter, James F.         1003 Tulip Tree House            453 332-0617
  5   Englert, Michael         224 Greenup St,                  735 423-4351
  6   Harding, Edward          2400 Central Parkway             645 871-6223
  7   Harrington, James T,     238 High St,                     837 871-4900
  8   Holland, Earl            3712 Drake Road                  324 561-4870
  9   Kuehnle, Karen           9900 Yale Ave,                   143 339-6731
 10   Owen, David J.           612 Knight Ridge Road            812 339-8770
 11   Schumann, Fritz W,       100 E, Miller Dr,                532 334-1873
 12   Sharpe, Sarah            7897 Providence St,              315 337-4662
 13   Sikes, William L,        3751 Clifton Ave,                632 241-8445
 14   Simpson, Jeremy          3509 Ludlow Ave,                 976 321-7362
 15   Stone, Betty             700 Vine St,                     545 321-9000
 16   Timmerman, Chuck         7900 Castleway Drive             812 984-9745
 17   Tuke, John               531 Remington Road               754 332-6742
 18   Yeagar, Patrick          4237 Mariemont Ave,              516 561-2145
 19   Zakon, Steven            3549 Keene St,                   534 332-6773
 20   Zealear, Mathew          2909 Fresno St,                  532 334-9008
                                                          ───────ADDRESSES
  08-Mar-88  06:00 PM
```

Query Record-Sort

The only difference between **R**ecord-Sort in the FORM window and in the SHEET window is that in the SHEET window you may need to specify the range to be sorted. As in the FORM window, the range to be sorted is called the Database range. You must enter in the **Q**uery Settings sheet the cell addresses of the Database range (with the SHEET **Q**uery Settings **B**asic **D**atabase command). Fortunately, if the database was generated in the FORM window, the Database range should already be designated correctly. If you need to specify the range to be sorted, you must include the field name headings in a sort operation.

The Query Settings Sheet

You can invoke the settings sheet for the SHEET **Q**uery commands by selecting **S**ettings from the main **Q**uery menu. This settings sheet is the same one that appears in the FORM window; in fact, the settings that are currently attached to the FORM window also reside in the **Q**uery **S**ettings sheet. If you make a change in the FORM **S**ettings, the same change is immediately reflected in the **Q**uery **S**ettings, and vice versa. Figure 15.28 shows the **Q**uery **S**ettings sheet for the Priority database. Notice that the sheet appears exactly as it did in the FORM window (see fig. 15.10A).

In 1-2-3 the Query key can repeat a database operation using the current settings. Symphony does not offer a Query key. With Symphony's settings sheets (and the way the **Q**uery menu is set up), a Query key is no longer necessary. Just by

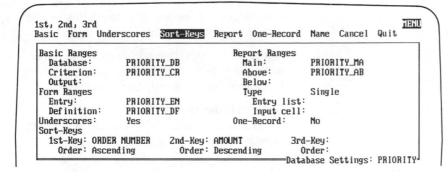

Fig. 15.28

The Query Settings sheet.

issuing one of the commands in the menu, you invoke a database operation using the latest settings.

Before you can execute the SHEET Query commands, you must set up the following three ranges:

1. The Criterion range specifying the search criteria

2. The Database range to be searched

3. The Output range where Symphony will write the output in the worksheet (not required for Find or Delete)

The Criterion and Database ranges are automatically specified in the database settings sheet when you generate the database. You will, however, need to enter the specific search criteria into the Criterion range in the spreadsheet. (See the "Query Find" section of this chapter for an example of how this is done.) The third range, Output, is used with the SHEET Query Extract and SHEET Query Unique commands.

All you need to specify for the Output range is a single row containing the names of the fields that you want copied; you do not need to include all the field names. You can specify a larger area for the Output range, but Symphony needs only the field names.

Ways of Searching for Records

Besides Record-Sort and Settings, Query is also the host command for a series of other subcommands. Here are these commands and their functions:

Find   Moves down through a database, locating the cursor at records that match given criteria (similar to issuing Criteria Use in a FORM window and then browsing through the resulting records)

Extract	Creates copies in a specified area of the worksheet of all or some of the fields in certain records that match given criteria
Unique	Similar to **Extract**, but recognizes that some of the records in the database may be duplicates; includes only unique records
Delete	Deletes all the records in a database that match given criteria and shifts the remaining records to fill in the gaps

Query Find

Suppose that you want to find in the Priority database all the records with a priority of 4. First, make sure that the Database range has been appropriately specified. To check the Database range, use the **Settings Basic Database** command to verify the range A34..G53.

Next, enter the selection criteria. Recall that the FORM window offers a **Criteria** command for entering and invoking criteria. The SHEET window does not have this command. Instead, you must manually enter the criteria in the Criterion range. For the current example, enter the number 4 in cell D30. Then make sure that the Criterion range is designated as A29..G30 in the **Query Settings** sheet. Figure 15.29 shows the highlighted Criterion range.

Fig. 15.29

The Criterion range.

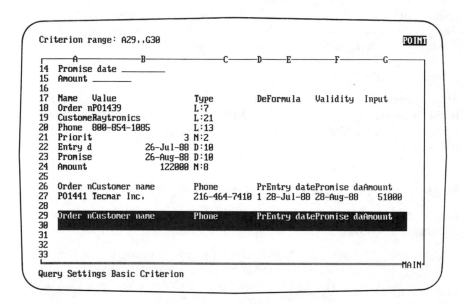

Now that the appropriate ranges have been specified, you can issue the **Query Find** command. Figure 15.30 shows what happens when you do. The cursor highlights the first record that conforms to the search criteria. By using the ↓ key, you can position the cursor at the next record that conforms to the criteria. If you continue to press ↓, you can browse through the records that conform to the search criteria. The ↑ key works in the opposite direction and moves you to the previous record that conforms to the criteria. The Home and End keys, respectively, take you to the first and last records that fit the search criteria. To end the **Find** operation and return to the **Query** menu, you can press either Enter or Esc.

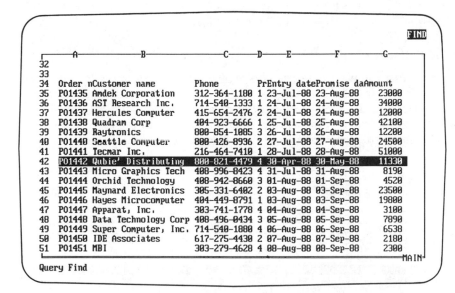

Fig. 15.30

Finding the first record that meets the selection criteria.

Note in figure 15.29 that when you manually enter criteria in the Criterion range, you must place numbers and labels below the appropriate field name. The same is not true for formulas. Formulas are written using relative addressing with reference to the first row of the database. Therefore, in formulas the addresses are important, not what field names they fall under. (Note: You cannot use the ? character to have Symphony automatically supply the address for you. You may recall that you can use this character in the FORM window.)

Suppose that you want to search the Priority database for every record in which the customer name begins with any letter after the letter *L*. The following Criterion ranges are equivalent:

Customer Name	Priority
@LEFT(CUSTOMER NAME,1)>"L"	
Customer Name	Priority
	@LEFT(CUSTOMER NAME,1)>"L"

Notice that the range name CUSTOMER NAME is used in the examples. When you are building a database in the FORM window, Symphony automatically creates range names for the first records directly below the field name headings; you should use these names to your advantage in the SHEET environment.

Query Extract

Let's say that you want to create copies of all the records in the Priority database in which the promise date occurs after September 3, 1988. The command you use to perform this kind of operation is **Query Extract**. Figure 15.31 shows the results. As you can see, the **Extract** operation copies to the area below the field names all the records that conform to the selection criteria.

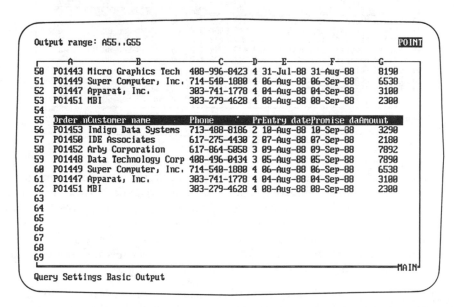

Fig. 15.31

Extracting the records that meet the selection criteria.

In figure 15.31, the Output range was set up manually because Symphony does not use the Output range in a FORM window. To create this Output range, use the Copy command to copy the field-name headings from the Database range or the Criterion range. When you enter the Output range in the **Query Settings**

Basic Output settings sheet, enter only the range of the field-name headings (A55..G55 in fig. 15.31). After specifying the Output range and entering the criteria in the Criterion range, you can extract the records.

The advantage of the Extract option is that it allows you to do detailed analysis on a database. You can use Extract to pull data from one or more records in a database and perform special processing on the subset. You must be careful, however, to designate the Database and Criterion ranges properly.

As mentioned earlier, the theoretical maximum number of records in a database is about 8,000, but the actual limit is much lower than that. If you are performing an Extract operation, you will require even more space for the Output range; this requirement further restricts the space you can devote to the database.

Always consider the requirements for the Output range and how they may limit the kind of Extract you can perform. With a fairly small database, this limitation is not a problem. The larger a database gets, however, the more you should keep an eye on the amount of RAM available. A frequent check of the SERVICES Settings command will tell you how much RAM is left and allow you to gauge the kinds of Extract operations that are possible with the available RAM.

Query Unique

Another type of search, which uses a variation of the Query command, selects all the *unique* records in a database. Query Unique can copy all the unique records from a database to a separate part of the worksheet. A popular way to use this command is to focus on specific fields in a database. To illustrate how this operation works, suppose that you want to get a listing of all the companies represented in your customer database, which is organized as shown in figure 15.32; all the records have a "Name" and a "Company" field.

As you can see, several companies are listed more than once in the database. To avoid copying duplicate records to the Output range, use the Unique option. The Unique option is set up like the Extract option, but the results can be quite different. Figure 15.33 shows how the Extract and Unique options work on the same Criterion range (J2..J3).

In this example, the Criterion range has only one field name in it ("Company"), and the cell below the field name has been deliberately left blank. For the Extract operation, this setup allows all the records in the database to meet the criterion. Therefore, the results of the Extract show copies of the company fields from every record in the database. The Unique operation, however, eliminates all the duplicate listings of the companies. The result of the Unique operation is a list of the individual companies in the customer database.

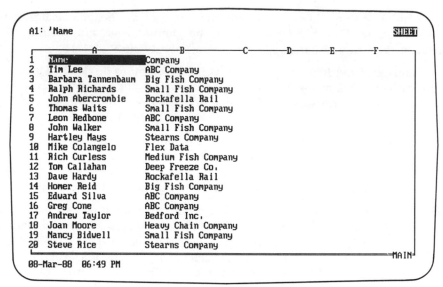

Fig. 15.32

A sample customer database.

```
A1: 'Name                                                           SHEET
     ┌─────A──────────┬──────B───────C─────D─────E─────F─┐
   1 │Name            Company                            │
   2 │Tim Lee         ABC Company                        │
   3 │Barbara Tannenbaum Big Fish Company                │
   4 │Ralph Richards  Small Fish Company                 │
   5 │John Abercrombie Rockafella Rail                   │
   6 │Thomas Waits    Small Fish Company                 │
   7 │Leon Redbone    ABC Company                        │
   8 │John Walker     Small Fish Company                 │
   9 │Hartley Mays    Stearns Company                    │
  10 │Mike Colangelo  Flex Data                          │
  11 │Rich Curless    Medium Fish Company                │
  12 │Tom Callahan    Deep Freeze Co.                    │
  13 │Dave Hardy      Rockafella Rail                    │
  14 │Homer Reid      Big Fish Company                   │
  15 │Edward Silva    ABC Company                        │
  16 │Greg Cone       ABC Company                        │
  17 │Andrew Taylor   Bedford Inc.                       │
  18 │Joan Moore      Heavy Chain Company                │
  19 │Nancy Bidwell   Small Fish Company                 │
  20 │Steve Rice      Stearns Company            ─────MAIN┘
 08-Mar-88  06:49 PM
```

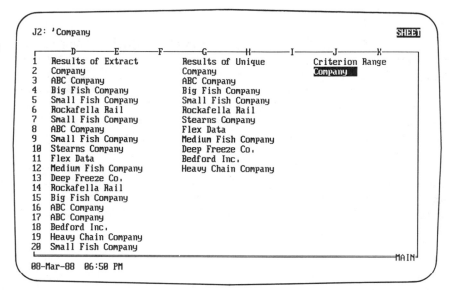

Fig. 15.33

Comparing Extract to Unique.

```
J2: 'Company                                                        SHEET
     ┌───D───────E──────F──────G──────H──────I─────J──────K─┐
   1 │Results of Extract     Results of Unique   Criterion Range│
   2 │Company                Company             Company        │
   3 │ABC Company            ABC Company                        │
   4 │Big Fish Company       Big Fish Company                   │
   5 │Small Fish Company     Small Fish Company                 │
   6 │Rockafella Rail        Rockafella Rail                    │
   7 │Small Fish Company     Stearns Company                    │
   8 │ABC Company            Flex Data                          │
   9 │Small Fish Company     Medium Fish Company                │
  10 │Stearns Company        Deep Freeze Co.                    │
  11 │Flex Data              Bedford Inc.                       │
  12 │Medium Fish Company    Heavy Chain Company                │
  13 │Deep Freeze Co.                                           │
  14 │Rockafella Rail                                           │
  15 │Big Fish Company                                          │
  16 │ABC Company                                               │
  17 │ABC Company                                               │
  18 │Bedford Inc.                                              │
  19 │Heavy Chain Company                                       │
  20 │Small Fish Company                         ─────MAIN┘
 08-Mar-88  06:50 PM
```

Query Delete

The last method used to search records is the **Delete** option, which removes unwanted records from a database. (This option is similar to the **Record-Sort Unique** operation in the FORM window, except the **Query Delete** option does not sort the database.) Figure 15.34 shows a portion of an Overdue Accounts database. Suppose that you want to purge all the paid accounts from your Overdue Accounts database, but only after you have verified that the accounts have been paid.

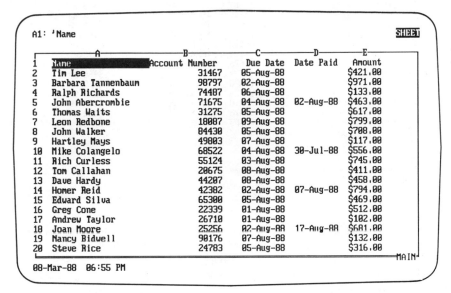

Fig. 15.34

An Overdue Accounts database.

First, extract all the paid records to verify their accuracy. To do so, use the Extract option with the Criterion range shown in figure 15.35. This figure also shows the results of the Extract. After you perform the Extract operation and review the results, you can use the same Criterion range for the Delete operation. After a confirmation step, the database appears as shown in figure 15.36. Notice that the Delete option removes the records that meet the criteria and closes up the gaps that are left in the database. Like the Find operation, the Delete operation does not require an Output range.

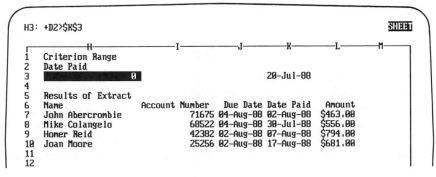

Fig. 15.35

The Criterion range and results of the Extract.

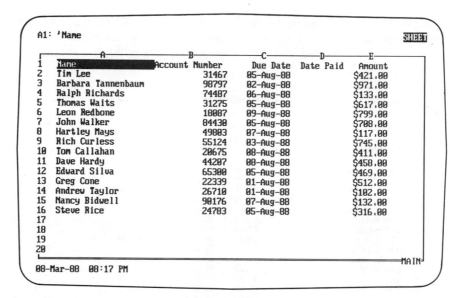

Fig. 15.36

After deleting the extracted records.

When you use the **Delete** option, make sure that you are deleting the correct records. The precautionary step of extracting them first is a good idea. This way you can verify that you have set up the right Criterion range. Once you have deleted the records, they are gone from RAM. But if you make a mistake with the **Delete** option and have not yet saved the file, you can regain the original database by bringing the file back from storage with the SERVICES **File Retrieve** command and writing over the current worksheet.

Query Parse

The final option offered in the **Query** menu is **Parse**. Although you may find other uses, **Query Parse** is principally designed to take data entered during a communications session and convert the data to a usable form. Because the use of **Query Parse** is so intimately connected with the COMM environment, **Query Parse** will be covered in Chapter 17.

Database Statistical Functions

Symphony's database statistical functions are similar to standard statistical functions, but the database functions have been modified to manipulate database fields. Like the standard statistical functions, the database statistical functions perform in one simple statement what would otherwise take several statements to accomplish. Because of their efficiency and ease of application, you should take advantage of Symphony's database functions. The functions include

@DCOUNT	Gives the number of items in a list
@DSUM	Sums the values of all the items in a list
@DAVG	Gives the average value of all the items in a list
@DMIN	Gives the minimum of all the items in a list
@DMAX	Gives the maximum of all the items in a list
@DSTD	Gives the standard deviation of all the items in a list
@DVAR	Gives the variance of all the items in a list

The general form of these functions is

@DFUNC(Database range,offset,Criterion range)

The Database and Criterion ranges are the same as those used by the SHEET Query commands and all the commands in the FORM window. You can use the standard settings for the Database and Criterion ranges (the ones in the database settings sheet that were used to produce the database), or you can specify different ranges. As usual, the Database range defines the database to be scanned, and the Criterion range specifies which records to select from the database. The offset, either 0 or a positive integer, indicates which field to select from the database records. A value of 0 means the first column; a 1, the second column; and so on.

An example that uses the database statistical functions involves computing the mean, variance, and standard deviation of the average interest rates offered by money market funds for a given week. If you are unfamiliar with the concepts of mean, variance, and standard deviation, refer to Chapter 5, where these concepts are explained.

Figure 15.37 shows a Money Market Returns database and the results of the various database statistical functions. The functions to find the maximum and minimum rates of return are also included.

The equations and their related statistics are

Statistic	*Formula*
Count	@DCOUNT(A3..B20,1,D13..D14)
Sum	@DSUM(A3..B20,1,D13..D14)
Mean	@DAVG(A3..B20,1,D13..D14)
Variance	@DVAR(A3..B20,1,D13..D14)
Std Dev	@DSTD(A3..B20,1,D13..D14)
Maximum	@DMAX(A3..B20,1,D13..D14)
Minimum	@DMIN(A3..B20,1,D13..D14)

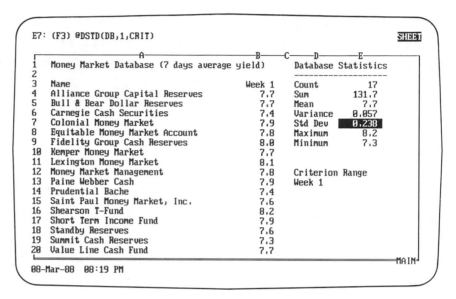

The results, as seen in figure 15.37, indicate that the mean return for the week for the 11 different money market funds is an annual percentage rate of 7.7 (cell E5). The variance is approximately .057 (cell E6), yielding a standard deviation of approximately .238 (cell E7). This standard-deviation figure indicates that about 68 percent of the money market funds are returning an annual rate of between 7.46 percent and 7.94 percent.

One std dev below mean = 7.7 - .238 = 7.46
One std dev above mean = 7.7 + .238 = 7.94

Summit Cash Reserves returns the lowest rate at 7.3 percent. The 7.3 figure comes from the @DMIN function used in cell E9. This value is approaching two standard deviations below the mean, computed as follows:

Two std devs below mean = 7.7 - (2 x .238) = 7.22

Because approximately 95 percent of the population falls within plus or minus two standard deviations of the mean, Summit Cash Reserves is close to being in the lower 2.5 percent of the population of money market funds for that week. (The 5 percent outside two standard deviations is divided by 2 because the population is assumed to be normal.)

Conversely, the Shearson T-Fund returns the highest rate: 8.2 percent. The @DMAX function determines the highest rate (cell E8), which is just over two standard deviations above the mean of the highest 2.5 percent of the population. Obviously, the database statistical functions can tell you a great deal about the database as a whole and how to interpret different values in it. These functions are also quite useful for printing database reports.

Database Reports

Symphony has a special feature for printing database reports. You can print advanced database reports, like mailing lists and form letters, or something as simple as a listing of your database as it appears in the spreadsheet. Depending on the criteria that you set up, the database report can include all or separate portions of a database; you can use SERVICES Print Settings to direct the report to the printer, a file, or a range within the worksheet.

In the first example, you will see how to use the database-reporting feature to print the entire Priority database to the printer. In the second, you will see how to print a portion of the database and direct it to a range within the current worksheet. In the final example, you will see how to print groups of database records, with each group placed on a separate page. The last example also shows you how to use database statistical functions with the reporting feature.

Printing the Entire Database

To print the entire Priority database, you must be familiar with two Report ranges: the Above and Main ranges. Symphony sets up both ranges automatically when you use the Generate command to create a database in a FORM window.

The Above Report Range

To access the Above range (and all the other Report ranges), select the Report option from the FORM Settings command menu. Then you must select one of four options: Main, Above, Below, or Type.

Figure 15.38A shows the FORM Settings sheet, and figure 15.38B highlights the Above range for the Priority database. As you can see, the Above range contains the same field-name headings as the Database and Criterion ranges. Symphony uses these field names for the column headings of the report. Symphony will print at the top of the database report, however, any text you put in the Above range. You can also use the SHEET Move and Insert commands to create an Above range that is deeper than one line. This feature is particularly useful for creating report titles.

The Main Report Range

The Main range is contained in the single row directly below the Above range in the spreadsheet (A27..G27) and is called PRIORITY_MA. This range contains the cells that are to be printed once for each record in the database report. If you locate the cursor on the values in the range, you can see that they refer to the fields in the first record of the Database range. For example, cell A27 contains +ORDER NUMBER.

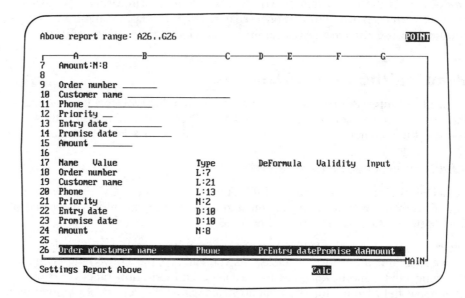

Fig. 15.38A

The FORM Settings sheet.

Fig. 15.38B

The Above range highlighted.

The final step before you use the SERVICES **Print** command is to enter selection criteria in the Criterion range. (Recall that you use the **Criteria Edit** command to enter selection criteria in a FORM window.) To print all the records in the database, make sure that you use the **Criteria Edit** command to delete any criterion records from the Criterion range.

Directing the Report to the Printer

To direct this report to the printer, select the SERVICES **Print Settings** command. The **Source** setting should be **Database**. When you select **Database**, you must tell Symphony which FORM **Settings** sheet to use. For this example, suppose that the name of the settings sheet is PRIORITY. Figure 15.39 shows the **Print Settings** with the **S**ource set to **D**atabase PRIORITY. The final step is to select **G**o from the SERVICES **P**rint menu. Symphony then produces the database report, a portion of which appears in figure 15.40.

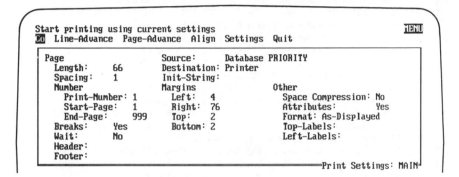

```
Start printing using current settings                              MENU
GO  Line-Advance  Page-Advance  Align  Settings  Quit

   Page                  Source:       Database PRIORITY
     Length:     66       Destination: Printer
     Spacing:    1        Init-String:
   Number                 Margins                Other
     Print-Number: 1        Left:   4              Space Compression: No
     Start-Page:   1        Right:  76             Attributes:        Yes
     End-Page:     999      Top:    2              Format: As-Displayed
   Breaks:       Yes        Bottom: 2              Top-Labels:
   Wait:         No                                Left-Labels:
   Header:
   Footer:
                                              Print Settings: MAIN
```

Fig. 15.39

The Print Settings sheet with the Source set to Database PRIORITY.

Notice that the column widths in the report appear just as they do in the database. To change the column widths in the printed report, you must also change the column widths of the database. Another alternative is to direct the report to a range in the spreadsheet with the column widths you like, and then print directly from that range.

Printing a Portion of a Database to a Range

If you want to print just a portion of a database, you must modify the Criterion range to select only the records you want. For example, suppose that you want to print all the records in the database whose "Amount" field is greater than $10,000. Use the FORM **C**riteria **E**dit command to enter +?>**10000** in the "Amount" field. Press PgUp and then issue the **C**riteria **U**se command to get the appropriate records.

Once you have entered the selection criteria, suppose that you want to direct the output to a range rather than the printer. In this case, set the SERVICES **P**rint **S**ettings **D**estination to **R**ange and enter an appropriate range. Figure 15.41 shows how the spreadsheet appears when the database report has been directed to a range. Notice that the results are long labels.

Creating Database Subtotals

Symphony gives you a way to create subtotals by using the database report feature with the database statistical function @DSUM. For example, suppose that you want to create a report with a separate page presenting each group of records for each priority in the Priority database. You also want the total dollar amount for each priority.

```
    Order nCustomer name        Phone        PrEntry datePromise daAmount
    PO1438 Quadram Corp         404-923-6666 1 25-Jul-88 25-Aug-88   42100
    PO1441 Tecmar Inc.          216-464-7410 1 28-Jul-88 28-Aug-88   51000
    PO1435 Amdek Corporation    312-364-1180 1 23-Jul-88 23-Aug-88   23000
    PO1436 AST Research Inc.    714-540-1333 1 24-Jul-88 24-Aug-88   34000
    PO1446 Hayes Microcomputer  404-449-8791 1 03-Aug-88 03-Sep-88   19800
    PO1440 Seattle Computer     800-426-8936 2 27-Jul-88 27-Aug-88   24500
    PO1453 Indigo Data Systems  713-488-8186 2 10-Aug-88 10-Sep-88    3290
    PO1450 IDE Associates       617-275-4430 2 07-Aug-88 07-Sep-88    2180
    PO1445 Maynard Electronics  305-331-6402 2 03-Aug-88 03-Sep-88   23500
    PO1437 Hercules Computer    415-654-2476 2 24-Jul-88 24-Aug-88   12000
    PO1444 Orchid Technology    408-942-8660 3 01-Aug-88 01-Sep-88    4520
    PO1452 Arby Corporation     617-864-5058 3 09-Aug-88 09-Sep-88    7892
    PO1439 Raytronics           800-854-1085 3 26-Jul-88 26-Aug-88   12200
    PO1448 Data Technology Corp 408-496-0434 3 05-Aug-88 05-Sep-88    7890
    PO1442 Qubie' Distributing  800-821-4479 4 30-Apr-88 30-May-88   11330
    PO1443 Micro Graphics Tech  408-996-8423 4 31-Jul-88 31-Aug-88    8190
    PO1451 MBI                  303-279-4628 4 08-Aug-88 08-Sep-88    2300
    PO1449 Super Computer, Inc. 714-540-1880 4 06-Aug-88 06-Sep-88    6538
    PO1447 Apparat, Inc.        303-741-1778 4 04-Aug-88 04-Sep-88    3100
    PO1448 STR Corporation      408-665-7893 4 03-Aug-88 02-Sep-88    5600
    PO1449 New York Systems     800-321-6745 4 03-Aug-88 02-Sep-88   21000
    PO1450 Ashe Electronics     317-665-8734 4 06-Aug-88 05-Sep-88    3670
    PO1451 Northwestern Data    412-436-9876 4 09-Aug-88 08-Sep-88    1295
    PO1452 Micro Labs           617-864-2321 4 12-Aug-88 11-Sep-88   10200
    PO1453 DataServe Inc.       714-553-6584 4 15-Aug-88 14-Sep-88    4500
    PO1454 Alton Industries     305-221-0976 4 18-Aug-88 17-Sep-88    3700
    PO1455 SPE                  800-999-3232 5 21-Aug-88 20-Sep-88   11700
    PO1456 Orange Computer      713-432-5643 5 24-Aug-88 23-Sep-88    5420
    PO1457 HAL Technology       317-882-7432 5 27-Aug-88 26-Sep-88    6000
    PO1458 Midwest Systems      317-456-9087 5 30-Aug-88 29-Sep-88    2400
    PO1459 Magnum Corporation   305-972-3456 5 02-Sep-88 02-Oct-88    7200
    PO1460 Romar Industries     412-665-4323 5 05-Sep-88 05-Oct-88    8200
    PO1461 Neville Electronics  303-884-2123 5 08-Sep-88 08-Oct-88    3700
    PO1462 McKee, Inc.          714-908-4632 5 11-Sep-88 11-Oct-88    7050
    PO1463 STR Communications   800-233-4126 5 14-Sep-88 14-Oct-88    4250
    PO1464 Easterwood, Inc.     713-921-7834 5 17-Sep-88 17-Oct-88    4300
    PO1465 Data Control         408-231-0503 5 20-Sep-88 20-Oct-88    6200
    PO1466 Becker Corporation   415-885-9193 5 23-Sep-88 23-Oct-88    4900
```

Up to this point, the two database report examples have required only a single pass through the database. Therefore, the FORM Settings Report Type command has been left at Single, the default setting. When you want to produce subtotals (or any other database statistics), however, you need to set the Report Type to Multiple. (Familiarity with the SHEET Range What-If command is helpful for understanding this example; see Chapter 4 for a discussion of this command.)

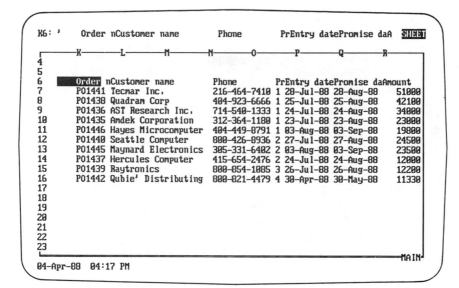

Fig. 15.41

Printing the database to a range.

Before you can set the report type to **Multiple**, you need to switch to the SHEET environment and build a small table of input values (what Symphony calls an Entry list) in an out-of-the-way area of the spreadsheet. Symphony will substitute the values in the Entry list into the Criterion range to produce subtotals for each priority. For example, you can use the **Range Fill** command to enter the values in cells C1..C4 in figure 15.42.

When you issue the **Settings Report Type Multiple** command, Symphony asks for the address of the Entry list you have created. For this example, type **C1..C4**. Symphony then asks for an Input cell, which is the cell where you want Symphony to substitute the values in the Entry list. You want to have Symphony substitute the values into the Priority column of the Criterion range, so enter cell **D33**.

At this point, you have almost all the settings for producing separate report pages. But you still need to enter the @DSUM function for printing subtotals. To enter the @DSUM function in the proper location, you need to know about the Below range.

The Below Report Range

The Below range, the final **Settings Report** range, is used to enter information at the end of a report. The Below range must be located directly below the Main range in the spreadsheet. When you create a database with the **Generate** command, Symphony automatically provides enough room to enter a Below range that is one row deep. Symphony does not, however, set up the address of this range; you must do that.

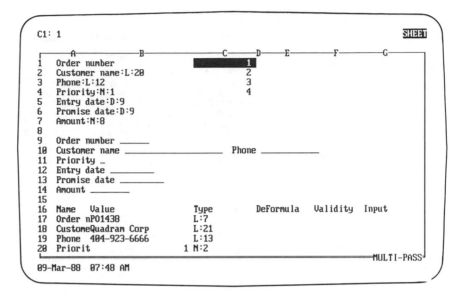

Fig. 15.42

Creating an Entry list (C1..C4).

Before you enter the address of the Below range, first decide how you want the bottom of the report to look. As you did for the Above range, you can use the SHEET **M**ove and **I**nsert commands to create a Below range that is deeper than one row. Suppose that you want a series of hyphens across the bottom of the report, with the subtotals below the hyphens. Figure 15.43 shows how the Below range (A28..G30) must appear.

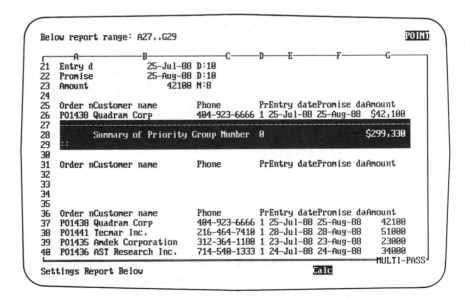

Fig. 15.43

A sample Below range.

The @DSUM function appears in cell G29. The actual function is

@DSUM(PRIORITY_DB,6,PRIORITY_CR)

The formula for cell D29 is +D33. Also, notice that the third line of the Below range contains the page-marker characters (::). To enter the marker in the Above range, shift to the DOC environment and enter the **P**age command.

Now that you have set the ranges (Above, Main, Below, and Entry), you must switch back to the FORM environment and enter the **P**rint command. The **S**ource for the reports is again **D**atabase, but this time the **D**estination is a **F**ile called MULTIPAS.PRN. Figure 15.44 shows how the report appears when you print MULTIPAS.PRN.

```
Order nCustomer name        Phone         PrEntry datePromise daAmount
PO1438 Quadram Corp         404-923-6666 1 25-Jul-88 25-Aug-88  $42,100
PO1441 Tecmar Inc.          216-464-7410 1 25-Jul-88 25-Aug-88  $51,000
PO1435 Amdek Corporation    312-364-1180 1 25-Jul-88 25-Aug-88  $23,000
PO1436 AST Research Inc.    714-540-1333 1 25-Jul-88 25-Aug-88  $34,000
PO1446 Hayes Microcomputer  404-449-8791 1 25-Jul-88 25-Aug-88  $19,800
--------------------------------------------------------------------
       Summary of Priority Group Number  1                     $169,900
```

Fig. 15.44

Printing separate pages with database subtotals.

```
Order nCustomer name        Phone         PrEntry datePromise daAmount
PO1440 Seattle Computer     800-426-8936 2 25-Jul-88 25-Aug-88  $24,500
PO1453 Indigo Data Systems  713-488-8186 2 25-Jul-88 25-Aug-88   $3,290
PO1450 IDE Associates       617-275-4430 2 25-Jul-88 25-Aug-88   $2,180
PO1445 Maynard Electronics  305-331-6402 2 25-Jul-88 25-Aug-88  $23,500
PO1437 Hercules Computer    415-654-2476 2 25-Jul-88 25-Aug-88  $12,000
--------------------------------------------------------------------
       Summary of Priority Group Number  2                      $65,470
```

Notice that the "Amount" field appears in the **C**urrency **0** format. To control the format of the display, simply change the format of the cells in the Main range. You may then need to widen the Amount column. If you see asterisks in the cell, select the SHEET **W**idth **S**et command.

Printing Mailing Labels

Printing mailing labels is simple once you are familiar with the basics of generating database reports. A good database for showing how to print mailing labels is the database of names and addresses that appears at the beginning of the chapter (see fig. 15.1).

To print mailing labels, you must change the position and contents of the Main range. The first step is to shift to the SHEET environment and go to an out-of-the-way area of the worksheet. Then enter the following formulas in three consecutive cells down a column, for example in K1..K3:

```
+FIRST&" "&LAST
+ADDRESS
+CITY&", "&STATE&" "&ZIP
```

As an alternative, instead of entering the preceding formulas, you can shift to a DOC environment and enter these lines:

```
&FIRST& &LAST&
&ADDRESS&
&CITY&, &STATE& &ZIP&
```

This slightly different structure is more in keeping with standard mail-merging conventions in which each field name is enclosed by ampersands and automatically concatenated.

The next step is to cancel the current Report ranges from the settings sheet, because Above and Below ranges are not needed. Switch back to the FORM window and select **Settings Cancel Report**. Enter the **Settings Report Main** command to designate the Main range. To print one-inch labels, you must include three blank lines below cell K3 (assuming you have six lines for each one-inch mailing label). Therefore, the Main range is K1..K6. Finally, to print labels, designate the SERVICES **Print Settings Source** as **Database** and the **Destination** as **Printer**. Figure 15.45 shows the results.

As a simple exercise to test your understanding of printing database reports, see if you can figure out how to print mailing labels by ZIP code. Hint: You need to use the **Multiple** pass option.

Printing a Form Letter

A final demonstration of Symphony's capability to print database reports is the form letter. Suppose that you are again dealing with the Priority database, and you want to send a letter to all the customers in the database whose records have been entered on or after August 7, 1988. An example of the letter follows:

Dear IDE Associates:

We are pleased to receive your order and have entered it as PO1450. Please use this number when you contact us about the status of your order. As promised, you should receive your chips on

09/07/88

Shamim Ahmad
Weatherly Street
Cincinnati, OH 45243

James F. Cotter
1003 Tulip Tree House
Belle Mead, NJ 13120

Michael Englert
224 Greenup St.
Newport, KY 11166

Edward Harding
2400 Central Parkway
New York, NY 02934

James T. Harrington
238 High St.
Boston, MA 02116

Earl Holland
3712 Drake Road
Columbus, OH 43987

Karen Kuehnle
9980 Yale Ave.
New Haven, CT 06785

David J. Owen
612 Knight Ridge Road
Baltimore, MD 34523

Fritz W. Schumann
100 E. Miller Dr.
Providence, RI 12344

Sarah Sharpe
7897 Providence St.
Miami, FL 61998

William L. Sikes
3751 Clifton Ave.
Nashville, TN 42378

Jeremy Simpson
3509 Ludlow Ave.
Las Cruces, NM 72814

Betty Stone
700 Vine St.
Dallas, TX 64824

Chuck Timmerman
7900 Castleway Drive
Indianapolis, IN 53747

John Tuke
531 Remington Road
Chicago, IL 85677

Patrick Yeager
4237 Mariemont Ave.
Des Moines, IA 63457

Steven Zakon
3549 Keene St.
Bangor, ME 12392

Mathew Zealear
2909 Fresno St.
Fresno, CA 43645

Fig. 15.45

Printing mailing labels.

If the status of your order changes, we will phone you at 617-275-4430. Please inform us if this number is not the correct number.

Sincerely,

Tom Perkins

The first step for producing this form letter is to enter its contents in an out-of-the-way area of the spreadsheet (or create a DOC window). To produce the preceding letter, move the cursor down to cell A200, switch to the DOC environment, and type the letter. Where you need variable information from the database, type the relevant field name enclosed by ampersands (&). Here is how the form letter should look:

Dear &CUSTOMER NAME&:

We are pleased to receive your order and have entered it as &ORDER NUMBER&. Please use this number when you contact us about the status of your order. As promised, you should receive your chips on

&PROMISE DATE&

If the status of your order changes, we will phone you at &PHONE&. Please inform us if this number is not the correct number.

Sincerely,

Tom Perkins

|::

Notice the page break (|::) at the end of the letter, which ensures that each letter is printed on a new page.

After entering the contents of the letter, you must designate the selection criteria for the records whose entry date is on or after August 7, 1988. Figure 15.46 shows the Criterion range (A29..G30) and the formula in the "Entry date" column.

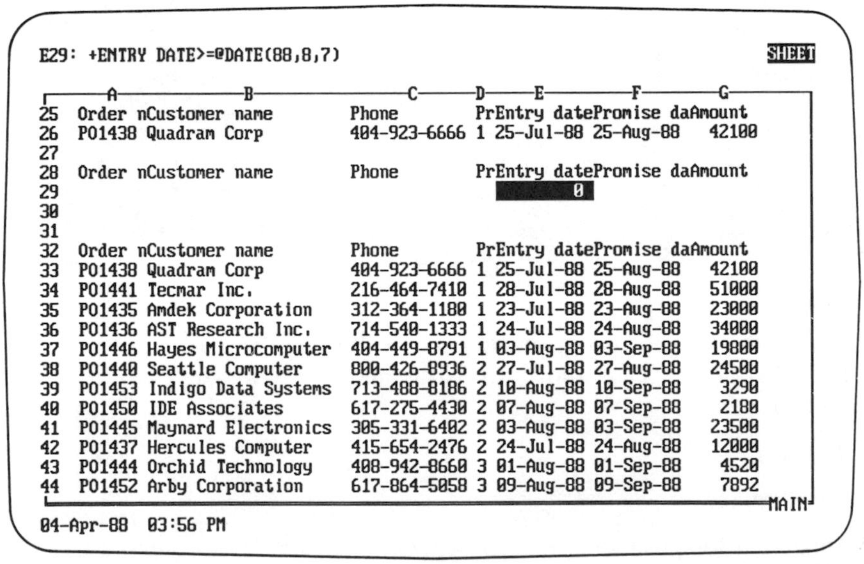

Fig. 15.46

The ENTRY DATE formula in the Criterion range.

```
E29: +ENTRY DATE>=@DATE(88,8,7)                                       SHEET

     ┌──A──────────B──────────────C──────D────E────────F────────G──────
     25  Order nCustomer name    Phone        PrEntry datePromise daAmount
     26  PO1438 Quadram Corp     404-923-6666 1 25-Jul-88 25-Aug-88   42100
     27
     28  Order nCustomer name    Phone        PrEntry datePromise daAmount
     29                                                    0
     30
     31
     32  Order nCustomer name    Phone        PrEntry datePromise daAmount
     33  PO1438 Quadram Corp     404-923-6666 1 25-Jul-88 25-Aug-88   42100
     34  PO1441 Tecmar Inc.      216-464-7410 1 28-Jul-88 28-Aug-88   51000
     35  PO1435 Amdek Corporation 312-364-1180 1 23-Jul-88 23-Aug-88  23000
     36  PO1436 AST Research Inc. 714-540-1333 1 24-Jul-88 24-Aug-88  34000
     37  PO1446 Hayes Microcomputer 404-449-8791 1 03-Aug-88 03-Sep-88 19000
     38  PO1440 Seattle Computer 800-426-8936 2 27-Jul-88 27-Aug-88   24500
     39  PO1453 Indigo Data Systems 713-488-8186 2 10-Aug-88 10-Sep-88 3290
     40  PO1450 IDE Associates   617-275-4430 2 07-Aug-88 07-Sep-88    2180
     41  PO1445 Maynard Electronics 305-331-6402 2 03-Aug-88 03-Sep-88 23500
     42  PO1437 Hercules Computer 415-654-2476 2 24-Jul-88 24-Aug-88  12000
     43  PO1444 Orchid Technology 408-942-8660 3 01-Aug-88 01-Sep-88   4520
     44  PO1452 Arby Corporation 617-864-5050 3 09-Aug-88 09-Sep-88    7892
     └                                                              MAIN
     04-Apr-88  03:56 PM
```

```
 ┌─────────────────────────────────────────────────────────────────┐
 │ Define ranges for database report                          MENU   │
 │ Basic  Form  Underscores  Sort-Keys  Report  One-Record  Name  Cancel  Quit │
 │ ┌─────────────────────────────────────────────────────────────┐ │
 │ │ Basic Ranges                        Report Ranges             │ │
 │ │   Database:      PRIORITY_DB           Main:      A200..I215   │ │
 │ │   Criterion:     PRIORITY_CR           Above:                  │ │
 │ │   Output:                              Below:                  │ │
 │ │ Form Ranges                            Type       Single       │ │
 │ │   Entry:         PRIORITY_EN            Entry list:            │ │
 │ │   Definition:    PRIORITY_DF            Input cell:           │ │
 │ │ Underscores:     Yes                 One-Record:   No          │ │
 │ │ Sort-Keys                                                     │ │
 │ │   1st-Key:            2nd-Key:              3rd-Key:          │ │
 │ │    Order:             Order:               Order:           │ │
 │ │                                  Database Settings: PRIORITY │ │
 │ └─────────────────────────────────────────────────────────────┘ │
 └─────────────────────────────────────────────────────────────────┘
```

Fig. 15.47

The settings sheet for printing the sample form letter.

The final step before using the **Print** command is to designate the Main range, A200..I215 for this example. This choice allows for the longest lines in the letter. If you choose a range that is narrower, say A200..C215, the lines will be truncated when you print the letter.

Figure 15.47 shows the settings sheet for printing the letter. Notice that the Above and Below ranges are left blank in this example.

If you want to send the letter directly to the printer, select (from the **Print** menu) **Printer** as the **Destination** and **Database** as the **Source**.

Chapter Summary

In this chapter, you have seen how to use Symphony's FORM window, database commands in the SHEET environment, and database statistical functions. You have also seen a demonstration of Symphony's special report-generating capabilities, which are a part of the FORM environment. In the next chapter, you will practice many of the database operations you saw in this chapter. In Chapter 20, you will find some examples of how to use the Symphony Command Language to help you build input forms and perform other FORM window operations.

16

Data Management Hands-On Practice

The previous chapter led you through the many different aspects of Symphony's data management: creating and modifying a database, sorting, searching, using database statistical functions, and producing reports. This hands-on practice session concentrates on data-management basics to get you up and running quickly. You will generate a database, enter data, sort the data, locate records according to different search criteria, and produce simple reports.

Figure 16.1 shows a sample data-entry form for the database you will be creating. This database tracks information about sales people for a company with regional sales divisions.

Creating the Database

Although FORM mode is Symphony's data-management environment, which you use to generate the database, you must first type your field names, types, and lengths in a SHEET or DOC window. To begin creating the database you will use for this practice session, follow these steps:

1. Load the Symphony program. A blank worksheet should be displayed, and you should be in SHEET mode.

2. Refer to figure 16.2 and enter the following labels:

In cell:	Enter:
A1	LAST NAME:L:15
A2	FIRST NAME:L:15

515

Fig. 16.1

A data-entry form.

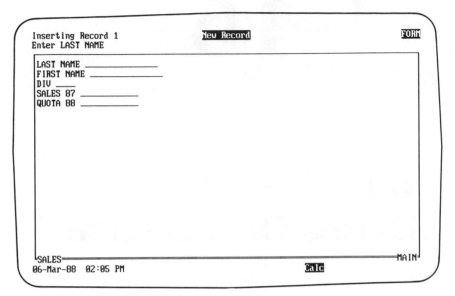

A3   DIV:L:4
A4   SALES 87:N:12
A5   QUOTA 88:C:12

Fig. 16.2

Typing the field names for the input form.

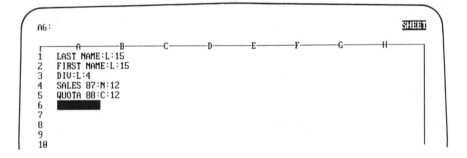

Now that you have entered the field names in the spreadsheet, Symphony's FORM environment takes over to generate the database and all the special database ranges.

1. Press the Type key (Alt-F10) and select **FORM**.

   Note: The message No Definition range defined displays in the control panel. Disregard this message; it will disappear as soon as you generate the database.

2. Select FORM **Generate**.

3. Choose **Label** as the default field type. (In this example, your choice doesn't really matter, because you specified the types for each field in the spreadsheet.)

4. Press Enter to accept the default field length. Again, what you choose doesn't matter, because you already indicated the specific lengths.

5. Enter **SALES** as the name for the Database settings sheet.

6. Specify the field-name range as **A1..A5**. Symphony instantly creates and displays the input form (see fig. 16.1).

As soon as you have an input form, you can begin entering data. Enter one record into the database.

1. Type **Peterson** in the LAST NAME field and press Enter.

2. Enter **Stewart** in the FIRST NAME field.

3. Enter **NE** (for Northeast) in the DIV field.

4. Enter **310000** in the SALES 87 field. Your screen should look like figure 16.3.

    Note: The cursor skipped past the QUOTA 88 field because you designated that field as computed (C). You will enter the formula for this computed field later.

```
Inserting Record 1            New Record                          FORM
Enter LAST NAME

 LAST NAME Peterson_____
 FIRST NAME Stewart_____
 DIV NE__
 SALES 87 310000_____
 QUOTA 88 _____
```

Fig. 16.3

Entering a new record.

5. Press the Ins key to insert the record. A blank data-entry form then appears.

It's a good idea to save the file after you have generated the database.

1. Select SERVICES File Save.

2. Enter **SALES** as the file name.

Viewing the Database Ranges

Symphony created several special database ranges in the spreadsheet when you issued the **Generate** command. Let's look at these ranges now.

1. Press the Switch key (Alt-F9) to return to SHEET mode. Look at everything Symphony created with the **Generate** command!

2. Press Alt-F9 to switch back to FORM mode.

3. Select FORM **Settings** to display the Database settings sheet, as shown in figure 16.4. Let's look at the Basic and Form ranges, one by one. Notice the range names (such as SALES_DB) that appear next to each range in the settings sheet. Symphony created these range names when generating the database.

Fig. 16.4

*The Database
settings sheet.*

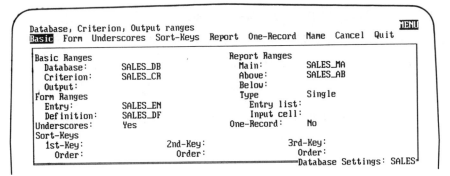

```
Database, Criterion, Output ranges                                    MENU
Basic  Form  Underscores  Sort-Keys   Report  One-Record  Name  Cancel  Quit

Basic Ranges                              Report Ranges
   Database:        SALES_DB                 Main:        SALES_MA
   Criterion:       SALES_CR                 Above:       SALES_AB
   Output:                                   Below:
Form Ranges                                  Type         Single
   Entry:           SALES_EN                   Entry list:
   Definition:      SALES_DF                    Input cell:
Underscores:        Yes                      One-Record:  No
Sort-Keys
   1st-Key:                    2nd-Key:                  3rd-Key:
    Order:                      Order:                    Order:
                                                  Database Settings: SALES
```

4. Select **Basic Database**. The Database range (SALES_DB or A28..E29) holds all the database records. Right now, you have only one record, but as you input more records, Symphony enters them into this range in the spreadsheet.

5. Press Enter to accept this range.

6. Select **Criterion**. The Criterion range (SALES_CR or A23..E24) is where selection criteria is entered when you search for a record or want a list of only certain records in the database.

7. Press Enter to accept this range.

8. Select **Quit Form Entry**. The Entry range (SALES_EN or A1..A7) should look familiar to you. This range holds the input form that you use for data entry.

9. Press Enter.

10. Select **Definition**. The Definition range (SALES_DF, or A14..H18) is where you will enter the formula for the computed field (QUOTA 88)

and where you can enter formats for date and numeric fields and indicate other special settings for the input form.

11. Press Enter.

12. Select **Quit Quit**.

Entering Formulas

As mentioned previously, QUOTA 88 is a computed field. Though you specified a computed field type when you generated the database, you haven't yet entered the formula. The 1988 quota should be 110 percent of the 1987 sales. You must enter this formula in the Definition range.

1. Switch to SHEET mode.

2. Go to the Definition range by pressing the GoTo key (F5) and entering **SALES_DF**.

3. Move the cell pointer to the Formula column in the QUOTA 88 row (cell E18), as shown in figure 16.5.

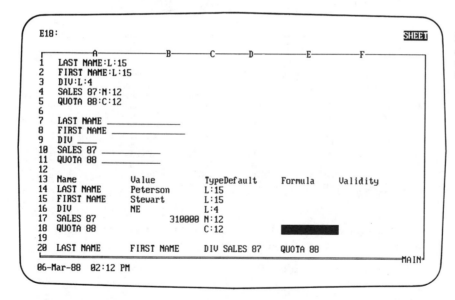

```
E18:                                                            SHEET
        A          B          C         D         E         F
 1   LAST NAME:L:15
 2   FIRST NAME:L:15
 3   DIV:L:4
 4   SALES 87:N:12
 5   QUOTA 88:C:12
 6
 7   LAST NAME  _____
 8   FIRST NAME _____
 9   DIV  ____
10   SALES 87 _____
11   QUOTA 88 _____
12
13   Name          Value          TypeDefault    Formula      Validity
14   LAST NAME     Peterson       L:15
15   FIRST NAME    Stewart        L:15
16   DIV           NE             L:4
17   SALES 87            310000   N:12
18   QUOTA 88                     C:12          ████████████
19
20   LAST NAME     FIRST NAME     DIV SALES 87   QUOTA 88
                                                            MAIN
06-Mar-88  02:12 PM
```

Fig. 16.5

Entering a formula in the Definition range.

4. Enter the formula **+B17*110%**.

   Note: Formulas always refer to cells in the Value column (column B).

5. Switch back to FORM mode.

Because you entered the first record before writing the formula, you need to recalculate the record. Record 1 should be displayed, so simply press the Calc key (F8). The figure 341000 appears in the QUOTA 88 field.

Entering Records

Enter a record and see how the quota is automatically calculated once you enter the 1987 sales.

1. Press PgDn to display a blank form.

2. Type **Jones** in the LAST NAME field and press Enter.

3. Enter **Robert** in the FIRST NAME field.

4. Enter **NW** (for Northwest) in the DIV field.

5. Enter **300000** in the SALES 87 field. Symphony automatically calculates QUOTA 88 and displays 330000 in that field.

6. Press Ins to insert the record.

Refer to figure 16.6 and enter the remaining records.

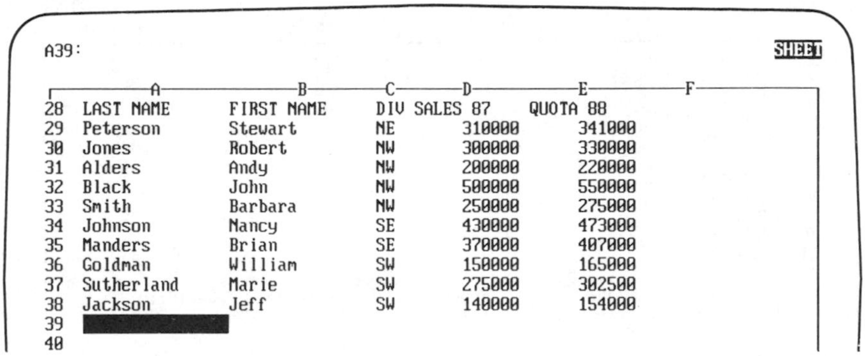

Fig. 16.6

The database records.

```
A39:                                                         SHEET
        ┌────A─────────B────────C───D──────────E─────────F───
     28 LAST NAME    FIRST NAME  DIV SALES 87   QUOTA 88
     29 Peterson     Stewart     NE     310000    341000
     30 Jones        Robert      NW     300000    330000
     31 Alders       Andy        NW     200000    220000
     32 Black        John        NW     500000    550000
     33 Smith        Barbara     NW     250000    275000
     34 Johnson      Nancy       SE     430000    473000
     35 Manders      Brian       SE     370000    407000
     36 Goldman      William     SW     150000    165000
     37 Sutherland   Marie       SW     275000    302500
     38 Jackson      Jeff        SW     140000    154000
     39 ████████████
     40
```

1. Type each row in figure 16.6 on a separate form. Remember to use the Ins key to insert the record.

2. Save and replace the file.

Maintaining the Database

Once you have generated a database and entered data into it, you need to keep the database accurate and up-to-date. At times, you will want to locate specific records so that you can edit the data or look up information. Having the data sorted in a meaningful order helps you organize and find information.

Sorting the Data

If you have ever had to sort anything manually, you know how tedious the process is. Fortunately, the computer is a star when it comes to sorting.

Sorting in Symphony is a two-step process. First, you must specify your sort key (the field by which you want to sort) in the settings sheet. Second, you must tell Symphony to perform the record sort.

Sort the SALES database by LAST NAME.

1. Select FORM Settings Sort-Keys 1st-Key. The screen temporarily switches to SHEET mode, and the cell pointer is sitting within the Database range.

2. Point to cell A28 in the LAST NAME column and press Enter.

3. Type **A** for Ascending order. As shown on your screen and in figure 16.7, the LAST NAME field is entered as the 1st-Key in the settings sheet.

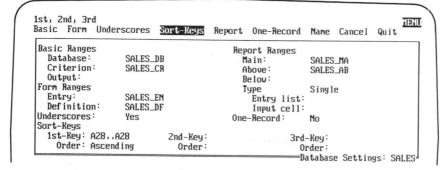

Fig. 16.7

The settings sheet with 1st-Key specified.

4. Select FORM Record-Sort All to sort all the records.

Browse through the records and notice how they are now arranged alphabetically.

1. Press Home to go to the first record.

2. Press PgDn and PgUp to look at the records.

3. Press End to go to the last record.

Finding a Record

If you have dozens, hundreds, or thousands of records in your database, you will need a faster way of going to a specific record than the PgDn and PgUp keys, even if the database is sorted. The **Criteria** command gives you that speed. You enter in a criterion record what you are seeking, and Symphony displays this record for you. You can then look up or update information in the record.

Because the SALES database is small (we knew you didn't want to type more than 10 records), you won't need to use the **Criteria** command to locate a record. But you can still get an idea of how this command would work on a larger database.

Use the **Criteria** command to look up Smith's 1988 quota.

1. Select FORM **Criteria** Edit. A blank criterion record displays.

2. Next to the LAST NAME field, enter **Smith** (see fig. 16.8).

Fig. 16.8

*Entering criteria in
a criterion record.*

```
Editing Criterion Record 1 of 1                          EDIT
Enter LAST NAME

LAST NAME Smith_____
FIRST NAME _____
DIV ____
SALES 87 _____
QUOTA 88 _____
```

3. Press PgUp to go back to the database.

4. Select FORM **Criteria** Use to invoke the criteria. The record for Smith displays. What is her quota?

The message (1 Match) displays in the control panel. This message tells you that only one record matches your search criteria. In other words, only one Smith is located in the database.

When a **Criteria** is in Use, as it is now, you can look only at the selected record or records. If you want to be able to view the entire database again, you must tell Symphony to **Ignore** the criteria.

1. Select FORM **Criteria** Ignore. Note that the (Match 1) message in the control panel has disappeared.

2. Press PgUp and PgDn to confirm that your entire database is now accessible.

In the previous example, you knew exactly how Smith was spelled, so you had no trouble locating the record. Sometimes, though, you may not be sure of the spelling. In that case, you would use a wildcard to help you locate the record. Let's say that you want to look up information for a salesperson whose name begins with a *J*.

1. Select FORM **Criteria Edit**. Notice that your last search criteria (Smith) is still there. You can type right over this criteria.

2. Next to the LAST NAME field, enter **J***. The asterisk is a wildcard that tells Symphony to accept all characters that follow the *.

3. Press PgUp.

4. Select FORM **Criteria Use**. The first record that matches the criteria appears on-screen, and the control panel displays the message (Match 1 of 3), as shown in figure 16.9.

5. Press PgDn to look at the three records.

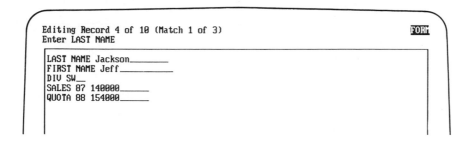

```
Editing Record 4 of 10 (Match 1 of 3)                         FORM
Enter LAST NAME

 LAST NAME Jackson_____
 FIRST NAME Jeff_____
 DIV SW__
 SALES 87 140000_____
 QUOTA 88 154000_____
```

Fig. 16.9

The first record that meets the criteria.

Deleting a Record

Jackson was the record you wanted to find. His 1987 sales were so bad, you want to fire him. Delete him from your database.

1. Press PgUp or PgDn to display Jackson's record. You can see how poor his 1987 sales were.

2. Press the Del key to delete the record.

3. Select **Yes** to confirm your intention.

Once you have deleted a record, it is gone forever.

Editing a Record

Editing a record in FORM mode is similar to editing a cell in SHEET mode. You can replace what is in the field by typing over the data, or you can use the Edit key (F2) to modify the contents.

Correct Johnson's last name to Johanson.

1. If necessary, press PgUp or PgDn to display Johnson's record.

2. With the cursor in the LAST NAME field, press the Edit key (F2).

3. Press the right-arrow key until the cursor is on the first n.

4. Type **a**. The record should look like figure 16.10.

5. Press Enter.

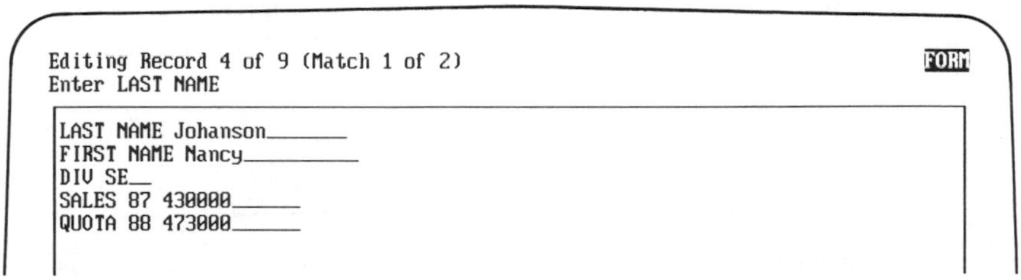

Fig. 16.10

After editing a
criterion record.

```
Editing Record 4 of 9 (Match 1 of 2)                          FORM
Enter LAST NAME

LAST NAME Johanson_____
FIRST NAME Nancy_____
DIV SE__
SALES 87 430000_____
QUOTA 88 473000_____
```

Creating Reports

To print a database report in Symphony, you specify the **Database** (not a **Range**) as the **Source**. The report will print in whatever order the database is currently sorted, using the criteria currently specified.

Printing the Default Report

Print the report that Symphony automatically set up for you when you generated the database. The default report will print all fields with the field names above each column.

Reports use the last criteria entered. Because you want the entire database to print, delete the criterion record before printing.

1. Select FORM **C**riteria **E**dit to display the criterion record.

2. Press the Del key to delete the record.

3. Select **Y**es to confirm.

4. Press PgUp.

Print the report.

1. Select SERVICES **P**rint **S**ettings **S**ource **D**atabase **SALES**.

2. Select **Q**uit to exit the **S**ettings menu.

3. Select **A**lign **G**o to print. Your report should look similar to figure 16.11.

4. Select **P**age to feed the paper out of the printer. (Some printers may require an additional **P**age before you can tear off the sheet.)

5. Select **Quit**.

28	LAST NAME	FIRST NAME	DIV	SALES 87	QUOTA 88
29	Alders	Andy	NW	200000	220000
30	Black	John	NW	500000	550000
31	Goldman	William	SW	150000	165000
32	Johanson	Nancy	SE	430000	473000
33	Jones	Robert	NW	300000	330000
34	Manders	Brian	SE	370000	407000
35	Peterson	Stewart	NE	310000	341000
36	Smith	Barbara	NW	250000	275000
37	Sutherland	Marie	SW	275000	302500

Fig. 16.11

The printed report.

Modifying the Report

To modify the report, you need to be familiar with the Report ranges Symphony automatically set up when it generated the database. The Above Report range (SALES_AB) consists of the report column headings, which by default are simply the field names. You edit this range if you want to change the content or alignment of the column headings. The Main Report range (SALES_MA) prints once for each record in the database. Each cell in this range references the appropriate field in the database. If you want to format the data in the report, this range is the one to change.

The report would look better if the numbers had commas and if the column headings above the numbers were aligned on the right. Format the numbers in the Main range to the **P**unctuated format.

1. Press Alt-F9 to switch to SHEET mode.

2. Press the GoTo key (F5) and enter **SALES_MA**.

3. Move the cell pointer to cell D21.

4. Select SHEET **F**ormat **P**unctuated.

5. Type **0** for the number of decimal places and press Enter.

6. Highlight the range D21..E21. Press Enter. Your screen should now look like figure 16.12.

The Above range is directly above the Main range. Right-align the column headings over the numbers.

1. Move the cell pointer to the cell containing SALES 87, cell D20.

2. Select SHEET **R**ange **L**abel-Alignment **R**ight.

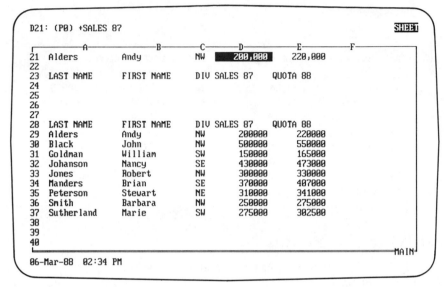

Fig. 16.12

Formatting data in the Main range.

3. Highlight the range D20..E20. Press Enter. Your screen should now resemble figure 16.13.

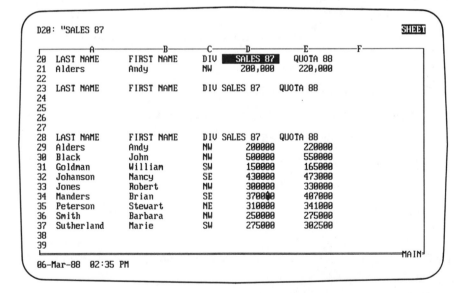

Fig. 16.13

Aligning labels in the Above range.

Print the report again. Symphony remembers that you have specified the **Database** as the **Source**.

1. Press Alt-F9 to switch back to FORM mode.

2. Select SERVICES **P**rint **G**o. Your report should look similar to figure 16.14.

	A	B	C	D	E	F
28	LAST NAME	FIRST NAME	DIV	SALES 87	QUOTA 88	
29	Alders	Andy	NW	200,000	220,000	
30	Black	John	NW	500,000	550,000	
31	Goldman	William	SW	150,000	165,000	
32	Johanson	Nancy	SE	430,000	473,000	
33	Jones	Robert	NW	300,000	330,000	
34	Manders	Brian	SE	370,000	407,000	
35	Peterson	Stewart	NE	310,000	341,000	
36	Smith	Barbara	NW	250,000	275,000	
37	Sutherland	Marie	SW	275,000	302,500	

Fig. 16.14

The printed results.

3. Select **P**age to feed the paper out of the printer. (Some printers may require an additional **P**age before you can tear off the sheet.)

Chapter Summary

In this hands-on practice session, you reviewed data-management basics in Symphony's FORM mode. You generated a database, entered data, sorted the data, located records according to different search criteria, and printed and modified simple reports.

Chapter 17 introduces you to Symphony's COMM environment for data communications.

PART VI

Symphony Communications Module

Includes

Communications

Communications Hands-On Practice

17

Communications

Because Symphony has the COMM window for data communications, you can use your personal computer for two-way communicating. For example, your personal computer can receive database information from a corporate mainframe or a minicomputer. You can also hook up to a time-sharing service to get the latest information on news, stocks, weather, and other current topics. Finally, you can link up with a friend's microcomputer to exchange Symphony models, information, or gossip.

Like many other functions in Symphony, the communications capability is surprisingly strong and rivals the power of many stand-alone packages. The program also has some weaknesses, however, of which you should be aware. For example, you cannot use Symphony's file-transferring capability in all situations; and unless you build macros to automate the process, sending and receiving messages between microcomputers can be slow and laborious. In general, though, you should be pleasantly surprised at the COMM window's power.

Symphony enables you to connect with many different kinds of computers; just follow the simple rules outlined in the next section, entitled "Guidelines for Successful Communications." The chapter then covers how to connect with an electronic bulletin board system so that you can copy public domain software programs. That section is followed by an explanation of how to communicate with another person's microcomputer if that person is also running Symphony. These discussions provide enough background to enable you to make good use of Symphony's communications environment.

Guidelines for Successful Communications

Symphony's COMM window is a powerful feature, but you can easily become discouraged with it if you run into early problems. The following guidelines give you some general background on Symphony's COMM window and let you know what you can expect from the program.

Modems and Acoustic Couplers

For successful communications through Symphony, you must have a modem or an acoustic coupler. (You can also connect two microcomputers with a serial cable, or you can hard-wire your computer to a mainframe or minicomputer, but these tasks are beyond the scope of this book.) A modem (MOdulator-DEModulator) is a device that converts digital signals in your computer into analog tones which travel over telephone lines. Modems can be external devices connecting the serial (RS-232) interface on your computer to a telephone cable, or they can be internal devices on a board that are directly connected to your computer and to a telephone line.

An acoustic coupler, which is another type of modem, requires that you place a standard telephone receiver in the rubber cradles of the coupler. Otherwise, acoustic couplers are hooked up like any other external modem. Because the most frequent problems with modems of either type are poor cable connections, take special precautions to make sure your connections are sound.

Asynchronous and Synchronous Transmission

A second important point is that Symphony supports *asynchronous communications transmission*. This term means that a clock in the computer is used to time the sampling of incoming data and the recording of the number of bits in each sample. The clock is set according to the transmission speed you specify (the baud rate or bits per second). In general, because the asynchronous transmission technique leaves most of the timing work up to the computer, this type of communication requires relatively inexpensive modems and is simple to use.

Most mainframe computers, however, use *synchronous communications transmission*. Under this kind of transmission, the modem provides a clock signal to detect the bits being received. A master-clock signal is also provided by the host computer to its attached modem. For purposes of timing, and for a variety of other reasons too complex to go into here, this type of transmission requires more complex and expensive modems.

What is the advantage of synchronous communications transmission? The major advantage is that you can transmit data faster. Usually low to medium speeds (0 to about 1200 baud) are associated with asynchronous transmission, while higher speeds (anything above 1200 baud) are achieved with synchronous transmission.

Perhaps in the future, Symphony will support synchronous communications transmission, but for now any computer with which you use Symphony to communicate must follow the asynchronous transmission method. Most systems designed to communicate with personal computers follow the asynchronous convention, so you should not have much trouble. You probably cannot communicate with a sophisticated mainframe, however, that is not normally used to communicate with microcomputers.

Protocol Methods

Symphony supports three different protocols for file transfer. *Protocol* is another name for the rules established for exchanging information between computers. A communications protocol is required to ensure that computers send and receive data accurately. You indicate the protocol method during program installation. Your choices are XMODEM/B and BLAST.

XMODEM protocol, developed by Ward Christensen, has become a standard in the microcomputer industry. When you are using Symphony's file-transfer capability, both computers must use XMODEM protocol.

B protocol is a special protocol that you can use with the CompuServe Information Service. Though CompuServe also supports XMODEM, the advantage to using B protocol is that file transfers are done completely through CompuServe. With XMODEM, you would have to tell both CompuServe *and Symphony* that you want to transfer a file. XMODEM and B protocols are offered as one selection in the Install program: XMODEM/B.

Symphony also supports BLAST protocol. If you are communicating with a mainframe that uses this protocol, you select this method. You cannot use BLAST to send files between two microcomputers.

Protocol Parameters

Once these specifics are clear to you, your next step for successful communications with Symphony is to make sure that you correctly set all the parameters for protocol. These parameters include baud rate, byte length, number of stop bits to be transmitted, and parity. Table 17.1 describes each parameter.

Normally, you don't have to worry about choosing the protocol parameters. They are usually specified by the computer you are trying to communicate with. A good general guideline, though, is always to match the two computers' settings for baud rate, byte length, stop bits, and parity.

Table 17.1
Protocol Parameters

Baud rate	Speed at which data is transmitted. Can vary between 0 and 9600, but most frequent settings are 300, 1200, and 2400.
Byte length	The number of bits (binary digits) to be transmitted in a byte. (Also called the word length.) Can be set to either 7 or 8 bits.
Stop bits	The number of bits following each data word. Asynchronous transmission usually requires the addition of stop bits. Choices are 1 or 2.
Parity	During parity checking, the individual On bits are added, and the total is an odd or even number. Choices are Odd, Even, or None.

Proper Driver Choice

The final step for successful communications is making sure that you have selected the proper driver set. The options you are given during installation are Hayes (and compatibles) and Popcom (and compatibles). If you don't have a Hayes or Popcom modem, check your modem's documentation to see if it is compatible with either of these brands. If so, you can make the appropriate selection.

Connection to a Bulletin Board System

One common use for a computer with a modem is to connect with an electronic bulletin board system (BBS). These electronic bulletin boards generally offer public domain software that you can download (copy) to your computer. Public domain software are programs (word processors, games, utilities, and so on) that are available to whoever wants them, free of charge. Sometimes you are requested to send the author a donation if you like the program, but payment is purely voluntary.

Most BBSs offer an electronic mail system through which you can send and receive messages from other BBS users, such as the World of Lotus or CompuServe. Thus, if you have a computer-related problem, you can leave a "help!" message; if you're lucky, a fellow computer guru will respond with a solution. This resource can be invaluable when you get stumped with a computer dilemma for which you can't find an answer. Many BBS users are quite experienced with computers and are therefore knowledgeable resources for you.

So how do you discover BBSs in your area? Your best bet is to contact a local computer users' group. Most of these groups have a bulletin board for their members or can steer you towards other BBSs. So your next question is, "How do I find out about local computer users' groups?" Magazines such as *Lotus* and *PC World* list users' groups on a regular basis.

To get started, you might want to try *PC Magazine*'s bulletin board. A variety of public domain software is available for anyone to download. You can even download a file that lists bulletin boards around the country. Call either 212-696-0306 or 415-598-9100.

Before you connect with a BBS, you must first find out what protocol parameters it uses. Your protocol must match the BBS's protocol. Most BBSs use the following parameters:

300, 1200, or 2400 baud
8-bit byte length
1 stop bit
No parity

Changing the Default Settings

Now that you are familiar with the standards required for the BBS, you are ready to select the first set of COMM window settings. Figure 17.1 shows the settings that appear when you select a COMM window and choose Settings from the main COMM menu. Lotus provides these default settings with the program.

```
Speed and type of transmission                                    MENU
Interface  Phone  Terminal  Send  Break  Handshaking  Capture  Login  Name  Quit

  Interface            Terminal                Send
    Baud:      110       Screen:    Window        EOL:       \m
    Parity:    None      Echo:      No            Delay:     0
    Length:    7         Linefeed:  No            Response:  \j
    Stop bits: 1         Backspace: Backspace     Format:    No
    Comm Port: COM1      Wrap:      Yes           Break:     60
  Phone                  Delay:     0           Handshaking
    Type:      Pulse     Translation:            Inbound:   Yes
    Dial:      60          (none)                Outbound:  Yes
    Answer:    15                              Capture:
    Number:                                      Range:     No
                                                 Printer:   No
                                          Communications Settings:
```

Fig. 17.1

The COMM Settings sheet.

Once you modify the settings sheet, you can store the settings in a communications configuration file (CCF) that you can retrieve whenever you want to use those settings. If you are using one of the popular information services (such as CompuServe), you can retrieve a communications configuration file included with Symphony Release 2.0. The CCF files included are ADP, COMPUSRV, DOWJONES, MCI, and SOURCE. These files are located on the Help and Tutorial disk (5 1/4-inch floppy) or the Program, Help and Tutorial disk (3 1/2-inch floppy). You can use the files as they are given to you, or you can modify them as needed.

To create new settings, your first step is to create a new settings sheet name. Select **N**ame from the **S**ettings menu, choose **S**ave, and give the new settings the name **BBS** (Bulletin Board System).

The Interface Settings

Now that you have named the new settings sheet, you are ready to change the Interface settings. When you select Interface from the main Settings menu, the following choices appear:

Baud **P**arity **L**ength **S**top-Bits **C**omm-Port

Most of these terms should already be familiar to you. When you select the **B**aud option, Symphony gives you these choices:

Menu Choice	Baud Rate
1	110
2	150
3	300
4	600
5	1200
6	2400
7	4800
8	9600

For this example, assume that you are using a 1200-baud modem, so select option **5**. When you select the **P**arity option from the Interface menu, Symphony gives you the choices of **1** (None), **2** (Odd), and **3** (Even). As was mentioned earlier, the bulletin board system requires that you choose option **1**, no parity.

For the **L**ength option, Symphony offers choices **1** (7 bits) and **2** (8 bits). To select a character length of 8 bits, choose **2**. Select **1** stop bit from the Stop-Bits menu. Finally, with the **C**omm-Port option, you indicate which communications port (either **1** or **2**) on your machine you are using. The default setting is COM1, but this choice depends on your hardware configuration. Figure 17.2 shows the COMM Settings menu after you have selected all the new Interface settings.

The Phone Settings

After selecting the Interface settings, your next logical step is to choose the **P**hone settings. When you select **P**hone from the **S**ettings menu, the following

```
┌─────────────────────────────────────────────────────────────────────────────┐
│ Speed and type of transmission                                         MENU   │
│ Interface  Phone  Terminal  Send  Break  Handshaking  Capture  Login  Name  Quit │
│ ┌───────────────────────────────────────────────────────────────────────┐   │
│ │ Interface          Terminal               Send                         │   │
│ │   Baud:      1200    Screen:    Window       EOL:      \n               │   │
│ │   Parity:    None    Echo:      No           Delay:    0                │   │
│ │   Length:    8       Linefeed:  No           Response: \j               │   │
│ │   Stop bits: 1       Backspace: Backspace    Format:   No               │   │
│ │   Comm Port: COM1    Wrap:      Yes          Break:    60               │   │
│ │ Phone                Delay:     0          Handshaking                  │   │
│ │   Type:      Pulse   Translation:             Inbound:  Yes             │   │
│ │   Dial:      60        (none)                 Outbound: Yes             │   │
│ │   Answer:    15                            Capture:                     │   │
│ │   Number:                                     Range:    No              │   │
│ │                                               Printer:  No              │   │
│ │                                    Communications Settings:             │   │
│ └───────────────────────────────────────────────────────────────────────┘   │
└─────────────────────────────────────────────────────────────────────────────┘
```

Fig. 17.2

After selecting new Interface settings.

choices appear:

Type   **D**ial-Time   **A**nswer-Time   **N**umber

The **P**hone settings you want depend on the kind of modem you are using. If your modem has an auto-dial feature, you can select **N**umber and enter the number for the bulletin board system. Symphony then dials the number for you when you tell the program to do so. If your modem is incapable of auto-dialing, however, you will have to dial the number yourself.

Assume for now that you have a Hayes Smartmodem with auto-dial and that you are calling from a business phone where you have to dial 9 to get an outside line before you dial the number. After Symphony dials the 9, you want the program to pause momentarily before entering the access number. By entering a series of commas between the 9 and the phone number, you can have Symphony pause for as long as you need. The length of the pause that a comma produces is difficult to gauge. But Lotus recommends five commas as a good starting point. For this example, enter the following string for **S**ettings **P**hone **N**umber:

9,,,,,6382762

You must also indicate the **T**ype of phone you are using. (Again, skip this option if your modem is incapable of auto-dialing.) If you have standard rotary-dial service, select **P**ulse. Select **T**one for push-button service.

Dial-Time is the maximum time in seconds that Symphony spends dialing a call and trying to make a connection after you issue **P**hone **C**all, the command that initiates calling. The default setting is 60 seconds, which normally works fine.

Answer-Time is the maximum number of seconds that Symphony spends answering a call when you issue **P**hone **A**nswer. The default here is 15 seconds, which is also sufficient under normal circumstances. **D**ial-Time and **A**nswer-Time work through a modem's auto-dial and auto-answer features, so don't worry about these commands if your modem does not have these features. Figure 17.3 shows the COMM settings after you have made all the **P**hone settings.

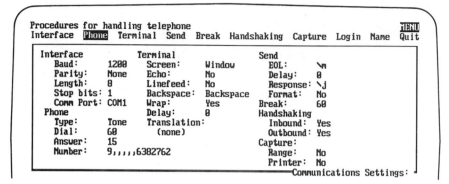

Fig. 17.3

After selecting new Phone settings.

The Terminal Settings

The next step is to designate the Terminal settings. These settings are used to match the characteristics of the COMM window in which you are working to the characteristics of the service (or computer) you are calling. In practice, you can make several of the Terminal settings after you have established a connection with the service. In some cases, you must see how the remote computer reacts to your input before you change the settings. In other cases, you can adjust the settings before you establish the connection. When you select Terminal from the main Settings menu, you can choose from these options:

Screen   Echo   Linefeed   Backspace   Wrap   Delay   Translation

The Screen option lets you eliminate the box that encloses the COMM window. Some remote computers require that you have a full 25-line display (specifically, when you are trying to emulate the VT 100 display terminal). Because you are trying to run a standard IBM PC/XT/AT or PS/2 connection in this example, however, leave this option set to Window, the default, rather than changing it to Full-Screen.

The Echo option controls whether the characters you type are displayed on-screen. Normally, you want to have your input displayed so that you can see whether it is correct. If you are connecting with a full-duplex system, you can leave the setting at No. Full-duplex systems "echo" the characters you type automatically, but half-duplex systems (which allow only one-way communication) do not. Therefore, the echo option is normally set to Yes for half-duplex systems.

If you are not sure whether the system you are working on is full- or half-duplex, you can set this option after you have established the connection. If you see two characters for every one you type, set the option to No. If you see no characters when you type, set Echo to Yes. If you see three characters for every character you type, your modem is probably also echoing characters. Turn off this feature on your modem and then set the Echo option to No.

Linefeed, the third Terminal option, is another option that you can set while you are connected to the remote computer. A few computers do not supply a linefeed. If your messages write over one another on the same line, you need to set Linefeed to Yes. In this example, assume that the remote system supplies a linefeed, so leave this option set to No.

The Backspace option determines where the Backspace key deletes. By default, whenever you press the Backspace key, the cursor moves one character to the left and erases the character in that space. By setting this option to Delete, you can have the Backspace key delete the character on which the cursor rests, and have all the characters to the right of the cursor shift one place to the left. Normally, you will leave this setting on the default, which is Backspace.

If long lines that you type or that are returned to you from the other computer do not wrap around to the next line, you need to set the Wrap option to Yes. The default is Yes, so you should keep this setting for the current example.

Use Delay to set the delay between transmissions of characters. The unit of measure is 1/128 of a second, and Lotus says that typical settings range from 30 to 60. You may find, however, that a smaller setting is sufficient. You must set this option by trial and error. (For the current example, we chose a setting of 10.) The Delay option is particularly important for slowing down the transmission of characters while you are logging onto another computer. A good indicator of the need to increase the delay is when the other computer appears to be losing the characters you send it. Of all the Terminal options, the Delay option requires the most experimenting. This option is one of the most important ones you have for controlling the interaction between your microcomputer and a remote computer system.

The next Terminal option is Translation, which you use to choose the current character-code translation table. You want to use this option when you are using an International character set to communicate with a remote computer, or if you are an expert user and have devised a special translation table. You have the following choices after selecting Translation:

Default   National   Custom   Generate

In most cases, including the current example, you will leave the option set to Default.

If you have attached the application add-in for DEC VT 100 terminal emulation, an additional Terminal option appears: VT100. This option gives you access to another settings sheet so that you can modify special screen characteristics (such as color, scrolling speed, cursor appearance) of a VT 100 terminal.

Figure 17.4 shows the COMM settings after you have set the Terminal settings. Only the Delay option has been changed from the default.

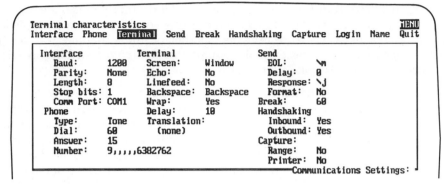

Fig. 17.4

After selecting new Terminal settings.

Setting Up a Log-in Sequence

Setting up a log-in sequence with a remote computer is one of the most interesting aspects of Symphony's COMM window. You have several options you can work with. One has already been mentioned, the **Settings Terminal Delay** command. The other options are part of the **Settings Login** command. Figure 17.5 shows the command menu and settings sheet that appear when you select **Login** from the **Settings** menu.

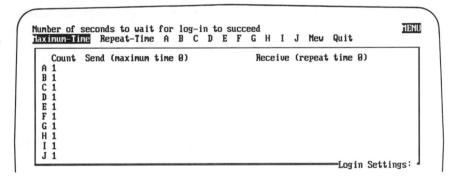

Fig. 17.5

The Settings Login command menu and settings sheet.

The **Login** menu is the place where you store strings to be sent to the remote computer (Send strings) and the responses you are expecting in return (Receive strings). Suppose that during the log-in sequence to a local bulletin board system, you expect the following sequence of events:

1. Once you get the CONNECT message, the BBS displays a series of messages and then asks What is your FIRST name?.

2. You respond with your first name and press Enter.

3. The BBS then returns the message What is your LAST name?.

4. You type your last name and press Enter.

5. The BBS asks you to Enter your password:.

6. You type your password and press Enter.

You are then logged onto the system and can send messages to other users, download files, and use any other services the BBS offers. (These services are usually displayed on a menu.)

Entering Send and Receive Strings

To automate this log-in sequence, you can enter Send and Receive strings in the Login menu. Figure 17.6 displays the finished log-in sheet. First, select the **A** option from the Login menu. When you do, Symphony shows you the following options:

Count   Send   Receive   Quit

In this remote system, you must receive something (the question What is your FIRST name?) before you can send anything. Therefore, A has no Send string. To enter the first Receive string, select Receive, then enter **What is your FIRST name?** after the prompt. This string is the one that you want to appear on the screen before Symphony transmits a Send string. In other words, when Symphony sees this string from the remote computer, the program will send the next string (B) automatically. You are finished with the **A** option, so select **Quit** from the **A** menu.

Select **B** to enter the next set of Send and Receive strings. To enter your first Send string, select **Send** and enter **Becky\013** (or use *your* first name followed by \013). The \013 signals the Enter key. Select Receive and enter **What is your LAST name?**. Then Quit from the **B** menu.

Select **C** and enter **Bridges\013** (or use *your* last name) as the **Send** string, and **Enter your password:** as the Receive string. Then **Quit** from the **C** menu.

The **D** option requires that you enter a Send string (enter **pass\013** or whatever your password is). You do not need a Receive string for this option.

You may have noticed that you never changed the Count option. The Count option designates the number of times you want to transmit the Send string. Because you needed to send each string only once, you left Count set to the default of 1 for this example.

Note: Some remote computers require that you send a series of Enters at the beginning of the log-in sequence. If so, enter **\013** for the A option and set the Count option to 3, 4, or however many Enters the remote computer expects.

The Maximum-Time Option

After selecting options **A**, **B**, **C**, and **D**, you must enter a value for the Maximum-

Time option of the **Login** menu. **Maximum-Time** refers to the maximum number of seconds that Symphony waits for the log-in sequence to succeed. This amount includes all the time needed for sending and receiving during the log-in sequence. The **Maximum-Time** will vary depending on how much sending and receiving you want to accomplish in the log-in sequence. For the current example, a good setting is 30 seconds. You can use a value as small as 10 seconds, but 10 seconds may not be enough time if the remote computer is slow in responding. If the **Maximum-Time** setting is reached before the log-in sequence is completed, Symphony interrupts the log-in sequence and issues an error message.

The Repeat-Time Option

You may also want to enter a value for the **Repeat-Time** option. The **Repeat-Time** value is the number of seconds that you want Symphony to delay between issuing a Send string and getting a Receive string from the remote computer. If, for example, Symphony issues a Send string and the bulletin board system responds immediately, Symphony issues the next Send string immediately. The other system may be slow, however, in responding to the Send string. You don't want Symphony to get ahead by sending another string before receiving a response to the first one. Therefore, you must set the **Repeat-Time** to allow the other computer enough time to respond. For the current example, a repeat time of 5 seconds works fine. (The time you require may be less if you are using a 2400-baud modem.)

Striking the right balance between too much and not enough time for the **Repeat-Time** requires some experimenting. Allowing extra time is not a problem if you have the **Maximum-Time** set high enough to allow the entire log-in sequence to be completed.

Figure 17.6 shows how the **Login** settings sheet appears after you have entered all the settings. Notice that the **Maximum-Time** and **Repeat-Time** appear above the Send and Receive columns, respectively.

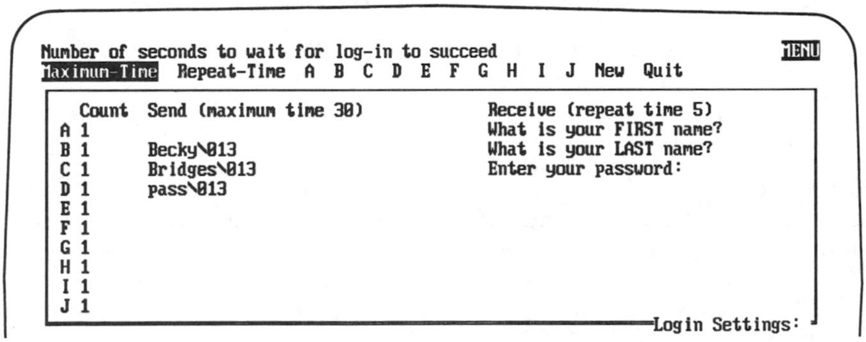

Fig. 17.6

After setting up the log-in sequence.

```
 Number of seconds to wait for log-in to succeed                    MENU
 Maximum-Time  Repeat-Time  A  B  C  D  E  F  G  H  I  J  New  Quit

    Count  Send (maximum time 30)        Receive (repeat time 5)
  A 1                                     What is your FIRST name?
  B 1      Becky\013                      What is your LAST name?
  C 1      Bridges\013                    Enter your password:
  D 1      pass\013
  E 1
  F 1
  G 1
  H 1
  I 1
  J 1
                                                      Login Settings:
```

Changing Handshaking Settings

Handshaking refers to whether Symphony uses XON/XOFF (Ctrl-Q/Ctrl-S) protocol when communicating with a remote computer. If, after the DOS TYPE command, you have used Ctrl-S to stop a file from displaying and used Ctrl-Q to start displaying again, you have used XON/XOFF. (Don't confuse XON/XOFF with the Christensen XMODEM protocol; the two are entirely different.) Most manufacturers adhere to the XON/XOFF standard, so most remote computers recognize the Ctrl-Q and Ctrl-S characters. Some computers have their own variations of handshaking protocol, however, and require different control characters. On a rare occasion you may have to disable Symphony's handshaking in order to communicate with one of these computers. Even if handshaking is disabled, however, you can still manually issue a Ctrl-S to stop the display (not the transmission) of a communications session, and then use Ctrl-Q to start the display again.

Symphony has two controls for **Handshaking: Inbound** and **Outbound.** (You access the **Handshaking** options from the **Settings** menu.) If you set **Handshaking Outbound** to **Yes,** you are indicating that Symphony can start and stop a remote computer's transmission by issuing XON/XOFF signals. Similarly, if you set **Handshaking Inbound** to **Yes,** the remote computer can stop Symphony's transmission by XON/XOFF signals. The default setting for both **Inbound** and **Outbound** is **Yes,** and you probably will not need to change these settings.

Starting Communications

Now that you have an understanding of most of the COMM settings, you are ready to start communications. You can change any of the COMM settings while you are in the middle of a communications session, so don't worry if you are not sure about a particular setting. Try the settings that you think are most appropriate, and change them one by one if they don't work properly.

Phoning

Let's return to the original example. Suppose that you have a Hayes Smartmodem with auto-dial, and you have entered a bulletin board system's access number in the **Settings Phone Number** setting. You are now ready to have Symphony dial the number for you. To do so, select **Phone** from the main COMM menu. The following menu choices appear:

   Call   Wait-Mode   Answer   Hangup   Data-Mode   Voice-Mode

When you select **Call** and press Enter, you should hear some strange beeping noises from the modem as it dials the number. A Dialing... message appears at the top of the screen. When Symphony makes a connection with the remote system, you should hear a high-pitched tone over the speaker. (If Symphony does not make the connection, an error message appears on the screen.) After a short while, the high-pitched tone stops, and you are ready to begin the log-in sequence.

Note: If your modem does not have an auto-dial feature, you have to dial the phone number yourself. When you hear the high-pitched tone over the receiver, flip the switch on your modem from Voice to Data, and you are ready to start the log-in sequence.

Starting the Log-in Sequence

After phoning the remote system, select **Login** from the main COMM menu. Symphony displays the letters A through J. You have already entered the log-in sequence for the current example in the **Settings Login** settings, so select **A**. Symphony now starts the log-in sequence by looking for Receive string A and displaying the message Logging in... at the top of the screen. If the **Login** settings you have chosen are working properly, you should not have to touch the computer again until you are completely logged into the remote computer.

Symphony continues sending strings until the program reaches an empty line in the **Login** menu. If your **Login** settings are not correct, however, you may have to halt the log-in sequence in midstream (by pressing Ctrl-Break followed by Esc) and enter the log-in sequence manually. If this situation occurs, enter a different value for the **Settings Terminal Delay** command and try logging in again.

Phone-and-Login

As an alternative to using the **Phone** command to dial the number and the **Login** command to begin your login sequence, you can use the COMM **Settings Name Phone-and-Login** command. Before invoking this command, though, you must create a named settings sheet containing all the correct interface parameters, the phone number, and the login sequence. Use the COMM **Settings Name Create** command to save and name the settings.

When you invoke the **Phone-and-Login** command, you will be prompted for a settings sheet name. Once you type the name or select the name from the list, Symphony retrieves the settings sheet, dials the number, and begins the login sequence. It's a powerful, time-saving command.

Copying to the Printer

While you are in a COMM window, you can have Symphony send to the printer a copy of all data that appears on the screen, including all the data sent by the remote computer and all the data you type. The command to initiate printing is **Settings Capture Printer**. When you have begun printing, the CAPTURE message appears at the bottom of the screen.

Once you have started copying to the printer, you can stop the procedure any time by using the Capture key (F4 on IBM PC/XT/AT and PS/2 computers and compatibles). To start copying again, press the Capture key a second time. You must also use the Capture key when capturing data in a range in the worksheet. (The Capture key is the only special-function key used in a COMM window.)

Capturing Data in a Range

After you have logged onto the bulletin board system and found some interesting data, you may want to capture that data in a range in Symphony. Captured data is stored in a worksheet as labels; therefore, you can immediately use the data in a DOC window. If you want to use the data as numbers, however, you must convert it to a usable form before you can perform calculations, make a graph, play "what if," and so on.

Before you can capture data, however, you must designate in the spreadsheet a Capture range where you want the data placed as it comes in. The Capture range can be located anywhere in the spreadsheet. Just make sure that the range you designate is large enough (both in width and length) to contain all the data you want to capture.

Suppose, for example, that a friend left you an electronic message on the bulletin board. To capture that data in a range in the Symphony worksheet, you must use the **Settings Capture Range** command with the Capture key. When you issue **Capture Range**, Symphony temporarily shifts to the SHEET environment so that you can enter a Capture range. A good technique is to make the Capture range a little larger than you think you need. Otherwise, if the Capture range gets full, you have to erase the Capture range (by using the **Settings Capture Erase** command), reset the Capture range to a larger size, reissue the bulletin board's command to read a message, and start capturing again.

As mentioned, you must use the Capture key to capture data in a COMM window. After you set the Capture range and want to begin capturing data, press the Capture key and choose **Range Yes** to initiate the process. When you have captured all the data you want, press the Capture key again, followed this time by **Range No**.

Converting Numbers to a Usable Form

When you have received numerical data from a remote computer, you need a way to convert the data to numbers so that you can use it in calculations, graphs, and the like. You have two ways to accomplish this conversion: use functions, such as @DATEVALUE, @TIMEVALUE, and @VALUE; or use the **Query Parse** command.

Setting the Capture Range Column Widths

Before you can convert the number data to a usable form, you must make sure that you capture the data properly. Suppose that you have captured the data that appears in figure 17.7, and you want to convert it for use in a graph.

```
A2:                                                              SHEET
    ┌─────A────────B────────C────────D────────E────────F─────┐
    1                 INTERNATIONAL BUSINESS MACHS
    2     ▉▉▉▉▉▉▉
    3   Cusip: 45920010        Exchange: N        Ticker: IBM
    4
    5     Weeks    Friday
    6     Date     Volume    High/Ask    Low/Bid   Close/Avg
    7    _____   _____   _____    _____   _____
    8
    9   06/01/88  4,315,400  108 3/4     105 5/8    107 7/8
    10
    11  06/08/88  8,216,000  109 1/4     103 3/8    105 3/4
    12
    13  06/15/88  7,536,000  105 1/2      99 1/8     99 1/2
    14
    15  06/22/88  7,490,000  108 1/2      99        105 1/4
    16
    17  06/29/88  4,677,500  106 1/2     102 3/4    105 3/4
    18
    19  07/06/88  2,200,500  107 1/2     104 5/8    105 3/4
    20                                                        MAIN
    └─────────────────────────────────────────────────────────┘
    08-Apr-88   11:49 AM
```

If you plan to use @functions to convert the data to a useful form, you should set the Capture range for this data as A1..E20. Because this Capture range is several columns wide, Symphony enters the data for Weeks Date, Friday Volume, High/Ask, Low/Bid, and Close/Avg in separate columns. Remember to indicate a Capture range that is wide enough if you want Symphony to maintain columnar separation.

In addition, if you use the @function method, you must set the column widths to conform to the data you are capturing. If you leave the columns set to the default width of 9, Symphony may not split the data where you prefer. The best way to determine the column widths for your data is to experiment. The column widths for figure 17.7 were set to the following:

Column	*Width*
A	9
B	13
C	12
D	12
E	12

If you plan to use the **Query Parse** method, you should set a Capture range that is one column wide, A1..A20. Then, all the data for each row will be written in one long label.

Using Functions To Convert Data

To use @functions to convert the data in figure 17.7 from labels to numbers, switch to a SHEET window and go to an out-of-the-way area of the worksheet. You can then use the following formulas to convert the data in row 9:

Variable	*Function*
Weeks Date	@DATEVALUE(A9)
Friday Volume	@VALUE(B9)
High/Ask	@VALUE(C9)
Low/Bid	@VALUE(D9)
Close/Avg	@VALUE(E9)

Once you have the formulas for the first row, copy them to succeeding rows. Then use the SHEET **Range Values** command to change the formulas in the out-of-the-way range to numbers and to copy them over the original label data.

Using Query Parse

The second technique for converting string data to numbers, the **Query Parse** command, is much easier than using functions. To use **Query Parse**, you must be familiar with the FORM window (see Chapter 15).

Suppose, once again, that you have captured the data in figure 17.7. But this time you are using **Query Parse**, so you need to capture the data in a one-column Capture range (A1..A20). One advantage to using **Query Parse** is that you don't need to determine beforehand how to split the data into separate columns.

The first step is to create a simple input form using a DOC (or SHEET) window. The best location for entering the fields for the input form is below or to the right of the captured data. Figure 17.8 shows how you enter the fields. The lengths for the variables are determined by the widths of the data fields. This method is necessary for **Query Parse** to work properly.

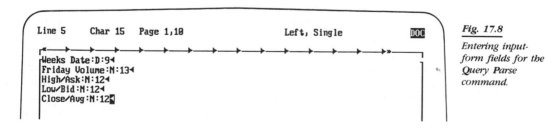

Fig. 17.8

Entering input-form fields for the Query Parse command.

Next, switch to a FORM window and use the **Generate** command, which causes Symphony to generate the input form and the important ranges for the database. You are now ready to issue the **Query Parse** command.

To enter the command, shift from a FORM to a SHEET window. When you issue **Query Parse**, Symphony asks you for the range to be parsed. Be sure to indicate all columns the data is displayed in (in this example, A1..E20) even though the data is contained in only one column. Although the Capture range may contain all kinds of unrelated data (such as titles and log-in sequences), Symphony conveniently discards all the lines that do not conform to the field definitions you supply. After you enter the range to be parsed, Symphony asks for a Review range. This range is where Symphony puts all the nonconforming lines. Choose an out-of-the-way place for the Review range. After you enter the Review range, Symphony executes the **Query Parse**. Figure 17.9 shows the results.

Fig. 17.9

The results of converting data with Query Parse.

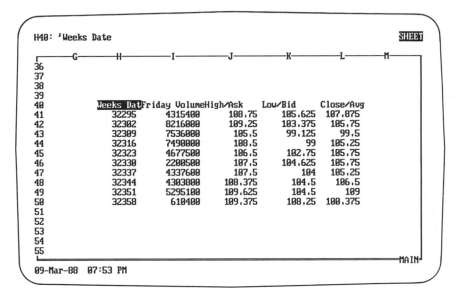

Saving Settings

Before you exit Symphony, make sure that you save your settings in a communications configuration file. To save the settings, issue the **Settings Name Save** command. Symphony then saves the settings to a .CCF file on the Symphony Program disk. After you have saved your settings, you can retrieve them by selecting the **Settings Name Retrieve** command. If you want Symphony to retrieve the settings for you automatically every time you boot the program, you can enter the name of the .CCF file in the SERVICES Configuration Communications command and select Update to save the new configuration. For more on modifying and updating the SERVICES Configuration menu, see Chapter 2.

Ending a Session

Each bulletin board system has its own command for logging off. For example, you may have to enter **x** to exit. If your modem has an auto-hangup feature, select **Phone Hangup** from the main COMM menu. This command causes Symphony to signal your modem to hang up the phone. If you do not have an auto-hangup, flip the switch on your modem from Data to Voice.

Communications with Another Microcomputer

At some point, you will probably want to use the COMM environment to communicate with another Symphony user. In fact, you should make a special point of trying this type of communication. Call up a friend who also has Symphony and try passing messages and data back and forth. You will learn a great deal about Symphony's COMM environment by experimenting.

Matching the Interface Settings

When you are communicating with another microcomputer, your first concern should be that you both have the same **Interface** settings. For example, if one modem is capable of being set at either 1200 or 300 baud, and the other modem can be set only at 300, both must be set at the lower rate. The settings for parity, length, and stop bits must also be the same.

When you are sending files back and forth by means of the **File-Transfer Send** and **File-Transfer Receive** commands (the commands for file transfer), Symphony temporarily modifies the **Interface** settings to accommodate the protocol. (For example, XMODEM protocol is 8-bit word length, no parity, and 1 stop bit.) When the file transfer is complete, Symphony adjusts the settings back to what they were originally. No specific action is required on your part.

Making the Connection

Once you have coordinated the **Interface** settings for both computers, you are ready to make the connection. Suppose that your friend is the caller, and you are the receiver of the call. After your friend uses the **Phone Call** command to dial your number, you use the **Phone Answer** command to have Symphony automatically answer the call. While Symphony is working, it displays the message Answering... at the top of the screen.

Just how long Symphony attempts to answer the call depends on the **Settings Phone Answer-Time** setting that you have entered. The default setting of 15 seconds is usually more than enough time when you know you are being called.

Because Symphony does not have a special indicator to let you know when you are being called, you have to rely on signals from your modem. If it is equipped with a speaker, you will begin to hear noises when someone is calling. If you are not in a COMM window, you must switch to one to issue the Answer command. (On modems that are not equipped with an auto-answer feature, the Answer command has no effect.) You can also have Symphony automatically answer the call for you regardless of what kind of window you are in. Simply set the **Phone Wait-Mode** command to **Yes**. This way, your modem automatically answers a call after a preset number of rings, determined by a setting on the modem.

If your modem is not equipped with the auto-answer feature, you should keep the modem set to Voice mode. Then when someone calls you, just flip the switch from Voice to Data. You should be ready to send messages at that point.

Sending Messages

After you have made the connection, you are automatically in a "chat" mode where everything you type is also seen on the other person's screen, and everything the other person types displays on your screen. If you want to send a longer message that you have previously typed in the SHEET or DOC environment, you can use the **Transmit-Range** feature.

When you enter the **Transmit-Range** command, Symphony temporarily shifts to the SHEET environment so that you can designate the range to be sent. *Note:* If your message stretches across several columns, make sure that you designate all the columns involved. If you point to only the first column (as you may do, because your message may be a long label), Symphony transmits only the first portion of the message. After you have designated the range and pressed Enter, Symphony immediately shifts back to the COMM environment and transmits your message.

In general, transmitting messages is awkward in Symphony, but you can automate the process. Chapter 20 shows how to use the Lotus Command Language to make sending messages a simple task.

Sending Ranges

You can also use the **Transmit-Range** command to send other data. For example, you may want to send a portion of an inventory spreadsheet or the latest figures you received on T-Bill auction rates.

When you use **Transmit-Range** to send ranges, you must make sure that you have selected the proper options for the **Settings Send** command. When you select **Settings Send**, Symphony returns the following choices:

End-of-Line   Delay   Response   Format

The End-of-Line option is used to enter an end-of-line terminator. Symphony uses the terminator between lines of data when you enter the **Transmit-Range** command. The end-of-line terminator is a three-digit ASCII control code (or letter equivalent) preceded by a backslash. For example, the most common end-of-line indicator is \013 (or its equivalent \m), the carriage-return character. This indicator is the default setting for Symphony and is the end-of-line terminator that you want for communicating with another Symphony user.

The **D**elay option sets the number of seconds you want Symphony to wait before sending consecutive lines of a range. The default setting is 0, the setting you want for communicating with another Symphony user. Some time-sharing services are slow to accept new data, however, and you may have to enter a delay time when sending a range to these services.

Sometimes you will want to have Symphony read a string from a remote computer before sending a data range. To have Symphony read the string, you must enter it in the **Response** setting. For example, suppose that the remote computer is running a line editor that is currently in EDIT mode. After you have sent a command to switch the editor from EDIT to INSERT mode, you want to have Symphony read the editor's response before sending a range. If the editor's prompt is INSERT, this string is what you enter in the **Response** setting. For the current example, leave the **Response** string blank. When you get into more sophisticated applications later, such as using the Lotus Command Language to send data ranges, you may want to include a **Response** string.

If you are transmitting a Symphony document, you can use the **Format** option to include (or not include) DOC mode's special symbols (hard tabs, hard returns, indents, page breaks, and format lines). If you enter **Format Yes**, these special symbols will be included with the document when you transmit it. If you enter **Format No**, the symbols will not be transmitted. When sending a document to another Symphony user, you probably want the word-processing symbols to be included.

Transferring Files

Symphony gives you two options for sending data back and forth between your computer and another Symphony user's machine. First, as described previously, you can use the **Transmit-Range** command for transmitting a portion of a file. Unfortunately, the receiving Symphony user must capture the data as lines of text when you transmit data this way. Second, you can use the **File-Transfer Send** and **Receive** commands. These commands are used to transfer entire files by means of Symphony's XMODEM file-transferring capabilities. One of the main advantages of XMODEM file transfer is that you keep the separation between cell entries. Another advantage is that error checking takes place while the file is being transferred.

When you issue the File-Transfer Send command to transfer a file to another Symphony user, Symphony first requests the name of the file you are transferring. (Remember that you are not limited to sending only Symphony files.) Suppose that the name of the file you select is SALES.WR1. After you enter this name, Symphony sends that name to the remote computer and displays the following message on your screen:

```
Sending file: SALES.WR1
Waiting for connection...
```

If the receiving user has already issued the File-Transfer Receive command, you will probably not see the second line of the message. Instead, Symphony will show some variation of the following message:

```
Sending file: SALES.WR1
1024 out of 2048 sent 0 errors corrected
```

As Symphony transmits the file, the numbers in the second line of the message are constantly updated to reflect the status of the transfer. Incidentally, the receiving user's screen shows the same messages with the word Sending replaced by Receiving.

With all the error checking that occurs, transferring a file takes a substantial amount of time; for example, transferring approximately 5,000 bytes takes three to four minutes. (The speed, however, depends on your baud rate.)

If the remote computer you are working with does not support XMODEM/B or BLAST protocol, you have to use Symphony's Settings Capture Range command to transfer a file from the remote computer to Symphony. Sometimes this technique is the only way to get data from a remote computer into Symphony. Because no error checking occurs when you are capturing data in a range, you may get some strange control characters mixed with your data. If you do, use the @CLEAN function to remove the control characters.

Chapter Summary

In this chapter, you have learned about Symphony's COMM window through two examples: accessing a bulletin board system and communicating with another Symphony user. In many ways Symphony's COMM window is quite sophisticated. Chapter 18 provides a hands-on practice session for working with Symphony's communications. And in Chapter 20, you will find some examples of how to use the Lotus Command Language to help streamline some of the COMM window operations. With these Command-Language additions, Symphony provides a powerful communications capability.

18

Communications Hands-On Practice

In the previous chapter, you read how you can use Symphony's COMM mode to connect with an electronic bulletin board system and with another microcomputer that is running Symphony. In this hands-on practice session, you will connect with the popular CompuServe Information Service. This time-sharing service offers current and historical information on a wide variety of subjects: financial news, stocks, weather, travel, and, of course, computers. You can even play games and go shopping while you are on-line!

In this session, you will access *The World of Lotus*, a special information service that Lotus Development Corporation has set up on CompuServe. With this service, you can leave messages about a problem you are having with Symphony, and then a Lotus employee, or perhaps another Symphony user, will offer help. The service also provides lists of other resources (magazines, books, and users' groups). In addition, you can download a variety of files to be used with Symphony: new drivers, add-in applications, worksheet templates, macros, utilities, and so on. These files are free; you pay only for your CompuServe connect time.

In this practice session, you will first modify the CompuServe communications configuration file that is included with Symphony Release 2.0 and create a login sequence to automate the process of logging onto CompuServe. Then once you connect with CompuServe, you will enter The World of Lotus, capture data in the spreadsheet so that you can read the data later, and download a small spreadsheet file.

This chapter makes the following assumptions:

- You have installed Symphony for communications and have indicated XMODEM/B protocol during installation.

- Your modem is installed.

- You have already set up a CompuServe account and have a user ID and a password.

- You know the local access number for CompuServe. (A phone list comes with your CompuServe information packet.)

Settings

With Symphony 2.0, Lotus includes communications configuration files for several popular information services, one of which is CompuServe. Because creating a communications settings sheet from scratch can be confusing to the novice "telecommunicator," you will appreciate that Lotus has made the settings for you. All you need to do is add the local CompuServe access number to the settings sheet. In addition, depending on your modem, you may have to change the baud rate.

Modifying a Communications Configuration File

If you copied all the Symphony disks to your hard disk, the CompuServe communications configuration file (COMPUSRV.CCF) should be in your Symphony directory. If you are working on 5 1/4-inch floppy disks, COMPUSRV.CCF is on the Help and Tutorial disk. If you have 3 1/2-inch disks, the communications configuration files are on the Program, Help and Tutorial disk.

First, load Symphony and retrieve the COMPUSRV.CCF file.

1. Load the Symphony program. A blank worksheet should appear, and you should be in SHEET mode.

2. Press the Type key (Alt-F10) and select **C**OMM to display a COMM window.

3. Select COMM **S**ettings **N**ame **R**etrieve.

4. Select **COMPUSRV.CCF** and press Enter. Your settings sheet should look like figure 18.1.

   Note: If COMPUSRV.CCF is not listed, you may need to switch disks or directories. If you are using a hard disk, make sure that the Symphony directory (the one with the program files) is displayed. If it's not, change the path. If you are using 5 1/4-inch disks, make sure that the Help and Tutorial disk is in drive A. If you are using

3 1/2-inch disks, the Program, Help and Tutorial disk should be in drive A. If you cannot locate COMPUSRV.CCF, you will need to enter the settings as shown in figure 18.1.

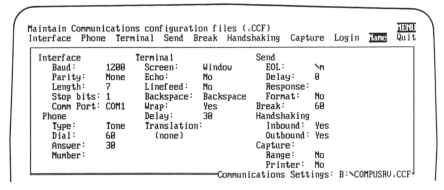

Fig. 18.1

The settings sheet for the CompuServe communications configuration file.

Enter your local CompuServe access number into the settings sheet.

1. Select COMM Settings Phone Number.

2. Enter the number.

   Note: If you are calling from a business phone that requires you to dial 9 to get an outside line, precede the phone number with 9,,,,,.

It's a good idea to designate a Capture range before you log onto CompuServe so that you can save information as it displays on the screen.

1. Select Capture Range from the Settings menu.

2. Specify the range **A1.A8192**. Your settings sheet should look similar to figure 18.2.

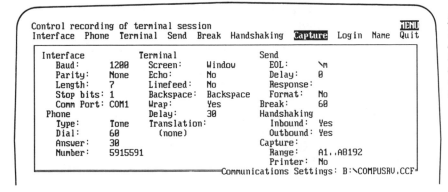

Fig. 18.2

The settings sheet after entering the local CompuServe access number and designating a Capture range.

Specifying a Capture range in the settings sheet automatically turns on the Capture; thus, as soon as you log onto the other computer, everything on your screen will be saved into the spreadsheet. Because you want to turn on the Capture in the middle of the session, turn Capture off now.

1. Press Esc until you are out of the COMM menu. Notice the CAPTURE message at the bottom of the screen.

2. Press the Capture key (F4).

3. Select **Range No**. The CAPTURE message disappears.

Make any other necessary changes to the sheet (baud rate, phone type, and so on).

Automating Your Log-in Sequence

CompuServe, like an electronic bulletin board system, requires you to answer a few questions to identify yourself after you connect. This process is called "logging on" or "logging in." To save yourself the trouble of entering your user ID and password each time you access CompuServe, you can create a log-in sequence that will automatically log on for you. The following sequence is required to log onto CompuServe:

1. You enter a carriage return, and CompuServe responds with Host Name:.

2. You type **cps** followed by Enter. CompuServe returns the message User ID:.

3. You type your user ID number and press Enter. CompuServe responds with Password:.

4. You type your password and press Enter.

Begin entering the Send and Receive strings into the log-in sheet. The first keystroke that CompuServe looks for after you connect is a carriage return. Thus, a carriage return, indicated by \013, is your first Send string.

1. Select COMM **Settings Login**. You then see the menu shown in figure 18.3.

2. Select **A Send**.

3. Enter **\013**.

4. Select **Receive**.

5. Enter **Host Name:**.

6. Select **Quit**.

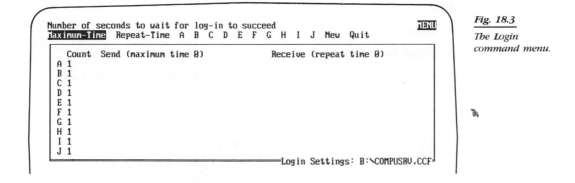

Fig. 18.3

The Login command menu.

Enter the next set of strings in the **B** option.

1. Select **B S**end.

2. Enter **cps\013**.

3. Select **R**eceive.

4. Enter **User ID:**.

5. Select **Q**uit.

Enter the next set of strings in the **C** option.

1. Select **C S**end.

2. Enter your user ID number (for example, **72106,2551**) followed by **\013**.

3. Select **R**eceive.

4. Enter **Password:**.

5. Select **Q**uit.

Enter the last Send string in the **D** option (You don't need to specify a Receive string after you enter your password.)

1. Select **D S**end.

2. Enter your password (for example, **ralph*morter**) followed by **\013**.

3. Select **Q**uit.

You should now enter values for the **Maximum-Time** and **Repeat-Time** options on the **Login** menu. Maximum-Time is the total amount of time (in seconds) that Symphony waits for the entire log-in sequence to succeed. Repeat-Time is the amount of time (in seconds) that Symphony waits between issuing a Send string and getting a Receive string.

1. Select **Maximum-Time**.

2. Enter **30**.

3. Select **Repeat-Time**.

4. Enter **5**. Your log-in sequence should look similar to figure 18.4.

Fig. 18.4

The log-in sequence.

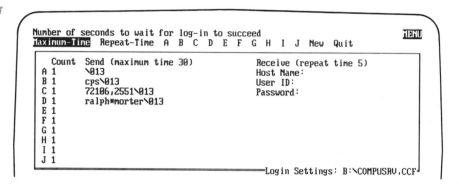

```
Number of seconds to wait for log-in to succeed                          MENU
Maximum-Time  Repeat-Time  A  B  C  D  E  F  G  H  I  J  New  Quit

   Count  Send (maximum time 30)           Receive (repeat time 5)
A  1      \013                             Host Name:
B  1      cps\013                          User ID:
C  1      72106,2551\013                   Password:
D  1      ralph*morter\013
E  1
F  1
G  1
H  1
I  1
J  1
                                    Login Settings: B:\COMPUSRV.CCF
```

5. Select **Quit** to go back to the **Settings** menu.

6. Select **Name Save** to save your modifications.

7. Press Enter to keep the same name (COMPUSRV.CCF) and select **Yes** to replace.

Connecting with CompuServe

If your modem does not have auto-dialing capability, you need to dial the number yourself. Turn your modem on, dial the number, and, after you connect, switch your modem from Voice to Data mode. If your modem does have an auto-dial feature, you can use a Symphony command to dial the number that you previously entered in the settings sheet. Make sure that your modem is turned on and follow these steps:

1. Select COMM **Phone Call**. The phone number you entered in the settings sheet appears.

2. Press Enter to dial CompuServe. If your modem has a speaker, you may hear your modem dialing the number. When your computer successfully connects with CompuServe, you will briefly hear a high-pitched tone and will see on your screen the message CONNECT.

Congratulations! You have successfully accessed a remote computer. You are now ready to begin the log-in sequence you created, and enter The World of Lotus.

1. Select COMM **L**ogin **A**. You will see CompuServe ask several
   questions (the Receive strings you specified), and the responses
   automatically fill in (the Send strings you entered). Eventually, you
   will get the CompuServe menu and a prompt to Enter choice !.

2. Enter **go lotus**. The World of Lotus menu appears, as shown in
   figure 18.5.

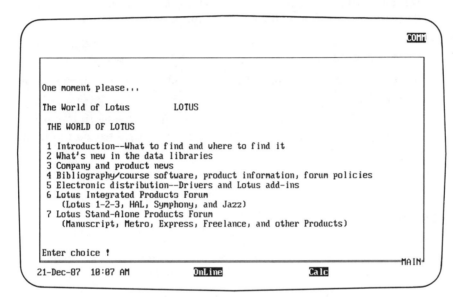

Fig. 18.5
The World of Lotus menu.

```
                                                              COMM

   One moment please...

   The World of Lotus            LOTUS

     THE WORLD OF LOTUS

     1 Introduction--What to find and where to find it
     2 What's new in the data libraries
     3 Company and product news
     4 Bibliography/course software, product information, forum policies
     5 Electronic distribution--Drivers and Lotus add-ins
     6 Lotus Integrated Products Forum
         (Lotus 1-2-3, HAL, Symphony, and Jazz)
     7 Lotus Stand-Alone Products Forum
         (Manuscript, Metro, Express, Freelance, and other Products)


   Enter choice !
                                                               MAIN
   21-Dec-87  10:07 AM         OnLine              Calc
```

Capturing Data in a Range

Because you are charged by the minute while you are logged onto an information
service, you may want to save information to a spreadsheet range so that you
can read the data after you have logged off. You have already indicated the
Capture range where the data will be stored in the spreadsheet. Use the Capture
key (F4) to indicate when you want to capture the data.

The World of Lotus has a section on commonly asked questions and answers
about Symphony. Capture these questions and answers in your spreadsheet.

1. Enter **4** to display the Bibliography menu.

2. Enter **2** to display the Product information menu.

3. Enter **2** to choose Symphony Q&A.

4. Press the Capture key (F4).

5. Select **Range Yes**. The CAPTURE message appears at the bottom of the screen. Everything that now appears on your screen will be stored in the previously specified spreadsheet range.

6. Enter **1** to choose Commonly asked questions and answers.

7. When you get the message Press <CR> for more !, enter **s** to scroll the text continuously, because you won't be reading it on-screen. If you simply press Enter here, CompuServe will pause after each screen, and you will have to continue pressing Enter.

8. When you reach the end of the list of questions, and CompuServe displays the message Last page !, press the Capture key (F4).

9. Select **Range No**. The CAPTURE message at the bottom of the screen disappears.

10. Press Switch (Alt-F9) to switch to SHEET mode. Notice the text that has been stored in the spreadsheet. (You can inspect it more closely after you have logged off.)

11. Press Alt-F9 to return to COMM mode.

Downloading a File

The World of Lotus contains a Data Library of files that you can download: worksheet templates, utilities, macros, and so on. Before you can download any of the files in the Data Library, you must first join the Lotus Integrated group.

1. Enter **go lotus** to go to The World of Lotus main menu.

2. Enter **6** to select Lotus Integrated Products Forum.

3. Enter **5** to select Join Lotus Integrated. You are prompted to enter your name.

4. Enter your name and confirm it.

5. Enter **4** to see the Data Libraries menu. The menu should look similar to figure 18.6.

6. Enter **12** for Communication Utils.

Use CompuServe's browse command to locate a file about redialing; then download this file.

1. Enter **2** to Browse thru Files. CompuServe asks you to Enter keywords or <CR> for all.

2. Enter **REDIAL**. CompuServe prompts Oldest files in days or <CR> for all.

3. Press Enter for all.

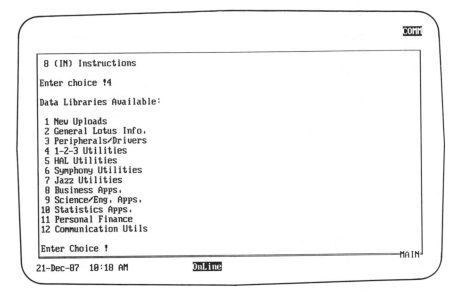

Fig. 18.6

The Data Libraries menu.

You are looking for the file called REDIAL.WRK. It's possible that this file will be the only one listed, but if not, follow the instructions on-screen to browse through the files. See figure 18.7 for a description of REDIAL.WRK. This file is small (approximately 2000 bytes), so it shouldn't take too long to download.

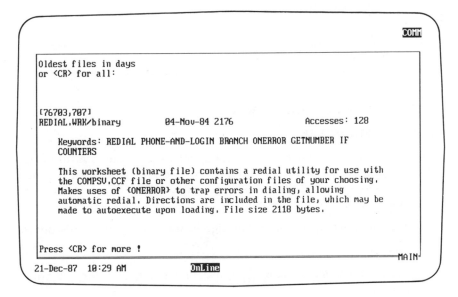

Fig. 18.7

A description of REDIAL.WRK.

1. If the message Press <CR> for more is displayed, press Enter.

2. When you get the message <CR> for disposition menu !, press Enter.

3. Enter **2** to download this file.

4. Enter **1** for XMODEM (MODEM7) protocol. The message Starting XMODEM transfer. Please initiate XMODEM transfer... appears, as shown in figure 18.8. This message is telling you to issue Symphony's **File-Transfer** command.

Fig. 18.8

The screen before you begin the file transfer.

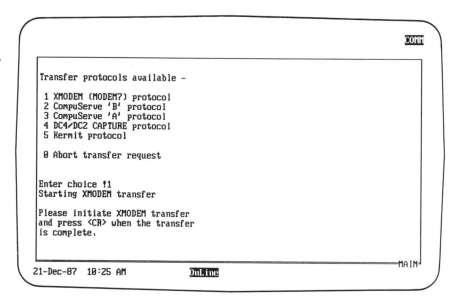

```
                                                              COMM

   Transfer protocols available -

   1 XMODEM (MODEM7) protocol
   2 CompuServe 'B' protocol
   3 CompuServe 'A' protocol
   4 DC4/DC2 CAPTURE protocol
   5 Kermit protocol

   0 Abort transfer request


   Enter choice !1
   Starting XMODEM transfer

   Please initiate XMODEM transfer
   and press <CR> when the transfer
   is complete.

                                                            MAIN
   21-Dec-87  10:25 AM            OnLine
```

5. Select COMM **File-Transfer Receive**.

6. Enter **REDIAL.WRK**.

As the file downloads, you will see a status message in the control panel that reads xx bytes received, 0 errors corrected, where **xx** is a number which will increase to the file size (in this case, 2176). When the file transfer is complete, log off of CompuServe.

1. Press Enter when the status message in the control panel disappears.

2. Enter **bye**.

3. Select COMM **Phone Hangup** to disconnect, and then turn off your modem.

Don't forget that while you were logged onto CompuServe, you captured the Symphony Q&As to the spreadsheet. You should save the spreadsheet to a file.

1. Press Alt-F9 to switch to SHEET mode.

2. Select SERVICES **F**ile **S**ave.

3. Enter **Q&A** for the file name. You can read or print this file later.

Retrieve the REDIAL worksheet you downloaded and see what it contains.

1. Select SERVICES **F**ile **R**etrieve.

2. Enter **REDIAL**.

This file contains a macro that will automatically dial and log into an information service.

Chapter Summary

In this practice session, you first modified the CompuServe communications configuration file (COMPUSRV.CCF) that is included with the Symphony program. You then used your modem to connect with CompuServe's computer and accessed a special information service called The World of Lotus. You used Symphony communications commands to capture data in a spreadsheet range and to download a small spreadsheet file. To help you fully understand this file, read the next chapter, "Creating and Using Macros."

PART VII

Symphony Macros and the Command Language

Includes

Creating and Using Macros

An Introduction to the Command Language

19

Creating and
Using Macros

Imagine a hand emerging from your computer and typing Symphony commands for you while you sit back and relax. This idea is what macros are all about. You can reduce multiple keystrokes to a two-keystroke operation with Symphony macros: Press two keys, and Symphony does the rest, whether you're formatting a range, creating a graph, or printing a spreadsheet.

This chapter introduces the concept of macros; explains how to create, use, and debug macros; and provides numerous examples that you can copy for your own applications.

What Is a Macro?

In its most basic form, a macro is simply a collection of keystrokes. A macro is like a storehouse of keystrokes. These keystrokes can be commands or simple text and numeric entries. You can use a macro rather than the keyboard to issue a command or to enter data in the Symphony spreadsheet.

If you are a Symphony novice, you may think macros are something to leave to Symphony gurus and computer programmers. This chapter shows you how easy macros are to build, however, and gives you a number of macros that you can create and use immediately. Even if you are new to Symphony, you can begin experimenting with macros.

The Elements of Macros

Once you have decided what you want a macro to do (for example, format a cell in currency format with 0 decimal places), follow four basic steps:

1. Enter the macro keystrokes in a spreadsheet cell.

2. Name the macro.

3. Invoke the macro, using the name you gave it.

4. Correct any errors in the macro, if necessary.

The following section, "Creating Macros," discusses the first two steps. The last two steps are explained in the sections entitled "Using Macros" and "Debugging Macros."

Creating Macros

Suppose that you want to create a simple macro that will format the current cell in the **Currency** format with **0** decimal places. If you execute this command manually, your keystrokes are (1) press the Menu key (F10), (2) select Format, (3) select **Currency**, (4) type **0**, (5) press Enter, and (6) press Enter again to format only the current cell.

You can create this macro in two different ways. You can either enter the macro into the worksheet exactly as you enter any other label (by typing all the characters), or you can use the Learn mode to have Symphony type in the macros for you. (Learn mode is discussed in the next section.) Here's how the macro would look in a spreadsheet cell:

    {MENU}fc0~~

{MENU} is the special macro keyword used to bring up the menu. The fc stands for **Format Currency**, and the 0 tells Symphony that you want no digits to be displayed to the right of the decimal.

At the end of the macro are two characters called tildes. When used in a macro, the tilde (~) represents the Enter key. In this case, the two tildes signal two presses of the Enter key. If you were entering this command from the keyboard, you would have to press Enter twice: after supplying the 0 for the number of decimals, and again to signal that the format applied to the current cell.

Symphony also uses symbols other than the ~ to represent keystrokes. For example, look at the following macro:

    {MENU}fc0~{END}{RIGHT}~

This macro is similar to the one just discussed, except that this version also causes the cell pointer to move. You can use this macro to format an entire row rather than just one cell. Notice the phrase {END}{RIGHT} in the macro. The {END} stands for the End key on the keyboard. The {RIGHT} represents the → key. {END}{RIGHT} has the same effect in the macro as these two keys would have if you typed them in sequence from the keyboard. The pointer moves to the next boundary between blank and nonblank cells in the row.

Symphony uses symbols like these to represent all the special keys on the IBM PC, AT, and PS/2 keyboards. In every case, the name of the function key (such as RIGHT for the →, or CALC for function key F9) is enclosed in braces. For example, {UP} represents the ↑ key, {TAB} stands for the Tab key, and {EDIT} represents the Edit (F2) key.

Table 19.1 shows the complete list of special key representations. If you are entering the keystrokes for the macro manually, you must use these representations to enter the keys or commands. If you are using Learn mode, Symphony will enter these representations for you as you press the corresponding keys or commands.

Table 19.1
Macro Key Representations

Function Keys

Representation	Corresponding Key
{ABS}	F3 in SHEET window
{CALC}	F8 in SHEET window
{CAPTURE}	F4 in COMM window
{CENTER}	Alt-F4 in DOC window
{DRAW}	Alt-F8
{EDIT}	F2 in SHEET and FORM windows
{ERASE}	F4 in a DOC window
{GOTO}	F5
{HELP}	F1
{INDENT}	F3 in DOC window
{JUSTIFY}	F2 in DOC window
{LEARN}	Alt-F5
{MENU} or {M}	F10
{SERVICES} or {S}	F9
{SPLIT}	Alt-F3
{SWITCH}	Alt-F9
{TYPE}	Alt-F10
{USER}	F7
{WHERE}	Alt-F2 in DOC window
{WINDOW}	F6
{ZOOM}	Alt-F6

Cursor-Movement Keys

Representation	Corresponding Key
{BIGLEFT}	Ctrl-←
{BIGRIGHT}	Ctrl-→
{DOWN}	↓
{END}	End
{HOME}	Home
{LEFT}	←
{PGDN} or {BIGDOWN}	PgDn
{PGUP} or {BIGUP}	PgUp
{RIGHT}	→
{UP}	↑

Other Special Keys

Representation	Corresponding Key
{BACKSPACE} or {BS}	Backspace
{BREAK}	Ctrl-Break
{DELETE}	Del
{ESCAPE} or {ESC}	Esc
{INSERT}	Ins
{TAB}	Tab
{?}	Causes macro to pause and wait for input from keyboard; macro resumes execution after you press Enter
~	Enter

Word-Processing Accelerator Keys

Representation	Corresponding Key
{AUTO}	Ctrl-J
{CASE}	Ctrl-X
{COPY}	Ctrl-C
{DLEFT}	Ctrl-T
{DLINE}	Ctrl-D
{DRIGHT}	Ctrl-Y
{DWORD}	Ctrl-Backspace
{FORMAT}	Ctrl-F
{MERGE}	Ctrl-O
{MOVE}	Ctrl-M
{NEXTPAGE}	Ctrl-PgDn
{PAGE}	Ctrl-N
{PASTE}	Ctrl-P
{REPLACE}	Ctrl-R
{SEARCH}	Ctrl-S
{TOPPAGE}	Ctrl-PgUp

Note that you must type a label prefix (such as an apostrophe) before any macro which begins with a nontext character (/, \, +, -, or any number). Otherwise, Symphony interprets the macro characters as numbers or commands, which it will immediately execute.

Because 240 characters is the maximum number of characters that can fit in a cell, you can type up to 240 characters for each macro in a single cell. If your macro contains more than 240 characters, you can continue typing in the cell directly underneath. (Do not leave a blank line, because the macro stops when it reaches a blank cell.) You may want to divide the macro into consecutive cells before the 240-character limit is reached. By placing different functions of a long macro on separate lines, your macro is easier to read. Compare the two macros in figure 19.1.

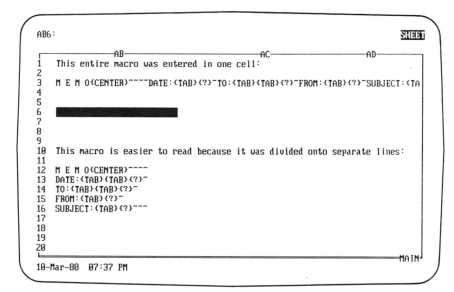

Fig. 19.1

Two macros compared.

Learn Mode

Instead of remembering what your keystrokes are and then entering them manually into a spreadsheet cell, you can use Symphony's Learn mode to record the keystrokes. Learn mode is similar to a tape recorder. Before you can turn on the tape recorder, though, you need to designate a range in the spreadsheet where you want Symphony to store the keystrokes. Use the SERVICES Settings Learn Range command and designate a cell or a column of cells (such as AA1..AA20) as the Learn range.

When you are ready to begin recording the keystrokes, press the Learn key (Alt-F5). The message Learn appears at the bottom of the screen. Now every key you press is translated into a macro command and stored in the Learn range. To enter the simple formatting macro discussed in the previous section, press F10, type **fc0**, and press Enter twice. To turn off the recording, press the Learn key (Alt-F5) again. The Learn message disappears.

If you look in your Learn range in the spreadsheet, you can see the same macro that you entered manually in the previous section:

{MENU}fc∅~~

The keys you pressed in Learn mode were automatically translated into the special macro representations (for example, ~ for Enter). You can see that using the Learn mode is by far the easier method.

Function Key Grammar

To specify more than one use of a special key, you can include repetition factors inside the braces of a special-key phrase. For example, you can use the following statements:

{PGUP 3}
{RIGHT JUMP}

These statements translate to: Press the PgUp key three times in a row, and press the right-arrow key the number of times indicated by the value in the cell with a range name JUMP.

Where To Put the Macros

The safest place to put your macros is in their own window, with a restrict range specified. This method keeps you from accidentally overwriting or erasing part of a macro as you create your model. Also, if you create a window for your macros, you can quickly move to them by pressing the Window key (F6).

You can create your macro window anywhere outside the active area of your model. Since most models rarely require more than 26 columns, column AA is a practical location for your macros. To create the window, use the SERVICES **W**indow **C**reate command. Enter MACROS as the window name, select SHEET as the window type, and press Enter to accept the entire screen as the area.

The next step is to restrict the range of the window. It's very important not to overlook this step or else you are defeating the main purpose of creating a window for your macros. With a restrict range specified you will not run the risk of accidentally destroying your macros when you make changes to your model. Select **R**estrict **R**ange and highlight the number of columns and rows you think you'll need for your macros. (You can always expand the range later if your need to.)

Documenting Your Macros

The macros that you create in this chapter are simple and don't require much explanation. But the more commands a macro executes, the more difficult it is to understand. Suppose that you have created a complex macro but have not looked at it for a month. Then you decide that you want to modify the macro. Without built-in comments, you might have a difficult time remembering what each step of the macro does.

That's where documentation comes in. Place comments next to each step of the macro so that you, or someone else, can determine exactly what the macro does. The best method is to place the comments in the column to the right of the macro next to the macro steps. For example, in the simple macro in figure 19.2, the macro name is in column AA, the macro itself is in column AB, and the comments are in column AC.

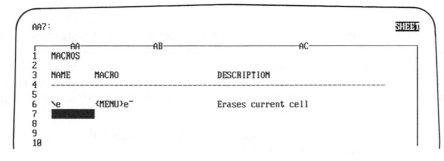

Fig. 19.2

A suggested macro layout.

Naming Macros

A macro that you have entered in the worksheet as a label (or a series of labels) must be given a name before you can invoke the macro. Ranges containing macros are assigned names just like any other range. Three different types of macro names are available.

One kind of macro name is a single alphabetic character, preceded by a backslash (\). For example, you might want to name the format macro \f. The second type of macro name can be up to 15 characters long (the standard limit for range names). Although the first method is easier and faster, use the second method if you like longer, more descriptive macro names. The third type of macro name is a number (1 through 10) preceded by a backslash. For example, you can name a macro \10.

Using Range Name Create

Suppose that you just built the macro shown in figure 19.3. Now you need to name this macro so that you can invoke it from the keyboard. You have decided to name the macro \d (for dollar). It is always a good idea to choose a name that in some way describes the macro. Obviously, creating descriptive one-letter names is difficult. In this case, for example, you could choose the name \d (for dollar) or \f (for format). You might want to name this macro \$, but because the symbol $ is not a letter, \$ is not a legal macro name.

Fig. 19.3

A sample macro.

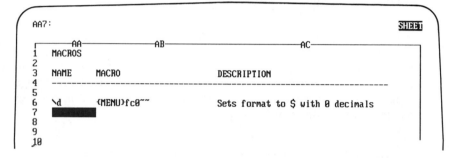

To assign the name, issue the command SHEET **Range Name Create**. Next, type the name you selected—**\d**—and press Enter. Finally, Symphony prompts you for the range to name. If the cell pointer is currently on cell AB6, which is where the macro itself is located, you can simply press Enter to assign the name to the cell. Otherwise, you must move the cell pointer to the appropriate cell, or type the cell coordinates from the keyboard.

Some macros require more than one row in the spreadsheet. For example, look at the simple two-row macro in figure 19.4.

Fig. 19.4

A simple two-row macro.

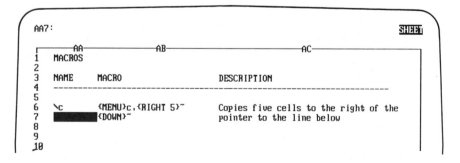

To name this macro, you need to assign a name to only the first cell in the range that contains the macro. In this case, you would assign the name \c to cell AB6. You can indicate the entire range, AB6..AB7, but it's not necessary.

Using Range Name Labels Right

Another way to name cells is with the SHEET **R**ange **N**ame **L**abels **R**ight command. This method works only if you have typed the macro names next to the keystrokes. The **L**abels **R**ight command allows you to name a range by using the contents of the cell immediately to the left as the range name. For example, suppose that you had created the macros in figure 19.5.

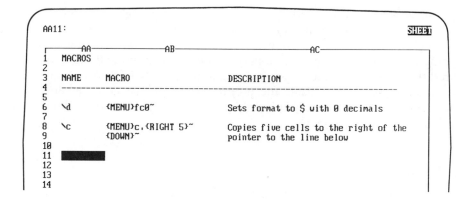

Fig. 19.5

Two sample macros.

With your cell pointer on cell AA6, you can name both macros at once with the SHEET **R**ange **N**ame **L**abels **R**ight command. When asked for the label range, highlight the range AA6..AA8. Symphony assigns the name \d to cell AB6, and the name \c to cell AB8.

If you are documenting your macros properly, you will already have the names in the sheet; therefore, using the **L**abels **R**ight option is a simple and convenient way to name all your macros simultaneously.

Executing Macros

You execute, or invoke, macros whose names consist of a backslash and a letter (for example, \d) by pressing the Macro key (usually the Alt key) and at the same time pressing the letter name of the macro. For example, if the macro you want to use is named \d, you invoke the macro by pressing Alt-D. The \ symbol in the name is a representation of the Alt key.

Macros you named with regular range names are invoked with the User key (F7). When you press the User key, a User indicator appears at the lower right corner of the screen. You can then enter the name of the macro you want to execute. As you type the characters in the name, they appear in place of the User indicator. If you enter a macro name longer than four characters, the name scrolls across the indicator.

If you assigned a number as the macro name (for example, \2), you invoke the macro by pressing the User key followed by the function key of the name (F2, in this case).

As soon as you issue the command, the macro starts to run. If the macro does not contain any bugs or pause instructions, it will continue to run until finished. You will be amazed at its speed. The commands are issued faster than you can see them.

You can store many macro keystrokes or commands in a single cell. Some macros that are especially long or include special commands must be split into two or more cells, like the example shown in figure 19.4. When Symphony starts executing a macro, the program continues in the first cell until all the keystrokes stored there have been used. Symphony then moves down one cell to continue execution. If that cell is blank, the program stops. If that cell contains more macro commands, however, Symphony continues reading down the column until reaching the first blank cell.

Automatic Macros

Symphony offers an exciting macro feature called automatic macro execution. This technique allows you to create a special macro that executes automatically when you retrieve the file that contains the macro. First you create this macro just like you do any other macro. Then you specify the macro's name in the SERVICES Settings Auto-Execute Set command.

An even more powerful feature is Symphony's capability to load a model automatically into the worksheet. Use the SERVICES Configuration Auto command and specify the name of the file you want Symphony to retrieve each time you load the program. Select Update to save the new configuration. If the file contains an autoexecute macro, the macro automatically executes when you load Symphony.

You can use these two automatic features to create completely self-contained programs in the Symphony worksheet. Pressing the Alt or User key is not required to start the macro in these cases. When combined with menus and the other useful macro commands, the automatic execution feature makes macros a remarkably user-friendly tool.

The section entitled "Some Simple Macros" provides an example of an auto-execute macro in an autoload file.

Debugging Macros

Although your macros will contain fewer errors if you write the macros automatically with Learn mode rather than type them yourself manually, sometimes a macro does not work perfectly the first time. Errors that cause the program to malfunction are called "bugs" and the process of eliminating them is called "debugging."

Common Errors

Like all computer programs, macros are literal creatures. They have no capability to discern an error in the code. For example, you can recognize immediately that {GOTI} is a misspelling of {GOTO}. But a macro cannot see the mistake. The macro tries instead to interpret the misspelled word and, being unable to, delivers an error message.

If you enclose in braces a phrase that is not a key name or a command keyword, Symphony returns the error message

```
Unrecognized key Range name{...}(A1)
```

where { ... } represents the invalid key name and (A1) tells you that the error occurred in cell A1.

Consequently, you must be extremely careful when you build your macros so that they have no errors. Even misplaced spaces and tildes can cause difficulty for Symphony. No matter how careful you are, however, some errors are going to slip through.

The biggest problem most beginners have with macros is forgetting to represent all of the required Enter keystrokes in the macros. This omission can lead to some dismaying results. For example, the missing ~ after the {RIGHT 5} in the macro in figure 19.6 causes the {DOWN} command to be included in the definition of the FROM range of the SHEET Copy command, instead of defining the TO range. The result of running this macro is shown in figure 19.7. As you can see, the SHEET Copy command in the macro stopped in the middle of its execution because of the missing tilde.

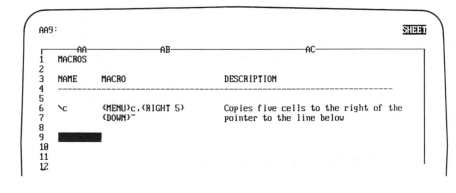

Fig. 19.6

A macro with a missing ~.

Fig. 19.7

The result of running the macro with the missing ~.

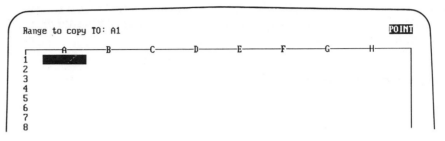

Another big problem with Symphony macros is that the cell references included in macros are always absolute. The references do not change when, for example, cells are moved about or deleted from the sheet. For example, this simple macro erases the contents of cell A6:

{MENU}eA6~

But suppose that you use the SHEET Move command to move the contents of cell A6 to B6. Because cell references in formulas automatically adjust when cells are moved, you might expect your macro to read:

{MENU}eB6~

If you try this example, however, you will see that the macro has not changed.

If you think about it for a second, this rigidity makes perfect sense. A macro is nothing but a label, and you wouldn't expect other labels to change when the sheet is changed. For example, if you created the label

A15A15A15A15

you wouldn't expect it to change to

C15C15C15C15

if you inserted two columns in the sheet to the left of column A. Macros are no different.

The absolute nature of cell references within macros is a strong argument in favor of using range names. A range name remains associated with the same range even if you move that range. Range names within macros (and other formulas) follow the cells to which the names apply, thus eliminating the absolute reference problem. Be careful, however, not to use range names that are also macro keywords or key representations. For example, do not create a range name called EDIT.

Stepping through a Buggy Macro

Like programs written in other programming languages, Symphony macros often need to be debugged before you can use them. Symphony has an extremely useful tool that helps make debugging much simpler: the Step function. When Symphony is in Step mode, all macros are executed one step at a time. Symphony literally pauses between each keystroke stored in the macro. Thus you can follow the macro's execution step by step.

Let's step through the buggy macro developed in figure 19.6. This macro was supposed to copy the contents of five cells to the next line. If you look at figure 19.7 to see the results of executing the macro, you see no indication that the second line has been included in the FROM range. All you know is that the macro ends with the program waiting for you to specify the TO range.

When you discover an error, you must first exit the macro and change to READY mode by pressing Ctrl-Break and Esc. When the mode indicator says READY, you can start debugging the macro.

But if you don't know what the macro's problem is, your next step is to enter Step mode and rerun the macro. To invoke the single-step mode, press Alt-F7. The message Step appears at the bottom of the screen. This message flashes Pause as soon as you press Alt-C to execute the \c macro. At this point, the macro moves forward only one step at a time. After each step, the macro pauses and waits for you to type a key before the macro proceeds to the next step. Although you can use any key to step through a macro, you may find the space bar the easiest.

As you step through the macro, you will see each command appear in the control panel. In this example, the \c macro was executed with the cell pointer in cell A1. Just before the error occurs, the control panel looks like the one shown in figure 19.8. Because the macro does not have a tilde (the Enter key) after the FROM range is specified, the TO range is included as part of the FROM range.

Thanks to single-step mode, you can easily pinpoint the error's location in the macro. Once you identify the error, you can exit Step mode by pressing Alt-F7 again. Abort the macro by pressing Ctrl-Break and Esc; then you're ready to repair the macro's error.

Editing the Macro

Fixing an error in a macro is as simple as editing the cell that contains the erroneous code. You don't need to rewrite or rename the cell. You need only to change the element in error.

In this example, first move the pointer to cell AB6, then press F2 to enter EDIT mode. Because the error is a missing ~, fixing the macro is easy. Just type ~ and press Enter.

Editing complex macros is no different from editing this simple macro. Just use Symphony's cell editor (F2) to correct the cell that contains the error.

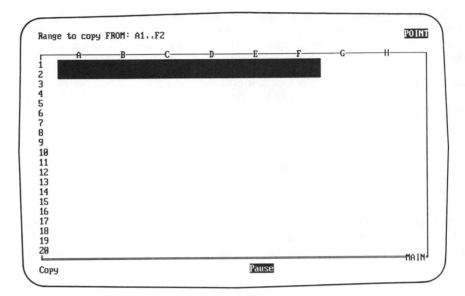

Fig. 19.8

*An extra line
included in the
FROM range.*

Some Simple Macros

Now that you have a feel for all the different macro commands available in Symphony, as well as a good general understanding of Symphony's work environments, you are probably thinking about ways you can use macros to speed up tasks you do frequently. To get you started, this section provides practical, yet simple, examples of macros for all of Symphony's different work environments.

Look through the following macros, select the ones you find most useful, and enter them in your macro library. To enter any of the macros in this section, you should follow the steps outlined in the previous sections. In summary, you will need to take these steps:

1. Enter the keystrokes, either manually or automatically (with Learn mode), in a spreadsheet cell.

   Note: Some of the macros contain special macro commands (for example, {?}) that you cannot enter with Learn mode, so you must enter these commands manually.

2. Name the macro with the SHEET **R**ange **N**ame **C**reate or **R**ange **N**ame **L**abels **R**ight command.

3. Invoke the macro with either the Alt or User key, depending on the type of name you gave the macro.

4. Debug the macro and correct any errors.

Utility Macros for Any Environment

You can use the following macros in any of Symphony's five environments because these macros all use commands invoked by the Services key. As you know, the SERVICES menu contains commands applicable to any work environment. The utility macros are listed in figure 19.9. Included are macros to save, retrieve, and print files.

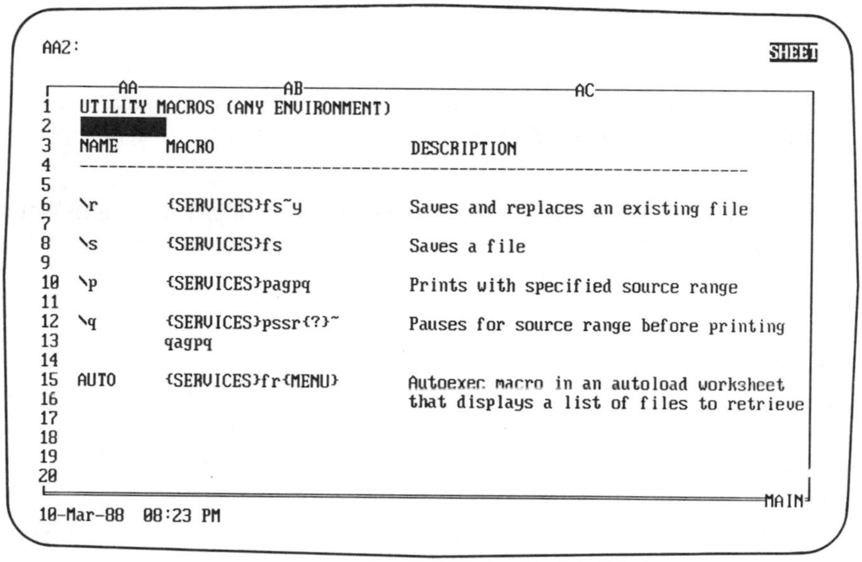

```
AA2:                                                           SHEET
       ┌───AA────────────AB──────────────────────AC──────────
      1 UTILITY MACROS (ANY ENVIRONMENT)
      2 ███████████
      3 NAME      MACRO              DESCRIPTION
      4 ─────────────────────────────────────────────────────────────
      5
      6 \r        {SERVICES}fs~y     Saves and replaces an existing file
      7
      8 \s        {SERVICES}fs       Saves a file
      9
     10 \p        {SERVICES}pagpq    Prints with specified source range
     11
     12 \q        {SERVICES}pssr{?}~ Pauses for source range before printing
     13           qagpq
     14
     15 AUTO      {SERVICES}fr{MENU} Autoexec macro in an autoload worksheet
     16                              that displays a list of files to retrieve
     17
     18
     19
     20
       └─────────────────────────────────────────────────MAIN┘
     10-Mar-88  08:23 PM
```

Fig. 19.9

Utility macros for any environment.

Save Macros

Normally, resaving a file with the same name takes five keystrokes. Because saving is so important, you should make the process as quick and painless as possible by creating save macros.

The save and replace macro (\r) is

    {SERVICES}fs~y

This macro displays the SERVICES menu, selects File Save, presses Enter to keep the same name, and selects **Yes** to replace.

You must be careful never to use this macro on a file you have not named yet. If you do, you will replace the first file in your directory with this new worksheet!

Consequently, you may want your save macro to stop before replacing the file. The macro

    {SERVICES}fs

displays the SERVICES menu and selects **File Save**. Then you can enter a name, or press Enter and type **Y** to save the file under the same name.

Print Macros

One of the first macros you will want to create is a printing macro. You will love the convenience of simply pressing two keys (such as Alt-P) to print. The following \p macro prints in DOC mode, or in any other mode as long as you have specified the **Source Range**:

```
{SERVICES}pagpq
```

This macro displays the SERVICES menu, selects the **Print** command, **Aligns** the paper, prints with **G**o, gives a **Page-Advance**, and selects **Quit** to leave the **Print** menu.

The \p macro prints the document with the current settings for margins, source range, headers, footers, and so on. If you want the macro to ask you for a **Source Range**, create the following macro:

```
{SERVICES}pssr{?}~
qagpq
```

which displays the SERVICES menu, selects the **Print** command, and selects Settings **Source Range**. The {?} pauses for you to enter a range; then the macro selects **Quit** to exit the **Settings** menu, **Aligns** the paper, prints with **G**o, gives a **Page-Advance**, and selects **Quit** to leave the **Print** menu.

When the {?} macro command pauses the macro so that you can enter the **Source Range**, you can enter the range by pointing and highlighting or by typing. As soon as you press Enter, the macro continues executing.

See Chapter 20 for a print macro that uses the Command Language to print multiple copies of a spreadsheet or document.

An Autoexecuting Macro

The first thing most of you probably do once you load Symphony is retrieve a file. By creating a file-retrieving macro and specifying it as an autoexecuting macro in an autoloading worksheet, you can have Symphony automatically display a list of file names from which you can choose.

Here's how it's done. First, in a blank spreadsheet, create the following macro:

```
{SERVICES}fr{MENU}
```

After displaying the SERVICES menu, this macro invokes the **File Retrieve** command and uses the Menu key to display the files in an alphabetical, multicolumn list. Give the macro a name such as AUTO. Specify the macro as autoexecuting by selecting the SERVICES **S**ettings **A**uto-Execute command. Enter **AUTO** for the range.

Also save the file with a name like AUTO. Specify this file as autoloading by selecting the SERVICES **C**onfiguration **A**uto command. Enter the name **AUTO**. Select **U**pdate to save the settings.

Now, whenever you load Symphony, you can simply point to the file you want to retrieve and press Enter.

Macros in the SHEET Environment

This section describes how to create macros that will draw lines (horizontal and vertical), sum a column of numbers, set column widths, and move the cell pointer during data entry. The macros are listed in figure 19.10.

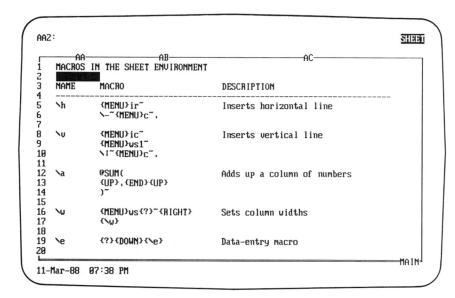

```
AA2:                                                            SHEET
      ┌─────AA────────────AB──────────────────────AC─────────
    1 │MACROS IN THE SHEET ENVIRONMENT
    2 │████████████
    3 │NAME      MACRO                  DESCRIPTION
    4 │─────────────────────────────────────────────────────────
    5 │\h        {MENU}ir~             Inserts horizontal line
    6 │          \-~{MENU}c~.
    7 │
    8 │\v        {MENU}ic~             Inserts vertical line
    9 │          {MENU}ws1~
   10 │          \!~{MENU}c~.
   11 │
   12 │\a        @SUM(                 Adds up a column of numbers
   13 │          {UP},{END}{UP}
   14 │          )~
   15 │
   16 │\w        {MENU}ws{?}~{RIGHT}   Sets column widths
   17 │          {\w}
   18 │
   19 │\e        {?}{DOWN}{\e}         Data-entry macro
   20 │
      └──────────────────────────────────────────────────MAIN┘
11-Mar-88  07:38 PM
```

Fig. 19.10

Sample macros for the SHEET environment.

A Macro To Draw Horizontal Lines

You can improve the legibility and appearance of your spreadsheets by adding dashed lines under column headings and above total rows. The \h macro assumes that you have not left a blank line for the dashed line, so the macro inserts a row before creating the dashed line.

```
{MENU}ir~
'\-~{MENU}c~.
```

This macro selects **I**nsert **R**ow from the SHEET menu, enters the repeating label (\-), selects SHEET **C**opy, presses Enter for the FROM range, and presses a period to anchor the TO range. Because your lines will vary in length, the macro stops so that you can highlight the number of cells into which you want to copy.

A Macro To Draw Vertical Lines

Vertical lines can also help you or another user read a large worksheet. The \v macro assumes that you are inserting the lines after the worksheet is completed; consequently, the macro begins by inserting a column.

```
{MENU}ic~
{MENU}ws1~
'\|~{MENU}c~.
```

In the first line, the \v macro selects **I**nsert **C**olumn from the SHEET menu. Then in the succeeding lines, the macro selects SHEET **W**idth **S**et, enters **1** for the column width, enters a vertical bar with the repeating-label prefix (\|), selects SHEET **C**opy, presses Enter for the FROM range, and presses a period to anchor the TO range. Again, the macro stops to let you define the length of the line.

A Macro To Sum a Column

Because adding up a column of numbers is a common spreadsheet task, the \a macro would be a perfect "addition" to your macro library.

```
'@SUM(
{UP}.{END}{UP}
)~
```

This summing macro begins the @SUM function, moves the pointer up one cell to the bottom of the column, anchors with a period, moves the pointer to the top of the column with {END}{UP}, ends the formula with a), and presses Enter.

The macro uses two shortcuts with which you may not be familiar. The first shortcut is to begin the range definition at the bottom rather than the top. This method is faster because the pointer needn't move all the way to the top and then back to the bottom. Thus, {UP} moves the cell pointer to the bottom of the column. {END}{UP} is the second shortcut employed by the macro. {END}{UP} highlights until reaching a blank cell, so the macro finds the top of the column of numbers (if no blank cells exist in the range you are summing).

The \a macro works only if the cell above the pointer contains a value or label. If the cell is blank, the macro sums the wrong range.

A Macro To Set Column Widths

Use the \w macro when you need to set the column widths of several consecutive columns.

```
{MENU}ws{?}~{RIGHT}
{\w}
```

This macro invokes the SHEET Width Set command, then pauses for you to enter a column width. The macro next presses Enter, moves the pointer to the next column to the right, and then automatically reexecutes. This automatic looping is accomplished by placing the macro name in braces, {\w}. This program, however, is what is called an infinite loop: it continues endlessly. So how do you stop it? Like you stop any macro—by pressing Ctrl-Break and Esc.

You can build similar macros for any command (such as formatting) that you want to repeat several times to consecutive columns or rows.

A Data-Entry Macro

Data entry often involves entering a series of numbers down a column. With the \e macro, your PC keyboard has some of the same convenience as an enhanced keyboard; you no longer need to toggle between numbers and arrows on the 10-key numeric keypad. You can turn Num Lock on to enter numbers, and the macro takes care of moving the cell pointer.

```
{?}{DOWN}{\e}
```

This macro pauses to let you enter data; moves the pointer down one cell; and loops back to the beginning, pausing for you to enter the next number.

Before invoking the macro, press the Num Lock key so that you can use the 10-key pad to enter numbers. When you are finished entering numbers in that column, press Ctrl-Break to stop the macro. Turn Num Lock off (or hold down the Shift key while pressing the arrows), and move the pointer to the next column. Then reactivate Num Lock and the macro.

If you enter data across rows, you can change the {DOWN} statement to {RIGHT}.

Macros in the DOC Environment

Because word processing often involves repetitive tasks, you will probably create a set of macros you use regularly and keep them in your macro library. Figure 19.11 illustrates some word-processing macros. You will see the need for other macros as you edit, and you can create them "on the fly" to speed up a repetitive editing process.

Fig. 19.11

Sample macros for the DOC environment.

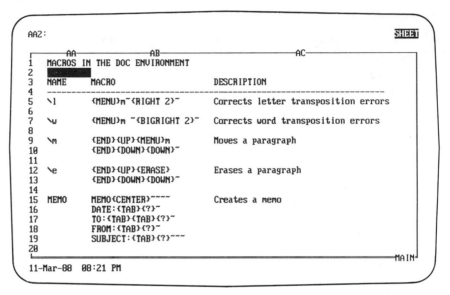

```
AA2:                                                           SHEET
      ┌──AA──────────AB───────────────────────AC─────────────
    1 │MACROS IN THE DOC ENVIRONMENT
    2 │████████
    3 │NAME    MACRO              DESCRIPTION
    4 │────────────────────────────────────────────────────────
    5 │\l      {MENU}m~{RIGHT 2}~  Corrects letter transposition errors
    6 │
    7 │\w      {MENU}m ~{BIGRIGHT 2}~  Corrects word transposition errors
    8 │
    9 │\m      {END}{UP}{MENU}m    Moves a paragraph
   10 │        {END}{DOWN}{DOWN}~
   11 │
   12 │\e      {END}{UP}{ERASE}    Erases a paragraph
   13 │        {END}{DOWN}{DOWN}~
   14 │
   15 │MEMO    MEMO{CENTER}~~~~    Creates a memo
   16 │        DATE:{TAB}{?}~
   17 │        TO:{TAB}{TAB}{?}~
   18 │        FROM:{TAB}{?}~
   19 │        SUBJECT:{TAB}{?}~~~
   20 │                                                     MAIN
      └──────────────────────────────────────────────────────
   11-Mar-88  08:21 PM
```

This section includes macros for correcting typing mistakes (transposing letters and words), moving a paragraph, erasing a paragraph, and creating a memo. Several Spelling Checker macros are also included, as shown in figure 19.12.

Fig. 19.12

Sample Spelling Checker macros.

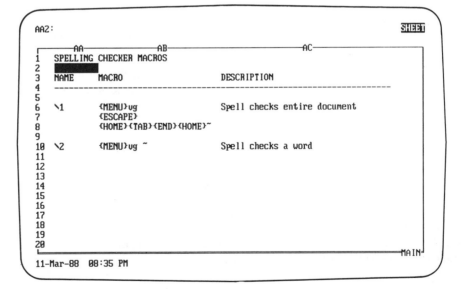

```
AA2:                                                           SHEET
      ┌──AA──────────AB───────────────────────AC─────────────
    1 │SPELLING CHECKER MACROS
    2 │████████
    3 │NAME    MACRO              DESCRIPTION
    4 │────────────────────────────────────────────────────────
    5 │
    6 │\1      {MENU}vg           Spell checks entire document
    7 │        {ESCAPE}
    8 │        {HOME}{TAB}{END}{HOME}~
    9 │
   10 │\2      {MENU}vg ~         Spell checks a word
   11 │
   12 │
   13 │
   14 │
   15 │
   16 │
   17 │
   18 │
   19 │
   20 │                                                     MAIN
      └──────────────────────────────────────────────────────
   11-Mar-88  08:35 PM
```

Letter-Transposition Macro

One common typographical error is transposed letters. For example, you may type *recieve* rather than *receive*. The \l macro uses the DOC Move command to correct the error.

```
{MENU}m~{LEFT}~
```

The \l macro displays the DOC menu, selects Move, presses Enter, moves the cell pointer to the left, and again presses Enter.

To invoke the macro, place the cell pointer on the second transposed letter and press Alt-L.

Word-Transposition Macro

Another useful macro for editing in a DOC window is the word-transposition macro, which enables you to transpose two words located next to each other. Like the letter-transposition macro just described, the word-transposition macro (\w) uses the DOC Move command to correct the error.

```
{MENU}m ~{BIGRIGHT 2}~
```

This macro selects DOC Move, presses the space bar to highlight the word, presses Enter, presses Ctrl-→ twice to move to the target location, and finally presses Enter.

The cell pointer should be on the first letter of the first transposed word when you invoke this macro with Alt-W.

Paragraph-Moving Macro

A paragraph is one of the most common blocks of text you move in a document. The \m macro highlights a paragraph and stops so that you can enter the target location.

```
{END}{UP}{MENU}m
{END}{DOWN}{DOWN}~
```

This handy macro moves the cell pointer to the beginning of the paragraph, selects DOC Move, moves the cell pointer to the end of the paragraph, and presses Enter. Remember that the {END}{UP} combination moves the cell pointer to the beginning of the paragraph, while {END}{DOWN} moves the cell pointer to the end of the paragraph. Note the extra {DOWN} in the macro. This instruction highlights the line after the paragraph, so that you won't have spacing problems after the move.

To invoke the paragraph-moving macro, press Alt-M with the cell pointer placed anywhere in the paragraph except on the first character. The macro executes until it reaches the Move TO where? prompt. At this point, you should move the cell pointer to the location in your document to which you want the paragraph moved. Finally, press Enter to complete the move operation.

Paragraph-Erasing Macro

Although Symphony Release 2.0 has accelerator keys for erasing words, lines, and parts of lines, you may want to create macros for deleting other blocks of text. The \e macro erases a paragraph.

```
{END}{UP}{ERASE}
{END}{DOWN}{DOWN}~
```

The macro moves the cell pointer to the beginning of the paragraph, presses the Erase key, highlights to the end of the paragraph, and presses Enter. Before invoking the macro, make sure the cell pointer is anywhere in the paragraph except the first character. This macro isn't much different from the paragraph-moving macro; the erasing macro simply substitutes {ERASE} for {MENU}m.

Memo Macro

The memo macro (MEMO) enters the constant headings (TO:, FROM:, and so on) of a memo and then pauses for you to enter the variable information.

```
MEMO{CENTER}~~~~
DATE:{TAB}{?}~
TO:{TAB}{TAB}{?}~
FROM:{TAB}{?}~
SUBJECT:{TAB}{?}~~~
```

The MEMO macro types and centers the word **MEMO**, presses Enter four times to get blank lines, enters **DATE:**, presses Tab, pauses for you to type, and presses Enter. These steps are repeated for each memo heading line. You may need to change this macro to conform to your company's memo format. If the memos are always from the same person, you can fill in the name next to FROM: instead of pausing the macro at that point.

Execute this macro by pressing the User key (F7) and entering **MEMO**.

Spelling Checker Macros

Once you have attached the Spelling Checker add-in, you can use either of the Spelling Checker macros shown in figure 19.12. The first one (\1) specifies the entire document for the spell-check range, while the second one (\2) checks only the current word.

```
\1     {MENU}vg
       {ESCAPE}
       {HOME}{TAB}{END}{HOME}~
```

The \1 macro selects **Verify G**o from the DOC menu, presses Esc to unanchor, moves the cell pointer to the beginning of the document, reanchors with Tab, highlights to the end of the document, and presses Enter.

    \2   {MENU }vg ~

The second Spelling Checker macro selects DOC **Verify G**o, presses the space bar to highlight the word, and presses Enter. This macro assumes that the cell pointer is at the beginning of the word you want to check and that a space follows the word.

You execute these two macros with the User key. For example, to invoke the first macro, press the User key (F7) and then press F1. After the macro has executed, the correction menu displays, and you can correct the spelling errors in the document. (*Note:* You will not see the correction menu if Spelling Checker finds no misspelled words.)

Macros in the GRAPH Environment

Some useful macros for the GRAPH environment are listed in figure 19.13. These examples include macros to view a graph, select and view one of many graphs, and print a graph.

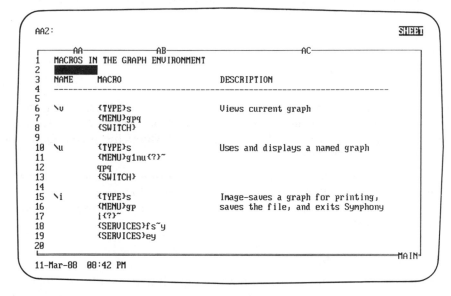

Fig. 19.13

Sample macros for the GRAPH environment.

Graph Preview Macro

Unlike 1-2-3, Symphony does not have a Graph function key that displays the current graph. In Symphony, you have to go to the menu—unless you create the \v macro:

```
{TYPE}s
{MENU}gpq
{SWITCH}
```

This preview macro changes the window type to SHEET, selects the **Graph Preview** command, exits the **Graph** menu with **Quit**, and switches window type.

You can execute the macro in any window type, because the first line begins by changing to a SHEET window. The last instruction in the macro switches you back to the window type you were in before executing the macro.

The macro pauses when the graph is displayed because this pause is an inherent part of the **Preview** command. Press any key to continue macro execution.

Choose-a-Graph Macro

When you have multiple graphs in a file, each graph has a name, and it takes quite a few keystrokes to load the graph settings and then look at the graph. The \u macro displays the list of graph names so that you can select the one you want, and then displays that graph.

```
{TYPE}s
{MENU}g1nu{?}~
qpq
{SWITCH}
```

This macro changes the window type to SHEET, selects **Graph 1st-Settings Name Use**, pauses to let you highlight the graph name, and presses Enter. Then the macro selects **Quit** to exit the **Settings** menu, **Previews** the graph, **Quits** the **Graph** menu, and switches window type.

The choose-a-graph macro is similar to the graph preview macro, except that the choosing macro allows you to select the graph before previewing. Like the preview macro, this macro pauses when the graph is displayed. Press any key, and the macro will continue executing.

Graph-Printing Macro

To print a graph, you need to save both the graph and the file and then exit Symphony. Use the \i macro when you have only one graph to print. (See the next chapter for a macro to print multiple graphs.)

```
{TYPE}s
{MENU}gp
i{?}~
{SERVICES}fs~y
{SERVICES}ey
```

The \i macro changes the window type to SHEET, selects **Graph Preview**, selects **Image-Save**, pauses to let you enter a file name, and presses Enter. Then the macro selects SERVICES **File Save**, presses Enter to keep the same name, selects **Yes** to replace, and selects SERVICES **Exit Yes** to leave Symphony.

The macro previews the graph so that you can make sure it is the one you want to print (press Ctrl-Break and Esc if you see the wrong graph). The macro assumes that you have previously saved the worksheet file. Also, this macro requires that you give the graph file a new name when you **Image-Save**. If you don't, the macro does not work.

Macros in the COMM Environment

Several simple COMM macros are listed in figure 19.14. These macros automatically dial a number in the spreadsheet, disconnect a call, log into a remote computer, and capture data to a printer during a communications session.

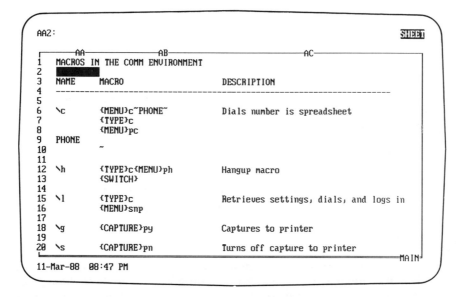

Fig. 19.14

Sample macros for the COMM environment.

Auto-Dialing Macro

The COMM environment does not limit you to dialing other computers. If you have a modem that can auto-dial, you can build a simple macro that dials a phone number in a spreadsheet cell. The \c macro is useful if you have a phone list in a spreadsheet or database. You must be in a SHEET window with the cell pointer on the number you want to dial before invoking this macro.

```
\c            {MENU}c~PHONE~
              {TYPE}c
              {MENU}pc
PHONE
                  ~
```

This macro selects **Copy** from the SHEET menu, presses Enter to copy from the current cell, enters **PHONE** as the range name to copy to, changes the window type to COMM, selects **Phone Call**, and presses Enter to dial the number. Notice the empty cell in the macro next to the word PHONE. This is the cell to which the phone number is copied. You should use the **Range Name** command to name this cell PHONE.

The auto-dialing macro is different from the other macros you have learned so far, because it is dynamic; a different phone number is copied into PHONE each time you invoke the macro.

If you use this macro to dial a person, you can pick up the phone as soon as the party answers. You can use the following hangup macro when you want to disconnect the call.

Hangup Macro

You can think of the hangup macro as a companion to the auto-dialing macro. You can use the \h macro to disconnect any call, whether the call was placed to another person or to a remote computer.

```
{TYPE}c{MENU}ph
{SWITCH}
```

The macro changes to a COMM window type, selects **Phone Hangup** from the COMM menu, and then switches back to the last environment you were in.

Log-in Macro

Symphony's **Phone-and-Login** command retrieves a communications settings sheet, dials the number, and logs into a remote computer. Even though this single command combines three separate commands, it still takes six keystrokes to execute. The \l macro executes in two.

```
{TYPE}c
{MENU}snp
```

This compact macro first changes the window type to COMM, then selects Settings **Name Phone-and-Login**. The macro stops at the point where you are asked to enter a communications configuration file name. You can select the name, and then the macro will dial the number and log in for you.

Capture Macros

When logged onto a remote computer, you may want to print what appears on your screen so that you have a hard copy record of your communications session. Most times, though, you don't want to print everything; you want to turn the printing on when important information displays and turn it off when menus and other unimportant messages appear. You can control printing with the \g and \s macros.

    \g   {CAPTURE}py

This simple macro presses the Capture key and selects **Printer Yes**.

    \s   {CAPTURE}pn

Conversely, the \s macro presses the Capture key and selects **Printer No**.

If you want to capture the data to a spreadsheet **Range** rather than to the **Printer**, substitute r for p in the two previous macros.

Macros for the FORM Environment

Simple macros to use in the FORM environment are listed in figure 19.15. These macros speed up searching and sorting in a FORM window.

Search Macros

To find records in a FORM window, you must complete a criterion record and instruct Symphony to use this criteria. The \c macro performs these commands automatically.

    {MENU}ce{?}~
    {PGUP}
    {MENU}cu

First, the macro selects **Criteria Edit** from the FORM menu and pauses for you to enter criteria. Then the macro returns to the database and selects **Criteria Use**.

When the criterion record displays and the macro pauses, use only the arrow keys to move between fields. If you press Enter, the macro continues executing before you have a chance to fill in the criteria.

Fig. 19.15

Sample macros for the FORM environment.

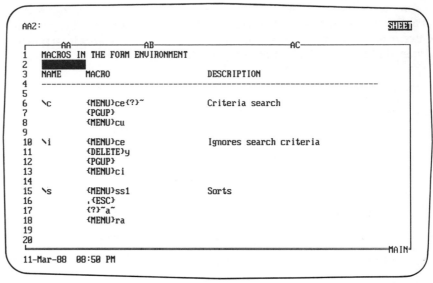

```
AA2:                                                              SHEET
        ┌──AA─────────────AB──────────────────────AC───────────────┐
       1│ MACROS IN THE FORM ENVIRONMENT                            │
       2│ ████████                                                  │
       3│ NAME      MACRO                    DESCRIPTION            │
       4│ ─────────────────────────────────────────────────────────│
       5│                                                           │
       6│ \c        {MENU}ce{?}~            Criteria search        │
       7│           {PGUP}                                          │
       8│           {MENU}cu                                        │
       9│                                                           │
      10│ \i        {MENU}ce                Ignores search criteria │
      11│           {DELETE}y                                       │
      12│           {PGUP}                                          │
      13│           {MENU}ci                                        │
      14│                                                           │
      15│ \s        {MENU}ss1               Sorts                   │
      16│           ,{ESC}                                          │
      17│           {?}~a~                                          │
      18│           {MENU}ra                                        │
      19│                                                           │
      20│                                                      ─MAIN┘
         │
         11-Mar-88  08:50 PM
```

After invoking this macro, you can look at only the records that satisfy the specified criteria. To see all the database records again, use the \i macro to **Ignore** the criteria.

```
{MENU}ce
{DELETE}y
{PGUP}
{MENU}ci
```

This macro selects Criteria Edit from the FORM menu, presses Del, confirms the deletion with **Yes**, returns to the database, and selects Criteria **Ignore**.

Note that the \i macro deletes the criterion record. Although this step is not mandatory, it is a good idea, because the criteria are *not* ignored during printing.

Sort Macro

Sorting requires two steps in Symphony. First, you specify the field by which you want to sort. Second, you perform the sort. The \s macro performs both steps.

```
{MENU}ss1
'.{ESC}
{?}~a~
{MENU}ra
```

The sort macro selects **S**ettings **S**ort-Keys **1**st-Key from the FORM menu, presses period then Esc, and pauses to let you point to the sort field. Then the macro specifies **A**scending order and selects **R**ecord-Sort **A**ll.

The second line of this macro contains a trick that is useful when you don't know whether a range is anchored. You can't just use the Esc key, because if the range isn't anchored, Esc cancels the command. But if you place a period before {ESC} in the macro, you can ensure that the range is indeed anchored before you press Esc to unanchor.

The Macro Library Manager

With Symphony Release 1.1 and higher releases, you also get an add-in application called the Macro Library Manager. With this add-in, if you have macros that you use in more than one worksheet, you do not need to create them in every worksheet. The Macro Library Manager allows you to create macros that are stored in a separate part of working memory (RAM) and can be invoked from any worksheet. Symphony saves the macros both to memory and to a disk file with a .MLB file extension. This way the macros are ready for you to invoke and are also saved permanently.

Symphony provides a different set of commands to manage these libraries of macros. After you create and debug the macros, you save the range containing the macros in a macro library, where they sit ready to be invoked from any worksheet. You can load a macro into memory and can retrieve a worksheet and invoke the macro. When you retrieve another worksheet, it does not wipe out the macro in that separate area of memory (nicknamed hyperspace at Lotus). When you save a worksheet range, however, Symphony erases the macro from the worksheet so that you can clear out any commonly used macros from any worksheet.

Accessing the Macro Library Manager

Because the Macro Library Manager is an add-in application, you must attach it before you can use it. Once the Macro Library Manager is attached, the SERVICES menu provides a new choice: **M**acros. Selecting that option brings up the Macro Library Manager commands. To attach the Manager, take the following steps:

1. Press SERVICES and select **A**pplication from the menu.

2. Select **A**ttach and then move the cell pointer to MACROMGR.APP to select it. (If you have a two floppy drive system, be sure that the Help and Tutorial disk [5 1/4-inch], or the Program, Help, and Tutorial disk [3 1/2-inch] which contains the .APP files, is in drive A.)

From then on, you just press SERVICES Macros whenever you need to access the Macro Library Manager menu.

Creating a Macro Library in Hyperspace

When you create a macro library, Symphony moves a range out of your worksheet and stores it in two places: RAM memory and a permanent disk file. The macro range can consist of any number of macros, and each library can contain up to 16,376 cells.

To save a range to a macro library, you call up the SERVICES menu and select Macros and then Save. Symphony prompts you for a file name under which to store the library, and a worksheet range to be stored. At this point you can also add a password to the library file. In its usual "last chance to back out" style, Symphony informs you if the library already exists on disk or in memory and asks whether you want to go ahead with the operation. If you respond Yes, Symphony erases from the worksheet the range and any range names contained in it and saves the new range to RAM (hyperspace) and to a disk file (for permanent storage). Symphony automatically adds the file extension .MLB to the file name you specify.

Ordinarily, however, when you are not creating or modifying the macro, you don't need or want to have it in the worksheet before putting it into hyperspace. You use the Macros Load command, which copies the macro library directly from disk to memory.

Invoking Macros from the Library

The macros contained in a library are callable from any worksheet even though you cannot "see" them. The big advantage, of course, is that you do not have to store multipurpose macros separately in every worksheet in which you need them.

Once a library is stored in memory (hyperspace), you call up a macro in the usual way. A macro stored in a pass-protected library does not require that you use the password to invoke the macro. The password protection is used only to prevent any unauthorized user from editing the macro.

If you try executing a macro whose range name is in your active worksheet and in one or more libraries, Symphony looks to the current worksheet first, and then to the libraries in the order in which they were loaded into memory. That order is the same order that appears in the control panel when you select Macros Edit, Remove, or Name-List. The program runs the first macro found with the selected name. For that reason, you should avoid using the same range name for macros in different libraries. Figure 19.16 shows the flow of macro libraries to and from hyperspace, disk, and worksheet.

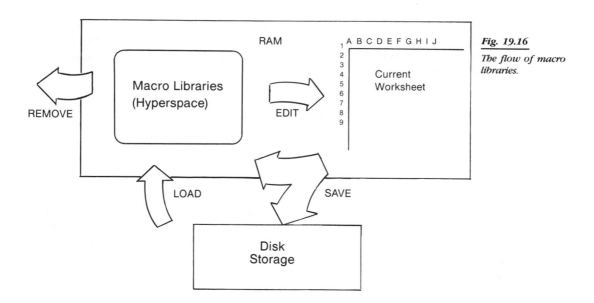

Fig. 19.16

The flow of macro libraries.

If you have forgotten what range names are contained in a library in memory, you can display a list of the names with the **Macros Name-List** command. This command is similar to the SHEET window's **Range Name Table** command except that only the range names are listed with Name-List. No cell range definitions are listed, because the library has no cell coordinates. After you indicate which library in memory you want, Symphony prompts you for a location in the worksheet to place the table. The table is simply a one-column listing of all the range names associated with that library.

Modifying a Library

When you need to modify or just look at a macro in a library, you must bring the library into your active worksheet. You do that with the **Macros Edit** command, which prompts you for the name of a library to copy from memory into the worksheet. You cannot bring a library directly from disk into the worksheet; the library must be loaded into memory first. If the library file is password-protected, Symphony prompts you for the password.

You may have ranges with the same names in the worksheet and in the library you are bringing in. Symphony has a way of resolving that conflict. The program prompts you to **Ignore** (and drop) any library range names that conflict with worksheet range names or to **Overwrite** the worksheet range name definitions with those from the incoming library. Again, the safe practice is to avoid the problem by naming your range names uniquely.

Symphony prompts you for a location in the worksheet to place the entire library. You will need an empty range of cells because Symphony overwrites whatever is there. Remember that Symphony copies the entire library. You cannot select only certain macros or ranges to load.

Removing a Macro

After you edit and test a macro library again, you will probably want to save the range back into a library, either the one from which it came or a new one. Use the **Macros Save** command to remove the range from the worksheet again.

At times, you may want to remove a library from memory entirely, perhaps to free up some memory for a larger worksheet or for other libraries. Symphony provides a **Macros Remove** command for that purpose. Note that this command does not erase the library file from the disk. To erase an .MLB disk file containing a macro library, use the normal SERVICES **File Erase** command, which now includes an additional option of **Macro-Library** files.

Using Range Names and Cell Coordinates

You must observe three important rules when creating and working with macro libraries:

1. Macro statements that use any worksheet menu commands (such as Copy, Move, and so on) cannot contain library range names. The statements must always refer to cells in the worksheet only. Look at the following statements contained in a library:

COPY_OUT	{GOTO}D1~{MENU}cOUT~~
COPY_IN	{GOTO}E1~{MENU}cIN~~
STATE_OUT	{GOTO}D3~+OUT~
STATE_IN	{GOTO}E3~+IN~
IN	999

   If the cell named OUT is in the current worksheet, and the cell named IN is only in the library but not in the worksheet, the COPY_OUT and STATE_OUT macros would work correctly, but COPY_IN and STATE_IN would not. They would stumble over the range name IN.

2. Formulas shouldn't cut across libraries or between a library and the worksheet. Range names or cell references in a formula in a library must refer to that library. Otherwise, the formulas evaluate as meaningless. Similarly, any cell references in a worksheet formula must not refer to cells or ranges in a library. Look at the following macros that are contained in a macro library; both FORMULA_IN and

FORMULA_OUT contain formulas (+IN and +OUT, respectively), and the cell named IN contains the label '{SERVICES}FB.

FORMULA_IN	{SERVICES}FB
FORMULA_OUT	{SERVICES}FB
IN	{SERVICES}FB

Again, the cell named OUT is in the worksheet and contains the label '{SERVICES}FB. FORMULA_IN works fine because the cell it refers to (IN) is contained in the same library. FORMULA_OUT does nothing; it is a formula referring to a cell in the worksheet, so the formula is blank in the macro library.

3. Command language statements can refer to cells in another library or in the worksheet. For example, {LET E2,IN} or {MENUBRANCH MENU1} work whether IN and MENU1 are range names in a library or in a worksheet.

Chapter Summary

By establishing the habit of creating macros for your most frequent Symphony tasks, you'll save time and increase efficiency. Think of the operations you perform most often, jot down the series of keystrokes needed to complete each operation, and begin your own macro library. As you become experienced in creating and using keyboard macros, begin experimenting with the Command Language. Turn to Chapter 20 and learn about Symphony's Command Language.

20

Introduction to the Command Language

In addition to Symphony's keyboard macro capabilities, the program contains a powerful set of commands offering many of the ingredients of a full-featured programming language. This set of commands is called the Symphony Command Language. With the Command Language, you can customize and automate Symphony for your worksheet applications.

In the preceding chapter, you learned how to automate keystrokes to save precious time by streamlining work functions. This chapter explains the various Command Language commands you can use to perform a variety of programming tasks. This chapter is not designed to teach programming theory and concepts, but rather to introduce you to the capabilities of programming with the Command Language.

If you have a burning desire to try your hand at programming, or you want to become your company's Symphony expert (creating models to amaze every department), or you are interested in developing template models to distribute on the open market, you should begin by reading this chapter.

Why Use the Command Language?

Programs created with the Command Language give you added control and flexibility in the use of your Symphony files. With the Command Language, you control such tasks as accepting input from the keyboard during a program, performing conditional tests, repeatedly performing a sequence of commands, and creating user-defined command menus.

601

You can use the Command Language as a full-featured programming language to develop custom worksheets for specific business applications. For example, by developing Command Language programs that teach users exactly how to enter and change data on a worksheet, you can ensure that data is entered correctly. With this type of program, novice users of an application do not have to be familiar with all Symphony commands and operations.

Using the Command Language is nothing mysterious. After learning the concepts and the parts of the Command Language discussed in this chapter, you'll be ready to develop programs that

- create menu-driven spreadsheet/database models

- accept and control input from a user

- manipulate data within and between files

- execute tasks a predetermined number of times

- control program flow

- set up and print multiple reports

- make intelligent decisions based on user input

- execute multiple programs based on decisions made within programs

As you become more experienced with the Command Language, you'll be able to take advantage of its full power to

- disengage or redefine the function keys

- develop a complete business system—from order entry to inventory control to accounting

- operate Symphony as a disk-based database system—limiting the size and speed of the file operation only to the size and speed of the hard disk

If you want to take Symphony to its practical limits, the Command Language is the proper vehicle, and your creativity can be the necessary fuel.

What Is the Command Language?

The Symphony Command Language is a set of more than 40 invisible commands. These commands are called invisible because, unlike the command instructions that you invoke through the Symphony menu and function keys, the Command Language commands cannot be invoked from the keyboard. You can use these commands only within Command Language programs.

The program in figure 20.1 illustrates how you can use the Command Language.

With commands such as MENUBRANCH and BRANCH, you can create custom menus to assist and prompt a user. The program in figure 20.1 begins by creating a range name wherever the user has positioned the cell pointer before invoking the program. The second line continues by displaying a custom help screen. The third line uses the MENUBRANCH command to display a menu with three options: select the next help screen, select the previous help screen, or return to the original cell-pointer position in the worksheet. The BRANCH command in the last line of the first two menu options causes the program to redisplay the menu after the user has selected either the next or the previous help screen.

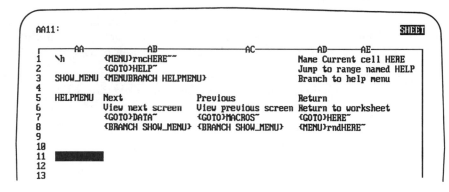

Fig. 20.1

Command Language program using MENUBRANCH and BRANCH.

As you read this chapter, you will learn about the commands for accepting input, for program control, for decision-making operations, for data manipulation, for program enhancement, and for file manipulation.

The Elements of Command Language Programs

The commands discussed in this chapter are used most often with the keyboard macros discussed in Chapter 19. In the examples that follow, you will see how to use macros with the Command Language to produce complete, efficient programs that take Symphony's macro capability far beyond simply automating keystrokes.

Command Language programs contain the Command Language commands and all the elements that can be included in macros. Programs can include the following:

- Keystrokes used for selecting Symphony commands (for example, {MENU}fcØ)

- Range names and cell addresses

- Keywords for moving the cell pointer (see Chapter 19 for a list of keywords)

- Keywords for function keys (see Chapter 19)

- Keywords for editing (see Chapter 19)

- Keywords for accelerator keys (see Chapter 19)

- Key representation for Enter: ~

- Command Language commands

Command Language Syntax

Like the keywords used in macros, all commands in the Command Language are enclosed in braces. Just as you must represent the right-arrow key in a macro as {RIGHT}, you must enclose a command such as QUIT in braces, as in {QUIT}.

Many commands, however, require additional arguments within the boundaries of the braces. The arguments that follow commands have a syntax similar to the grammar used in Symphony @functions. The general format of commands that require arguments is

{COMMAND argument1,argument2, . . . ,argumentN}

An argument can consist of numbers, strings, cell addresses, range names, formulas, and functions.

The command and its arguments are separated by a space, and, for most commands, arguments are separated by commas (with no spaces). As you study the syntax for the specific commands described in this chapter, keep in mind the importance of following the conventions for spacing and punctuation. For example, when you use the BRANCH command to transfer program control to a specific location in the program, you must follow the word BRANCH with the cell address or range name indicating where the program should branch.

Creating, Using, and Debugging Command Language Programs

With Command Language programs, as with macros, you must keep several considerations in mind to ensure that your programs are efficient and error-free. You begin by defining which actions you want the program to perform and determining the sequence of actions. Then you develop the program, test it, and, if necessary, debug it.

If you have created keyboard macros, you have a head start toward creating Command Language programs, which share many of the conventions used in keyboard macros. If you haven't experimented with Symphony macros, you should do so before you try to develop Command Language programs. You also might want to review Chapter 19's detailed discussions of creating, using, and debugging macros, because many of the concepts are related to Command Language programs. The following paragraphs contain a brief overview of macro creation.

Like keyboard macros, Command Language programs should be carefully planned and positioned on the worksheet. Create a window for your Command Language programs, specifying a restrict range so that changes to your worksheet will not affect your programs.

You enter Command Language programs just as you enter macros—as text cells. You must precede with a label prefix any line that begins with a nontext character, such as /, \, (, +, -, so that Symphony does not interpret the characters that follow as numbers or commands.

After you have decided where to locate your program and have begun to enter program lines, keep several considerations in mind.

First, remember to document your Command Language programs as you would document macros—to the right of each program line. Because Command Language programs are usually more complex than macros, documenting each line is essential. A documented program is easier to debug and change than an undocumented one.

Second, remember that you must name Command Language programs in the same way that you name macros. Refer to Chapter 19's section on "Naming Macros" for a review of the three types of macro names. Enter the program name in the cell directly to the left of the program's first line. Use Symphony's SHEET **Range Name Labels Right** command to name your Command Language program. If you want the program to be invoked automatically as soon as you open the worksheet file, specify the macro as an autoexecuting macro with the SERVICES **Settings Auto-Execute** command.

After you have developed and started to run your program, you may need to debug it. Like macros, Command Language programs are subject to such problems as missing tildes (~), misspelled keywords, or the use of cell addresses that remain absolute in the program but have changed in a worksheet application. You can solve the cell-address problem by using range names in place of cell addresses wherever possible.

To debug Command Language programs, you use Symphony's Step mode as you would for simple keyboard macros. Before you execute the program, press Alt-F7 to invoke Step mode. Then execute your Command Language program. Press any key or the space bar to activate each operation in the program. When you discover the error, press Alt-F7 to turn off Step mode, press Esc, and edit your program.

The Command Language Commands

Using the power of the program's Command Language, you can make Symphony applications easier to use; you can enhance the features of Symphony's regular commands; and you can customize Symphony for special worksheet applications. In the following sections, the Command Language commands are grouped into six categories: accepting input, program control, decision-making operations, data manipulation, program enhancement, and file manipulation.

Commands for Accepting Input

The {?}, GET, GETLABEL, GETNUMBER, and LOOK commands provide for all possible types of input into a Symphony worksheet (see table 20.1). You can also use these commands to provide the operator with a more user-friendly interface than that of Symphony's standard commands and operations. For example, you can use these commands to create prompts that help the user enter data more easily and quickly. These commands also make it easy to perform simple validity checks on the input before storing it in the spreadsheet.

Table 20.1
Commands for Accepting Input

Command	Description
{?}	Accepts any type of input
{GET}	Accepts a single character into <location>
{GETLABEL}	Accepts a label into <location>
{GETNUMBER}	Accepts a number into <location>
{LOOK}	Places first character from type- ahead buffer into <location>

The {?} Command

The {?} command causes the program to pause while you enter any type of information. During the pause, no prompt is displayed in the control panel; you can move the cell pointer, thus directing the location of the input. The program continues executing after you press Enter. The format for the {?} command is simply

{?}

For example, the following one-line program combines macro commands and a Command Language command to create a file-retrieve program:

{SERVICES}fr{?}

This program displays all files in the current drive and then pauses to accept input from you. In this instance, you can either type the name of a viewed file or simply move the cell pointer to a file name and press Enter.

The GET Command

The GET command places a single keystroke into a target cell. The keystroke can then be analyzed or tested in a number of ways, and the results of these tests can be used to determine the flow of the program. The format for the GET command is

{GET location}

This command accepts a single keystroke into the range defined by *location*. In the example shown in figure 20.2, the GET statement traps individual keystrokes in a cell named STROKE. Line 2 evaluates STROKE. If the keystroke in STROKE is the letter Q, the file is saved automatically. If STROKE contains any other keystroke, {SERVICES}fs~y is ignored. In either case, control is passed to line 3 of the program, which places the cell pointer in cell F25.

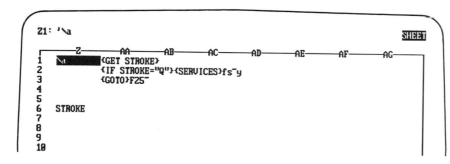

Fig. 20.2

Using the GET command to trap keystrokes.

A more involved use of GET is shown in figure 20.3. Suppose that you are writing an inventory program and want to prompt the user to make a one-keystroke choice to enter data on premium- or regular-quality widgets. Figure 20.3 shows the program you might use in such an application.

In this example, the GET command is used to pause the program while the user enters a single letter from the keyboard; the command then stores that entry in a cell named CODE. Notice that the program enters the user-prompt in the cell named MAIN. If you want a prompt to appear in the control panel rather than in the spreadsheet, you must use the GETLABEL or GETNUMBER command.

The GETLABEL Command

The GETLABEL command accepts any type of entry from the keyboard, and enters it as a label. For example, you can type a telephone number without having to first type a label prefix. The prompt (which must be a string enclosed in quo-

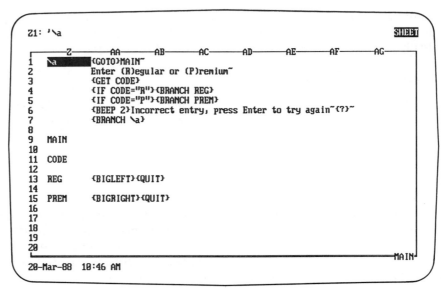

Fig. 20.3

Using the GET command to allow one-character input.

tation marks) is displayed in the control panel, and the entry is placed in the target cell as a label when you press the Enter key. The format for the GETLABEL command is

{GETLABEL prompt,location}

where *location* is the cell in which the program places the label.

In the example in figure 20.4, the GETLABEL statement displays a prompt and accepts a label date into cell AA19. Line 2 places in cell AA20 a formula that converts the label date to a numerical date and then formats the cell to appear as a date.

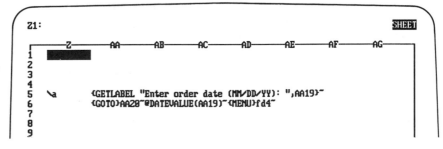

Fig. 20.4

Using the GETLABEL command to allow input of a label date.

Figure 20.5 shows how to use GETLABEL with the IF, BRANCH, and BEEP commands (discussed later in this chapter) to prompt for a part description.

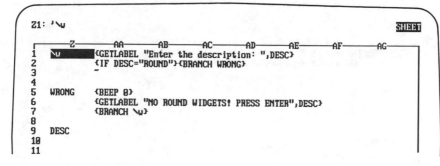

Fig. 20.5

*Using the
GETLABEL
command with
other commands
for more complex
string input.*

You can add a second GETLABEL command to this program so that if you make
an incorrect entry, an error message displays, and the program pauses until you
press any key. Remember, however, that whatever you enter in response to the
prompt is stored in DESC.

The GETNUMBER Command

The GETNUMBER command accepts only numerical entries. The format for the
GETNUMBER command is

{GETNUMBER prompt,location}

The *prompt* (which must be a string enclosed in quotation marks) is displayed
in the control panel, and the numerical entry is placed in *location* when you
press Enter.

In the example in figure 20.6, the GETNUMBER statement displays a prompt
and accepts a numerical entry into cell AB10. Line 2 then copies that numerical
entry into the next available row in column A (the @COUNT function finds the
next open row in column A).

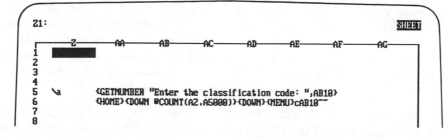

Fig. 20.6

*Using the
GETNUMBER
command for
numerical input.*

Figure 20.7 shows how you can use GETNUMBER in an inventory program. Here
GETNUMBER prompts for a part number. If the user does not enter a number
between 0 and 9999, the program first will display the message
INVALID PART NUMBER! PRESS ENTER and then will prompt the user to enter
another number.

Fig. 20.7

Using GETNUMBER in an inventory application.

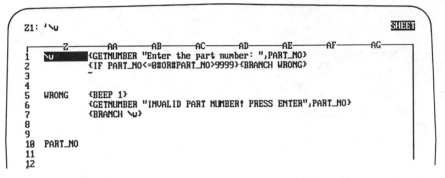

The LOOK Command

The LOOK command checks Symphony's type-ahead buffer. The general form of the command is

  {LOOK location}

If any keys have been pressed since program execution began, LOOK places the first keystroke in the target cell *location*. The LOOK command frequently is used to interrupt processing until you press a key.

When the LOOK command is executed, the keyboard type-ahead buffer is checked, and the first character is copied into the indicated location. Thus, you can type a character at any time, and the program will find it when the LOOK command is executed. You can then test the contents of location with an IF statement. Because the character is not removed from the type-ahead buffer, you must make provisions to use the character or dispose of it before the program ends or needs keyboard input.

In the program in figure 20.8, the LOOK statement examines Symphony's type-ahead buffer and places the first keystroke in the cell named STROKE. If no keys have been pressed, the LOOK statement blanks the cell, leaving only a label prefix. Although program execution is not halted by this statement, lines 2 and 3 of the sample program force the program to pause. Line 3 forms a looping structure until a key is pressed, satisfying the IF condition in line 2. This application is the most common use of the LOOK statement. (For more information, see the discussions of the IF and BRANCH commands.)

As a simple test of the LOOK command, try the example in figure 20.9. This program causes the speaker to beep until you press any key. Each time the LOOK command is encountered, Symphony checks the keyboard buffer and copies into location INTERRUPT the first character found. Then an IF statement checks the contents of INTERRUPT and branches accordingly. The GETLABEL command at the end serves to dispose of the keystroke that interrupted the loop.

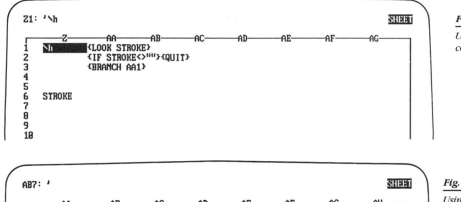

Fig. 20.8

Using the LOOK command.

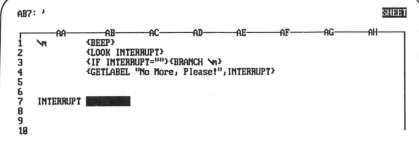

Fig. 20.9

Using the LOOK command to stop a beeping program.

The LOOK command is more helpful when you have built a lengthy program to process, such as a stock-portfolio database, and you want to be able to stop processing at certain points in the program. You can enter a LOOK command, followed by an IF statement similar to that in figure 20.9, at several places in the program. Then, if you press a key, the program stops the next time a LOOK is executed. If you do not touch the keyboard, the program continues processing. In this example, the LOOK command is preferable to the GET command, which always stops the program to wait for an entry.

Commands for Program Control

The commands shown in table 20.2 (BRANCH, MENUBRANCH, MENUCALL, RETURN, QUIT, ONERROR, BREAKOFF, BREAKON, WAIT, DISPATCH, DEFINE, and RESTART) allow varying degrees of control in Symphony programs. These commands, used alone or in combination with decision-making commands, afford you specific control of program flow.

The BRANCH Command

The BRANCH command causes program control to pass unconditionally to the cell address indicated in the BRANCH statement. The general format of the BRANCH command is

{BRANCH location}

Table 20.2
Commands for Program Control

Command	Description
{BRANCH}	Program continues at \<location\>
{MENUBRANCH}	Prompts user with menu found at \<location\>
{MENUCALL}	Like MENUBRANCH except that control returns to the statement after the MENUCALL
{RETURN}	Returns from a program subroutine
{QUIT}	Ends program execution
{ONERROR}	Traps errors, passing control to \<branch\>
{BREAKOFF}	Disables Ctrl-Break key
{BREAKON}	Enables Ctrl-Break key
{WAIT}	Waits until specified time
{DISPATCH}	Branches indirectly via \<location\>
{DEFINE}	Specifies cells for subroutine arguments
{RESTART}	Cancels a subroutine

The program begins reading commands and statements at the cell location indicated in *location*. Program control does not return to the line from which it was passed unless directed to do so by another BRANCH statement.

In the example in figure 20.10, line 1 places the cell pointer in cell R34 and then enters an @COUNT function. Line 2 passes program control to cell F13, regardless of any commands that may follow the BRANCH command (in either the same cell location or the cell below). The program then reads commands beginning in cell F13.

BRANCH is an unconditional command unless it is preceded by an IF conditional statement, as in the following example:

```
{IF C22="alpha"}{BRANCH G24}
{GOTO}S101~
```

(The IF statement must be in the same cell to act as a conditional testing statement.) For more information, see "The IF Command."

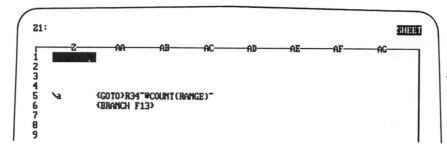

Suppose, for example, that three separate companies are under your corporate umbrella, and that you have written a program for adding and modifying records in a corporate personnel database. Figure 20.11 shows a portion of such a program. Depending on how the user of the program responds to the prompt Enter Company (R, A, or C):, you want the program to branch to a different place in the program and prompt the user further for data specific to that company.

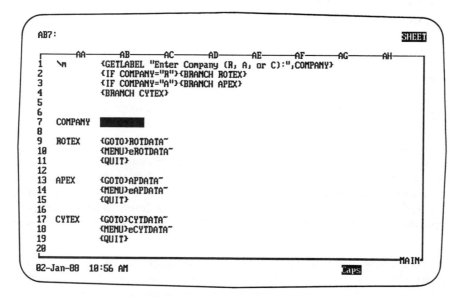

Fig. 20.11

Using BRANCH in a database application.

The BRANCH statements in the \m program cause the flow of program execution to shift to the different company routines. In this example, the BRANCH statements are coupled with IF statements to shift execution conditionally, depending on the user's response. After the program executes a company routine, the QUIT statement at the end of the routine causes program execution to stop.

You may prefer that execution return to the \m program or to another program after completing the company routine. You can arrange this setup in one of two ways: (1) you can replace the QUIT statements at the end of the company routines with {BRANCH \m} statements to return to \m; or (2) you can replace the BRANCH statements in \m with subroutine calls (discussed later in this chapter) and then include in the subroutine a BRANCH to the point where execution should continue.

You need to remember two important points about BRANCH statements. First, they cause a permanent shift in the flow of statement execution (unless you use another BRANCH statement). Second, BRANCH statements are most often used in combination with IF statements.

The MENUBRANCH Command

The MENUBRANCH command defines and displays in the control panel a menu-selection structure from which you can initiate as many as eight individual programs. You select the appropriate menu item as you would make a selection from a Symphony command menu, by either highlighting the selection and pressing Enter or by typing the first letter of the selection. The form of the MENUBRANCH command is

{MENUBRANCH location}

The *location* is the range where the menu is located. The menu invoked by the MENUBRANCH command consists of one to eight consecutive columns in the worksheet. Each column corresponds to one item in the menu. The upper left corner of the location named in a MENUBRANCH statement must refer to the first menu item; otherwise, you receive the error message Invalid use of Menu macro command.

Each menu item consists of three or more rows in the same column. The first row is the menu option name. If the length of the option name exceeds 80 characters, Symphony truncates the option name to 40 characters. Be careful to choose option names that begin with different letters. If two or more options begin with the same letter, and you try to type the first letter to access an option, Symphony selects the first option found with the letter you specified. That option may not be the one you intended.

The second row in the menu range contains descriptions of the menu items. The description is displayed in the bottom row of the control panel when the cell pointer highlights the name of the corresponding menu option. Each description may contain up to 80 characters of text. The description row must be present, even if it is blank.

The third row begins the actual program command sequence. Once the individual programs have been executed, program control must be directed by statements at the end of each individual program.

No empty columns can exist between menu items; the column immediately to the right of the last menu item must be empty. You can supplement the Symphony menu structure by creating a full-screen menu (for enhancement purposes only).

In figure 20.12, the MENUBRANCH statement produces a menu structure that begins in cell AB4. The individual programs begin in row 6 in each cell. Each of these programs must contain a statement to continue once the main task has been completed. For example, suppose that you are using the corporate personnel database and that you have entered the program shown in figure 20.12.

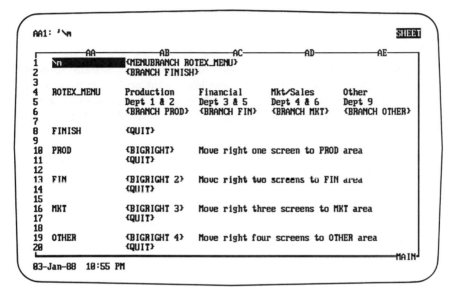

Fig. 20.12

A program using the MENUBRANCH command.

When the MENUBRANCH statement is executed, Symphony displays in the control panel the menu beginning at cell ROTEX_MENU. (***Note:*** You must use the **SHEET Range Name Labels Right** command to assign the name ROTEX_MENU to the cell in which the label Production resides. Production is the first menu item.)

The top line of the control panel contains a description of whatever menu item is currently highlighted. For instance, when you move the cell pointer to Financial, the capsule description Dept 3 & 5 appears.

Now suppose that you want to select the second menu item (Financial). As mentioned previously, you select it the same way you do any Symphony menu item, by pressing Enter after you've positioned the cursor on your choice, or by typing the first letter of the menu item. After you've selected Financial from the menu, the next statement to be executed is {BRANCH FIN}.

If, instead of selecting a menu item, you press the Esc key, Symphony stops displaying the menu items and executes the next program command after the MENUBRANCH command, {BRANCH FINISH}.

Modeling Tip: If you have a multilevel menu structure, you can make the Esc key function as it does in the Symphony command menus (backing up to the previous menu). After the current MENUBRANCH command, place a BRANCH to the previous level's MENUBRANCH. When you press the Esc key, this BRANCH backs you up to the previous menu.

The MENUCALL Command

The MENUCALL command is identical to the MENUBRANCH command except that Symphony executes the menu program as a subroutine (see the subsequent discussion of subroutines). Once the individual menu programs have been executed, program control returns to the cell immediately below the cell containing the MENUCALL statement. The format of the MENUCALL command is

{MENUCALL location}

Suppose that you replace the MENUBRANCH command in figure 20.12 with a MENUCALL. The results are shown in figure 20.13.

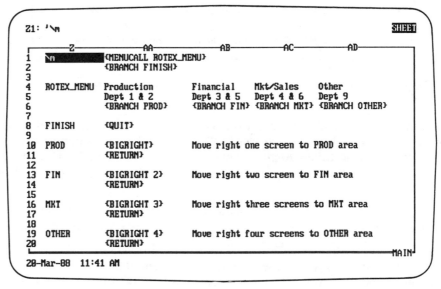

Fig. 20.13

Using the MENUCALL command in place of MENUBRANCH.

When you use a MENUCALL, Symphony returns to the statement immediately following the MENUCALL whenever it reads a blank cell or a {RETURN}. For example, suppose that you select the Financial menu option, which causes Symphony to branch to FIN. The first statement in FIN moves the cell pointer two screens to the right. When Symphony encounters the RETURN statement, though, the flow of execution shifts back to the statement following the MENUCALL, which is the {BRANCH FINISH} statement.

Keep in mind that pressing Esc has the same effect with MENUCALL as it does with MENUBRANCH. Execution shifts to the statement following the MENUCALL statement. But you can use the Esc key technique to back up to previous menus only if you want this technique to also apply when the MENUCALL command finishes executing.

The advantage of MENUCALL is that you can call the same menu from several different places in a program and continue execution from the calling point after the MENUCALL is finished. You enjoy this advantage whenever you use subroutines.

Subroutines

The MENUCALL statement should give you some feel for calling subroutines. Quite a bit more, however, can be involved in calling standard (nonmenu) subroutines.

A subroutine is an independent program that can be run from within the main program. Calling a subroutine is as easy as enclosing the name of a routine in braces ({SUB}). When Symphony encounters a name in braces, the program passes control to the named routine. Then, when the routine is finished (when Symphony encounters a blank cell or a {RETURN}), program control passes back to the command in the cell below the cell that called the subroutine.

Why use subroutines? You can duplicate a simple subroutine by using two BRANCH commands. But by using a subroutine, you can execute the subroutine from any number of locations within the main program.

The RETURN Command

The RETURN command indicates the end of subroutine execution and returns program control to the cell immediately below the cell that called the subroutine. When Symphony reads the RETURN, execution returns to the main program (or other subroutine) at the location after the subroutine call. Do not confuse RETURN with QUIT, which ends the program completely. You can use RETURN with the IF statement to return conditionally from a subroutine. The form of this command is

{RETURN}

In figure 20.14, line 1 places the cell pointer in AA101 and then calls the subroutine SUB. After SUB is executed, the RETURN command passes control to the next command after the subroutine call, which places the cell pointer in

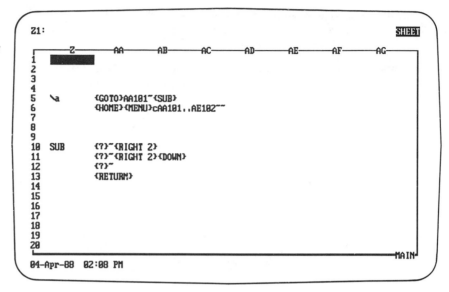

Fig. 20.14

Using the RETURN command.

the Home position and then copies the range of cells entered by the subroutine into the range whose upper left corner is identified by the Home position.

Symphony also ends a subroutine and returns to the calling routine when the program encounters, while executing the subroutine, a cell that either is blank or contains a numeric value. Although this method of returning from a subroutine works, the RETURN command is preferred because it documents the fact that a particular set of macro keywords and Command Language instructions is intended to be a subroutine.

The QUIT Command

The QUIT command forces the program to terminate unconditionally. Even without a QUIT command, the program terminates if it encounters (within the program sequence) a cell that is empty or contains an entry other than a string. It is good practice, however, to always put a QUIT statement at the end of your programs to indicate that you intend execution to stop. (Conversely, do not put a QUIT command at the end of a program that you intend to call as a subroutine.) The form of the QUIT command is

{QUIT}

In the following example, the QUIT command forces the program sequence to terminate unconditionally:

{HOME}{SERVICES}fs~y {QUIT}

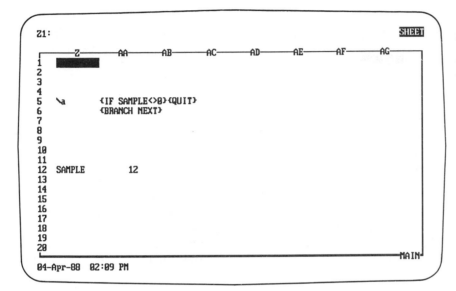

Fig. 20.15

Using the QUIT command with an IF statement.

When QUIT is preceded by an IF conditional testing statement, as in figure 20.15, termination of the program depends on the IF statement.

The ONERROR Command

The processing of Command Language programs is normally interrupted if a system error (such as Disk drive not ready) occurs during execution. By sidestepping system errors that would normally cause program termination, the ONERROR command allows programs to proceed. The general format of the command is

{ONERROR branch,[message]}

The ONERROR command passes program control to the cell indicated by *branch*; any errors can be recorded in the message cell (*[message]*). (The second argument is optional.)

As a general rule, you should always make sure that the program executes your ONERROR statement before an error occurs. Therefore, you may want to include an ONERROR statement near the start of your programs. Because you can have only one ONERROR statement in effect at a time, you should take special precautions to write your programs so that the right message appears for each error condition.

In figure 20.16, the ONERROR statement acts as a safeguard against leaving drive A empty or not closing the drive door. If an error occurs, program control passes to the cell named ERROR (AA8). This cell contains a GETLABEL statement that prompts you to correct the error.

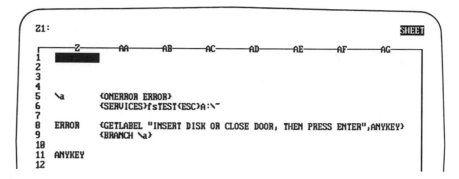

Fig. 20.16

Using the ONERROR command to prompt users to close the drive door.

The best place to put an ONERROR statement is directly above the program line that you think may cause an error. For example, suppose that your program is about to copy a portion of the current spreadsheet to a disk file, using the SERVICES **F**ile **X**tract command. A system error will occur if the drive is not ready or the disk is full. Therefore, you should include a strategically placed ONERROR command (see fig. 20.17).

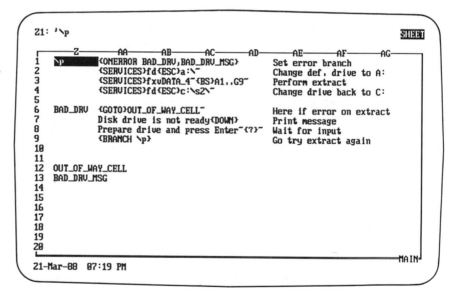

Fig. 20.17

Using an ONERROR statement to retry disk access.

In this example, the ONERROR statement causes the program to branch to a cell called BAD_DRV if an error occurs. A copy of the error message that Symphony issues is entered in a cell called BAD_DRV_MSG. Then, the first statement in the BAD_DRV routine moves the cell pointer to an out-of-the-way cell (cleverly called OUT_OF_WAY_CELL). Next, the message Disk drive is not ready is entered in the spreadsheet, followed by Prepare drive and press Enter.

The program pauses for you to press Enter. Finally, the program branches back to \p to try again.

Ctrl-Break presents a special problem for the ONERROR statement. Because Ctrl-Break causes an error condition, the ONERROR statement is automatically invoked. Therefore, a good technique when you plan to use the ONERROR statement is to disable Ctrl-Break after you have debugged your program. (See the following discussion of the BREAKOFF command.) By disabling Ctrl-Break, you can prevent the confusion that might arise with an untimely error message.

The BREAKOFF Command

The easiest way to stop a program is to issue a Ctrl-Break command. But Symphony can eliminate the effect of a Ctrl-Break while a program is executing. By including a BREAKOFF command in your program, you can prevent a user from stopping the program before its completion. Before you use a BREAKOFF statement, however, you must be certain that the program has been fully debugged.

The BREAKOFF command disables the Ctrl-Break command during program execution. The form of the BREAKOFF command is

    {BREAKOFF}

BREAKOFF is used primarily to prevent a user from interrupting a process and destroying the integrity of data in the spreadsheet. You do not need to use BREAKOFF unless you are developing extremely sophisticated programs; but, in such applications, BREAKOFF can be an important safeguard against user-caused problems.

The BREAKON Command

To restore the effect of Ctrl-Break, use the BREAKON command. The form of this command is

    {BREAKON}

You will probably want a simple one-line program that issues a BREAKON, just in case something happens to your original program during execution. You may also want to make sure that the last statement in your program before QUIT is BREAKON.

Because any Ctrl-Break commands in the keyboard buffer are executed as soon as the BREAKON command is executed, be sure that the BREAKON is at a place where the program can safely stop. Figure 20.18 demonstrates how you can use the BREAKOFF and BREAKON commands.

The WAIT Command

The WAIT command causes the program to pause until, or for, an appointed

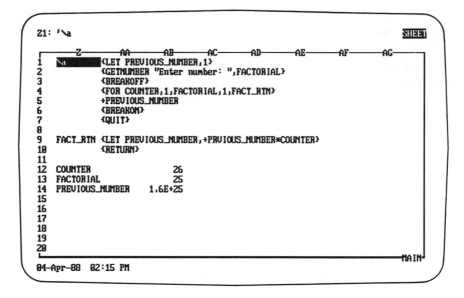

Fig. 20.18

Using the BREAKOFF and BREAKON commands.

```
Z1: '\a                                                      SHEET
      ─Z──────AA──────AB──────AC──────AD──────AE──────AF──────AG──
 1   \a          {LET PREVIOUS_NUMBER,1}
 2               {GETNUMBER "Enter number: ",FACTORIAL}
 3               {BREAKOFF}
 4               {FOR COUNTER,1,FACTORIAL,1,FACT_RTN}
 5               +PREVIOUS_NUMBER
 6               {BREAKON}
 7               {QUIT}
 8
 9   FACT_RTN {LET PREVIOUS_NUMBER,+PREVIOUS_NUMBER*COUNTER}
10               {RETURN}
11
12   COUNTER              26
13   FACTORIAL            25
14   PREVIOUS_NUMBER   1.6E+25
15
16
17
18
19
20
      ────────────────────────────────────────────────────────MAIN
 04-Apr-88  02:15 PM
```

time. The general form of the WAIT command is

{WAIT argument}

where *argument* specifies the appointed time or the time to elapse. The WAIT statement in figure 20.19 allows the message to be displayed for 5 seconds.

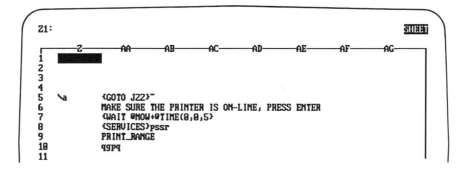

Fig. 20.19

Using the WAIT command to display messages.

```
Z1:                                                          SHEET
      ─Z──────AA──────AB──────AC──────AD──────AE──────AF──────AG──
 1
 2
 3
 4
 5   \a          {GOTO J22}~
 6               MAKE SURE THE PRINTER IS ON-LINE, PRESS ENTER
 7               {WAIT @NOW+@TIME(0,0,5)}
 8               {SERVICES}pssr
 9               PRINT_RANGE
10               qgpq
11
```

The serial-time-number must contain a date plus a time. If you want the program to wait until 6:00 P.M. today to continue, you can use the expression {WAIT @INT(@NOW)+@TIME(18,00,00)}. To make the program pause for 50 seconds, use the expression {WAIT @NOW+@TIME(00,00,50)}.

The DISPATCH Command

The DISPATCH command is similar to the BRANCH command. The DISPATCH command, however, branches indirectly to a location specified by the value contained in the location pointed to by the argument. The form of the command is

{DISPATCH location}

The *location* given as the DISPATCH argument should contain a cell address or range name that is the destination of the DISPATCH. If the cell referred to by location does not contain a valid cell reference or range name, an error occurs, and program execution either stops with an error message or transfers to the location in the current ONERROR command.

The DISPATCH location must be a cell reference or range name that points to a single cell reference. If the location is either a multicell range or a range that contains a single cell, the DISPATCH acts like a BRANCH statement and transfers execution directly to location.

In figure 20.20, the DISPATCH statement selects the subroutine to be executed, based on the input in the cell NUMBER generated by the GETLABEL statement. The string formula in the DISPATCH command concatenates the word SUB and the menu selection number entered by the user. Because the name of every subroutine begins with the word SUB, the DISPATCH command passes program control to the subroutine specified by the user.

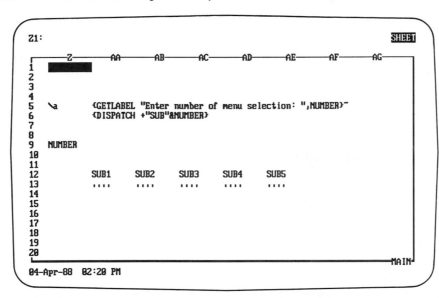

Fig. 20.20

An example of the DISPATCH command.

The DEFINE Command

An important subroutine feature of Symphony is the capability of passing arguments, using the keyword version of the subroutine call only. A subroutine called with arguments must begin with a DEFINE statement that associates each argument with a specific cell location. The form of the subroutine call with arguments is

{DEFINE loc1:Type1,...}

where *loc1*, *loc2*, and so on are names or cell references for the cells in which to place the arguments passed from the main program. You can use one or more arguments, separated by commas. *Type* is either STRING or VALUE and is optional; if not present, the default is STRING.

If an argument is of type STRING, the text of the corresponding argument in the subroutine call is placed in the indicated cell as a string value (label).

If an argument is of type VALUE, the corresponding argument in the subroutine call is treated as a formula, and its numeric or string value is placed in the argument cell. An error occurs if the corresponding argument in the subroutine call is not a valid number, string, or formula. You do not, however, have to put a string in quotation marks or have a leading + sign in a formula that uses cell references.

Suppose that you have an application where you must repeatedly convert strings to numbers and display the numbers in Currency format. Rather than enter the same code at several different places in the program, you decide to write a subroutine. Figure 20.21 shows how the subroutine might appear. (The SHEET **Range Name Labels Right** command has been used to define all the range names in this example.)

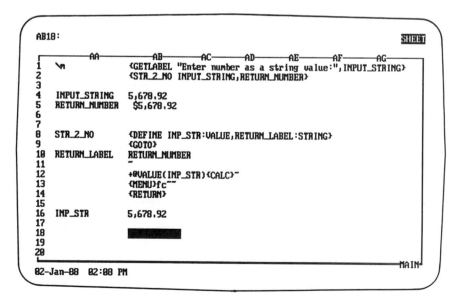

Fig. 20.21

An example of a subroutine call with parameters.

The first statement in the program is a GETLABEL statement that reads a string value into the cell named INPUT_STRING. Line 2 calls a subroutine named STR_2_NO and passes the arguments INPUT_STRING (the name of the cell containing the input string) and RETURN_NUMBER (the name of the cell where the formatted number is to be stored).

The STR_2_NO subroutine begins with a DEFINE statement, which defines where and how the arguments passed to the subroutine from \m are to be stored. Any subroutine that receives arguments passed from its calling macro must begin with a DEFINE statement.

The DEFINE statement in STR_2_NO specifies two cells, INP_STR and RETURN_LABEL, that will hold the two arguments passed from the caller. Note that if the number of arguments in the subroutine call does not agree with the number of arguments in the DEFINE statement, an error occurs.

The DEFINE statement specifies that the first argument in the subroutine call is to be evaluated and its value placed in INP_STR. Because the first argument is the cell reference INPUT_STRING, the value in cell INPUT_STRING—the string "5,678.92"—is placed in INP_STR.

The DEFINE statement specifies that the text of the second argument in the subroutine call is to be placed into cell RETURN_LABEL as a string. Because the text of the second argument is RETURN_NUMBER, the string RETURN_NUMBER is placed in cell RETURN_LABEL.

The cell containing the second argument is located in the body of the subroutine. This technique is used to allow the subroutine to return a value to a location designated by the caller. In this example, the location RETURN_NUMBER is passed to the subroutine as a string value. The subroutine uses the passed value as the argument of a {GOTO} statement that places the cell pointer on the output cell. This technique is one of two primary ways to return information to the calling routine. The other way to return information is to place it in a specified cell that is used every time the subroutine is called.

After the subroutine places the cell pointer on the output cell, the subroutine continues by converting the string in INP_STR to a number and placing the resulting numeric value in the output cell.

Passing arguments to and from subroutines is important if you want to get the most from Symphony's subroutine capabilities. Subroutines with arguments simplify program coding and make the resulting macros easier to trace. Subroutine arguments are almost essential when you are developing a subroutine to perform a common function that you will use again and again. They are also one of the trickiest parts of the Symphony Command Language.

The RESTART Command

Just as you can call subroutines from the main program, you can also call one subroutine from another. In fact, as Symphony moves from one subroutine to the next, the program saves the addresses of where it has been. This technique is called stacking, or saving addresses on a stack. By stacking, Symphony can trace its way back through the subroutine calls to the main program.

If you decide that you don't want Symphony to return by the path it came, you can use the RESTART command to eliminate the stack. In other words, the RESTART command allows a subroutine to be canceled at any time during execution. You will not need to use this command until you are an expert at writing Command Language programs. Once you reach this point, though, this command is invaluable. The RESTART command is normally used with an IF statement under a conditional testing evaluation. The format for RESTART is

{RESTART}

Figure 20.22 illustrates how you can use RESTART to prevent a user from omitting data in a database. This example combines the GETLABEL, GETNUMBER, and BRANCH commands to produce a simple database application for entering product information. GETLABEL and GETNUMBER prompt the user for product data; if the product item number and price are omitted, RESTART prevents the user from continuing to enter new data; in the last line, BRANCH loops to repeat the process for entering a new record.

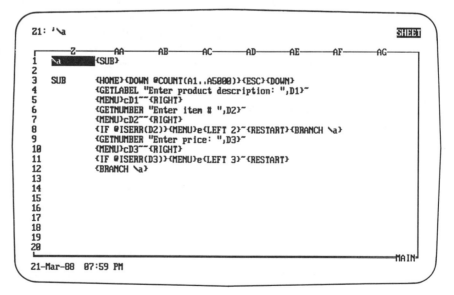

Fig. 20.22

Using RESTART in a database application.

```
Z1: '\a                                                    SHEET
        Z      AA       AB      AC     AD     AE     AF     AG
1    \a         {SUB}
2
3    SUB        {HOME}{DOWN @COUNT(A1..A5000)}{ESC}{DOWN}
4               {GETLABEL "Enter product description: ",D1}~
5               {MENU}cD1~~{RIGHT}
6               {GETNUMBER "Enter item # ",D2}~
7               {MENU}cD2~~{RIGHT}
8               {IF @ISERR(D2)}{MENU}e{LEFT 2}~{RESTART}{BRANCH \a}
9               {GETNUMBER "Enter price: ",D3}~
10              {MENU}cD3~~{RIGHT}
11              {IF @ISERR(D3)}{MENU}e{LEFT 3}~{RESTART}
12              {BRANCH \a}
13
14
15
16
17
18
19
20
                                                          MAIN
21-Mar-88  07:59 PM
```

Let's look at the program, line by line. The first line simply begins the subroutine (named SUB) in cell AA3. The subroutine begins by determining exactly where to move the cell pointer in the product database. Notice that @COUNT is used in AA3 to count the number of records in the database. After the cell pointer moves to an empty cell, line AA4 prompts the user for a product description and enters this data in cell D1. The Copy command in AA5 copies the product description to the appropriate cell in the database.

The commands in AA6 through AA11 prompt the user for the product item number and price, copy the data to the appropriate locations in the database, and check that the item number and price have been entered. Cell AA8 checks to make sure that item numbers are entered. If the data has not been entered, the RESTART command clears the stack, allowing the subroutine to be canceled. If a user forgets to include a number, the program prompts the user to reenter product information. Cell AA11 checks for price data. If price information is omitted, RESTART again clears the stack, allowing the subroutine to be canceled.

Decision-Making Commands

The Command Language's decision-making commands, shown in table 20.3, give you the capabilities of true programming languages such as BASIC. With these three commands (IF, FOR, and FORBREAK), you can test for numeric and string values. The IF command provides the kind of conditional logic available in many high-level languages. FOR and FORBREAK offer a conditional looping capability, allowing you to control how many times a group of commands is activated.

Table 20.3
Decision-Making Commands

Command	Description
{IF}	Conditionally executes statements after IF
{FOR}	Activates a loop (loop count is placed in <counter>)
{FORBREAK}	Terminates a FOR loop

The IF Command

The IF statement uses IF-THEN-ELSE logic to evaluate the existence of certain numeric and string values. Commonly used to control program flow and enable the program to perform based on criteria provided by the user, the Command Language's IF command is the functional equivalent of the IF command in BASIC. The form of the IF command is

{IF condition}{true}
{false}

If the logical expression (*condition*) is true, then the remaining commands on the same line are executed. (These commands ordinarily include a BRANCH command to skip the {false} statements.) If the expression is false, execution skips the commands after the IF command on the current line and continues on the next line.

As the following examples illustrate, IF statements can check for a variety of conditions, including the position of the cell pointer, a specific numeric value, or a specific string value. In figure 20.23, for example, the IF statement checks to see whether the current location of the cell pointer is row 200. If it is, program control is passed to cell AA8, where a QUIT command is executed. If the cell pointer is not on row 200, the cell pointer moves down a row, accepts input, then branches back to cell AA5, where the IF statement again checks to see whether the cell pointer is located on row 200.

Fig. 20.23

Using IF to check the cell pointer.

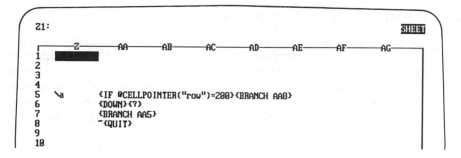

Figure 20.24 illustrates how you can use IF to evaluate a cell's value. The IF statement evaluates the value in cell R18. If cell R18 contains a negative value, the program converts that value to 0, and program execution is halted. If the value in cell R18 is 0 or greater, line 2 replaces the value in cell R18 with the value representing the equation (R18*.55).

Fig. 20.24

Using IF to evaluate a cell value.

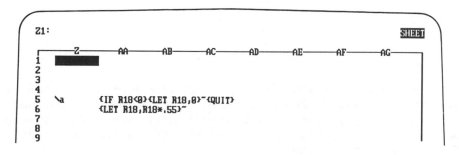

The IF command can also evaluate a string value entered by a user. You can, for example, develop IF statements that complete certain operations depending on whether the user enters *Y* (Yes) or *N* (No).

Suppose, for example, that you want to test the value in a single-cell range called NEW_RECORD. If the value in NEW_RECORD is *Y* (for Yes), you want to add a new record to a database. Otherwise, you want to modify an existing record in the database. Your program will include the following statements:

```
{IF NEW_RECORD="Y"}{BRANCH NEW_ROUTINE}
{BRANCH MOD_ROUTINE}
```

The first line is contained in a single cell. The part of the cell following the IF portion is called the THEN clause. The THEN clause is executed only if the result of the logical test is true. In this case, the THEN clause contains the keyword BRANCH, followed by the range name NEW_ROUTINE. (BRANCH is often used with IF.) The program branches to NEW_ROUTINE if the value of NEW_RECORD is equal to Y (or y—the test is not case-sensitive).

The second line contains the ELSE clause, which is executed only if the result of the logical statement in the IF statement is false (because the THEN clause contains a branch to NEW_ROUTINE). In most cases you will want the THEN clause to branch to a subroutine or another part of the program. If the program statements in the THEN clause do not transfer control, the line below the IF statement (the ELSE clause) is executed after the statement(s) in the THEN clause. Thus, the program will execute both the THEN and the ELSE clauses if the IF statement is true. In this example, the ELSE clause also contains a BRANCH statement, but the range to branch to is called MOD_ROUTINE.

The FOR Command

The FOR command is used to control the looping process in a program by calling a subroutine to be executed a certain number of times. FOR enables you to define the exact number of times the subroutine will be executed. The form of the FOR command is

```
{FOR counter,start,stop,step,routine}
```

The FOR statement contains five arguments. The first argument is a cell that acts as the *counter* mechanism for the loop structure. The second argument is the starting number for the counter mechanism; the third, the completion number for the counter mechanism. The fourth argument is the incremental value for the counter mechanism; and the fifth, the name of the subroutine. Arguments 2, 3, and 4 can be values, cell addresses, or formulas. Arguments 1 and 5, however, must be range names or cell addresses. Because multiple loops are permitted, you need to be careful of the logical flow of multiple looping structures.

Notice how FOR is used in the simple example in figure 20.25. FOR in the first line of the program controls how many times the program loops to format a column of values. The FOR statement begins by using the range named COUNT, located at AA5, as a counter to keep track of how many times the program should loop. The second argument, 1, is the start-number for the counter; the next argument, 5, is the stop-number. The program keeps track of the looping process by comparing the counter to the stop-number and stops executing if the counter value is larger than the stop-number. The FOR statement's next argument, 1, is the step-number; this number is the value by which the counter is to be incremented after each loop. The last argument, FORMAT, is the name of the routine to be executed.

Fig. 20.25

Using FOR to control the number of loops in a formatting program.

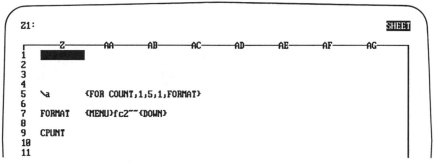

The FORBREAK Command

If you want to end the processing of a FOR command based on something other than the number of iterations, such as a conditional test, you can use the FORBREAK command. When you use this command, Symphony interrupts the processing of the FOR command and continues execution with the command following the FOR.

Data Manipulation Commands

The LET, PUT, CONTENTS, and BLANK commands allow precise placement of data within worksheet files. These commands, which are listed in table 20.4, function similarly to such menu commands as Copy, Move, and Erase but provide capabilities that go beyond simple copy, move, and erase operations.

The LET Command

The LET command places a value or string in a target cell location without the cell pointer having to be at the location. LET is extremely useful, for example, for placing criteria in a database criterion range. The form of the LET command is

{LET location,expression}

This command places the value of *expression* in *location*.

Table 20.4
Data Manipulation Commands

Command	Description
{LET}	Places value of expression in <location>
{PUT}	Puts value into col, row within range
{CONTENTS}	Stores contents of <source> to <destination>
{BLANK}	Erases the cell or range

In the program in figure 20.26, the LET statement in line 1 is executed only if the condition in the IF statement is true, and the LET statement in line 2 is executed only if the condition is false. Line 1 places a label in a cell, whereas line 2 places a value representing the formula (in the program) in a cell.

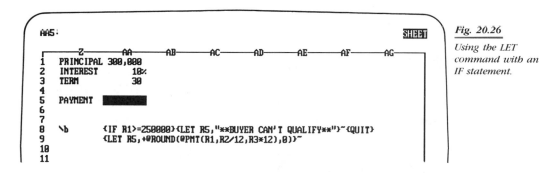

Fig. 20.26

Using the LET command with an IF statement.

Figure 20.27 shows how to use LET in an application that takes a master file and saves it under a new name, that of a client code number. The program begins with a GETLABEL statement that prompts you for a client code number and places the number in cell B3. The LET statement then duplicates the client code number in the cell named CODE, which lies within the program in AA7.

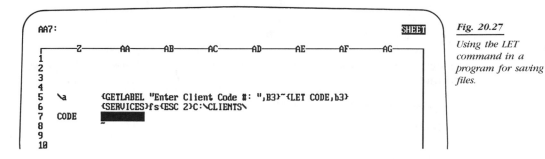

Fig. 20.27

Using the LET command in a program for saving files.

You can use a string value with the LET command. In fact, you can even use a string formula. For example, if the cell named FIRST contains the string "Robert", and LAST holds the string "Hamer", the statement

{LET NAME,FIRST&" "&LAST}

stores "Robert Hamer" in NAME.

Like the DEFINE command, the LET command allows you to specify :STRING and :VALUE suffixes after the argument. The STRING suffix stores the text of the argument in the location, whereas the VALUE suffix evaluates the argument as a string or numeric formula and places the result in the location. When a suffix is not specified, LET stores the argument's numeric or string value if the argument is a valid formula; otherwise, the text of the argument is stored. For example:

{LET NAME,FIRST&" "&LAST:VALUE}

stores "Robert Hamer" in NAME, whereas

{LET NAME,FIRST&" "&LAST:STRING}

stores the string *FIRST&" "&LAST* in NAME.

You can duplicate the LET command by moving the cell pointer to the appropriate location with {GOTO} and entering the appropriate value into the cell. The LET command, however, has the major advantage that it does not disturb the current location of the cell pointer. You can also use the SHEET **R**ange **F**ill command to enter numbers, but not to enter string values. Overall, the LET command is a convenient and useful means for setting the value of a cell from within a program.

The PUT Command

The PUT command places a value in a target cell location determined by the intersection of a row and a column in a defined range. The form of the PUT command is

{PUT range,col,row,value}

The PUT statement contains four arguments. The first argument defines the *range* into which the value will be placed. The second argument defines the *col*umn offset within the range; the third, the *row* offset within the range. The fourth indicates the *value* to be placed in the cell location. Argument 1 may be a range name or cell address. Arguments 2, 3, and 4 may be values, cell references, or formulas.

For example, this PUT statement

{PUT TABLE,S1,S2,ARG4}

places the contents of the cell named ARG4 in the range named TABLE at the intersection defined by the values in cells S1 and S2.

Figure 20.28 shows the results of different variations of this command. Keep in mind that the row and column offset numbers follow the same conventions followed by functions (the first column is number 0, the second is number 1, and so on).

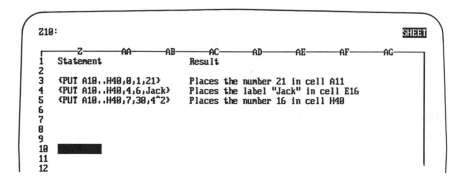

Fig. 20.28

Using the PUT command to enter numbers and labels.

The CONTENTS Command

The CONTENTS command stores the contents of a source cell in a destination cell, optionally assigning an individual cell width and/or cell format. If width or format are not specified, the CONTENTS command uses the column width and format of the source location to format the string. The form of the CONTENTS command is

{CONTENTS destination,source,[width],[format]}

For example, the following CONTENTS statement:

{CONTENTS THERE,HERE,11,121}

places the contents of the cell named HERE in the cell named THERE, gives the individual cell a width of 11, and formats the entry as a full international date (121). The number used for the format number in this statement (121) was taken from the list of CONTENTS command format numbers that appears in table 20.5. This table also supplies the format numbers for the other examples in this section.

Suppose that you want to copy the number 123.456, which resides in cell A21, to cell B25, and change the number to a string while you copy. The statement for this step is

{CONTENTS B25,A21}

The contents of cell B25 will be displayed as the string 123.456 with a left-aligned label-prefix character.

Table 20.5
Numeric Format Codes for CONTENTS Command

Code	Destination String's Numeric Display Command
0	Fixed, 0 decimal places
1-15	Fixed, 1 to 15 decimal places
15-31	Scientific, 0 to 15 decimal places
32-47	Currency, 0 to 15 decimal places
48-63	Percent, 0 to 15 decimal places
64-79	Comma, 0 to 15 decimal places
112	+/- Bar Graph
113	General
114	D1 (DD-MMM-YY)
115	D2 (DD-MM)
116	D3 (MMM-YY)
121	D4 (Full International)
122	D5 (Partial International)
119	D6 (HH:MM:SS AM/PM time format)
120	D7 (HH:MM AM/PM time format)
123	D8 (Full International time format)
124	D9 (Partial International time format)
117	Text format
118	Hidden format
127	Current window's default display format

Next, suppose that you want to change the width of the string when you copy it. Rather than have the string display as 123.456, you want it to display as 123.4. To get this result, change the statement to

{CONTENTS B25,A21,6}

This second statement uses a width of 6 to display the string. Symphony truncates the least significant digits of the number to create the string. If the number cannot be displayed in the specified width using the specified format, Symphony places a string of asterisks (*****) in the cell instead. (This method works just like Symphony's normal spreadsheet formatting commands.)

Finally, suppose that you want to change the display format of the string while you copy it and change its width. The following command changes the display format to **Currency 0**:

{CONTENTS B25,A21,5,32}

The result of the statement is the number $123.

In the following examples of the CONTENTS command with 123.456 as the number in cell A21, the width of column A is 9, and the display format for cell A21 is Fixed **2**.

{CONTENTS B25,A21}	Displays the number 123.46 in cell B25, using the Fixed **2** format.
{CONTENTS B25,A21,4}	Uses a width of 4 and the Fixed **2** format. The result is ****.
{CONTENTS B25,A21,5,0}	Displays the number 123 in cell B25, using the Fixed **0** format.

The CONTENTS command is rather specialized but very useful in situations that require converting numeric values to formatted strings. CONTENTS can convert long numeric formulas to strings, using the Text format. This application is particularly useful for debugging purposes.

The BLANK Command

The BLANK command erases a range of cells in the spreadsheet. Although this command works similarly to the SHEET Erase command, using BLANK in your Command Language programs has a few advantages. BLANK is faster than SHEET Erase because BLANK works outside the menu structure. The form of the BLANK command is

{BLANK location}

where *location* is the range to be erased.

In the example in figure 20.29, the BLANK statement erases RANGE1. Line 2 executes the {BLANK RANGE2} statement only if the conditional IF statement tests true.

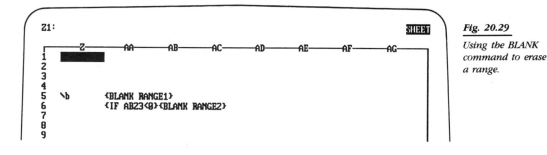

Fig. 20.29

Using the BLANK command to erase a range.

Program Enhancement Commands

The commands shown in table 20.6 (BEEP, PANELOFF, PANELON, WINDOWSOFF, WINDOWSON, INDICATE, RECALC, RECALCCOL, PHONE, and HANDSHAKE) can "dress up" your program or recalculate a portion of your worksheet. With your skillful placement, these commands can add the polish that a solid program structure needs in order to become a smooth, easy-to-use application. This catchall group of maintenance-oriented commands includes commands to sound your computer's speaker, control the screen display, selectively recalculate portions of the spreadsheet, and invoke communications commands. Two commands in this group (WINDOWSOFF and PANELOFF) can increase significantly the execution speed of large Command Language programs.

Table 20.6
Program Enhancement Commands

Command	Description
{BEEP}	Sounds one of the computer's four beeps
{PANELOFF}	Suppresses display of control panel
{PANELON}	Displays control panel
{WINDOWSOFF}	Suppresses redisplay of current window
{WINDOWSON}	Enables redisplay of current window
{INDICATE}	Resets control panel indicator to <string>
{RECALC}	Recalculates a specified portion of the worksheet row by row
{RECALCCOL}	Recalculates a specified portion of the worksheet column by column
{PHONE}	Phones a remote computer
{HANDSHAKE}	Sends single-line messages to a remote computer

The BEEP Command

The BEEP command activates the computer's speaker system to produce one of four tones. Each argument (1 through 4) produces a different tone. The BEEP command is commonly used to alert a user to a specific condition in the program or to draw the user's attention. The form of the BEEP command is

　　{BEEP [number]}

or

　　{BEEP}

The following BEEP statement:

　　{IF A35>50}{BEEP 2}

produces a sound if the condition presented in the IF statement is true. If the statement is false, program control passes to the next cell below the IF statement.

The PANELOFF Command

The PANELOFF command freezes the control panel, prohibiting the annoying display of program commands in the control panel during program execution. You can use this command effectively to display messages in the control panel, regardless of the cell pointer's current location. Be aware, however, that the PANELOFF command prevents the display of prompts from GETLABEL and GETNUMBER statements. The form of the PANELOFF command is

{PANELOFF}

In figure 20.30, the PANELOFF command in line 1 suppresses the control panel's display of the Copy command that follows in line 2.

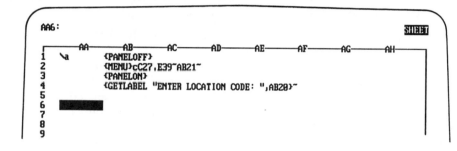

Fig. 20.30

Using PANELON with GETLABEL.

The PANELON Command

The PANELON command unfreezes the control panel. This command is commonly used immediately before a GETLABEL or GETNUMBER command. The form of the PANELON command is

{PANELON}

In figure 20.30, the PANELON command reactivates the control panel so that the prompt for the GETLABEL statement is displayed.

The WINDOWSOFF Command

By using the WINDOWSOFF command, you can freeze the lower part of the screen and have just the control panel show the changes that occur as a result of the commands activated in your program. The WINDOWSOFF command freezes the current screen display, regardless of whether the program is executing. WINDOWSOFF is particularly useful when you are creating applications that will be used by novice Symphony users. WINDOWSOFF enables you to display only those screen changes that the user must see, freezing other changes that might confuse a beginner. The form of the WINDOWSOFF command is

{WINDOWSOFF}

In this example:

{WINDOWSOFF}
{MENU}cS24~Z12~ {CALC}

the WINDOWSOFF command prevents the automatic screen-rebuilding associated with the SHEET Copy command and the Calc key.

Using the WINDOWSOFF and PANELOFF commands can have a significant effect on program execution time. In one complex application, use of the WINDOWSOFF and PANELOFF commands to freeze the screen reduced execution time by 50 percent, from 5 to 2 1/2 minutes. Speed improvement depends, of course, on the particular application.

You can use WINDOWSOFF with PANELOFF to create a graph "slide show" for business meetings. These commands allow you to display a sequence of graphs uninterrupted by intervening worksheet screens.

The program in figure 20.31 demonstrates how to use the WINDOWSOFF and PANELOFF commands to eliminate screen shifting and to reduce execution time for such a presentation. The PANELOFF and WINDOWSOFF commands in AB1 suppress redrawing of the window and panel. Lines AB2 through AB8 display four different graphs, turning the window display on and off as needed. (Windows must be turned back on before each preview so that the graph can be seen.) In line AB9, the PANELON command restores redrawing of the panel. The program ends in line AB10 by returning the worksheet display with the cell pointer located at the Home position.

Fig. 20.31

Using WINDOWSOFF and PANELOFF for a graphics slide show.

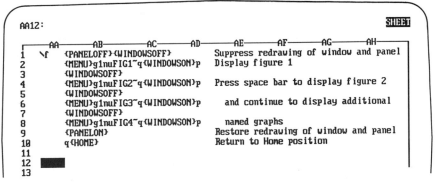

Be aware that if something goes wrong with your program while the WINDOWSOFF command is in effect, you can get into trouble. Unless you have a simple one-line program already preset for issuing the WINDOWSON command (see the following section), you may have to reboot Symphony and start your application all over again to recover the use of the screen. Therefore, it is wise to develop and test your programs without the WINDOWSOFF and WINDOWSON commands; add these commands to the debugged and tested program.

The WINDOWSON Command

The WINDOWSON command unfreezes the screen, allowing display of executing program operations. This command is commonly used to allow display of the Symphony menu structures. The form of the WINDOWSON command is

{WINDOWSON}

In figure 20.31, the WINDOWSON command is used throughout the program so that the graphs can be seen when you preview.

The INDICATE Command

The INDICATE command alters the mode indicator in the upper right corner of the Symphony screen. This command is commonly used to provide custom indicators. The INDICATE command accepts a string argument of up to seven characters. If the string is longer, Symphony uses only the first seven characters. When you use the INDICATE command, you have to enter a string. You cannot use a cell address or range name. The form of the INDICATE command is

{INDICATE string}

Suppose, for example, that you want to display the message START in the upper right corner of the screen. You can use the following INDICATE command:

{INDICATE START}

Unless you clear your indicator, using the command

{INDICATE}

displays the START message until you exit Symphony.

To blank out the indicator completely, you can use the command

{INDICATE ""}

The RECALC and RECALCCOL Commands

Two macro commands, RECALC and RECALCCOL, allow you to recalculate a portion of the worksheet. This feature can be useful in large spreadsheets where recalculation time is long and where you need to recalculate certain values in the worksheet before you proceed to the next processing step in your macro. The commands for partial recalculation have the form

{RECALC location,condition,iteration-number}

and

{RECALCCOL location,condition,iteration-number}

in which *location* is a range or range name that specifies the cells whose formulas are to be recalculated. The *condition* and *iteration-number* arguments are optional.

If you include the condition argument, the range is recalculated repeatedly until condition has a logical value of TRUE (1). The condition argument must be either a logical expression or a reference to a cell within the recalculation range that contains a logical expression. If condition is a reference to a cell outside the recalculation range, then the value of condition, either TRUE (1) or FALSE (0), will not change, and condition will not control the partial recalculation.

If you include the iteration-number argument, you must also specify the condition argument (the value 1 makes condition always TRUE). The iteration-number specifies the number of times that formulas in the location range are to be recalculated.

The RECALC and RECALCCOL commands differ in the order in which cells in the specified range are recalculated. The RECALC command performs the calculations by row—all the cells in the first row of the range, then all the cells in the second row, and so on. The RECALCCOL command performs the calculations by column—all the cells in the first column of the range, followed by all the cells in the second column, and so on. In both commands, only cells within the specified range are recalculated.

Use RECALC to recalculate the range when the formulas in the range refer only to other formulas in rows above or to the left of themselves in the same row in that range. Use RECALCCOL to recalculate the range when formulas in the range refer only to other formulas in columns to the left or to cells above themselves in the same column.

Just a word of caution here: You may have to use CALC if formulas in the range refer to other formulas located below and to their right, or if formulas refer both to cells in rows above and to the right and to cells in columns below and to the left.

You need to include in the range only those cells you want to recalculate. The formulas in the recalculation range can refer to values in cells outside the range; however, those values are not updated by RECALC or RECALCCOL.

When either the RECALC or RECALCCOL command is executed, the partial recalculation occurs immediately. The results do not appear on-screen, however, until the screen is redrawn. Program execution may continue for some time before a command that updates the screen is executed. In the interim, the recalculated numbers, although not visible on-screen, are available for use in calculations and conditional tests.

If the program ends, and you want to be sure that the recalculated numbers are on-screen, use the PgUp and PgDn keys to move the window away from and back to the recalculated range. The act of looking away and back again updates the screen and displays the current values in the recalculated range.

You may need to use CALC, RECALC, or RECALCCOL after commands such as LET, GETNUMBER, and {?}. You do not need to recalculate after invoking Symphony commands such as SHEET Copy and Move; Symphony automatically recalculates the affected ranges after such commands, even during program execution.

Caution: Recalculating a portion of the worksheet can cause some formulas (those outside a recalculated range that reference formulas within the range) to fail to reflect current data. If this situation occurs in your application, be sure to perform a general recalculation at some point before the end of your program.

The PHONE Command

The PHONE command allows you to phone a remote computer without having to switch to a COMM window. The general form of this command is

{PHONE phone-number-string}

Figure 20.32 shows an example of how to use the PHONE command. Notice that the phone-number-string is the range name PHONE_NO. You can also use a string formula for the argument.

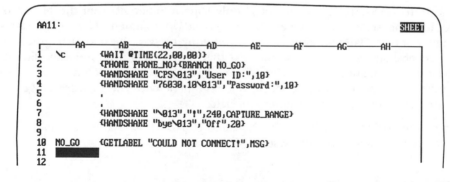

Fig. 20.32

A program that uses the PHONE and HANDSHAKE commands.

Notice the BRANCH statement that follows the PHONE statement in cell AB2. If Symphony is unable to make a connection, the program executes the statement following the PHONE command in the same line (in this case, {BRANCH NO_GO}). If a connection is made, however, the next statement that Symphony executes is on the line below the PHONE statement.

The HANDSHAKE Command

You can also send single-line messages to a remote computer without having to switch to a COMM window. The command to send messages is HANDSHAKE, and its general form is

{HANDSHAKE send-string,receive-string,seconds,capture- location}

The *send-string* is the string you want to send; the *receive-string* is the string you expect from the remote computer in response to the send-string. The third argument is the number of *seconds* that you want to allocate for sending the send-string and receiving the receive-string. This number is the maximum amount of time you want Symphony to take to complete the transaction. Symphony moves immediately to the next statement when the receive-string is read. The final argument, *capture-location*, indicates where you want Symphony to save the text that precedes the receive-string (but not including the receive-string).

Suppose that after establishing a connection, you want to send all the log-in messages and menu responses for calling up the stock information on the remote system. The HANDSHAKE statements in figure 20.32 show how you might do this.

In the first HANDSHAKE statement, notice that the *send-string* argument includes the string CPS followed by the decimal ASCII code for the Enter key (\013). *Note:* Do not forget the decimal ASCII code, or the HANDSHAKE statement will not work properly.

Although the second HANDSHAKE statement is similar to the first, the second HANDSHAKE sends the User ID number and receives the next prompt from the remote computer; the next prompt is a prompt to enter the password.

The third HANDSHAKE statement is only slightly different from the first two. Because this statement includes a *capture-location* argument, issuing this statement from a COMM window causes Symphony to save the text that precedes the receive string (in this case the text that precedes "!") on the same line in the capture-location. In practice, you will rarely need to include a capture-location argument. Do not confuse this argument with the Capture range required for capturing large amounts of data.

The combination of the WAIT, PHONE, and HANDSHAKE statements makes the delayed accessing of remote systems quite easy.

File Manipulation Commands

Eight commands give Symphony the capability of opening, reading, writing, and closing a sequential data file containing ASCII text data. This capability allows Symphony applications to read and write files used by other business applications. Although the SERVICES File Import command provides a limited capability to manipulate foreign files, the file manipulation commands shown in table 20.7 provide a capability equal to the sequential file commands in BASIC or other programming languages.

Table 20.7
File Manipulation Commands

Command	Description
{OPEN}	Opens file for reading, writing, or both
{CLOSE}	Closes a file opened with {OPEN}
{READ}	Copies specified characters from the open file to <location>
{READLN}	Copies next line from file to <location>
{WRITE}	Copies a string to the open file
{WRITELN}	Copies a string plus a carriage-return, line-feed sequence to the open file
{SETPOS}	Sets a new position for the file pointer
{GETPOS}	Records file pointer position in <location>
{FILESIZE}	Records size of open file in <location>

Warning: The file manipulation commands are programming commands. To read from and write to foreign files successfully, you must understand exactly how these commands work and how the sequential files you are manipulating are organized. If you write to a file containing another application, be sure to back up the file before trying to write to it from within Symphony.

If you keep this warning in mind, this group of commands can open up the world of outside files to your Symphony applications. If you need to process external data files, these commands make it possible to do the job with Symphony.

The OPEN Command

The OPEN command opens a disk file, providing access so that you can write to or read from that file. The form of the OPEN command is

{OPEN filename,access mode}

The *filename* argument is a string, an expression with a string value, or a single-cell reference to a cell that contains a string or a string expression. The string must be a valid DOS file name or path name. A file in the current directory can be specified by its name and extension. A file in another directory may require a drive identification, a subdirectory path, or a complete DOS path in addition to the file name and extension.

The *access-mode* argument is a single character string that specifies whether you want to read only ("R"), write only ("W"), or both read from and write to the file ("M").

"R" (Read)	Read access opens an existing file and allows access with the READ and READLN commands. You cannot write to a file opened with Read access.
"W" (Write)	Write access opens a new file with the specified name and allows access with the WRITE and WRITELN commands. Any existing file with the specified name is erased and replaced by the new file.
"M" (Modify)	Modify access opens an existing file with the specified name and allows access with both read (READ AND READLN) and write (WRITE and WRITELN) commands.
"A" (Append)	Append access opens an existing file and positions the file pointer at the end of the file. Append access allows access with WRITE and WRITELN commands.

Note that Symphony allows only one file to be open at a time. If you want to work with more than one file in your application, you must open each file before using it and then close it again before opening and using the next file. Note also that the "M" (Modify) argument cannot create a new file.

The OPEN command succeeds if it is able to open the file with the access you requested. If the OPEN command succeeds, program execution continues with the cell below the OPEN command. Any commands after the OPEN statement in the current cell are ignored.

The OPEN command fails with an ERROR if the disk drive is not ready. You should use an ONERROR command to handle this contingency.

If the access mode is Read or Modify, but the file does not exist on the indicated directory, the OPEN command fails, and program execution continues with the commands after the OPEN command in the current cell. You can place one or more commands after the OPEN command in the same cell to deal with the failure. The most common practice is to place a BRANCH or a subroutine call after the OPEN to transfer to a macro that handles the failure.

Here are some examples (with explanations) of the OPEN command:

{OPEN "PASTDUE","R"}{BRANCH FIXIT}

> Open the existing file named PASTDUE in the current directory for reading. If the file cannot be opened, branch to the routine FIXIT.

{OPEN "C:\DATA\CLIENTS.DAT",w}

> Open the new file named CLIENTS.DAT in drive C, subdirectory DATA, for writing.

{OPEN FILE,m}{BRANCH RETRY}

> Open the file whose name is in cell FILE for Modify access. If the file cannot be opened, branch to the routine RETRY.

Figure 20.33 shows an example of using all the file commands except the READ and WRITE commands (which are similar to READLN and WRITELN). The program named \o uses the OPEN command to open a user-specified file. This program illustrates how to deal with `Disk drive not ready` and `File not found` errors. After the program prompts you for the file name and access mode, an ONERROR command sets the error jump to the routine that handles such problems as the drive not being ready. Next, the OPEN command is used with the BRANCH command. This BRANCH handles such problems as a `File not found` error.

The CLOSE Command

The CLOSE command closes a currently open file. If no file is open, the CLOSE command has no effect. CLOSE does not take an argument. The CLOSE command is particularly important for files that you are writing or modifying. You can lose the last data written to a file that you don't close. The form of the CLOSE command is

{CLOSE}

Under most circumstances, Symphony automatically takes care of a file that you do not close, but you should make it a practice to use CLOSE when you are finished using any file opened with OPEN. Better safe than sorry. Use of the CLOSE command is illustrated in the program labeled \c in figure 20.33.

The READ Command

The READ command reads a specified number of characters from the currently open file, beginning at the present file pointer location. The form of the READ command is

{READ bytecount,location}

Fig. 20.33

A program that uses the file manipulation commands.

```
Z1: '\o

     Z——AA————————AB————————AC——AD——AE——AF——AG——AH——AI——AJ——
1    \o {GETLABEL "Enter file name: ",FILE}              \w {GETLABEL "Enter text to write: ",BUFFER}
2       {GETLABEL "R, W, or M access mode: ",A}             {WRITELN BUFFER}{WRITERR}
3       {ONERROR NOTREADY, MESSAGE}
4       {IF A="R"}{OPEN FILE,R}{BRANCH OPENERR}
5       {IF A="W"}{OPEN FILE,W}{BRANCH OPENERR}         \s {GETNUMBER "Enter file position: ",FILEPOINTER}
6       {IF A="M"}{OPEN FILE,M}{BRANCH OPENERR}            {SETPOS filepointer}{notopen}
7
8
9    \r {READLN BUFFER}{READERR}                        \g {GETPOS FILEPOINTER}{NOTOPEN}
10
11
12   \c {CLOSE}{NOTOPEN}                                \f {FILESIZE SIZE}{NOTOPEN}
13
14
15   A
16   MESSAGE
17   FILE
18   BUFFER
19   CHAR
20   FILEPOINTER
21   SIZE
22
23   OPENERR      {GETLABEL "Could not open file.",CHAR}
24
25   NOTREADY     {GETLABEL "DISK DRIVE NOT READY.",CHAR}
26
27   READERR      {GETLABEL "READ FAILED. No file open, or (W)rite access",CHAR}
28
29   WRITERR      {GETLABEL "WRITE FAILED. No file open, or (R)ead access",CHAR}
30
31   NOTOPEN      {GETLABEL "No file open",CHAR}
32
```

in which *bytecount* is the number of bytes to read, and *location* is the cell to read into. READ places the specified number of characters from the file into the location cell as a label. Bytecount can be any number between 1 and 240, the maximum number of characters in a Symphony label. If bytecount is greater than the number of characters remaining in the file, Symphony reads the remaining characters into location. After the READ command finishes, the file pointer is positioned at the character following the last character read.

For example, the statement

{READ NUM,INFO}

transfers information from the open file into the cell location named INFO. The amount of information transferred is determined by the contents of the cell named NUM, which can contain either a value or a formula.

The READ command is useful primarily when you want to read a specific number of characters into the buffer. A data file that contains fixed-length records, for example, is read conveniently by the READ command with bytecount equal to the record length.

You should not use READ with ASCII text files from a word processor or text editor. Such files generally have variable length lines terminated with a carriage-return, line-feed sequence and are read better with the READLN command. Although figure 20.33 does not contain an example of the READ command, READ is used much like the READLN in the figure's \r program.

The READLN Command

The READLN command reads one line of information from the currently open file, beginning at the file pointer's current position. The READLN command form is

{READLN location}

The characters read are placed in the cell *location* in the current spreadsheet. For example, the statement

{READLN HERE}

copies a line from an open file into the cell named HERE. The line will be determined by the SETPOS command. (SETPOS is discussed later in the chapter.)

Use READLN to read a line of text from a file whose lines are delimited by a carriage-return, line-feed combination. You would, for example, use READLN to read the next line from an ASCII text file. ASCII text files are created with Symphony's SERVICES **Print Settings Destination File** command. Also referred to as print files, these files are assigned the .PRN file extension by Symphony. READLN is best suited to reading files that are print images. The program labeled \r in figure 20.33 illustrates the use of READLN.

Using READ and READLN
If you attempt to read past the end of the file, if no file is open, or if the file was opened with Write access, the READ or READLN command is ignored, and program execution continues in the same cell. Otherwise, after the READ or READLN command is completed, program execution continues on the next line. You can thus place a BRANCH or subroutine call after the READ or READLN to handle the problem of an unexecuted READ or READLN statement.

The WRITE Command

The WRITE command writes a string of text to the currently open file. The WRITE command has the form

{WRITE string}

The *string* argument can be a literal string, a range name or cell reference to a single cell that contains a string, or a string expression. Because WRITE does not place a carriage-return, line-feed sequence at the end of the string, you can use multiple WRITE commands to concatenate text on a single line. WRITE is well suited to creating or updating a file that contains fixed-length database records. Although figure 20.33 does not contain an example of the WRITE command, this command is used in much the same way as is the WRITELN command in the \w program in that figure.

If the file pointer is not at the end of the file, Symphony overwrites the existing characters in the file. If the file pointer is at the end of the file, Symphony extends the file by the number of characters written. And if the file pointer is past the end of the file (see the discussion of the SETPOS command), before writing the characters, Symphony extends the file by the amount indicated.

The WRITELN Command

The WRITELN command is identical to the WRITE command except that WRITELN places a carriage-return, line-feed sequence after the last character written from the string. The WRITELN command form is

{WRITELN string}

WRITELN is useful when the file being written or updated uses the carriage-return line feed to mark the end of its lines or records. In many applications, you can use several WRITEs to write a line to the file, then a WRITELN to mark the end of the line. The WRITELN command is illustrated in the \w program in figure 20.33.

The SETPOS Command

The SETPOS command sets the position of the file pointer to a specified value. The form of the command is

{SETPOS file-position}

File-position is a number, or an expression resulting in a number, that specifies the character at which you want to position the pointer. The first character in the file is at position 0, the second at position 1, and so on.

As an example, suppose that you have a database file with 100 records which are each 20 bytes long. To access the first record, you can use the commands

{SETPOS 0}
{READ 20,buffer}

To read the 20th record, you can use the commands

{SETPOS (20-1)*20}
{READ 20,buffer}

Nothing prevents you from setting the file pointer past the end of the file. If the file pointer is set at or past the end, and a READ or READLN command is executed, the command does nothing, and program execution continues with the next command on the same line (error branch). If the file pointer is set at or past the end, and a WRITE or WRITELN command is executed, Symphony first extends the file to the length specified by the file pointer, and then, starting at the file pointer, writes the characters.

Warning: If you inadvertently set the file pointer to a large number with SETPOS and write to the file, Symphony attempts to expand the file and writes the text at the end. If the file will not fit on the disk, the WRITE command does nothing, and program execution continues with the next command on the same line (error branch). If the file will fit on the disk, Symphony extends the file and writes the text at the end.

If a file is not currently open, SETPOS does nothing, and execution continues with the next command on the same line as the SETPOS command. Otherwise, when the SETPOS command is completed, execution continues on the next line of the program. You can thus place a BRANCH command or a subroutine call after the SETPOS command to handle the problem of an unexecuted statement. SETPOS is illustrated in the \s program in figure 20.33.

The GETPOS Command

The GETPOS command allows you to record the file pointer's current position. The form of this command is

{GETPOS location}

The current position of the file pointer is placed in the cell indicated by *location*, where location is either a cell reference or a range name. If location points to a multicell range, the value of the file pointer is placed in the upper left corner of the range.

The GETPOS command is useful if you record in the file the location of something you want to find again. You can use GETPOS to mark your current place in the file before you use SETPOS to move the file pointer to another position. You can use GETPOS, for example, to record the locations of important items in a quick-reference index. GETPOS is illustrated in the \g program in figure 20.33.

The FILESIZE Command

Another file-related command, FILESIZE, returns the length of the file in bytes. The form of the command is

{FILESIZE location}

The FILESIZE command determines the current length of the file and places this value in the cell referred to by *location*. Location can be a cell reference or range name. If location refers to a multicell range, the file size is placed in the cell in the upper left corner of the range. FILESIZE is illustrated in the \f program in figure 20.33.

A Command Language Application

Although Symphony's **Print** menu provides most of the capabilities needed for a variety of worksheet printing tasks, you cannot use the **Print** menu to print multiple copies of a single report automatically. To print multiple copies of the same report, you must repeatedly select the commands for aligning paper and beginning the print operation. With Symphony's Command Language, you can create a program to accomplish these tasks. And you can enhance the program by adding help screens and prompts that will help users solve problems that may occur during the print operation.

Figure 20.34 illustrates a Command Language program for printing multiple copies of a report. Notice that this program includes 10 of the commands discussed in the previous sections of this chapter. These commands include

- Commands for accepting input: GET, GETNUMBER, and LOOK

- Commands for program control: BRANCH, MENUCALL, and BREAKOFF

- Decision-making commands: IF and FOR

- Program enhancement Commands: BEEP and PANELOFF

Fig. 20.34

A Command Language program that prints multiple copies.

```
Z1: '\p                                                          SHEET
       Z         AA        AB        AC        AD        AE        AF        AG
1    \p        {GETNUMBER "Enter number of copies: ",STOP}~
2              {IF @ISERR(STOP)}{BEEP}{BRANCH \p}
3              {PANELOFF}{BREAKOFF}{GOTO}MSG_SCRN~
4              {WINDOWSOFF}{FOR COUNT,1,STOP,1,PRINT}~{BEEP 3}{WINDOWSON}
5
6    COUNT
7    STOP
8    INTERRUPT
9    MESSAGE
10
11   PRINT     {LOOK INTERRUPT}
12             {IF INTERRUPT="{MENU}"}{BRANCH ABORT}
13             {SERVICES}pagpq
14
15   ABORT     {BEEP 2}{GET MESSAGE}~
16             {MENUCALL MSG}
17             {QUIT}
18
19   MSG                         - PRINT JOB ABORTED AT YOUR REQUEST -
20             Press Enter to end macro execution (printer may not stop immediate
21             {CALC}{RETURN}
22
23
24
25
```

In the program's first line, the GETNUMBER command lets you enter the number of copies to be printed. For example, if you want three copies, you would enter **3** in response to the prompt Enter number of copies:. Then the

GETNUMBER command stores the number in the range STOP (cell AA7). Notice the companion error-checking routine for GETNUMBER in the program's second line (AA2).

In line 3, PANELOFF prevents movement on the control panel (so that you won't be distracted); BREAKOFF disables Ctrl-Break; and a message screen (with the range name MSG_SCRN) is incorporated into the worksheet. This message screen informs you that the print job is in progress and explains what to do if something goes wrong (see fig. 20.35). Notice that cell AJ9 in figure 20.35 uses a string formula to tell you how many copies are to be printed.

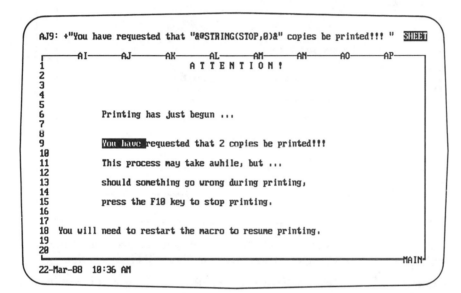

Fig. 20.35

The message displayed by the print program.

As you can see from figure 20.34, two additional range names (INTERRUPT and MESSAGE) appear in lines 8 and 9, respectively. The PRINT subroutine contains a LOOK statement followed by an IF statement, both of which use the range INTERRUPT. Two other subroutines, ABORT and MSG, are used also. (The range to be printed must be predefined.)

When you run the program, the following actions take place. First, the prompt Enter number of copies: is displayed in the control panel. After you enter a number, a message screen similar to the one shown in figure 20.35 appears. The string formula in cell AJ9 is updated with the value entered in STOP, confirming the number of copies to be printed. You are told to wait a while and to press F10 if you want to interrupt the print operation. At this point, printing begins.

Now let's see how the procedure to cancel printing works. Suppose that you requested the wrong number of copies to be printed. As soon as you press F10, the computer beeps, the menu message – PRINT JOB ABORTED AT YOUR REQUEST – appears in the control panel, and you are instructed to press Enter to end macro execution (see fig. 20.36).

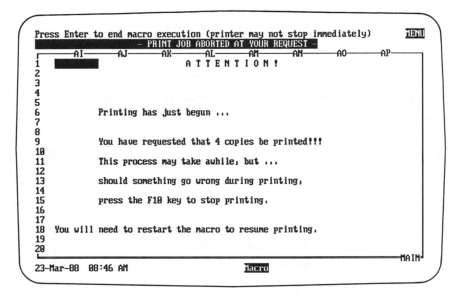

Fig. 20.36

Message showing that the print job has been aborted.

```
Press Enter to end macro execution (printer may not stop immediately)    MENU
                     - PRINT JOB ABORTED AT YOUR REQUEST -
        AI      AJ      AK      AL      AM      AN      AO      AP
 1 ▮▮▮▮▮▮▮▮              A T T E N T I O N !
 2
 3
 4
 5
 6            Printing has just begun ...
 7
 8
 9            You have requested that 4 copies be printed!!!
10
11            This process may take awhile, but ...
12
13            should something go wrong during printing,
14
15            press the F10 key to stop printing.
16
17
18   You will need to restart the macro to resume printing.
19
20                                                                       MAIN
   23-Mar-88   08:46 AM                    Macro
```

How did all these steps occur? The essential elements in this method of stopping the program are the LOOK and IF statements in the PRINT subroutine.

LOOK checks the type-ahead buffer to see whether anything was typed during program execution. If something was typed, the first character is copied into the range named INTERRUPT. If a function key was pressed, the name representation for that function key is stored in INTERRUPT. In this program, each time LOOK is executed, Symphony checks INTERRUPT to see whether anything is stored there. For instance, if you had pressed F10, {MENU} would be stored in INTERRUPT.

INTERRUPT is then evaluated by the IF statement, which indicates that if INTERRUPT contains the string {MENU}, the program should branch to the subroutine ABORT; otherwise, the program should print the worksheet. Note that you must press F10 to stop printing. Pressing any other key causes a false condition in the IF statement, and the print routine is executed. Because both LOOK and IF are part of PRINT, these two commands are executed whenever the FOR statement executes the loop; INTERRUPT is checked on every pass.

When program control next moves to ABORT, no additional reports are printed. ABORT causes the computer to beep and issues the GET command to clear the keyboard buffer (LOOK doesn't do this). ABORT then displays the menu message stored in MSG. Because {MENUCALL MSG} is used, the {RETURN} in the MSG subroutine sends the program back to ABORT when you press Enter. Because the cell after {MENUCALL MSG} is blank, the program ends.

Figure 20.37 shows what happens if you press F10 during program execution. Because you pressed F10, the range name INTERRUPT contains the string {MENU}. Notice that the range name MESSAGE also contains {MENU} (GET put the string there). Because {MENU} has already done its job with LOOK and is now useless, MESSAGE is nothing more than the "wastebasket" where GET sends all unwanted characters.

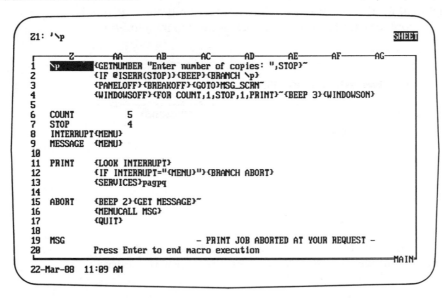

Fig. 20.37

The print program after the F10 key has been pressed.

This example is a sophisticated program for a special application that uses many Symphony capabilities, including string formulas and keyword commands. You will probably want to use this program if you occasionally print multiple copies of long reports (or even if you print multiple copies of short reports).

Other Command Language Programs

The following examples include some Command Language programs that you can use in Symphony's SHEET, GRAPH, COMM, and FORM environments.

A Copy Program To Skip Columns or Rows

Worksheets are often easier to read if you separate data with empty rows or columns. Unfortunately, this format makes it difficult to copy. You could create a long, slow macro program that copies across blank cells and then goes back and erases the cells that should be blank. By specifying your FROM range in a different way, however, you can simply use the Copy command, without having to go back and erase anything. Because this "trick" requires a bit of math, you can create a program that will do the calculation and copying for you.

Figure 20.38 contains the skipping copy program. In the first line, the GETNUMBER command asks you how many copies you want to make, and stores your response in a cell named COPIES. The second line invokes the SHEET Copy command. Line 3 recalculates the formula in the cell named NUMBER (the next macro line). The formula calculates how many cells down the pointer should highlight for the FROM range. (The formula multiplies the number of copies by 2 and subtracts 1.) The final two lines of the program finish the Copy command.

Fig. 20.38

A copying program that skips rows between multiple copies.

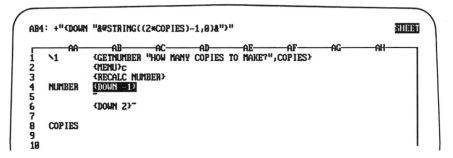

```
AB4: +"{DOWN "&@STRING((2*COPIES)-1,0)&"}"                        SHEET

         AA        AB        AC        AD        AE        AF        AG        AH
  1     \1        {GETNUMBER "HOW MANY COPIES TO MAKE?",COPIES}
  2               {MENU}c
  3               {RECALC NUMBER}
  4     NUMBER    {DOWN -1}
  5
  6               {DOWN 2}~
  7
  8     COPIES
  9
  10
```

This version of the program skips rows. If you need to copy to every other column, change the {DOWN} instructions to {RIGHT} instructions.

A Program To Image-Save a Series of Graphs

The graph-printing macro in Chapter 19 was designed to print a single graph. If you want to print more than one graph in a file, use the program in figure 20.39. This program displays the graph menu (line 1), has you select which graph you want to print, and previews the graph so that you can make sure you chose the correct one (line 2), and invokes the Image-Save command and pauses for you to enter a file name for the graph (line 3). In line 4, the program asks if you want to print another graph and stores your response in a cell named ANSWER. If you answer **Y** for Yes (line 4), the program branches to the cell named ANOTHER and then prompts for the next graph (line 5). If you don't answer **Y**, the file is saved with the same name (line 6), and you are exited from Symphony (line 7).

After you run this program, all your graphs are saved in .PIC files, and you can load the PrintGraph program to print the graphs.

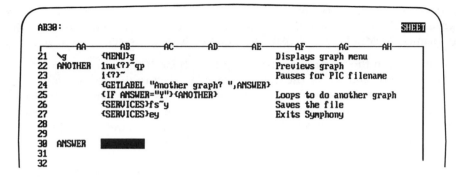

Fig. 20.39

A program to image-save a series of graphs.

A Program To Auto-Dial

If you have a spreadsheet or database file of phone numbers, you can create several programs that automatically dial each number in the list. Figure 20.40 shows an auto-dialing program. The \d dialing program dials the telephone number on which the cell pointer is located, while the \h hang-up program disconnects the call when you are finished, moves the pointer to the next number, and then reactivates the \d program.

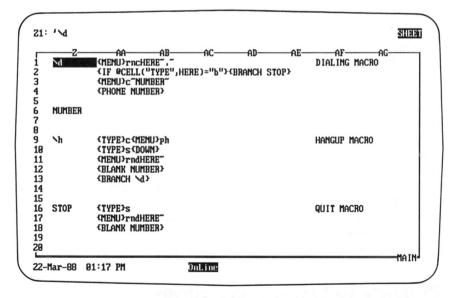

Fig. 20.40

A program that includes auto-dialing and auto-hang-up macros.

The first line of \d assigns the range name HERE to the current cell. Line 2 uses the IF command to test whether the cell is blank. If so, the program branches to the STOP subroutine. STOP deletes the range name HERE, erases the number in NUMBER, and quits the program's execution.

If the current cell is not blank, however, the third line in the \d program is executed. This line copies the telephone number (the current cell) into the cell named NUMBER. Line 4 dials the number with the PHONE command.

The first line in the \h program hangs up the phone. The second line switches to SHEET mode and moves the pointer down one cell to the next number. The next two lines are housekeeping commands that delete the range name HERE and erase the last number from the cell named NUMBER. Note that the program uses the Command Language BLANK command, which is faster than the SHEET Erase command. The last line of the hang-up program branches back to the dialing program.

A Program To Redial

If you frequently get a busy signal when dialing an electronic bulletin board or information service, you can use the redialing program in figure 20.41 to redial continuously until you connect. All you have to do is press Esc if you get a busy signal (or no answer), and the macro dials the number again. This program assumes that you have entered the phone number into the communications settings sheet.

Fig. 20.41

A program to redial a telephone number.

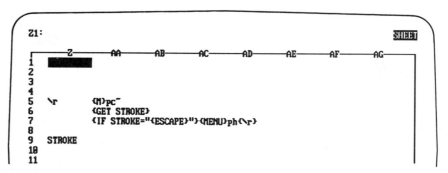

The first line of the program dials the number. The second line, {GET STROKE}, puts the next keystroke you type into a cell named STROKE. The IF statement tests the contents of the STROKE cell. If you pressed Esc, then the program hangs up the phone and branches to the beginning of the program and dials again. If you pressed any other key, the macro ends.

A Program To Create Entry Forms

A program that will help you make more efficient use of the FORM environment is one for building entry forms. Figure 20.42 shows a looping macro that takes field name, type, and length information and builds a range that is ready for the FORM Generate command.

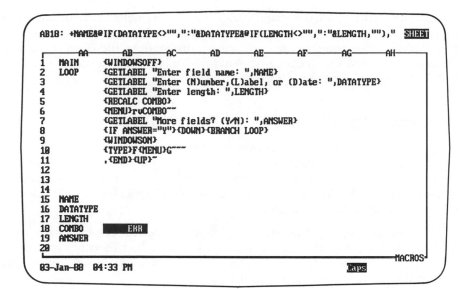

Fig. 20.42

A program to generate a database.

The first line of the macro uses the WINDOWSOFF command to eliminate the shifting of the screen when data is entered.

The range name LOOP marks the place in the code to which the macro will branch each time after entering in the spreadsheet all the information associated with a field name. The cell named LOOP contains the first of three GETLABEL commands. The first GETLABEL retrieves the field name and places it in a cell called NAME. (NAME and all the other cells used as the target location cells for the GETLABEL commands are listed below the macro.) The second GETLABEL gets the field type designation, and the third GETLABEL, the field length. The RECALC statement is then used to recalculate the cell called COMBO, which is a concatenation of NAME, TYPE, and LENGTH (including the appropriate colons) when those fields contain entries. The RECALC statement is essential here, or else the formula will reflect the entry from the previous loop.

The formula stored in the cell named COMBO is

+NAME&@IF(DATATYPE<>"","":"&DATATYPE&@IF(LENGTH<>"","":"&LENGTH,""),"")

This formula concatenates the TYPE and LENGTH strings to the NAME string only if TYPE and LENGTH contain entries. Otherwise, just the NAME string should appear in COMBO. *Note:* Do not leave spaces in the formula for documentation purposes, or the formula generates a syntax error message.

After the RECALC command statement, the next statement uses the SHEET **R**ange **V**alues command to copy COMBO to the cell where the cursor is currently positioned. As you recall, the **R**ange **V**alues command converts the formula to an actual value as the command copies from one location to another.

Next, another GETLABEL command asks whether more fields exist for this input form. The IF statement that follows the GETLABEL asks whether the answer is Y. If that choice is entered, the statements to the right of the IF are executed. Otherwise, the next line is executed. Window display is turned back on and the GENERATE command then creates the database.

Programs for Changing Default Values

Symphony lets you specify one default value for each field in your database so that if most of your records contain a certain value, you don't have to enter this value into each record. Sometimes, though, you have several values that appear frequently in a field. With some simple macros, you can quickly change the default values on-the-fly as you enter data.

Defaults are specified by entering the value in the Default column of the database's Definition range. For this example, let's assume the two values commonly used in a City field are San Francisco and San Jose. The default cell for the City field in this sample database is in cell D12.

```
\1      {LET D12,San Francisco}
        {CALC}{ESC}

\2      {LET D12,San Jose}
        {CALC}{ESC}
```

The first program, \1, puts San Francisco into D12 and recalculates so that the new default is reflected. The second program, \2, puts San Jose into D12. Because the LET statement is used to place the values, you can execute these programs at any time in any window environment. When you want to activate a new default, press the User key (F7) followed by the appropriately numbered function key (F1 or F2 in this example).

Chapter Summary

As you work with the Symphony Command Language, you soon will discover that your powerful spreadsheet program has an extremely potent programming language.

Although Symphony's Command Language makes many things possible, be aware of some practical limitations. For example, because Symphony is RAM-based, you must limit the size of your files. In addition, Symphony may not always execute programming commands with lightning speed. A trade-off of capabilities almost always exists; the most difficult applications may take a good deal of time to execute.

If you are an adventurer who wants to develop efficient, automated, customized models, and if you can live with the programming limitations, the Command Language is for you. This chapter has provided the groundwork for developing such models. As you become more experienced with the Command Language, turn to other Que publications for help in becoming an expert Command Language programmer.

Troubleshooting Section

This section addresses many of the problems you can encounter while using Symphony, and offers a variety of creative solutions. First-time users of Symphony will find that this section can help them untie knots that seem hopelessly snarled but are really only minor inconveniences when understood correctly.

Experienced users will undoubtedly derive even greater benefit from the problems and solutions presented here. As your use of the program becomes increasingly complex and sophisticated, so do the problems and errors that you encounter. Although first-time users face problems that momentarily seem insurmountable, the most perplexing problems in using Symphony are those faced by power users who push the program to its limits.

We suggest you use this section in two different ways:

1. Read the entire section after you have read the rest of the book and have begun to use Symphony; or use the same method segment-by-segment. Most people learn Symphony in segments—learning how to build a simple spreadsheet before learning to incorporate complex formulas and functions; learning how to create and edit documents; later learning how to print reports and create graphs; and much later, perhaps, learning how to create and use macros or to use the program's database management and communications capabilities. You can use this troubleshooting section the same way: after you learn the basics of one area of the program, read through the applicable portion of the troubleshooting section. Reading this section before you encounter problems will help you to avoid those problems.

2. Refer to this section as you encounter problems. The section is arranged to provide easy reference. The running heads at the upper right corner of the right-hand pages contain the name of the general area of problems covered on that page (for example, SPREADSHEET PROBLEMS). As each problem is introduced, a more specific designation (for example, DATA ENTRY PROBLEM #1) appears in the left margin, followed by a brief description of the problem. A quick scan of the heads and the margins will take you to the area that describes your problem. Using this section as a reference will be even easier, of course, if you have already read the material, as recommended previously. As an additional aid, a separate Troubleshooting Cross-Reference Index is provided at the end of this section.

The topics in the troubleshooting section are arranged in the following order:

1. *Installation*: You should read this section before you install Symphony. Some potentially disastrous installation problems cannot be remedied—they can only be avoided. Some installation problems, however, can be corrected after they occur. This section covers both initial installation problems and subsequent problems, such as those encountered when you later decide to create and use your own driver sets or install different printers.

2. *Spreadsheet*: This section covers problems in the basic spreadsheet environment—the environment in which you will probably encounter your first problems and surprises.

3. *Commands:* This section covers the use of Symphony commands in the spreadsheet.

4. *Functions*: This section solves a variety of basic and highly complex problems associated with Symphony's built-in @functions.

5. *File operations*: This section particularly addresses problems encountered while transferring and combining data from different files, using different directories, and saving and retrieving files.

6. *Windows*: If not used properly, windows can create more problems than they solve. This section helps you use Symphony's window feature more effectively.

7. *Word processing*: This section covers the problems you might face when working in Symphony's DOC mode.

8. *Printing*: Printing is a troublesome area for most users, who struggle to "get their reports to look exactly like they're supposed to look." This section answers many printing problems and provides many creative and useful tips.

9. *Graphing:* The wide variety of graphing options makes this area as complex as printing. This section helps you through the maze.

10. *Data management:* This area is possibly the most troublesome one of all. Many of the highly sophisticated database management systems (DBMS) on the market are much more powerful than Symphony's data management. Nevertheless, Symphony's capabilities are considerable, complex, and unfamiliar to many users, who enter this area reluctantly. Once you do start to use Symphony's database capabilities, you quickly and frequently encounter problems. Overcoming these problems, with the help of this section, can open doors to a much more extensive and rewarding use of Symphony.

11. *Communications:* Most of the problems you'll have in telecommunications have nothing to do with Symphony. That fact doesn't make these problems any easier to deal with. This section gives you useful solutions to communications problems.

12. *Macros:* Macros and the Symphony Command Language are among Symphony's most powerful features. This area is one that many users have fun with because they can learn a little at a time, building their skills slowly. As the skills build, so do the problems. This section helps you with many of those problems.

The troubleshooting reference section cannot be, and is not meant to be, a comprehensive listing of all Symphony problems. This section sometimes echoes and reinforces the explanations given elsewhere in the book. More often, this section extends your knowledge and your skills beyond the commentary given elsewhere. The ultimate solver of problems must be you, the individual user, but this section can help by solving specific problems and by showing a pattern of creative thinking for solving problems as they occur.

Troubleshooting Installation

Problems with Drivers

DRIVER PROBLEM #1:

You can't print, and you can't display graphs on a color monitor.

EXPLANATION: The program requires a file, called a driver set, that describes the equipment used in your system. This file must have the extension .SET. When you execute Symphony, the program looks for a file (called LOTUS.SET) containing the driver set. The Program disk contains an initial driver set called LOTUS.SET. This driver set uses a Universal Text Display driver that works with almost any display but has no support for printers and can't display graphs.

SOLUTION: Run the Install program and follow the prompts to describe your computer system. If you don't give the driver set a special name, Install names it LOTUS.SET.

Note: If you use different displays on your computer system, you may need several driver sets. You can use Install to set up different driver sets and give them individual names. To tell the program to use a driver set other than LOTUS.SET, specify the name of the driver .SET file when you execute the program.

For example, if you run Install and name a driver set COLOR.SET, you must specify this name whenever you run a Symphony program. Instead of typing *symphony* (or *access* or *pgraph*) at the DOS prompt, type *symphony color* (or *access color* or *pgraph color*).

If you always use the same display with your system, let Install name your driver set LOTUS.SET. Then you can forget about it when you execute Symphony.

DRIVER PROBLEM #2:

When loading Symphony, the system hangs with a blank screen, forcing you to reboot.

EXPLANATION: The default Universal Text Display driver works with almost any display. If you have a color monitor, however, and try to start the program with a driver installed for a monochrome monitor, or vice versa, you hang the system.

SOLUTION: First, if the driver set is not called LOTUS.SET, make sure that you specified the proper driver set when you executed Symphony. Suppose, for example, that LOTUS.SET is set for monochrome and that you have the color-monitor driver in a file called COLOR.SET. Be sure to specify COLOR when you use a color monitor. If you are using LOTUS.SET, rerun Install and check the driver set.

If the driver set seems to be correct, test to see if the original driver set on the Program disk runs correctly. If you execute the program from the hard disk, put the Program disk in drive A and, at the C : > prompt, type

SYMPHONY A:LOTUS

If the original driver set runs correctly, you can be certain that you specified an incorrect driver set and must rerun Install. If the computer still hangs, the problem must involve the switch setting for the math coprocessor.

ALTERNATE EXPLANATION: Two sets of switches located within an IBM Personal Computer tell the computer what kind of monitor you have, how much memory and how many floppy disk drives you have, and so on. The XT contains one set of switches. Although the AT has no switch settings, its SETUP program serves the same purpose.

One of the switch settings on the PC or XT tells the computer whether you have a math coprocessor chip installed. This special chip can perform math functions many times faster than the regular microprocessor in your computer. In most cases, a computer with a math coprocessor executes faster than a computer without one. The amount of time saved in a worksheet recalculation depends on the kinds of calculations in the worksheet. In a PC, XT, or PS/2 Model 25 or 30, the math coprocessor is an 8087 chip; in an AT or PS/2 Model 50 or 60, it is an 80287 chip; in a PS/2 Model 80 it is an 80387.

If you do not have a math coprocessor, but the switch settings indicate that you do, the system hangs as soon as you try to run the program.

You may have owned a PC for years and not been aware that this switch setting was not set properly, because your computer operates correctly as long as you do not run programs that try to use the math coprocessor. Some editions of the *IBM Guide to Operations* show the switch settings reversed.

ALTERNATE SOLUTION: If you do not have a math coprocessor, set the switch indicated in your guide to the ON position, even if the guide states otherwise.

If you have an AT, run its SETUP program, making sure that you have not indicated that you have a math coprocessor if none is installed. If you have a Personal System/2, this type of error cannot occur because no switch settings or SETUP programs exist.

DRIVER PROBLEM #3:

You have access to several printers and plotters that you use occasionally for printing worksheets and graphs, but keeping track of all the driver sets for these different configurations is difficult.

EXPLANATION: Symphony lets you use only the printers and plotters in your driver set. If you put all your output devices in different driver sets, you must remember which driver set to use whenever you execute the program.

SOLUTION: Do not set up different driver sets for each printer or plotter. Put all the printers and plotters in one set.

You must use more than one driver set only when you change either the physical display or the way Symphony displays information, which is an option with some display systems. (With a Hercules card, for example, you can display text as either 25×80 or 38×90.)

If you switch equipment and use different printers and plotters, you can install them all in one driver set. Whenever you specify a text printer, Install asks whether you have another printer. If you sometimes attach another printer to your system, answer **Yes** and then select the other printer. You can complete this step for as many as four different printers that you might attach to your computer. Repeat the step for any printers or plotters that you might attach to your computer for printing graphs.

Because the program does not expect more than one printer or plotter to be used at a time, you can install more than one, even when only one is attached. Then, while you're working in Symphony, use the SERVICES Configuration **Printer Name** command to select the printer currently attached to your computer. If the printer you choose as the default printer is to remain the default, you must select **Update** from the SERVICES Configuration menu. This command saves the defaults to disk; then, whenever you start Symphony, the same defaults are in effect.

If you attach printers to different ports on your computer, you must use the SERVICES Configuration Printer Type command to tell Symphony which printer interface to use. Parallel printers usually are Parallel 1. If you have more than one parallel-printer port, you must specify the one to which the printer is connected. If you use a serial printer, you must specify which serial port (interface) you're using (usually Serial 1). If you use a local area network, and printed output is redirected to another computer, you may have to specify DOS Device LPT1: to LPT4:.

In PrintGraph, use **Settings Hardware Printer** to specify the printer or plotter. Symphony then lists all the graph printers and plotters that you included in your driver set (see fig. T.1). Use **Settings Hardware Interface** to specify the correct LPT or COM port. After you make the changes, use **Settings Save** to make the new settings the default.

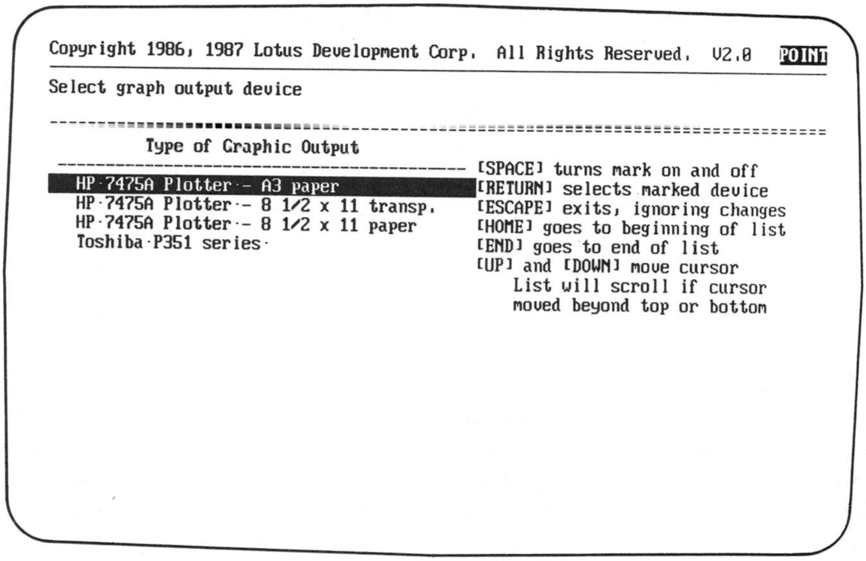

```
Copyright 1986, 1987 Lotus Development Corp.  All Rights Reserved.  V2.0  POINT

Select graph output device
--------------------------------------------================================================
          Type of Graphic Output
---------------------------------------------- [SPACE] turns mark on and off
  HP 7475A Plotter - A3 paper                  [RETURN] selects marked device
  HP 7475A Plotter - 8 1/2 x 11 transp.        [ESCAPE] exits, ignoring changes
  HP 7475A Plotter - 8 1/2 x 11 paper          [HOME] goes to beginning of list
  Toshiba P351 series                          [END] goes to end of list
                                               [UP] and [DOWN] move cursor
                                                    List will scroll if cursor
                                                    moved beyond top or bottom
```

Fig. T.1

A list of all graph output devices in the driver set.

Troubleshooting the Symphony Spreadsheet

Problems with Data Entry

DATA ENTRY PROBLEM #1:

After you type a label that starts with a number, the program beeps and puts you in EDIT mode.

EXPLANATION: When you begin typing information in a cell, Symphony changes the SHEET mode indicator in the screen's upper right corner to either LABEL or VALUE. If the first character you type is a number or a symbol used in a formula, the program assumes that you are typing a value. If you then type any character that is invalid for a value entry and press Enter, Symphony beeps, moves the cursor to the first character the program rejects, and switches to EDIT mode.

SOLUTION: To type a label such as *353 Sacramento Street*, you must first type a label prefix, such as an apostrophe ('), so that Symphony knows you are working with a label. If you forget to enter the prefix, and Symphony beeps, press Home and insert the apostrophe.

If the label is a valid numeric entry, instead of an error you'll get a numeric calculation that you don't want. For example, if you type *842-7162* as a telephone number, Symphony evaluates the entry as a formula and displays -632Ø. Edit the field to change it from a number to a label.

DATA ENTRY PROBLEM #2:

When you finish writing a complex formula, Symphony beeps and switches to EDIT mode. If you can't find the error immediately, you have to press Esc. You lose the entire formula and have to start again.

EXPLANATION: When you type an invalid formula, the program refuses to accept the entry and switches to EDIT mode. You must provide a valid entry before you can continue.

SOLUTION: Make the formula a valid entry by converting it to a label: press the Home key, type an apostrophe, and press Enter. Then you can work on the problem until you find and correct the error. Or you can work on another part of the worksheet and return to the formula later.

One common reason for Symphony rejecting a formula is the use of an unnamed range name. If you forgot to create a range name, convert the formula to a label, create the range name, and then edit the formula to remove the label prefix.

Note: Here is a method for debugging complex formulas. For example, suppose that you enter this formula in a cell:

@IF(@ISERR(A1/A2),@IF(A2=0),0,@ERR),A1/A2)

When you press Enter, Symphony beeps and switches to EDIT mode. If the error isn't obvious, you are stuck. You cannot exit EDIT mode unless you either fix the error or press Esc, erasing the contents of the cell. But because the program accepts anything as a label, you can insert a label prefix at the beginning of the entry and then press Enter. Then copy the formula to another cell and work on the formula until you find the error.

In this case, begin by eliminating the compound @IF from the formula. To do so, copy the formula to a blank cell (a work area) and then erase the middle @IF statement, replacing it with a 0 (zero):

@IF(@ISERR(A1/A2),0,A1/A2)

Because this formula works, the problem must be in the @IF statement that you erased. Again, copy the original formula to the work area. Now delete everything except the middle @IF:

@IF(A2=0),0,@ERR)

You can see that you should erase the right parenthesis that follows A2=0. Make the change and test it:

@IF(A2=0,0,@ERR)

When this segment works, erase the work cell and correct the original formula:

@IF(@ISERR(A1/A2),@IF(A2=0,0,@ERR),A1/A2)

You may write formulas that are longer and more complex than this example. To debug them, simply convert them to labels and test them, one part at a time.

Problems with Circular References

CIRCULAR REFERENCE PROBLEM #1:

The CIRC indicator suddenly appears after you enter a formula.

EXPLANATION: Whenever the worksheet is recalculated and a CIRC indicator appears at the bottom of the screen, Symphony is warning you about a circular reference. Circular references are formulas that refer to themselves, either directly or indirectly. Because they usually are errors, you should correct circular references as soon as they occur.

An example of the most common direct circular reference is shown in figure T.2. In this example, the @SUM function includes itself in the range to be summed. Whenever the worksheet recalculates, this sum increases.

Fig. T.2

A direct circular reference.

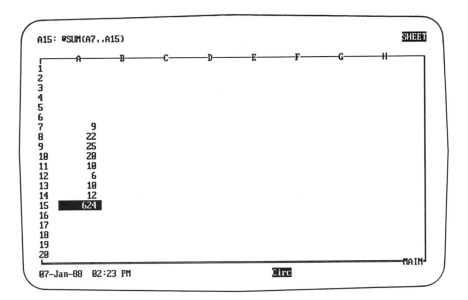

SOLUTION: Change the @SUM formula to include the cells through A14, but excluding A15; the CIRC indicator will disappear.

CIRCULAR REFERENCE PROBLEM #2:

The CIRC indicator appears after you enter a formula, but the formula does not refer to itself.

EXPLANATION: Symphony is warning you about an indirect circular reference, which is tricky to find and to fix. No formula refers to itself, but two or more formulas refer to each other. For example, each formula in figure T.3 seems reasonable, but A1 refers to A3, A2 refers to A1, and A3 refers to A2. You have no way of evaluating these formulas. The numbers increase whenever the worksheet recalculates.

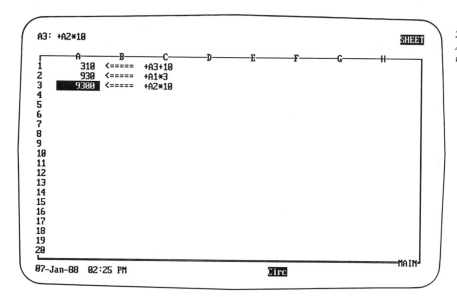

Fig. T.3

An indirect circular reference.

SOLUTION: If you can't find an obvious reason for the CIRC indicator, use SHEET Settings to find the cell location of the circular reference (see fig. T.4). If, after looking at the formula in the cell, you still cannot find the problem, write down the formula and check the contents of every cell referenced. You eventually will track down the problem.

ALTERNATE EXPLANATION: @CELL("width") can cause an annoying circular reference if you use the cell address that contains this function to determine the width of the column that contains the formula. For example, if cell C9 contains the formula:

@CELL("width",C9..C9)

it is considered a circular reference.

ALTERNATE SOLUTION: Because all the cells in the column must be the same width, change the formula to refer to another cell in the same column:

@CELL("width",C8..C8)

Fig. T.4

SHEET Settings showing a circular reference.

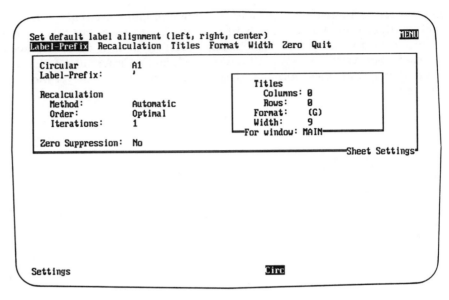

```
 Set default label alignment (left, right, center)              MENU
 Label-Prefix  Recalculation  Titles  Format  Width  Zero  Quit

   Circular         A1
   Label-Prefix:    '
                                           Titles
   Recalculation                            Columns: 0
     Method:        Automatic               Rows:    0
     Order:         Optimal                 Format:    (G)
     Iterations:    1                       Width:      9
                                           For window: MAIN
   Zero Suppression: No
                                                    Sheet Settings




   Settings                         Circ
```

CIRCULAR REFERENCE PROBLEM #3:

You have a formula that is supposed to be a circular reference, and you don't know how many times to recalculate to get the correct answer.

EXPLANATION: Even deliberate circular references can be a problem. Figure T.5 shows a profit calculation in which total profit depends on the amount of the executive bonus, but the bonus is based on profits—a legitimate circular reference. Every time Symphony recalculates, the profit figure comes closer to the right answer. The problem lies in knowing how many recalculations you need. The general answer is that you must recalculate until the change in the results is insignificant.

SOLUTION: You can recalculate manually if you have a one-time calculation and a small worksheet. Use @ROUND to set the required precision. In figure T.5, the bonus is rounded to whole dollars. Then press F8 (Calc) to calculate the worksheet until the profit number does not change. In the example shown in figure T.5, you must calculate the worksheet five times before the profit figure stops changing.

If the numbers change often, and you want to recalculate automatically, use the macro in figure T.6 to recalculate the profit information until PROFIT is equal to OLD PROFIT in cell F5. Figure T.6 shows the result of executing the macro. In most cases, cell F5 would be hidden. This macro works because RECALC proceeds row-by-row, and F5 is above PROFIT. If OLD PROFIT were below PROFIT, this macro would not work because the two numbers would always be the same and the macro would stop at the first RECALC.

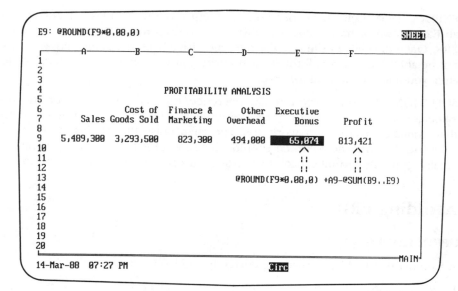

Fig. T.5

*A deliberate
circular reference*

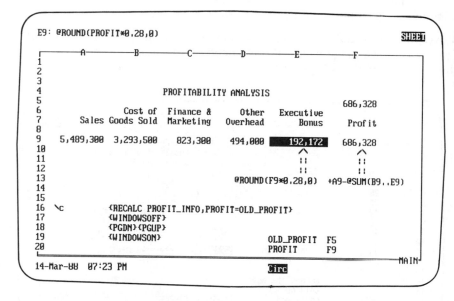

Fig. T.6

*A macro that
automatically
solves a circular
reference.*

CIRCULAR REFERENCE PROBLEM #4:

An ERR is created in one of the cells in an intentional circular reference, which causes all the cells in the circular reference also to return ERR. You remove the source of the ERR, but the remaining cells continue to show an ERR.

EXPLANATION: Cells that depend on a cell which returns an ERR will also return an ERR. If two or more cells with ERR refer to each other, the result is always ERR. Once the cells in the circular reference have been contaminated, you may not be able to eliminate all the ERRs no matter how many times you recalculate after you correct the original error.

SOLUTION: First break the circular reference; then correct the error and recalculate. The fastest way to break the circular reference is to copy the cells that evaluate to ERR to a work area and then erase the original cells. Next calculate the worksheet, which should cause the ERR indicators to disappear. Finally, copy the formulas back to the original cells and erase the work area.

Avoiding ERR

ERR PROBLEM #1:

A formula that had been working correctly suddenly changes to ERR.

EXPLANATION: A valid formula can be destroyed by certain subsequent entries. When Symphony can't evaluate part of a formula, the program changes that part of the formula to ERR, and the result is ERR.

Moves, deletions, and certain entries can destroy or invalidate a formula. If you move a cell or a range to a cell referenced in a formula, the program replaces the reference with ERR (see fig. T.7).

Fig. T.7

Moving cells turns a formula to ERR.

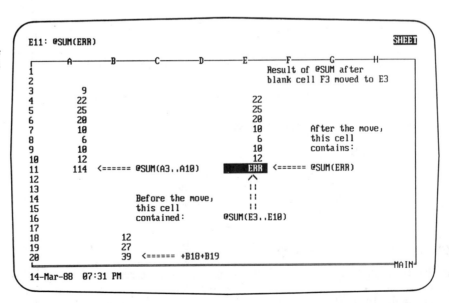

SOLUTION: If you want to move a *value* into a cell after you refer to that cell in a formula, you cannot use the SHEET Move command. Instead, you must use SHEET Copy to copy the cell and then erase the original cell.

If you want to move a *formula* to a cell after you have referred to the cell in a formula, you again cannot use the SHEET Move command. Instead, you must use SHEET Copy, following these four steps:

1. Edit the formula to convert it to a label.

2. Copy the label to the cell.

3. Edit the label to convert it back to a formula.

4. Erase the original cell.

You have to convert the formula to a label to prevent relative cell references from changing when you copy the formula.

If you want the cell references to change when you copy the formula to its new location, just copy the cell as a formula.

ERR PROBLEM #2:

Formulas change to ERR after you delete a row or a column somewhere else in the worksheet.

EXPLANATION: Although you seldom deliberately delete a row or column containing information used in formulas, deleting such information accidentally is not unusual. The SHEET Delete Rows or Columns command deletes the entire row or column in the window without giving you a chance to inspect the entire row or column; you can see only the usual screenful of cell entries. Information contained in the row or column may be somewhere off-screen. Figure T.7 shows a formula (in cell B20) before row 18 was deleted. Figure T.8 shows the effect of deleting the row; the referenced cell changes to ERR.

SOLUTION: Avoid this problem by checking the worksheet carefully before you delete rows or columns. To check a row, move the cell pointer to the row and then press End ← and End → to move to the beginning and end of the row in the active window. Use End ↓ and End ↑ to move to the end and beginning of the column in the window.

Even this method is not foolproof. A formula can legitimately refer to a blank cell in a row or column that is completely blank. Perhaps the cell will contain data that has not yet been entered. If you delete this blank row or column, the formula that refers to the cell in that row or column changes to ERR.

The most foolproof way to avoid this error is to

1. Save the worksheet.

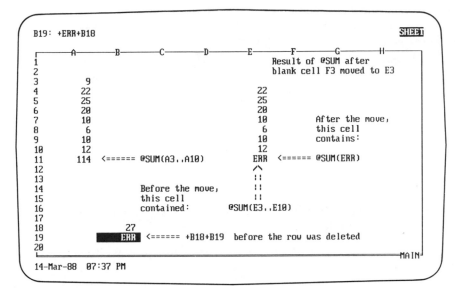

Fig. T.8

Deleting cells turns a formula to ERR.

2. In a blank cell, put an @SUM formula that sums the entire active area (from A1 to {END}{HOME}).

3. Delete the row or column and, if recalculation is set to Manual, calculate the worksheet.

If your @SUM formula changes to ERR, you know that somewhere a cell changed to ERR when you deleted the row or column. Search the worksheet until you find the ERR. If the formula is in error, correct it. If the deleted row or column is needed, then retrieve the worksheet you saved before the deletion.

ERR PROBLEM #3:

String formulas change to ERR after you erase a cell or a range.

EXPLANATION: With numeric formulas, it usually does not matter whether a cell contains a number or a string or whether it is blank. Blank cells and cells containing strings are treated as zeros in numeric calculations.

String formulas, however, are not as forgiving as numeric formulas. A string formula results in ERR if any referenced cell is blank or contains numeric values. If you erase a cell used in a string formula, the string formula changes to ERR. This change may be acceptable if you plan to enter new data in the cell. Figure T.9 shows some examples of numeric and string formulas.

SOLUTION: If you are sure that you will complete the blank cells before you print the worksheet, nothing needs to be done. In fact, you should leave the ERR to remind you that data is missing.

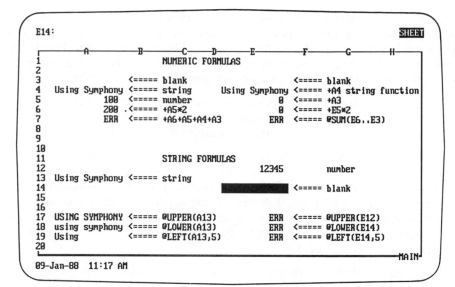

Fig. T.9

Blank cells and numbers cause ERR in string functions.

If the data is optional, you must trap the possible error in the formula. You can test for a null string in the cell before referencing the cell in the formula. A blank cell is treated as though it contains a null string (""). For example, the formula

　+A1&B1

concatenates the strings in A1 and B1 if both contain strings. If A1 always contains a string and B1 can be blank, change the formula to

　+A1&@IF(@CELL("type",B1..B1)="b","",B1)

If A1 is either blank or a number, the result is ERR, and the program warns you that something is wrong. If B1 is blank, no error occurs, and the formula equates to the contents of A1.

Here's another formula that behaves in a similar manner:

　+A1&@S(B1..B1)

The @S function avoids errors, filtering out anything that is not a string. This formula works if B1 contains a label or number, or is blank.

Problems with Memory Management

MEMORY PROBLEM #1:

While working on a large worksheet, you run out of memory.

EXPLANATION: Symphony Release 1.1 solved part of the problem by providing an improved method of memory management for blank cells. But running out of memory is still one of the most common problems in Symphony. People tend to keep building bigger and more complex worksheets. These users eventually run out of memory and then have to redesign the entire worksheet.

SOLUTION: You have several options to avoid running out of memory. But because none of these methods is foolproof, use SERVICES Settings to check available memory while you build large worksheets.

Proper worksheet design is the best way to avoid memory problems. Don't try to put an entire accounting system into one worksheet. And don't try to use one worksheet for all your product-line forecasts, even if the worksheets for all the product lines are identical. Instead, build separate worksheets based on a single template. Not only do properly designed worksheets save memory; they also speed recalculation. (The larger the worksheet, the longer you must wait whenever you recalculate.)

Sophisticated analysis models can require a dozen or more separate worksheets. Each of these worksheets can either print a detailed report or (for a smaller, consolidated report) extract data to be combined into a summary report. Use the SERVICES File Combine Add command to consolidate worksheets into a summary report.

ALTERNATE SOLUTION: Another way to avoid memory problems is to make sure that your computer has the maximum amount of memory. If you want to build large worksheets, you need at least 640K, the maximum amount of memory that normal programs can use. Memory has become so inexpensive that most of the new computers on the market, including the IBM Personal System/2, include at least 640K of standard memory. If your computer comes with 256K, you can add 384K for as little as $100 to $150.

Because Symphony users wanted to build increasingly larger worksheets, Lotus (working with Intel and Microsoft) developed the LIM expanded memory specification (EMS). This hardware and software specification lets a program use memory that exceeds the 640K limit. To use expanded memory, a program must know about EMS. Although you cannot use EMS with older programs, you can use as many as four megabytes of expanded memory with Symphony Release 1.1 (and later releases). Because a normal memory board doesn't work with more than 640K, however, you must buy a special memory expansion board designed to be an EMS board.

Expanded memory works in both the PC (and compatibles) and the AT (and compatibles). AST Research, Inc., has devised an extended EMS called EEMS. Both EMS and EEMS boards provide the same expansion capabilities for Symphony worksheets.

Using expanded memory does not solve all memory problems. Although certain parts of worksheets—labels, formulas, decimal numbers, and integers larger than 32,767—use expanded memory, everything else must be in regular memory (up to 640K). And you must have four bytes in regular memory for every cell stored in expanded memory. You can have a maximum of approximately 100,000 individual cell entries before you run out of conventional memory, which means that you can run out of memory and still have megabytes of expanded memory that you have not used (and cannot use).

ALTERNATE SOLUTION: Because formulas take up more space than numbers, you can use formulas to build a worksheet and then, using the SHEET Range Values command, convert the formulas to numbers. Use this method with any numbers that will not change when you update the worksheet. (Be sure to save the original template with the unconverted formulas, in case you later discover that you need the formulas.)

Because the results of the SHEET Range What-If command are numbers, not formulas, you can save memory by converting large tables of formulas to data tables. Then repeat the SHEET Range What-If command to recalculate the tables if the values in the input cells change. Do not use this technique in a large worksheet if you frequently need to recalculate the data table—it could take several minutes or even hours.

ALTERNATE SOLUTION: The shape of the active area also can affect the total amount of memory used by the worksheet. The active area is defined as a rectangle starting in cell A1 and ending in the last row and last column that (1) contains either data or a range format, or (2) is unprotected. For example, a worksheet with a value in G3 and a format in A12 has an active area from A1 to G12. A worksheet with cell AF4 unprotected and a label in B300 has an active area from A1 to AF300.

Although Lotus says that the memory-management scheme for Symphony Release 1.1 (and later releases) uses no memory for empty cells, this statement does not appear to be true. For example, putting the number 1 in cells A1, A2, B1, and B2 uses 32 bytes of memory. Putting the number 1 in cells A1, A8192, IV1, and IV8192 uses 65,536 bytes of memory. (In fact, simply formatting or unprotecting those four cells uses 65,536 bytes—even though you enter no data at all in the worksheet.)

If memory is a problem, keep the shape of the occupied cells in your worksheet as small as possible. To move the cursor to the lower right corner of the active area of any worksheet, press End then Home. You may be surprised to discover that a stray entry is costing you quite a bit of memory.

ALTERNATE SOLUTION: If you frequently move, insert, and delete rows and columns when you build large worksheets, you may run out of memory. When you move data or delete rows and columns, not all the memory is recovered. You usually can recover the memory by saving the worksheet and retrieving it again.

Troubleshooting Symphony Commands

Problems with Range Names

RANGE NAMES PROBLEM #1:

A range name that was valid suddenly results in an ERR.

EXPLANATION: Moving and deleting cells and ranges can change formulas to ERR (see the "Avoiding ERR" problems). These operations also cause the loss of range names. Both ranges and range names are identified by the upper left corner cell and the lower right corner cell. If you move a cell or a range of cells to one of these corner cells, the range name is lost. Suppose, for example, that you are working with the range name table shown in figure T.10A. After a few move and delete operations, your range name table changes (see fig. T.10B). As you can see, you have lost only those range names in which the cells in the upper left or lower right corners were affected.

SOLUTION: Although both ranges and range names are lost in the same manner, using range names provides an easy way to audit these errors. Keep a current range name table in all your worksheets. After you make any changes, re-create the range name table and look for blank cells next to range names.

CAUTION: If you lose a range name and then save and later retrieve the file, something strange happens—the lost range names no longer are lost. Any cell that was erased or had data moved into it, however, is changed to cell IV8192. As an example, figure T.10C shows the figure T.10B worksheet after the file has

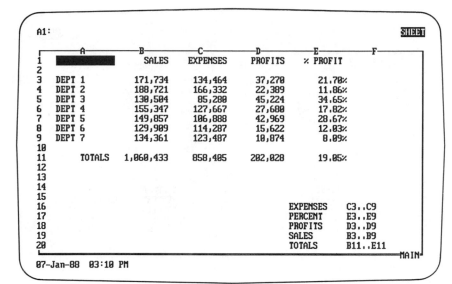

Fig. T.10A

A range name table.

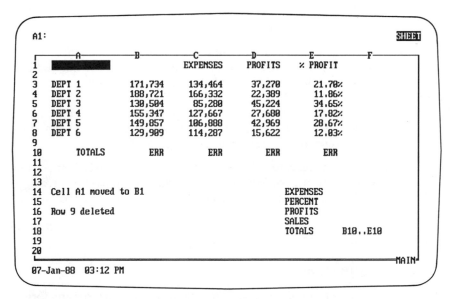

Fig. T.10B

The range name table after moving and deleting.

been saved and retrieved. The effect on macros that use these range names can be disastrous.

To avoid these problems, frequently create a range name table and check the table and the worksheet carefully for blank cells, ERR, or IV8192.

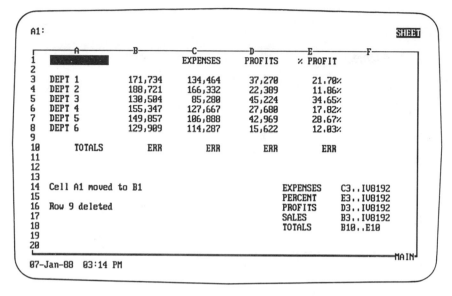

Fig. T.10C

The range name
table after the file
is saved and
retrieved.

```
A1:                                                                    SHEET
┌─────────A────────B────────C────────D────────E────────F──────────────┐
│ 1  ▓▓▓▓▓▓▓▓▓▓▓▓▓          EXPENSES  PROFITS  % PROFIT                 │
│ 2                                                                     │
│ 3  DEPT 1        171,734  134,464   37,270    21.70%                  │
│ 4  DEPT 2        188,721  166,332   22,389    11.86%                  │
│ 5  DEPT 3        130,504   85,280   45,224    34.65%                  │
│ 6  DEPT 4        155,347  127,667   27,680    17.82%                  │
│ 7  DEPT 5        149,857  106,888   42,969    28.67%                  │
│ 8  DEPT 6        129,909  114,287   15,622    12.03%                  │
│ 9                                                                     │
│10     TOTALS       ERR       ERR      ERR       ERR                   │
│11                                                                     │
│12                                                                     │
│13                                                                     │
│14  Cell A1 moved to B1               EXPENSES   C3..IU8192            │
│15                                    PERCENT    E3..IU8192            │
│16  Row 9 deleted                     PROFITS    D3..IU8192            │
│17                                    SALES      B3..IU8192            │
│18                                    TOTALS     B10..E10              │
│19                                                                     │
│20                                                                 MAIN│
└──────────────────────────────────────────────────────────────────────┘
    07-Jan-88  03:14 PM
```

RANGE NAMES PROBLEM #2:

A valid formula seems to change automatically to an incorrect cell reference.

EXPLANATION: Range names also can cause formulas to change incorrectly. For example, a common convention with macros is to name the current cell HERE, move the cell pointer wherever it's needed to complete the macro, and then return the cell pointer to HERE. This process can cause problems if you reassign the range name HERE instead of first deleting the range name. When you reassign a range name to a different cell or range, any formulas that refer to the old cell or range change to refer to the new cell or range.

In figure T.11A, cell A10 is named HERE, and the formula in A12 refers to A10. Figure T.11B shows the same worksheet after the name HERE has been reassigned to refer to C10. Notice that the formula in A12 now refers to C10.

SOLUTION: To avoid this problem, always use SHEET **Range Name Delete** before you use SHEET **Range Name Create** to reassign a range name.

RANGE NAMES PROBLEM #3:

A range name looks correct in the range name table, but the macros and formulas that refer to the named range do not work properly.

EXPLANATION: This problem occurs when you use a range name that is also a cell address. If you set up a complex report and give the individual pages the range names P1, P2, and P3, the printed report will contain only the cells P1,

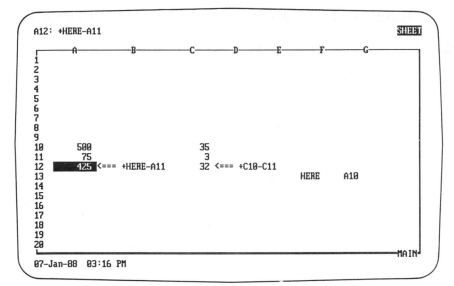

Fig. T.11A

*A formula using
the range name
HERE.*

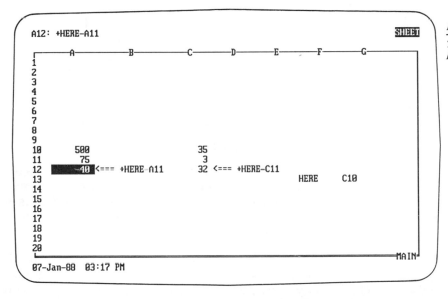

Fig. T.11B

*The formula after
HERE is reassigned.*

P2, and P3. If you give a macro the range name GO2 and then {BRANCH GO2},
the macro will branch to cell GO2 and, probably, stop at a blank cell.

SOLUTION: Never name a range with a combination of one or two letters and
a number. Don't even use a range name such as TO4; a range name that is not
a valid cell address in the current version of Symphony may be a valid cell address
in a future release.

Problems with Relative and Absolute Addressing

ADDRESSING PROBLEM #1:

After you copy a formula to other cells, the copied formulas are incorrect—the addresses are wrong.

EXPLANATION: One of Symphony's handiest built-in features is the automatic formula adjustment for relative cell addressing when a formula is copied. Relative addressing is so natural and automatic that after a while you no longer think about it.

For example, consider the following formula in cell A4:

+A1+A2-A3

When the cell pointer is positioned in A4, the program displays this formula on the top line of the control panel. You think of the formula as

Add the contents of A1 and A2 and subtract the contents of A3.

If you copy the formula from A4 to B4, it becomes

+B1+B2-B3

This result, which is exactly what you would expect after you have gained some experience in using Symphony, depends on what is called relative addressing. Each formula is stored with addresses relative to the cell that contains the formula. Internally, Symphony interprets the formula in A4 as:

Add the contents of the cell three rows up and the cell two rows up and subtract the contents of the cell one row up.

This formula is the same one originally in A4 and copied into B4.

You occasionally do not want the cell references to change when you copy a formula. If you copy the cell references as relative addresses, you get the wrong formula. In figure T.12, for example, the formula for % OF TOTAL SALES was written in C2 and copied to C3..C13. The relative addressing adjustment changes the formula in C3 from +B2/B14 to +B3/B15.

SOLUTION: Specify an address as absolute when you write the formula, not when you copy it. To make an address absolute, precede the column and the row by a dollar sign ($). If you use the pointing method to specify a range or a cell address, make the address absolute by pressing the Abs key (F3) when you point to the cell. If you type a cell address manually, make the address absolute by pressing F3 after you type the address.

The formula in C2 should be +B2/$B$14. When you copy this formula, the relative address (B2) changes, but the absolute address ($B$14) does not change. The results of the correct formulas are shown in column G.

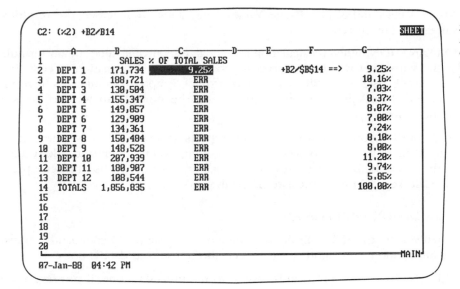

Fig. T.12
*ERRs after copying
a formula with
relative cell
addressing.*

Problems with Recalculation

RECALCULATION PROBLEM #1:

As your worksheets become larger, recalculation becomes annoyingly slow.

EXPLANATION: Whenever you add or change a cell, Symphony recalculates the entire worksheet. At first, this recalculation is almost instantaneous, and you can ignore the delay. As you add formulas and include more complex formulas and string functions, the delay increases noticeably and becomes annoying. Your work can slow down dramatically if you add data to many cells in a large worksheet.

SOLUTION: The first solution is to change recalculation to manual by using the SHEET Settings Recalculation Method Manual command. You experience no delay the next time you make an entry, because no recalculation occurs. To warn you that the information in some of the cells may be incorrect, the Calc indicator appears at the bottom of the screen. Also check to determine whether Recalculation is set to Optimal. Depending of the application, this setting may provide faster recalculation.

Press the Calc key (F8) when you want the program to recalculate the worksheet. The Calc indicator disappears until you make another entry.

RECALCULATION PROBLEM #2:

When you print reports after you have updated the worksheet, some of the data is incorrect. You may have a similar problem when you use the SERVICES File

Xtract Values and SHEET Range Values commands. In all cases, the resulting values are not current.

EXPLANATION: When recalculation is manual, the current values of any formula in the worksheet may be incorrect if you change the information in cells that the formula uses. Generally, you cannot expect Symphony commands to recalculate the worksheet (even when getting the correct answer requires a recalculation).

SOLUTION: If you use a macro to print reports, to extract data as values, or to convert formulas to values with the SHEET Range Values command, add {CALC} to the macro before it executes the commands. If you don't use a macro, press the Calc key (F8) to recalculate manually.

RECALCULATION PROBLEM #3:

When you use the SERVICES File Combine Add (or Subtract) command to transfer information from another worksheet, the transferred data is not current.

EXPLANATION: This problem is related to the preceding one. If you save a file that recalculates manually and later combine all or part of that file into another worksheet, the current values of the formulas may be incorrect (even if the current worksheet is set for automatic recalculation).

The SERVICES File Combine Add and Subtract commands use the current values of the formulas in the source file. Unless these formulas are recalculated, the values combined with the File Combine Add and Subtract commands may be incorrect. On the other hand, the File Combine Copy command brings formulas, not current values, into the worksheet. Therefore, when you use that command, you do not have to be concerned about whether the source file has been recalculated.

SOLUTION: In this case (unlike the preceding problem, in which you can calculate the worksheet immediately before executing the command), you must calculate the source worksheet before saving it. If you use a macro to save your worksheet, add {CALC} to the macro before it saves the file. If you don't use a macro, recalculate manually by pressing the Calc key (F8) before you save the file.

RECALCULATION PROBLEM #4:

You want to see only a few values on a large worksheet that takes a long time to recalculate, but you are spending an inordinate amount of time recalculating.

EXPLANATION: On large, complex models that can take several minutes to recalculate, you almost always use manual recalculation. If you build or change the model or enter data in one section, however, you often want to see the current values in only that area. Continually pressing the Calc key (F8) causes you to lose time while you wait for the program to recalculate the entire worksheet.

SOLUTION: You can recalculate only part of a worksheet in one of several ways.

To recalculate a single cell, simply edit the cell. Press the Edit key (F2) and then press Enter.

To recalculate a range of cells, copy the range to itself. Figure T.13 shows a range that is part of a large worksheet. To recalculate the cells in only the range BC65..BH75, copy the range BC65..BH75 to BC65. All the cells in the range recalculate when Symphony copies them to themselves.

```
BC65: @SUM(D3..D48)                                              SHEET

     --BB------BC------BD------BE------BF------BG------BH--
59              Summary Totals from the Budget Detail
60              ----------- This Year ----------      ------ Next Year -----
61
62              Actual    Budget   Forecast  Variance  Budget    Budget
63              YTD       YTD      Full Year  YTD       YTD       Full Year
64
65   Region 1   125,876   100,900   167,415  (24,976)  163,800   218,400
66   Region 2   114,056    98,600   151,694  (15,456)  155,600   207,467
67   Region 3   122,868   133,600   163,414   18,732   195,000   260,000
68   Region 4   112,611   124,600   149,773   11,989   180,900   241,200
69   Region 5   106,903   115,400   142,181    8,497   168,900   225,200
70   Region 6   104,307    85,800   138,728  (18,507)  138,000   184,000
71   Region 7   118,989   140,700   158,255   21,711   200,200   266,933
72   Region 8   125,247   101,300   166,579  (23,947)  163,900   218,533
73   Region 9   148,397   131,500   197,368  (16,897)  205,700   274,267
74
75   Totals    1,079,254 1,032,400 1,435,407 (46,854) 1,572,000 2,096,000
76
77
78                                                               MAIN

09-Jan-88  02:58 PM
```

Fig. T.13

A range that is part of a large worksheet.

To recalculate part of a worksheet inside a macro, use the macro commands RECALC and RECALCCOL.

RECALCULATION PROBLEM #5:

Because your worksheet is large, you keep recalculation on manual and use the partial-recalculation methods described in the preceding solution. But the partial recalculation *sometimes produces incorrect results.*

EXPLANATION: When you recalculate the entire worksheet, Symphony uses optimal calculation as the default. In other words, Symphony only recalculates those formulas that are affected by changes. And unless you change the recalculation order to **R**owwise or **C**olumnwise, Symphony always calculates a cell after calculating the results of all the cells to which that cell refers (this order is called the "natural order" of recalculation). This step avoids problems that occurred in older spreadsheet programs, which could calculate only across rows or down columns. With natural-order calculation, formulas can be anywhere in the worksheet; with other calculation methods, formulas are correct after one recalculation only when they refer to cells above or to the left of the cell being recalculated. Formulas that refer to a cell address below and to the right of the cell being recalculated are known as forward references.

The worksheet shown in figure T.14A contains forward references and shows the formulas before any recalculation. Figures T.14B and T.14C show the results of different methods of recalculation. Certain combinations produce correct results, but others are incorrect.

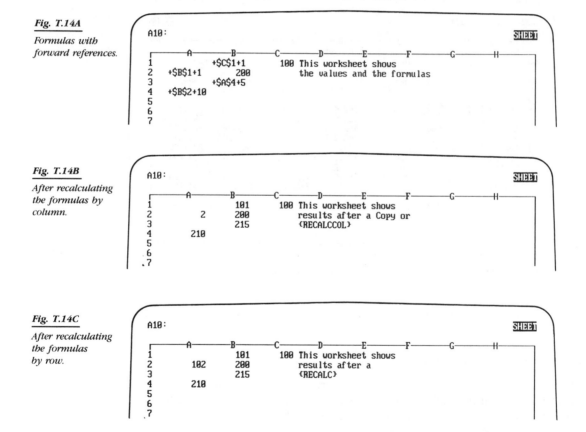

Fig. T.14A

Formulas with forward references.

Fig. T.14B

After recalculating the formulas by column.

Fig. T.14C

After recalculating the formulas by row.

Figure T.14B shows the results after a Copy or RECALCCOL recalculates the formulas by column. The formula in A2 is incorrect because it was calculated while cell B1 still contained a value of 1. Later, column B was calculated, and cell B1 became 101, but it was too late to change the value in A2. The other formulas are correct.

Figure T.14C shows the results after a RECALC recalculates the formulas by row. The formula in B3 is incorrect because it was calculated while cell A4 still contained a value of 10. Later, row 4 was calculated, and cell A4 became 210, but it was too late to change the value in B3. The other formulas are correct.

SOLUTION: No complete solution to the problem exists. The only way to get complete natural-order recalculation is to recalculate the entire worksheet. If you know the structure of the data and the formulas, however, you can make sure that you get the correct answer from partial recalculation.

First, be sure to recalculate all the cells that are referenced by the formulas in the area you want to recalculate. Suppose, for example, that you want to re-calculate part of a large worksheet (see fig. T.15). If you change the discount rate in BA60 and then recalculate the range BD65..BD75, you'll get an incorrect answer because the average discounts are not recalculated. To get the correct answer, recalculate the range BC65..BD75. (Note that you do not have to include cell BA60 in the recalculation because that cell contains a number and is not affected by a recalculation.)

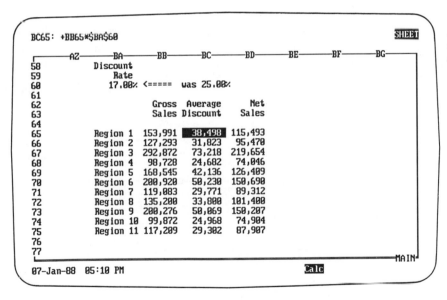

Fig. T.15

A range that is part of a large worksheet.

Try to avoid forward references in the area in which you want partial recal-culation. If no forward references are present, the partial recalculations can work.

If you cannot avoid forward references, you can still get the correct answer if you pay attention to how partial recalculation proceeds. When you copy a range or use RECALCCOL, the program recalculates each cell, starting at the upper left corner of the range and continuing down each column. When it reaches the bottom of each column, Symphony starts recalculating at the top of the next column in the range.

If you use RECALC, the program recalculates each cell, starting at the upper left corner of the range and continuing across each row. When it reaches the right-most cell of each row, Symphony starts recalculating at the leftmost cell in the next row.

The following rules apply to partial recalculation:

1. If you use Copy or RECALCCOL for a partial recalculation, the results may be incorrect for a formula that refers to another formula which is either in a column to its right or below it in the same column.

2. If you use RECALC for a partial recalculation, the results may be incorrect for a formula that refers to another formula which is either in a row below it or to its right in the same row.

3. Formulas that refer to cells containing values are correct using any recalculation method.

If you must use partial recalculation on a range with forward references, the only solution involves more than one recalculation. You must RECALC or RE-CALCCOL once for every nested forward reference in the range. A nested forward reference is a formula that refers forward to a formula that refers forward (and so on) to a cell. Figure T.16 shows a series of forward references. Each RECALC resolves one additional forward reference.

Fig. T.16

A series of forward references.

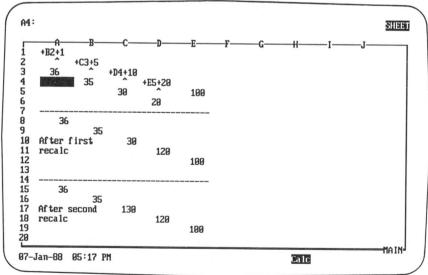

After you have determined how many nested forward references you need to recalculate, add that number of RECALC or RECALCCOL statements to your macro.

Miscellaneous Problems

DATA DESTRUCTION PROBLEM #1:

You use the SHEET Move command to move a range of cells, and you end up losing data.

EXPLANATION: The SHEET Move command does not insert the cells you are moving; it copies over the cells at the TO location.

SOLUTION: Insert rows and/or columns to hold the moved cells *before* issuing the Move command.

DATA DESTRUCTION PROBLEM #2:

You combine data from two files with the SERVICES File Combine Copy command, and you lose data.

EXPLANATION: The File Combine Copy command brings in the specified range or file beginning at the cell pointer location. If any data is in the area, this data will be overwritten with the data from the other file.

SOLUTION: First, save the file so that you can recover the original file if anything unexpected happens. Then position the cell pointer where you want the data to begin and make sure that you have sufficient room for the data. Then you are ready to issue the SERVICES File Combine Copy command.

DATA DESTRUCTION PROBLEM #2:

Occasionally, by making a mistake with SHEET Copy, Move, or Delete, you destroy part of the worksheet and then must painstakingly reconstruct it.

EXPLANATION: Unlike modeling languages and statistical-analysis packages, spreadsheets such as Symphony do not separate the model from the data. (The model is composed of formulas and macros that do not change. The data is the numbers that you continually enter and change.) When you use Symphony to enter data, you risk accidentally changing the model as well.

SOLUTION: Always keep a backup copy of all worksheets. (Keep two or three backup copies of critical worksheets.) Then, if you destroy a worksheet, you can recover it from the backup file.

You can use the Protection option to prevent the worksheet from being destroyed. Protected cells cannot be changed. If you try to change a protected cell, the program beeps and displays the warning message `Protected cell` but does not change the contents of the cell.

Use the SHEET **R**ange **P**rotect Allow-Changes command to unprotect the cells you want to change. After you have completed the worksheet and are ready to use it, turn on the protection feature by issuing SERVICES **S**ettings **G**lobal-Protection **Y**es before you enter data.

TEMPLATE PROBLEM #1:

At the beginning of every month, you must carefully erase all the data from the past month to prepare for the new month. If you leave old data, the information for the new month will be incorrect.

EXPLANATION: This problem is related to the preceding one. Because Symphony does not distinguish between the model and the data, the program can't present a blank model for the next month's data.

SOLUTION: Although Symphony can't distinguish between the model and the data, you can. Build a model, or template: a worksheet that contains all necessary formulas, formats, and macros but no data. Save this worksheet and make a backup copy. Then use this model every month to start the new month. After you've added data to the file, always be sure to save it under a name different from that of the template. For example, you might name a budget template BUDGET. Retrieve BUDGET every month, saving it as BUD0888 in August 1988; BUD0988 in September 1988; and so on.

ALTERNATE SOLUTION: Rather than use the SHEET **E**rase command to erase each range of data, use the SERVICES **F**ile **C**ombine **S**ubtract command. First, save the file and, with the file still on the screen, place the cell pointer in cell A1. Then issue the SERVICES **F**ile **C**ombine **S**ubtract command and combine the same file. All values will be subtracted from themselves, leaving zeros in the data entry cells. Formulas and labels remain unchanged.

Troubleshooting Functions

FUNCTIONS PROBLEM #1:

You get apparent rounding errors, even when you have not rounded off.

EXPLANATION: When you use formats such as Fixed, Punctuated, and Currency with a fixed number of decimal places, Symphony keeps the number to 15 decimal places but rounds off the display. Figure T.17A shows the formula results without any formatting, while figure T.17B shows the apparent rounding errors resulting after the cells are formatted with 0 decimal places.

SOLUTION: To avoid such rounding errors, use the @ROUND function to round off numbers to the same precision shown in the display (see fig. T.17C).

FUNCTIONS PROBLEM #2:

You get ERR when you try to combine numbers and strings.

EXPLANATION: Although Symphony has a full complement of string functions, you cannot mix strings and numbers in the same function. Figure T.18A shows the effect of trying to build an address by using words from strings and a number for the ZIP code.

SOLUTION: Use the @STRING function to convert a number to its equivalent string (see fig. T.18B). Then you can use the converted number in a string function.

693

Fig. T.17A

Formula results without formatting.

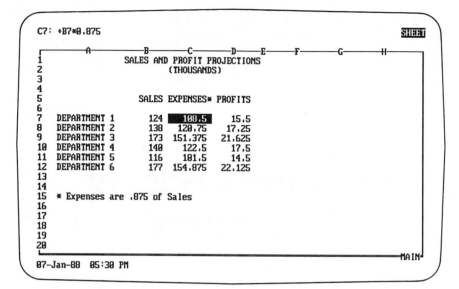

```
C7: +B7*0.875                                          SHEET
          A          B         C        D    E    F      G        H
1                   SALES AND PROFIT PROJECTIONS
2                        (THOUSANDS)
3
4
5                    SALES EXPENSES* PROFITS
6
7    DEPARTMENT 1     124    100.5      15.5
8    DEPARTMENT 2     138    120.75     17.25
9    DEPARTMENT 3     173    151.375    21.625
10   DEPARTMENT 4     140    122.5      17.5
11   DEPARTMENT 5     116    101.5      14.5
12   DEPARTMENT 6     177    154.875    22.125
13
14
15   * Expenses are .875 of Sales
16
17
18
19
20                                                          MAIN
07-Jan-88  05:30 PM
```

Fig. T.17B

Apparent rounding errors after cells are formatted.

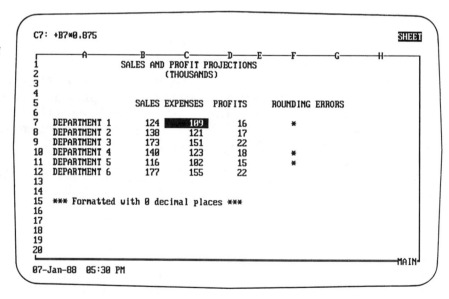

```
C7: +B7*0.875                                          SHEET
          A          B         C        D    E    F      G        H
1                   SALES AND PROFIT PROJECTIONS
2                        (THOUSANDS)
3
4
5                    SALES EXPENSES  PROFITS    ROUNDING ERRORS
6
7    DEPARTMENT 1     124    109       16          *
8    DEPARTMENT 2     138    121       17
9    DEPARTMENT 3     173    151       22
10   DEPARTMENT 4     140    123       18          *
11   DEPARTMENT 5     116    102       15          *
12   DEPARTMENT 6     177    155       22
13
14
15   *** Formatted with 0 decimal places ***
16
17
18
19
20                                                          MAIN
07-Jan-88  05:30 PM
```

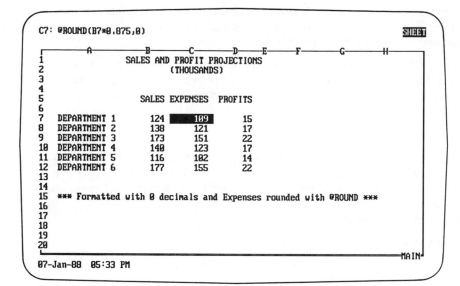

Fig. T.17C

Rounding errors eliminated by @ROUND.

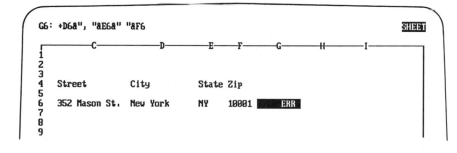

Fig. T.18A

An error when numbers mix with strings.

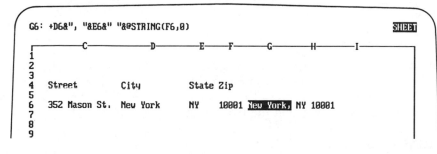

Fig. T.18B

A function that converts a number to a string.

FUNCTIONS PROBLEM #3:

You want to use string functions on a field, but you are not sure whether a number or a string will be entered in the field.

EXPLANATION: All functions work on either strings or numbers, but not on both. If you don't know what a cell contains, and you guess incorrectly, you risk getting ERR or an incorrect result.

SOLUTION: You can test a cell to see whether it contains a number or a string and then, depending on the contents of the cell, use the appropriate functions. Suppose, for example, that you want to concatenate the contents of A1 and B1. The formula is

+A1&B1

The ampersand (&), which is a string concatenation operator, causes an error if either A1 or B1 is blank or contains a number. Let's assume that you are sure that A1 contains a string but that you don't know whether B1 contains a string, a number, or is blank. To concatenate B1 to A1 only if B1 contains a string, use the following formula:

+A1&@S(B1)

The @S function (a filter) does nothing if the cell contains a string, but returns a null string if the cell does not contain a string. The formula therefore results in either A1 (if B1 does not contain a string) or in A1&B1 (if B1 contains a string).

To concatenate the contents of B1 regardless of whether it contains a number or a string, you need a more complex formula (see fig. T.19).

Fig. T.19

A formula that handles numbers, strings, or blank cells.

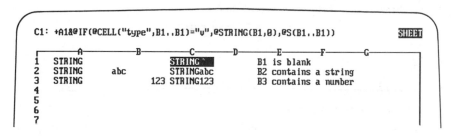

In the formula in the control panel of figure T.19, if the type is "v" (for value), the contents of the cell are converted to a string. If the cell is blank, the @S function filters it out, and the cell is ignored. If the cell contains a string, the @S function does nothing, and the two strings are concatenated.

FUNCTIONS PROBLEM #4:

Your averages are returning incorrect results.

EXPLANATION: The @AVG function adds up the values in the specified range and divides by the number of nonblank cells in that range. If the range contains any labels, they will be counted in the total number of nonblank cells, and the average will be incorrect.

SOLUTION: Never include labels (such as the dashed line at the bottom of the column) in your average range. You can see in figure T.20A that Example #1 includes the dashed line in the range to average and results in an incorrect average. Example #2 specifies the correct range (no labels included). Also, make sure that cells which appear blank don't have a space entered in them, because a space in a cell is considered a label. You can tell if a cell contains a space by placing the cell pointer in the cell and looking in the control panel. If you see an apostrophe, a space is there. Use SHEET Erase to erase the space. Example #3 in figure T.20B has a space entered into one of the cells in the average range, so the total is incorrectly divided by 3. The average range in Example #4 contains a cell erased with the SHEET Erase command, so the total is correctly divided by 2.

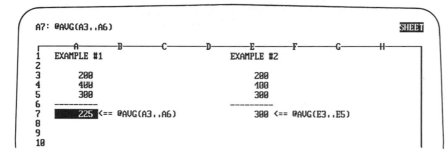

Fig. T.20A

Including labels in a range to average.

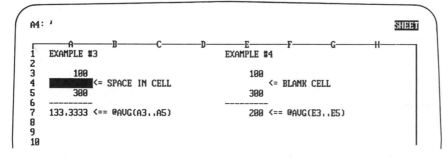

Fig. T.20B

Including cells with spaces in a range to average.

FUNCTIONS PROBLEM #5:

You enter a formula using @CELL—for example, @CELL("type",B25)—and ERR displays as the result.

EXPLANATION: The @CELL function requires that the cell be specified as a range. The @CELLPOINTER, @S, and @N functions also have this requirement.

SOLUTION: You can specify a range for a single cell in two ways. You can indicate the range the standard way (for example, B25..B25), or you can precede the cell address or range name with an exclamation point (!B25).

Troubleshooting File Operations

FILE PROBLEM #1:

Your hard disk contains so many files that finding the files you want is difficult; whenever you perform a file operation, long delays occur.

EXPLANATION: A single hard disk can hold hundreds—even thousands—of files. If that many files were placed in one subdirectory, however, keeping track of them would be impossible. And DOS slows down significantly if you have more than approximately 112 or 224 files (depending on which version of DOS you use) in one subdirectory.

If you try to put all the files in the root directory, DOS reaches an absolute limit and won't let you save additional files.

SOLUTION: Set up separate subdirectories for different applications and users.

The default directory should contain the subdirectory of files that you use most often. To specify the name of this subdirectory, use the SERVICES Configuration File command.

To reach files in other subdirectories, use the SERVICES File Directory command. This command changes the directory until you either use SERVICES File Directory again or return to the default directory by quitting and reentering Symphony.

FILE PROBLEM #2:

You want to retrieve a file that is not in the default directory, but you don't remember which directory contains the file.

EXPLANATION: You can see only the files in the current directory. The file you want is in another subdirectory, but Symphony does not list all the disk's subdirectories.

SOLUTION: Select SERVICES File List and, depending on the type of file you're looking for, choose **Worksheet**, **Print**, **Graph**, or **All**. Symphony displays a list of all files of that type and all subdirectories on the current directory. To search forward through a chain of directories, move the cursor to the directory you want and press Enter. To search backwards through the chain of directories, use the Backspace key. When you locate your file, use the SERVICES File Directory and/or File Retrieve commands to retrieve the file. For ASCII files, use SERVICES File Import.

ALTERNATE SOLUTION: Attach the DOS add-in application and use the SERVICES DOS command to suspend Symphony temporarily and return to DOS. This method makes the DOS TREE command available to you; you can use the TREE, CD, and DIR commands to find the subdirectory and file that you want.

After you have located the file, return to Symphony by typing **exit** at the DOS prompt. Then you can use the SERVICES File Directory and/or SERVICES File Retrieve commands to read the file.

FILE PROBLEM #3:

While building a large file, you fear making a mistake that will destroy part of the file and cost you hours of work.

EXPLANATION: Sooner or later, everyone destroys part or all of an important file. The greater your proficiency in Symphony, the larger and more complex the files you can build—and the more disastrous the errors you can make.

SOLUTION: Once you destroy the file, you may not be able to restore it. The only solution may be to avoid the problem by preparing for it.

You can best prepare for this problem by saving your file frequently when you make many changes or write macros. Be sure to save the file under a different name. (If you were to use the same file name, you might save the file two or three times after making a disastrous error before discovering the error.)

If you are developing a worksheet, for example, save it under a name that includes a sequence number (such as BUDGET1, BUDGET2, BUDGET3, and so on). When you reach BUDGET10 and have done some testing, you can consider erasing BUDGET1. At least once during each development session, save the file to a floppy disk. This backup copy is an additional safeguard.

If you enter data in a file daily, save the file under a name that includes the date (BUD0809 or BUD0810, for example).

Remember that time spent storing data is minimal compared to the time you might have to spend reentering lost data and rebuilding lost macro-driven files.

FILE PROBLEM #4:

Some of the formulas brought in by SERVICES File Combine Copy are meaningless.

EXPLANATION: Using SERVICES File Combine Copy is similar to using SHEET Copy within a worksheet. The same rules about relative addressing apply in both instances. If you combine (pull in) part of another worksheet that contains formulas which refer to cells in the combined area, the formulas stay the same in relation to the cells to which they refer. If you combine formulas that refer to cells outside the combined area, however, these formulas become references to cells somewhere else in the current worksheet. These formulas may become meaningless, leading to incorrect results.

For example, figure T.21 shows the result of combining the data in J10..K15. Because the formula in K10 refers to cell G10, which is a blank cell in this worksheet, the result in K10 is 0. In the original worksheet, the corresponding cell contained a price, and the formula gave a correct result.

Fig. T.21

Meaningless formulas after a File Combine.

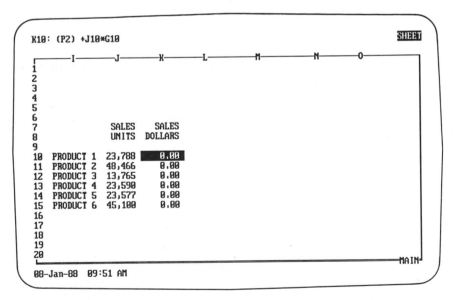

SOLUTION: You can use SERVICES File Combine Add to combine into the current worksheet the values from another worksheet. The formulas in the other worksheet are converted to numbers. If you don't want any of the formulas from the other worksheet, simply use SERVICES File Combine Add for the entire range. If you want some of the formulas from the other worksheet, first use File Combine Copy to get the formulas. Then, to get the numbers, use File Combine Add on a different range.

SERVICES File Combine Add, however, has pitfalls of its own. As Symphony executes the command, the program checks each cell in the current worksheet. If a cell is blank or contains a number, the corresponding value from the file being combined is added to that cell. If the cell in the current worksheet contains a formula, Symphony skips that cell, regardless of what the corresponding cell in the file being combined may contain. And File Combine Add brings in only numeric values—not strings.

FILE PROBLEM #5:

You use SERVICES File Combine Add and get old values.

EXPLANATION: Before combining, File Combine Add automatically converts to values any formulas in the range to be combined (even if you select the Formulas option). If the file is set for manual recalculation and was saved without a recalculation, some of the formulas may not reflect current values.

SOLUTION: If you intend to use a worksheet later for file combining (adding or subtracting), always calculate the worksheet before saving it.

FILE PROBLEM #6:

After you use SERVICES File Import Numbers to read in an ASCII file, some of the information is lost, and some of it looks scrambled.

EXPLANATION: File Import Numbers works only when the data in the ASCII file is in a precise format. Each field must be separated by commas or spaces, and each string must be enclosed in double quotation marks. Symphony ignores data that is not in this format but imports whatever data the program finds and recognizes as numbers. Ordinarily, the result is a useless mess.

SOLUTION: Using SERVICES File Import Text, read in the ASCII data as a series of long labels. Then use SHEET Query Parse to separate the data into individual cells that Symphony can use.

FILE PROBLEM #7:

To save a backup copy, you use SERVICES File Directory to change the directory to A:\ and then use SERVICES File Save to save the file. Later, you notice that the file was not saved on drive A.

EXPLANATION: When you save a file, Symphony remembers the entire path that was last used to save the file or, if you haven't saved the file, to retrieve it. The program does not consider the current directory. Even when you change the directory before you execute a SERVICES File Save, you still save the file in the original directory.

Suppose, for example, that your file BUD0810 was read from the default directory: C:\SYMPHONY.

You change the directory to A:\ and then use SERVICES File Save. Symphony ignores the fact that the current directory is A:\ and displays the default path:

```
Enter save file name: C:\SYMPHONY\BUD0810
```

The file is saved again in C:\SYMPHONY.

SOLUTION: Clear the entire old path explicitly by pressing Esc and retyping the file name. Because you gain nothing by changing the current directory, leave it alone and include drive A in the file name. In this example, after you use SERVICES File Save, you'll see the prompt:

```
Enter save file name: C:\SYMPHONY\BUD0810
```

Pressing Esc once displays:

```
Enter save file name:
```

At this prompt, type **A:\BUD0810** and then press Enter. The file is saved on drive A.

Caution: The next time you save this file, Symphony will save it on drive A unless you reverse the process and type the old path in drive C.

FILE PROBLEM #8:

When you try to retrieve a password-protected file, you get an error message, `Incorrect password`. You cannot retrieve the file.

EXPLANATION: You must enter the password exactly as you assigned it, including the same capitalization. In other words, passwords are case-sensitive.

SOLUTION: Try entering the password in all uppercase and then all lowercase letters.

Troubleshooting Windows

WINDOW PROBLEM #1:

You've divided the screen into two windows with the SERVICES **W**indow **P**ane command. You no longer want the second window, but when you delete it, the first window is still only half the screen width (see fig. T.22).

EXPLANATION: Deleting a window does not change the size of any existing windows.

SOLUTION: Select the SERVICES **W**indow **L**ayout command and highlight the entire screen to make the window full-screen again.

ALTERNATE SOLUTION: The Zoom key (Alt-F6) will also make the window full size, but this solution is temporary. The window returns to its previous size when you turn off the Zoom (Alt-F6) or when you display another window with the Window key (F6) or the SERVICES **W**indow **U**se command.

WINDOW PROBLEM #2:

When typing in a DOC window you have created, you get the error message `Not enough room in Restrict range`, and you can't type anymore. When inserting rows in a SHEET window you get a similar message, `Selected range not within Restrict range`.

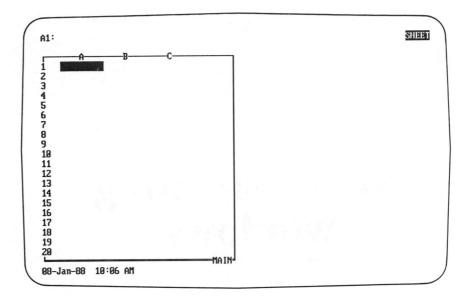

EXPLANATION: If you have specified a restrict range for a window, you will encounter these error messages when you try to go beyond that range.

SOLUTION: Expand the window's restrict range with the SERVICES Window Settings Restrict Range command.

WINDOW PROBLEM #3:

When you press the Window key (F6) to move between windows, you are unable to go to one of your windows.

EXPLANATION: The Window key will not move to hidden windows, so at some point you must have hidden the elusive window with the SERVICES Window Hide command.

SOLUTION: Use the SERVICES Window Use or Window Expose command to retrieve the hidden window.

WINDOW PROBLEM #4:

You don't like the order in which the Window key (F6) displays your windows.

EXPLANATION: The window order corresponds to the order in which the windows were created, unless you have used the Window Use command. Window Use changes the order of the window stack by placing after the current window the window you specify.

SOLUTION: Decide what order you would prefer. Check to see which window is current (displayed with a double line at the bottom of the window). Issue the SERVICES Window Use command and select the window that should succeed the current window. Repeat the command for each window that you want to reorder. For example, in figure T.23, the Window key moves in a clockwise direction from MAIN to 1, to 2, to 3. If you want to reverse the order, place the pointer in the MAIN window and select SERVICES Window Use 3. Then put the pointer in window 2 and select SERVICES Window Use 1.

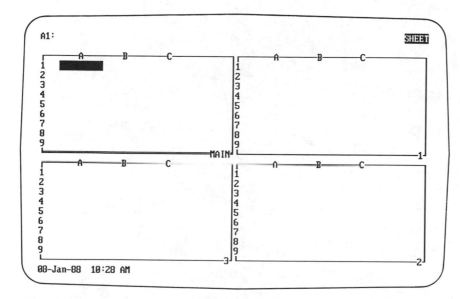

Fig. T.23

A sample window layout.

WINDOW PROBLEM #5:

You have a window that is less than full-screen size, and you don't like where the window is placed on the screen.

EXPLANATION: By default, windows are anchored where you create them. But you can move them.

SOLUTION: To move a window, select SERVICES Window Layout. The window will appear highlighted. Press the Scroll Lock key. When you press the cursor movement keys (arrows, PgUp, PgDn, Ctrl-right arrow, and Ctrl-left arrow) the highlighted window will move. Press Enter when you are satisfied with the location.

WINDOW PROBLEM #6:

You have created many different windows in a file, each with specific restrict ranges. Though the windows allow you to organize your data effectively, you sometimes find it too restrictive, because you cannot look at the entire worksheet without continually hitting the end of each window's restrict range.

EXPLANATION: If you restrict the range of every window, including the default window MAIN, you can never move freely through the entire worksheet.

SOLUTION: Leave the MAIN window with the default restrict range of the entire worksheet (A1..IV8192). You can hide the window with SERVICES **Window Hide** until you need to use the window. Then you can display it with **Window Use** or **Window Expose**.

Troubleshooting Word Processing

WORD-PROCESSING PROBLEM #1:

When you change the tab settings in a format line, the text does not move to these new tab stops.

EXPLANATION: You can configure Symphony Release 2.0 for two types of tabs: hard and soft. If you choose hard tabs, as in figure T.24A, a tab character is inserted when you press the Tab key. When you retrieve the file later, the text will move to new tab stops when you change the settings. If you choose soft tabs, as in figure T.24B, the tab character is not saved in the file. Instead, spaces are inserted where the tab character was, and additional spaces are not inserted when you change tab settings. The earlier versions of Symphony do not support hard tabs at all.

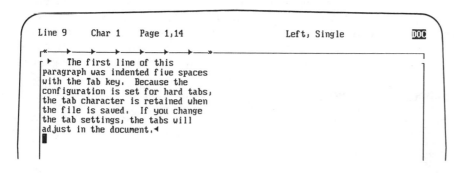

Fig. T.24A

With configuration set for hard tabs.

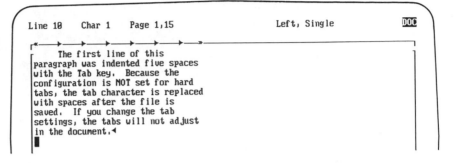

Fig. T.24B

With configuration not set for hard tabs.

```
Line 10    Char 1    Page 1,15                    Left, Single           DOC
┌─►──►──►──►──►──►──»────────────────────────────────────────────────┐
┌       The first line of this
│ paragraph was indented five spaces
│ with the Tab key.  Because the
│ configuration is NOT set for hard
│ tabs, the tab character is replaced
│ with spaces after the file is
│ saved.  If you change the tab
│ settings, the tabs will not adjust
│ in the document.◄
  ▌
```

SOLUTION: Use the SERVICES Configuration Document Hard-tabs command and specify **Yes.**

WORD-PROCESSING PROBLEM #2:

You get the message `Cannot alter this area of document` when you try to edit in a DOC window.

EXPLANATION: The text you are trying to edit was entered in a SHEET window. Symphony DOC mode lets you edit text that was created in SHEET mode only if the text was entered as a left-aligned label in the leftmost column of the window. If the text is in the leftmost column but is centered, right-aligned, a repeating label, or a value, you cannot edit it. An asterisk displays in the control panel when you place the cursor on a noneditable line.

SOLUTION: Switch to SHEET mode and use the Edit key (F2) to edit these cells.

WORD-PROCESSING PROBLEM #3:

As you are entering new text, the words do not wrap to the next line.

EXPLANATION: Automatic wordwrap only works in Insert mode. If you forget to turn Overtype mode off when editing, the new text will not wrap. Also, word-wrap is turned off if you have set Justification to None.

SOLUTION: Turn Overtype mode off by pressing the Ins key. The `Ovr` indicator at the bottom of the screen will disappear. Or, change the justification with the DOC Format Settings Justification command. If justification was turned off in a format line you created, edit it with the DOC Format Edit Current Justification command. You may need to press the Justify key (F2) to realign the paragraph.

WORD-PROCESSING PROBLEM #4:

The Backspace key deletes but leaves a blank space where the character was; the text to the right of the cursor does not shift to the left as the text usually does.

EXPLANATION: In Insert mode, the Backspace key deletes to the left of the cursor and slides text at the right of the cursor to the left to close up the space where the deleted character was. In Overtype mode, the Backspace key deletes to the left of the cursor and leaves the space open. Figure T.25 shows how blank space is left after backspacing a word in Overtype mode.

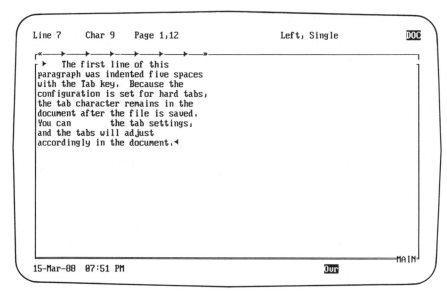

Fig. T.25

After backspacing a word in Overtype mode.

SOLUTION: Turn Overtype mode off by pressing the Ins key. The `Ovr` indicator at the bottom of the screen will disappear. Press F2 to justify the paragraph and remove the spaces.

WORD-PROCESSING PROBLEM #5:

Symphony doesn't seem to be paying attention to the number of spaces you insert. Sometimes when you put in one space, Symphony adds another when it justifies the paragraph. Other times, when you press two spaces, Symphony subtracts one. If you want more than two spaces, Symphony will not let you have more than one or two.

EXPLANATION: Symphony has spacing rules it follows when justifying your paragraphs. If a word contains no vowels and ends with a period (*Mr.*, for example), Symphony allows only one space after the period. If a word has at least one vowel and ends with either a period, question mark, or exclamation point, *and* the next word begins with a capital letter, Symphony puts two spaces after the period. If the next word is not capitalized, only one space is inserted.

SOLUTION: If you need more or fewer spaces than Symphony's justification rules permit, you can use hard spaces to override the rules. Unlike soft spaces, hard spaces are not altered during Symphony's paragraph justification. Instead of entering the space or spaces as you normally do, press the Compose key (Alt-F1) and press the space bar twice. A raised dot appears on the screen. Repeat this process for each space.

WORD-PROCESSING PROBLEM #6:

When you type a capital letter or number followed by a period at the left margin, these characters slide to the left of the margin. For example:

Things to Do

1. Go to the bank.

2. Call about insurance.

EXPLANATION: Symphony assumes that if you type letters or numbers followed by a period or colon, you want a hanging indent—characters that stick out to the left of a line. Hanging indents are often used for creating outlines.

SOLUTION: Control the left margin with the **Print** settings rather than the document **Format** settings. First, set the left margin so that no room exists for hanging characters. In other words, set the document's left margin to 1 with the DOC Format **Settings** Left command. Second, control the left margin in the print settings sheet with the SERVICES **Print Settings Margins Left** command.

WORD-PROCESSING PROBLEM #7:

You can't seem to get the Indent key (F3) to work properly. The text doesn't wordwrap to where you want it.

EXPLANATION: The Indent key wraps text to wherever the Indent key was pressed (that is, where the indent symbol appears).

SOLUTION: Use the space bar or Tab key to position the cursor where you want the text to wrap to; then press the Indent key. Let's look at two examples. To indent the first paragraph in figure T.26, you press the Tab key followed by the Indent key at the beginning of the paragraph. In the second paragraph, you press the Tab key before the hanging characters (1 .). After the period, you press the space bar twice and the Indent key once.

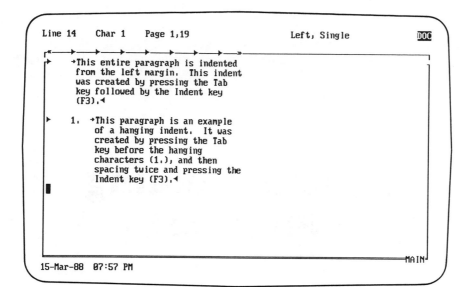

Line 14   Char 1   Page 1,19   Left, Single   DOC

    →This entire paragraph is indented
     from the left margin. This indent
     was created by pressing the Tab
     key followed by the Indent key
     (F3).◄

     1. →This paragraph is an example
          of a hanging indent. It was
          created by pressing the Tab
          key before the hanging
          characters (1.), and then
          spacing twice and pressing the
          Indent key (F3).◄

                                          MAIN
15-Mar-88 07:57 PM

Fig. T.26

*Indenting
paragraphs.*

Troubleshooting Printing

PRINTING PROBLEM #1:

Sometimes when you print, you get about 10 blank lines in the middle of the page.

EXPLANATION: Symphony keeps track of the number of lines on the page whenever it prints. If the final page of the report ends on line 35, for example, Symphony knows there are 31 lines left on the page. But if you use the form-feed button on your printer or use the printer knob to roll the paper out manually, Symphony doesn't know it. The program thinks you are still on line 35 even though you are back on line 1. The next time you print, Symphony inserts a page break where the program thinks the end of the page is, but this spot is the middle of the page.

SOLUTION: After you have manually adjusted the paper to the top of the page, use the SERVICES **P**rint **A**lign command to tell Symphony the printer is now at the top of the page.

ALTERNATE SOLUTION: Don't use the printer controls to feed out the paper. Use the SERVICES **P**rint **P**age-Advance or **L**ine-Advance commands to eject the paper. With this method, Symphony will always know on what line number on the page the print head is.

PRINTING PROBLEM #2:

When you print a document, the right ends of some lines are truncated.

EXPLANATION: Symphony looks at two sets of margins when printing a document: the margins in the document format settings and the margins in the print settings. The print margin settings are added to the format margin settings when the document is printed. The print settings right margin must be greater than the sum of the left margin in the document format settings, the left margin in the print settings sheet, and the right margin in the document format settings. If the right margin in the print settings is less than this sum, some (or all) of your lines will be cut off when you print.

SOLUTION: It doesn't hurt to make the print settings right margin a very large number; it just needs to be greater than the sum of all the other margins. Therefore, when printing a document, use the SERVICES **Print Settings Margins Right** command and type a large number, such as 240, the maximum.

PRINTING PROBLEM #3:

You have specified double-spacing in the print settings sheet, but the document is still single-spaced when it prints.

EXPLANATION: When you are printing from a DOC window, the document format settings have priority over the print settings. Therefore, whatever spacing is specified in the document format is used when the document is printed.

SOLUTION: Use the DOC **Format Settings Spacing 2** command to double-space the document before printing.

PRINTING PROBLEM #4:

Even though you specified top and bottom margins of 0, several blank lines still appear at the top of the page.

EXPLANATION: Symphony considers the top margin to be the number of lines from the top of the page to the header line. Whether or not you enter a header, Symphony reserves one line for the header and two lines for the space between the header and body text. Likewise, three lines are reserved at the bottom for the footer.

SOLUTION: If you need every line on the page for your report, select SERVICES **Print Settings Page Breaks No** so that the headers, footers, and page-break margins are suppressed.

ALTERNATE SOLUTION: If you would like to fit more lines on the page but would like to have top and bottom margins, you can enter an initialization string for your printer to condense the print vertically by printing more than 6 lines per inch. You would also need to change the page length. For example, the init-string for 8 lines per inch on an Epson RX-80 is \027\065\009. You would set the corresponding **Page** Length to 88 (8 lines per inch * 11-inch page).

PRINTING PROBLEM #5:

The footer is not printed on the last page of your multipage report.

EXPLANATION: Symphony does not automatically advance to the top of the next page when it finishes printing. Therefore, Symphony does not print the footer on the last page until you tell the program to advance to the next page or until you exit the program.

SOLUTION: Do not use the form-feed button on your printer to eject the last page. Instead, use the SERVICES **Print Page**-Advance command; the paper will advance, and the footer will print.

ALTERNATE SOLUTION: Put a hard page break on the last line of your Source range. Use the DOC **Page** command to insert the page-break symbol in the first column, last row, of the Source range.

PRINTING PROBLEM #6:

You have a multiple-page report that spans different sections of the worksheet. Specifying all the different print ranges is a laborious task.

EXPLANATION: The program remembers only the last print range specified. If a report has multiple print ranges, you must specify each one whenever you print the report.

SOLUTION: Give each page or print range a descriptive name (PAGE1, PAGE2, and so on). Then create a macro that prints each range (see fig. T.27).

Fig. T.27

A simple print macro.

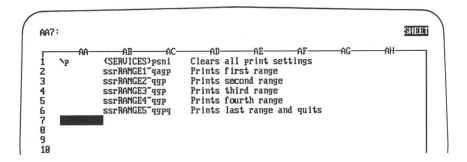

PRINTING PROBLEM #7:

Your print macro usually works as you want it to, but after you change the print options (to print a different report), the standard reports print incorrectly.

EXPLANATION: Symphony remembers the print settings from the last report you printed. If you print a special report on wider paper—or with different margins, headers, footers, and print initialization strings, for example—these settings affect the next report that you print with the macro.

SOLUTION: Use the SERVICES **P**rint **S**ettings **N**ame **C**reate command to create a print settings sheet containing the particular settings needed to print the report. At the beginning of your print macro, use the SERVICES **P**rint **S**ettings **N**ame **U**se command to retrieve this settings sheet before printing.

ALTERNATE SOLUTION: At the beginning of your print macro, use the SERVICES **P**rint **S**ettings **N**ame **I**nitial-Settings command to reset all printer options to their defaults and to clear everything else (see the first line of fig. T.27). Then have the macro specify the printer options you want. In this way, you can include in one worksheet several print macros that won't interfere with one another.

PRINTING PROBLEM #8:

After you have made changes to the worksheet, your reports sometimes print data that is not current.

EXPLANATION: In manual recalculation mode, Symphony prints the worksheet as of the last recalculation.

SOLUTION: If you specify the printing options manually, press the Calc key (F8) before you start the **P**rint command. If you use a macro to print, begin the macro with {CALC}.

PRINTING PROBLEM #9:

When you set up your print ranges, you considered margins and the six lines reserved for headers and footers. But the program occasionally skips a page between pages.

EXPLANATION: You can use one of two methods to skip to the next page when you print reports: you can specify a long report and let Symphony skip automatically to a new page whenever it prints a full page or encounters a page-break code, or you can specify individual print ranges for each page and use the **P**age-Advance command to tell the program to skip to the next page. Under certain conditions, the two methods conflict, and both send a page break to the printer, which results in a blank page.

With top and bottom margins of 0, you can have a one-page print range of as many as 60 lines. If Symphony encounters a print range of exactly 60 lines, the program automatically tells the printer to skip to the next page. If your macro also sends a page break, you get a blank page.

SOLUTION: Either restrict your print ranges to 59 lines (minus the number of lines for top and bottom borders) or do not issue a **P**age-Advance command after a 60-line page.

PRINTING PROBLEM #10:

You do not want to print certain information that's in the middle of a print range.

EXPLANATION: Suppose that you've documented assumptions, shown intermediate results that clarify a calculation, and added comments to make your worksheets easier to understand. You may not want to include this information in your final printed reports.

SOLUTION: This problem has several solutions. Select those that best meet your needs.

Two solutions skip only rows:

1. You can specify multiple print ranges that skip any rows you do not want printed. (This method is practical only if you use a macro to print and if you do not add comments after completing the worksheet.)

2. You can use a special label prefix, the vertical bar (|), to tell Symphony not to print a row. (This symbol is located on the Backslash key.) Whenever Symphony sees this label prefix in the leftmost cell of a row in a print range, the program skips that row. Except for printing, this label prefix and the left-aligned label prefix (') act in the same way. The contents of the cell are displayed normally.

Or to skip one or more columns in the middle of a print range:

3. Use the SHEET Width Hide command to hide the column before you print it. Then, after you have printed the range, "unhide" the column by selecting SHEET Width Display.

PRINTING PROBLEM #11:

You want to print a report twice. But instead of starting at page 1, the second copy begins with the next page number of the first copy.

EXPLANATION: With Symphony, you can build a report from many separate sections of a worksheet. If you use page numbers in headers or footers, every page starts with the next page number because the program assumes that you are producing one report.

SOLUTION: Issue the **Align** command after a **Page-Advance** command to instruct Symphony to start again at page 1. Because **Align** also tells the program that you have adjusted the paper to the top of the page, always issue the **Page-Advance** command before the **Align** command to prevent your pages from being misaligned. Another way of changing the page number is with the **Print Settings Page Number Print-Number** command. Enter the first page number that you want printed in the header or footer.

PRINTING PROBLEM #12:

You don't want to bother specifying individual print ranges for a long report.

EXPLANATION: If your report is more than five pages long, setting up the range names, settings sheets, and writing the macro to print the report can be a tedious process. And if the report will grow longer as time passes (if it contains year-to-date details, for example), you want to avoid having to continue adding range names and settings and then changing the macro.

SOLUTION: Let Symphony automatically break up your report. Symphony forces a page break after every full page and automatically inserts any headers or footers that you specify. If you specify borders, Symphony prints them on every page; you simply specify one print range.

Symphony also splits vertically a report that is too wide to print on a single page. The program prints as much material as possible on one page and then prints the "right side" of the report on separate pages. You can leave these pages separate or tape them together to make a wide report.

PRINTING PROBLEM #13:

You let Symphony handle page breaks automatically, but the program separates information that you want kept on one page.

EXPLANATION: When you specify a long report and let the program separate it automatically into pages, every page has the same number of print lines. But the report may contain information that you do not want separated: paragraphs of explanation, or multiple-line descriptions of accounts, for example.

SOLUTION: Leave the report as one print range, and insert page-break characters manually wherever you want a page to end. To insert a page-break character, move the cell pointer to the cell in the leftmost column of the row at which you want to start a new page. Then use the DOC **P**age command to instruct Symphony to insert a row above the cell pointer and put a page-break character (|::) in the cell. Or you can insert a row in the spreadsheet and type the page-break character (|::) into a cell.

PRINTING PROBLEM #14:

When you used the DOC **P**age command to specify a page break, the command inserted a row through a macro, spreadsheet, or database in the same row as the print range.

EXPLANATION: Symphony inserts a page break by inserting a row across the entire window. The blank row is inserted through anything that spans that row.

SOLUTION: Rather than use DOC **P**age to insert a page break, indicate where you want the new page by typing the page-break character as a label.

In the leftmost column of the row where you want the new page, type the page-break character—a vertical-bar label prefix followed by two colons (|::). Symphony treats this label as a page-break character, except that no blank row is inserted in the worksheet. Remember that you must type the page-break character in a blank line in your print range because the row with the page-break character does not print.

ALTERNATE SOLUTION: Restrict the range for the window containing your print range so that inserted rows won't affect other areas of the file. Use the SERVICES **Window Settings Restrict Range** command.

PRINTING PROBLEM #15:

You used the **Print Settings Init-String** command to tell the printer to print compressed print. But the report wraps to a new line after 72 characters, even though additional space remains on the line.

EXPLANATION: The **Init-String** command indicates how many characters are printed per inch. The number of characters printed on each line is specified in the margin settings.

SOLUTION: Whenever you change the print pitch, change the right margin. With a default left margin of 4 and a default right margin of 76, the 72-character print line matches the standard 72 data characters that Symphony displays on the screen.

If you change the line spacing to something other than six lines per inch, you also must change the **Page Length** to match the new setting.

Troubleshooting
Graphing

GRAPHING PROBLEM #1:

Because your worksheet uses many different graphs, selecting the graph ranges and other specifications is a slow, tedious process.

EXPLANATION: Symphony has one current active graph in each window. To use many different graphs in one worksheet, you must spend time specifying each one separately.

SOLUTION: Although the program has only one current active graph in a window, you can save a library of graphs within the worksheet. Use the SHEET Graph 1st-Settings Name Create command (or the GRAPH 1st-Settings Name Create command) to save the settings under a name you choose. Then enter the specifications for that graph.

Repeat the process for each graph, giving each a different name. Then, to recall any graph, issue the SHEET Graph 1st-Settings Name Use command (or GRAPH 1st-Settings Name Use) and either type the name of the appropriate graph or point to its name in the list of graph names. If you are working in a GRAPH window, you can use the GRAPH Attach command to view a named graph.

When you save the worksheet, the graph names and settings are saved also. Be sure to save the worksheet; if you forget to save, the names and settings will be lost.

GRAPHING PROBLEM #2:

You are creating and naming graphs, and your settings for the different graphs get all mixed up.

EXPLANATION: The SHEET **Graph 1st-Settings Name Create** command (or GRAPH **1st-Settings Name Create**) assigns the name to whatever *current* settings are displayed on the settings sheets. If you've created one graph and then change the settings before you name the next graph, the changes you make are recorded in the first graph.

SOLUTION: First name your graph, then change your settings, rather than the other way around.

GRAPHING PROBLEM #3:

You don't like the patterns used by some of the graph ranges.

EXPLANATION: Symphony has a fixed set of patterns for each graph range (X, and A through F). By default, the A-range is assigned pattern 2; the B-range, pattern 3; and so on. You may find that looking at two particular patterns next to each other, however, strains your eyes (see fig. T.28A).

Fig. T.28A

Patterns for the A-range and B-range.

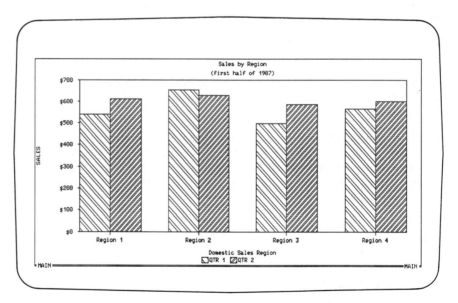

SOLUTION: Use the SHEET **Graph 1st-Settings Hue** command (or GRAPH **1st-Settings Hue**) to assign different patterns to the data ranges. Figure T.28B shows the graph with the A-range specified with hue 1, and the B-range with hue 7.

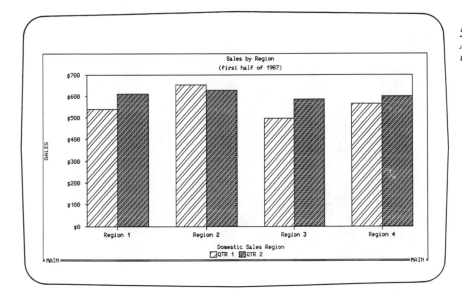

Fig. T.28B

A graph specified with hues 1 and 7.

GRAPHING PROBLEM #4:

You want to separate the bars in your graphs, but the program automatically puts them side by side.

EXPLANATION: In a bar graph with multiple ranges, each graph range touches the one next to it even if ample room exists to separate them.

SOLUTION: You can specify a range of blank cells (or zeros) as a dummy graph range. Symphony displays this dummy range as a bar with zero height, which is the same as a space between the bars. The bar graph in figure T.29 shows that the A and C ranges, which contain data, are separated by B and D ranges of blank cells.

GRAPHING PROBLEM #5:

You are graphing data (in thousands) in which numbers higher than 1,000 represent millions. Symphony automatically scales the data and adds the deceiving notation (Thousands) to the Y-axis.

EXPLANATION: This problem can be extremely confusing. Symphony assumes that all the numbers you graph represent units. If the largest numbers are greater than 1,000, Symphony automatically scales the numbers into thousands and adds the notation (Thousands) to the Y-axis. You cannot stop this automatic scaling.

If you graph information that is already in thousands (or millions, or more) in the worksheet (such as you might find on a financial statement), the (Thousands) indicator on the graph will be incorrect.

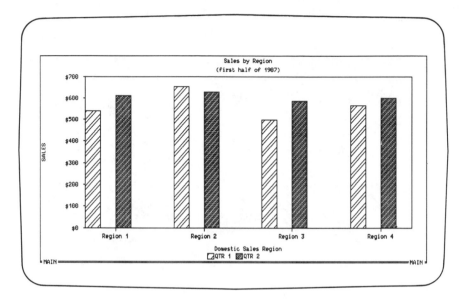

Fig. T.29

Adding spaces to the graph with blank B- and D-ranges.

Figure T.30A shows a table of sales data for the first three quarters. The numbers are in thousands of dollars. Note that one of the numbers in the table (in cell D5) is larger than 1,000. Figure T.30B shows the graph of this data with the incorrect Y-axis labels.

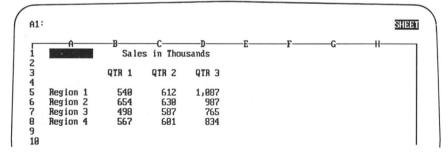

Fig. T.30A

Data with numbers in thousands.

SOLUTION: Although you cannot stop the automatic scaling, you can change the data to be in thousands (for example, add three zeros to each cell). Then the graph will be labeled in millions rather than thousands (see fig. T.30C).

GRAPHING PROBLEM #6:

Your graph's X-axis ranges overlap.

EXPLANATION: You can fit only a limited number of X-axis labels or numbers on a graph before they start to overlap (see fig. T.31A).

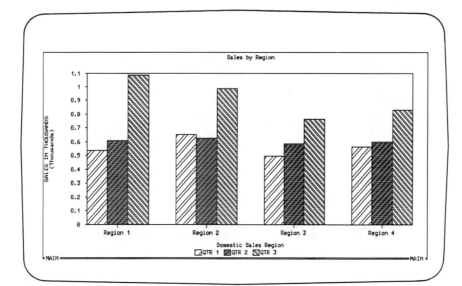

Fig. T.30B

*An incorrect
scaling notation.*

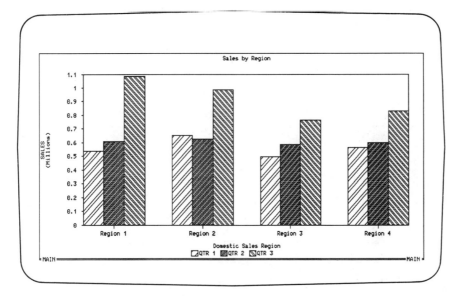

Fig. T.30C

*Correctly labeled in
millions.*

SOLUTION: Use the GRAPH 2nd-Settings Other Skip command (or SHEET Graph 2nd-Settings Other Skip) to skip a specific number of X-axis entries between the entries displayed on the graph. Figure T.31B shows the graph after Skip 2 is specified.

Fig. T.31A

Overlapping X-axis labels.

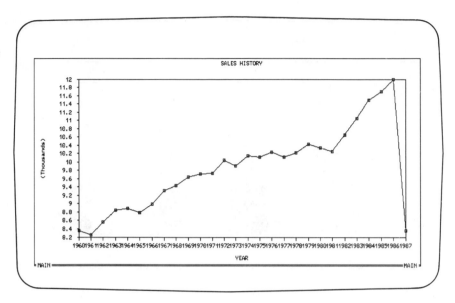

Fig. T.31B

Skipping every second X-axis label.

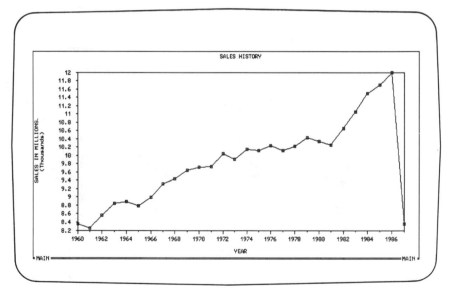

GRAPHING PROBLEM #7:

After waiting 30 minutes while a graph prints, you discover an error and must print the graph again.

EXPLANATION: This problem is a common one. The graph display does not show exactly what the printed graph will look like. For example, the display doesn't show the different type fonts you can specify for the text portion of your graph. And you can easily overlook missing legends or incorrect data on the display.

SOLUTION: Speed up the process of printing a graph by specifying the lowest possible density for your printer. Select **Settings Hardware Printer** from the PrintGraph menu to look at a list of all the printers and densities you included in your driver set (see fig. T.32). Most printers have at least two densities; some have three or four. Depending on the density, the difference in print time for one full-page graph can be a few minutes or an hour or more. Although the lowest density may not be acceptable for printing material that you show to someone else, you can use the low density for a quick test print.

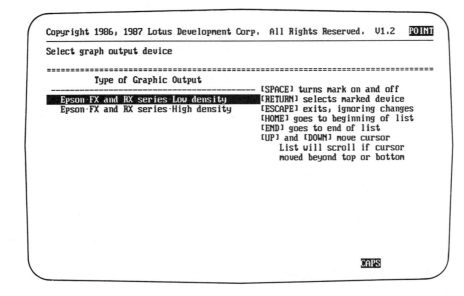

Fig. T.32

Choosing a low-density graph to speed printing.

Or you can get a quick test print by specifying an unusually small size. To do so, choose **Settings Image Size Manual** from the PrintGraph menu and then specify a small **Width** and **Height** for the test print. To produce a graph that covers one-sixteenth of a page, for example, specify a Width of 2.345 inches and a Height of 3.5 inches. These numbers are half the sizes that you would specify for a half-page graph.

When you are confident that the graph is correct, print it full-size in the print density you want.

GRAPHING PROBLEM #8:

Your pie chart looks like someone blew it up with a stick of dynamite. Every piece is exploded (see fig. T.33A).

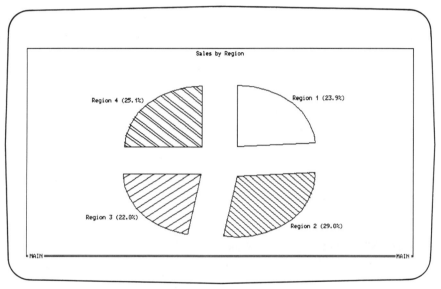

Fig. T.33A

A pie chart with all slices exploded.

EXPLANATION: Pie charts use the A-range for the graphing values, and the B-range for the shading/exploding codes. If a value in the B-range is over 100, the pie piece will be separated from the rest of the pie—that is, it will be exploded. If all values in the B-range are over 100, all pieces of the pie will be exploded. If you didn't mean to explode sections of the graph, you probably had a B-range left over from another graph.

SOLUTION: In a SHEET window, cancel the B-range with the SHEET **Graph 1st-Settings Cancel Entire-Row B** command. In a GRAPH window, use the GRAPH **1st-Settings Cancel Entire-Row B** command. If you want shading in your pie segments, set up a B-range with values between 1 and 7 (see fig. T.33B).

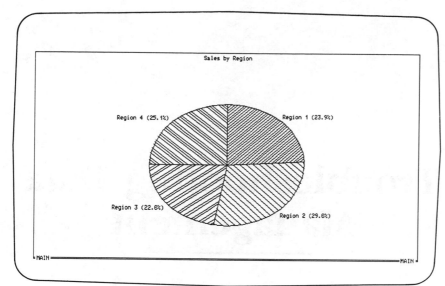

Fig. T.33B

After canceling the B-range and resetting for shading.

Troubleshooting Data Management

DATA MANAGEMENT PROBLEM #1:

You enter a criterion, but all the records are selected.

EXPLANATION: When you choose SHEET Query Find, Extract, Unique, or **De**lete, or FORM Criteria Use, Symphony uses the criterion as a filter to select records from the database. If the criterion is not exact, these **Q**uery commands do not work correctly.

SOLUTION: Issue the FORM Settings **B**asic Criterion command (or SHEET **Q**uery Settings **B**asic Criterion). When Symphony highlights the old range, check it carefully, looking for the following errors:

1. *Does the Criterion range contain any blank rows?* (See fig. T.34.) This error is the most common one in Criterion ranges that select all records. Each row is a separate selection test; if a record in the database passes any one test, that record is selected. Because a blank row has no tests, all records are selected. Make sure that only the field names and the rows containing criteria are highlighted.

2. *Do any compound tests use #NOT# or <> (not equal)?* These compound tests, which can be extremely tricky, can produce results that are just the opposite of the results you are trying to produce. Here is an example of an erroneous compound test:

   +B5<>100#OR#B5<>200

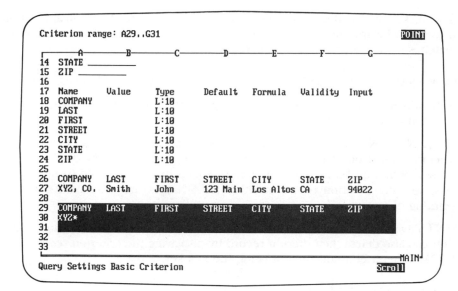

The purpose of this test is to select all records except those in which the value in column B is either 100 or 200. This written statement makes sense, but the effect of the test (the formula) is to select all records in which the value in column B is anything but 100 or 200. If the value is 100, it passes the test because it is not 200; if the value is 200, it passes the test because it is not 100. The correct way to write the test is

  +B5<>100#AND#B5<>200

DATA MANAGEMENT PROBLEM #2:

You enter a criterion, but none of the records is selected.

EXPLANATION: Each field in a criterion record (or a row in a Criterion range) can be a separate test. To be selected, a record must pass all the tests in the same criterion record or row. If you write the selection tests incorrectly, it may be impossible for a record to pass all of them. This problem is most common when you use the #AND#, #OR#, and #NOT# operators in your selection tests.

SOLUTION: Carefully check the selection tests in your criterion records or range for tests such as:

  +NUMBER>100#AND#NUMBER<0

This test tells Symphony to select records only when the value is both greater than 100 and less than 0. Because this result is impossible, no records are selected.

Also, make sure that the test's format matches the data in the field you are testing. If you use label matches or string functions on numeric data, or if you use number matches on strings, nothing is selected.

DATA MANAGEMENT PROBLEM #3:

You printed a database report, and not all records printed, even though you selected FORM Criteria Ignore.

EXPLANATION: Symphony uses the spreadsheet Criterion range as a filter to select records from the database. Criteria Ignore only affects the display of records in FORM mode. Even though you specified that you wanted to ignore the criterion, the criterion is still in effect for SHEET Query commands and the printing of reports.

SOLUTION: Use SHEET Erase to erase the criterion from the Criterion range. You can also delete the criterion record by displaying the criterion record with FORM Criteria Edit and then pressing the Del key.

DATA MANAGEMENT PROBLEM #4:

A SHEET Query Find command works correctly, but SHEET Query Extract (or Unique) does not.

EXPLANATION: Because Find does not use the Output range, unlike Extract and Unique, something must be wrong with that range.

SOLUTION: The field names in the Output range must match the field names in the database. If the names do not match, Symphony selects the correct records but does not copy any fields to the Output range. To ensure that the field names match, copy them from the database.

DATA MANAGEMENT PROBLEM #5:

When you Extract records, you get the message Too many records for Output range, and only some of the records that should have been extracted are displayed in the Output range.

EXPLANATION: As your database grows, the output from Extract commands grows also. When you define an Output range, you can define the number of rows that you want Symphony to use. If the output of the Extract (or Unique) command contains more records than you have specified, the Query stops, and you get an error message.

SOLUTION: Specify as the Output range only the row containing the field names. Symphony treats this specification as allowing the use of as many rows as necessary for Extract or Unique.

If you use this solution, however, be sure not to put anything below the Output range. If you do, you will lose valuable data; the next time you issue an **Extract** or **Unique** command, Symphony will erase everything below the field names before copying the selected records. (The program will even erase data that is far below the area needed for copying in the selected records.)

ALTERNATE SOLUTION: Enlarge the size of the Output range and then rerun the **Extract**.

DATA MANAGEMENT PROBLEM #6:

You inserted more records into your database, but these new records are not sorted according to the sort key you have specified.

EXPLANATION: Sorting records involves two steps. First, you use FORM **Settings Sort-Keys** (or SHEET **Query Settings Sort-Keys**) to specify the sort key, then you perform the **Record-Sort**. The sort key is stored in the settings sheet, so you only need to make this specification once. You must still use **Record-Sort**, however, after new records are added to the file.

SOLUTION: After adding new records to a database, issue the FORM **Record-Sort** command.

DATA MANAGEMENT PROBLEM #7:

You print a database report, but the column widths are not correct, and some of the columns display asterisks.

EXPLANATION: When you generate a database, Symphony sets column widths for each field according to the field length you specified. Symphony uses the column widths of the current window when printing reports. If you are not in your FORM window when you issue the SERVICES **Print** command, Symphony uses the column widths of whatever window you are in.

SOLUTION: Make sure that before you issue the SERVICES **Print** command you are in the FORM window in which you created the database.

DATA MANAGEMENT PROBLEM #8:

You specified two sort keys, and you no longer want the second key. The Backspace and the Esc keys, however, won't clear the key.

EXPLANATION: Once you have specified a sort key, the only way to clear it is with the **Cancel** command.

SOLUTION: In a SHEET window, issue the SHEET **Query Settings Cancel Sort-Keys** command. In a FORM window, use the FORM **Settings Cancel Sort-Keys** command. All sort keys will be cleared, and you will then need to reenter the **1st-Key**.

Troubleshooting Communications

COMMUNICATIONS PROBLEM #1:

You are unable to connect with a remote computer. When you dial the number, you either get garbage on the screen, never connect, or immediately disconnect.

EXPLANATION: The Interface settings (baud, parity, length, stop bits) for the remote computer must exactly match yours. If they are not identical, you will not be able to communicate successfully.

SOLUTION: Double-check your Interface settings. When in doubt, use 1200 baud, no parity, 8-bit word length, and 1 stop bit. Most information services and electronic bulletin boards use these settings.

ALTERNATE EXPLANATION: It's possible that too much static on the phone lines is preventing a good connection.

ALTERNATE SOLUTION: If the problem lies in the phone lines, take these steps:

1. Try dialing again later.

2. Try connecting at a lower baud rate (300 or 1200). Higher baud rates are more sensitive to static.

3. If you are dialing another computer user, have the other user call you.

4. Use another long-distance carrier. Some carriers have more static than others. By dialing 10288 before the phone number, you can access AT&T's lines.

COMMUNICATIONS PROBLEM #2:

You try to use the COMM Settings Interface command, but Symphony won't let you change any of the options.

EXPLANATION: When you installed Symphony, you indicated that you did not plan to use communications. You are not allowed to change the Interface settings if you have not installed Symphony for communications use.

SOLUTION: Run the Install program and answer **Yes** when asked Do you plan to use communications?.

COMMUNICATIONS PROBLEM #3:

You are on-line with another PC user, and you connected with the following settings: 1200 baud, even parity, 7-bit word length, and 1 stop bit (see fig. T.35). Though you were successful in connecting and typing messages back and forth, you were not able to transfer a file successfully.

```
Terminal characteristics                                          MENU
 Interface  Phone  [Terminal]  Send  Break  Handshaking  Capture  Login  Name  Quit
 ┌──────────────────────────────────────────────────────────────────────┐
 │ Interface            Terminal                    Send                  │
 │   Baud:      1200      Screen:     Window          EOL:      \m        │
 │   Parity:    Even      Echo:       No              Delay:    0         │
 │   Length:    7         Linefeed:   Yes             Response: \j        │
 │   Stop bits: 1         Backspace:  Backspace       Format:   No        │
 │   Comm Port: COM1      Wrap:       Yes             Break:    60        │
 │ Phone                  Delay:      10            Handshaking           │
 │   Type:      Tone      Translation:                Inbound:  Yes       │
 │   Dial:      60          (none)                    Outbound: Yes       │
 │   Answer:    15                                  Capture:              │
 │   Number:    5915591                               Range:    No        │
 │                                                    Printer:  No        │
 └───────────────────Communications Settings: C:\SYMPHONY\BBS.CCF─────────┘
```

Fig. T.35

Sample communications settings.

EXPLANATION: Successful telecommunications require that both computers use the same protocol settings. You were able to connect because you both had specified 7 bits, even parity, and 1 stop bit. During file-transfer operation, however, Symphony automatically changes these settings to 8 bits, no parity, and 1 stop bit. If the other PC's communications program isn't also using these settings during file transfer, you will not be able to transfer files.

SOLUTION: If you plan to transfer files, you and the other user should specify 8 bits, no parity, and 1 stop bit for your Interface settings.

COMMUNICATIONS PROBLEM #4:

When you are using the Phone-and-Login command, the log-in starts before the connection is made, and the system hangs with a WAIT message. But if you phone and log in separately, everything works fine.

EXPLANATION: With the Phone-and-Login command, Symphony dials the number and then waits for the `Online` indicator to display at the bottom of the screen before starting the log-in sequence. If the `Online` message is displayed before dialing, Symphony prematurely starts the log-in sequence.

SOLUTION: This premature display of the `Online` message is usually caused by an incorrect switch setting in the modem. If you have a Hayes 1200 modem, switch 6 must be in the off (open) position. If you have a Hayes 1200B modem, switch 3 must be off (open).

COMMUNICATIONS PROBLEM #5:

When you are connected to a remote computer, everything you type appears twice (for example, `HHEELLLLOO`).

EXPLANATION: You are communicating with a full-duplex computer that automatically sends back to you the characters you type. In addition, Symphony is also displaying the characters you type. The result is that every character you type appears twice (an echo).

SOLUTION: Change the Echo setting on your settings sheet to No (COMM Settings Terminal Echo No). See figure T.35.

COMMUNICATIONS PROBLEM #6:

When you are connected to a remote computer, you can't see anything you type.

EXPLANATION: You are communicating with a half-duplex computer that does not send back to you the characters you type. In addition, Symphony is not displaying the characters you type.

SOLUTION: Change the Echo setting on your settings sheet to Yes (COMM Settings Terminal Echo Yes).

COMMUNICATIONS PROBLEM #7:

When you are connected to a remote computer, the Enter key moves the cursor back to the beginning of the same line; the cursor doesn't move down to the next line.

EXPLANATION: The Enter key is giving a carriage return but not a line feed. The Linefeed setting controls whether a linefeed is given.

SOLUTION: Change the Linefeed setting on your settings sheet to Yes (COMM Settings Terminal Linefeed Yes). See figure T.35.

Troubleshooting Macros

MACRO PROBLEM #1:

You write a macro. When you try to execute it with the Alt key, nothing happens.

EXPLANATION: You must use a precise name format for macros invoked with the Alt key. The range name must be exactly two characters: the first is a back-slash; the second, a letter (from A to Z). If you name your macro anything else, Symphony cannot execute it with the Alt key. You must use the User key for other types of macro names.

SOLUTION: Use SHEET **R**ange **N**ame **C**reate to check the macro's range name. Symphony lists, in alphabetical order, all the range names in the worksheet. Range names that start with a backslash are at the end of the list. If you don't see the macro's range name listed, you haven't named your macro. Even experienced programmers make this seemingly trivial mistake, which is the most common reason a macro won't work.

If the range name is in the list, make sure that you have included the backslash. For example, although the letter A is a valid range name, it is not a valid name for a macro that is used with the Alt key.

Another common error is to use a slash (/) rather than a backslash (\) when you name a macro. If the range name is on the list, check carefully to make sure that the name starts with a backslash.

If the macro name is listed and looks valid, highlight it and press Enter. Symphony highlights the range with that name. The range should contain only one cell—the first cell of the macro. The contents of the macro must be a label or a string-valued function. If the cell is blank or contains a numeric value, the macro will not work.

MACRO PROBLEM #2:

After you write a few macros, you move some data. The macros now refer to the wrong addresses.

EXPLANATION: Macros are not like formulas; the addresses in macros do not change automatically when you move data that is used by the macro. In fact, a macro is nothing more than a label. Symphony does not adjust the contents of labels when you move data, because the program does not know that labels contain addresses.

SOLUTION: *NEVER* use cell addresses in macros. Always give range names to all the cells and ranges you use in macros, and use these range names in the macros. Then, if you move these ranges or insert and delete rows and columns, the range names will adjust automatically, and the macro will continue to refer to the correct cells and ranges.

MACRO PROBLEM #3:

Your macro seems to work correctly, but after you execute the macro, the display is wrong.

EXPLANATION: Symphony does not update the display or recalculate the worksheet during certain macro commands. Figure T.36A shows a macro (\a) that has just been executed. Although the contents of cell A1 should be 100, the cell is blank. And although the worksheet is set for automatic recalculation, the Calc indicator is on.

Fig. T.36A

The macro does not update the display.

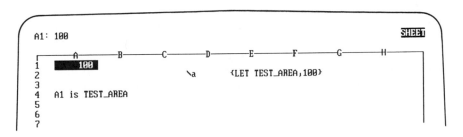

SOLUTION: To display the update, add a tilde (~) to the end of the macro. If you add a tilde to the macro shown in figure T.36A, Symphony displays 100 as the contents of A1, and the Calc indicator vanishes (see fig. T.36B). Other macro commands such as RECALC and RECALCCOL require other commands that force Symphony to update the display. The PgDn-PgUp key combination (in a macro, use {PgDn} and {PgUp}) is the easiest way to accomplish this update (refer to fig. T.6).

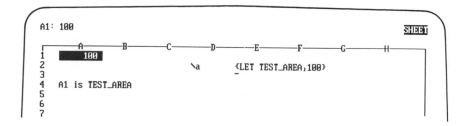

Fig. T.36B

Placing a ~ at the end of the macro.

MACRO PROBLEM #4:

Although the logic of your macro appears correct, the macro never works properly. Critical values do not seem to be current, even when recalculation is on automatic.

EXPLANATION: On a large worksheet, macros would execute slowly if Symphony recalculated the entire worksheet after every macro command. Symphony seldom recalculates the worksheet while a macro executes. If critical values change during execution, the macro uses the old values—not the current ones.

SOLUTION: Determine which cells and ranges must be recalculated to make the macro work correctly and then add RECALC or RECALCCOL statements to the macro where necessary. A complete worksheet recalculation with {CALC} works also but usually is extremely slow.

The macro shown in figure T.37A tests incorrectly for a valid entry. In this macro, GETNUMBER finds the old value because the test in IP_TEST (cell C12) is not updated after GETNUMBER. To correct the problem, add a RECALC command to the macro (see fig. T.37B). In this case, a tilde works if the worksheet is set for automatic recalculation. A RECALC or RECALCCOL is required in manual recalculation mode.

In figure T.37b, the macro branches to PROCESS if the test in C12 is 1 (true) and branches to ERROR_ROUTINE if the test is not 1 (false). These routines will perform whatever processing you need in your worksheet.

MACRO PROBLEM #5:

You need to change a macro that you wrote earlier, but you can't remember how it works.

EXPLANATION: This common problem surprises users when they first start to work with macros. After having painstakingly written, tested, and debugged a macro, you use it successfully in your worksheet. Because you wrote the macro, you know exactly what it does and how it operates. When you have to change it, you are amazed that you can't remember how it works.

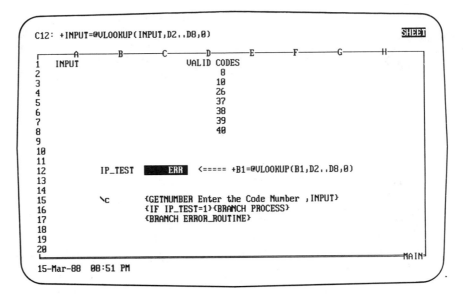

Fig. T.37A

A macro that requires recalculation to work correctly.

```
C12:  +INPUT=@VLOOKUP(INPUT,D2..D8,0)                              SHEET
        A        B        C        D        E        F        G        H
   1  INPUT                      VALID CODES
   2                                  8
   3                                 10
   4                                 26
   5                                 37
   6                                 38
   7                                 39
   8                                 40
   9
  10
  11
  12          IP_TEST      ERR      <===== +B1=@VLOOKUP(B1,D2..D8,0)
  13
  14
  15          \c           {GETNUMBER Enter the Code Number ,INPUT}
  16                       {IF IP_TEST=1}{BRANCH PROCESS}
  17                       {BRANCH ERROR_ROUTINE}
  18
  19
  20                                                              MAIN
  15-Mar-88  08:51 PM
```

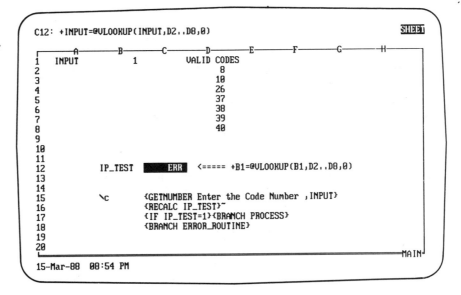

Fig. T.37B

Adding a RECALC statement to the macro.

```
C12:  +INPUT=@VLOOKUP(INPUT,D2..D8,0)                              SHEET
        A        B        C        D        E        F        G        H
   1  INPUT     1                VALID CODES
   2                                  8
   3                                 10
   4                                 26
   5                                 37
   6                                 38
   7                                 39
   8                                 40
   9
  10
  11
  12          IP_TEST      ERR      <===== +B1=@VLOOKUP(B1,D2..D8,0)
  13
  14
  15          \c           {GETNUMBER Enter the Code Number ,INPUT}
  16                       {RECALC IP_TEST}~
  17                       {IF IP_TEST=1}{BRANCH PROCESS}
  18                       {BRANCH ERROR_ROUTINE}
  19
  20                                                              MAIN
  15-Mar-88  08:54 PM
```

Even people who write Symphony macros for a living have this problem. They write the macro quickly but have difficulty figuring it out a few months later.

SOLUTION: Structure and document your macros carefully and consistently. Keep each macro short, and design it to perform only one operation. Instead of trying to cram the entire macro onto one line, keep each line of macro code short. Put all the range names to the left of the cell with that name, and put comments to the right of each macro statement. Write your comments in plain language, and explain why the macro does what it does.

To make your macros easy to read, use upper- and lowercase letters consistently. Always use lowercase letters for menu commands, and uppercase letters for range names and functions. Macro keywords can be either upper- or lowercase, but be consistent in all your macros. (For example, all keywords in this book are uppercase.)

As you can see from the following example,

```
\h    {MENU}rncHERE~~{GOTO}HELP~{?}{ESC;
rb{GOTO}HERE~{MENU}rndHERE~
```

a poorly constructed, undocumented macro is confusing. This macro is a sub-routine that provides the operator with a page of help text (at the range name HELP). When the operator reads the information and presses Enter, the macro returns the cursor to range name HERE (its position before the macro executed).

Figure T.38 shows the same macro code after its structure has been improved and documented.

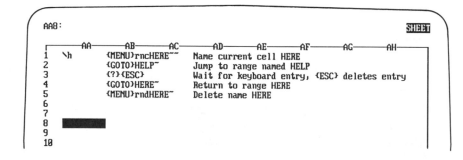

Fig. T.38

A well-constructed macro.

MACRO PROBLEM #6:

Although your macro seems correct, it starts to beep in the middle of some commands and puts some commands as a label in a cell.

EXPLANATION: The macro may look correct, but Symphony is not interpreting the macro in the way you anticipated. Either something is missing, or the macro contains extraneous keystrokes.

SOLUTION: This problem commonly occurs if you forget to include tildes (to indicate Enter) in a macro. You can use one of two methods to find errors:

1. Press Alt-F7 to put macro execution in single-step mode. When you execute the macro, Symphony executes only one keystroke and then

waits for you to press any key. When you press a key, you signal the program to execute the next macro keystroke. As you watch the macro execute in slow motion, you usually can see exactly where the error lies. (With some macros, this single-step approach can be painfully slow.)

2. Play "computer" and execute the macro manually. First, print the macro; then replay it from the keyboard, doing exactly as the macro indicates, keystroke-by-keystroke. Unless the problem is a recalculation problem that happens only during macro execution, you will find the error if you follow the script faithfully. If the macro works when you execute it manually, change recalculation to manual and try again.

ALTERNATE SOLUTION: You may have created a range name with the same name as a macro key name (such as {MENU} or {TYPE}). If you make this mistake, Symphony uses the range name rather than the function of the key. Consequently, if you name a cell MENU, Symphony will never display the menu invoked with the F10 key. If you are having trouble with your macro, look at your range names and check them against a list of macro key names (see fig. T.39).

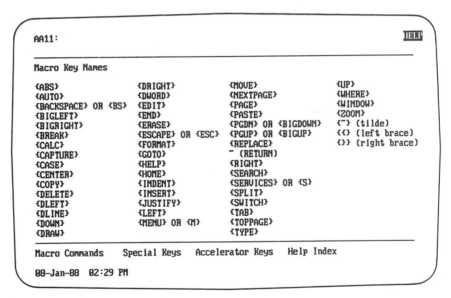

Fig. T.39

A list of macro key names.

MACRO PROBLEM #7:

You have written a series of handy macros for your worksheet, but you can't remember all their names.

EXPLANATION: You can name 26 macros (A to Z) for execution with the Alt key, 10 macros for execution with the function keys, and an unlimited number of macros with regular range names. Even remembering 20 or more macros in several worksheets boggles the mind.

SOLUTION: Use menus to execute macros. Menus are easier to learn than many of the macro keywords. You can have a large macro-driven worksheet with hundreds of macros, only one of which (\m, for example) is executed from the keyboard. You use this one macro to bring up the main menu. A series of hierarchical menus can contain any number of macros, each of which can have any valid range name. (Only macros executed from the keyboard require special names that start with a backslash.)

If you use more than five macros, even if they are for your own use only, put them in a menu so that you won't have to remember their names.

MACRO PROBLEM #8:

You wrote a macro containing an error. The macro destroyed your worksheet.

EXPLANATION: A macro can do anything that you can do from the keyboard. A macro can erase all or part of the worksheet, quit Symphony, and erase a file on the disk. If you don't prepare for possible catastrophic errors, you can lose hours—even days—of work.

SOLUTION: Always save your worksheet before you test a macro. Then, if the macro destroys something, you still have the data on disk. If part of the macro saves the file, make sure that you first save it with a different name. Saving the file is futile if the macro erases most of the worksheet and then saves the destroyed file with the name of the original file.

In fact, using a macro to save a file automatically is so dangerous that you should save your files manually until you are completely familiar with macro programming and the Lotus Command Language. Some people believe that it is too dangerous to ever do file saves from a macro.

A

Installing Symphony

Before you can use Symphony, you need to complete the following "maintenance" operations: (1) initialize the original Program disk; (2) make backup copies of all the disks; (3) copy COMMAND.COM to the disks; (4) install the Symphony disks to run with your equipment; and (5) prepare data disks.

The Symphony package contains nine 5 1/4-inch disks or five 3 1/2-inch disks. The 3 1/2-inch disks have about twice the capacity of the 5 1/4-inch disks, so some of the 3 1/2-inch disks have the same files as two of the 5 1/4-inch disks:

5 1/4-inch disks	*3 1/2-inch disks*
Program disk	Program, Help, and Tutorial disk
Help and Tutorial disk	Master Library and Tutorial Lessons disk
Tutorial Lessons disk	
Master Library disk	PrintGraph with Translate disk
PrintGraph Program disk	
Translate disk	Install disk
Install disk	Speller and Outliner Add-Ins disk
Speller and Outliner Add-Ins disk	
Speller Dictionary disk	

The instructions in this chapter assume that you have the 5 1/4-inch disks. If you are installing Symphony from the 3 1/2-inch disks, consult this table to decide which disks to use.

743

Installing Symphony on a Hard Disk

Installing Symphony on a hard disk consists of two steps: creating a subdirectory to store the Symphony program files and copying the files from the floppy disks to the hard disk. This section describes those steps.

These instructions assume that your computer's hard disk is designated drive C. Some hard disks, however, are identified by a different letter, such as D or E. If necessary, substitute the appropriate letter for C as you follow these instructions.

Creating a Symphony Subdirectory

To create a subdirectory for your Symphony program, first make certain that C is the current disk drive. Do so by entering **c:** and pressing Enter. Then type **cd** and press Enter to make the root directory the current directory. (Unless noted otherwise, you must press Enter after each of the commands in this section.)

To create your directory, enter

md symph

If an existing subdirectory or file already has the name SYMPH, DOS issues the error message Unable to create directory. If you see that error message, choose a different name for your Symphony directory.

Copying the Program Files

Before you begin copying the Symphony program files from the floppy disks to the hard disk, make the Symphony subdirectory the current directory by entering

cd symph

(Remember to use the appropriate name if you have chosen a name other than SYMPH.)

Insert the 5 1/4-inch Program disk or the 3 1/2-inch Program, Help, and Tutorial disk in drive A, and then enter

copy a:*.* c:/v

When the DOS prompt (C>) reappears, indicating that the copying is finished, remove the disk from drive A. Repeat these steps with all the disks in the Symphony package.

Using Symphony on a Floppy Disk System

Symphony is easy to use on a floppy disk system because the Program disk contains the necessary program and data files for all operations except printing graphs, which requires use of the PrintGraph disk (see Chapter 13). The Help and Tutorial disk gives access to the help screens and the tutorial, although the tutorial lessons are on the Tutorial Lessons disk. (If your computer has two 3 1/2-inch disk drives, you benefit from their higher capacity: you need not change disks just to access the Symphony help screens.) The Install disk and the Master Library disk are necessary for creating and saving driver sets so that you can run Symphony with your equipment. The Translate disk contains the files for converting Symphony files to and from other programs. The Speller and Outliner Add-Ins disk and the Speller Dictionary disk (5 1/4-inch disks only) give you access to two new applications: a Spelling Checker and a Text Outliner.

Here is the general procedure for preparing and then using the disks that come with your Symphony package:

1. Run the initialization program to record your name and company name on the original Symphony Program disk. This step is mandatory before you can use Symphony.

2. Make backup copies of all Symphony disks.

3. Add the DOS COMMAND.COM file to all the disks.

4. As explained in the "Installing Drivers" section, install the backup copies of the following four disks:

   Symphony Program disk

   Help and Tutorial disk (5 1/4-inch only)

   PrintGraph Program disk

   Install disk

5. Use the backup copy of the Symphony Program disk for booting and accessing the Symphony program; use the backup copies of your other disks as needed.

6. Refer to the Customer Assurance Plan that comes with the disks for directions on how you can get a replacement for lost or destroyed disk(s).

Initializing Symphony

Before using the Symphony program and before making backup copies of your Symphony disks, you must run an initialization program. This program records your name and company name on the original Symphony Program disk.

To run the initialization procedure, follow these steps:

1. With the A> on the screen, insert the original Symphony Program disk (5 1/4-inch) or Symphony Program, Help, and Tutorial disk (3 1/2-inch) in drive A.

2. Type **init** and press Enter.

3. Press Enter to begin. When prompted, fill in your name and company name.

Making Working Copies of the Symphony Disks

Before you begin, format nine 5 1/4-inch disks or six 3 1/2-inch disks, depending on which type of system you are using. Label the disks, giving them the same names as the original disks.

Place one of the original Symphony disks in drive A and the corresponding blank disk in drive B. Enter

copy a:*.*b:/v

and press Enter. When the DOS prompt reappears, repeat the COPY command for the rest of the original Symphony disks.

When you have copied all the Symphony disks, find a safe place for all the original Symphony disks and use your backup copies.

Installing Drivers

You need to install driver programs to tailor Symphony for your particular computer system. The drivers are programs that reside in files on the Master Library disk. These files store information about your specific system—the display, printer, plotter, modem, and so on. You can create one or many driver files, depending on your needs. If, for example, you want to run Symphony on an IBM Personal Computer that is capable of displaying graphics in multicolor, and also run the program on a COMPAQ which displays graphics and text in one color, then two separate driver files will enable you to run Symphony on both computers whenever you like.

When you make your driver selection, review carefully the options. Whether or not your system can display graphs and text at the same time, and in color, depends on a number of factors—the type of monitor(s) you are using, color cards, and so on.

Some equipment selections enable you to view text and graphics only at different times on the screen—what Lotus calls Toggle mode. An IBM color monitor with a color card, for example, will display graphs and text in color, but not at the same time. Some dual monitor combinations, on the other hand, enable you to view color graphs on one screen and text on the other at the same time (Dual mode). Finally, other equipment options permit you to view simultaneously graphs in single color and text on the screen (Shared mode).

Many figures in this book display both graphs and text (spreadsheets, database, and documents) on the same screen. These figures were shot from equipment capable of displaying both but only in single color—an example of Shared mode.

Before you begin to run the Install program, prepare a list of the kinds of equipment you plan to use. First, Symphony has to know what kind of display hardware you have. For example, a color monitor uses graphics control characters that are different from those for a monochrome monitor equipped with a Hercules Graphics Card displaying regular black-and-white graphs. Second, Symphony needs to know what kind of printer(s) you have. Third, Symphony asks you to indicate the graphics printer(s) or plotter(s), if any, you plan to use. And finally, Symphony needs information about your modem so that you can use the Symphony communications feature. A complete list of driver options is presented in figure A.1.

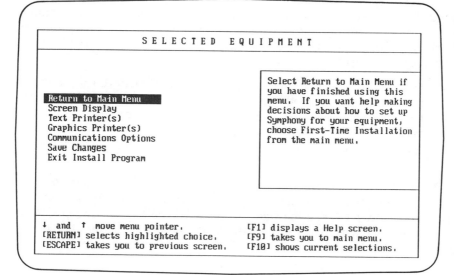

Fig. A.1

A list of driver options.

To select drivers, you need to consider not only the kinds of equipment required to run Symphony, but also the optional equipment that you can use. As mentioned in Chapter 1, the required hardware for running Symphony is the following:

- The IBM Personal Computer, XT or AT, PS/2, or compatibles, with at least 384 kilobytes (384K) of RAM required for each (512K with Spelling Checker)

- Two floppy disk drives or one floppy drive and one hard disk drive

- A monochrome monitor or a graphics monitor (single color or multicolor)

The following optional equipment enables you to use all of Symphony's features:

- Printer (parallel or serial port)

- Modem or acoustic coupler

- Additional monitor

In addition, if you have an add-on memory board (which can bring your system up to a maximum of 640K of RAM) or an expanded memory board (allowing use of up to 4 megabytes of RAM), you can use more of Symphony's worksheet area.

With Symphony's window capability, a dual monitor system will enhance your ability to integrate Symphony's environments (spreadsheet, word processing, graphics, data management, and communications).

When installing drivers, you must provide information for all required equipment, but you can select only the sections for the optional equipment you will be using. If, for example, you are not going to use a plotter or modem, the Symphony Install program allows you to skip the steps for adding these pieces of equipment to the driver set. Following is the procedure for selecting drivers to run Symphony with your equipment:

1. Load the Install disk. Then, at the prompt, type **install**. (A> is the prompt for systems with two disk drives, and C> is the prompt for hard disk drive systems.) You don't have to load the Install disk for a hard drive system. If all the Symphony files have been copied to the Symphony subdirectory, type **install** and press Enter at the DOS C> prompt.

2. Begin the Install process. If you have a system with two disk drives, you must replace the Install disk with the Master Library disk when Symphony gives you the signal to do so. If you have a hard disk drive system, be sure that you start the Install process from the directory that contains your Symphony files.

3. Choose **First-Time** installation the first time around. Follow the step-by-step directions that appear on the screen for creating and naming the driver. If you are creating only one driver, you may use the default driver name "Lotus." If you are creating two or more drivers, you must name each driver.

4. Follow the directions for placing the driver(s) on the backup copies of the Symphony Program disk and the PrintGraph disk.

Once you have completed installing your Symphony disks, they should be ready to run with your equipment. You can also use the Install program to modify a driver set that you have previously created and to create additional driver sets if needed. One use for additional driver sets is for running Symphony with different systems containing different monitors—one with a color monitor and one with a monochrome monitor, for example.

Configuring the Printer and the Data Disk

After drivers are installed, you must set the configuration for the printer and the default drive for disk storage. Symphony helps in this process by saving certain default settings from session to session. Lotus provides a default configuration for all settings, but you may want to change some of Lotus's choices.

You access the settings for the printer by issuing the **Configuration Printer** command from the SERVICES menu. (Symphony menus and the **Configuration** command are discussed in Chapter 2; printer settings are discussed in Chapter 11.) Access the setting for the default drive for disk storage by choosing the **Configuration File** command from the SERVICES menu. The default drive for transferring data to and from disk storage is drive A. You may have to change this drive assignment if you have a hard disk system.

Preparing Data Disks

The final step in getting started in Symphony is preparing data disks. For those who are unfamiliar with preparing blank disks, you must properly format these disks before you can use them to store the data entered in worksheets. Symphony enables you to format a blank disk without having to exit from the program by using the DOC application add-in feature (discussed in Chapter 2).

B

Symphony Release 2.0: New Commands and Features

This appendix lists the commands that Release 2.0 has added to the Symphony program, as well as the new features that are available.

New Spreadsheet Commands

Command	*Function*
SHEET Settings Recalculation Order Optimal	The new Optimal option turns on minimal recalculation so that Symphony recalculates only the cells that are affected by changes.
SHEET Settings Zero	The Zero command "hides" the contents of all cells with a value of zero.
SERVICES Configuration Other International Negative	With the Negative command, you can choose how negative numbers will display—in parentheses or with a leading minus sign.

New Database Features

A database can now have up to 256 fields in either the SHEET or FORM environment.

An existing database is much easier to modify (see "New Database Commands").

New Database Commands

Command	Function
FORM Field Move	Move repositions a field in the input form.
FORM Field Insert	Insert adds a new field to the input form and in the database ranges.
FORM Field Delete	Delete removes a field from the input form and some of the database ranges.

New Word-Processing Features

You can now see page breaks and page numbering on-screen. Page breaks are indicated in the window borders, so that you can instantly see where the page will break before printing. The page and line numbers appear in the control panel at all times. Although the Where key (Alt-F2) is still functional, the new page orientation features make it redundant.

Paragraphs automatically reformat after you make editing changes. As you insert and delete characters, the paragraph remains aligned with the margin settings.

You can undelete text using the Paste accelerator key, Ctrl-P.

Print attributes (such as underlining) are easier to enter. When you press Ctrl-B to begin an attribute, a menu of print attributes displays in the control panel. You can choose the appropriate attribute from the menu. Print attribute codes do not display in your text; the attributed text appears on your screen as underlined, low intensity, or colored, depending on your monitor.

With the new Hard-tabs option, you can change the tab stops in the format line, and existing tabs in the document automatically adjust to the new settings.

You can use wildcard and special characters in Search and Replace operations. Release 2.0 allows the following symbols in your Search or Replace strings:

Wildcard string:	Symphony finds:
\?\	Any character
\&\	Any letter or number
\a\	Any letter
\A\	Any uppercase letter
\#\	Any number

Special symbol:	Symphony finds:
\~\	Carriage-return character
\^\	Tab character
\:\	Page-break character
\-\	Space, tab, or hard space
	Backslash character

In addition, two add-in programs are included for use with the DOC environment: Spelling Checker and Text Outliner.

New Word-Processing Commands

Command	Function
SERVICES Configuration Document Hard-tabs	Hard-tabs Yes inserts tab symbols, rather than spaces, when you press the Tab key.
DOC Verify	If the Spelling Checker application is attached, the Verify option appears on the DOC menu. This option checks the spelling in your document.

Short-cut, or "accelerator," keys are offered for most commands. Here's a list of these accelerator keys:

Command	Function
Ctrl-J	AUTO (turns auto-justification on/off)
Ctrl-B	BEGIN (begins print attribute)

Ctrl-X	CASE (converts capitalization of characters)
Ctrl-C	COPY (copies text)
Ctrl-T	DELETE LEFT (deletes text to start of line)
Ctrl-D	DELETE LINE (deletes current line)
Ctrl-Y	DELETE RIGHT (deletes text to end of line)
Ctrl-Backspace	DELETE WORD (deletes previous word)
Ctrl-F	FORMAT (inserts format line)
Ctrl-O	MERGE (inserts merge character)
Ctrl-M	MOVE (moves text)
Ctrl-PgDn	NEXT PAGE (moves cursor to next page)
Ctrl-N	PAGE (inserts page break)
Ctrl-P	PASTE (inserts last deleted text)
Ctrl-R	REPLACE (replaces text with specified text)
Ctrl-S	SEARCH (searches for specified text)
Ctrl-E	STOP (ends print attribute)
Ctrl-PgUp	TOP PAGE (moves cursor to top of page)

New Communications Features

Symphony Release 2.0 includes five configuration files for communicating with popular information services. You can use the files as they are given to you, or you can modify them as needed. The .CCF files included are ADP, COMPUSRV, DOWJONES, MCI, and SOURCE.

An application add-in for DEC VT100 terminal emulation is also included.

New Communications Commands

Command	*Function*
COMM Settings Send Format	When Format is set to Yes, the DOC format characters (for example, carriage returns, format lines, print attributes) will be transmitted.

COMM Settings Terminal VT100

When the VT100 application add-in is attached, this new menu option appears, and a new settings sheet appears at the bottom of the screen.

Other New Features

Macro Keynames

Macro keynames, corresponding to the new accelerator keys in the word-processing environment, are available to use in your macros:

Command	Function
{AUTO}	Turns auto-justification on/off
{CASE}	Converts capitalization of characters
{COPY}	Invokes the DOC Copy command
{DLEFT}	Deletes to left end of line
{DLINE}	Deletes line
{DRIGHT}	Deletes to right end of line
{DWORD}	Deletes word
{FORMAT}	Inserts format line
{MERGE}	Inserts merge character
{MOVE}	Invokes the DOC Move command
{NEXTPAGE}	Moves cursor to next page
{PAGE}	Inserts page break
{PASTE}	Inserts last deleted text
{REPLACE}	Invokes the DOC Replace command
{SEARCH}	Invokes the DOC Search command
{TOPPAGE}	Moves cursor to top of page

Translate Program

Three additional conversion formats are offered in the Translate program: DCA (IBM revisable-format Document Content Architecture), Multiplan (SYLK TM), and Open Access (SIF).

Index

#AND# operator, 182, **729**
#NOT# operator, 182, **729**
#OR# operator, 182, **729**
1st-Settings Cancel command, 396
1st-Settings Cancel Entire-Row B command, **726**
1st-Settings Cancel Entire-Row Graph command, 397
1st-Settings Format command, 407
1st-Settings Hue command, 400, 402, 417, **720**
1st-Settings Legend command, 401
1st-Settings menu, 386
1st-Settings Name Create command, **719-720**
1st-Settings Name Delete command, 395
1st-Settings Name Use command, **719**
1st-Settings Range menu, 398, 406
1st-Settings Type menu, 413
1st-Settings Type Stacked-Bar graph, 403
2nd-Settings Other Origin command, 393
2nd-Settings Name Delete command, 395
2nd-Settings Other Aspect command, 414
2nd-Settings Other command, 415, 428
2nd-Settings Other Grid command, 412
2nd-Settings Other Skip command, 406, **723**
2nd-Settings X-Scale command, 391
2nd-Settings X-Scale Format Other command, 428
2nd-Settings Y-Scale command, 391, 426
2nd-Settings Y-Scale Exponent command, 427
2nd-Settings Y-Scale Format Other command, 428
2nd-Settings Y-Scale Type Automatic-Linear command, 426
2nd-Settings Y-Scale Type command, 425
< (less than) operator, 181
<= (less than or equal to) operator, 181
< > (not equal) operator, 181
= (equal) operator, 181
> (greater than) operator, 181
>= (greater than or equal) operator, 181
? command, 606-607
@ functions, 155-208, 297, 545-547, *see also* Symphony functions
@@ function, 191
@LN function, 157
@MAX formula, 101
@MID function, 194
{-B} hidden Section-begin marker, 350
{B} Section-begin marker, 350
{E} Section-end marker, 350
{N} Nonprinting heading marker, 350

A

Above report range, 503
ABS function, 156
absolute addressing, 127-128, 130-132
    problem, 684

absolute reference errors in macros, 578
accelerator keys
    DOC window
        Auto (Ctrl-J), 252, 287
        Begin (Ctrl-B), 252
        Case (Ctrl-X), 252
        Copy (Ctrl-C), 252, 272
        Delete Left (Ctrl-T), 252, 269
        Delete Line (Ctrl-D), 252, 269
        Delete Right (Ctrl-Y), 252, 269
        Delete Word (Ctrl-Backspace), 252, 269
        Format (Ctrl-F), 252, 295
        Merge (Ctrl-O), 252
        Move (Ctrl-M), 252, 270
        Next Page (Ctrl-PgDn), 252
        Page (Ctrl-N), 252, 292
        Paste (Ctrl-P), 252, 269, 272
        Replace (Ctrl-R), 252, 278, 281
        Search (Ctrl-S), 253, 278, 280
        Stop (Ctrl-E), 253
        Top Page (Ctrl-PgUp), 253
accepting input Command Language commands, 606-611
Access System menu, 24, 31-35, 224, 430
ACOS function, 160
acoustic couplers, 532
Action Eject command, 438
Action Pause command, 438
add-in word processing applications, 321-358
addressing
    absolute, 127-132
    cells, 127-133, 187
    mixed cell, 130-133
    relative, 127-132
ADP file, 536
advanced
    FORM window features, 481-491
    graph topics, 421-428
alphanumeric keyboard, 53-54
Alt (Macro) key, 575, **735**
Alt-F1 (Compose) key, 250, 258, **710**
Alt-F2 (Where) keys, 250
Alt-F3 (Split) key, 250
Alt-F4 (Center) key, 250
Alt-F5 (Learn) key, 571-572
Alt-F6 (Zoom) key, 38-40, **703**
Alt-F7 (Step) key, 605
Alt-F8 (Draw) key, 38, 423-425, 437
Alt-F9 (Switch) key, 38-39, 50
Alt-F10 (Type) key, 31, 36, 38, 50, 248, 334, 350, 482
AMERICAN.LEX file, 327
analysis, what-if, 18-19, 111-113
anchoring cells, 116
AND to combine record selection criteria, 476-477
annuity, 168-169
Answer command, 550

All bold listings in the index are in the troubleshooting section.

Application
command, 214, 595
menu, 45-46, 322, 333
Application Attach command, 322-333
Application Clear command, 334
Application Detach command, 323, 334
applications
integrating, 10-14, 17-18
Macro Library Manager, 595
PrintGraph, 429-440
Spelling Checker, 22, 29, 321-332
Text Outliner, 22, 29, 332-357
approximate matching record labels, 479
matching record labels, 479
arguments, 155-162, 175
CELL function table, 189-190
ASCII files
converting WordStar to, 225-226
copying, 222
ASCII/LICS characters, functions used with, 199-201
ASIN function, 160
aspect
cells, 187-191
ratio in graphs, 414
asynchronous communication transmission, 22, 532-533
ATAN function, 160
ATAN2 function, 160
Attach command, 46, 474, 491, **719**
attaching
graphs, 449-451
settings sheets, 474
Spelling Checker, 322-323
Text Outliner, 333-334
Attribute command, 341, 347-348
attributes for printing, 308-310
Attributes Global Non-Printing command, 354
AUTO command, 755
auto-dial
Command Language program, 655-656
macro, 592
Auto-Justify command, 285, 287-288
automatic exit, 50-51
automatic
macros, 576
paragraph justification, 287
recalculation, 150-151
overriding scale in graphs, 391
scale settings changing in graphs, 390-391
scaling labels, 426-428
spelling correction, 324
auxiliary dictionaries, 327-331
available memory check, 79
AVG function, 163, **696**

B protocol, 22, 533
backing up files, **699-700**
backslash (\), 83
Backspace key, 259
backup copies
disks, 743, 745
files, 214
bar graphs, 442-443
crosshatching, 399-400

Bar-Graph format, 146
batch printing graphs, 438
baud rate, 532, 534
BEEP command, 636-637
Below report range, 507-508
blank
inserting columns and rows, 119-121
strings eliminating spaces, 197
BLANK command, 635
BLAST protocol, 22, 533
Boldface italic print attribute, 253
Boldface italic subscript print attribute, 253
Boldface italic superscript print attribute, 253
Boldface italic underline print attribute, 253
Boldface print attribute, 253
Boldface subscript print attribute, 253
Boldface superscript print attribute, 253
Boldface underline print attribute, 253
braces ({}), 604
misplaced in macros, 577
BRANCH command, 611-614
BREAKOFF command, 621
BREAKON command, 621
bulletin board connection, 534-535
byte length, 534

CALC command, **715**
calculating mean, 163
Cancel command, **731**
capital letter beginning sentence with, 324
capitalization Spelling Checker menu, 326
Caps Lock key, 55
capture macro, 593
carriage returns, 264
CASE command, 755
catalog of settings sheets, 394-395, 474
CD command, **699**, 744
CELL function, 188-190, **671**, **697**
arguments table, 189-190
cell pointer, 16, 259
moving, 59-63
restricted movement, 149-150
CELLPOINTER function, 191, **697**
cells
addressing, 127-133, 187
entering in formulas, 86
anchoring, 116
column width, 187
coordinates in macro libraries, 598-599
copying, 124-126
determining the aspect, 187-191
format, 187
freezing, 148-150
hiding, 147
highlighting, 116
label prefix, 187
moving, 237-238
contents of, 114-116
pointing to, 116-118, 122
printing formulas, 374-376
protecting, 239-242
before copying, 217
range names, 99-100

All bold listings in the index are in the troubleshooting section.

references, 134-135
referring to indirectly, 191
type of, 187
CHAR function, 200
characters
changing in text, 259
erasing, 259
and editing, 267
inserting in text, 258-259
international sets, 25
label-prefix, 82
LICS, 200
moving cursor one, 260-261
replacing in string, 195
translation, 227
check available disk space, 210
choose a graph macro, 590
CHOOSE function, 174-175
CIRC message, 152
circular references, 152-153
problems, **670-674**
CLEAN function, 201, 552
Clear command, 46
clearing the screen, 330
clipboard, 269
CLOSE command, **645**
CODE function, 201
code number of LICS characters, 201
color in pie chart graphs, 416-417
COLS function, 191
column-by-column recalculation, 151-152
columns
adjusting width, 136-137
changing to rows, 103-104
deleting in worksheet, 122-124
headers, 82-84
hiding, 136
to prevent printing, 368
inserting blank in worksheet, 119-121
restoring hidden, 136
setting width
macro, 585
of capture range, 546-547
summing with SHEET window macros, 584
width of cell, 187
combining files, 216-219
COMM
menu, 535, 543-544, 549
window, 531-552
changing default settings, 535-539
macros, 591
auto-dialing, 592
capture, 593
hangup, 592
log-in, 592-593
Command Language, 27-28, 601-**659**
elements of programs, 603-604
label prefixes, 605
syntax, 604
window, 605
Command Language commands
accepting input commands, 606-611
CONTENTS, 198
data manipulation, 630-635
decision-making commands, 627-630
file manipulation, 642-649

program
control commands, 611-627
enhancement, 635-642
Symphony Release 2.0
{AUTO}, 755
{CASE}, 755
{COPY}, 755
{DLEFT}, 755
{DLINE}, 755
{DRIGHT}, 755
{DWORD}, 755
{FORMAT}, 755
{MERGE}, 755
{MOVE}, 755
{NEXTPAGE}, 755
{PAGE}, 755
{PASTE}, 755
{REPLACE}, 755
{SEARCH}, 755
{TOPPAGE}, 755
{?}, 606-607
{BEEP}, 636-637
{BLANK}, 635
{BRANCH}, 611-614
{BREAKOFF}, 621
{BREAKON}, 621
{CALC}, 715
{CLOSE}, 645
{CONTENTS}, 633-635
{DEFINE}, 623-625
{DISPATCH}, 622-623
{FILESIZE}, 649
{FORBREAK}, 630
{FOR}, 629-630
{GETLABEL}, 607-609
{GETNUMBER}, 609
{GETPOS}, 649
{GET}, 607
{HANDSHAKE}, 642
{IF}, 627-629
{INDICATE}, 639
{LET}, 630-632
{LOOK}, 610-611
{MENUBRANCH}, 614-616
{MENUCALL}, 616-617
{ONERR}, 619-621
{OPEN}, 643-645
{PANELOFF}, 637
{PANELON}, 637
{PHONE}, 641
{PUT}, 632-633
{QUIT}, 618-619
{READLN}, 647
{READ}, 645-647
{RECALCCOL}, 639-641, **687-690**, **736-737**
{RECALC}, 639-641, **687**, **690**, **736-737**
{RESTART}, 626-627
{RETURN}, 617-618
{SETPOS}, 648-649
{WAIT}, 621-622
{WINDOWSOFF}, 637-639
{WINDOWSON}, 639
{WRITELN}, 648
{WRITE}, 647-648
Command Language programs, see also *programs*, 650-658
auto-dial, 655-656

All bold listings in the index are in the troubleshooting section.

changing default values, 658
creating, 604-605
    entry forms, 656-658
debugging, 604-605
documenting, 605
image-save series of graphs, 654
printing multiple copies, 650-653
redial, 656
skipping columns or rows, 653-654
using, 604-605
COMMAND.COM file, 743, 745
commands see also Symphony commands and Command
    Language commands
    cut-and-paste, 114-124
    DOS
        CD, **699**, 744
        COPY, 214, 744, 746
        DIR, **699**
        ERASE, 220
        MD, 744
        RENAME, 223
        TREE, **699**
        TYPE, 365
    invisible, 602
    Move and formulas, 115-116
    print attributes, 253-254
    selecting with cursor or keys, 98
    Settings Name Create, 544
    SHEET window, 97-154
    Symphony Release 2.0, 751-753
communications, 531-552
    asynchronous transmission, 22, 532-533
    automating log-in sequence, 556-558
    between computers, 549-552
    capturing data ranges, 545-548, 559-560
    configuration file (CCF), 535-536
    connecting with CompuServe, 558-563
    converting data with @ functions, 547
    downloading files, 560-563
    ending a session, 549
    getting started, 543
    hands-on practice, 553-563
    log-in sequence, 540-543
    modifying configuration files, 554-556
    new features, 754-755
    overview, 22-23
    parsing data, 547-548
    problems, **732-734**
    protocol, 533
    sending
        data received to printer, 544-545
        messages, 550
        ranges, 550-551
    settings, 554-558
    synchronous transmission, 532-533
comparing strings, 196
complex bar graphs, 398-403
CompuServe, 22-23
    connecting with, 558-563
COMPUSRV file, 536
Configuration Auto command, 576
Configuration Document Auto-Justify Yes command, 287
Configuration Document command, 281, 291
Configuration Document Hard-tabs command, **708**, **753**
Configuration Document Justification command, 282, 285
Configuration Document settings command, 254-258

Configuration Document Spacing command, 289
Configuration Document Tabs command, 289
configuration file, 21, 254-255, 292
    modifying communications, 554-556
    Spelling Checker, 331
Configuration File command, 221-222, **698**, 749
Configuration menu, 43-45, 255, **666**
Configuration Other Application Set command, 322, 334
Configuration Other File-Translation command, 222
Configuration Other File-Translation Generate Current
    command, 226
Configuration Other File-Translation Generate Save command,
    226
Configuration Other International command, 138-139
Configuration Other International Currency command, 141
Configuration Other International Date command, 205
Configuration Other International Negative command, 142,
    751
Configuration Other International Punctuation command,
    142-143
Configuration Other International Time command, 145, 207
Configuration Printer Auto-LF command, 363
Configuration Printer command, 374-375, 377, 749
Configuration Printer Init-String command, 363, 373-374
Configuration Printer Margins command, 363, 370-371
Configuration Printer Name command, 363, **666**
Configuration Printer Page-Length command, 292, 363
Configuration Printer settings command, 362-363
Configuration Printer Type command, 363, **667**
Configuration Printer Wait command, 363
Configuration Settings command, 225
Configuration Update, 248
Configuration Window Type command, 248
configurations
    data disks, 749
    printer, 749
    PrintGraph, 430-433
    saving settings, 548
    settings, 43-45
connecting to bulletin boards, 534-535
CONTENTS command, 198, 633-635
control panel, 63-65
converting telecommunicated numbers to usable form, 545
Copy command, 83, 124-135, 214, 272, 345, 366, 496, 653,
    675, **690**, 744, 746, 755
copying
    ASCII files, 222
    between windows, 237
    cells, 125-126
    contents of spreadsheets, 219
    data, 124-135
    formulas, 233-235
    LICS files, 222
    outline sections, 345
    program files, 744
    protecting cells before, 217
    text, 219
    values, 104
COS function, 160
COUNT function, 163, 166
Create command, 39
creating and printing graphs hands-on practice, 441-455
Criteria Edit command, 475-476, 504-505, **730**
Criteria Ignore command, 475-476, 480, **730**
Criteria Use command, 474, 476-477, 505
Criterion Edit command, 477

All bold listings in the index are in the troubleshooting section.

criterion range, 477-480
crosshatches in pie chart, 414-415
CTERM function, 172-173
Ctrl-B (Begin Attribute) keys, 253
Ctrl-Break keys, 32, 51
Ctrl-E (End Attribute) keys, 253
Ctrl-P (Paste) key, 268
Currency format, 141-142
cursor movement, 258-267, 303-304
    keys, 59-63, 260-268
    line to line, 262
    named lines, 265-267
    next hard carriage return, 264
    next screen, 262-263
    one character at a time, 260-261
    specific lines or pages, 264-265
    top of page or next page, 264
    word to word, 261-262
    selecting commands, 98
custom character-translation table, 227
cut-and-paste commands, 114-124

D

data
    copying, 124-135
    destruction problems, **691**
    disks configuring, 749
    editing, 89-91
    erasing range of cells in spreadsheet, 635
    form, 10-11
    input in paused program, 606-607
    managing, 19-20
    parsing communications, 547-548
    placing value
        in defined range, 632-633
        or string in target cell location, 630-632
    retrieving from specified ranges, 179-180
    sending to printer data received, 544-545
    sorting database, 521
    storing source cell in destination cell, 633-635
    transferring between computers, 549-552
data entry
    macro, 585
    problems, **668-669**
data management, 459-513
    functions, 174-180
    hands-on practice, 515-527
data manipulation Command Language commands, 630-635
Data-Labels command, 409-411
databases, 462-470, 515-517
    adding
        fields, 490
        new records, 469
    creating, 462-470, 515-517
        reports, 524-527
        subtotals, 505-507
    deleting records, 470, 523
    editing records, 523-524
    entering
        and revising records keys, 466-468
        formulas, 519-520
        records, 520
    finding records, 521-523

maintaining, 520-524
manipulating, 459-462
    groups of records, 491-500
modifying
    previous records, 469
    records, 469-470
    reports, 525-527
new features, 752
organization of, 461
overview, 19-20
printing
    default report, 524-525
    portion to a range, 505
problems, **728-731**
querying, 462
reports, 503-509
sorting, 462, 470-474, 521
statistical functions, 500-502
undoing changes to records, 469
viewing ranges, 518-519
date and time arithmetic, 201-208
Date format, 144-145
DATE function, 202-203
dates
    converting, 202-203
    displaying, 204-205
    entering in worksheet, 144-145
    extracting, 204
    functions, 202-205
DATEVALUE function, 203, 547
DAVG function, 501
DAY function, 204
day extracting from date, 204
DCA files, 756
DCOUNT function, 501
DDB function, 174
debugging
    formulas, 147
    macros, 576-579
decision-making Command Language commands, 627-630
defaults, 485-486
    directory, 221
    field length or type, 465
default settings
    changing interface, 536
    changing phone, 536-537
    COMM window, 535-539
    PrintGraph, 452
    terminal, 538-539
    text justification, 84
DEFINE command, 623-625
Definition range, 486-487
    modifying, 484-485
Del key, 342, 480
Delete Columns command, **675**
Delete
    command, 114, 122-124, 342, **691**
Delete Global Columns command, 124
Delete Global command, 122
Delete Row command, 330, 482, **675**
deleting
    fields, 491
    files, 220-221
    graph settings, 395
    GRAPH window, 423
    print settings sheets, 375, 377

All bold listings in the index are in the troubleshooting section.

range names, 100
records, 499-500
rows, 238-239
windows, 38-39
depreciation, 173-174
Destination Printer command, 372
Detach command, 46
dictionaries
adding words to, 326
AMERICAN.LEX, 327
auxiliary, 327-331
PERSONAL.LEX, 327
viewing in spreadsheet, 329
Dictionaries Set command, 328
DIR command, **699**
directories
changing, 221
creating, 744
default, 221
font, 432
graph, 432
disks
backup copies, 743, 745
checking space 210
Help and Tutorial, 72-74, 536
Program, 743
Speller and Outliner Add-Ins, 333
storing macro libraries, 596
Symphony Program, 71
Tutorial, 68-72
DISPATCH command, 622-623
displaying
dates, 204-205
DOC window, 249
graphs, 383-428
in color, 401-403
files, 211
Macro Library files, 211
multiple settings, 48
negative numbers, 141
nonSymphony files, 211
numeric punctuation, 138
on-screen, 63-68
print files, 211
time, 207
worksheet files, 211
DLEFT command, 755
DLINE command, 755
DMAX function, 501
DMIN function, 501
DOC
command menu, 251
function keys *see keys*
menu, 24, 249-251, 260, 267, 295
mode, 350-352, 354
switching with OUTLN mode, 350
DOC window, 10, 247-299, 365-366, 369
display, 249
format settings, 255
hands-on practice, 301-319
integrating with other windows, 297-298
DOC window macros, 585-586
letter-transposition, 587
memo, 588
paragraph-erasing, 588
paragraph-moving, 587-588

word-transposition, 587
documenting
Command Language programs, 605
errors, 192
macros, 573
documents, 10, 301-307
creating with outline, 350-355
format lines, 314-315
formatting, 281-289, 307-310
including spreadsheet in, 310-313
indenting sections, 293
moving cursor to beginning or end, 264
outlining existing, 352-354
printing outlined, 354-355
spell-check, 323-332
typing, 301-303
varying format of text, 293
DOS command, **699**
DOS.APP file, 430
double-declining-balance depreciation, 174
DOWJONES file, 536
drawing horizontal lines macro, 583-584
drawing vertical lines macro, 584
DRIGHT command, 755
drivers
file, **664**
installing, 746-749
Universal Text Display, **664-665**
DSTD function, 501
DSUM function, 501, 505, 509
DVAR function, 501
DWORD command, 755

E

edit checks on fields, 488-489
EDIT mode, 84, 89-91, 326, 336, 579
editing
format lines, 294-297
macros, 579
spreadsheet data, 89-91
text, 267-278
End key, 21, 261
pointing with, 117-118
Entry range, 481-483
Erase
command, 21, 114, 117-119, 124, 220, 251, 258, 261, 268, 292, 491, **692**, **697**, **730**
key, 21
erasing
blocks of text erasing, 268-269
characters, 259
entire worksheet, 118-119
text, 267-278
ERR
function, 185-186
message, 87
problem, **674-677**
error-trapping functions, 185-187
errors
correcting typing, 304-307
documenting, 192
in macros, 577-578
Esc key, 51, 98, 116-117
EXACT function, 196

All bold listings in the index are in the troubleshooting section.

Exit command, 34, 47
EXP function, 157
Expanded Memory Specification (EMS), 81
exploded pie chart graphs, 417
Expose command, 39
extensions of file names, *see* file name extensions
Extract command, **730-731**
extracting
    records, 496-497
    strings, 194-195

F

F1 (Help) key, 72-73
F2 (Edit) key, 89-91, 200, 238, 330, 341, 579, **708**
F2 (Justify) key, 250, 256, 269-270, 287-288, 293
F3 (Abs) key, 134-135
F3 (Indent) key, 250, 293, **710**
F4 (Capture) key, 545
F4 (Erase) key, 251, 254, 261-262, 268, 292
F5 (GoTo) key, 102, 150, 251, 266, 337, 350
F6 (Window) key, 38-39, 135, 271, 274, **703-704**
F7 (User) key, 575-576, 658
F8 (Calc) key, 91, 150-151, **715**
F9 (Services) key, 31, 42, 213
F10 (Menu) key, 31, 47, 98, 102-103, 251, 260, 323, 471
FALSE function, 192
Field command, 490
Field Delete command, 491
Field Insert command, 752
Field Move command, 481, 483, 752
fields,
    adding to database, 490
    changing format, 490
    computing, 486-487
    default length, 465
    deleting, 491
    edit checks on, 488-489
    field names, 461
        range, 465
    transforming, 487-488
    type of, 464
    value checks on, 489
    type default, 465
File Bytes command, 210
File Combine Add command, 216-219, **678**, **686**, **701**
File Combine command, 38, 219, 267, 298
File Combine Copy command, 216-219, **686**, **691**, **700-701**
File Combine Copy Named-Area command, 276
File Combine Subtract command, 216, **686**, **692**
File
    command, 209
    menu, 42-43, 210-228
File Directory command, 221, **698-699**, **701**
File Erase command, 220-221, 598
File Import command, 222-223, 225
File Import Numbers command, **701**
File Import Structured command, 222-223
File Import Text command, 222-223, 330, **701**
File List command, 211, **699**
File List Worksheet command, 211
file management, 210-228
file manipulation Command Language commands, 642-649
file name extensions, 209-210

.APP, 210
.CCF, 210
.CTF, 210
.DCT, 328
.MLB, 210, 595
.PIC, 210, 397, 429-430, 654
.PRN, 210, 226-227, 365
.SET, 664
.WR1, 210, 226
file names, 28, 209-210
File operations, 209
    problems, **698-702**
File Retrieve command, 27, 213-215, 274, 276, 500, **699**
File Save command, 23, 27, 38, 47, 212-214, 274, 276, 375, **701-702**
File Table command, 211-212
File Xtract command, 215, 219, 278, 620
File Xtract Formulas command, 215
File Xtract Values command, 215, **685-686**
File-Transfer Receive command, 549, 551-552
File-Transfer Send command, 549, 551-552
File-Translate command, 224
files
    ADP, 536
    AMERICAN.LEX, 327
    and windows, 37-38, 210
    backing up, **699-700**
    close currently open file, 645
    combining, 216-219
    COMMAND.COM, 743, 745
    communications configuration (CCF), 535-536
    COMPUSRV, 536
    configuration, 21, 254-255, 292
    converting WordStar to ASCII, 225-226
    copying
        program, 744
        text, 272-278
    DCA, 756
    deleting, 220-221
    displaying, 211
    DOS.APP, 430
    DOWJONES, 536
    downloading, 560-563
    driver set, **664**
    finding, **699**
    importable file extensions, 223-224
    importing, **701**
    length of file in bytes, 649
    LOTUS.SET, **664-665**
    MACROMGR.APP, 595
    making backup copies of, 214
    MCI, 536
    moving text within same, 269-272
    opening disk file, 643-645
    OUTLINER.APP, 333
    password-protecting, 241-242
    PERSONAL.DCT, 327-328, 330
    printing, 365
        macro, 582
    reading, 645-647
    record file pointer's current position, 649
    retrieving macro, 582-583
    saving macro, 582
    set file pointer to specified value, 648-649
    SIF, 756
    SOURCE, 536

All bold listings in the index are in the troubleshooting section.

SPELLER.APP, 322
storage and retrieval, 212-214
SYLK TM, 756
SYMPHONY.CNF, 43, 254, 292
table, 211-212
    in separate, 243
transferring, 222-227, 551-552
    Symphony files to WordStar, 225-227
    WordStar files to Symphony, 225-226
    with XMODEM, 551
    write string of text to open file, 647, 648
files table, 211-212
FILESIZE command, 649
financial functions, 166-174
FIND function, 192-194
Fixed command, 143-144
floppy disk system installation, 745-746
fonts
    choosing for graphs, 434-435
    directory, 432
footers, **714**
    setting for printing, 369-370
FOR command, 629-630
FORBREAK command, 630
form
    feeds, 438-439
    letters printing, 510-513
FORM
    menu, 470-471, 474
    window, 10-12, 459-460, 462-468, 472, 480, 503, 510,
        548
        advanced feature, 481-491
    macros, 593-595
Format command, 137-140, 203, 391, 490, 755
    DOC Format Edit Current Justification command, 708
    DOC Edit Current Reset command, 258
    DOC Format Justification None command, 331
    DOC Format Location command, 352
    DOC Format Outline-Section command, 353
    DOC Format Settings, 254-258
        changing, 307-308
        DOC window, 255
        guidelines, 256-258
    DOC Format Settings Auto-Justify command, 269-270,
        272, 287
    DOC Format Settings command, 21, 255-258, 281, 285,
        291
    DOC Format Settings Justification command, 282, 284,
        464, 708
    DOC Format Settings Justification None command, 357,
        482
    DOC Format Settings Left command, 370-371, 710
    DOC Format Settings Spacing command, 289, 369, 713
    DOC Format Settings Tabs command, 289
    DOC Format Use-Named command, 297
    SHEET Format Fixed command, 159
    SHEET Format Other Hidden command, 26, 147
    SHEET Format Punctuated command, 142-143
    SHEET Format Time command, 145, 207
    SHEET Settings Format Other Hidden command, 147
    SHEET Settings Format Punctuated command, 142-143
    SHEET Settings Format Time command, 145
format lines, 281-285, 289, 294-297
    and @, 297
    in documents, 314-315

formats
    Bar-Graph, 146
    Currency, 141-142
    Date, 144-145
    Fixed, 143-144
    General, 140-141
    Hidden, 147
    international, 25
    Literal, 146-147
    of field changing, 490
    Percent (%), 144
    punctuation, 142-143
    Recalculation, 150
    Scientific, 146
    Time, 145-146
    Titles, 148-150
    Zero, 147
formatting
    cell, 187
    documents, 281-289, 307-310
    outline, 347-348
    spreadsheets, 313
    worksheet, 137-153
forms, special input, 481
formulas
    @MAX, 101
    @SUM, 101
    and Move command, 115-116
    connecting text strings, 85
    copying, 233-235
    debugging, 147
    entering, 233-235, 311-313
        cell addresses in, 86
        in database, 519-520
        in spreadsheet, 82, 85-88
    relating to values, 85
    using in record selection criteria, 475-476
freezing cells, 148-150
frequency distributions, 109-111
full-duplex, 538
function keys, 38, 56-59
functions, *see also* Symphony functions
    @, 155-208, 545-547
    arguments, 155-160
    ASCII/LICS, 199-201
    data management, 174-180
    date, 202-205
    depreciation, 173-174
    error-trapping, 185-187
    financial, 166-174
    logical, 180-188
    mathematical, 156-160
    overview, 24-25
    problems, **693-697**
    special, 188-192
    statistical, 160-166
    string, 192-199
    Symphony, 87
    time, 205-207
    trigonometric, 160
future value of annuity, 168-169
FV function, 168-169

All bold listings in the index are in the troubleshooting section.

G

General command, 140-141
Generate command, 463-465, 476, 478, 481-482, 491, 503, 548, 656
GET command, 607
GETLABEL command, 607-609
GETNUMBER command, 609
GETPOS command, 649
Go command, 368
GoTo (F5) key, 21, 264-265
grammar function key, 572
Graph 1st-Settings Cancel Entire-Row B command, **726**
Graph 1st-Settings Hue command, **720**
Graph 1st-Settings Name Create command, **719-720**
Graph 1st-Settings Name Use command, **719**
Graph 2nd Settings command, 388
Graph 2nd-Settings Other Skip command, **723**
Graph 2nd-Settings Titles command, 388
Graph
    command, 383, 385-386, 422
    menu, 384, 387, 390, 397
GRAPH window, 10, 12-14, 383-384, 387, 422-425
    deleting, 423
    macros, 589-591
        graph printing, 590-591
        choose a graph, 590
        graph preview, 590
graphs, 10, 383-428, 441, 447-449
    adding
        grids, 412
        labels, 388-390
        titles, 388-390
    adjusting size and orientation, 433-434
    advanced topics, 421-428
    aspect ratio, 414
    attaching, 449-451
    bar graph crosshatches, 399-400
    batch printing, 438
    changing
        automatic scale settings, 390-391
        to nonzero origin, 393
    choosing
        fonts, 434-435
        page size, 437
        range-colors, 435-437
    complex bar, 398-403
    controlling lines and symbols, 408-409
    data labels, 409-411
    deleting settings, 395
    directory, 432
    displaying, 383-428
    fitting to scales, 392
    formatting numbers, 391
    grids adding, 412
    hiding parts, 428
    high-low-close-open, 419-421
    line, 404-412
    named, 447-451
    overriding automatic scale, 391
    overview, 20
    pie chart, 412-417
    preview macro, 590
    printing, 429-440, 451-455, **725**
        and exiting, 439-440
    files, 34
    macro, 590-591
    problems, **719-727**
    recalling settings, 393-396
    resetting settings, 396-397
    saving
        for printing, 397, 451-452
        settings, 393-396
    selecting files to print, 437
    simple bar, 385-397
    special command options, 425
    stacked-bar, 403
    types of, 384-428
    using, 447-449
        legends, 401
    viewing, 387
    what if, 423
    XY, 417-419
guidelines for format settings, 256-258

H

half-duplex, 538
hands-on practice
    communications, 553-563
    creating and printing graphs, 441-455
    data management, 515-527
    DOC window, 301-319
    SHEET window, 229-244
HANDSHAKE command, 642
handshaking, 543
hangup macro, 592
hard disk system installing Symphony, 744
hard space, 258
hardware requirements, 15
Hardware menu, 432
headers, 82-84
    setting for printing, 369-370
headings (outlines)
    changing levels, 345-347
    editing, 341
    for outlines, 334-336
    hiding and exposing, 337, 339
    inserting additional, 341
    removing from, 342
Help and Tutorial disk, 72-74, 536
Help Index, 72-74
Hide command, 39
hiding
    and exposing headings keys, 339
    columns, 136
    parts of graphs, 428
hierarchical menus, 32
high-low-close-open graphs, 419-421
highlighting
    cells, 116
    misspelled words, 324-326
HLOOKUP function, 175-179
Home key, 149
HOUR function, 207
hours extracted from time, 207
hyperspace, 596
hyphenated words, 324

All bold listings in the index are in the troubleshooting section.

I

IF
    command, 627-629
    function, 181-188
Image menu, 433, 435
Image settings for printing graphs, 433
Image-Save
    command, 654
    series of graphs Command Language program, 654
Image-Select command, 437
importing files, **701**
indenting
    changing outlines, 349-350
    sections of documents, 293
INDEX function, 179-180
INDICATE command, 639
indirect cell reference, 191
initializing
    string sending to printer, 373-374
    Symphony, 746
input, 607-611
input forms, 463-465
    creating special, 481
    using multiple, 491
Ins key, 334, 341
Insert Columns command, 120
Insert
    command, 114, 119-121, 334, 336, 341, 503, 508
    mode, 258-259, 293, 296
Insert Global command, 119, 121
Insert Row command, 19, 120, 162, 330, 479
inserting
    hard space, 258
    rows, 238-239
Install program, 34
installing
    drivers, 746-749
    problems, **664-667**
    Symphony, 743-749
    floppy disk system, 745-746
    hard disk system, 744
INT function, 157
integer convert dates to, 202-203
integrating
    applications, 10-14, 17-18
    DOC window with other windows, 297-298
interest rate periodic, 172
interface
    card for printing, 432
    changing settings, 536
Interface
    command, 536
    matching settings, 549
internal rate of return, 169-171
international character set, 25
invisible commands, 602
Invoke command, 46
IRR function, 169-171
    sporadic cash flow problem, 170
    value returned unreasonable problem, 170
ISERR function, 186-187
ISNA function, 186-187
ISNUMBER function, 187-188
Isolate command, 39

ISSTRING function, 187-188
Italic print attribute, 253
Italic subscript print attribute, 253
Italic superscript print attribute, 253
Italic underline print attribute, 253
iterations in recalculation, 152-153

J-K

Join command, 343-344
justification, **709-710**
    paragraphs, 282-289
    setting, 282-285
Justify command, 269-270, 272, 287-288, 293
Justify Paragraph command, 250

keynames new macro, 755
keypad (numeric), 54-55
keys
    Abs (F3), 134-135
    Alt, **735**
    Backspace, 259
    Begin Attribute (Ctrl-B), 253
    Calc (F8), 91, 150-151, **715**
    Caps Lock, 55
    Capture (F4), 545
    Center (Alt-F4), 250
    Compose (Alt-F1), 250, 258, **710**
    Ctrl-Break, 32, 51
    cursor movement, 59-63, 260-268
    Del, 342, 480
    Draw (Alt-F8), 38, 423-425, 437
    Edit (F2), 89-91, 200, 238, 330, 341, 579, **708**
    editing outlines, 341
    End, 21, 117-118, 261
    End Attribute (Ctrl-E), 253
    Enter (represented by tilde [~]), 568
    entering and revising database records, 466-468
    Erase (F4), 21, 251, 254, 261-262, 268, 292
    Esc, 51, 98, 116-117
    function, 56-59
    GoTo (F5), 21, 102, 150, 251, 264-266, 337, 350
    Help (F1), 72-73
    hiding and exposing headings in outlines, 339
    Home, 149
    Indent (F3), 250, 293, **710**
    Ins, 334, 341
    Justify (F2), 250, 256, 269-270, 287-288, 293
    Learn (Alt-F5), 571-572
    Macro (Alt), 575
    Menu (F10), 31, 47, 98, 102-103, 251, 260, 323, 333, 464, 471
    new word-processing shortcut, 753-754
    Num Lock, 55
    Paste (Ctrl-P), 268
    period (.), 116
    Scroll Lock, 55
    selecting commands, 98
    Services (F9), 31, 42, 213
    slash (/), 47, 98
    special combination, 59
    Split (Alt-F3), 250
    Step (Alt-F7), 605
    Switch (Alt-F9), 38-39, 50

All bold listings in the index are in the troubleshooting section.

Tab, 337
Type (Alt-F10), 31, 36, 38, 50, 248, 334, 350, 482
User (F7), 575-576, **658**, **735**
Where (Alt-F2), 250
Window (F6), 38-39, 135, 271, 274, **703-704**
Zoom (Alt-F6), 38-40, **703**
keystrokes
    collection of, 567
    recording macro, 571-572

L

LABEL mode, 82
label prefixes, 187, 605, **668**
    (|), **716**
    characters, 82, 84
labels
    adding to graphs, 388-390
    entering, 230-232, 311-313
        in spreadsheet, 82-84
    naming ranges from adjacent, 100
    repeating, 197
        on multipage printouts, 372-373
Learn mode, 27-28, 571-572
LEFT function, 194-195
legends in graph, 401
LENGTH function, 195
LET command, 630-632
letter-transposition macro, 587
LICS
    characters, 200-201
    copying files, 222
line graphs, 404-412
Line-Marker Assign command, 297
Line-Marker command, 265-266
lines
    controlling in graphs, 408-409
    erasing and editing, 267-268
    format, 281-285, 289
    moving cursor, 262-267
Literal format, 146-147
locating one string within another, 192-193
lock key indicators, 55-56
LOG function, 157
log-in
    automating sequence, 556-558
    macro, 592-593
    sequence, 540-544
logarithmic scale override, 425-426
logging off communications, 549
logical functions, 180-188
    and strings, 184-185
    table, 180
logical
    operators, 181-182
    statements, 181-185
Login menu, 540-542
LOOK command, 610-611
lookup table, 175-179
Lotus Command Language *see Command Language*
Lotus International Character Set (LICS), 25, 199
LOTUS.SET file, **664-665**
LOWER function, 196
lowercase conversion of strings, 196

M

macro key representation table, 569-570
macro keynames, 755
macro libraries, 28, 596-599
Macro Library Manager, 595-596
MACRO window, 572
MACROMGR.APP file, 595
macros, 27-28, 567-599
    automatic, 576
    COMM window, 591
        auto-dialing, 592
        capture, 593
        hangup, 592
        log-in, 592-593
    common errors in, 577-578
    debugging, 576-579
    DOC window, 585-586
        letter-transposition, 587
        memo, 588
        paragraph-erasing, 588
        paragraph-moving, 587-588
        word-transposition, 587
    documenting, 573
    editing, 579
    errors,
        absolute reference, 578
        omitting tilde (~), 577
        placing braces, 577
    executing, 575-576, 579
    file retrieving, 582-583
    FORM window
        search, 593-594
        sort, 594-595
    GRAPH window, 589
        choose a graph, 590
        graph preview, 590
        graph printing, 590-591
    invoking, 575-576
        from library, 596-597
    naming, 573-575
        with range names, 100
    placing in windows, 572
    printing files, 582
    problems, **735-741**
    recording keystrokes, 571-572
    saving files, 581-582
    SHEET window
        data-entry, 585
        drawing lines, 583-584
        setting column widths, 585
        summing a column, 584
    Spelling Checker, 588-589
    tilde (~) key, 568
    using, 567-599
    utility macros for any environment, 581-583
Macros Edit command, 597
Macros Load command, 596
Macros Name-List command, 597
Macros Remove command, 598
Macros Save command, 598
mailing labels printing, 509-510
Main report range, 503-504
maintaining database, 520-524
Maintenance Add command, 328

All bold listings in the index are in the troubleshooting section.

Maintenance command, 329
managing
    data, 19-20, 459-513
    files, 210-228
manipulating database, 459-462
manual recalculation, 150-151
margins, **710-713**
    setting, 289-291, 370-371
markers
    page break (::), 292
mathematical
    function, 156-160
    operators, 86-87
    relationship in models, 18-19
MAX function, 163
maximum values, 163
Maximum-Time setting, 541-542
MD command, 744
mean, 163-165
median, 164
memo macro, 588
memory
    checking available, 79
    limitations, 78-81
    management problems, **677-679**
Menu key, 333, 464
MENUBRANCH command, 614-616
MENUCALL command, 616-617
menus
    1st-Settings, 386
    1st-Settings Range, 398, 406
    1st-Settings Type, 413
    Access System, 24, 31-35, 224, 430
    Application, 45-46, 322, 333
    COMM, 535, 543-544, 549
    command, 24, 31, 47
    Configuration, 43-45, 255, **666**
    Delete, 123
    DOC, 249-251, 260, 267, 295
    File, 42-43, 210-228
    FORM, 470-471, 474
    Format, 139-147
    Graph, 384, 387, 390, 397
    Hardware, 432
    hierarchical, 32
    Image, 433, 435
    Login, 540-542
    Name, 375
    New, 46
    OUTLN, 335, 340
    Print, 43, 227, 363-364, 377, 505, 650
    PrintGraph, 439-440
    Query, 492-493
    Range, 99-113, 387, 390, 398
    SERVICES, 31, 35-47, 79, 106, 209-210, 214, 227, 249,
        255, 278, 368, 595-596, 749
    Settings, 46, 433, 436, 438, 470-471, 536, 538, 540, 543
    Spelling Checker, 326
        correction, 324-325
    sticky, 50-51
    Symphony, 31-51
    TYPE, 50
    Verify, 323
    Verify Settings, 331
    Window, 36, 38
    window TYPE, 31

MERGE command, 755
merging outline sections, 343-344
MIC file, 536
MIN function, 163
minimum values, 163
MINUTE function, 207
misspelled words
    deleting, 329
    highlighting, 324-326
mixed cell addressing, 130-133
MOD function, 159-160
models of mathematical relationships, 18-19
modems, 532
modes, 164
    all windows, 66
    DOC, 350-354
    EDIT, 84, 89-91, 326, 336, 579
    indicators, 65-68
    Insert, 258-259, 293, 296
    LABEL, 82
    Learn, 27-28, 571-572
    OUTLN, 337, 350-354
    Overstrike, 258-259, 293, 296
    Overtype, **709**
    POINT, 86, 125
    Shared, 383
    SHEET, 89, 356
    for specific windows, 67
    Step, 579, 605
    VALUE, 86
Modify command, 329
modifying
    macro libraries, 597-598
    outline, 340-350
MONTH function, 204
Move command, 114-118, 267, 269-270, 336, 345, 483, 491,
    503, 508, 675, **691**, 755
multiple input forms, 491

N

N function, 199, **697**
NA function, 185-186
Name
    command, 331, 394
    menu, 375
Name Create command, 395
Name Initial-Settings command, 396
Name Reset command, 395
Name Retrieve command, 331
Name Use command, 394-395, 422
named graphs, 447-451
naming, 28-29
    files, 28, 209-210
    line-markers, 265-266
    macros, 573-575
    print settings sheets, 375, 377
    ranges, 28, 99-103
    settings sheets, 28, 473
natural recalculation, 151-152
negative numbers, 141
net present value, 166-167
New
    command, 118-119

All bold listings in the index are in the troubleshooting section.

menu, 46
new features
    communications, 754-755
    database, 752
    Symphony Release 2.0, 751-756
    translate program, 756
    word processing, 752-754
New Yes command, 330
Next command, 375, 474
NEXTPAGE command, 755
nonblank entries, 163
nonzero origin in graphs, 393
NOW function, 205
NPV function, 166-167
Num Lock key, 55
number of
    investment time periods, 172-173
    time periods of annuity, 169
numeric format codes for CONTENTS command table, 634
Numbering Delete-Numbers command, 352, 354, 357
Numbering Renumber command, 352
numbers
    converting
        telecommunicated to usable form, 545
        to strings, 197-199
    displaying in outlines, 337
    entering, 232-233
        in spreadsheet, 82, 84
    filling ranges with, 108-109
    formatting in graphs, 391
    random, 158
    removing from outline, 352
    rounding, 158-159
    serial, 202
numeric
    keypad, 54-55
    values converting to string values, 199

O

offset-number, 175
on-screen prompts, 490
ONERR command, 619-621
OPEN command, 643-645
operations of File, 209
operators
    #AND#, 182, 729
    #NOT#, 182, 729
    #OR#, 182, 729
    < (less than), 181
    <= (less than or equal to), 181
    <> (not equal), 181
    = (equal), 181
    > (greater than), 181
    >= (greater than or equal), 181
    complex logical, 182
    mathematical, 86-87
    order of precedence, 87
    simple logical, 181-182
    string, 86-87
optimal recalculation, 151-152

OR to combine record selection criteria, 477
ordinary annuity, 168
organization of database, 461
orientation of graphs, 433-434
OUTLINER.APP file, 333
outlines, 332-357
    changing
        heading levels, 345-347
        indentation, 349-350
    copying sections, 345
    creating document with, 350-355
    cursor-movement keys, 337
    displaying numbers in, 337
    editing
        headings, 341
        keys, 341
    formatting, 347-348
    from existing document, 352-354
    headings, 334-336
        hiding and exposing, 337, 339
        inserting additional, 341
    merging sections, 343-344
    modifying, 340-350
    moving
        around in, 337
        sections, 345
    printing, 339-340
    removing
        headings, 342
        numbers, 352
    table of contents from, 356-357
    text, 265
OUTLN
    menu, 335, 340
    mode, 337, 350-352, 354
        switching with DOC mode, 350
    window, 332-334
overall-string, 193
Overstrike mode, 258-259, 293, 296
Overtype mode, 709
overview
    communications, 22-23
    databases, 19-20
    functions, 24-25
    graphs, 20
    security, 25-27
    spreadsheets, 16-19
    Symphony, 9-30
        Release 2.0, 29
    windows, 23
    word processing, 21-22

P

page break (::) marker, 292, 512, 717
Page command, 292, 509, **714**, **717**, 755
Page Length command, **718**
page size for graphs, 437
Page-Advance command, **715-716**
pages
    aligning, 716

All bold listings in the index are in the troubleshooting section.

controlling length, 292
moving cursor, 264-265
setting length, 374
Pane command, 39
PANELOFF command, 637
PANELON command, 637
paper advancing in printer, 438
paragraphs
    automatic justification, 287
    erasing
        and editing, 267-268
        macro, 588
    justifying, 282-289
    moving
        cursor to beginning or end, 262
        macro, 587-588
parameters protocol, 533-534
parity, 534
password-protecting files, 241-242, **702**
PASTE command, 755
pausing printer, 438
payment per period, 171-172
Percent (%) format, 144
periodic
    investment interest rate, 172
    payments, 171-172
period (.) key, 116
PERSONAL.DCT file, 327-330
phone settings, 536-537
Phone Answer command, 549
Phone Call command, 549
Phone command, 536, 543, 641
Phone Hangup command, 549
Phone Wait-Mode command, 550
Phone-and-Login command, **733-734**
PI function, 160
pie charts, 412-417, 444-446
PMT function, 171-172
POINT mode, 86, 125
pointing, 116-118, 122
population statistics, 164
precedence of operators, 87
present value of annuity, 168
Preview command, 387, 406
Previous command, 375, 474
Print Align command, 369-370, 377, **712**
print
    attributes, 308-310
        commands, 253-254
    current date (@) special character, 369-370
    file, 365
Print
    command, 340, 368, 504, 509, 513, **715**, **731**
    menu, 43, 227, 363-364, 377, 505, 650
Print Go command, 354, 364, 377
Print Line-Advance command, 377, **712**
print options
    setting, 368-370
print page number (#) special characters, 369-370
Print Page-Advance command, **712**, **714**
print ranges
    designating, 368
    specifying, **717**

Print Settings command, 222, 362-363, 375, 377, 503-504
Print Settings Destination Erase command, 365
Print Settings Destination File command, 330, 365, 377
Print Settings Destination Printer command, 365
Print Settings Destination Range command, 365, 377
Print Settings Init-String command, 373-374, **718**
Print Settings Margins command, 370-371
Print Settings Margins Left command, **710**
Print Settings Margins No-Margins command, 365
Print Settings Margins Right command, **713**
Print Settings Name command, 375
Print Settings Name Create command, **715**
Print Settings Name Delete command, 375
Print Settings Name Initial-Settings command, **715**
Print Settings Name Reset command, 377
Print Settings Name Use command, 375, **715**
Print Settings Other Format command, 374
Print Settings Other Left-Labels command, 372-373
Print Settings Other Top-Labels command, 372-373
Print Settings Page Length command, 292, 374
Print Settings Page Length setting command, 265
Print Settings Page Number command, 369
Print Settings Page Number Print-Number command, **716**
Print Settings Page Number Start-Page command, 370
print settings sheets, 355, 375, 377
Print Settings Source Cancel command, 355
Print Settings Source command, 510
Print Settings Source Range command, 226, 354, 368, 372
print size controls, 373-374
Print Source Range command, 357
printers
    advancing paper, 438
    configuring, 749
    controlling, 377
    pausing, 438
    selecting, 431
    sending
        initializing string, 373-374
        reports to, 504-505
PrintGraph, 429-440
    changing settings, 453-454
    configuration, 430-433
    menu, 439-440
    program, 34
PrintGraph settings sheet, 431
printing
    and exiting graphs, 439-440
    cell formulas, 374-376
    form letters, 510-513
    form feeds, 438-439
    graphs, 429-440, 451-455, **725**
        changing PrintGraph settings, 453-454
        default PrintGraph settings, 452
        files, 34
        Image settings, 433
        selecting files, 437
    hiding columns to prevent printing, 368
    mailing labels, 509-510
    multiple copies Command Language program, 650-653
    outlined document, 354-355
    outlines, 339-340
    problems, **664-666**, **712-718**
    repeating labels on multipage printouts, 372-373

All bold listings in the index are in the troubleshooting section.

reports, 366-368, 378-382
saving graphs, 397
setting headers and footers, 369-370
specifying interface card, 432
spreadsheets, 361-382
to a file, 365
to a range, 365-366
top of page marker, 438-439
word-processing documents, 361-382
problems
    absolute addressing, **684**
    circular reference, **670-674**
    communications, **732-734**
    data
        destruction, **691-692**
        entry, **668-669**
    database, **728-731**
    ERR, **674-677**
    file operations, **698-702**
    functions, **693-697**
    graphing, **719-727**
    installation, **664-667**
    macros, **735-741**
    memory management, **677-679**
    printing, **664-666**, **712-718**
    range names, **680-683**
    recalculation, **685-690**
    relative addressing, **684**
    spreadsheet, **668-679**
    Symphony commands, **680-692**
    template, **692**
    windows, **703-706**
    word processing, **707-711**
Program disk, 743
Program Help and Tutorial disk, 536
programs
    alerting user with a tone, 636-637
    branching to location directed by argument, 622-623
    calling one subroutine from another, 626-627
    Command Language, 650-658
    control
        Command Language commands, 611-627
        program flow, 627-629
        to specific cell address, 613-614
    controlling looping process in programs, 629-630
    creating Command Language, 604-605
    custom mode indicators, 639
    debugging Command Language, 604-605
    elements of Command Language, 603-604
    end of subroutine execution, 617-618
    enhancement Command Language commands, 635-642
    freezing bottom of the screen, 637-639
    Install, 34
    interrupting FOR command, 630
    menu
        program as subroutine, 616-617
        selection of multiple, 614-616
    moving between, 32
    pausing
        for specified time, 621-622
        while data input, 606-607
    phoning remote computer, 641

preventing user from using Ctrl-Break, 621
PrintGraph, 34
proceeding after system error, 619-621
program control to specific cell address, 611-612
recalculating portions of worksheet, 639-641
restoring use of Ctrl-Break, 621
sending single line messages to remote computers, 642
subroutine call with parameters, 623-625
terminate unconditionally, 618-619
turning off display of commands, 637
turning on display of commands, 637
unfreezing bottom of the screen, 639
prompts changing on-screen, 490
PROPER function, 196
protecting
    cells, 239-242
        before copying, 217
    ranges, 104-107
    worksheets, 25-27
protocols, 22
    B, 22, 533
    BLAST, 22, 533
    parameters, 533-534
    XMODEM, 22, 533
    XON/XOFF (Ctrl-Q/Ctrl-S), 543
punctuation
    controlling numeric display, 138
    format, 142-143
PUT command, 632-633
PV function, 168

Q

Query
    command, 491, **728**, **730**
    menu, 492-493
Query Delete command, 498-500
Query Extract command, 496-497, **730**
Query Find command, 493-495, 499, **730**
Query Parse command, 223, 545, 547-548, **701**
Query Record-Sort command, 473, 492
Query Settings Basic Criterion command, **728**
Query Settings Basic Database command, 492
Query Settings Cancel Sort-Keys command, **731**
Query Settings command, 492, 494
Query settings sheet, 492-493
Query Settings Sort-Keys command, **731**
Query Unique command, 497
querying database, 462
Quit command, 51, 364, 618-619

R

RAM
    effect of worksheet size, 78-81
    storing macro libraries in, 596
RAND function, 158
random numbers, 158

All bold listings in the index are in the troubleshooting section.

Range
 command, 386
 menu, 99-113, 387, 390, 398
Range Distribution command, 109-111
Range Fill command, 108-109, 111, 200, 226, 507
Range Label-Alignment command, 84
Range Name command, 99-103
Range Name Create command, 99-100, 276, 574, **682**, **735**
Range Name Delete command, 100, **682**
Range Name Labels command, 99-100
Range Name Labels Right command, 575, 605, 624
Range Name Reset command, 100
Range Name Table command, 100
range names, 28, 99-103
 in macro libraries, 598-599
 problems, **680-683**
 unnamed, **669**
Range Protect Allow-Changes command, 106, 692
Range Protect command, 26-27, 104-107, 218
Range Protect Prevent-Changes command, 106
Range Transpose command, 103-104
Range Values command, 104, 200, 547, 657, **679**, **686**
Range What-If 2-Way command, 113
Range What-If command, 19, 111-113, **679**
ranges, 91-93, 100, 175
 Above report, 503
 Below report, 507-508
 capturing data in, 545-560
 colors choosing for graphs, 435-437
 criterion, 477-480
 Definition, 486-487
 deleting names, 100
 describing, 191
 designating, 93
 field names, 465
 filling with numbers, 108-109
 Main report, 503-504
 modifying
  Definition, 484-485
  Entry, 481-483
 naming from adjacent labels, 100
 pointing to, 117-118
 printing, 365-366, 505
 protecting, 104-107
 restricting, 37, 264, 269, 272
  in windows, 41-42
  MACRO window, 572
 retrieving data from specified, 179-180
 sending, 550-551
 setting width of captured columns, 546-547
 shape of, 92
 specifying records to be sorted, 492
 table of names, 100
 totalling, 161-162
 viewing database, 518-519
RATE function, 172
READ command, 645-647
READLN command, 647
RECALC command, 639-641, **687**, **690**, **736-737**
RECALCCOL command, 639-641, **687-690**, **736-737**
recalculating spreadsheets, 243
recalculation, 151-153
 changing order of, 151-152
 problems, 685-690
 speed, 81
Recalculation format, 150
Receive strings, 541-542
Record Sort command, 471-473, **731**
records, 461
 adding new, 469
 approximate matching labels, 479
 criteria for selection, 474-477
 deleting, 470, 499-500
  from database, 523
 editing in database, 523-524
 entering, 466-468, 520
 extracting, 496-497
 finding in database, 521-523
 manipulating groups of database, 491-500
 modifying
  and deleting while searching, 480-481
  before placing in database, 469-470
  previous database, 469
 searching for, 474-497
  with wildcards, 480
 selecting unique, 497
 sorting range, 492
 undeleting, 469, 500
 using
  AND to combine criteria for selection, 476-477
  formulas in criteria for selection, 475-476
  OR to combine criteria for selection, 477
redial Command Language program, 656
redisplaying windows, 39
references
 cells, 134-135
 circular, 152-153
regression line, 418
relative addressing, 127-132
 problems, **684**
remainders, 159-160
removing
 macro libraries, 598
 unwanted LICS characters, 201
 windows, 39
RENAME command, 223
REPEAT function, 197
Repeat-Time setting, 542
repeating labels or strings, 197
repetition in headers, 83
Replace command, 21, 278, 280-281, 755
REPLACE function, 195
replacing text, 278-281, 316-318
reports
 creating in databases, 524-527
 database, 503-509
 entering data at end, 507-509
 examples of printing, 366-368
 modifying in database, 525-527
 printing database default report, 524-525
 sending to printer, 504-505
Reset menu, 433
RESTART command, 626-627
restoring hidden columns, 136

All bold listings in the index are in the troubleshooting section.

Restrict Range command, 572
restricted
    cell pointer movement, 149-150
    ranges, 37, 264, 269, 272
results of printing reports, 378-382
retrieval of files, 212-214
return
    internal rate, 169-171
RETURN command, 617-618
reverse video, 92, 116
RIGHT function, 194-195
ROUND function, 158-159, **672**, **693**
rounding numbers, 158-159
row-by-row recalculation, 151-152
rows
    changing to columns, 103-104
    deleting, 238-239
        in worksheet, 122-124
    headers, 82-84
    inserting, 238-239
        blank in worksheet, 119-121
ROWS function, 191

S

S function, 199, **696-697**
sample statistics, 164
Save menu, 433
saving
    auxiliary dictionaries, 330-331
    configuration settings, 548
    files macro, 581
    graphs for printing, 451-452
    part of worksheet file, 215
scales
    changing Y-Axis width, 426
    fitting graphs to, 392
    logarithmic override, 425-426
scaling labels automatically, 426-428
scatter plots, 417
Scientific format, 146
scientific notation, 140
screens
    clearing, 330
    display, 63-68
    moving cursor to next, 262-263
Scroll Lock key, 55
search and replace strings character in DOC window, 279
Search command, 21, 260-261, 278, 280-281, 755
search macro, 593-594
search-string, 193
searching
    for records, 474-481, 493-497
        modifying and deleting while searching, 480-481
    for strings, 279-281
    for text, 278-281
    with wildcards, 279
SECOND function, 207
section markers, 350
security overview, 25-27

Select Configuration Other International Negative command, 141
Select Name command, 536
selecting
    criteria of records, 474-477
    from list, 174-175
    printer, 431
    unique records, 497
Send strings, 541-542
sentences
    capitalizing first word, 324326
    erasing and editing, 267-268
separate segments of header or footer (|) special character, 369-370
serial number, 202
    from time values, 206
SERVICES menu, 31, 35-47, 79, 106, 209-210, 214, 227, 249, 255, 278, 368, 595-596, 749
SETPOS command, 648-649
setting
    margins, 289-371
    page length, 374
    print options, 368-370
    spacing, 289-291
    tabs, 289-291
settings
    communications, 554-558
    configuration, 43-45
    displaying multiple, 48
    format, 255-258
    Justification, 282-285
    matching Interface, 549
    Maximum-Time, 541-542
    recalling graph, 393-396
    Repeat-Time, 542
    resetting graph, 396-397
    saving graph, 393-396
Settings commands, 38, 79, 430, 497, **671**, **678**
    COMM Settings Capture Erase command, 545
    COMM Settings Capture Printer command, 544
    COMM Settings Capture Range command, 545, 552
    COMM Settings Interface command, **733**
    COMM Settings Login command, 540
    COMM Settings Name Create command, 544
    COMM Settings Name Phone-and-Login command, 544
    COMM Settings Name Retrieve command, 548
    COMM Settings Name Save command, 548
    COMM Settings Name Use command, 473
    COMM Settings Phone Number command, 537, 543
    COMM Settings Send command, 550
    COMM Settings Send Format command, 754
    COMM Settings Terminal Delay command, 540, 544
    COMM Settings Terminal Echo Yes command, **734**
    COMM Settings Terminal Linefeed Yes command, **734**
    FORM Settings Basic Criterion command, 477-479, **728**
    FORM Settings Basic Database command, 471-494
    FORM Settings Cancel Report command, 510
    FORM Settings Cancel Sort-Keys command, **731**
    FORM Settings Form Definition command, 485
    FORM Settings Form Entry command, 482
    FORM Settings Report command, 503
    FORM Settings Report Main command, 510

All bold listings in the index are in the troubleshooting section.

FORM Settings Report Type command, 506
FORM Settings Report Type Multiple command, 507
FORM Settings Sort-Keys command, **731**
FORM Settings Underscores No command, 484
PrintGraph Settings Hardware Interface command, **667**
PrintGraph Settings Hardware Printer command, **667, 725**
PrintGraph Settings Hardware Size-Paper command, 437
PrintGraph Settings Image Size Manual command, **725**
PrintGraph Settings Save command, **667**
SERVICES Settings Auto-Execute command, 605
SERVICES Settings Auto-Execute Set command, 576
SERVICES Settings Global-Protection command, 26-27, 106, 218, 332
SERVICES Settings Global-Protection Yes command, **692**
SERVICES Settings Learn Range command, 571
SERVICES Settings Security Unlock command, 27
SHEET Settings Format command, 138-139, 141-142
SHEET Settings Format Currency command, 141
SHEET Settings Format Date command, 144
SHEET Settings Format Other Hidden command, 147
SHEET Settings Format Punctuated command, 142
SHEET Settings Format Time command, 145
SHEET Settings Recalculation command, 150-153
SHEET Settings Recalculation Method Manual command, **685**
SHEET Settings Recalculation Order Optimal command, 751
SHEET Settings Titles Both command, 149
SHEET Settings Titles command, 148-150
SHEET Settings Width command, 136-137
SHEET Settings Zero command, 147, 751
Settings menu, 46, 433, 436, 438, 470-471, 536, 538, 540, 543
settings sheets, 24, 35, 47-50, 138-139
    attaching, 474
    catalogs, 394-395, 474
    naming, 28, 473
    Print, 355
    PrintGraph, 431
    Query, 492-493
    Spelling Checker, 327-328, 331
Shared mode, 383
SHEET
    menu, 84, 97-99
    mode, 89, 356
SHEET window, 10, 12, 77-96, 383-384, 387, 463, 472, 491-493, 547
    commands, 97-154
    hands-on practice, 229-244
    macros
        data-entry, 585
        drawing horizontal lines, 583-584
        drawing vertical lines, 584
        summing a column, 584
    setting column widths, 585
    simple bar graph, 385-386
    with other windows, 93-96
shortcut keys new word-processing commands, 753-754
SIF files, 756
simple bar graphs, 385-397
    adding titles and labels, 388-390
    data range, 387

SHEET window, 385-386
SIN function, 160
skipping columns or rows Command Language program, 653-654
slash (/) key, 47, 98
SLN function, 173
sort macro, 594-595
sorting database, 462, 470-474
SOURCE file, 536
spacing setting, 289-291
special
    characters, 369-370
    combination keys, 59
    command options for graphs, 425
    functions, 188-192
speed of recalculation, 81
spell-check
    automatic correction, 324
    documents, 323-332
    spreadsheets, 331-332
Speller and Outliner Add-Ins disk, 333
SPELLER.APP file, 322
Spelling Checker, 22, 29, 321-332
    attaching, 322-323
    configuration file, 331
    correction menu, 324-325
    invoking, 322-323
    macros, 588-589
    menus, 326
    settings sheet, 327-328, 331
spreadsheets, 10, 77-91
    and expanded memory, 81
    changing, 237-239
    commands, 97-154
    copying contents, 219
    editing data, 89-91
    entering
        data, 82-88
        formulas, 82, 85-88
        labels, 82-84
        numbers, 82, 84
        string formulas, 88
    formatting, 313
    including in document, 310-313
    large, 242-243
    memory limitations, 78-81
    overview, 16-19
    printing, 361-382
    problems, **668-679**
    recalculating, 243
    spell-checking, 331-332
    viewing dictionaries in, 329
SQRT function, 157, 166
stacked-bar graphs, 403
standard deviation, 164
statements, logical, 181-185
statistical functions, 160-166
    database, 500-502
STD function, 164-166
Step mode, 579, 605
sticky menus, 50-51
stop bits, 534

All bold listings in the index are in the troubleshooting section.

storing
    files, 212-214
    format lines, 294-297
straight-line depreciation, 173
Strike-through print attribute, 253
strings
    and logical functions, 184-185
    comparing, 196
    conversions, 196-199, 203, 206
    eliminating blank spaces, 197
    extracting, 194-195
    finding length of, 195
    formulas entered in spreadsheets, 88
    function, 192-199, **693**, **695-696**
    locating one within another, 192-193
    operators, 86-87
    Receive, 541-542
    repeating, 197
    replacing characters in, 195
    search, 193
    searching for, 279-281
    Send, 541-542
    start-number, 193
    values converting to numeric values, 199
subdirectories, **698**, 744
Subscript print attribute, 253
subtotals in databases, 505-507
SUM function, 87, 101, 161, 162
sum-of-the-years'-digits depreciation, 173
Superscript print attribute, 253
switching between 1st-Settings and 2nd-Settings sheets, 390
SYD function, 173
SYLK TM files, 756
symbols in graphs, 408-409
Symphony
    disks making working copies, 746
    display area, 63-68
    entering, 33-34
    environments, 10-11
    exiting, 33-34
    files transferring to WordStar, 225-227
    initializing, 746
    installing, 743-749
    keyboard, 51-63
    menus, 31-51
    overview, 9-30
    Program disk, 71
    Release 2.0 new features, 751-756
Symphony Command Language *see Command Language*
Symphony commands
    1st-Settings Cancel, 396
    1st-Settings Cancel Entire-Row B, **726**
    1st-Settings Cancel Entire-Row Graph, 397
    1st-Settings Format, 407
    1st-Settings Hue, 400, 402, 417, **720**
    1st-Settings Legend, 401
    1st-Settings Name Create, **719-720**
    1st-Settings Name Delete, 395
    1st-Settings Name Use, **719**
    1st-Settings Type Stacked-Bar, 403
    2nd-Setting Other Origin, 393
    2nd-Settings Name Delete, 395

2nd-Settings Other, 415, 428
2nd-Settings Other Aspect, 414
2nd-Settings Other Grid, 412
2nd-Settings Other Skip, 406, **723**
2nd-Settings X-Scale, 391
2nd-Settings X-Scale Format Other, 428
2nd-Settings Y-Scale, 391, 426
2nd-Settings Y-Scale Exponent, 427
2nd-Settings Y-Scale Format Other, 428
2nd-Settings Y-Scale Type, 425
2nd-Settings Y-Scale Type Automatic-Linear, 426
Action Eject, 438
Action Pause, 438
Answer, 550
Application, 214, 595
Application Attach, 322-333
Application Clear, 334
Application Detach, 323-334
Attach, 46, 474, 491, **719**
Attribute, 341, 347-348
Attributes Global Non-Printing, 354
Auto-Justify, 285, 287-288
Cancel, **731**
Clear, 46
Configuration Auto, 576
Configuration Document, 281, 291
    settings, 254-258
Configuration Document Auto-Justify Yes, 287
Configuration Document Hard-tabs, **708**
Configuration Document Justification, 282, 285
Configuration Document Spacing, 289
Configuration Document Tabs, 289
Configuration File, 221-222, 698, 749
Configuration Other Application Set, 322, 334
Configuration Other File-Translation, 222
Configuration Other File-Translation Generate Current, 226
Configuration Other File-Translation Generate Save, 226
Configuration Other International, 138-139
Configuration Other International Currency, 141
Configuration Other International Date, 205
Configuration Other International Negative, 142
Configuration Other International Punctuation, 142-143
Configuration Other International Time, 145, 207
Configuration Print Type, **667**
Configuration Printer, 374-375, 377, 749
    settings, 362-363
Configuration Printer Auto-LF, 363
Configuration Printer Init-String, 363, 373-374
Configuration Printer Margins, 363, 370-371
Configuration Printer Name, 363, **666-667**
Configuration Printer Page-Length, 292, 363
Configuration Printer Type, 363
Configuration Printer Wait, 363
Configuration Settings, 225
Configuration Update, 248
Configuration Window Type, 248
Copy, 83, 124-135, 272, 345, 366, 496, 653, **675**, **690**
Create, 39
Criteria Edit, 475-476, 504-505, **730**
Criteria Ignore, 475-476, 480, **730**
Criteria Use, 474, 476-477, 505

All bold listings in the index are in the troubleshooting section.

Criterion Edit, 477
Data-Labels, 409-411
Delete, 114, 122-124, 342, **691**
Delete Columns, **675**
Delete Global, 122
Delete Global Columns, 124
Delete Row, 330, 482, **675**
Destination Printer, 372
Detach, 46
Dictionaries Set, 328
DOS, 699
Erase, 21, 114, 117-119, 124, 251, 258, 261, 268, 292,
    491, **692**, **697**, **730**
Exit, 34, 47
Expose, 39
Extract, **730-731**
Field Delete, 491
Field Insert, 490
Field Move, 481, 483
File, 209
File Bytes, 210
File Combine, 38, 219, 267, 298
File Combine Add, 216-219, **678**, **686**, **701**
File Combine Copy, 216-219, **686**, **691**, **700-701**
File Combine Copy Named-Area, 276
File Combine Subtract, 216, **686**, **692**
File Directory, 221, **698-699**, **701**
File Erase, 220-221, 598
File Import, 222-223, 225
File Import Numbers, **701**
File Import Text, 222-223, 330, **701**
File List, 211, **699**
File List Worksheet, 211
File Retrieve, 27, 213-215, 274, 276, 500, **699**
File Save, 23, 27, 38, 47, 212-214, 274, 276, 375, **701-**
    702
File Table, 211-212
File Xtract, 215, 219, 278, 620
File Xtract Formulas, 215
File Xtract Values, 215, **685-686**
File-Transfer Receive, 549, 551-552
File-Transfer Send, 549, 551-552
File-Translate, 224
Fixed, 143-144
Format, 137-140, 203, 391, 490
Format Create, 289, 295
Format Currency, 141-142
Format Date, 144, 204
Format Edit, 289
Format Edit Current Justification, **708**
Format Edit Current Reset, 258
Format Fixed, 159
Format Justification None, 331
Format Location, 352
Format Other Hidden, 26, 147
Format Outline-Section, 353
Format Punctuated, 142
Format Settings, 21, 255-258, 281, 285, 291
Format Settings Auto-Justify, 269-270, 272, 287
Format Settings Justification, 282, 284, 464, **708**
Format Settings Justification None, 357, 482
Format Settings Left, 370-371, **710**
Format Settings Spacing, 289, 369

Format Settings Spacing 2, **713**
Format Settings Tabs, 289
Format Time, 145, 207
Format Use-Named, 297
General, 140
Generate, 463-476, 478, 481-482, 491, 503, 548, 656
Go, 368
Graph, 383, 385-386, 422
Graph 1st-Settings Cancel Entire-Row B, **726**
Graph 1st-Settings Hue, **720**
Graph 1st-Settings Name Create, **719-720**
Graph 1st-Settings Name Use, **719**
Graph 2nd-Settings, 388
Graph 2nd-Settings Other Skip, **723**
Graph 2nd-Settings Titles, 388
Hide, 39
Image-Save, 654
Image-Select, 437
Insert, 114, 119-121, 334, 336, 341, 503, 508
Insert Columns, 120
Insert Global, 119, 121
Insert Row, 19, 120, 162, 330, 479
Interface, 536
Invoke, 46
Isolate, 39
Join, 343-344
Justify, 269-270, 272, 287-288, 293
Justify Paragraph, 250
Line-Marker, 265-266
Line-Marker Assign, 297
Macros Edit, 597
Macros Load, 596
Macros Name-List, 597
Macros Remove, 598
Macros Save, 598
Maintenance, 329
Maintenance Add, 328
Modify, 329
Move, 114-118, 267, 269-270, 336, 345, 483, 491, 503,
    508, **675**, **691**
Name, 331, 394
Name Create, 395
Name Initial-Settings, 396
Name Reset, 395
Name Retrieve, 331
Name Use, 394-395, 422
New, 118-119
New Yes, 330
Next, 375, 474
Numbering Delete-Numbers, 352, 354, 357
Numbering Renumber, 352
Page, 292, 509, **714**, **717**
Page Length, **718**
Page-Advance, **715-716**
Pane, 39
Phone, 536, 543
Phone Answer, 549
Phone Call, 549
Phone Hangup, 549
Phone Wait-Mode, 550
Phone-and-Login, **733-734**
Preview, 387, 406
Previous, 375, 474

All bold listings in the index are in the troubleshooting section.

Print, 340, 368, 504, 509, 513, **715**, **731**
Print Align, 369-370, 377, **712**
Print Go, 354, 364, 377
Print Line-Advance, 377, **712**
Print Page-Advance, **712**, **714**
Print Settings, 222, 362-363, 375, 377, 503-504
Print Settings Destination Erase, 365
Print Settings Destination File, 330, 365, 377
Print Settings Destination Printer, 365
Print Settings Destination Range, 365, 377
Print Settings Init-String, 373-374, **718**
Print Settings Margins, 370-371
Print Settings Margins Left, **710**
Print Settings Margins No-Margins, 365
Print Settings Margins Right, **713**
Print Settings Name, 375
Print Settings Name Create, **715**
Print Settings Name Delete, 375
Print Settings Name Initial-Settings, **715**
Print Settings Name Reset, 377
Print Settings Name Use, 375, **715**
Print Settings Other Format, 374
Print Settings Other Left-Labels, 372-373
Print Settings Other Top-Labels, 372-373
Print Settings Page Length, 292, 374
Print Settings Page Length setting, 265
Print Settings Page Number, 369
Print Settings Page Number Print-Number, **716**
Print Settings Page Number Start-Page, 370
Print Settings Source, 510
Print Settings Source Cancel, 355
Print Settings Source Range, 226, 354, 368, 372
Print Source Range, 357
problems, **680-692**
Query, 491, **728**, **730**
Query Delete, 498-500
Query Extract, 496-497, **730**
Query Find, 493-495, 499, **730**
Query Parse, 223, 545, 547-548, **701**
Query Record-Sort, 473, 492
Query Settings, 492, 494
Query Settings Basic Criterion, **728**
Query Settings Basic Database, 492
Query Settings Cancel Sort-Keys, **731**
Query Settings Sort-Keys, **731**
Query Unique, 497
Quit, 51, 364
Range, 386
Range Distribution, 109-111
Range Fill, 108-109, 111, 200, 226, 507
Range Label-Alignment, 84
Range Name, 99-103
Range Name Create, 99-100, 276, 574, **682**, **735**
Range Name Delete, 100, 682
Range Name Labels, 99-100
Range Name Labels Right, 575, 605, 624
Range Name Reset, 100
Range Name Table, 100
Range Protect, 26-27, 104-107, 218
Range Protect Allow-Changes, 106, **692**
Range Protect Prevent-Changes, 106
Range Transpose, 103-104
Range Values, 104, 200, 547, 657, **679**, **686**

Range What-If, 19, 111-113, **679**
Range What-If 2-Way, 113
Record Sort, 471-473
Record-Sort, **731**
Replace, 21, 278, 280-281
Reset, 433
Restrict Range, 572
Save, 433
Search, 21, 260-261, 278, 280-281
Select Configuration Other International Negative, 141
Select Name, 536
Settings, 38, 79, 430, 497, **671**, **678**
Settings Auto-Execute, 605
Settings Auto-Execute Set, 576
Settings Basic Criterion, 477, 479, **728**
Settings Basic Database, 471-472, 494
Settings Cancel Report, 510
Settings Cancel Sort-Keys, **731**
Settings Capture Erase, 545
Settings Capture Printer, 544
Settings Capture Range, 545, 552
Settings Form Definition, 485
Settings Form Entry, 482
Settings Format, 138-139, 141-142
Settings Format Currency, 141
Settings Format Date, 144
Settings Format Other Hidden, 147
Settings Format Punctuated, 142
Settings Format Time, 145
Settings Global-Protection, 26-27, 106, 218, 332
Settings Global-Protection Yes, **692**
Settings Hardware Interface, **667**
Settings Hardware Printer, **667**, **725**
Settings Hardware Size-Paper, 437
Settings Image Size Manual, **725**
Settings Interface, **733**
Settings Label-Prefix, 84
Settings Learn Range, 571
Settings Login, 540
Settings Name Phone-and-Login, 544
Settings Name Retrieve, 548
Settings Name Save, 548
Settings Name Use, 473
Settings Phone Number, 537, 543
Settings Recalculation, 150-153
Settings Recalculation Method Manual, **685**
Settings Report, 503
Settings Report Main, 510
Settings Report Type, 506
Settings Report Type Multiple, 507
Settings Save, **667**
Settings Security Unlock, 27
Settings Send, 550
Settings Sort-Keys, **731**
Settings Terminal Delay, 540, 544
Settings Terminal Echo Yes, **734**
Settings Terminal Linefeed Yes, **734**
Settings Titles, 148-150
Settings Titles Both, 149
Settings Underscores No, 484
Settings Width, 136-137
Settings Zero, 147

All bold listings in the index are in the troubleshooting section.

Symphony Release 2.0 commands
  Configuration Document Hard-tabs, 753
  Configuration Other International Negative, 751
  Field Insert, 752
  Field Move, 752
  Settings Recalculation Order Optimal, 751
  Settings Send Format, 754
  Settings Zero, 751
  Verify, 753
Tables Outline, 340
Tables Table-of-Contents, 356
Terminal, 538-539
Transmit-Range, 550-551
Unique, **731**
Update, 43-44, 255
Use, 39
Verify, 322
Verify Go, 324
Verify Maintenance, 330
Verify Maintenance Add, 329
Verify Maintenance Delete, 329
Verify Maintenance Modify, 329
Verify Settings Dictionaries Set, 328
Verify Settings Options, 324
Width, 137
Width Display, 136, **716**
Width Hide, 136, 368, **716**
Width Restore, 136-137
Width Set, 136-137, 491, 509
Window, 23
Window Create, 148, 249, 398, 572
Window Delete, 38-39, 137, 210, 423
Window Expose, **704**, **706**
Window Hide, 39, **704**, **706**
Window Layout, 39-40, **703**, **705**
Window Pane, 41, **703**
Window Settings, 39, 423
Window Settings Borders, 63
Window Settings Restrict Range, **704**, **718**
Window Settings Type, 50
Window Use, **703-706**
Windows Settings Restrict, 106-107, 269
Symphony functions, 87
  @@, 191
  @ABS, 156
  @ACOS, 160
  @ASIN, 160
  @ATAN, 160
  @ATAN2, 160
  @AVG, 163, 696
  @CELL, 188-190, **671**, **697**
  @CELLPOINTER, 191, **697**
  @CHAR, 200
  @CHOOSE, 174-175
  @CLEAN, 201, 552
  @CODE, 201
  @COLS, 191
  @COS, 160
  @COUNT, 163, 166
  @CTERM, 172-173
  @DATE, 202-203
  @DATEVALUE, 203, 547
  @DAY, 204

@DDB, 174
@ERR, 185-186
@EXACT, 196
@EXP, 157
@FALSE, 192
@FIND, 192-194
@FV, 168-169
@HLOOKUP, 175-179
@HOUR, 207
@IF, 181-188
@INDEX, 179-180
@INT, 157
@IRR, 169-171
@ISERR, 186-187
@ISNA, 186-187
@ISNUMBER, 187-188
@ISSTRING, 187-188
@LEFT, 194-195
@LENGTH, 195
@LN, 157
@LOG, 157
@LOWER, 196
@MAX, 163
@MID, 194
@MIN, 163
@MINUTE, 207
@MOD, 159-160
@MONTH, 204
@N, 199, 697
@NA, 185-186
@NOW, 205
@NPV, 166-167
@PI, 160
@PMT, 171-172
@PROPER, 196
@PV, 168
@RAND, 158
@RATE, 172
@REPEAT, 197
@REPLACE, 195
@RIGHT, 194-195
@ROUND, 158-159, **672**, **693**
@ROWS, 191
@S, 199, **696-697**
@SECOND, 207
@SIN, 160
@SLN, 173
@SQRT, 157, 166
@STD, 164-166
@STRING, 197-198, 693, **695-696**
@SUM, 87, 161-162
@SYD, 173
@TAN, 160
@TERM, 169
@TIME, 206
@TIMEVALUE, 206
@TRIM, 197
@TRUE, 192
@UPPER, 196
@VALUE, 197-199, 547
@VAR, 164-166
@VLOOKUP, 175-179
@YEAR, 204

All bold listings in the index are in the troubleshooting section.

database functions
@DAVG, 501
@DCOUNT, 501
@DMAX, 501
@DMIN, 501
@DSTD, 501
@DSUM, 501, 505, 509
@DVAR, 501
File Import Structured, 222-223
time, 145
SYMPHONY.CNF file, 43, 254, 292
synchronous communications transmission, 532-533
syntax of Command Language, 604
system reqirements, 15

T

Tab key, 337
tab settings, 289-291, **707-708**
table of contents from outline, 356-357
tables
custom character-translation, 227
logical function, 180
lookup, 175-179
macro key representation, 569-570
numeric format codes for CONTENTS command, 634
putting in separate files, 243
range names, 100
translation, 226
Tables Outline command, 340
Tables Table-of-Contents command, 356
TAN function, 160
telecommunications *see communications*
template problems, **692**
TERM function, 169
Terminal command, 538-539
test variable, 175
text
changing characters, 259
copying, 219
to another file, 274-278
within same file, 272-274
editing, 267-278
entering, 258-267
erasing, 267-278
inserting
characters, 258-259
print attributes commands, 253
justification default settings, 84
moving, 315-316
within same file, 269-272
outlining, 265
replacing, 278-281, 316-318
searching for, 278-281
strings connected by formulas, 85
unerasing, 269
varying formats of, 293
wordwrap, 258-259
Text Outliner, 29, 332-357
tilde (~)
in macros, 568
omitting in macros, 577

time
and date arithmetic, 201-208
converted from string, 206
displaying, 207
extracting, 207
function, 145, 205-207
today, 205
values to serial numbers, 206
Time formats, 145-146
TIMEVALUE function, 206
titles added to graphs, 388-390
Titles format, 148-150
top of page marker, 438-439
TOPPAGE command, 755
totalling ranges, 161-162
transferring files, 222-227, 551-552
translating
characters, 227
program new features, 756
Translate utility, 35, 222-225
translation tables, 226
Transmit-Range command, 550-551
TREE command, **699**
trigonometric functions, 160
TRIM function, 197
troubleshooting section, **661-741**
TRUE function, 192
tutorial, 34, 71
Tutorial disks, 68-72
TYPE
command, 365
menu, 50
window menu, 31
type-ahead buffer, 610-611
types of graphs, 384-428

U

undeleting records, 500
Underline print attribute, 253
underscores, 484
unerasing text, 269
Unique command, 731
Universal Text Display driver, **664-665**
unnamed range names, **669**
unprintable LICS characters, 200-201
Update command, 43-44, 255
UPPER function, 196
uppercase converting strings to, 196
Use command, 39
User key, **735**
utilities
Translate, 35, 222-225
utility macros, 581-583

V

value checks on fields, 489
VALUE
function, 197-199, 547

All bold listings in the index are in the troubleshooting section.

mode, 86
value returned unreasonable problem, 170
values
    copying, 104
    entering, 311-313
    finding maximum or minimum, 163
    from formulas, 85
    key, 174
    looking up, 175-179
    net present, 166-167
VAR function, 164-166
Verify
    command, 322, 753
    menu, 323
Verify Go command, 324
Verify Maintenance Add command, 329
Verify Maintenance command, 330
Verify Maintenance Delete command, 329
Verify Maintenance Modify command, 329
Verify Settings Dictionaries Set command, 328
Verify Settings menu, 331
Verify Settings Options command, 324
viewing graphs, 387
VLOOKUP function, 175-179

W

WAIT command, 621-622
what-if
    analysis, 18-19, 111-113
    graphs, 423
Width command, 137
Width Display command, 136, **716**
Width Hide command, 136, 368, **716**
width of columns
    adjusting, 136, 137
Width Restore command, 136-137
Width Set command, 136-137, 491, 509
wildcards searching with, 279, 480
Window command menu, 36
Window Create command, 148, 249, 398, 572
Window Delete command, 38-39, 137, 210, 423
Window Expose command, **704**, **706**
Window Hide command, 39, **704**, **706**
Window Layout command, 39-40, **703**, **705**
Window menu, 38
Window Pane command, 41, **703**
Window Settings command, 39, 423
Window Settings Restrict Range command, **704**, **718**
Window Settings Type command, 50
Window Use command, **703-706**
windows, 35-42, 236-237
    and files, 37-38, 210
    changing
        from one GRAPH window to another, 422
        shape and size, 40-41
    COMM, 531-552
    Command Language, 605
    copying between, 135, 237
    deleting, 38-39
    DOC, 10, 247-299, 365-366, 369

FORM, 10-12, 459-460, 462-466, 468, 472, 480, 503, 510, 548
    function keys for, 38, 56-59
    GRAPH, 10, 12-14, 383-384, 387, 422-425
    MACRO, 572
    modes, 66-67
    OUTLN, 332-334
    overview, 23
    placing macros in, 572
    problems, **703-706**
    redisplaying, 39
    removing, 39
    restricting ranges in, 41-42
    SHEET, 10, 12, 77-96, 383-384, 387, 463, 472, 491-493, 547
Windows command, 23
Windows Settings Borders command, 63
Windows Settings Restrict command, 106-107, 269
WINDOWSOFF command, 637-639
WINDOWSON command, 639
word processing, 247-299
    add-in applications, 321-358
    new features, 752-754
    overview, 21-22
    problems, **707-711**
    printing documents, 361-382
word-transposition macro, 587
words
    adding to dictionary, 326, 328-329
    capitalizing first in sentence, 326
    deleting misspelled, 329
    erasing and editing, 267
    moving cursor one, 261-262
WordStar files
    converting to ASCII, 225-226
    transferring to Symphony, 225-226
wordwrap, 258-259, 708
working copies of Symphony disks, 746
worksheets, 10
    deleting columns or rows, 123-124
    entering dates, 144-145
    erasing entire, 118-119
    files saving, 215
    formatting, 137-153
    inserting blank columns or rows, 119-121
    protecting, 25-27
    worksheet size, 78-81
WRITE command, 647-648
WRITELN command, 648

X-Y-Z

XMODEM file transfer, 551
XMODEM protocol, 22, 533
XON/XOFF (Ctrl-Q/Ctrl-S) protocol, 543
XY graphs, 417-419

Y-Axis scale width, 426
YEAR function, 204

Zero format, 147

All bold listings in the index are in the troubleshooting section.

More Computer Knowledge from Que

SELECT QUE BOOKS TO INCREASE
YOUR PERSONAL COMPUTER PRODUCTIVITY

IBM PS/2 Handbook

by Richard Dalton

The hot new book on IBM's hot new microcomputers! Richard Dalton, founding editor of The Whole Earth Software Catalog, presents an overview of Personal System/2 hardware, including technical information on each model, tips on integrating PS/2 with other machines, and discussions of PS/2 software. This book helps you understand the differences between PS/2 models, decide which machines best suit your needs, and get the most out of your hardware investment. IBM Personal System/2 is the new standard in microcomputers, and Que's *IBM PS/2 Handbook* will help you with your hardware purchasing decisions!

Managing Your Hard Disk

by Don Berliner

Que's *Managing Your Hard Disk* introduces innovative techniques to bring your hard disk to peak performance. Storing and retrieving "libraries" of information is simple when you follow this book's easy-to-understand instructions. *Managing Your Hard Disk* will show you proper backup procedures, ways to activate menu programs, and strategies for using programs that normally won't run on a hard disk. If your personal computer utilizes a hard disk, you need Que's *Managing Your Hard Disk*!

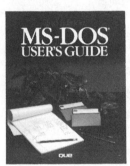

MS-DOS User's Guide, 2nd Edition

by Chris DeVoney

Gain control over your operating system with Que's *MS-DOS User's Guide*, 2nd Edition. This new edition updates DOS guru Chris DeVoney's popular text with information through MS-DOS 3.2. The perfect combination of beginning tutorial, advanced guide, and lasting reference, this book is designed to meet your changing DOS needs. Even after you've mastered MS-DOS, you will use the comprehensive Command Reference section to look up DOS commands. *MS-DOS User's Guide*, 2nd Edition, is an absolute necessity for all users of MS-DOS!

Using PC DOS, 2nd Edition

by Chris DeVoney

The best-selling guide to PC DOS is now even better! DOS master Chris DeVoney has updated *Using PC DOS*—the Que classic that covers every aspect of the IBM operating system. Critically acclaimed, *Using PC DOS* is a combination of beginning tutorial and lasting reference, now covering PC DOS through version 3.3. This new 2nd Edition adds up-to-date information on IBM's PS/2 computers and shows how to work with 3 1/2-inch disks. Also featured is a comprehensive beginning tutorial and the popular Command Reference, an easy-to-use consolidation of essential DOS commands. No IBM microcomputer user should be without a copy of *Using PC DOS*, 2nd Edition!

REGISTRATION CARD

Register your copy of *Using Symphony*, 2nd Edition, and receive information about Que's newest products. Complete this registration card and return it to Que Corporation, P.O. Box 90, Carmel, IN 46032.

Name _____ Phone _____

Company _____ Title _____

Address _____

City _____ State ____ ZIP _____

Please check the appropriate answers:

Where did you buy *Using Symphony*, 2nd Edition?
- ☐ Bookstore (name: _____)
- ☐ Computer store (name: _____)
- ☐ Catalog (name: _____)
- ☐ Direct from Que
- ☐ Other: _____

How many computer books do you buy a year?
- ☐ 1 or less
- ☐ 2-5
- ☐ 6-10
- ☐ More than 10

How many Que books do you own?
- ☐ 1
- ☐ 2-5
- ☐ 6-10
- ☐ More than 10

How long have you been using Symphony?
- ☐ Less than 6 months
- ☐ 6 months to 1 year
- ☐ 1 to 3 years
- ☐ More than 3 years

What influenced your purchase of *Using Symphony*, 2nd Edition?
- ☐ Personal recommendation
- ☐ Advertisement
- ☐ In-store display
- ☐ Price
- ☐ Que catalog
- ☐ Que mailing
- ☐ Que's reputation
- ☐ Other: _____

How would you rate the overall content of *Using Symphony*, 2nd Edition?
- ☐ Very good
- ☐ Good
- ☐ Satisfactory
- ☐ Poor

How would you rate *Part I: Understanding and Getting Started with Symphony*?
- ☐ Very good
- ☐ Good
- ☐ Satisfactory
- ☐ Poor

How would you rate *Part VII: Symphony Macros and the Command Language*?
- ☐ Very good
- ☐ Good
- ☐ Satisfactory
- ☐ Poor

How would you rate the *Troubleshooting Section*?
- ☐ Very good
- ☐ Good
- ☐ Satisfactory
- ☐ Poor

How would you rate the *Hands-On Practice Sessions*?
- ☐ Very good
- ☐ Good
- ☐ Satisfactory
- ☐ Poor

What do you like *best* about *Using Symphony*, 2nd Edition?

What do you like *least* about *Using Symphony*, 2nd Edition?

How do you use *Using Symphony*, 2nd Edition?

What other Que products do you own?

For what other programs would a Que book be helpful?

Please feel free to list any other comments you may have about *Using Symphony*, 2nd Edition.

_____

_____

_____

_____

FOLD HERE

_____
_____
_____
_____

Place
Stamp
Here

Que Corporation
P.O. Box 90
Carmel, IN 46032

ORDER FROM QUE TODAY

Item	Title	Price	Quantity	Extension
67	Managing Your Hard Disk	$19.95		
807	Using PC DOS, 2nd Edition	22.95		
806	IBM PS/2 Handbook	19.95		
96	MS-DOS User's Guide, 2nd Edition	21.95		

**Prices and charges are for domestic orders only.
Non-U.S. prices might be higher.**

Book Subtotal _____

Shipping & Handling ($2.50 per item) _____

Indiana Residents Add 5% Sales Tax _____

GRAND TOTAL _____

Method of Payment:

☐ Check　　☐ VISA　　☐ MasterCard　　☐ American Express

Card Number _____ Exp. Date _____

Cardholder's Name _____

Ship to _____

Address _____

City _____ State _____ ZIP _____

If you can't wait, call **1-800-428-5331**, ext. 888 and order TODAY.

All prices subject to change without notice.

FOLD HERE

‾‾‾‾‾‾‾‾‾‾‾‾‾‾‾‾‾‾‾‾‾‾‾

‾‾‾‾‾‾‾‾‾‾‾‾‾‾‾‾‾‾‾‾‾‾‾

‾‾‾‾‾‾‾‾‾‾‾‾‾‾‾‾‾‾‾‾‾‾‾

‾‾‾‾‾‾‾‾‾‾‾‾‾‾‾‾‾‾‾‾‾‾‾

Place
Stamp
Here

Que Corporation
P.O. Box 90
Carmel, IN 46032